Core Management for HR Students and Practitioners

For our respective wives, Ann, Jill and Judy,
for their support and love

Core Management for HR Students and Practitioners

Second edition

Peter W. Winfield, Ray Bishop and Keith Porter

ELSEVIER
BUTTERWORTH
HEINEMANN

AMSTERDAM BOSTON HEIDELBERG LONDON NEW YORK OXFORD
PARIS SAN DIEGO SAN FRANCISCO SINGAPORE SYDNEY TOKYO

Elsevier Butterworth-Heinemann
Linacre House, Jordan Hill, Oxford OX2 8DP
200 Wheeler Road, Burlington MA 01803

First published 2000
Reprinted 2001
Second edition 2004

British Library Cataloguing in Publication Data
A catalogue record for this book is available from the British Library

Library of Congress Cataloguing in Publication Data
A catalogue record for this book is available from the Library of Congress

ISBN 0 7506 5827 4

Every effort has been made to contact Copyright holders requesting permission to reproduce
their illustrations in this book. Any omissions will be rectified in subsequent printings if
notice is given to the Publisher

For information on all Butterworth-Heinemann publications
visit our website at: www.bh.com

Composition by Genesis Typesetting Limited, Rochester, Kent
Printed and bound in Italy

Contents

About the authors

Peter W. Winfield, BA, MA, PG.Dip.L, Dip. PM, Cert.M, FCIPD, MCIM, Winston Churchill Fellow, is a former IPD course director at Croydon Business School, and has experience as a senior HR manager in the public sector. Currently, he is programme manager for employment law courses at Malpas Flexible Learning Ltd, a visiting lecturer at the University of Leicester, Faculty of Law, and HR/employment law adviser to private clients. Peter Winfield is an external examiner for CIPD and Masters' programmes at a number of institutions, as well as a freelance writer, trainer and consultant.

Ray Bishop, BA (Hons), Post grad. Cert Ed., is a senior lecturer at London Metropolitan University where he has taught on a number of professional, undergraduate and higher national business programmes. He also spent 15 years working for various organizations in a management services role.

Keith Porter, BA, MSc., Dip. PM, FCIPD, is a freelance lecturer, trainer and consultant. He teaches Human Resource Management and Human Resource Strategies on management programmes at Birkbeck College, University of London and on CIPD programmes at various institutions. A registered Investors in People adviser, he has helped many organizations to achieve the Standard and has worked extensively as a performance management consultant, notably with schools. As a trainer, he specializes in the design and delivery of management development programmes.

Preface

This book has been written to provide a comprehensive coverage of the CIPD's Core Management syllabus: Managing People, Managing Activities and Managing in a Business Context, which all providers of the Institute's Professional Education Scheme (PES) must follow. This scheme was introduced by the CIPD in September 1999. The authors have also attempted to extend a number of sections, notably Chapter 7 on corporate strategy (this forms the basis for the new Human Resource Strategy Common Module). Several chapters provide materials that will aid those preparing to study People Management and Development (previously Core Personnel & Development), and the Generalist Electives. The text is also an aid for students on BA Business Studies programmes, HNC/D and Certificate and Diploma in Management Studies, and will also be of assistance to MBA first-year students.

There are, however, further secondary aims. These are to stimulate self-reflection for purposes of completing coursework as well as contributing to the process of continuous professional self-development (CPD) as well as to generate critical thinking about some of the skills required in the HR profession and those that are likely to be assessed in any formal programme of study.

The authors hope that the reader will find the text written in a student-friendly style, making the concepts, theories and their practical application easy to grasp. Throughout the book will be found cross-references to other chapters and sections. This is because of the overlap and important linkages between the subjects. Indeed, the study of HR Management is a complex matter and to divide it into three neat compartments is artificial and misleading, although convenient. For that reason the reader will not only find the cross-referencing helpful, but some subjects repeated in other parts of the book with a particular emphasis placed on them, depending on the part of the syllabus to which it is referenced. For example, the study of power and authority is first considered in Chapter 3 (Managing People) where it helps define management and leadership styles and the basis of relationships between people at work; in Chapter 4 (Managing Activities) it is used to illustrate the basis on which managers manage; and in Chapter 9 (Managing in a Business Context) it is used to show how the political system functions.

An extensive range of books are recommended in the **Further reading** sections at the end of each chapter, but in addition to those texts shown students should consult the publications available from the CIPD.

Acknowledgements

The authors would like to express their sincere thanks to the following persons who have contributed in various ways to the text of this book:

Moira French for her wise counsel and helpful ideas with Part Two, Managing Activities.

Olivia Rahman for her valuable ideas and corrections to Chapter 12, The Legal Context.

Also Richard Barr (Director of Business Support, Springboard Housing Association), Hilaire Gomer, Mark Naylor, Graeme Hoyle of Crawley College and Paul Sinnott (Barclays Bank plc).

Extracts from the fortnightly award-winning HR news magazine, *Personnel Today*, appear by kind permission. *Personnel Today* is part of an HR portfolio which includes *Training, Employers' Law* and *Occupational Health* magazine. It reaches 40 000 senior HR and training managers across the UK's public and private sectors.

Introduction

Aim of the book

Why another introductory text on core human resource management when the student is so spoilt for choice? Simply, because the authors feel there is a continuing need for such a book. Their combined experience tells them no matter how many books are published on the subject there are few that satisfactorily combine all the necessary elements. These are breadth and depth of coverage, practical management exercises and case studies, exam questions to further help students, a narrative that is both fully referenced to relevant theories and concepts, but also supplied with practical examples. Also, a list of useful website addresses at the end of each chapter. Finally, a text that is up to date, readable and can link with other study materials/lectures easily. The authors believe that this book fulfils these aims.

Core Management for HR Students and Practitioners is based on the professional standards introduced by the IPD (now CIPD) in summer 1999, and which correspond to N/SVQ level 4/5. As you will see from the Preface, this book is specifically aimed at students following the CIPD's Core Management programme, but also at students on other management courses. The CIPD's Standards for Core Management will undergo changes beginning in summer 2003, although the contents of this book will remain relevant for the first part of the CIPD's Professional Education Scheme beyond that date.

Advice for students on answering examination questions is availabe via our website. Simply visit the page dedicated to this book at: www.bh.com/management/Winfield.

A lecturer's resource pack is also available, located on the web. Lecturers should contact Butterworth-Heinemann Customer Services Department, Linacre House, Jordan Hill, Oxford OX2 8DP, Tel: 01865 474000, for the password to this site. The resource pack includes a grid to the CIPD Core Management syllabus, lesson plan ideas, diagrams from within the text for use as OHPs, and sample worked answers.

A complementary text covering the Managing Information part of the CIPD's Core Management is available separately.

What are the specific learning outcomes of reading this book?

What is the *rationale* of this book? Throughout this book the authors have emphasized the complex and overlapping nature of HR management work. Its rationale is therefore to link and draw together the many strands of the subject to form a cohesive narrative, but simultaneously to provide a strong descriptive and analytical treatment of the individual subjects. By such an approach it is hoped that a thorough understanding of not only 'what' constitutes HR core management, but also 'how' it can be applied to best effect will be accomplished.

Part One
Managing People at Work

Learning outcomes

To understand and explain:

- The behaviour of individuals in work organizations – the causes, benefits, difficulties and changes in behaviour
- The learning and developmental process of individuals and how this can be harnessed in the workplace for mutual benefit
- The nature of work, attitudes to work, new patterns of work and the changing nature of the psychological contract
- The causes of stress and its symptoms, prevention and elimination in the workplace
- How issues of quality and ethics impact on the workplace and work systems
- The sources, types and applications of power in the workplace
- The methods of influence and conflict resolution in the workplace
- The importance, systems, methods, techniques and skills associated with recruitment and selection
- Motivational theories and their effective practical application, particularly in respect of job design
- The sources and types, acquisition, practice and development of leadership, and the distinguishing of leadership with management and
- How performance can be improved, managed and rewarded, as well as poor performance improved and managed effectively.

Introduction to Part One

The purpose of this part of the book is to examine the various dimensions of individual behaviour at work which can enable a manager to subsequently deploy and use those human resources to best effect. What cannot be understood cannot be used effectively. The overarching aim is therefore, to remedy any defects in that understanding. For that reason (and for the purpose of passing exams and assignments too) there is a great deal of discussion here about how various theories and concepts can be practically applied in the workplace.

The areas of study and research that inform much of the materials used in Part One are found in the behavioural sciences – a study of the reasons and patterns of human behaviour. A specialist study of behaviour is psychology, which provides the underpinning of several areas of study in the book, particularly in Chapter 1 and to a lesser extent in Chapter 3, but particularly in Section 14.6 of Chapter 14. Also, a source of the materials is sociological research – a study of the way in which people interact in groups, institutions and in wider society. Conclusions in the book have been drawn about why certain types of behaviour can manifest themselves in the workplace, the trends and changes detected in behaviour and what predictions can be made about behaviours in particular environmental situations. Social behaviour in groups is also addressed in Part Two of the book, Section 4.4.

Understanding how and why people behave in the way they do enables the manager to do a number of things:

- To select, induct, develop and deploy people in jobs which are best suited to their 'psychological profile' and provide mutual benefits
- Therefore, an understanding of their motivation needs can be attempted with implications for designing and implementing appropriate rewards and incentives. These, in turn can be used to recruit, retain, stimulate and develop individuals.

There are further aims for the informed and knowledgeable manager:

- To design and implement jobs, work systems and performance goals that will motivate the individuals
- To predict poor and good performance
- To take remedial action to halt poor performance and enhance good performance before clear evidence of either is apparent to the uninformed manager
- To construct styles of leadership appropriate to the variables indicated in this list.

This Part of the book attempts to address all of these issues, and more.

1 Individual differences

As we reflect about the human problems in industry, it becomes obvious that they are really manifestations of certain undesirable 'forms of behaviour' . . . a term which in our usage embraces not only overt actions or activities, such as how well a person does a job, but also covert aspects such as attitudes. The variability in any given form of behaviour should not be assumed to be a fortuity, but rather should be assumed to be the consequence of some combination of factors.[1]

Chapter objectives

In this chapter you will:

● Examine the sources, structure, behavioural application and measurement of:
  – social perception and attribution
  – personality
  – intelligence and
  – values and attitudes
● Assess how these differences in individuals are part of behaviour in the workplace and
● Identify some of the issues relating to individual differences and vulnerable groups.

Case study

The selection interview

The MD's working week was, as usual, extremely busy and stressful. The whole of Monday was 'blocked out' for interviewing candidates for the new post of Customer Services Manager for the Midlands region. Selection would be based on an application form and one interview. Three months after the successful candidate had started work he was dismissed for poor performance and misconduct. He had seemed 'so right' for the job; he had attended the same school as the MD's son and according to the application form had achieved three 'A' levels at grade B, he spoke with a Birmingham accent which would 'go down well with the customers', and the MD had assessed his personality as 'forthright, assertive and resilient'.

However, within weeks the new manager had proved himself to be uncooperative, a racist and a sexist bully, poor at acquiring new knowledge, and weak in spotting problems before they 'blew up'. When they did, he became sullen and started to drink at lunchtimes, sometimes to excess. Furthermore, he lost his temper with several important customers.

What functions of this manager's psychological make-up do you think the MD had failed to evaluate properly?

Feedback

The superficial nature and lack of preparation of the selection process meant that the MD relied too much on 'hunches' and similarities between himself and the candidate. The psychological profile of the candidate had been totally ignored in respect of his:

- **Personality** (he was a bully and short-tempered, which the MD had interpreted as 'assertive'; also, the MD had failed to identify his inclination towards depression which was exacerbated by drinking alcohol. Had the MD bothered to obtain references?)
- **Social perception framework** (his harassment of colleagues on the basis of their sex and race suggested he perceived women as sex objects and black people as inferior).
- **Attitudes** (his harassment and bullying suggested a prejudicial attitude towards women and black people).
- **Intelligence** (his poor ability to learn new behaviours, remember important information, discern and solve problems. Had the MD been over-impressed by the candidate's alleged academic prowess and his verbal fluency?)

All these psychological functions will be examined in this chapter.

Chapter introduction

Edgar Schein[2] has correctly said that human nature is 'elusive', yet to understand and isolate elements of it and evaluate and measure it are critical success factors for employers who aim to have a successful employment relationship with their workforce. This relationship can be categorized by using the former Employment Department's definition of 'human resource planning':

A strategy for the selection (appointment), utilization (deployment and work performance), improvement (training and development) and preservation (retention by offering attractive and fair rewards/incentives) of the workforce.

Unfortunately, for employers human nature is also highly complex and individual; no one person has the same make-up of social perceptions, social origins, personality, intelligence and attitudes. This chapter will examine all these factors and draw conclusions about some of the ways employers can use this understanding to improve their people management. The critical individual differences of motivation, job satisfaction and potential to lead will be discussed in Chapter 3. The links between individual learning, training and development, and performance will also be examined in Chapter 3. As the opening quotation points out, it is all these variable factors, and more, that cause individual behaviours. The difficulty for people managers is not only understanding them in isolation, but seeing how they all interact uniquely for every organizational participant.

The sources of human behaviour have been argued over by theorists for centuries. The debate still rages whether human personality and intelligence in particular are determined by a unique genetic structure inherited from parents (the biological source or origins in 'nature'), or by the situational upbringing of the individual (the sociological source or origins in 'nurture'). Furthermore, whichever source of behaviour you subscribe to, there is also the well-documented evidence that as society develops so do individuals in terms of their psychological make-up (see Figure 1.1).

Exercise

The following are examples of widely but not completely accepted social standards:

(i)   All people are equal irrespective of gender, race, religion, disability or age.
(ii) Gay men and lesbians should be given equal rights with heterosexuals, and should not be discriminated against for their sexuality.
(iii) Women priests should be ordained in the same way as male priests.

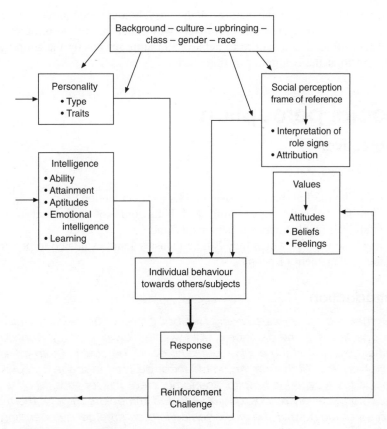

Figure 1.1. Individual differences and behaviour.

(iv) Employers should be constrained in acting towards employees as they see fit by employment protection legislation, (e.g. rights to maternity/paternity leave/pay or to claim unfair dismissal).

Take each one of these examples – compare how they would have been received by each generation dating back to the year 1700.

Feedback

Acceptance of these social standards by society has not changed uniformly over time, but at different rates depending on the issue. Number (iv) became widely acceptable in the twentieth century, and number (i) acceptable in the latter half of that century. Numbers (ii) and (iii) are arguably, still not accepted by a minority of people in society. Moreover, everybody in the UK will have a unique set of views and behaviours towards these four situations.

The problem is identical for employers – how to establish the truthful beliefs, feelings, motives, abilities, attitudes, prejudices and likely behaviour in a disparate workforce. Where a 'profile' of information can be determined about individuals and their likely behaviours in groups, employers can predict behaviours and construct organizational scenarios which will make the best use of their workforce.

A critical variable in determining success will be the power that underpins the employment relationship. For example, an organization which seeks to coerce its workers for little financial gain and with poor job satisfaction will fail. However, one that relies on the power of money (resource power) but which offers poor job satisfaction may be storing-up problems of poor employee loyalty. As we will see in Chapters 2 and 3 these factors and others will constitute the nature of the 'psychological contract' between employer and employee. The danger is that employers will either ignore the information or misinterpret it. This will lead to a failure to achieve the aims set out by the Employment Department referred to at the beginning of this section.

1.1   Social perception

Objectives

In this section you will:

- Examine the link between visual and social perception
- Identify the sources, structure and behaviours of individual perceptual frames of reference, intelligence and personality and
- Examine ways in which they can be measured and evaluated to provide information for the management of people.

1.1.1   Introduction

A father and his son were driving to a ball game when their car stalled on the railroad tracks. In the distance a train whistle blew a warning. Frantically, the father tried to start the engine, but in his panic, he couldn't turn the key, and the onrushing train hit the car. An ambulance sped to the scene and picked them up. On the way to the hospital, the father died. The son was still alive, but his condition was very serious, and he needed immediate surgery. The moment they arrived at the hospital, he was wheeled into an emergency operating room, and the surgeon came in, expecting a routine case. However, on seeing the boy, the surgeon blanched and muttered, 'I can't operate on this boy – he's my son'.[3]

What do you make of this grim riddle? It is common for people to take at least a few minutes before they get the answer. Is the surgeon the boy's real father and the driver the adopted father or the father a priest? The answer is that the surgeon is the boy's mother.

As Hofstadter points out, the social assumption about the surgeon is made in 'default', that is, a solution to a problem or the most plausible assumption about a situation or person is arrived at automatically based on our expectations. These will be determined by what life has taught us to expect so that a 'frame of reference' is constructed by which we judge the people and things around us. The same process of 'perception' applies to visual perception. Look at Figures 1.2–1.4. What do you see?

Figure 1.2. What do you see (1)?

Figure 1.3. What do you see (2)?

Figure 1.4. What do you see (3)?

An assessment of what is seen in the figures will vary according to whether you looked at the prominent figure or the background in Figures 1.2 and 1.3. Both can be interchanged so that in Figure 1.2 you see an obscured disc or a funny-shaped face; in Figure 1.3 you see a vase or two faces. We are only capable of seeing one answer to a problem in isolation, just as we only see one shape. In Figure 1.4 do you see a beautiful young woman dressed in Edwardian style wearing a 'choker' or an old woman with a hooked nose and wearing a shawl? These ideas are based on the German Gestalt school of learning and psychological development, the word 'Gestalt' meaning 'whole' or 'form'. It is, indeed, easier for us to group things together to form a pattern according to their key characteristics, and to group information into patterns so that we can more easily make sense of them.

What has this to do with people management? In the same way that we perceive visual data or a story or information associated with a problem, we also perceive people with whom we interact in the same way. **Social perception** is a dynamic and interactive process which we are all subject to on an involuntary basis; it is not a skill, but a psychological process. Skill is involved where we must discover the truth behind a situation or the appearance of an individual. Every minute of each day of our lives our senses are bombarded with thousands of pieces of information from the words spoken to us, what is right or wrong, the time, the environment, instructions, and so on. A lot of this information is received by more than one sensory organ, for example a conversation with someone is detected and interpreted by hearing, vision, and possibly touch or smell. We can only make sense of this mass of information by using previous knowledge of similar situations or of people in order to mentally organize the incoming data and thus respond appropriately. Something which is new or unique stands out and attracts our attention, but anything which is familiar will be catagorized in accordance with previous perceptions of the same or similar situations or people. As with Figures 1.2 and 1.3 we will identify and perceive the primary shape first and then look for the detail to substantiate our initial perception (primacy effect).

Thus, by default we can misperceive the situation or the person, just as we assumed the injured boy's father was the surgeon because we assumed a surgeon would also be a man and not a woman.

Exercise

In the light of what we already know about social perception what key functions of people management could be affected by the process?

Feedback

● Recruitment and selection, particularly interviews.
● Performance appraisal or pay review interviews and decisions – for example, the most recent behaviour which the appraiser has observed will taint the objectivity of the appraisal interview (recency effect).
● Disciplinary or grievance interviews and decisions.
● Equal opportunities and discrimination.
● Training and development, for example about roles and levels of trainability of trainees.

1.1.2 The influences on the individual's social perception

These can be summarized in Figure 1.5. The importance of cultural differences and upbringing can be demonstrated in the Muller–Lyer illusion (Figure 1.6). Segall *et al*[4] showed that those brought up in a 'Western' culture perceived the top line to be shorter than the bottom one, but those such as African tribespeople whose culture was not rich in straight lines and right-angles saw the two lines to be equal in length.

1.1.3 Stereotyping

The most powerful influence which social perception can have in the workplace is through our inclination to stereotype others. The perceptual framework that we establish as we mature is used as a benchmark against which we evaluate everything else. According to

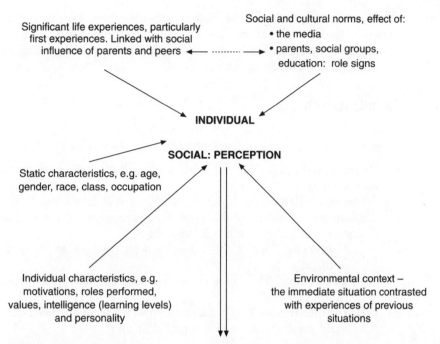

Figure 1.5. The individual's perceptual framework by which all other persons and situations will be judged.

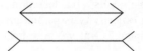

Figure 1.6. The Muller–Lyer illusion.

Taguiri[5] stereotyping is 'the general inclination to place a person in categories according to some easily and quickly identifiable characteristics such as age, sex, ethnic membership and then to attribute to them qualities believed to be typical of members of that category'.

Our perceptions lead us towards creating stereotypical images that we find psychologically comfortable. By this process we can easily over- or underestimate individual and intergroup differences. Clues will be looked for in the person(s) with whom we are in contact to see if they conform to our own frame of reference. These can be typified as 'role signs', and can include colour of skin, gender, age, accent as well as colour of hair, style of attire, facial hair, school background or height and size. Some role signs we may interpret negatively, others positively, but psychologically we will place the person in a 'pigeon hole'. The greater the conformity to our own frame of reference, the greater the likelihood that we will identify with that person favourably. The opposite is also true and we may attribute to that person a whole personality because he or she fits the frame of reference of someone from the past who looked similar. Research shows that poorly prepared interviewers can decide in less than 4 minutes on the acceptance or rejection of a candidate by comparing them to his or her frame of reference of the ideal candidate. The MD in our opening case study seems to have fallen into the same trap. Selective perception is linked to Thorndike's (1913) identification of the 'halo' and 'horns' effect. Small pieces of information of either a positive (halo) or negative (horns) nature can determine whether or not we identify with that individual. Combined with our attitudes this can lead to holding a prejudice and subsequently unlawfully and unfairly discriminating against someone (see Section 1.2.4 and Chapter 11).

1.1.4   Attribution theory

Essentially this is concerned with our search for rules to explain behaviour. Heider (1944) suggests that there are two types of attribution: dispositional and situational.

● **Dispositional attribution:** Here we attribute behaviour to the personal make-up of the individual, whereas
● **Situational attribution:** Is where behaviour will be attributed to external factors. To illustrate the usefulness of this process for managers the three categories of attribution evaluation must also be taken into account:
  (i)   **Consensus:** This is the extent to which people in the same situation behave identically.
  (ii) **Consistency:** This is the extent to which the individual behaves in the same way over a period of time.
  (iii) **Distinctiveness:** This is the extent to which the individual behaves in the same way in different situations over a period of time.

Summary

In this section we have introduced the important concept of social perception – a psychological process influenced by social learning and upbringing which accounts for why human beings see each other in the way they do. Not only does this help explain subsequent human behaviour, it raises questions about avoiding inappropriate or inaccurate perception of others and equipping ourselves with the skills and techniques to overcome the subjectivity involved. The task to ensure that objectivity is paramount in human relations is the subject of the issues discussed in Chapter 3. But we now turn to other individual differences that also affect human behaviour.

Exercise

Read the following scenario and decide whether the manager would attribute A's behaviour to disposition or the situation:

● **Scenario 1:** Employee A is late for work in the morning, but all other employees have good timekeeping (low consensus). A is regularly late for work nearly every morning (high consistency). A is also late returning from lunch and for internal meetings (low distinctiveness).

Feedback

It would be reasonable to attribute this behaviour to A's disposition, about which the manager can take remedial action to solve the problem.

1.2   Personality

Objectives

In this section you will:

● Examine the various theories of personality
● Identify the applications of personality measurement through questionnaires and
● Identify the characteristics of personality questionnaires

1.2.1   Introduction

Personality is the dynamic organization within the individual of those psycho-physical systems that determine his unique adjustments to his environment.[6]

This definition summarizes the complex interaction of beliefs, thoughts and behaviour that typify how individuals are perceived by others and by themselves. The individual's behaviour can then be classified according to style, such as 'outgoing' or 'inward looking'. Our personality as the learned Professor Hans Eysenck[7] has noted, is unique to each one of us, and when combined with other attributes such as intelligence leads to measurable performance in work. The key reason for studying personality is that if one accepts it can be defined and measured, then employee personality, the organization and jobs can be matched to acquire a perfect 'fit'.

Indeed, personality can determine good or bad work performance, including the critical ability to work successfully alongside and with other people. With the growth of teamwork, changing work pressures and systems, workplace stress, and the importance of leadership, the personality of managers is of concern to employers.

Our difficulty is that a great deal of contention exists about the nature of personality and ways in which it can be evaluated. Most people use adjectives to describe personality according to stereotypical traits, such as 'lazy', 'fastidious', 'cheerful' and so on. We tend to 'cluster' aspects of a personality by referring to an easily identifiable pattern or 'type' that depends on crude physical, racial as well as behavioural characteristics, such as 'women with blonde hair are dumb', 'fat people are jolly', 'foreigners are untrustworthy', and so on.

1.2.2   Development of personality

Most accept that personality is formed by a combination of what is inherited (origins in 'nature'), and environment, upbringing and social experiences (origins in nurture):

- **Nature:** Heredity (genetic inheritance): Determines physical characteristics, special abilities (intelligence) and emotional reactivity
- **Nurture:** Environmental: Exposure to unique family experiences, culture, e.g. gender roles and societal role models, values, traumatic events
- **Maturation:** Socialization (peer groups, work colleagues and early adult experiences)

1.2.3   Theories of personality

Theories of personality can be divided into two main approaches.

Idiographic (individualistic)

This involves studying each person in their own right and the ways in which they function. Idiographic literally means self-report. Vernon has termed these intuitive or subjective theories because they involve compiling a profile of the individual, which records their individual traits. Personality, as well as being an inherited function, is also one derived from the way people are treated. Through this social process we develop an understanding about ourselves. The theme of the 'looking-glass self' was developed by G. H. Mead.[8] For example, if our behaviour stimulates a response of dislike, fear and distrust this may be the desired response and we will enhance our personality traits that reinforce this behaviour. Also, the opposite would be true.

In the same category as idiographic is the humanistic theory of personality. This emphasizes the positive nature of 'human beings' and 'self-actualization', proponents being

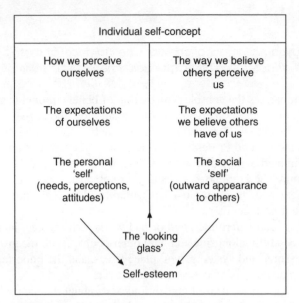

Figure 1.7. Roger's theory of self-concept.

Abraham Maslow and Carl Rogers. The latter developed the 'self-theory' derived from client-centred therapy (Figure 1.7). It is constructed by:

- **Self:** A person evaluates every experience in relation to his or her self-concept, and wants to behave in ways consistent with their self-image (that is, the image portrayed to others. Self-concepts include:
  - How we perceive ourselves including evaluations of the 'looking-glass self'
  - The image we feel others have of us (what people think of us) and what we believe others expect of us
  - How we expect to be seen
  - Actual experiences (interactions with others with whom we identify).
- **Self-esteem:** The degree to which we like or dislike ourselves.
- **Ideal self:** What the individual would like to be.

The closer the ideal self is to the real self, the more fulfilled is the individual. Peoples' innate motivation towards personal growth and happiness is the rationale for Rogers' theory. The individual can come to terms with their true self and the expectations of others. The difficulty in applying this theory to work environments is that exercising one's own preferred personal characteristics to obtain a personally harmonious self-concept is seldom, if ever, permitted in work organizations, where behaviour is closely prescribed. Indeed, one of the themes of this book is that the workplace and work systems closely control the individual to specified norms of behaviour.

Nomothetic (law giving)

By this approach human personality can be ordered into patterns to allow comparison with those of others. Vernon calls them 'inferential theories' because through scientific, objective analysis inferences can be made about personality and ordered into traits using factor analysis. Personality probably has an hereditary basis and can be determined by stable characteristics.

The most widely accepted theory is that based on personality traits. There is an assumption that personality can be described by a number of continuous dimensions or scales, each representing a trait, such as 'emotional stability', 'aggressiveness', or 'creativity'. A trait refers to any observable human characteristic in which one individual differs from another in a relatively permanent and characteristic way. The factor analysis is used to determine basic traits and determine ways of measuring them.

The so-called 'father' of the modern study of personality is Hans Eysenck, who developed a 'hierarchical' approach to the subject, which can be summarized in Figure 1.8.

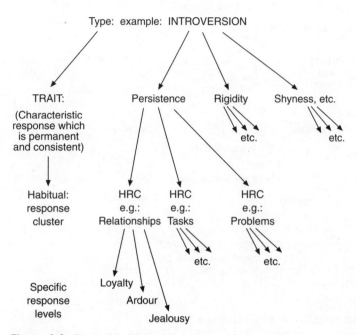

Figure 1.8. Eysenck's hierarchical theory of personality.

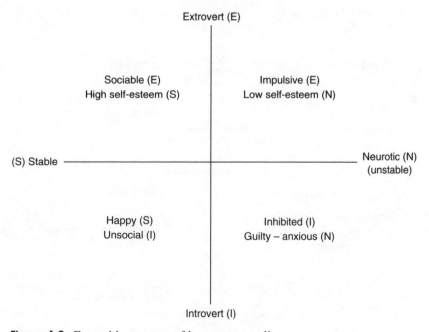

Figure 1.9. Eysenck's structure of human personality.

Personality types separate into two dimensions:

- **extrovertism** (outgoing)–**introvertism** (reserved and inward-looking), and
- **neuroticism** (instability)–**stability** (easy with people and adaptable)

There is interdependence between these dimensions so that in reality it will be difficult to find someone who is wholly an extrovert, for example.

Traits of the extrovert

Expressiveness/openness   Practicality

Activity and energy   Risk taking

Extrovert ← Identification

Impulsiveness   Sociability

Irresponsibility

Traits of the introvert

Inactivity   Carefulness

Inhibition   Control

Introvert ← Rigidity

Unsociability prefers own company or of a few people   Responsibility

Reflectiveness/thinker

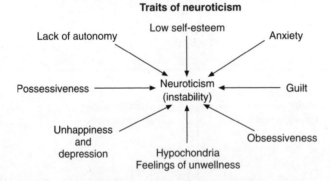

Traits of neuroticism

Lack of autonomy   Low self-esteem   Anxiety

Possessiveness ——— Neuroticism (instability) ← Guilt

Unhappiness and depression   Obsessiveness

Hypochondria Feelings of unwellness

Traits of emotional stability

Good self-esteem   Calm/resilient

Capable of autonomy   Freedom from guilt/anxiety

Stability

Happiness   Casualness/adaptability

Sense of health/wellbeing

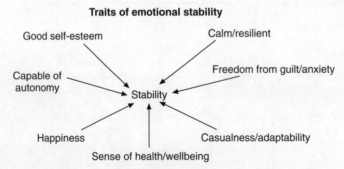

Figure 1.10. Clusters of personality traits (Eysenck, after C. J. Jung).

You will see from Figures 1.8 and 1.9 that personality traits tend to 'cluster' together normally in a compatible way. For example, someone who is impulsive is also likely to be sociable and enjoy taking risks. It is unlikely that the controlled, inhibited person will also like the continuous company of people. These clusters are shown in Figure 1.10.

1.2.4   Measuring personality

The first point to make is that the methods should not be described as 'tests' because a test implies a right or a wrong answer. Individual personality is unique and each of us will have our own personality profile; it may be inappropriate for a particular organization or type of work, but that is not saying it is 'wrong'. For this reason the term 'questionnaire' should be used.

Two principal methods of profiling personality can be employed:

- **Rating scales** based on observable behaviour by a rater, but subject to over-generalizations, subjectivity and bias.
- **Personality inventories.** These are very widely used in employee selection and development. They require the 'subject' to answer a series of related questions which are designed to generate a spontaneous response which truly reflects preferences for behaviour in a number of given scenarios. The profile of each 'subject' can be compared with all others. For this reason completion of this 'paper and pencil' questionnaire must be within a strict timetable and under controlled conditions. The results, once collated and evaluated, can be scored to give a profile of personality traits, and thus enable a prospective employer to typify the personality of the subject. Many are based on the work of Eysenck and more recently Cattell, who identified sixteen and twenty-one personality factors (traits). Cattell distinguished between:
  (i)   Source traits – which are at the root of observed behaviour, and
  (ii) Surface traits – which are superficial and detectable patterns of behaviour having their origins in source traits.

Look at Figure 1.10. Neuroticism as defined by Eysenck would be a surface trait for Cattell, and the qualities which make neuroticism (e.g. emotional instability, terseness, timidity, etc.) would be source traits. However, not all of Cattell's sixteen factors 'compress' to give 'E' and 'N' dimensions.

Exercise	Judge for yourself whether you are an introvert or extrovert. Answer 'yes' or 'no' to the questions in Figure 1.11. Work quickly, do not hesitate in answering and be honest!

Feedback	Answering 'yes' to the following questions: 1, 2, 4, 5, 6, 7, 10, 11, 12, 17, 19, 20, 21, 22 and 23

indicates that you are more extrovert than introvert. Answering 'yes' to the following questions:

3, 8, 9, 13, 14, 15, 16, 18

indicates you are more introvert than extrovert. The position is reversed if you answered 'no' to any of these questions.

Similar questionnaires include the extensively used and popular battery of methods used by the consultancy Saville and Holdsworth, the Personal Style Inventory used for competency-based selection and development produced by Hogan and Champagne (1979),

		Yes	No	
1	Do you long for excitement?			
2	Are you usually carefree?			
3	Do you stop and think things over before doing anything?			
4	Do you generally do and say things quickly without stopping to think?			
5	Would you do almost anything for a bet?			
6	Do you do things on the spur of the moment?			
7	Do you like going out a lot?			
8	Generally do you prefer reading to meeting people?			
9	Do you prefer to have a few but special friends?			
10	When people shout at you, do you shout back?			
11	Can you usually let yourself go, and enjoy yourself at a lively party?			
12	Do other people think of you as being lively?			
13	Are you mostly quiet when you are with other people?			
14	If there is something you want to know about would you rather look it up in a book than talk to someone about it?			
15	Do you like the kind of work that requires attention to detail?			
16	Do you hate being with a crowd who play jokes on one another?			
17	Do you like doing things in which you have to act quickly?			
18	Are you slow and unhurried in the way you move?			
19	Do you like talking to people so much that you never miss a chance of talking to a stranger?			
20	Would you be very unhappy if you could not see lots of people most of the time?			
21	Would you say that you were fairly self-confident?			
22	Can you easily get some life into a rather dull party?			
23	Do you like playing jokes on others?			

Figure 1.11. Personality type exercise – introvert or extrovert?

and the Myers–Briggs Type Indicator widely used in the USA. The dimensions used in the latter are:

Extrovert – Introvert (E or I)
Sensing or Intuitive (S or N)
Thinking or Feeling (T or F)
Perceiving or Judging (P or J)

The results are collated into sixteen personality types. For example, ISTP would indicate the individual is a careful, logical thinker, who can successfully apply this to real-life situations, but may over concentrate on one thing at a time.

1.2.5   Personality theory applied to people management

The ability to predict how an individual will respond to a whole range of situations in the workplace is a powerful resource and it is hardly surprising that employers have put so much effort (and trust) in techniques to profile personality and subsequent behaviours. Some of these behaviours will be long-term in their effect such as leadership, management of employees, dealing with customers, generating ideas or handling stress. The latter is explored in Section 2.4, particularly the notion of stress-prone personalities (types A or B). Others will be of short-term importance, e.g. can they handle an emergency or a crisis?

The growth of management systems which emphasize commitment, loyalty, teamwork and quality (such as human resource management) require a personality 'fit' with job, fellow-workers and organizational systems. This is particularly important where the employer is constructing a strong culture that requires conformity to certain patterns of values, beliefs and behaviour.

The nomothetic approach to typifying personality naturally appeals to employers because it emphasizes the relative stability and possible measurement of personality. There would be little point in evaluating someone's personality if it were constantly changing.

Specific applications of personality to work situations

- **Health and safety:** The Health and Safety Executive has reported that personality traits are connected with workplace accidents.[9] Extroverts who are too confident are just as equally likely to cause accidents as are neurotics who are indecisive and can make unintentional errors. The emphasis should be on carefully selecting the individual to the risk situation. For example, in one situation strict adherence to the rules may be the safest approach, but in other situations a flexible approach could be the best.
- **Authoritarianism:** This person is likely to have personality traits that include deference to others in authority, intellectual rigidity, exploitative and superior behaviour to 'subordinates'. Inflexibility is another likely trait as well as a strict adherence to orders. Clearly, the organization and work should match this type of person, but the risk is that coupled with other personality traits, such as inflexibility in the face of new ideas or knowledge (dogmatism) and certain attitudes can lead to bullying (see Section 1.4).
- **Risk propensity:** The greater the possession of a trait for taking risks, the greater will be this individual's enjoyment of working in a volatile environment requiring quick decision making. Clearly, this would suit some employers in financial dealing, selling, or entrepreneurial jobs, but not in those where careful adherence to details, rules and systems is necessary.
- **Working in teams:** Team role theory argues that people contribute to teams in two ways: they perform functional and team roles. The former relate to technical or specialist expertise, 'whereas team roles relate to the type of contribution that they can make to the internal workings of teams'.[10] These roles and Belbin's typology are fully discussed in Section 4.4. However, as Tony Manning in a report for ACAS shows, team role theory does not adequately provide a framework for individual personality. He has argued that the so-called 'Big Five' model of personality can provide that framework linked to the Belbin roles (see Section 4.4).
  - (i) **Extroverts** – Those involved in coordinating team activities, influencing and shaping the actions of team members, investigating resources for the team (if necessary with a network of connections) and the team worker who conscientiously ensures the functions of the team are completed.
  - (ii) **Tender or tough-minded** – Those who are tender-minded will be conscientious and anxious to have the team's work completed according to specification. Also, this is true of those who put ideas into practice. The tough-minded are better suited to being coordinators, shapers, innovators of ideas, resource investigators and those who monitor and evaluate performance of the team.
  - (iii) **Conscientiousness or spontaneous** – The conscientious worker will prefer structure and order and is best-suited to coordinating, implementing ideas, occupying a team worker role, and monitoring-evaluating.

(iv) **Anxiety or Stable** – The emotional nature of the anxious person means that he/she is suited to the role of the completer – finisher and team worker, and to some extent the resource investigator because of the desire to contribute and complete the work of the team. Stability translates into resilience in the face of pressure and for this reason the coordinator, shaper, resource investigator and, partly, the monitor-evaluator.

(v) **Openness – Closure to learning from new experiences** – The former is required in the coordinator, shaper, plant, resource investigator and monitor-evaluator.

All of the above are directly relevant to leadership types/styles, discussed in Section 3.3.

Summary

The assessment of personality has been systematically undertaken since the First World War when it was used to predict the behaviour of officers in the front line. The same rationale is behind employers' desire to profile the personality of job candidates today: Will the individual 'fit' and will their personality help or hinder them to provide high-quality, consistent performance? In this section we have examined the theoretical framework of human personality, covering definitions, theoretical approaches to categorization and measurement. We have also examined several personality-related issues for the selection, promotion and roles of individuals at work. It must be emphasized that despite massive research and evidence on the subject controversy still continues about the efficacy of measuring personality and the application of results to people management. Performance at work is the product of the individual's motivation, the quality of leadership and the type of work available, but also other individual factors such as intelligence and attitudes; also, preferences for learning discussed in Chapter 3.

1.3   Intelligence – attainment, abilities and aptitudes

Definition:

It seems to us that in intelligence there is a fundamental faculty, the alteration or the lack of which is of the utmost importance for practical life. This faculty is judgement, otherwise called good sense, practical sense, initiative, the faculty of adapting one's self to circumstances. To judge well, to comprehend well, to reason well, these are the essential activities of intelligence.

(Binet and Simon, 1905)

Section objectives

In this section you will:

● Explore the meaning of intelligence and the numerous controversies surrounding the subject
● Examine the meaning of human intelligence and
● Identify methods of intelligence testing in the workplace.

1.3.1   Introduction

Underlying these definitions is the acceptance that intelligence is a 'cognitive' faculty, that is, a function of the brain which permits individuals to think logically and rationally, to reason new solutions to new problems based on previous knowledge. However, at this point there remains disagreement about how intelligence can be catagorized or measured.

First, there is the practical difference between **attainment** and **ability**. The former can be measured fairly easily because it evaluates what someone can already do or that which they already know. Traditional educational exams are the common method to measure attainment. The difficulty for employers is whether someone with a body of knowledge or skill can apply it successfully in the workplace. This is proven application of that knowledge or skill. Practical and applied tests can be used to evaluate ability.

Second, a sharper difference exists between **ability** and **aptitudes**. The latter includes having the potential to learn, develop and apply skill/knowledge in the future. Tests have also been developed to measure this faculty, but have generated controversy for their theoretical basis and application, such as the eleven-plus test.

The third difference of opinion concerns the **nature of intelligence**. The view of Spearman (1904) was that all individuals possess a general intelligence factor ('g') in varying amounts. This enables a person to succeed at a wide variety of tasks, but which also includes some special abilities. Burt and Vernon (1950–1970) developed this notion by identifying a range of independent specific mental abilities (ISMA), such as:

Verbal abilities – comprehension
                 – writing
                 – articulation
                 – reasoning

A contrary view was developed by Thurstone (1938) who argued that intelligence *could* be broken down into a number of primary mental abilities (PMAs) such as:

- Spatial
- Perceptual speed
- Number facility
- Verbal comprehension
- Word fluency
- Memory
- Inductive reasoning.

However, further research has shown that there are links between these variables, giving some support for the notion of a general level of intelligence. Some, such as Gardner (1983), argue there is no such thing as one type of intelligence, but six, each dependent on one another:

- Linguistic
- Logical-mathematical
- Spatial
- Musical
- Bodily kinaesthetic
- Personal.

In Western society the first three tend to be highly valued, but Gardner suggests a broader view of intelligence would be beneficial.

Fourth, and the most controversial, is the **source of intelligence**. Is it inherited from parents (*nature*) or is it a product of our environment and upbringing (*nurture*)? Most academics now agree that some aspects of intelligence are inherited, but opinions differ on the relative contributions. Numerous studies have compared the intelligence of twins separated at birth, the effect of diet, emotional trauma and parental protection with varying results. Research does seem to show that an inclination towards leadership in adult life is connected with a disrupted or traumatic childhood, such as the death of a parent.

Finally, there is the disputed question over the existence of our **quotient of 'emotional intelligence'** (EQ) raised by Goleman.[11] The essence of EQ is that modern organizations are placing greater pressure on their managers to make the correct decisions and so emotions must not only adapt to the environment but also be used for organizational purposes. Crucially, the ability to think clearly to make the decisions is equally due to our cognitive skills as it is to our emotions. This concept links firmly with the competency framework discussed in Chapter 2. EQ can, therefore, be of greater importance to organizations than the 'hard' technical skills required in many jobs.

Emotions seem an unpredictable and nebulous source of decision making, but it is the focused ability to apply them that is the key. Human emotions are the source of individual initiative and creativity. Rather than acting as a counterweight to sound, rational judgements, leading neurosurgeons believe they can stimulate exact thinking and appropriate judgements. According to Goleman the main components of EQ are:

- Self-awareness
- Emotional management
- Self-motivation
- Empathy
- Managing relationships
- Communication skills
- Personal style of interaction with others.

These components are also assessed in the context of leadership in Chapter 3. Self-awareness and control, arguably, are the most important. Goleman argues that without these the ability to manage relationships is undermined. More recently, Goleman has refined the components listed above into four 'domains' each of which builds upon the former: self-awareness, self-management, social awareness and relationships management. These are key to understanding yourself *and* others to do what is appropriate in any given situation.

Dulewicz and Higgs[12] have demonstrated that evidence exists to support Goleman's contention. More importantly, perhaps, there are valid and reliable means of measuring EQ. The implications are profound for developing managerial competencies and leadership discussed in Chapters 2 and 3 respectively.

1.3.2   Intelligence tests

The requirements of an effective test are the same as those discussed for personality and are fully discussed in Section 3.2. The first and most commonly used is based on the work of Binet (1881) and Stanford and Terman (1986). Binet's original measurement was based on the proposition that a 'dull' child was like a 'normal' child except 'retarded' in mental growth, so in a comparative test the 'dull' child would perform like a 'normal' but younger child. A scale of mental age was constructed by comparing the child's mental age (MA) compared to the child's chronological age (CA). Terman's work produced an age-graded test. A child's mental age could be evaluated by examining the number of questions answered successfully at each age level. By this method an index of intelligence – the intelligence quotient (IQ) – could be established; so:

$$IQ = \frac{MA}{CA} \times 100 = \text{(an IQ of 90–110 would be a normal distribution score)}$$

Wechsler intelligence tests

This test is now extensively used for verbal reasoning and timed performance. Example questions are:

Verbal: Comprehension: 'What is the advantage of having a health and safety policy'?

Digit span: The numbers '7–5–6–3–9' are repeated backwards to test memory.

Performance: Picture completion: The missing part of an incomplete picture must be identified and named. This will test visual alertness.

Work sample tests

General intelligence tests can be used to evaluate reasoning, analytical ability, decision making, or specific abilities such as problem solving. Batteries of tests can be used to evaluate all aspects of intelligence, but the most commonly used in employee selection are the verbal reasoning and numerical ability tests. (Learning is examined in Chapter 3.)

Summary

In this section we have examined the unique differences between people's social perception frames of reference, intelligence and personality. By measuring and evaluating these functions of an individual's psychological makeup organizations can take steps to carefully select, manage, develop, and predict behaviours. As we will see from Section 4.4 this can be extended to managing people in groups, and in Chapter 3 we apply this knowledge to the construction of people management systems and techniques.

1.4   Attitudes

It's not the ability to do the job that counts, it's whether they've got the right attitude.

Supervisor in a car factory

Section objectives

In this section you will

- Examine the definition, formation and outcomes of attitudes
- Identify the link between attitudes and prejudice and discrimination
- Examine the process of attitude change and measurement and
- Identify some of the trends connecting attitudes and work.

1.4.1   Introduction

It is impossible to directly observe someone's attitudes, yet they play an increasingly critical part in the job selection, promotion and development processes. Employers enthusiastically seek job candidates who will have the 'right attitude' to the organization and the job. With the appropriate attitude, some will argue, they can be developed, nurtured and moulded into the ideal employee.

What is an attitude? It can be said to have a number of properties:

- It is a disposition towards other persons, inanimate objects or ideas or abstract concepts, that is, a mixture of **feelings, knowledge** and a predisposition to **behave** towards them if given the opportunity to do so.
- It is relatively permanent. As we will see, our attitudes are based on our individual value system; this is not something which can be changed easily but is rooted in the essential way we see the world around us.
- An attitude can be positive or negative, and we may attribute attitudes to other people. For example, employees who scrupulously take their allotted lunch break of one hour to the full may be perceived by their manager to have a 'negative attitude' to their work. Alternatively, the attitude of someone to those of the same political persuasion may be a positive one.
- Attitudes permit people to construct an orderly framework of recognition and behaviour based on the life-standards determined by their central values.

The first of these properties could be translated into three sequential statements:

'What I know' (or rather what I think I know) – that is, our cognitive beliefs, which are rational and logical to us, about someone or something.

$\downarrow$

'What I feel' – that is, my positive or negative feelings about someone or something (an affectation).

$\downarrow$

'How I will act' – predisposition to behave towards someone or something.

(Based on the work of Kelvin, 1970)

1.4.2   Formation of attitudes

There are two principal formative influences:

- **Explicit or social learning:** We have seen from Section 1.1 that the interaction we enjoy with others such as parents, siblings, adults, and teachers has enormous impact on us. Through their praise, acceptance or criticism and punishment (reinforcement) we learn which sets of behaviours and beliefs are to be adopted and those which should be rejected. As a way of adapting to this learning environment, children will copy and so identify with their parents' values and day-to-day behaviour. These values are general beliefs about our world and the standards by which we behave. Capital beliefs are those which are central to our behaviour, such as the existence of God, evil, sin, right and wrong, and so on. Parents who have positive or negative attitudes about certain types of people, for example those who are racist, are likely to pass on these same attitudes to their children. However, the effect of social learning and the process of maturation into adulthood may cause the child to rebel against these attitudes in later years.
- **Social influence:** From the association with others throughout our life we comply with or conform to prevailing attitudes. This is particularly true when we are subject to the influence of groups and at times of change. The strength of influence conveyed by placing someone in a group or team has been relied upon by a growing number of employers to nurture an identifiable team ethos, often associated with quality, collaborative work, commitment and loyalty to the organization. These values are compatible with employers who adopt human resource management (HRM) strategies. It is also manifest when employers are attempting structural or culture change. One of the most difficult outcomes to achieve is for employees to 'let go' from previous values and adopt new ones.

1.4.3   **Attitudes and prejudice**

Prejudice is a negative attitude towards individuals or groups because of one or more characteristics, such as colour of skin or accent. The prejudicial attitude will be formed on the basis of what the individual believes and feels about these people. It will lead to a predisposition to act towards them in a way that is consistent with the beliefs and feelings. However, we seldom have the power and the opportunity to put these prejudices into practice. When we do it will manifest itself as discrimination. **Discrimination** amounts to treating someone less favourably because of some characteristic such as sex, race, colour of skin, age, education, class, etc.

However, some will not put into practice what they believe for a number of reasons; normally these will be competing or stronger attitudes based on central values. For instance, a self-proclaimed male sexist may not discriminate against a woman because his value system determines that he must treat everybody in a decent and fair way.

PREJUDICE + POWER = DISCRIMINATION

The interaction of personality and attitudes in highly prejudiced people:

Work by Lewin (1945) and Adorno (1950) shows that people who are highly prejudiced towards groups of people identified by particular characteristics tend to have authoritarian personalities. Employers can predict the behaviours of this type of prospective employee through the use of personality questionnaires and attitude measurement (discussed later in this section). Figure 1.12 summarizes the psychological interactions and processes involved with this type of person.

For employers there are clear implications in evidence of bullying and harassment. The more introverted is the individual with the authoritarian personality and prejudiced attitude, the more likely it is that he or she can be conditioned to adopt the values of the dominant group. This can be witnessed in the behaviour of hooligans, fascist groups and political extremists. The most infamous historical figure to fit within the biographical details and process in Figure 1.12 is, of course, Adolf Hitler. (The strategies which employers can implement to deal with discrimination are discussed in Chapter 11.)

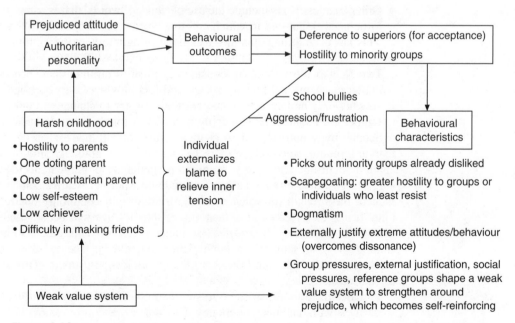

Figure 1.12. Psychological interactions and processes in the construction of values and attitudes.

1.4.4   Attitude change

People strive to maintain 'cognitive consistency', that is, a psychological balance between the three attitudinal elements: beliefs, feelings and actions, **and** between different attitudes. Where there is a conflict between these the individual will experience uncomfortable psychological tensions. There are two theoretical approaches to understanding these conflicts that can assist employers in managing attitude change.

As a means of changing attitudes **communication** can be successful, but only where it is **persuasive**. According to Osgood and Tannenbaum[13] the **congruity principle** is relevant where the person is exposed to persuasive communication. It is essential that **both** the source of the communication and the message itself are congruent with each other in order to be persuasive.

Exercise

Manager (A) has to convince employee (B) that a new system of work (C) must be introduced in order to speed up work outputs. B has a lot of respect for A, but is highly sceptical about C. What factors do you think would get B to take a more positive attitude towards C?

Feedback

- It is argued by researchers that the strongest attitude is likely to change the least, so B's positive attitude towards A must be capitalized upon.
- Source characteristics: Following on from the first point the credibility, attractiveness, trustworthiness and expertise of A will be important. (You will see from Section 3.1 that persuasion is a method of influence likely to work under expert and/or charismatic power.)
- If A's position or workload would appear to suffer as a result of C this would enhance A's argument and be more likely to convince B.
- It is for these reasons that individuals are more likely to be influenced by their peers with whom they identify.
- The characteristics of the message will be important. Where B does not believe in the message a two-sided argument, representing the advantages and disadvantages is more likely to induce attitude change.
- Other characteristics include the use of 'loaded' words, that is, a message, which appears to be neutral, but one in which emotive words are used to identify with the 'audience'. This has been a long-standing technique of agitators and revolutionary orators.[14]

Two final points should be considered. First, is attitude change necessary? For many workplace systems and policies to succeed it is only necessary for there to be compliance. It may not only be impractical and expensive to try to change attitudes, but also unethical to tamper with something so deeply part of someone's personal make-up.

Second, why not use fear to change someone's attitude? There is evidence that 'high fear' information can make a more lasting effect on attitudes. Traditionally, this has been applied to health and safety training, particularly to prevent accidents. But Festinger (1957) has shown that a change of attitude will not necessarily come about through fear. Indeed, the strength (or valence) of the training will commonly decline over a period of time. If it is then repeated too many times the message will become valueless. Festinger's theory of 'cognitive dissonance' is concerned with contradictory information, which challenges what someone believes (their cognition). The tension experienced by the individual will persist until there is a psychological adjustment. This tension is described as 'dissonance'.

The idea of 'bribing' smokers to stop is unlikely to change attitudes, but some will stop smoking at work and take the money. This type of response was observed by Festinger and Carlsmith[15] in college students asked to perform a very boring task. Dissonance theory predicts that cognitive dissonance will arise when a person is forced to behave in a certain way, but cannot justify the behaviour in terms of their own beliefs and feelings. The college students were paid $20 or $1 to tell other students waiting to perform the task that it was really interesting. Of course, quite the opposite was true. Festinger and Carlsmith found that the students who were paid $1 to lie rated the task themselves as interesting whereas the students who were paid $20 rated it as boring.

How can this be explained? Where there is sufficient external justification (e.g. $20), little dissonance is experienced and the person does not have to change their attitude. However, where the external justification is weak (e.g. $1) internal justification is sought to eliminate the dissonance caused by feeling the task is boring, but telling someone else quite the opposite. As Aronson (1969) has suggested, the value system of the person who is lying must be one whereby lying is an improper thing to do, otherwise no justification would be sought to behave in that way. Furthermore, as Brehm and Cohen[16] have shown, the person must be committed to that attitude otherwise dissonance is unlikely to occur.

1.4.5   Measuring attitudes

Surveying attitudes provides employers with useful information:

- What the workforce thinks and feels about its work, the workplace, the management style employed, the rewards offered and other key employee relations information.
- Information on the subsequent behaviour of employees in given situations.
- How the image and culture of the organization is seen by the workforce.
- The types of issues that would be important to employees when managing change.

There are a number of ways to measure attitudes: Structured *self-reports* or *questionnaires* which can systematically assess beliefs and assumptions are the most widely used methods. All staff surveys and opinion questionnaires are a form of attitude measurement, but some are anchored against a scale of measurement, such as the Thurstone Scales, the Likert Scales and the Semantic Differential Scales. All self-reporting is time-consuming and potentially expensive. As with all measurement techniques, there is room for sampling error, low response levels, misleading questions, a poor range of questions to sample different attitudes, and inaccurate analysis and classification of results.

1.4.6   Attitudes and work

No, the office is one thing, and behind me, and when I come home . . . I leave the office behind me . . .'

Wemmick, clerk to Mr Jaggers, in conversation with Pip,
from Charles Dickens' *Great Expectations*

Many surveys and commentators inform us that attitudes to work are changing. European Commission-funded research conducted by the University of London in 1998 showed that people aged 18–30 have attitudes towards work which require reciprocal behaviour by employers.[17] The changing nature of work, flexibility, temporary careers, the risk of redundancy and the long working-hours culture of the UK are all factors that concern the younger worker. If employers want flexibility and high performance, then workers want flexible hours to accommodate their lives outside work and commensurate rewards too. Indeed, another survey in 2002 into the state of the psychological contract also showed younger workers want employers to provide training and development, career opportunities and skills enhancement rather than many years of personal stagnation.[18]

Many respondents to the University of London survey, dissatisfied with the reality or prospect of long hours, were not prepared to exclude all else in order to deliver performance in a job that could have a short lifespan. There now seems to be a broad acceptance of the decline of lifelong careers with one employer, but the subsequent insecurity and demands for peoples' needs to be reciprocally met by employers is a growing challenge.

However, it is important to remember that there is little evidence to show that employees' attitudes bear any relation to their productive output, as opposed to attention to detail, quality and behaviours. High producers are just as often dissatisfied with their working conditions as are low producers, particularly where financial gain is achieved based on volume, such as in piecework. Obviously, this 'instrumental' approach to work coupled with low morale can result in poor attendance, high turnover and industrial conflict, particularly when the labour market offers plentiful work. Several of these matters are discussed in the next chapter.

1.4.7   Attitudes, work and discrimination

Women

The traditional attitude of men to women in the workplace has subordinated women to a secondary role. The 'glass ceiling' discussed in Section 11.4 is the product of stereotypical views of women that they are less committed to the organization, will leave to have a family, can deal with pressure less successfully than men, and may actually threaten the dominant position of men in the organizational hierarchy. In addition, there is a tendency in some men to view women in a sexist light, and this can have damaging implications for harassment. Traditionally, women have been segregated into lower-paid jobs with poorer career structures. The increase in flexible working discussed in Chapter 2 has partly encouraged this trend by making part-time and temporary working more common. It has also enabled many women to balance the conflicting roles of employee and child rearer/homemaker.

Finally, it is important to remember that evidence exists to show that in professional and managerial positions some women are very defensive of having obtained these jobs in the face of competition from men and, therefore do not encourage or promote other women to similar positions.

People with disabilities

Everybody has a disability in the sense that we have certain functions or tasks that we cannot perform through lack of bodily function, skill, knowledge and/or opportunity. However, as we discuss in Sections 11.4 and 12.13, 'disability' has a common legal meaning in the light of legislation passed to promote equal opportunities and prevent discrimination in respect of people with specified 'medical' disabilities. After the Second World War the 'normalization' of the disabled into fully productive roles in society became accepted, but occupational and societal segregation has remained a reality for many with both physical and mental impairments. In our discussion of the term 'intelligence' the word ability is used to denote the function to develop and apply new skills or knowledge. The risk in using the word 'disability' or 'disabled' is that negative assumptions can be made about those for whom these words would normally apply. People's traditional social perceptions and attitudes are a strong source of irrational prejudice and discrimination. Even where seriously physically disabled persons may at one time have been excluded from the labour market the changing nature of the workplace, technology, home working and aids for the disabled mean that full integration *should* now be enjoyed.

People from ethnic minorities

The definitions used when discussing black people or those from ethnic groups remains both wide and controversial. The labour market and legal issues are discussed in Chapters 8 and 12 respectively. What is an undisputed fact is that black people (to use a generic term) suffer discrimination in society because of the prejudices and the discrimination of those in positions of power in the workplace. As we have examined earlier in this section, the stereotypical perceptions of and attitudes towards black people is often based on misinformation and negative attitudes held by people who will often reject dissonant information to the contrary.

Age

While the number of people aged between 50 and 65 years in work has risen in recent years, a significant proportion of those in this age group are excluded from the labour market, particularly once they have been made redundant. There seems to be no logical reason for this exclusion other than social attitudes that discriminate against older persons, and a convenient means of short-listing job candidates. Studies have shown that older workers are more likely to show stronger commitment to work than younger workers, and have a lower incidence of absences and turnover. Indeed, many employers recognize that older workers can be more knowledgeable, experienced and reliable with good interpersonal skills, but there is a general perception that they are less adaptable and willing to work inconvenient hours.[19]

Exercise

You have the task of introducing a no-smoking policy into a company that has many employees who smoke cigarettes throughout the day. Several have been smoking for several years. The company is keen to encourage a healthier lifestyle in its workforce and would like you to try to change attitudes towards smoking. You will also consider simply imposing a ban in the offices (but not in other parts of the workplace) and disciplining those who break it. As an inducement you will offer a £50 bonus to those who can stop smoking at work. How would the theory of cognitive dissonance apply to your plan of action?

Feedback

Naturally, you will try persuasive communication using the techniques described earlier in this section. But you will also attempt to 'educate and inform' the workforce using some methods which will induce a high fear factor about smoking. On its own this is only likely to have part-success. Persuasive communication must also be used. It will be necessary to first measure the type and strength of employee attitudes. Thereafter, the attitude change must be tackled in an integrated way, with reinforcement carried out over several months. The reasons are shown in Figure 1.13.

Summary

Understanding the importance and elements of peoples' attitudes at work will heighten management's ability to construct appropriate employment strategies and practices. It will also inform employers about the boundaries of change that can be extended. To obtain true employee commitment and loyalty in organizations buffeted by volatile markets and intense competition requires change management that can convince people to adapt, and if necessary to change attitudes. In this section we have examined those elements of attitudes and attitude change which employers should understand in order to achieve such an objective.

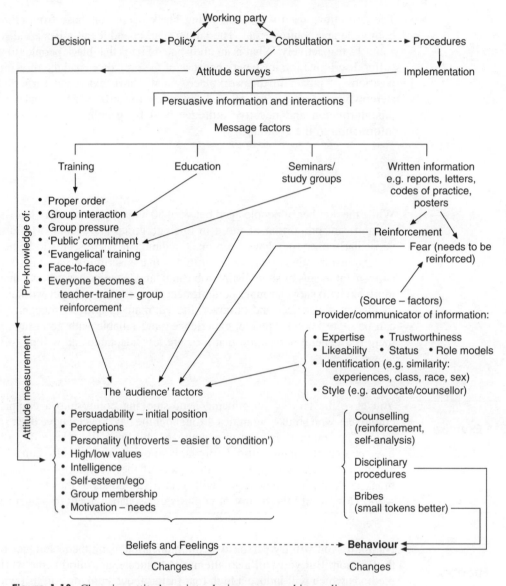

Figure 1.13. Changing attitudes – introducing a no-smoking policy.

Case
study

Twenty-First Century Communications

You are the newly appointed personnel manager for the company ('21CC'). You have been asked to address three unrelated problems:

1 The rising number of complaints of sexual harassment including some bullying, some of which have resulted in losing cases of sex discrimination at the employment tribunal.

2 The drawing-up of a systematic recruitment and selection process with full training for those involved. Currently, no managers involved in selection have been trained and do not have to follow any company procedures when interviewing.

3 The complaints from managers that the quality of all trainees is so poor that they have to correct almost every piece of work. Appraisal results are poor. The managers want extra training for all new entrants in this grade and disciplinary action taken against those who 'fail to come up to scratch'. In conversations with supervisors you hear the same story along the lines: 'Most people in this company don't have the right attitude'.

You do not believe these three problems are unrelated, but are all linked to four aspects of human behaviour: social perception, personality, intelligence and attitudes.

Task:
Under each one of these sub-headings list the issues or points which need to be addressed.

1 Social Perception

Feedback

- The harassment of female employees may be linked to stereotypical views of male employees about females.
- Perhaps women are segregated into specific roles in the company which reinforces stereotypes.
- The lack of recruitment and selection systems and methods is probably resulting in interviewers applying their own frames of reference to job candidates resulting in stereotyping.
- This in turn may result in the appointment of managers with sexist views and unsuitable trainees, but who conform to the 'halo' effect at the point of selection.
- It is also possible that the 'horns' effect is operating because managers state that the work of 'all' trainees is unsatisfactory, and that every piece of work requires remedial work. Is this really true?

2 Personality

- The personality of some managers involved in the harassment could be authoritarian.
- They could also be dogmatic in type, meaning they will not be open to new ideas about the dignity of all employees irrespective of sex.
- Personality should be a factor of selection. The use of personality questionnaires should be considered as an integral part of the new selection system.

3 Intelligence

- The new selection process requires the use of some form of intelligence test which is directly relevant to the work involved, such as a verbal or numerical reasoning test.
- Tests for trainability and potential should be considered as well as attainment.

4 Attitudes

- The attitudes of managers, supervisors and other employees with staff responsibilities towards bullying and harassment needs to be assessed and monitored. Attitudes surveys can be used and training specifically targeted towards attitude change over a period of time. Carefully applied methods to overcome dissonance must be used.

- An attitudinal profile of high-performing, conscientious employees should be prepared and used as the benchmark for recruiting and selecting new staff. The company needs employees with the appropriate attitude towards quality and high performance. This should link with the action taken under points 1–3.
- Unacceptable behaviour and conduct specified in the company's disciplinary procedures should include that which could be manifest through the spoken word as well as actions. The behaviour of employees must conform to acceptable standards. Supervisors should be given training in selecting, leading and changing the behaviour of employees. (These issues are dealt with in Chapter 3.)

In brief

As we pointed out at the beginning of this chapter, individual behaviour is complex, unique in sources and pattern to the individual, and therefore difficult to predict. However, understanding the individual differences that comprise human behaviour is a highly useful resource for the people manager. Without that knowledge he or she cannot hope to begin to understand why workers will behave in the way they do. More importantly, though, managers can use a variety of methods and techniques to observe, measure, evaluate and monitor different aspects of behaviour such as personality, intelligence or attitudes. A battery of methods is now available for use in selection, promotion, training and advancement. This knowledge base can only be effectively used in the context of the broad organizational context of work, the way it is organised and its meaning for individuals. It is to these issues that we next turn.

Examination questions for this chapter are given in Appendix 2.

References

1 McCormick, E. J. and Tiffin, J. (1974) *Industrial Psychology.* George Allen and Unwin Ltd.
2 Schein, E. H. (1980) *Organizational Psychology.* Prentice Hall.
3 Hofstadter, D. R. (1982) *Metamagical Themas.* Basic Books (Perseus).
4 Segall, M. H., Campbell, D. T. and Herskovits, M. J. (1966) *The Influence of Culture on Visual Perception.* Bobbs Merrill.
5 Taguiri, R. (1958) Social preference and its perception. In *Person, Perception and Interpersonal Behaviour* (eds Taguiri, R. and Petrullo, L.). Stanford University Press.
6 Allport, G. W. (1937) *Personality.* Holt.
7 Eynseck, H. (1990) In Foreword to Furnham, A., *Personality at Work – The role of individual differences in the workplace.* Routledge.
8 Mead, G. H. (1934) *Mind, Self and Society.* University of Chicago Press.
9 Health and Safety Executive (1998) *In Health and Safety.* September 1998.
10 Manning, A. (1999) Teamwork, team roles and personality. *ACAS Abstracts.*
11 Goleman, D. (1996) *Emotional Intelligence – Why it can matter more than IQ.* Bloomsbury Publishing; and Goleman, D., Boyakzis, R. and Mckee, A. (2002) *The New Leaders: Transforming the Art of Leadership into the the Science of Results.* Little, Brown.
12 Dulewicz, V. and Higgs, M. (1998) Soul researching – emotional intelligence. *People Management,* 1 October, 42–45.
13 Osgood, C. E. and Tannebaum, P. H. (1955) The principle of congruity in the prediction of attitude change. *Psychological Review* **62**, 42–55.
14 Hovland, C. I., Janis, I. L. and Kelley, H. H. (1953) *Communication and Persuasion.* Yale University Press.
15 Festinger, L. and Carlsmith, J. M. (1959) Cognitive consequences of forced compliance. *Journal of Abnormal and Social Psychology* **58**, 303–310.
16 Brehm, J. W. and Cohen, A. R. (1962) *Explorations in Cognitive Dissonance.* Wiley.
17 Lewis, S. *et al.* (1998) *Futures on Hold.* University of London Institute of Education survey for European Commission.

18 Industrial Relations Services – Employment Review 757, *Employment Trends*. 5 August 2002.
19 Kodz, J., Kersley, B. and Bates, P. (1999) *The Fifties Revival*. Institute of Employment Rights Report 359.

Further reading

Greenfield, A. (1997) *The Human Brain*. Weidenfeld and Nicolson.
Kolb, D. A., Rubin, I. M. and Osland, J. (1991) *Organizational Behaviour – An Experiential Approach*. Prentice Hall.
Luthans, F. (1995) *Organizational Behaviour*. McGraw-Hill.
Thomson, R. and Thomson, A. (2002) *Managing People*. Butterworth-Heinemann.

Web-site addresses

British Psychological Society: http://www.bps.org.uk/index.cfm
Chartered Institute of Personnel and Development: http://www.cipd.org.uk
Eurolink Age: http://www.eurolinkage.org
Office for National Statistics: http://www.ons.gov.uk
Policy Studies Institute: http://www.psi.org.uk

2 People at work

My father-in-law worked as a coachbuilder for London Transport; he rose at 6 am for 40 years. He never had leave during his children's or grandchildren's infancy, he never had a sabbatical, nor was he offered flexi-time. He enjoyed just eight years of full-time leisure before dying.

Into the next century it may become rare to work full-time for a business for as long as 10 years. If the revolution in the workplace does happen . . . people (will) have a series of different working arrangements depending on their age and circumstance.

The key word used again and again is flexibility. Firms looking for loyalty from valued staff must be prepared to allow a much more flexible approach to styles of working.

(Hilaire Gomer, Flexible revolution focuses on workplace as means to an end.
The Sunday Telegraph, 24 January 1999, p. A3)

Chapter objectives

In this chapter you will:

- Obtain an understanding of how the world of work has been undergoing a rapid transformation involving flexible patterns, systems and methods
- Examine the meaning of the 'psychological contract' and the implications of the changes to it
- Identify the importance of integrating added value to services and products, quality systems, and competencies for the management of people
- Examine the importance of identifying and removing workplace stress and
- Relate these issues to the successful management of people.

Chapter introduction

Case study

Occ-shift

In 1987 a new management consultancy offering a broad range of services called Occ-Shift was set up. The name of the company was supposed to reflect the change in occupational patterns away from 'permanent' careers with one or two employers, and a five-day working week 9 a.m. to 5 p.m. According to the company's marketing information, work was undergoing a revolution to 7-day, 24-four hour operations, with short assignments with different employers, based on the individual's marketability (skills, knowledge, expertise). Motivation could be maintained through challenging work and attractive pay and benefits.

In 1992 with the recession in the UK in full swing Occ-Shift embarked on a sporadic programme of 'downsizing'. By 1995 over 30 per cent of the workforce had gone, most of them made compulsorily redundant.

From 1993 onwards the relative profits of Occ-Shift remained stubbornly weak. Its reputation for quality started to suffer. But with the economy picking up, staff turnover increased. A new managing director decided to survey staff feelings. What he found shocked him. Over 70 per cent of the 'survivors' (as one manager described the workforce) now distrusted senior management and were fearful of losing their jobs and, therefore did not take risks in case they went wrong and were placed on the list for the next round of redundancies. Furthermore, they felt powerless in the face of annual 'cuts' and that the company had failed to deliver their part of the implicit agreement that hard work and loyalty would be rewarded with security of employment and fair pay and treatment. Fifty per cent of staff felt 'guilty' that they had survived the trauma of redundancy. A big impact on quality was the stress now experienced by most junior and middle management because of overwork.

With the 'aftershock' of 11 September 2001 producing a down-turn in Occ-Shift's business, the MD said he would not repeat the mistakes of 1992–95.

What had gone wrong?

The experience of Occ-Shift shows that the trend in the 1990s of organizations 'delayering' levels of management and generally 'downsizing' their workforce had caused lasting problems with their remaining workers. For many individuals their employer had ripped up the 'psychological contract' if not the legal employment contract. The 'survivors' were largely cynical and watchful of placing themselves in jeopardy of redundancy. Many had become demotivated by the experience. Their responses can be categorized as:

- Seeing the changes as an opportunity to prove themselves in an adverse situation and secure further rewards.
- Believing no risks should be taken to raise their profile in the organization. The 'ostrich sticking its head in the sand syndrome'.
- Fighting back – to 'punish' the employer for reneging on the psychological contract, for example by sabotaging work.
- Making amends for the withdrawal of the employer from the implicit agreement by which the employee will proportionately reduce their contribution.
- Leaving the employer by resigning, preferably moving to a competitor to 'punish' the employer.

The experience of Occ-Shift is not an uncommon one. Some of its general causes and solutions are discussed in this chapter.

2.1 The new employment relationship – the psychological contract

Section objectives

In this section you will:

- Understand the meaning of the term 'psychological contract', and its implication for the management of people at work
- Examine how the psychological contract has been undergoing a transformation in the context of the changing world of work

- Understand the definition 'work orientations' and their implications for the management of people at work and
- Identify the elements of the new psychological contract.

2.1.1   Introduction

It is a truism to state that the nature of work at the beginning of the new millennium continues to change. And yet many of the reasons why people work and what they look for once in employment remain unaltered. The relationship between worker and employer can be described not only in the sense of a legal contract but also in terms of a psychological one.[1] The psychological contract is a set of unwritten reciprocal obligations that exist between worker and employer that determine how they will behave towards each other. Since the beginning of the modern employment relationship in the early part of the twentieth century these obligations or expectations can be typified as hard work, trustworthiness and loyalty on the part of the individual, with fair terms and conditions, job security and fair treatment (including prospects of financial/career advancement) provided by the employer.[2]

The psychological contract is crucial in maintaining a managerial climate in which the organization can flourish.[3]

2.1.2   Work orientations – the meaning of work

A work orientation is a 'frame of reference' through which workers define the meaning of work. It will determine their levels of work satisfaction, a willingness to engage in conflict and cooperation with management; they are rooted in individual social experiences such as class, upbringing, social and physical environment and subsequent personal expectations. To understand how and why people behave the way they do at work we must evaluate the 'meaning' of work to them. In modern industrial society for many work is a source not only of money but also a significant part of their inner life. This contention has been significantly influenced by the work of Max Weber[4] who argued that capitalist society should be based on a rational, organized system of work, but not one where impersonal logic and bureaucratic rules should eliminate human inventiveness. Nevertheless, coupled with the Victorian emphasis on the religious and moral imperative of hard work the 'Protestant work ethic' has taken hold in industrial societies and still exerts a very strong influence today. Feelings of guilt, moral inadequacy and social exclusion accompany those who are unable to find work that matches their perceived social status. Occupation is a powerful label in terms of social prestige, irrespective of how intrinsically unpleasant the work may be to the jobholder.

2.1.3   Alienated labour

In 1844 Karl Marx first postulated his ideas that as society changed to place greater capital resources in the ownership of the few it removed from individual workers their traditional ability to control the work process, if not the product of their labour. Modern industrial systems determined both of these and according to Marx subordinated the worker as a dehumanized 'commodity of labour'. This economic perspective based on the wage relationship between worker and employer is linked to the undermining of work as a social process. As control of work is taken out of the hands of the individual so the work he or she performs becomes external to his or her self-perception; this results in a feeling of 'alienation' from him- or herself as work loses any intrinsic meaning.

Blauner[5] has identified four kinds of alienation:

- Powerlessness – No control over the work process
- Meaningless work – No sense of purpose in the performance of work
- Isolation – Lack of sense of belonging to any group or entity
- Self-estrangement – No sense of self-expression, e.g. skill, innovation or creativity

There exists a clear correlation between motivation and work orientations which are discussed later in this section. Earliest theories of motivation drew on developing patterns of work in industrialized centres of production. What Marx called an instrumental orientation towards work can be linked to economic (extrinsic) motivation, that is, a motivation to work simply to earn money to live. Henry Ford established the first large-scale industrialized production system at his Detroit plant in the USA. By 1918 it was employing up to 18 000 workers, including several welfare psychologists to counsel workers who had become 'alienated' by the unremitting moving assembly line. Ford was the first to fully adopt the ideas of F. W. Taylor[6] who advocated a 'scientific management' of people and capital resources. Taylor developed this by carefully observing work tasks and isolating the separate actions, which comprised the whole task performance. Having identified specific actions he could then set optimum times for the completion of each part of the task; this led to time and motion study, a practice taken up in 1919 by the Gilbreths who perfected models of work study. Taylor believed that approaching the organization and performance of work in a 'scientific' (i.e. a systematic and rational) way would not only increase efficiency and therefore production, but also the workers' capacity to maximize earnings. In practice, this led to the 'intensification' of work as more and more employers adopted a 'Taylorist' approach to factory work.

Workers were employed to complete short, simple but specific tasks which fitted into a mass production process. This 'specialization' of work seemed to confirm the worst predictions of Marx that workers would feel increasingly alienated by such pressures; unable to control their work volumes or to see how their small task fitted into the whole job, unable to communicate with co-workers, often deafened by the noise of the production line, and allowed only specific breaks for visits to the toilet or to eat and rest. Workers not only became increasingly alienated from themselves but were antagonistic to work and their employer. Thus, the scene was prepared for a century of industrial conflict between mass production employers and workers. (Conflict is examined in Section 6.2. Early management systems are also discussed in Section 4.1.)

It is easy in retrospect to condemn such relatively simplistic and dehumanizing aspects of work organization, but for decades they were seen as the best way to increase wealth. Today they continue to strongly influence modern workplaces and work systems.

Attempt the questions at the end of this section. They raise issues about the nature of work and attitudes towards it.

2.1.4 Worker orientations in the Fordist era

In 1956 Dubin[7] refined three types of orientation:

(i) **Instrumental:** Workers adopt a 'calculative' relationship with their employer whereby work is a means to an end. Money earned from work provides the means to support a meaningful way of life outside work that is treated as no more than a necessity. There is little or no identification with the work process or outputs. Industrial workers, particularly those in a 'Fordist' work environment, are most likely to adopt such an orientation. Arguably, many process work systems, such as mass retailing and call centres, have jobs with many 'Taylorist' and 'Fordist' characteristics.

(ii) **Bureaucratic:** With the rise of a salaried class of workers, so this type of orientation grew. Workers adopt a commitment to the employer who reciprocates with not only status, job security and protected income, but also a degree of involvement in the organization. Public sector workers have traditionally demonstrated this orientation with their ethos of service to the community, but since the 1980s various forces have undermined it.

(iii) **Solidaristic:** This orientation is based on the questionable definition of work as a group activity, with the emphasis on loyalty to the group rather than the maximization of extrinsic rewards. Examples are found in any small workplace or where small work teams operate. For many years, in sectors of the economy solidaristic orientations operated alongside instrumentality so that loyalty was collectively directed towards a trade union, but with the decline in union density in traditional industries this link has been broken. However, employers have capitalized on this fact; provided the values of the group are directed towards work achievement this can benefit the employer, who may seek to enhance this type of orientation and link it to a bureaucratic one so that team work and quality systems operate side by side.

Although the class and regional perspectives that informed Dubin's work have disappeared or have significantly altered, there remains proof that such orientations persist, albeit in an altered state. Goldthorpe[8] undertook one of the most influential studies in 1966 (and with Lockwood in 1968) resulting in the study: *The Affluent Worker*. The authors questioned whether car manufacturing employees were conditioned by the technology of their working environment in a way that 'liberated' them from the more unpleasant tasks associated with manufacturing jobs. Instead, they found that workers engaged in production systems organized along 'Taylorist' and 'Fordist' lines became alienated from their work, which induced tiredness, boredom and dissatisfaction. The principal orientation of these workers was an instrumental one. This was particularly true of the 1960s compared to earlier periods because consumer goods (such as washing machines, televisions, cars and foreign holidays) were becoming newly available to the 'working classes', and work was still 'a means to an end' to obtain them. There was more to enjoy **outside** work as the twentieth century came to a close, challenging employers to channel orientations away from a purely instrumental goal.

Even if we accept these categorizations of orientations as truly reflecting why people work and how they react to it, questions should be asked about a number of variables that can affect them; examples: cycles in the economy, life cycles (e.g. age and domestic responsibility), and changes in social norms and customs. Unemployment in the 1980s and 1990s can be strongly contrasted to the relatively high employment in the 1950s, 1960s and late 1990s. Although industrialized workers, particularly those semi-skilled or unskilled, have been affected more than any other group, the effects of globalization and economic and industrial restructuring have impacted on all groups in society. This has placed the traditional psychological contract under enormous strain and led to questions about a new orientation towards the meaning of work. You should also read Section 8.5 on globalization for a complete perspective.

2.1.5   Post-Fordism – the end of the psychological contract?

Numerous studies have been carried out since 1990 into the state of the psychological contract. Most have shown that job cuts and various strategies to reduce costs have left employees feeling distrustful of employers. Integral to employers' strategies in manufacturing has been 'lean' organizational structures and production systems, but in its broader application it has also come to imply 'mean'. By this we mean that through 'downsizing' and 'rightsizing' the organization is reduced to absolute minimum levels of resources, equipment and raw materials. In its wake has come reduced levels of supportive management, longer hours of work, and pressures on individuals which often go beyond the bounds of personal coping.

A study carried out in 2002 showed a sharp disparity between employers and employees in their perceptions of each other and low levels of employee trust. Whereas 73.3 per cent of senior HR managers said full trust between employers and employees could never be obtained, 45 per cent of employees said they did not fully trust their employer. Perhaps even more disturbingly, 60 per cent of employers admitted that truly they did not treat their workforces as their most important asset, mirrored by the 50 per cent of employees who believed their employer would dispense with their services once they were no longer useful. Evidence also supports the results of other surveys of employers that there are still strong age preferences in recruitment and that wholesale flexible and family-friendly work regimes are too costly and inconvenient to introduce.[9]

'UK employee apathy hits business profits'

by Ross Wigham

Personnel Today: Tuesday, 10 September 2002, page 11.

'Levels of commitment in the UK are significantly lower than in most of its global competitors and have a negative impact on profitability.

A new International Survey Research (ISR) report shows that fewer than six out of ten UK employees want to stay with their current employer or recommend it as a good place to work.

The research covered more than 360,000 staff from the world's top 10 economies.

Just 59 per cent of UK employees viewed their firm in a favourable light with only China (57 per cent) and Japan (50 per cent) having worse figures. Better performers included France: 67 per cent, USA: 67 per cent and Germany: 74 per cent.

The research also found that levels of staff commitment had a direct impact on the bottom line. Over three years of the study, profit margins among companies viewed favourably by staff rose by 20.6 per cent, but firms with less committed employees experienced a fall of 1.38 per cent.

Roger Maitland, deputy chairman of ISR said that the quality of leadership in an organization was vital to empower staff and make them feel more committed.

"Committed employees are more likely to stay with an organization, go the extra mile for the company and put maximum effort into their work."

Maitland blames poor leadership. He said: "Too often in the UK, the people at the bottom of an organisation are alienated from those at the top."

He added: "Employees see their leaders as lacking both intellectual capital and emotional intelligence."

2.1.6   A new psychological contract

Rose[10] and other writers have shown that while evidence for the existence of the work ethic in the UK has been overstated, arguments showing its decline are similarly exaggerated. It is much more likely that orientations to work are undergoing a change which reflect the nature of economic society. Standards of living have never been higher, yet since 1945 working hours (notwithstanding the introduction of the Working Time Regulations in 1998) have never been longer.

Identify the reasons why working hours and work pressures have been increasing for employees.

- Pressures from senior management for efficiency savings and improved productivity
- Tighter working deadlines
- Domestic and global competitive pressure
- A society increasingly operating on a 24-hour day, 7 days a week
- Staff absences and turnover
- Demands for high-quality standards from customers
- High regulatory standards and because
- Managerial and supervisory grades are committed to their work because of work culture and a need to meet financial commitments.

(From Kodz, Kersley and Strebber.[11])

A new breed of employee is emerging in a reaction to the ruthless cost-cutting measures of post-1980s businesses. As loyalty is no longer rewarded, individuals are taking charge of their own destinies and with the breakdown of the old employment relationships, 'Me plc' has become the latest catchword. But how will companies cope with the contract culture they have helped to create?

The changing nature of the psychological contract has raised three questions, the answers to which are only partly available:

- Will there be a continuing growth of flexible forms of work, e.g. self-employment and peripheral work?
- What are the implications for worker–employer relationships of the breakdown in the traditional psychological contract?
- What steps can employers take to reconstruct a new psychological contract?

The answer to the first question is partly answered by the 2002 Labour Force Survey.[12] This shows that in the last ten years full-time self-employment has fallen from 2.6 million to 2.5 million (total: 2.5 m workers). Part-time work has remained constant at 5.3 per cent of all workers (total: 7 m workers), although this is one area of the 'flexible workforce' which is projected to grow by 2 million jobs between now and 2010, and will be mainly filled by women. But, even here, the incidence of part-time working varies considerably across different sectors. Home-working and portfolio work (i.e. those with more than one principal source of income) has increased from 3 per cent to 5 per cent (total: 1.1 m workers). This must be placed in the context of a growing total labour force of 28.2 million workers, of which 93 per cent are permanent workers and 75 per cent are full-time.

These figures do not represent an arrest of the trend in outsourcing, contracting-out and peripheral work, but merely show the effects of the upturn in the economy from the mid-1990s onwards and an 'evolutionary change on the margins' of the workforce.[13] Indeed, the former probably accounts for the willingness of some to become self-employed. We should also take into account the growth in the public sector since the end of the 1990s. Predictions that unprecedented changes would occur in the labour market have, to date, proved false.

This could also be said of a new work paradigm; work and the workplace are evolving, but to state that there has been a wholesale transformation within the last 25 years is going too far. However, the current economic climate holds many dangers, and particularly since 2001 employers have been either laying-off employees or 'hoarding' them despite unfavourable economic conditions. In fact, it is the peripheral workers who have suffered as employers protect their core employees. This mirrors the theory of flexibility discussed in Section 2.3 below.

This leads us to the second question. The alleged rupture of the traditional psychological contract has been caused by longer-term strategic decisions impacting on ways of managing human resources. Three examples can be cited:

- Research shows workers in the City of London and Dublin believe there is 'no future development opportunities within the company they currently work for'. In addition, 'more than 60 per cent don't feel their skills are being used to the optimum within their current role ... the challenge for HR is in retaining "star" players in the current market ...'.[14]
- The Working Britain Survey shows that in 1992 61 per cent of older workers and women were '*completely*' or '*fairly*' satisfied with work, but in 2002 this had fallen to 48.6 per cent.[15]
- Reed Recruitment Group reports that in 2001–2002 45 per cent of 2800 workers, including professionals, surveyed said trust in their managers had fallen in the last year.[16]

What are the consequential effects? The Institute of Employment Studies cites the following:

- Increased employee absence and turnover
- Low employee morale, commitment and loyalty
- Lower productivity, performance and quality
- Greater risks of accidents
- Enhanced health risks for employees
- Detrimental effect on the family and social lives of employees
- Reduced opportunities for job progression, career enhancement, promotion and training for those unwilling to participate in a long hours culture
- Risk of alienation from work colleagues.

From this analysis we must be careful not to conclude that the traditional psychological contract has been seriously damaged. The CIPD's 'Pressure at Work and the Psychological Contract' (Guest and Conway, 2002) showed that despite a decline in worker job satisfaction, particularly in the public sector, most have maintained a sound level of commitment towards their employer. This can be partly explained because many workers no longer expect or want a *long-term career* with their current employer. Also, trust levels are fairly high *vis-à-vis* their immediate manager, although it remains low in respect of senior management.

Third, there have been success stories despite the gloomy picture. In these examples a new psychological contract has been forged out of painful experiences in the recent past. They are introduced as part of collaborative change management processes, and can include performance management systems involving new role definitions, meeting training and development needs, open consultation and communications, effective leadership and management styles, and establishing fair rewards and incentives, both financial and career-related. All these must increasingly address individual needs for family-friendly and flexible work regimes.

Summary

In this section we have assessed how the psychological contract has been under strain because lifelong patterns of work have been undergoing enormous changes. The instrumental orientations dominant among many workers in both industry and service sectors have only strengthened in circumstances where employers have been perceived to break the contract. This has grave implications for employers who blindly make cuts and changes to the workforce without involving them in these decisions. The answer is to support the psychological contract by alternative means when those traditionally relied upon are no longer available.

2.2   People competencies and roles

Section objectives

In this section you will:

● Examine the meaning of adding value in terms of human resource activities
● Relate adding value to performance management and quality systems

2.2.1   Introduction

One of the most significant influences on organizations in recent years has been the requirement to improve the quality of its products and services. Political policy and shifts in economic activity to the services have meant that organizations operating in this sector, both public and private, have found that standards of performance by employees are paramount to continued funding and commercial survival respectively. The term 'adding value' has been used to cover those work systems and methods which can improve the cost-sales ratio through means such as customer satisfaction. A system, which has grown in application throughout the 1990s, has been performance management, which focuses people performance on specific business objectives and combines a number of supports such as training and development, appraisals and pay. A further dimension to improving the quality of workers' contribution has been the growth of competencies as a way of identifying specific qualities held by successful workers and the requisite performance outcomes. One of the most important competencies in contemporary workplaces is leadership of others to work towards new standards of excellence.

2.2.2   Adding value

The challenge for all parties to the employment relationship is how to add value to the organization. In other words, how can the workforce be managed to provide optimum performance? Rather than concentrate on the inputs of performance e.g., time, money, effort, training, setting objectives and measuring them, adding value is more concerned with the outputs of performance, such as improvements in quality and sales, reductions in costs and prices in relation to the inputs, problems solved and applied innovation, and an increase in customer base. The employer of a large multidisciplinary workforce or an independent professional 'portfolio' worker are equally faced with this same challenge – 'What to do to prosper?'[17]

The process of obtaining added value from employees

Organizations that have succeeded in adding value have sought to ensure that all the workforce works towards enhanced customer satisfaction, irrespective of operating in the public or private sectors. Whatever their job, they are encouraged to be salespeople for the organization. The HR (or personnel department) has a key role to play here 'selling' its services to internal customers based on 'service-level agreements', and developing strategies for the whole workforce to add value. The Human Resource Planning process is essential for this role to be executed properly. HR Planning permits policies and practices to be developed directly (vertically) from business objectives but integrated (horizontally) so that they represent a cohesive strategem. With the introduction of age discrimination legislation in 2006 organizations must also establish effective succession planning.

2.2.3   Performance management and competencies

According to Lawson,[18] performance management is 'about the arrangements organizations use to get the right things done successfully'. By aspiring to ever-greater levels of organizational performance employers have turned to a variety of methods to deliver this aim. In isolation or in combination, traditional approaches have included the effective selection of people, work study, management by objectives, total quality management (TQM), and performance-related pay, to name but a few. The modern approach to performance management combines the process of linking people with the resources offered by capital, equipment and technology (Figure 2.1).

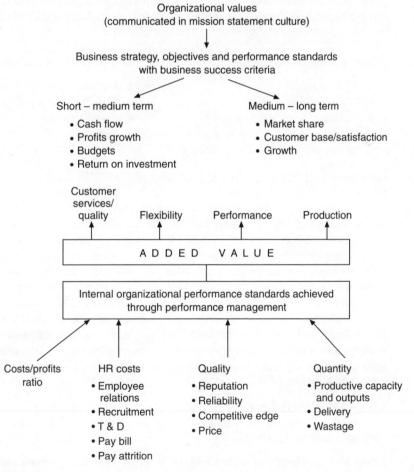

Figure 2.1. Business objectives and the link with performance management (partly based on Lawson[18]).

The concerns expressed about the paucity of management skills during the 1980s led to a number of initiatives, including the Management Charter Initiative (MCI) and National Vocational Qualifications (NVQ). McClelland first used the term 'competency' in respect of management performance in his work on motivation. The original definition was of 'an underlying characteristic of an individual which is causally related to effective or superior performance in a job'. In other words, what a person in a given situation should be able to do. The Learning Skills Council defined 'competence' as 'an action, behaviour or outcome which the person should be able to demonstrate'. That is, the task that a person who works in a given occupational area should be able to carry out in terms of their behaviour in a given position.

Although competency is a term used most widely in respect of management, for which special management competencies have been developed, it does also apply to professional and vocational behaviours, which, once identified, can be developed, e.g. effective communications or leadership. The rationale for competencies is that in the relatively small manufacturing and product sector of the economy the quality differentiation can be insignificant, but in the dominant service sector quality customer satisfaction is crucial to success or failure. The behaviour of people at work is therefore what counts.

It is easy to be confused between the term 'competencies' first used in the USA meaning examining **actual performance** in the job which can be measured and improved by training, and the meaning given in the UK describing behaviours which are **naturally present** in the individual (natural or in-built competencies) which can be combined with those acquired by the employee through learning, training and development.

Key natural competencies:	Key acquired competencies can comprise:
● Agreeableness ● Conscientiousness ● Openness to experience and ● Attitudes (e.g. any prejudices) ● Intelligence (e.g. potential, ability to learn)	● Knowledge (e.g. professional) ● Skills (e.g. in a particular job) ● Awareness (e.g. of a particular job, profession

Every job to which competencies are applied will have a specific **framework** of competencies that are relevant to that job, and to the organization in question. This framework can be consolidated into an individual **competency profile**. Organizations will 'cluster' behavioural competencies together, but the danger is that in doing so a number of surface and core personality traits may be muddled for different individuals (see Section 1.2). The competencies can be identified individually using a number of methods such as an analysis of the competencies of good and poor performers, repertory grid or critical incident techniques, some of which overlap. The result should be half a dozen core competencies each with different levels. Once the levels are established key result areas can be established. These are statements of behaviour translated into performance outputs required of the jobholder. Jobs can typically have a range of eight to ten key result areas. These are then incorporated into the main part of a job specification.

Example

Core competency: Leadership: At the recruitment stage these are identified as natural competencies, that is, the candidate must already possess the leadership competency to varying levels as required:

Level 1:   Can lead a number of teams of professional accountants and managers
Level 2:   Can lead one project team comprising professional accountants and managers
Level 3:   Can lead non-professional members of a work team.

A key result area for Level 1 would be: 'prepares business plans to maximize team members' expertise and customer contracts'.

Problems

Once competent does this imply there is no further need for training or development? Which competencies should be rewarded financially and through other means more than others?

The traditional method of assessing the successful application of competencies has been through performance appraisal, but the subjectivity, poor methodology and inadequate training of both appraiser and appraisee present in many appraisal schemes means that in isolation the outcomes are often dysfunctional. As we have seen, an appraisal process as part of a performance management system is the best method. Assessment can focus on the competencies required in the job using the competency profile. In practice this may be incorporated into the job specification. The performance outputs should be clearly identified and measurable criteria used for the assessment. The difficulty in linking pay to such a system is that care must be taken not to award performance-related pay for personality traits. Performance (achievement of outputs) should, of course, be awarded although it is based on the application of certain competencies. Competency-based pay (CBP) will reward the possession of certain competencies. This is similar to skills-based pay which rewards the gaining of new vocational skills. The result of the combination of PRP and CBP is a form of 'person-based pay'.

Examples

Performance-related pay bonus for:
Creating £60 000 worth of business in one month in excess of targets by 50 per cent.

Competency-based pay for effectively demonstrating two key competencies:
1 **Competency:** negotiation
  Behavioural indicator: identifies and builds on common ground
2 **Competency:** Determination and persistence
  Behavioural indicator: sees other people's point of view but demonstrates repeated efforts to convince them to accept his arguments.

2.2.4   Quality

It is widely estimated that the costs of attracting a new customer are four to five times higher than retaining a current one. In some industries the costs are much higher. The shift to the service sector, intense competition and the emphasis on customer satisfaction over the past two decades has meant that organizations are seeking to add value in terms of the quality of customer service as well as product. Major customers (including organizations buying-in services or components from other firms) increasingly insist on consistent quality standards. In human resource terms performance standards are often focused on these outcomes and are seen as part of quality management systems. Different quality systems are discussed in Chapter 6.

Summary

In this section we have looked at the growing importance of quality and competence in jobs, particularly the growth in the service sector where customer satisfaction is paramount. This, in turn, depends on the quality of the organization's people – their attitudes, skills, and expertise; in other words, their level of competence to carry out the tasks involved within a culture of continuous improvement. The key dimension that ensures success or failure is the standard of supervisory and managerial leadership, which is discussed fully in Sections 3.3 and 4.1.

2.3   Flexibility and the new work paradigm

In this section you will:

- Examine new patterns of flexible working
- Assess the impact of flexibility on people management
- Identify the advantages and disadvantages of flexibility to employers and workers and
- Examine the importance of business ethics in people management.

2.3.1   Introduction

In this section we will be looking at the ways in which the organization and regime of work have become more 'flexible', and the impact on individuals and employers alike. Probably the biggest change in people management since the beginning of the twentieth century is still underway caused by global and national trends. Although it should not be over-stated, it has disrupted the conventional notion of there being just a few ways of working such as a job for life with one employer, and being engaged on work which does not change substantially over time. As we will see, a new paradigm of work is now a reality.

2.3.2   The effect of technology

Because capitalist society is stimulated by competitive pressure there is always the need to improve productivity and the variety as well as quality of goods. Marx believed that the mechanization of work was a natural outcome of the mobilization of capital in a modern industrial setting. He saw a constantly changing relationship between 'technical capital' (machinery, equipment, plant) and 'human capital' (the workers), where the intensification of the former would always subordinate the latter. His theme was consolidated by the work of Braverman[19] who contended that 'Taylorist' and 'Fordist' systems of work involving fragmentation and specialization of work, rationalization and mechanization ultimately lead to the degradation of work and de-skilling of workers. (See also the Technological context discussed in Chapter 13.)

The arguments against industrialized production systems have been criticized by Robert Blauner[5] who believed that technology could 'liberate' and energize workers by constantly upgrading skills to keep pace with its modernization. Moreover, as technology developed the worker would no longer be required to undertake the more monotonous and simplistic tasks, but could develop a higher range of work skills which would banish feelings of alienation and low self-esteem. Alienation and subsequent workplace conflict are, according to this theory, only stages in the development of a complex industrial society.

What then accounts for the historic lowest strike rate in the UK at the end of the 1990s? According to the Organization for Economic Cooperation and Development (OECD) the UK had the seventh lowest strike rate of twenty-four OECD countries in a ten-year period (1987–1997). Does this represent a vindication of Blauner's views? Probably not; in Section 2.4.3 we examine the changing context for work, which is discussed in detail in Part Three of this book. Blauner's work has, in turn, been criticized, and contrary arguments developed by other writers, notably, Woodward,[20] Wedderburn and Crompton (1972) and Salaman (1981). In particular, it has been noted that technology alone cannot provide the answers why people behave the way they do at work. Also, different industries involve distinct work processes and technology, which coupled with their own history and employee relations systems, produce very different worker attitudes and behaviours. Woodward, for example, found that management–

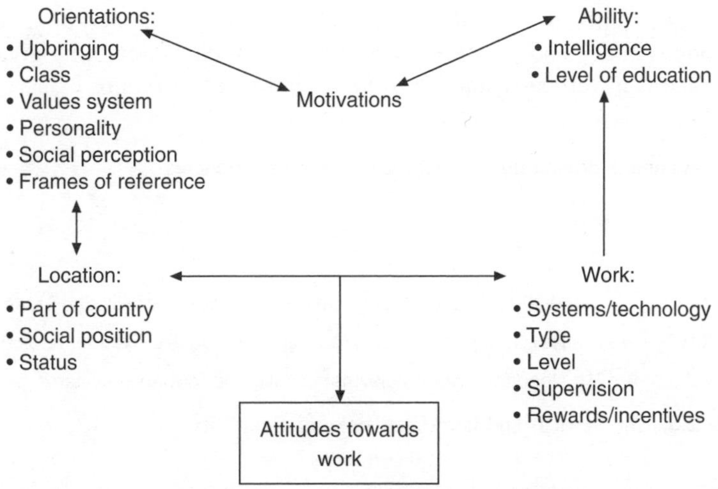

Orientations:
• Upbringing
• Class
• Values system
• Personality
• Social perception
• Frames of reference

Motivations

Ability:
• Intelligence
• Level of education

Location:
• Part of country
• Social position
• Status

Work:
• Systems/technology
• Type
• Level
• Supervision
• Rewards/incentives

Attitudes towards work

Figure 2.2. Summary of factors which influence attitudes towards work.

worker relations appeared to be better in the process industries (e.g. chemicals, technology, engineering) than in mass batch production industries typified by motor manufacturing. That is not to say that process workers do not maintain an instrumental approach to work. Evidence shows that they do, but the potential conflict is moderated by a relative satisfaction with their work provided requisite factors are also present. These factors are summarized in Figure 2.2.

2.3.3 The changing world of work

As we have seen in Section 2.1 the labour market and the nature of work within it continue to change over time. One of the key changes has been the growth of flexibility at all levels of work. Naturally, as business environments become more volatile and competitive, employers are under pressure to exploit whatever opportunities exist to adjust their capacity to meet these commercial demands. Together with new forms of work technology employers have incorporated flexibility into their organizations, and with it new forms of complementary people management, some of which we examined in Section 2.2.

One key effect of the changes described above has been the decline of the dual labour market system. A labour market is simplistically a means by which the demand for labour can be met by supply and the interaction of the one upon the other. The internal labour market operates within the workplace, enabling both demand and supply changes to be satisfied from within the existing workforce. External labour markets, by contrast, are situated outside the enterprise at the local, regional, national and, for some occupations, international level. The changes in economic and organizational structures in the 1980s have forced employers in highly competitive markets to realign internal labour markets to provide workers with a range of skills and competencies to meet changing commercial pressures. The external labour market, with its increasing rates of female participation, has reorientated itself to an economy dominated by the service sector. This, in turn, has changed the temporal nature of employment to include atypical forms of employment such as part-time and temporary jobs, home-working, performance-only contracts and annualized hours contracts. The last type of contract involves the employee being hired on a contract whereby they agree to work a total number of hours in a year for the employer, but at dates and times when there is a particular demand for work. Another version of this type of contract is the zero-hours contract whereby no guaranteed maximum hours will be worked; the employee may work as little as a handful or as much as several hundred hours depending on peaks and troughs in demand for staff. From the description of flexibility given here it is possible to see that it is vertically and horizontally linked as in Figure 2.3.

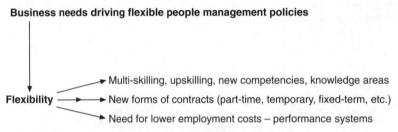

Figure 2.3. The vertical and horizontal links of flexibility.

Blyton[21] has identified four types of flexibility which match this typology:

(i)   **Functional flexibility:** This involves broadening job boundaries and skill definitions to improve productive capacity. As we have seen, it is stimulated by technical and organizational change, and has been introduced in the public sector more than in the private sector. Because of the harmonization of terms and conditions between traditional 'blue-collar' and 'white-collar' employees it is dangerous to state that this type of flexibility has been more evident among non-manual employees, but increasingly production workers have functional flexibility schemes included as part of collective agreements between unions and employers. For much of the 1980s and 1990s the common assumption was that professional workers were not associated with functional flexibility. However, this would be a mistaken view because an increasing number of professionals are required to possess a broad range of skills and competencies including project management, IT skills, people skills, general management and risk management.[22] Functional flexibility reflects the reality that for many employers the key is what the individual **can do** based on critical thinking rather than their level of **knowledge**. Functional flexibility involves developing and relating **competencies** in key fields to the needs of the organization which can be applied without the constraints of traditional imaginary or physical demarcation lines. In redesigning jobs the boundaries of those jobs can be extended to encompass a range and depth of individual skills. To succeed, however, there must be extensive investment in training and development to upgrade and maintain those skills.

(ii) **Numerical flexibility:** This embraces a broad spectrum of ways in which the employer can easily manage the headcount of the workforce through establishing different contractual regimes for different types of worker. This typifies above all other types of flexibility the matching of demand and supply, and for this reason has been criticized because it treats people as a commodity. Typically, low pay and poor terms and conditions are associated with numerical flexibility. Different forms of legal relationships can be established to limit the long-term relationship between employer and worker, such as a temporary, part-time work, subcontracting, and self-employment. The use of contract labour has become common in the large manufacturing and service organizations, and particularly in the public sector because of the policy of compulsory competitive tendering and market testing. As you will see from discussion of Figure 2.4, numerical flexibility is closely associated with internal peripheral and secondary labour markets because of the implications for poor job security.

(iii) **Temporal flexibility:** This can be an extension of numerical flexibility, but reflects an independent response to pressures for flexibility by organizing working time according to organizational needs. Examples: shift working, overtime, short-time working, flexi-time, annualized and zero-hours contracts. Arguably, most employers adopting both numerical and temporal flexibility have a short-term perspective, as Hendry[23] points out.

(iv) **Financial flexibility:** There are two dimensions to this type of flexibility. Primarily it reflects pay systems that are specifically designed or adapted to facilitate flexibility in the recipient workforce. Examples include:

- Performance-related pay: to improve performance and quality
- Team-based pay: to promote team working and a collaborative style of working
- Skills-based pay: to promote and reward upskilling in the workforce
- Competency-based pay: similar to skills-based pay, but can be used to reward the application of appropriate competencies at work
- Gainsharing and profit pay: to directly link profitability to employee performance
- Employee shares schemes: primarily to link rewards to employee loyalty
- Individually negotiated contracts with individual/job-related terms and conditions.

All these pay systems reflect a new orthodoxy[24] of providing rewards and incentives which are based upon the contribution of the employee and the organization's ability to pay, rather than the old orthodoxy of incremental pay systems designed to reward length of service. Most of the systems do not directly link effort or easily measurable works inputs and therefore have been more prevalent among managerial, professional and administrative workers.

The second dimension to financial flexibility lies in the benefits flexibility itself brings to the organization. The very existence of functional, numerical and temporal flexibility, coupled with the output-related pay systems, some of which yield tax advantages for employer and employee alike, all combine to give the employer choice in how, where and when human resources can be used.

Atkinson[25] was one of the first exponents of a new regime of work in the 1980s. His model reflects the dual labour market theory, and can be shown diagrammatically in Figure 2.4.

- **Core workers:** These represent the most valued workers to the organization who traditionally would be 'employed' on standard, full-time, open-ended (permanent) contracts of employment. Theoretically, at least they would enjoy relatively stable and secure employment with a package of pay and benefits concomitant with their position and industrial sector. Because core workers are supposed to be the most valued part of the organization's human resources it is argued that investment in training and development should be relatively high, so that they can operate as functionally flexible workers. In return, there would be well-developed levels of commitment and loyalty towards their employer, although evidence shows that with professional workers this is often displaced towards the respective profession or professional work group (bureaucratic orientation).
- **The first peripheral group:** Traditionally, these too would be full-time workers who undertake semi-skilled or less critical work for the organization. Temporal flexibility is used here so that they will be employed on part-time, temporary or fixed-term contracts. The career prospects, pay, terms and conditions, training and status of these workers reflects their secondary importance to the organization in functional terms.

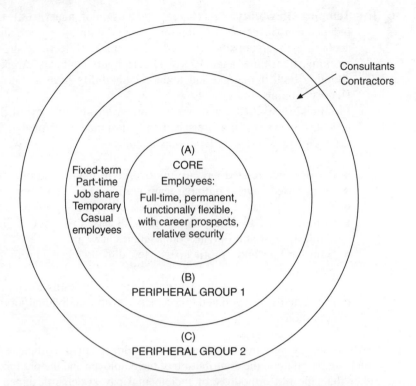

(A)   Represents internal labour market. Terms and conditions will be harmonized; pay related to performance, competence, skill, profits and value-added.

   Examples: Managers, engineers, technicians, craft/skilled operatives, supervisors.

(B)   Represents external labour market, but close to the organization. Probably less skilled and qualified than core. Higher turnover, shorter periods of employment, less training than core employees. Little chance of career.

   Examples: Clerical workers, secretarial staff, stores, driving and manual jobs.

(C)   Distanced workers:
   • Consultants and agencies undertaking specialist functions in management, IT, training and R & D. Fixed-term or performance-related service contracts.
   • Contractors and subcontractors undertaking cleaning, catering, maintenance, security, distribution, some specialist/professional services, e.g. law, engineering and medical.
   Contract by tender.

Figure 2.4. John Atkinson's model of the flexible firm (Institute of Manpower Studies, 1984).

● **The second peripheral group:** These workers will constitute a mixture of employees and contracted or subcontracted labour. They will be specifically used to perform certain types of work or to complete contractual assignments. Those on government training schemes have been placed in this subcategory, including Modern Apprenticeships and New Deal participants.

● **External workers:** Not part of the organization's human resources, but perceived more as a service which can be contracted easily and swiftly to undertake particular assignments. Some of these will be long-term, such as subcontractors hired to deliver a specific maintenance service such as security, cleaning, catering or transport. Others may be employed for relatively short periods of time and on an individual basis such as consultants for training, advisory work or systems analysis.

2.3.4

The reality of flexibility

Whether flexibility is a new management phenomenon has been disputed. In particular, the Atkinson model of the flexible firm was criticized by Anna Pollert[26] as 'old wine in new bottles'; in other words, as practices which had been growing over many decades, but which were being erroneously reformulated into a new predetermined strategy. The popularity of flexibility in the 1980s as a new 'strategy' was criticized by those who argued that employers were adopting flexible working practices in a wholly *ad hoc* and pragmatic way, using parts of the models discussed earlier in this section, but without a conscious long-term plan. Indeed, it is true that evidence now points to the fact that employers will continue to exploit the opportunities in the labour market and in society as a whole to introduce flexibility, rather than as a human resource centred or long-term business strategy. However, the 'Atkinson model' provides a helpful framework for understanding flexibility.

Critics of strategic flexibility have argued that there has been no wholesale segmentation of the workforce; indeed, as we shown in Section 2.1.6 this is true. But, in the last two decades there *has* been a transition towards a more 'flexible' workforce, and temporary work has been one growing manifestation whenever employers perceive economic difficulties ahead. The UK had 700 000 temporary workers, including those on fixed-term contracts, in 2002, many of whom worked for or were placed by agencies. An increasing tendency has been for employers to hire on a permanent basis many temporary workers once they have shown they are reliable. At the time of writing the EU is pursuing controversial draft legislation to protect temporary agency workers from less favourable treatment compared to 'permanent' employees.[27] See Section 12.12.

Homework and telework

This type of work has increasingly moved away from traditional craft or manual skills carried out at home to teleworking. The 'distanced' worker is connected to the employer via a telephone line and their computer. Although in excess of 2 million people now telework (of which nearly half a million are homeworkers) in the UK and the numbers grow each year, as with other forms of atypical working we must now ascribe to it something which is replacing traditional commuting to work with 'hot desking'. *Labour Market Trends* (October 2002) shows that of the homeworking teleworkers 27 per cent are in professional/technical occupations and 24 per cent are in administrative/secretarial jobs. Nevertheless, many organizations have pursued cost-savings by moving technology-based jobs, e.g. software processing, ticketing and financial data processing, to countries such as India, the Philippines and Indonesia where infrastructure and labour costs are lower. Teleworking is also discussed in Chapter 13.

Equal opportunities and the 'work–life balance'

Paradoxically, with the arrival of the 24-hour, 7-day week society that is increasingly reliant upon technology and instant communications, individuals demand relief from long work hours to spend more time engaged in leisure and with their families. The government has recognized this by introducing significant legislative rights for working parents and carers in the Employment Act 2002 (see Section 12.15). Added to these pressures is increasing evidence that the absence of a work–life balance can disadvantage employers. The Department for Trade and Industry says that £370 million costs are added to industry per annum through staff absences caused by stress at work. In 2002 the Minister of State for Employment, Alan Johnson, said 'Business needs to be smarter when it comes to beating these problems. Work–life balance policies such as flexible working, job-sharing and employee benefits do not require a huge cash investment – just a fresh approach.'[28]

Indeed, several studies show that family-friendly policies do enhance financial performance. Such policies normally involve one or several of the following:

- Parental leave
- Paternity leave and adoption leave
- Term-time working
- Flexitime, job-share and part-time or irregular working hours
- Creches or help with childcare
- Special leave for caring for dependent relatives or career breaks
- Providing a work regime that permits employees to work hours where home-life and work can be sensibly balanced
- Developing a culture where employees taking advantage of these policies are not 'marginalized', but are valued.[29]

As we have seen in Section 2.1, employee trust and commitment can be significantly improved by such measures. However, there are those who strongly argue that there is a difference between theory and reality; Robert Taylor argues that there is a 'huge gap in take-up between the offer of flexible working and its actual practice. Employees are often reluctant to step forward ... for fear of damaging their career prospects.' Others argue against employers having any form of social responsibility because family-friendly flexibility is a burdensome cost to be avoided.[30] Certainly, the main impact is upon female workers, who dominate part-time working and are the main applicants/beneficiaries of family-friendly policies.[27]

Two other dimensions must not be overlooked when examining numerical and temporal flexibility. It has had a double impact on members of ethnic minorities. Much of the low-paid part-time and temporary work is filled by members of this group, who are historically three times as likely as their white counterparts to be unemployed.[31]

An effect is also felt by those with disabilities. It is estimated that 70 per cent of the 2 million persons with a disability became disabled at work. Moreover, disabled people are at least 50 per cent more likely to be unemployed than their non-disabled counterparts, mainly because of stereotypical perceptions of this group held by employers. With the introduction of family-friendly policies this *may* encourage employers to see that with the help of advances in technology, functional and temporal flexibility can be suited to those with disabilities. However, the general opening up of the labour market to the disabled is more likely to be initiated by legislation, such as the Disability Discrimination Act 1995, but truly accomplished by culture change in the workplace.

MG Rover

In practice

Flexible working has helped MG Rover to transform itself from facing closure and losing £187 million per annum to making profits within four years. Morale has remained good despite a huge shortfall in profits.

One of the main factors under-pinning this turn-around has been to persuade 3,500 production workers of the need for working time accounts (WTA).

Under the new deal workers can build up a maximum 20 hours uptime, where 75 per cent is banked and the remaining 25 per cent is paid for.

If, at the end of three years, workers still have outstanding uptime, the company will pay for it and wipe the slate clean. The limit on downtime, where employees owe time to the company, is also 200 hours.

Extensive communications is used to explain the way the scheme works. Line managers and union officials are encouraged to sort out local disagreements on the spot. The success of this is demonstrated by a sharp reduction in the number of issues now dealt with by the formal grievance procedure. A hands-on approach is also encouraged when rewarding exceptional performance.

A sense of involvement in the company is fostered through 60 per cent of the business being held in shares by the employees. Ownership may partly explain why attendance is now running at 97.5 per cent.

Extract from: '*Driving through flexible changes*', Guy Sheppard[32]. *Personnel Today*, 29 October 2002, p. 13.

2.3.5   New forms of work organization

The influences identified in this chapter have led to a changing workplace which is more reliant on new technology, flatter management structures and a flexibility combining functional diversification, financial innovation and new forms of contracting with employees and distanced workers, although most workers are still 'permanent' full-time employees. The scope of organizations adopting flexible strategies is broad, and includes about a half of large enterprises. They include companies such as Coca-Cola, Renault, Rover, Motorola, the Japanese inward-investment companies, the banking and insurance sector, and several parts of the public sector. Particularly in car manufacturing, employers have coupled flexibility with new production techniques (such as 'just-in-time' methods), quality systems, high added-value goods/services and employee relations policies which include 'human resource management' practices such as effective communications, team work and team-based rewards. In the UK these flexible human resource policies have been traditionally less consensual than in countries such as Germany, Japan and the Nordic countries. Nevertheless, we can summarize the characteristics of the new work paradigm associated with flexibility in the exercise below.

Exercise

List the respective advantages and disadvantages of flexibility to employers and employees:

Feedback

Employer – advantages

- Control of costs
- Increased/improved performance and productivity – improved quality (functional)
- Reduced rates of overtime and other unit labour costs (e.g. fewer or nil pension contributions, statutory sick and maternity pay, National Insurance contributions)
- Outsourcing – distancing: reduction in total headcount of workforce – lower fixed costs and paybill
- Numerical: where employers believe they can hire and fire relatively easily they will be more inclined to employ more workers, thus generating a more active labour market(?) Positive impact on groups traditionally disadvantaged in the labour market, e.g. ethnic groups, people with disabilities(?)
- Reduced absenteeism
- Optimum use of workforce – less risk of idle time. Time itself becomes more manageable. Improved deployment of labour. Harmonization of terms (e.g. between 'blue' and 'white collar' employees)
- Core workforce feel valued – improved employee/industrial relations
- Functionally flexible employees – lifelong training and development possible. Also traditional job demarcations broken down permitting job enrichment and job satisfaction to accrue

- Organization becomes more adaptable – able to respond to external events and pressures. This in turn enables it to compete more strongly in global markets. A long-term strategy can be developed.

Employer – disadvantages

- Numerical
  - (i) Possibility of complex pay and conditions arrangements including different types of contracts. Together with temporal, the logistics of organizing a complex workforce.
  - (ii) Unreliability of workers (low morale, no commitment, poor attendance, time-keeping and attitude)
  - (iii) Over-reliance on non-committed workers not in core – impact on quality, service delivery and product specification. Long-term impact on reputation, profitability.

- Temporal
  - (i) Disinclination of workers to work payback hours in annualized hours or flexitime schemes.
  - (ii) Quality of supervision
  - (iii) Difficulties in organizing shift cover
  - (iv) Complexity – scheduling of work and communications

- Functional
  - (i) Opposition from trades unions or individuals unwilling to change
  - (ii) Requires a change or adaptable work culture
  - (iii) Training and development – costs
  - (iv) Rewards and incentives – costs to remain competitive
  - (v) Health and safety training, regulations and costs

- General:
  - (i) Costs of induction, introduction of new systems, different training systems – loss of economies of scale
  - (ii) Inappropriateness of the type of flexibility selected with organizational culture, structure and systems.

Advantages – employees

- Choice – can plan for different working patterns, hours, etc.
- Variability in employer and assignment (particularly the 'portfolio worker')
- Family-friendly work policies, benefits and conditions
- Enhanced job satisfaction, commitment and earnings
- Variable work – opportunities for job rotation, enrichment
- Different pay sources (e.g. competency-based pay, performance-related pay, etc.)
- Enhanced training and development with functional flexibility
- To be part of the core workforce – status

Disadvantages – employees

- On call – disruption, irregular working patterns (particularly with zero or annualized hours contracts)
- Unsocial hours and long hours
- Insecurity and poor pay, terms and conditions (particularly in the peripheral sectors). Causes stress where one or two incomes are essential – see Section 2.5
- Few benefits (peripheral sectors)
- Reduced employment rights, particularly for those with short periods of employment or compulsory classed as self-employed (e.g. agency workers)

- Reduced control and personal direction
- More pressure, stress and anxiety
- Less job satisfaction – specialization – job enlargement
- Certain categories of households contain adults with jobs in the more vulnerable flexible sectors
- Social isolation of those working at home or teleworking

The new organization of work

From the discussion in this chapter about the restructuring of work we can see that Bramham's view[33] of flexibility evidenced by eight forms of flexibility is an accurate one:

(i)   Training and development bringing skills flexibility and relevant competencies.
(ii)   Occupation – job flexibility by which individuals move from job to job or employer to employer rather than enjoy lifelong employment with one employer.
(iii)   Mobility – closely linked with (ii); the ability and willingness of the individual to move geographical location to obtain work.
(iv)   Working time reflecting different patterns of work across 24 hours and 7 days a week.
(v)   Organization flexibility reflecting less bureaucratic and hierarchical structures, possibly leading to matrix structures including project team working.
(vi)   Numerical – the power of the employer to increase and decrease the numbers of workers (employees and non-employees) quickly and easily.
(vii)   Financial – wage and salary cost flexibility arising from (iv)–(vi).
(viii) Attitude – the state of mind of workers to the practice of flexibility. For this reason employers who have been most successful in applying new forms of flexibility have recognized the key importance of organizational culture. Without a supportive culture to maintain full flexibility many employers can only fall back on selective (and often exploitative) forms of flexibility such as numerical flexibility. The practical implications of this concept of flexibility can be summarized as follows.

The flexible organization

What should be the strategy for the flexible organization? Some of the following elements must be present:

- First, the organization focuses on its 'core' activities. Horizontal links with other employers are forged for subcontracting and outsourcing purposes. These collateral services are, in fact, critical to the final product or service, e.g. components, parts, transport, cleaning, catering and other ancillary services.
- Second, organizational structure and systems must complement and support flexibility. The emphasis is placed on horizontal communication and a broad dissemination of information. This permits small self-managing (autonomous) or part-managing teams to operate and take more responsibility. There is less emphasis on vertical communication typified by hierarchical structures.

What of the critical part specifically played by human resources? Priority must be given to education, training, skills, experience, good communication skills and the ability to work in unstructured situations with a relatively high degree of personal responsibility. This freedom for individual initiative is known as 'intrapreneurship' because the organization turns inwards to develop and motivate its people in order to make its external activities more successful as work activities are not so clearly delineated as previously. In turn, this has implications for HR policy areas:

● Recruitment and selection: Managing a diverse group of employees requires different recruitment and selection methods, with contractual terms related to type, skill/ability and expertise of the worker. For the core employee selection methods must be relatively sophisticated to identify the individual's competencies, expertise, attitude and personality. The importance of a 'fit' between the employee, the job, the organization and its dominant culture is critical if flexibility is to succeed.

● Training and development: This must reflect the different groups of workers and their specific needs. For the core it will be the springboard for functional flexibility, and therefore the emphasis is likely to be placed on competencies, continuous self-development and the links to performance management or an appraisal system. Selection methods will help identify potential that can be developed over time. For peripheral workers training in key organizational systems and health and safety may be important.

● Human resource planning: The impact of the diversity of a flexible workforce must be carefully planned for in terms of hours of work, temporal variations, skills supply, training and development plans, volume of output matched by labour requirements and remuneration and benefits to match the market values of the different groups of workers. All this must be assessed in the context of the organization's business plans, culture and the external PESTEL factors.

● Remuneration and benefits: This policy must be carefully constructed to recruit and retain appropriate workers to meet the business and HR strategy. Pro-rata arrangements may be made to differentiate core and peripheral workers, e.g. those in the core receive a full range of benefits, whereas the peripheral workers receive only minimal benefits such as access to the canteen. The employer must balance the divisive nature of such a policy with the pay costs involved. The trend for many employers has been to adopt harmonized terms and conditions for all workers, except those in the secondary peripheral groups. Finally, decisions must be made about the level of financial participation (e.g. through employee share schemes) and performance pay (e.g. performance-related pay). Each pay system (e.g. shares, benefits, performance-related pay, skills-based pay) must be selected to achieve specific objectives such as tax-breaks, generation of commitment and improved motivation, and linked to future individual potential/contribution.

2.3.6   The new workplace ethics

A business must have a conscience as well as a counting house.

Sir Montague Burton – founder of the Burton menswear chain of shops

With the growth of new business and working practices in the 1980s, so business ethics received renewed attention from academics and employers alike. Ethics can be expressed in terms of an organization's mission statement that expresses its values, although it can be broadened to apply to an organization's:—

● Economic and financial systems
● Strategy and policies
● Functional operations, such as human resources, sales, R&D, etc. and
● Individual employee conduct (e.g. the abuse of power by managers over individuals, 'whistleblowing'.

In societal terms many organizations now embrace the concept of 'Corporate social responsibility'. This is broadly supported by managers on the grounds that the greater the corporate engagement with those affected by business activities, the better will be the performance of those organizations.

Business ethics originate from professional ethics such as medicine or law or human resources (as exemplified by the CIPD's Code of Professional Standards), and coupled with contemporary beliefs in how best to manage people. In the late twentieth century business ethics have incorporated the following:

- Concepts of employee participation and involvement in the workplace associated with the HRM movement
- People's changing attitudes towards work and their concern for fair treatment
- Global concerns for ethical management of people to avoid exploitation
- Public awareness and concern for ecological matters and
- Public expectations and concern about management corruption (linked to the Nolan Committee's Report on Standards in Public Life).

Business ethics often focus on five interdependent elements that cover the quality of products, information, management, decision making and treatment of employees and clients. As far as the workforce is concerned they are given responsibility for all resources and their use and there is mutuality of support typified by the stakeholder movement. This is important where freedom to be innovative and take control is exemplified by 'empowerment' and self-managed team work.

Ethics is therefore a mixture of the altruistic and self-interest. For those interested in people management the key is fair, open and effective management. In 1997 the Convention of Scottish Local Authorities published a code of conduct for their officials based on the seven principles of public life:

- Selflessness
- Integrity
- Objectivity
- Accountability
- Openness
- Honesty
- Leadership.

This was augmented by a section on the rights of employees, as well as on political neutrality, disclosure of information, corruption, conflicts of interest and appointments.[34]

Those organizations that are most enthusiastic about ethical management are likely to have also embraced the concept of 'stakeholding' (see Chapters 7 and 14). This, like many management concepts, has a range of meanings in practice. At one level it can denote no more than granting shares to the workforce, but at another level it includes a plurality of financial, emotional and practical investment by all those parties that might have such an interest. In defining stakeholding it is difficult to separate it practically from ethical considerations; the following models of stakeholding all contain different standards of ethics:

- **Long-term profit-generated stakeholding:** Rather than focus on short-term profit maximization to please shareholders the company takes investment decisions to generate higher workforce morale and commitment, and/or to make its products ecologically sound. These pay-forward costs will yield dividends in the long term through added-value employment practices, customer loyalty or even by not having to mount expensive 'firefighting' exercises with pressure groups or trades unions.
- **Stakeholding based on cooperative relationships:** By fostering collaborative relationships with employees, subcontractors and suppliers there is a build-up of trust, commitment and focused working involving open communications. This leads to a

climate of honesty and problem solving; in terms of groups this would be called 'synergy' – the product of all the constituent parts being greater than if they contributed without stakeholding. This approach conforms to the Kantian (after Kant) perspective of HRM ethics wherefore individuals must be accorded dignity, but pure self-interest was unethical.

Example

The Centrica Group employs 35 000 people. It has a policy of ethical treatment of employees, which embraces specific programmes that include equal opportunities, employee rewards, trade union recognition and involvement, family-friendly practices, robust communications/consultation systems and a developing policy on 'whistleblowing'. More broadly, it undertakes community and charitable works as well as having a wide-ranging environmental policy. The business believes all of this has helped to grow profits and improve employee morale and trust; the practical benefits include lower turnover and improved recruitment candidates.[35]

Case study

Problem at the town hall

Only your second week of working at the local council and already you're not sure whether you made the correct move, especially so soon after obtaining your CIPD diploma. As the new HR policy officer you have been asked by the Director of Personnel and Equal Employment Opportunities (PEEO) to lead a multi-disciplinary team to recommend a new ethical employee relations policy. A very expensive firm of consultants has told the Chief Executive it is what the council needs and the elected councillors agree with this view. But the problem is that there is no money in the budget for consultants to work up the new policy, so it must be completed in-house.

The Director of PEEO has told your team that the council has been appearing too frequently in the local and national newspapers. In the last six months articles have appeared about:

● Members of staff who are Muslims being refused time off for religious holidays and subsequently winning large amounts of compensation at the employment tribunal
● Police investigations into council officers who allegedly gave preferential treatment to bids from contractors for council work in return for cash
● The high absenteeism rate for the council's staff, which is one of the worst in the country
● The near-fatal accidents in the council's direct labour grounds maintenance department involving mechanical diggers
● The warning from the Equal Opportunities Commission that the council's recruitment and selection practices still include word-of-mouth recruitment and poor interviewing training
● Also, interviews have been given by trade union representatives to local newspapers about bullying at work.

As the person responsible for drafting the recommendations for the Director of PEEO you set yourself the task of outlining the key headings in the new policy and the practical steps that might be taken to implement it. What key headings and subsequent practical steps will you identify?

Draft ethical employee relations policy

Key headings:	Practical steps:
Values, fairness and equality	Appoint, promote and reward on merit. Revise equal opportunities policy. Train all members of staff in equal opportunities – enforce and discipline those who act in breach of the policy. Introduce anti-harassment and victimization rules. A policy of diversity will be pursued. References will be drawn up incorporating ethical practices, and will be truthful and open. All recruitment, selection, appraisal and training and development practices will be monitored, reviewed and updated. The council will adopt good practice in respect of recruitment, selection, promotion, career development, redundancy, redeployment and early retirement.
Honesty in all relationships	Make information about pay and terms/conditions transparent. Ensure all tasks are legal – checks and procedures. Train, reward, communicate openly, enforce standards of proberty. Do not cheat employees; create a culture where dishonesty is unacceptable.
To look after the physical and mental well-being of all staff and contractors	Promote and enforce a rigorous health, safety and welfare policy. Outlaw all forms of discrimination, victimization, harassment, bullying and intimidation. Create motivational environment through leadership, management style, fair rewards, incentives and training/development. Positive health programmes will be introduced, including employee assistance programmes, counselling and health screening.
To nurture and respect all members of staff	Respect all religious, ethnic and cultural differences. Respect and promote collective representation of employees through trades unions and works councils. Establish fair, effective and speedy grievance and disciplinary and complaints machinery. Promote a mutually supportive legal and psychological contract. Corruption will be punished. Disclosure of wrong-doing to senior management will be supported. Flexible working will be used to mutual benefit. Family-friendly practices will be introduced that go beyond provisions in the 2002 Employment Act.

The organizational culture must be transformed over time to recognize there is mutual advantage for the council, its staff and the public in recognizing the contribution of human resources. A Corporate Social Responsibility Policy will be formulated and an annual report published.

Summary

In this section we have explored what flexibility and the way it is permeating all parts of the world of work mean. The trends of flexibility have now been underway for three decades, but it is unlikely that the pace will slacken due to intensifying global competitive pressures and the changing make-up of the labour market. Employers have used flexibility as a short-term means to survive recession and to generate interim increases in profits and lower costs. But the lesson of this approach is that in the medium to long term problems are likely to multiply. We have seen that there is an ethical approach which uses flexibility to enhance employee performance based on competencies, improving skills and work applications, and thereby improve worker motivations. By this route employers will reap the benefits of value-added products and services.

2.4   Stress management

Case study

Taresh's problem

Failure to replace staff who have left the service department in which Taresh works has meant he has had to bear an ever-increasing workload. Management has promised him help in due course, but for the time being he must manage two after-sales service areas plus his own.

Taresh enjoys his home and social life, but the demands of the job have made him too tired to join his friends at badminton or cricket for their regular twice-weekly games. He finds himself getting short-tempered at home, irritable and annoyed by the frequent headaches and stomach pains which he now suffers because they slow him down, when he feels he should be putting more energy into his job, not less. Taresh describes how he feels to his brother-in-law in the following words: 'My head feels like a pressure cooker, ready to burst when I'm at work. When I'm at home I feel so tired I do nothing, but sit around and when I do go to bed I wake up at four in the morning, and can't get back off to sleep'.

Question

What would you advice Taresh to do? What will happen if Taresh doesn't stop working so hard or the company fails to give him help very quickly?

The advice

Taresh has a number of options. First, he must talk to his managers and convince them that he cannot cope for much longer. A replacement must be found to cover the second area or he must be given assistance. Could Taresh be trained to effectively manage his workload? Without these measures Taresh's stress will get worse. He is already suffering from the classic physical and emotional signs of stress and anxiety. The early waking is also sign of depression. Overtiredness will mean poor attention to detail and quality, the risk of accidents and errors, and subsequent damage to his employer's business. These are strong arguments against doing nothing. If matters do get worse there is a risk to Taresh's long-term health. He is also showing social signs of stress such as irritability. His social and home life are suffering and this is bound to cause feelings of guilt, anger and frustration. Ultimately, if Taresh were to suffer a mental breakdown after giving his employer several warnings he could take legal action against them for failing to look after his health.

As we will see from this section, the new work paradigm has a number of serious consequences for workers caught up in long or stressful working situations.

In this section you will:

- Examine the meaning and definitions of workplace stress
- Examine the symptoms, causes and effects of workplace stress and
- Relate these to possible steps to eliminate or reduce stress in the workplace.

2.4.1   Introduction: what is stress?

The word stress is commonly used in a negative sense so that the result for the individual is *distress*. We use the term to describe a wide range of situations, such as overwork, the illness of a loved one, taking an exam or driving test, being late for an important appointment or forming new relationships. Where the word stress is used it will have a negative connotation equating to strain, but the word eustress can be used where a non-threatening positive stimulus is described (*eu* from the Greek word meaning 'good').

Stress can be defined as the 'wear and tear' on our bodies as we experience the day-to-day challenges that face us. As we respond to these challenges the eustress that we experience can stimulate us into action: to develop new ideas, to rise to a challenge or motivate us to pursue an objective with fresh energy. But it can also have negative and damaging results which can have a lasting detrimental effect on the individual. The theme of this section focuses on the premise that managers should be able to construct working environments that eliminate or substantially reduce stress, but which also enhance stimuli for eustress. The former will reduce work performance, but the latter should induce more effective performance.

The subject matter can be divided into three overlapping approaches:

- It is concerned mainly with peoples' responses or symptoms
- The environmental causes of that stress which we will refer to as stressors
- The interaction between the two can be understood by the process of managing stress which involves monitoring, appraising and coping strategies.

Stress is essentially a psychological condition induced by external conditions that release or restrict certain chemicals in the brain; this, in turn can lead to a psychological change in the individual resulting in a change of behaviour. The worst cases of human stress are experienced when the individual has no power, or believes he or she has no power to change the stressful environment in which they are placed. In 1929 Walter Cannon described this as the '*fight or flight*' syndrome whereby human beings still behave in ways which link us to our earliest origins. When we are faced with danger (for example, a heavy workload, a bully at work or a new set of people to work with), we either 'fight': that is, we attempt to rise to the challenge, or we engage in 'flight': we back off, give up, or attempt to avoid or leave the workplace. In the last example, absenteeism is commonly a psychological symptom of stress.

In the work context, stress can be caused by '. . . a job being poorly matched to a worker's abilities, aggravated by insufficient control over that job and inadequate support and training'.[36]

2.4.2   Definitions of stress

Stress has been recognized as a human condition since the time of the ancient Greeks, and took on its present meaning as a person's response to an external stimulus in the early twentieth century. The earliest definitions equated human stress with strain or load placed on objects associated with equations used in engineering and physics, but in 1926 the *Harvard Business School Review* highlighted human stress caused by 'monotony and lack of interest (which) tell on a man mentally, morally and physically'. According to Hans Seyle (1946) there are three stages in the experience of stress:

- **Alarm.** The individual has lowered resistance when he or she is in a state of psychological equilibrium which permits the individual to co-exist comfortably within the environment. The individual subsequently receives an external stimulus which is initially alarming – this stimulates their defence mechanisms.
- **Resistance.** The individual adapts to the stimulus – this permits him or her to eventually return to a state of psychological equilibrium. However, if the stimulus continues to alarm the individual or the defence mechanism does not work the individual will reach:
- **Exhaustion.** When the willingness and ability to adapt to the stimulus collapses. This will result in 'giving up' or resigning oneself to the inevitable and lead to damage to psychological and physical health (see Figure 2.5).[36]

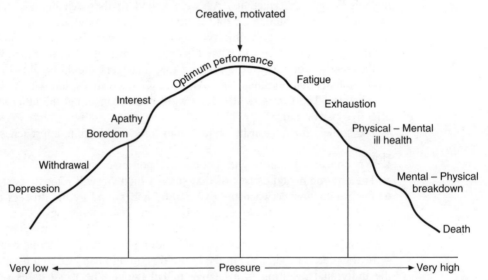

Figure 2.5. The general adaptation syndrome: behavioural analogue (adapted by Cooper and Cartwright).[37]

Hence, the individual may very quickly feel:

Somnolent
Torpid
Relaxed
Energized
Struggling (and finally)
Smashed

Another way of defining stress is as a harmful process through which individuals pass, some very quickly, others over a more protracted period of time. This accurately reflects the true meaning of stress not simply as one or more symptoms, but also the process of interaction between the individual and his or her environment. This approach can be linked to the model put forward by Professor Cary Cooper and Tom Cummings (Figure 2.6).[38]

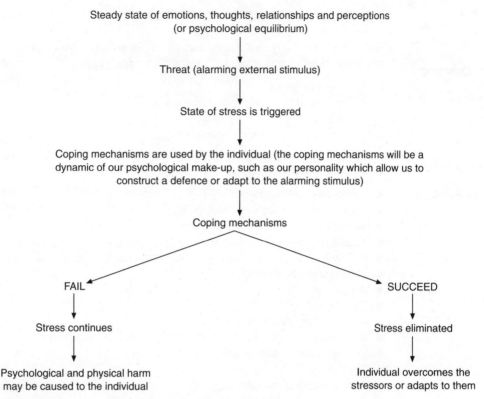

Figure 2.6. The Cooper–Cummings stress adjustment model.

Stress is the reaction people have to excessive pressures or other types of demand placed upon them. It arises when they worry that they cannot cope . . . effects are usually short-lived and cause no lasting harm . . . (but) where pressures are intense and continue for some time, the effects of stress can be sustained and far more damaging, leading to longer term psychological problems and ill health.

Health and Safety Executive[39]

    Many writers have emphasized that stress is a dynamic interaction not only between the work environment and the individual but also with the individual's real and perceived ability to cope with that stimulus. For example, Sheffield University have shown that the cause of symptoms associated with stress in several subjects was in fact rooted in subconscious problems. The cause of depression in 'Bill' when he accepted additional management responsibilities was found to be delayed reaction to his father's death when the subject was only seventeen years of age. Therapy counselling subsequently helped 'Bill'. This approach to defining stress reflects the view of the Freudians who believe that work-related stimuli simply trigger latent conflicts in the individual which can be satisfactorily dealt with in therapy.

    Scientifically, the question of stress is riddled with imprecision; this means that universal guidelines are not available to employers on how to define the causes of stress nor how to identify, avoid and eliminate it. In Chapter 1, we discussed the interaction of individual personality with environmental stressors which exemplifies this tension.

2.4.3   The common symptoms of stress

Write down as many symptoms and effects of stress as you can identify under these four headings. Feedback is provided on the following pages.

1 Physical symptoms
2 Psychological and emotional symptoms
3 Social effects for the individual
4 Changes in the individual's behaviour

1 Physical symptoms

- Headaches and migraine
- Backache and other muscular pain
- Insomnia
- Gastric disorders including excessive acid, indigestion, flatulence and stomach pain
- Tightening of muscles leading to nausea, breathing difficulties and fainting
- Constipation or diarrhoea
- Dry mouth
- Tiredness
- Excessive or diminished appetite
- In females, complicated or excessive pre-menstrual tension
- In males, impotence or reduced sexual drive

Excessive physical symptoms:

- Hypertension which Friedman and Rosenman[40] have linked with coronary disease.
- Ulcers
- Cardio-vascular problems, e.g. coronary thrombosis
- Heart disease (linked with excessive work hours)

There is increasing evidence that workplace stress undermines the body's immune system making it more susceptible to viruses and bacterial infection. Research work is continuing on the association between persistent stress and the propensity to develop different kinds of cancers. In extreme cases, stress can kill. In Japan, which has traditionally had a culture of long work hours, the term *karoshi* is used to describe death by overwork. The Japanese Ministry of Labour now receives hundreds of applications for compensation from bereaved families because of karoshi.

2 Psychological and emotional

Feelings of:

- Anxiety and tension
- Irritability
- Depression
- Crying
- Fear (e.g. of disapproval)
- Poor concentration
- Obsessively rehearsing matters
- Persecution
- Distrust
- Anger
- Poor relaxation – inability to 'switch off' after work has finished

'Burnout' has the long-term effect of reducing a person's ability to function at a certain level of activity and mental concentration. A long period of recovery with the use of various therapies may be needed to partly restore the individual's previous capabilities. Ultimately, a complete mental breakdown can occur.

3 Social effects

Inability to:

- Work as a team member
- Control temper and emotions
- Articulate clearly
- Write legibly and cogently

A subsequent rise is likely in intra-organizational conflict.

4 Behavioural effects

Increasing dependence on:

- Smoking (linked with quantative work overload)
- Irrational and unpredictable mood swings
- Refusal to obey instructions or to carry out work properly
- Suicide attempts
- Absenteeism from work
- Poor standards of work
- Attempts at sabotage
- Procrastination
- Nervous habits
- Quickened gestures and habits (e.g. talking, walking, eating)

These symptoms will not necessary follow in this order. There is support for the view that stress affects individuals with increasing levels of severity:

Level 1:	Temporary stress	Heart rate increases, respiration increase, blood pressure rises. Metabolic rate increases.
Level 2:	Prolonged level I Symptoms	Irritability, anxiety, tension. Inability to concentrate, restlessness.
Level 3:	Pronounced Disorders	Headaches, stomach disorders, chest pains.
Level 4:	Chronic stress	Ulcers, strokes, alcoholism, drug addiction, Heart attack, psychosis.[41]

Exercise

Under each of the four headings below identify six negative implications for the organization. Feedback is given below.

1 Physical

- Poor performance – lack of attention to detail
- Fall in quality and quantity of work
- Reliance on co-workers and temporary replacement
- Absenteeism – need to cover work
- Loss of business through individual's incapacity or reduced productivity

2 Psychological and emotional

- Effective communications undermined
- Irrational judgements made about others
- Valuable time wasted
- Withholding information from others
- Short but frequent periods of absence from workstation
- Accidents

3 Social

- Likelihood of conflict
- Deterioration in work patterns
- Deterioration in team/workforce morale
- Inability to fulfil dual roles (e.g. manager and leader, manager and coach or mentor) (this will also affect roles outside work – see Section 2.4.4).
- Low morale
- Withdrawal from the normal social networks present in the workplace leading to isolation

4 Behavioural

- Poor problem solving and decision making
- Over-reaction to situations – alienating colleagues and customers
- Accidents in the workplace
- Backlogs of work
- Increase in rumours, grudges and minor disputes
- Turnover of employees
- Requests for early retirement
- Early release on ill-health grounds.

The effect of employee stress on the effectiveness of British employers

- Fifty million working days are lost each year due to stress-related illness, and this costs industry £370 million.[42]
- Half a million UK workers say they have been made unwell due to work-related stress.[43]
- Seventy-six per cent of managers are suffering from work-related stress, with the main causes being lack of time, excessive workload, poor support and lack of control over work.[44] The length of the working day is fifth in order of causation. Working-time statistics are unclear as to the exact average working hours of managers and workers, but it seems that in the UK they are longer than in any other EU country.
- One estimate is that more than 50 per cent of workers operate at high speed or to tight deadlines for at least 25 per cent of their working day. Ten per cent of workers say they have been subjected to intimidation at work.[43] Indeed, in another survey, 45 per cent of respondents said that harassment and bullying was their key complaint about work, whereas 23 per cent cited new working practices and only 2 per cent health and safety.[45]
- Public sector workers suffer from high stress levels due to lack of resources – Their absence rate is 12.9 days per year, nearly a third higher than private sector workers, and research shows much of it is stress-related. (*Personnel Today*, 10 September 2002, p. 17)
- In one survey over 40 per cent of employers were unaware of existing resources in their organizations that could address stress, but 40 per cent of respondents had already taken *some* steps to reduce levels of stress.[44]

The cumulative costs of workplace stress, therefore, are having a detrimental effect on the economy as a whole. Insurance, re-training, recruitment, pension, legal and health service costs are all increasing as a result.

Finally, anxiety disorders and depression can be termed an impairment under the 1995 Disability Discrimination Act where they relate to a 'well-recognized clinical disorder'. The potential high costs of litigation by employees suffering from stress are now causing employers to adjust working practices and budgets.

In 2000 there was a 120 per cent increase in the number of employees successfully suing their employers for stress.

In 1995 the High Court ruled that John Walker's employer, Northumberland County Council, was legally liable for John's second nervous breakdown caused by pressure of work because it was reasonably foreseeable. The Council should have taken reasonable steps to relieve him of some work and they were negligent in not doing so. However, the Council was not negligent in respect of John's first breakdown which had also been caused by overwork. Nevertheless, dozens of stress-related claims will follow the precedent established by the Walker case that the employer can be liable for the work induced stress caused to an employee.

In summer 1999 the county court awarded £67 000 compensation to Beverley Lancaster who suffered panic attacks and depression due to stress contributed to by her employer, Birmingham City Council.

Personnel Today, 8 July 1999, p. 3

Disability discrimination is also discussed in Chapter 12.

2.4.4   Causes of workplace stress

Workplace stress and its causes remain a controversial subject. There is, however, a clear relationship between the individual's propensity for stress and defence mechanisms and the organizational environment. Below we discuss the individual both as victim and the cause of stress.

Role stress

You only have to think of the roles that you (the 'focal person') occupy in all the different aspects and stages of your life, such as child, parent, manager, disco-dancer, gardener, club secretary, friend and colleague to appreciate that individuals fulfil dozens of roles in their lifetime. Many will be occupied concurrently, and several of these in the workplace. Performing too many of these roles or being uncomfortable with having to adopt a particular role can cause or exacerbate stress.

Charles Handy[46] states that our performance of a particular role depends on two variables: The forces in the **individual**, i.e. personality, attributes, skills, self-concept and preferences; and the forces in the **situation**, e.g. organizational culture, systems, norms of behaviour, behaviour of others in the role set (i.e. with whom the focal person interacts), the exercise of power by others, workloads, opportunities to make decisions, take responsibility, exercise authority and so on.

According to Handy, in performing our various roles we are subject to a number of deficiencies in how we act out those roles:

● **Role ambiguity** – Uncertainty on the part of the focal person about what role she or he should be performing. For example, the focal person receives inadequate guidance from a manager.

- **Role incompatibility** – For example, the focal person has difficulty in ethically reconciling two roles such as a devout Christian with the exploitative policies of his or her employer.
- **Role conflict** – Here, for example two roles are concurrently performed (and although they are clear and have no ambiguity in themselves), it is impossible for the focal person to adequately devote sufficient time to more than one. The conflict between domestic responsibilities (e.g. parent or partner) is frequently quoted as a common example.
- **Role overload** – This occurs when the number of roles which the focal person is asked to perform simply become excessive and outside the ability of the individual to manage at the same time. This is different from work overload.
- **Role underload** – Those employers with a self-concept that is not matched by responsibility may experience a feeling that they are not being used to the full.

In addition to performing several roles, a number of life experiences which have a deep emotional impact on people can cluster together at one particular time to cause stress. The individual has the feeling that they cannot cope because events are out of their control at the very time when they need stability.

Traditionally, most attempts to construct a methodology of stress causation, symptoms and coping strategies have used the 'individual differences' model. For example, Cooper's stress factors place individual differences at their centre in dynamic relation to job and organizational factors outlined in Figure 2.7.

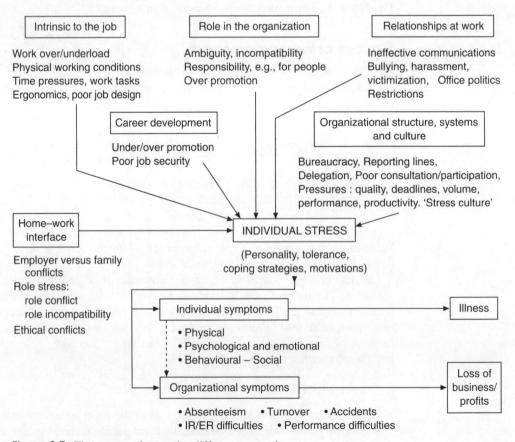

Figure 2.7. The causes of stress by different categories.

Stress and personality

Of specific relevance to understanding the interaction between the individual's personality and stress is the differentiation in the types of personality identified by Meyer Friedman and Ray H. Rosenman[40] based on work by Von Dusch (1868) and Dunbar (1943). The Type A personality will manifest itself by the individual constantly seeking achievement in a shorter timescale. Type B personality results in an opposite pattern of behaviours.

The relevance for the employers in determining the 'types' of personality is predicting whether a job candidate will be prone to stress. Selection devices are being continually refined to ensure that the 'best fit' occurs between the individual and the job and the organization. The increase in the use of psychometric testing, personality questionnaires and assessment centre techniques supports this view. A great deal of research exists which correlates personality type with success in job performance. For example, a job such as air traffic controller suits the Type A personality; consequently there is a high degree of stress present for Type B controllers because they are unsuited to the nature of the job (see Sections 1.2. and 3.2).

Figure 2.8 demonstrates heart rate for three jobs: **Postman/woman** (Type B), **Cycle Courier** (Type B) and **Doctor** (Type A). The system was developed by Ashridge Management College[47] to establish which jobs had built-in stressors. Increased heart rate is to be expected in jobs involving physical work like the postman, but not the GP's, yet you will see the GP's heart rate fluctuates sharply throughout the day. The most stable of the profiles belongs to the cycle courier.

2.4.5 The hardy personality

This concept has been developed in an attempt to explain why some people (whether Type A or Type B) develop ill health under stress and others do not. Kobasa (1979) has shown that 'hardiness' can be illustrated through resilience to pressure and the ability to control the effects of the contextual environment. A person with a 'hardy' personality will be open-minded, have a clear purpose in life, know the stressors present and develop coping mechanisms using a repertoire of techniques. This will enable the individual to enjoy a state of psychological equilibrium identified by Seyle. The concept of the 'Hardy' Personality can be successfully compared with the idea of *stress inoculation* devised by Cameron and Meichenbaum (1982) which supposes that a person can conceptualize stressors in their life and a subsequent programme of coping.

Employers should, however, be aware that the workplace itself can stimulate the manifestation of typical Type A behaviour through *rewards* and *stimulants* such as:

● Praise from the manager for working hard and putting in long hours
● Explicit and implicit pressure from the manager to 'go that extra mile'
● Bullying and harrassment which the individual seeks to displace by various avoidance behaviour ranging from working harder to absenteeism
● Competitive peer pressure
● Demands for 'flexibility'
● Performance-based pay systems based on high performance standards
● Skills and competence-based pay which encourages aspirations for further training and personal improvement
● Job overload including tight deadlines and quality demands
● A stress culture

The Marxist[48] view is that it is convenient for employers to displace the problem of the stressful working environment on the individual:

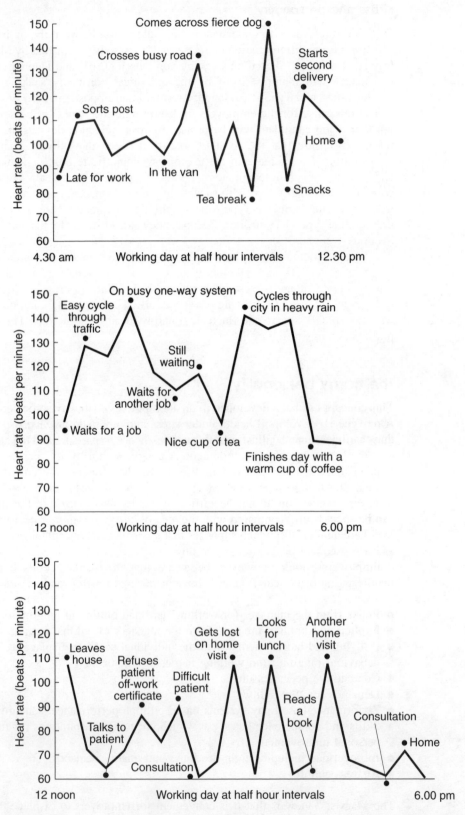

Figure 2.8. Jobs with in-built stressors. (Copyright: *The Guardian*, 8 January 1995, pp. 5–7)

By redefining the issue in terms of the stress faced by employees instead of poor pay and conditions imposed by employers, the new management theories ensure that management keeps the initiative ... Work is being intensified, but calling this stress suggests that the problem is at least partly the fault of the employees as though the real problem of overwork were just a weakness, or a mental health problem on their part.

All the possible main causes will now be considered as part of the solutions to stress.

2.4.6   Managing stress at work

As we have seen already there is no simple formula for identifying who will be affected by stress or what specific work situations will provide an unusually high degree of stressors. We can, however, isolate three variables which can combine to give rise to stress:

- The **work environment** (culture, management style, peer pressure and physical working conditions).
- Certain **occupations** are more stressful than others (this may be due to danger, effort, high levels of concentration, or boredom, monotony and fatigue).
- A person may be more prone to stress in certain situations according to their **personality**.

The combination of all three has led to the increase in methodical selection techniques (testing, *et al.*) which can bring higher than average predictive validity and reliability to selection decisions and so bring about a fit between the individual and the job (see Section 3.2).

Difficulties continue to arise where this carefully planned approach is not attempted. Many organizational responses, therefore are typified by too little too late, or at best a reactive strategy which attempts to minimize damage. In this section we outline steps which an organization and the individual can take to prevent and effectively respond to stress.

The organization

First, an organization should establish a strategy for managing stress as part of an employee health and performance improvement policy. This will involve maintaining careful records and statistics on turnover, absenteeism, accidents, grievances and production and quality indices. Where factors causing stress are identified they should be controlled and at best eliminated. For individuals stress should be reduced and prevented. Stress is, of course, a fact of working life and not all stress can be eliminated, but an organization that fails to recognize it as a problem and attempt remedial action will suffer a multitude of self-induced problems, not least the mismanagement of its 'greatest asset' – its people.

Job design

The individual's job is the most common cause of workplace stress. The way in which the job is organized into separate tasks and interrelates with other jobs is discussed in Chapter 3. This checklist does, however, cover the key inputs to removing high-volume, repetitive and meaningless activities which can cause stress.

- Analysing jobs to ensure there are manageable workloads. Use appraisal and performance review methods to re-work priorities. Use temporary and permanent adjustments to alleviate work overload. Many workers who have to deal with frenzied periods of activity, experience stress for this reason.
- Difficult or unrewarding work should be equitably spread between workers.

- Analysis and action to improve job characteristics.
- Job enlargement (an increase in tasks of the same level) should be avoided because this can lead to work overload.
- Consider job rotation (to avoid boredom, or to temporarily transfer the worker from a stressful situation, e.g. a person who deals with customer complaints).
- Plan jobs to have a meaningful pattern of interlocking tasks, so there is semblance of an overall task with a degree of completion (task significance), to avoid alienation.
- The work cycle itself should not be too long or too short.
- Job enrichment should be introduced where feasible (increased opportunities for enjoying variety and exercising discretion, judgement and achievement). Work by Karasek shows that although management jobs may be more stressful than non-management jobs, those with high levels of work tasks but low levels of autonomy can find work more stressful.
- Maximum feedback should be available to the worker so he or she knows how they are doing.

I suppose I was made redundant because I made poor quality cars. But in seventeen years, not once did management ask me for my ideas on how I could do the job better . . . Not once!

Car assembly worker, Company name withheld

Employee Assistance Programmes (EAPs)

These have proved to be a popular part of many employers' welfare strategies to help overcome or avoid employee stress. In the UK the market is now worth in excess of £42 million and over two million employees and their families are covered by an EAP. They were originally developed in the USA, and can provide a confidential personal counselling service on work and personal difficulties. Some employers will have the resources to operate their own in-house service, but many others use professional organizations which specialize in this type of work. Ideally, the EAP should take a holistic view of the employee so that he or she can seek advice on almost any issue. Anonymity is critical to assure users that it is not a shortcut for management to obtain personal information on workers. Counselling can be provided out of hours over the telephone, but ideally it should be given face to face. Employers are increasingly establishing EAPs when undergoing periods of change. As Professor Cary Cooper has pointed-out, EAPs do not solve the problem of stress, they cannot improve job satisfaction, help with autocratic leadership or a destructive culture. However, they can enable workers to talk through problems with trained counsellors getting personal insight and maybe practical solutions, but more employers should consider using EAP's as well as other initiatives.

Other measures

- Introduce measures to improve the **ergonomics** of a job such as preventing long periods of sitting or standing, or working in isolation. Alleviating extremes of temperature, ventilation and lighting will also help. In 1979 Oldham and Brass[49] found that moving workers from their small conventional offices into open-planned offices without interior walls or partitions produced mixed blessings of lower levels of concentration, a reduced sense of task identity and opportunities to forge friendships.
- Technology can confuse and overwhelm: training and familiarization systems should be established. Electronic mail and text-messaging should be used with care.

- The interface between the worker and their work should be clarified where neccessary. Work roles should be made clear to avoid role ambiguity and conflict (through clear job descriptions, competency profiles, communication and training).
- As part of health and safety audits any physical aspect of the work environment which causes stress should be investigated and remedied where practicable. The employer should attempt to construct a work environment that fulfils 'Quality of Work Life' (QWL) objectives (see Section 3.4).

Individual coping mechanisms

As well as the organizational steps it is important to remember that individuals can help themselves. Those particularly at risk should, according to Toffler (1971), establish 'stability zones'. These are ideas, places, things or people/organizations wherein or wherefrom the individual can obtain 'buffers' from the day-to-day stressors around them. An idea may be a deeply held religious or ethical belief, a person or partner, an object might be a hobby. They enable the individual to replace lost physical and mental energy. It is, therefore critical that employers recognize the need for employees to use these stability zones. Obvious examples are a weekend break and a proper lunch-break.

Further helpful aids include time-management, training in assertiveness and training in positive thinking that can include leadership skills. Delegation and physical exercise are also practical ways to deal with stress. Some of these issues are dealt with in Chapter 3.

The clear message from this analysis is that the problem of stress in the workplace has been growing at an alarming rate, and now threatens to seriously damage the health of a large proportion of the workforce and organizational effectiveness. However, for the first time in a number of years there are signs that employers and individuals are recognizing the need to take serious preventative as well as remedial action.

Summary

In brief, in this section we have defined workplace stress and differentiated between 'strain' and 'eustress'. The latter has a number of incremental stages with specific symptoms. The practical impact on the workplace can be very damaging. This is one reason why employers are turning to selection devices such as personality questionnaires to ensure that new staff are not especially stress prone. We have also examined the place of role stress and the interaction of personality and job environment. To help avoid and resolve stress job design is a critical preventative factor where it can provide the job holder with appropriate levels of autonomy, variety and manageable workloads. We finally examined the role of Employee Assistance Programmes and personal coping strategies.

Case study

Boxford Call Centre

There is growing concern that call-centre jobs will migrate to places such as India unless costs and investment in human capital are managed better. Some 6000 call centres exist in the UK employing half a million people (1.7 per cent of the working population).[50] Staff turnover varies according to location: in one survey 75 per cent of West Midlands employers reported turnover above 24 per cent, whereas in the north-east most employers reported a 70 per cent turnover rate. For customer service representatives their median average salary is around £13,500 p.a.[51]

The job of a customer services adviser (**csa**) at Boxford is twofold: selling and either answering bill enquiries, dealing with equipment/service breakdowns, or querying repairs and selling. The csa's are trained for only one of these jobs and remain doing this work for the rest of their working lives at Boxford. Each csa works in a confined space of about 1.5 m × 1.0 m. In front of the csas is a console which shows how many calls are waiting to be answered; up to ten calls may be waiting at any one time and these are shown by flashing yellow lights. All information about the customer can be instantly called-up on a computer screen using a keyboard, both of which are also in front of the operator.

Each csa is given a one-day training programme before starting work. Strict performance standards are enforced that specify:

- Each call should be closed (that is finished) within three minutes.
- The language used to customers must be appropriate to the business in hand.
- The conversation with the customer must not include any unnecessary social pleasantries or 'chit-chat'.
- Certain key words must be used to customers, such as 'Sir' or 'Madam'. If the customer has a tendency to ramble in describing their problem, the csa must interrupt them and ask: 'Is the problem related to . . . (sir)?
- Calls are regularly monitored in two ways:
  - All calls are automatically monitored so that a daily record is maintained of the number of calls taken by each csa (these should amount to on average eighty calls per day) and their duration.
  - Any one of the six supervisors can listen-in to a call without prior notice to the csa concerned.

Nearly all csas work six days a week.

Stress among csas

Turnover at Boxford has been gradually increasing over the last two years. Absenteeism in 1999 was running at 20 per cent per week, now it is 30 per cent per week. Every member of staff who returns from sick leave which has exceeded five days in three months is interviewed by a member of the personnel department. The department's annual report on absenteeism shows that the most common complaints are migraines, stomach upsets, colds, 'flu and backache. The conclusion is that a high proportion of absences are not genuine, but that the real reason is that staff want a break from boring work. Do you agree with this analysis? What should be done to manage the absence problem?

Feedback

Contrary to the view of the personnel department, a high proportion of the csas could be suffering from physical symptoms of stress.

The management of Boxford call centre should take immediate steps to verify the analysis, and if shown to be incorrect, take steps to implement a stress management strategy. First, the data should be re-assessed by:

- Conducting **exit interviews** which are structured to obtain objective, truthful information.
- **Performance appraisals** which highlight the causes and symptoms of stress. Management and supervisors may need training in adopting a **management style** which encourages more openness, trust and sharing of information. This should link with strong leadership.

- Staff consultation and information systems to facilitate **feedback** to management.
- Staff surveys (e.g. on attitudes, on suggestion schemes and on organizational climate).
- Staff training should be improved.

The stress management strategy should include:

- **Job design**, particularly **job rotation** (selling and customer enquiries rotated). Also the **ergonomics** of csas must be assessed, this should include enlarging the workstation area, building in regular breaks away from the workstation and providing areas for group socialization to take place, such as coffee areas.
- The **technology** should be made less threatening. The number of calls waiting to be answered should either be reduced (more csas) or held without flashing lights so that they are still answered automatically.
- The **targets** for answering calls should be reassessed.
- The strict limitations on the type of **language** use should be lifted.
- **Monitoring** results should be openly discussed with all csas.
- **Rewards** and **incentives** should be installed for employees performing at an optimum level (which is set at a level obtainable without undue pressure).
- Team leaders should 'walk the job' more often and obtain direct feedback from employee rather than rely on surveillance techniques. They should attempt to become 'leaders', and 'supervisors' less.
- Stress management should include monitoring and assessing employee health. If necessary a comprehensive **Employee Assistance Programme** should be introduced.
- Social and recreational facilities should be considered.
- Flexible and 'family-friendly' working practices should be considered, e.g. part-time work, term-time work or flexitime.
- The whole culture of Boxford should change.

Examination questions for this chapter are given in Appendix 2.

References

1 Argyris, C. (1960) *Interpersonal Competence and Organisational Effectiveness*. Tavistock Publishing.
2 Schein, E. (1965) *Organisational Psychology*. Prentice Hall.
3 McGregor, D. (1960) *The Human Side of Enterprise*. McGraw-Hill.
4 Weber, M. (1905) *The Theory of Social and Economic Organisation* (translated by Henderson, A. M., and Parsons, T. (1947)). Oxford University Press.
5 Blauner, R. (1964) *Alienation and Freedom*. University of Chicago Press.
6 Taylor, F. W. (1911) *The Principles of Scientific Management*. In *Job satisfaction – Challenge and response in modern Britain* (ed. Weir, M.) (1974). Fontana/Collins.
7 Dubin, R. (1956) Industrial workers' worlds: a study of the 'central life interests' of industrial workers. *Social Problems*, 3.
8 Goldthorpe, J. H. (1966) Attitudes and behaviours of car assembly workers: a deviant case and a theoretical critique. *Br. J. Soc.*, **17**, 227–244.
9 *Survey by Human Resources and Ceridian Centrefile* (October 2002). Human Resources. Haymarket Management Publications.
10 Rose, R. (1985) *Reworking the Work Ethic*. Batsford.
11 Kodz, J., Kersley, B. and Strebbler, M. (1998) *Tackling a Long Hours Culture*. Institute for Employment Rights.
12 *Labour Force Survey* (Autumn 2002) Stationery Office.

13 Overell, S. (2002) *Personnel Today*, 9 April.

14 Reade, Q. (2002) CitiPeople Index – Morgan McKinley. *Personnel Today*, 11 June.

15 *Personnel Today*, 29 October, 2002.

16 *Personnel Today*, 29 October 2002.

17 Mezzacappa, K. (1997) *The Link Between Human Resources and Customer Bonding*. Financial Times/Pitman Publishing.

18 Lawson, P. (1995) Performance management: an overview. In *The Performance Management Handbook* (ed. Walters, M.) pp. 1–14. Reproduced with permission of the publishers: The Institute of Personnel and Development, IDP House, Camp Road, London SW19 4UX.

19 Braverman, H. (1974) *Labor and Monopoly Capital: The Degradation of Work in the Twentieth Century*. Monthly Review Press.

20 Woodward, J. (1972) The structure of organizations. In *Writers on Organisations* (eds Pugh, D. S., Hickson, D. J., and Hinings, C. R.). Penguin.

21 Blyton, P. (1993) The search for workforce flexibility. In *The Handbook of Human Resource Management* (ed. Towers, B). Blackwell.

22 Leveson, R. (1996) Can professionals be multi-skilled? *People Management*, 29 August, 36–38.

23 Hendry, C. (1994) *Human Resource Management: A strategic approach to employment*. Butterworth-Heinemann.

24 Armstrong, M. (1996) *Employee Reward*. Institute of Personnel and Development.

25 Atkinson, J. (1984) Manpower strategies for flexible organisations. *Personnel Management*, August. Institute of Personnel Management.

26 Pollert, A. (1987) The flexible firm – A model in search of reality (or a policy in search of a practice)? *Warwick Papers in Industrial Relations*, **19**. University of Warwick.

27 *Working in Britain Survey* (2002) Economic and Social Research Council.

28 Department of Trade and Industry 'Work – life campaign'. (2002) *Equal Opportunities Review*, No. 108, August, 4.

29 Dex, S. and Smith, C. (2002) *The Nature and Pattern of Family-friendly Employment in Britain*. Marston Book Services.

30 Lewis, J. (2002) *Personnel Today*, 11 June.

31 *Survey on Flexible Working* (1994, 1996 and 1998). Equal Opportunities Commission.

32 Sheppard, G. (2002) *Personnel Today*, 29 October.

33 Bramham, J. (1994) *Human Resource Planning*. Institute of Personnel and Development.

34 Convention of Scottish Local Authorities Code of Conduct (1997) *Industrial Relations Services Employment Trends 629*, April, 5.

35 Corporate accountability. (2002) *Industrial Relations Survey, Employment Trends. Employment Review 756*, 22 July.

36 Cox, T. (1997) TUC Conference on health and safety.

37 Cooper, C., and Cartwright, S. Mental health and stress in the workplace, based on the work of Hans Seyle (1946).

38 Cummings, T. and Cooper, C. L. (1979) A cybernetic framework for the study of occupational stress. *Human Relations*, **32**, 395–419.

39 Health and Safety Executive (1995) *Stress at Work – A guide for employers*. HSE Books.

40 Friedman, M. and Rosenman, R. H. (1974) *Type A Behaviour and Your Heart*. Knopf.

41 Slavery, L. K. (1985) Stress and the employee. *LODJ*, **7**, 2.

42 Department of Trade & Industry 'Work – life campaign' research (2002).

43 Health and Safety Executive (2002) *Working on Stress*. October.

44 Health and Safety Executive contract research report (2001) *Baseline measurements for the evaluation of the work-related stress campaign*. Roffey Park Institute.

45 Industrial Relations Review survey (2002) *Personnel Today*, 10 September.

46 Handy, C. (1993) *Understanding Organisations*. Penguin.

47 *The Guardian*, 8 January 1995, 5–7.

48 *Living Marxism* (1995) Issue 87, November.

49 Oldham, G. R. and Brass, D. J. (1979) Employee reactions to an open-planned office – A naturally occurring quasi experiment. *Administrative Science Quarterly*, **28**, 542–556.

50 *Personnel Today*, 17 September 2002.

51 Pay and Benefits Review. (2002) *Industrial Relations Services Employment Review*, 23 September 2002, 19.

Further reading

Baret, C., Lehndorff, S. and Sparks, L. (eds) (2000) *Flexible Working in Food Retailing.* Routledge.

Belbin, M. (1997) *Changing the Way We Work.* Butterworth-Heinemann.

Carroll, M. and Walton, M. (1997) *Handbook of Counselling in Organizations.* Sage.

CIPD (2003) *Sustaining success in difficult times (psychological contract).* CIPD.

Clarke, J. (2002) *Stress – A Management Guide.*

Clutterbuck, D. (2003) *Managing the Work–life Balance.* CIPD.

Cortada, J. (1998) *Rise of the Knowledge Worker.* Butterworth-Heinemann.

Earnshaw, J. and Copper, C. (1996) *Stress and Employer Liability.* Institute of Personnel and Development.

Economic and Social Research Council (2000) *Working in Britain 2000.*

Jex, S. M. (1998) *Stress and Job Performance.* Sage.

Johnson, M. (1997) *Teleworking.* Butterworth-Heinemann.

Kirton, G. (2000) *The Dynamics of Managing Diversity: A Critical Approach.* Butterworth-Heinemann.

Petrick, J. A. and Quinn, J. F. (1997) *Management Ethics.* Sage.

Pettinger, R. (1997) *Managing the Flexible Workforce.* Financial Times/Pitman.

Stredwick, J. and Ellis, S. (1998) *Flexible Working Practices – Techniques and Innovations.* Institute of Personnel and Development.

Tobin, R. (2000) *Handling Employees' Problems.* Kogan Page.

Wainwright, D. and Calnan, M. (2002) *Work stress – The making of a modern epidemic.*

Web-site addresses

Centre for Economic Performance: http://www.cep.lse.ac.uk
Citizens Advice Bureaux: http://www.nacab.org.uk
Department for Work and Pensions: http://www.dwp.gov.uk
Eurolink Age: http://www.eurolinkage.org
Industrial Society – See: Work Foundation
Institute for Employment Studies: http://www.employment-studies.co.uk
International Stress Management Association: http://www.isma.org.uk
Labour Force Statistics: http://www.statistics.gov.uk
Labour Research Department: http://www.lrd.org.uk
Manpower: http://www.manpower.co.uk
Office for National Statistics: http://www.ons.gov.uk
Stress UK: http://www.stress.org.uk
Stress Management Webring: http://www.agenda.fsnet.co.uk/stress.htm
Work Foundation: http://www.workfoundation.org.uk
Workplace Bullying: http://www.successunlimited.co.uk

3 Optimizing the people contribution

For many organizations, the effective recruitment of new skills required for changing business needs was a real issue that needed to be tackled during the hype surrounding the dot-com start-ups. One of the key challenges was the need to entice people from attractive, smaller, innovative web companies.

Many of the featured organizations are seeking employees . . . to be able to adapt to working in a constantly changing environment, an uncertain market, and for companies where work roles often have blurred boundaries.

The financial organization's e-business initiative not only offers a number of different terms and conditions to its parent organization in an attempt to attract the type of talent the business requires, but also to cater specifically to the e-business environment. In particular, the e-business initiative offers employees with these skills benefits such as a £3000 development allowance and a company performance-related bonus.

Recruitment and performance measurement within the financial e-business initiative is conducted against a defined set of behaviours linked to the business environment. The recruitment team (at Sainsbury's) is looking for potential employees with appropriate experience and an attitude that fits the company's culture.

The e-business can only thrive with a motivated and loyal workforce who believe in the company and the quality of its output and/or products. At BT employee buy-in is achieved by emphasizing the benefits e-business provides for individuals as well as the business.

Constant change and the threat of redundancies in an e-business environment can undermine staff confidence and can make boosting staff morale a priority. The key at Sainsbury's 'to You' centres around sharing information and celebrating success. Such things are easily overlooked, so the company seeks to ensure managers reinforce these leadership practices.

Several of the case study organizations have provided employees with technological support to help them adapt to new working practices and acquire the necessary skills to work in the new environment.

A recurring theme throughout all the case studies is the challenge of getting the people bit right. HR issues permeate all the key issues. Effective recruitment and retention schemes need to be developed to secure talent and keep staff motivated and loyal. HR must also develop comprehensive training and development programmes to support employees through the technological and cultural changes that accompany the shift to e-business.

(Selected extract from 'E-Business: What are the human implications of transformation?' by Claire McCartney, Roffey Park, specially prepared for 'Personnel Today' 17 September 2002.)[1]

<table>
<tr><td>

Chapter objectives

</td><td>

In this chapter you will:

- Obtain an overview of a number of ways in which the contribution of people in the organization can be maximized, particularly by reference to:
- Examining the exercise of power and influence, recruiting and selecting for the right 'fit', leadership, motivation, development, and managing individual and team performance.

</td></tr>
<tr><td>

Chapter introduction

</td><td>

Like the Holy Grail or the Philosopher's Stone, those responsible for getting optimum performance from people down the ages have sought ways to do this with maximum effect and minimum trouble, but never quite found the answer. Modern organizations have never spent as much time and other resources on this question. In this chapter we will be examining some of the key issues in pursuit of this aim. The specific topics such as performance management and leadership, motivation and addressing poor performance are seldom addressed in a single analysis. In the article extract above from the Roffey Park report both the necessity for and the advantages of such a coordinated approach are illustrated. In this chapter we will be addressing the underpinning issues raised in the article.

- Motivation – The use of rewards and incentives, and understanding what needs employees have
- Leadership – The power on which effective leadership is based and the styles adopted to maximize people commitment and performance
- Recruitment and selection – To maximize the 'fit' between employee and organization, and the importance of comprehensive induction.
- Performance management – Providing the culture, systems and methods to generate and reward high performance, as well as effectively manage poor performance
- Nurturing, developing and growing an effective workforce.

</td></tr>
</table>

3.1   The use of power at work – control or commitment?

<table>
<tr><td>

Section objectives

</td><td>

In this section you will:

- Examine the difference between power, authority and influence
- Obtain a knowledge of the various sources of power and the reciprocal behaviours of workers and
- Examine how this information can be applied to the management of people at work.

</td></tr>
</table>

3.1.1   Introduction

The rationale for this book besides helping students pass their exams is to lay out in cogent form the numerous theories, ideas about how best to manage human resources and their practical application to the workplace. This rationale is informed by the simple assumption that management does have a 'right' to manage people in the same way that other resources such as money or equipment can be managed. There are concepts and rules which constrain the activities of management such as ethics (see Section 2.3), law (see Chapter 12), external factors such as labour markets (Chapter 8), and social forces and trades unions (see Chapters 9 and 11). However, despite this, capitalist society as a whole has developed with the notion that 'management has a right to manage'. Indeed, we can see from Chapter 12 employment law continues to be based on the dominance of this presumption.

Yet much of this chapter is concerned with the never-ending task of managers to motivate, lead and generally nurture their human resources. In other words, although management has the ultimate right to determine the day-to-day and future activities of the organization a reciprocal arrangement exists with the people who work for them to support such a system. Without their acceptance organizations could not function effectively. The basis on which the 'right to manage' is legitimized is because the organization run by a small group of managers is recognized as beneficial in some way to society or a part of society. Although there may be conflicting interests there are greater interests which are of a mutual nature to uphold such a right.[2]

Modern management techniques involve coercive and controlling systems, but management can also construct participative systems that maximize human contribution and thereby grow commitment and motivation. In an effort to explain the power relationship, which underpins these different ways of managing, our first difficulty is that the word 'power' is in itself a pejorative word. Lord Acton, a Victorian historian, said 'Power tends to corrupt, and absolute power corrupts absolutely', adding that 'great men are nearly always bad men'.[3]

A definition of power: 'The capacity of someone to alter another's behaviour'.

The definition implies that left to make his or her own choices about behaviour the person would have done something else. Today we emphasize that power does not always mean directing people away from their natural inclinations but directing their behaviour using different incentives and rewards. This raises the distinction between:

- **Authority:** The status which can legitimize power (e.g. the manager can give instructions but no one else) and
- **Influence:** The application of the power so that it has some practical effect (e.g. the manager can grant a pay rise) so that compliance occurs.[4]
- **Compliance,** as Etzioni[5] has pointed out, is the 'major element of the relationship between those who have power and those over whom they exercise it'. However, the types and strength of power exercised, the degree of authority and the reciprocal compliance will depend upon the structures, systems and culture of the work organization. Pfeffer[6] has shown that there are a number of variables that will generate conflict in the exercise of organizational power such as:
- Competition for resources – The scarcer they are, the greater the opportunity for conflict as different individuals and groups aspire to their possession.
- Incompatible technologies that do not have an effective interface. Questions arise such as whose fault is it that they are not compatible? Who will change theirs to provide an interface? Who will pay for it?
- Goal incongruity – variable goals and standards to achieve them, for example one manager wishes to approach a problem using a particular solution, which conflicts with the goals, or solutions of another manager.
- Conflicting links and interdependence – the normal day-to-day work functions of one employee will impact on the work of another and thereby cause disagreements. Wherever shared boundaries exist – work or domestic – there is a risk of conflict.

Power relationships in organizations

According to Etzioni the type, size, complexity and effectiveness of the organization enhances the need for compliance in its workforce.[5] The power used to influence will include physical, material, and symbolic rewards and deprivations. Organizations tend to allocate these means systematically and strive to ensure that they will be used in conformity with the organizational norms. So, not all power is the same but neither is the reason for compliance.

Etzioni's comparative model expresses the types of power typified by organizations, but what of the individual power sources used by individuals in organizations? These power sources require a number of supporting features to any power-based relationship.

Relativity of power

For someone to exercise power over another that power must have **salience**. So, if A tries to exercise power over B, then B must be influenced by A's power otherwise it is valueless. If A seeks to bribe you for £5 then this sum of money must be sufficient for you to do what A wants. For a manager, as his or her workforce change so their salience will alter depending upon who make-up their **power constituency**. This assumes that A has a **domain of power** over B. The domain is the accepted power constituency; for example, manager A tries to instruct B to do something, but B works in another department and will only be told what to do by his or her own manager – B does not come within A's power domain. What if B is one of A's own staff? B may very reluctantly follow A's instructions, but this does not mean the **balance of power** is completely one-sided in favour of A. B may have the power to hit back in some way, even by taking a day's absence when most needed by A.

Individuals when exercising their own sources of power must be aware of these key contextual features of the power relationship. What are these power sources? French and Raven,[7] as well as Handy[4] have identified a range of power sources as follows:

Power source (French and Raven)	Handy
Physical power	**Coercive**

This is based on physical force or the threat of force. It is seldom practised at work, but some bad managers, bullies and those who intimidate, victimize and harass others all practise this type of power. Once used the perpetrator may feel he or she needs to continue to exercise this power source or suffer the same fate. Institutions based on this power source include prisons, some schools and hospitals. The most common manifestation at work is during industrial disputes when there might be a lockout, strike, picket line or demonstration. The use of physical power must be the power source of last resort. Bullying, harassment (physical or sexual) and some forms of victimization are manifestations of physical power. However, the culture of an organization can reflect physical power where individuals feel they cannot speak out because of an implicit rather than explicit threat of some form of unofficial or official punishment.

Resource power	**Reward**

Arguably the traditional method of influencing people at work is the opportunity to give them what they want in return for appropriate behaviour. So, adequate work equals pay, high-quality work or harder work equals higher pay or a bonus. Some would say this amounts to no more than a bribe, and there is evidence to show that money is not a good motivator (this is discussed in Section 3.4 of this chapter). However, possession of a valued resource is a very strong basis for influencing others and for that reason Etzioni termed this 'calculative' power, because the person calculates that it is worth behaving in the way desired for the resource offered. To be effective there must be control over the resource in question, and the potential recipient must desire that resource.

In negotiations between management and trades unions management must have the power to grant or withhold, say, a pay increase, and the trades union(s) must want the pay increase for their members. Moreover, the union(s) must be able to withdraw its members from the workplace to go on strike, but the management continues to desire their continued working. This classic conflict of power has been the root of many industrial disputes whereby resource power and physical power sources of two parties come into direct conflict. (See also Chapter 9.)

Position power   **Legitimate power**

This source of power is based on the role or position that someone occupies in the organization. It is not the individual who personally possesses the power source but rather the power goes with the job. However, most managers will at least need resource power to support position power. Also, the organization must back the individual with power sources designed to generate compliance with the instructions given by the person in that 'position', such as a staff handbook, disciplinary procedures, etc. For these reasons this power source is commonly found in bureaucracies. Incompetent managers will often fall back on position power to ensure compliance, although they may first use any resource power they possess; this could include information, rights of access to networks or premises, e.g. car park.

Expert power   **Specialist**

Because of their expertise or knowledge or skill this person will enjoy this type of power. It requires no sanctions because others will follow instructions or heed the words of this person because they respect him or her for their expertise, so it is a power source that can only be enforced by the recognition of those over whom it is applied. If it is questioned the individual may need to fall back on other sources of power. Traditionally, the professions have enjoyed this type of power base, but unfortunately, only seldom does the personnel/ HR function.

Personal power   **Charismatic**

Quite the opposite source from position power. Here it is the individuals themselves who represent the power source through the strength of their personality or some personality trait. It is less resented than other power sources and does not require secondary sources of power such as resource power. For this reason many aspiring leaders in organizations would prefer to depend on this power source than all others. It is a particular but not universal element that makes up competent leadership. In non-bureaucratic organizational structures this type of power source and leadership based on it can flourish.

Negative power or reflective power

Everybody has the latent power to disrupt or to prevent something from happening, no matter how apparently insignificant in the organization. For example, a clerk 'loses' important papers on purpose, a secretary 'accidentally' shreds a crucial fax, the disgruntled manager blocks or filters information.

These power sources, either singularly or in combination, can induce many types of response. Effective management is about using leadership qualities and sound motivational methods based on relevant power sources to generate behaviours which are mutually beneficial. The preferred behaviours are 'identification' and 'internalization'. The former involves the individual employee adopting new ideas or behaviours because they admire or identify with the source, normally personal and expert power sources. The latter will involve the individual adopting them because they perceive them as their own, but this requires high-quality leadership. Finally, the individual will comply, normally because they believe it is in their best interests to do so, be it a reward or the avoidance of punishment. The notion of leaders using fear, convention, rewards, respect and trust are taken up again in the next section of this chapter.

Summary

In this section we have examined different sources of power, the affect of authority and influence, and the application of power at work. Society now demands that expressions of power in the workplace must not breach norms of behaviour. This means that managers must exercise power with care, particularly physical and negative power. Managers who purport to be leaders must hone the application of resource, charismatic and expert power, because it is these power sources which will produce responses from employees that equates to high performance, commitment, trust and cost-effectiveness. The search and hiring of this type of employee is now examined.

3.2 Recruitment and selection of human resources

Section objectives

In this section you will:

● Examine the meaning of efficient, effective and fair recruitment and selection
● Examine the systematic process of recruitment and selection and induction and
● Explore in depth key selection methods, such as interviewing and testing.

3.2.1 Introduction: what is recruitment and selection?

Perhaps the first question that should be asked in this part of the chapter is 'why recruitment and selection?' The answer seems simple: To fill a vacancy that has arisen. However, before rushing to fill a vacancy by bringing in someone from outside the organization should conduct an analysis of the situation that may show this is unnecessary.

First, an organization should have an effective Human Resource Planning (HRP) system, which will help determine its future people requirements alongside and integral to business objectives, work systems and technology used. HRP will also enable the employer to effectively assess labour turnover, particularly where exit analysis shows reasons for staff leaving. There is also little point in hiring someone using expensive selection techniques if the job is to be shortly changed or phased out. If this were expected could an internal transfer carry out the tasks in the meantime? On the other hand, could someone be hired with a view to the job changing in the near future?

Second, rather than externally recruit could an existing employee be transferred, promoted or retrained to undertake the work? From our discussion of the changes to work in Chapter 2 we have seen that promotion possibilities have significantly declined in the last twenty years; so the opportunity to take on new and perhaps more responsible work could be welcomed by a number of employees.

Third, what analysis has been undertaken to identify the reason why the previous post-holder left? Is there are a high incidence of turnover in that department or in the whole organization? Some of the 'push' reasons for staff turnover are:

● Poor management/leadership
● Employer branding – poor image
● Bullying/harassment

- Poor working conditions
- Lack of career development
- Lack of personal development – all of which lead to low morale

Some of the 'pull' reasons for staff turnover are:

- Improved pay and terms and conditions
- Better career and developmental prospects
- More attractive corporate image
- Easier commuting

Again, there is little point in embarking on expensive recruitment if the new post-holder will leave quickly as did the last job incumbent.

Lastly, two key issues must be addressed if the organization decides to go ahead and recruit externally – job analysis must be undertaken to ensure the written recruitment/job specifications are accurate. This matter is discussed under 'job design' in Section 3.4. Also, the recruitment and selection process must be revalidated to ensure it is capable of producing the best group of candidates, and ultimately the best candidate selected for the job. This brings us back to the question of what is meant by recruitment and selection.

According to Lewis recruitment is 'the activity that generates a pool of applicants, who have the desire to be employed by the organization, from which those suitable can be selected', and selection is 'the activity in which an organization uses one or more methods to assess individuals with a view to making a decision concerning their suitability to join the organization, to perform tasks which may or may not be specified'.[8]

The term 'recruitment' has also been extended not only to cover the supply of a pool of candidates for selection, but also those tasks associated with bringing the selected candidate into the organization through issuing the contract of employment for example. See Figure 3.1.

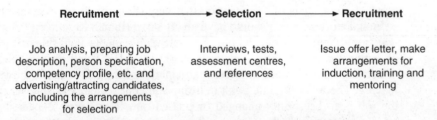

Figure 3.1. The relationship between recruitment and selection.

The organization must commit itself to the achievement of a number of critical success factors in recruitment and selection if the best person is to be selected. These factors are:

- The process must be **systematic:** that is, carried out in a logical fashion and consistently in line with the organization's policies, systems, Human Resource Plan and with business objectives.
- **Fairness.** Ethical and legal considerations must be complied with. The way in which recruitment/selection is carried out says a lot about the organization and prospective employees will be aware of the messages conveyed by the way the process is managed.

Organizational culture will influence any ethical practices, which may be enshrined in a code or policy on ethics. A key dimension is to act fairly within the law, especially concerning equal opportunities so as not to unlawfully discriminate. In Chapter 11 we will examine the legal obligations on employers and the originating employment statutes. The Equal Opportunities Commission and the Commission for Racial Equality have issued codes of practice and guidance booklets on applying equal opportunities practices to recruitment and selection. There is also a Code of Practice and Guidance which accompanies the Disability Discrimination Act 1995. Furthermore, codes of practice published by the CIPD should be followed, as should the numerous specialist ACAS handbooks. Fairness is also examined in the context of tests later in this section.

- **Efficiency:** This means using the resources of time, money, reputation and human resources to best effect. Having a systematic plan provides a blueprint for the exercise. An organization that employs someone on an annual salary of £30000 can mean an investment of nearly half a million pounds sterling, including employment costs, over a 10-year period. Numerous publications, such as those produced by such bodies as the CIPD will help guide the inexperienced recruiter.
- **Effectiveness:** Obtaining the right person using the optimum resources available must be the paramount objective. Moreover, ineffective recruitment can lead to a poor 'fit' between the employer and the new employee causing an induction crisis and under-performance. Not selecting the best candidate is a waste of money and could cause financial losses and otherwise to the employer. What is required therefore here is the optimum fit of the person, the organization, and the job.

In order to obtain the best 'fit' the selection devices used must be valid and reasonable:

- **Validity:** Any technique or method used must provide the employer with accurate results. There is little point in using an interview technique that does not enable the employer to select the best candidate. Furthermore, there is no point in paying for the use of expensive selection methods, such as tests if they do not measure the attributes or skills or competencies that you wish to measure in the candidates and those which are relevant to the job. A selection method which is valid will measure what it is supposed to measure.
- **Reliability:** Having found and used the most fair, efficient and effective methods and techniques which are valid the employer should be able to use them consistently over time. This means that using them on more than one occasion will provide the employer with results that are consistent and comparable with the results arising out of use on the last occasion.

3.2.2   First steps in recruiting

We have already discussed job analysis earlier in this section, but should remind ourselves that the key outcome from the process has traditionally been the job description, which most organizations still continue to use. The job description will contain:

- Key facts about the job
- Clusters of related facts and tasks
- Details of the main responsibilities
- A summary of the main purpose of the job
- Details of responsibilities and tasks grouped under key areas of activity and showing importance and frequency.

ACAS[9] have provided helpful advice on what should constitute a well-written job description:

- **Main purpose of job:** This should be written in one sentence, and at most two for complex jobs.
- **Main tasks of the job:** The objective here is not to detail every last possible task in minute detail, but to give the reader an accurate picture of the principal tasks and areas of responsibility. Some organizations use the term 'key accountability areas', examples being: 'resources management', 'people management', or 'training duties'. Each description should commence with an active verb such as 'writing', 'filing' or 'selling'. Too many job descriptions are written in vague terms such as 'managing', 'maintaining' or having an 'overview', and with little idea of outputs. A well-written task description could be:

'Telephoning potential customers to sell insurance policies A, B and E.
Importance: High.
Frequency: Continuous.
Authority to Act: High.'

This task starts with an (a) input (i.e. active verb): 'telephoning', then identifies the focus of the (b) action required: potential customers (this will usually be an adjective or noun) and finish with (c) output: to sell insurance.

Example

(a) 'Devise . . . (b) a system of record keeping . . . (c) which can be used to effectively monitor absenteeism'.   (Importance: Very important)
                    (Frequency or time-scale: To be completed by August 2002)

The tasks or key responsibilities should be clustered around the key accountability areas.

Finally, the **scope of the job** should be indicated. This will inform the reader of the importance and impact of the job. This can be done by describing the value of technology, materials or equipment used, the range of people supervised and the impact of the job on customers and the business. Information such as the author of the job description, the date of preparation, date of review and location of the job in the structure of the organization should always be included. A structure chart can help illustrate the last point.

In addition, information such as fluctuations in job demands, physical/social environments, membership of relevant groups, training required, and assessment methods could be included.

The job description is, therefore a synopsis of the job; it tells the reader where the job fits in with the total work system and gives specific information on what, when and where the tasks should be carried out.

Contractual matters

HRP requirements may mean the job is temporary, part-time, job-share or based on annualized hours. Whatever form the tenure and hours worked takes, these type of contracts which aid numerical and temporal flexibility should not be chosen for the wrong reasons. Our discussion of flexibility in Chapter 2 shows that some employers may exploit these types of flexibility for short-term financial reasons. Between 1999 and 2002 new legal measures, mainly emanating from the EU, were formulated and introduced to protect workers on fixed-term contracts, engaged in part-time work and other types of atypical work.

The person specification

This is the second of the two key documents and derives partly from the job description. It is a profile of the ideal person to fill the job, but without producing characteristics that could never be fulfilled. For this reason it is wise to show a desirable profile (i.e. ideal) and an **essential** (i.e. minimum) one, as well as an **unacceptable** profile. One candidate may possess characteristics which span both profiles; for example, she possesses the **desirable** qualifications, but her experience meets only **essential** criteria. In recent years person specifications have been criticized for failing to provide a benchmark as to what the candidate can actually do rather than a broad psycho-social profile. This is rather unfair because the person specification is designed specifically to produce just that; once established the use of selection methods can be adopted to evaluate what the candidate can or cannot do. It is one reason why competency profiles have become so popular in recent years.

Judge for yourself on the usefulness of the person specification by examining the best-used models in Table 3.1.

The information on the ideal and essential person characteristics can be ascertained by correlating the profiles of different employees and their performance standards, obtained through performance appraisals. Using a software package, the characteristics can be isolated and constructed in accordance with different jobs.

It is important to remember that unnecessary requirements are not simply a question of putting the wrong person into a job, but can be discriminatory too. For example, specifying unjustifiable requirements for gender, race, physical ability (direct discrimination), or height, size, first spoken-language or residence (indirect discrimination).

Furthermore, you should note that there are several aspects of the traditional person specifications which could lead the employer very easily into breaching the Disability Discrimination Act 1995. In the Seven-Point Plan elements 1, 5 and 7, and in the Five-fold Grading System element 1, clearly need modification to avoid references to

Table 3.1 The person specification – two models

Alec Rodger's Seven Point Plan

1 Physical make-up – health, appearance, bearing and speech
2 Attainments – education, qualifications, experience
3 General intelligence – intellectual capacity
4 Special aptitudes – mechanical, manual dexterity, facility in use of words and figures
5 Interests – intellectual, practical, constructional, physical active, social, artistic
6 Disposition – acceptability, influence over others, steadiness, dependability, self-reliance
7 Circumstances – any special demands of the job, such as ability to work unsocial hours, travel abroad, etc.

John Munroe-Frazer's Fivefold Grading System or Framework

1 Impact on others – physical make-up, appearance, speech and manner
2 Acquired qualifications – education, vocational training, work experience
3 Innate abilities – quickness of comprehension and aptitude for learning
4 Motivation – individual goals, consistency and determination in following them up, success rate
5 Adjustment – emotional stability, ability to stand up to stress and ability to get on with people

---

The amount of detail included in the specification will vary according to the job involved, but will not always increase with the level of the post; some quite junior posts can have important requirement in 'impact on other people', for example.

physical appearance and activity, for example, unless these are justifiable requirements of the job.

Before moving to the next stages of recruitment decisions must be taken on matters such as contractual status, pay and benefits, status, location and mobility.

Competency profile specification

Competencies have already been discussed in Chapters 2 and 3. Suffice here to say that these profiles are proving to be a popular and reliable alternative to the person specification. The big advantage is that they allow the selector to break down particular characteristics into different competencies. For example, the person specification might require someone with good judgement, but what does this mean? Without careful definition different selectors might interpret it differently. The broad 'natural' competency of 'judgement' could be first defined and then given a number of behavioural outcomes; so that judgement becomes:

Ability to make qualitative decisions: Behaviour:

● Employee makes decisions which avoid or cause problems; or
● Employee maximizes the role and input of all resources by making decisions and applying problem-solving techniques; or
● Employee can deal with decision making and problem solving under pressure without losing consistency and quality.

Clearly, this gives selectors a great deal more to specifically work with, and they can construct interview questions and other selection measurements which directly address the needs of the organization and the job.

3.2.3   Recruitment methods

These can be summarized in Figure 3.2, which shows the range of selection methods. It is probable that the HR function will be responsible for managing the total process, but increasingly in devolved organizational structures line management has a major contribution, and even a controlling role to play. A decision must also be taken on whether all or part of the function should be outsourced. One survey shows nearly 80 per cent of private sector firms and 43 per cent of public sector employers outsource some part of the recruitment/selection process.[10] The most common outsourced functions are advertising, screening interviews, testing and executive search – sometimes referred to as 'head-hunting'. The advantages of doing so are the expertise of the agency or consultancy in their particular field, the anonymity of the client/employer until final interview, and the cost-effectiveness of giving the task to a specialist. The latter will prevent valuable in-house resources from doing something which they are not trained to provide. However, disadvantages include excessive costs, particularly executive search. The norm for most employers when recruiting non-executive staff is to use employment agencies for temporary workers, and recruitment agencies for advertising and specialist services such as CV scanning. The final decision to appoint must always be kept in-house.

Advertising

There are two means by which a new employee can be attracted:

● **Internally** by means of a search or 'trawl' of potential candidates (used in the public sector and in large corporations). This gives an opportunity for staff to be transferred for

Recruitment and selection methods

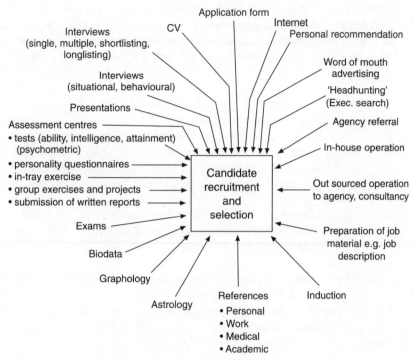

Figure 3.2. Recruitment and selection methods.

experience and training purposes. In addition there is internal advertising which in effect 'ring-fences' jobs so that existing employees can apply for promotion and transfer. This provides career 'headroom' which has significantly slumped due to 'downsizing'; it has a clear motivational effect and helps retain employees who might otherwise leave for a better job elsewhere. This method can also be used for internal redeployment of persons who are selected for redundancy from their own posts.

- **Externally** advertising in local, national or specialist newspapers, magazines or journals. Of limited use is radio, cinema and television, mainly due to costs and the imprecision of the market targeted. Other methods include:

(i)   Employment and recruitment agencies which have grown in popularity
(ii)   Open days, exhibitions of careers fairs
(iii)   Careers advisory services for local areas, universities or adults
(iv)   Training providers operating under New Deal and Modern Apprenticeships for young people.
(v)   Unsolicited letters and casual callers, or those responding to locally placed adverts.

External advertising enables the employer to work towards achieving a 'diverse' workforce through using flexible recruitment methods.

It is very inadvisable to use 'word-of-mouth' recruiting, say through present employees because this could perpetuate the current make-up of the workforce and give rise to indirect sex or race discrimination.

The source and method of attraction chosen will depend upon the type of vacancy that exists and how quickly it must be filled, the resources available to fill it, the difficulties in attracting good calibre candidates, the location of the job, and the history of failure/success in using different methods. Monitoring, therefore plays an important part of the process, not least to ascertain the equal opportunities dimension at every stage.

Assuming that a decision to advertise externally has been taken, a time scale for filling the vacancy determined and responsibilities for particular tasks allocated, the objectives of the advertisement must now be decided upon. Generally, they should follow the acronym ADIDA:

A – Attract attention: in a competitive sellers' market this could be difficult
D – Deter inappropriate applicants
I – Interest should be generated in the reader so they read all the advert
D – Desire should subsequently be aroused in the reader to apply for the job. This will be achieved by presenting relevant information that attracts the reader while leaving them wanting to learn more. Marketing the organization will also help 'sell' the job.
A – Action, therefore follows. The reader becomes an applicant. To facilitate this the advert should tell the reader exactly what they have to do to find out more about the job/organization and/or to apply.

To achieve these objectives the designer of the advert should define the target readership based on the job description and person specification or competency profile and produce text and graphics which can best convey the relevant message of attraction. At the same time balance this against the resources available and determine a budget maximum. Finally, monitor all information relevant to the process.

Exercise

What information should be monitored and analysed about the success or otherwise of the job advert?

Feedback

The analysis should be based on the different mediums chosen (e.g. newspaper, journal, etc.) and the different dates and locations of the medium used. The data can then be broken down into:

- Numbers responding
- Numbers requesting further details
- Numbers applying
- Numbers differentiated by sex, race, disability, age, home location
- Successfully shortlisted candidates and source of successful candidate, and finally,
- The cost-effectiveness of each medium used based on the above data.

A key decision to be made before advertising is the method of application: application form or curriculum vitae? Thereafter shortlisting will take place.

3.2.4   The interview

The selection interview is one of the great controversial techniques that has a central part in people management, despite heavy criticism and much evidence that it is prone to misuse and over-reliance. In Chapter 1 we examined the effect of social perception and stereotyping in interviewing. However, there are techniques that will make optimum use of the selection interview as a useful tool. There are many useful acronyms for remembering a basic structure for the interview; one that is very helpful is **PPAASS:**

P = Purpose: The interviewer(s) should have a clear idea and plan as to the reason for the interview, the objectives to be achieved and the role of the members of the interview 'panel'. To increase objectivity there should preferably always be at least two interviewers, although in practice, particularly at 'screening' interviews, this will be difficult.

P = Preparation: This represents the detailed arrangements before the actual interview begins. The exact role and interaction of the panel members must be decided in advance so that each member knows the order of questions, who will cover which questions including areas to be probed, and the procedure for the interviews. Indeed, will only one person conduct the interview or will two or more be involved? It is usual with panels of two or three members to have a representative from the HR function, the line manager involved and someone from the department or area in which the new employee will work.

Every interview must have a clear beginning, middle and an end. The reception arrangements must be carefully organized and the interviewing environment be prepared, including room layout. Where someone with a disability has indicated the requirement for special needs these should be organized beforehand. This will also cover greeting the candidate and informing him or her of the purpose of the interview, the role of each panel member, the duration of the interview, that there will be note taking during the interview, and that there will be an opportunity for them to ask questions.

A = Activation: This is arguably, the most important part of the interview. The interviewer's job is to 'activate' the interview – in other words, to generate a dialogue between themselves and the candidate, and in particular to get the candidate talking. Interviewers can use body language which is discussed under **'Attention'**, but they fail or succeed by using carefully chosen questions. There are a number of questions that can be used:

● Closed: These require a 'yes' or 'no' answer.

   Example: Q: 'Did you enjoy your last job?'
              A: 'No'.

● Direct: These require limited information to be given.

   Example: Q: 'What is your manager's name?'
              A: 'Appean Sharma'.

● Open: These require more than a one-word answer and frequently a well-phrased open question can generate a lot of information.

   Example: Q: 'Where did you obtain your CIPD qualification?'
              A: 'Through Malpas Flexible Learning Ltd.'
   Example: Q: 'Tell me what you find interesting about working in transport management'.
              A: 'Well, firstly I like the ability to visit different sites, and then there is the problem-solving to get the vehicles moving . . . (*and so and so on*)'.

You would have straight away detected a big difference in the type of open questions used. Indeed there is a large choice facing the interviewer. Some are too wide for the situation and the candidate; the 'tell me' type of question should only be used to relax the interviewee and get them talking, and to introduce a specific topic about which the interviewee knows something. Interviewees should do around 80–85 per cent of the talking in a selection interview. The second question asked could have equally elicited a very short answer such as 'I don't like transport management', or 'the travelling'. This is why interviewers should be prepared to have a range of questions at their fingertips. There is every advantage in having a list of preprepared questions covering all the key areas to be probed, but an effective interviewer will not just rely on them. Remember Rudyard Kipling's maxim:[11]

I keep six good serving men
(They taught me all I knew);
Their names are What and Why and When
And How and Where and Who.

- Probing: This is where the probing question is so useful. This type of question provides a clear focus to unsatisfactory answers. The interviewer can follow up leads or pull out and confirm a key piece of information buried in a long waffly answer.

    Example questions: 'Could you give me a recent example of that?'
    'What exactly did that entail?'
    'And how did they react to that idea?'

- Repeat or Playback: This enables the interviewer to clarify and confirm by relaying back the answer to the interviewee in some fashion.

    Example questions: 'Are you telling me you found it difficult to work with Mr Norgate?'
    'So, your idea is to . . . ?'

- Hypothetical: These questions will involve putting a scenario or idea or problem to the interviewees and asking them to explain their views, solutions or ideas. They are particularly useful when evaluating competencies. However, they must be used carefully so that they are reasonably within the interviewee's scope of answering otherwise they will lose confidence and 'dry up'.

Other questions used are the 'leading' question, which involves asking the interviewee something which leads him or her into giving a predictable answer. Again they must be used carefully. This type of question is similar to the forced-choice question which should only be used in special circumstances; an example would be: 'Do you prefer working in London or in Manchester?' As a general rule the 'multiple question' must be avoided because it involves wrapping two or more questions into one and will confuse the interviewee as well as the interviewer!

Interviewers should not 'fire' questions at interviewees as if the interview were an interrogation; this does not prevent the pace of the interview being brisk and the interviewee feeling challenged by a number of tightly grouped questions. A candidate who is too complacent and comfortable is unlikely to let their guard drop and the interviewer may find little or no truth in the answers provided.

In addition to questioning, the interviewer would be expected to use a number of **summaries** at the close of sections of the interview and try to link one part of the interview with the next. Where two or more board members are involved each should have a specific time-slot to pose questions with an opportunity to follow up later; a tennis-match should be avoided where one question is asked by one interviewer, and then by the next and so on.

A=Attention: This aspect of the interview involves the controlled use of body language. Although estimates differ, some argue that communication is made up of 55 per cent non-verbal signals such as body language, 38 per cent inflection and intonation in voice and only 7 per cent in the literal meaning of the words. The effectiveness of the interviewer's body language will obviously depend on their training, the interview environment (such as the distance between seats) and the interviewee's sensitivity to it. Through their body language the interviewer can signal to the interviewee their understanding of what they are saying and in turn encourage or discourage him/her from talking freely or closing up through fear of ridicule, boredom or disinterest on the part of the interviewer. Eye contact should be maintained at about an 80 per cent efficiency rate, and the gaze move around the top half of the face and not fix on the eyes or some other facial feature such as a mole!

Furthermore, 'open' body language is said to encourage openness by the interviewee. It would include not crossing legs, not having crossed legs turned away from the interviewee, not having closed palms nor having a posture which is seated away from the interviewee. 'Mental stroking' involves psychological encouragement involving nodding occasionally and briefly smiling or the interviewer changing their facial expression. Nothing will discourage the interviewee from talking more than a blank expression on the face of the interviewer.

Finally, body language and activation permit the interviewer(s) to **control** the interview. Without that the interviewer or the chairperson of the interview board cannot steer the interview through the planned stages. If an interviewee is overtalkative by using obvious methods of control such as saying: 'I'm afraid I must stop you there . . .' an interviewer can also simply cross their legs and move their body posture away from the interviewee and reduce eye contact frequency down to say 50 per cent. This links **activation** and **attention** so the interviewer can assert control.

S=Summary or rather summaries. We have partly dealt with this under Activation, but it is important to remember that a summary by the chairperson of the interview board at the end of the interview will allow other board members to ask any outstanding questions and the interviewee to add anything they may have omitted or badly explained earlier in the interview.

S=Structure. A point that is dealt with under preparation, but also the interviewer(s) should check at the end of the interview the following:

● Did the interviewer(s) refrain from interrupting each other?
● Did the interviewer(s) refrain from demonstrating to the interviewee how well or badly they were doing? (This will mislead the interviewee who may either 'give up' or believe they no longer have to try hard depending on the interpretation of the message.)
● Was there an appropriate close to the interview?
● Did the interviewee know what would happen next, e.g. when would they hear the decision of the interview board or when the next stage of the selection process would commence?

Exercise

Telephone interviewing has increased in recent years. Identify some of the dis/advantages of this type of interviewing:

Advantages:

● Cost effective
● Equitable tool
● Minimum interpersonal characteristics interfere with objective assessment
● Task focus – competency interviewing enhanced
● Less opportunity to stereotype and discriminate

Disadvantages:

● No non-verbal communication
● Reduced opportunity to control interviewee
● Interviewee can read from script
● Poor rapport established at beginning of possible job
● One-to-one interview, absence of panel interview heightens subjectivity

Competency-based interviewing

Using the competency profile as a basis for the interview an employer can conduct two types of interview:

- **A situational interview:** This will place the interviewee in a series of hypothetical situations that are described by the interviewer or are contained in a case study, whereupon he or she will be asked how they would handle the situations. Questions should be designed to show how well the interviewee can plan, organize, problem-solve or cope with pressure. In some situations a virtual (verbal) role-play can be constructed between interviewee and interviewer.

  Example question: 'Half your workforce have phoned in sick on Monday morning. An urgent job must be completed by the end of the day. Clearly, not all scheduled work requirements can be completed. How would you deal with the situation?'

- **A behavioural interview:** The interviewee will be asked to recall specific examples from their past to illustrate what and how they coped with particular work situations. The premise for this approach is the well-established technique that past behaviour is a good predictor of future human behaviour. The questions used are useful at the start and at the end of interviews because probing can be based on the interviewee's own experiences and are, thus, less threatening.

  Example question: 'What's the most difficult problem you have encountered in the last six months?'

3.2.5   The use of technology

The use of technology is a marked feature of recruitment and selection over the past decade. Well-established systems and techniques such as the face-to-face interview may not, however disappear overnight in the UK. In a study conducted by Industrial Relations Services in 2002[12] it was found that in management recruitment although 80 per cent of private and public sector organizations surveyed use the web for job advertising, but 5 per cent say it is effective as a recruitment tool. 'Traditional' media advertising was most favoured, followed by recruitment agencies. To dismiss the use of technology in UK recruitment and selection would, however, be wrong. Other surveys report a big surge in the use of online recruitment. The Recruitment Confidence Index[13] reveals that over 50 per cent of employers are using on-line recruitment (a three-fold increase since 1999). This covers employers in all types of sectors. As managers become more skilled at using the technology both confidence and usage will increase. Most use comes by operating their own corporate sites.

Online recruitment – advantages

- Marketing the employer's brand – its organization, products or services.
- Applicants can interrogate the home page and download organizational information.
- A candidate can be profiled and short-listed or rejected using an automated system, thus reducing time-scales incurred through the use of paper-driven systems, but improving recruitment productivity.
- Ability of employer to stay in touch with a potential candidate.
- Targeted recruitment and establishment of a talent pool within months.
- Assists in achieving global recruitment.
- Choice of several well-established agencies on-line.

Online recruitment – disadvantages:

- Cultural barriers (e.g. language) can be difficult to overcome for applicants and recruiters.
- Sectors of the community are far less likely to have access to a computer than others. (In the EU only 25 per cent of Internet users are female.)
- In some sectors applicants prefer face-to-face recruitment (e.g. the medical profession).
- Difficulties in identifying special needs or disabilities on-line.
- The way the 'technology' works will put off some people; others may not be computer-literate.
- 'Off-the-shelf' systems may not be appropriate for the recruiting employer.

In the USA most large organizations use the Internet to post jobs online, and the majority use some form of advanced online CV 'mining' or intelligent search tools. Although the use of video-links for interviewing are still in their infancy such a system would further reduce costs, e.g. travelling expenses, and allow recruiters to temporarily close a link if they needed to consult written information or with each other before continuing the interview. A clear disadvantage is that only a small part of the candidate would be visible.

Online assessment in other forms, e.g. psychometric testing, is also underdeveloped, but a large proportion of *The Times* 1000 companies use technology in some form of selection, although this may constitute having candidates take tests at a computer rather than use paper and pencil, e.g. GlaxoSmithKline. There are many arguments for and against this development; some of these are legal, such as compliance with all eight data protection principles (Data Protection Act 1998).

3.2.6   Assessment centres and tests

Assessment centres are not necessarily a physical place, but can be a process of selection which is centred at one location. The assessment centre approach involves using a battery or range of selection tools that simulate the relevant attributes, skills and competencies required in the job. For that reason assessment centres are normally used for selection including promotion (using internal or external candidates), although increasingly they are used for training and development as well as performance assessment. The basic concept is that because interviews are such a poor predictor of performance and tend to concentrate on past or current work, it is necessary to use selection tools that increase predictive validity and, therefore focus on assessing potential.

Figure 3.3 shows the relative levels of predictive validity and reliability for a range of selection tools. You will note that a single interview conducted by an untrained interviewer will have little more predictive validity than tossing a coin as a means of deciding on the selected candidate. Before exploring the functions of an assessment centre the term's validity and reliability should be defined; using a selection test is the best example:

Reliability

Where the same test is administered to the same person on two separate occasions (but using differently worded questions) the results should be very similar unless something has changed the individual. The reliability of assessment centres is much greater than single interviews. There are two other ways of looking at reliability. First, ask yourself this question: 'If you were to interview twenty-five job candidates over a two-week period could you guarantee that each 45-minute interview would be conducted with the

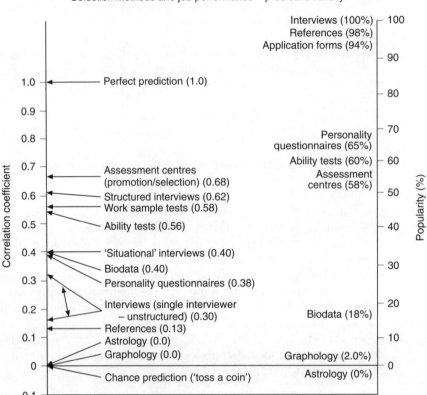

Figure 3.3. Selection methods and job performance – predictive validity and usage.

same degree of precision, skill, attention and pitch of questions as all other interviews?' Your answer is probably 'no', in which case there is poor reliability attached to those interviews.

Validity

This shows the extent to which the test is providing useful information. There are five types of validity. Arguably, predictive validity is the most important in selection, but the importance of each type will depend upon the reasons for the use of the test.

- **Face validity:** This is the extent to which the test looks appropriate and relevant to the person taking the test. If the test candidate takes the test seriously the results are more likely to be accurate and valid.
- **Predictive validity:** This is the extent to which the results of the test will correspond to some other future measure. In the case of predicting performance in a job the results of several tests can be compared to actual performance of the employee later in time. The closer the correlation between test results and performance, the greater will be the predictive validity of the test. Aptitude tests would be the best example of test usage.
- **Concurrent validity:** This is the extent to which the results achieved on a test correspond with those of another measure applied at or about the same time. So, using test A with a totally different test B would give you the concurrent validity.

- **Construct validity:** This is the extent to what the test measures what it is supposed to measure. For example, if the test is for verbal fluency that is what should be measured.
- **Content validity:** This is the extent to which the test measures something which is relevant. If a test is supposed to measure intelligence it should measure elements of intelligence that are relevant.

The tools used in an assessment centre can vary widely depending on its purpose. There are a number of required features of an effective assessment centre system:

- Small groups of candidates (between five and eight) should be used. This makes the selection exercises more manageable and allows for good interaction between them.
- A detailed and multi-dimensional analysis of the jobs and ideal/essential job-holders must be prepared on which the exercises used can be based.
- Where relevant, competency profiles must be prepared.
- The assessors are carefully and fully trained.
- Feedback is given to the candidates. This can be partly given at the second interview stage half-way through the process and allows self-selection whereby the candidate decides to pull out of their own volition when they perceive that the job is not for them.

As you can easily envisage, the use of assessment centres is a costly and time-consuming business; the average duration being two to five days. For this reason most employers will limit their use to filling senior or vital jobs. For other posts the employer may simply rely on one or two interviews, a personality questionnaire and two or three tests (see Section 1.2).

Using tests

Many selection tests are known as **psychometric tests.** This simply means that the test will enable an evaluation of the candidate's psychological functions to take place which will then be ordered and described by a numerical scale or category using statistical formulation. In other words, applying mathematics to psychological data and representing the results statistically. It is vital to note that using tests cannot turn the selection process into a mechanical process without errors. However, you will see from Figure 3.3 that it can provide reliable and valid outcomes, which should be combined with the results of other selection methods. This is one reason why the interview remains important despite its poor results when used in isolation. Using more than one interview can help with screening, giving feedback, picking up and probing information that has come to light through testing (or other assessment centre methods).

Before using a test the employer must be certain that it is appropriate to do so, and not just following a fad. In particular, an employer should look for a sound and proven methodological basis for the test, particularly validity and reliability. Also, the test supplier should be able to show clearly the norm references for the test. A norm is the average or normal performance that you would expect to see in people for whom the test was designed. The raw scores can be standardized to achieve this (statistically known as the coefficient). So, if you wished to use a test to select for a senior personnel manager post you would expect to see evidence of the norm references of the test in selecting for that type of test. The only way the test publisher can do that is to evaluate its effectiveness using 'dummy runs' with appropriate management-level test candidates.

A key factor that an employer would be expected to check is the test being free of sex or cultural bias. If the test is not free of these distortions then the results of the test will be skewed and biased against one sex or against those from ethnic groups; this is known as having 'adverse impact'. The easiest way in which a test can be biased is through the use of language. If language used in the test is of a colloquial nature those from different cultures, even from different parts of the UK, may not understand or may misinterpret the questions and produce low scores. Purchasing or hiring a test should involve receiving a test manual from the publishers, which gives evidence of all of these issues being satisfactorily addressed.

3.2.7   The final stages

References

Despite there being practically no validity in job references, and even less so in personal references, many organizations still have to use them to confirm basic information about candidates, such as dates of employment, status and salary.

Personal or academic references are useful for school- or college-leavers where they have little job history and where qualifications are an important part of the candidate's application, e.g. confirming the possession of the CIPD qualification for a post in a personnel department.

Medical references can be obtained under certain provisions of the Data Protection Act 1998, although employers must ensure that they do not breach the Disability Discrimination Act 1995 in turning away someone who may have an impairment classified under the Act.

Legally, work references must be accurate, honest and not be misleading.

Where the recruitment and selection is thorough, meaning several interviews and an assessment centre system used there will be a high consensus amongst managers and employees that a particular individual should be appointed – So, no one can say X or Y should not be appointed . . . With a flat structure based on project team work and the application of high quality skills it is absolutely key that we get the right person . . . We are investing for the future . . .

Senior manager at Goldman Sachs plc[14]

Offering the job to the successful candidate

The job offer should always be made in writing and the signatory of the letter ensure they have checked all the details as accurate. The job description should not be attached to the offer letter otherwise it will be arguably a part of the contract of employment. The job description is usually legally deemed to represent reasonable management instructions and therefore must possess a degree of flexibility for management to alter it reasonably from time to time without there being a breach of contract. These matters and those relating to the statement of principal terms and conditions are discussed in Chapter 12.

Induction

Effective induction is vital, not least because in the first three months of an employee's service there occurs the so-called 'induction crisis', and only after one year does stability occur. Staff turnover in the first three months can easily be 20–25 per cent. Effective selection can reduce turnover, but it can be wasted without properly planned and implemented induction. This can include the management of relocation, handling the new employee's domestic difficulties and the provision of information prior to the employee starting work. Finally, having sufficient time to complete the induction process, good management support and full information is crucial for success.

Induction is a systematic process to enable the new employee to 'fit' into his or her job and the organization as soon as possible. This will be achieved by becoming familiar with:

- The people he or she will work with (and needs to communicate with)
- The work environment
- The job (including career and training plans) and
- The organization (culture, structures and systems).

Exercise

Produce a short-list of things an induction process should cover.

Feedback

- Key information on 'housekeeping', work systems and environment
- Aims/objectives of immediate work group
- The role of the new employee – personal work objectives and standards
- Key internal and external contacts – all these matters help assist 'familiarization' and 'survival'
- Recreational and rest facilities
- Counselling, first-aid and medical facilities
- Health and safety including fire evacuation and
- Familiarization with services, trade unions, staff clubs and environment.

Summary

In this section we have examined the sometimes lengthy and expensive process of recruitment, selection and induction. For this reason it is necessary to ensure that the process is handled fairly, efficiently and effectively. By doing so it should produce results which are valid and reliable. Ultimately, it provides the right employee with a 'fit' for the job and the organization. Optimum performance may then be provided by the employee, but only with the right leadership, motivation and performance management. The different steps of the process can be summarized in Figure 3.4.

3.3   Leadership at work

Leadership – The ability to get others to do what they don't want to do and like it!

Harry S. Truman – President of the USA 1945–1953:

When the best leader's work is done the people say . . . 'we did it ourselves'!

Lao-Tzu – adviser to the Emperors of China in the fifth century BC

Leadership is about having a set of values and believing in them, but it is also having foresight, knowledge and intuition, especially about people. Leaders cannot expect others to believe in them if they do not believe in themselves.

Margaret Malpas – Founder of Malpas Flexible Learning Ltd (largest provider of CIPD flexible learning programmes in the UK)

(A) Vacancy created

QUESTIONS:

Does the vacancy need filling?
Does the job vacancy need redesigning?
Does the job need re-evaluating?
Is the job part of a restructuring?
Is the job likely to be made redundant?
Can you do without filling this job vacancy?

Do you have any form of business plan linked to your human resource plan?
If so, does this tell you anything about the way the vacancy must be filled or the job changed?

↓

(B) Conduct job analysis – Review the person specification, job description, job specification or competency profile

↓

(C) Confirm the terms and conditions of employment. Are you clear about the contract you will issue to the new emloyee?

↓

(D) Agree your methods of recruitment and selection. Make these as cost-effective as possible

↓

(E) Decide whether applicants will need to complete application form or CV

↓

(F) Identify sources of applicants – target them – attract them – choices – use:

- Internal sources: e.g. promotion
- External sources: advertisements – newspapers, journals
- Use consultants, agencies or specialist recruitment services

↓

(G) Set-up a monitoring and review process

Figure 3.4. The recruitment and selection process.

Section objectives

In this section you will

- Examine and assess different approaches to leadership and
- Examine their application to different work situations.

3.3.1   Introduction

Few topics in management theory have received as much attention as leadership, and therefore perhaps it is difficult, if not impossible, to define it. The acknowledged expert on the subject, Warren Bennis, says he has come across over 350 definitions and the elements that constitute effective leadership are 'hazy'.[15] However, a glance at the sample of definitions used above and in this section will show that there are common factors. First, they imply getting people to act in a way without threatening or coercing them; this results in the leader 'making things happen' as John Harvey-Jones has said.[16] This is done by calling upon a range of personal qualities, competencies and aptitudes to convince people to behave in certain ways of their own volition. By this route people believe in themselves and the leader, and so will credit success to themselves as well as the leader. As we will see from the discussion of motivation theories in the next section, there is nothing which motivates people better than success – a feeling of achievement, recognition, self-development and the opportunity to do even better next time. Power sources used will be charismatic, expert and resource.

Implicit in the definition of leadership is the ability to motivate. As Edgar Schein points out: '. . . any analysis of motivation and human nature inevitably leads to a discussion of how leaders (or managers) should handle followers'.[17] The two can therefore be muddled if we are not careful. Concentrating on motivation may seem the obvious thing to do, but ask yourself how many managers you know have attempted to motivate others but, in practice, have failed? This may be because they do not have the level of self-development and self-awareness necessary to have acquired and used the appropriate leadership qualities to create the optimum work environment that motivates. Supermen and superwomen are not required, but too few managers in the UK have the training and self-development to lead effectively. In the USA ten times the resources are put into this management discipline than in the UK.

3.3.2   Are leaders born or made?

This leads us to the question whether leaders can ever be developed in the face of historical evidence that many effective leaders seem to be born with innate aptitudes for it? In fact, it is the list of historical figures such as Churchill, Napoleon, or Gandhi who lead us away from the notion of developed leadership. Most of the historical leaders were male politicians or military people or both, and present a limited basis for analysing modern leadership in early twenty-first-century organizations, although those such as Churchill were great 'situational' leaders. There are, of course, many examples of female leaders, but they often have to exercise their leadership qualities in ways dominated by male characteristics. Examples are Joan of Arc dressing in male armour, Margaret Thatcher being known as the 'iron lady' or Golda Meir, who was called 'the best man in my cabinet' by the Israeli prime minister.

Historical figures do illustrate, however, that certain abilities can typify a so-called 'strong' leader:

● Good in a crisis by directing, leading by example and managing resources.
● Take effective decisions, if necessary under pressure.
● Act consistently with stated views or aims.
● Enjoy credibility with 'followers'.
● Prepared to defend 'followers' and take responsibility for their actions.
● Effectively convey a vision and related objectives. This is different from establishing an ideology, which is pursued no matter what the consequences will be.
● Communicate a vision effectively and often very simply to construct an attractive image for 'followers'. Charles Handy calls this the 'helicopter factor' – the ability to take an overview of the issues or problems, to 'see the wood from the trees' and so discern what is important and what is not.[4]

- Possess good persuasive communication skills. You will note from Chapter 1 that this helps attitude change.
- Possess charisma – more a personality trait than an ability, but nevertheless an effective source of power to influence. The constituency over which this source of power is applied must, however, be receptive to the charisma of the leader. Like communicating a message, the leader's personality must stimulate the follower's conscious as well as sub-conscious needs.
- Finally, generate success.

Each one of these abilities or in combination can be used to liberate 'followers' or to dominate them. This is one reason why a number of female leaders have adopted typical male characteristics of leadership ('macho-management') in the belief that this will demonstrate that women can lead just as well as men. Also, the difference between many historical leaders and today's corporate leaders is that in the past the leader was the 'hero' of their time; today and in the future it is the 'followers' who must be the heroes. Obviously, leadership operates within the social culture of its times. Nowadays, we expect a more 'democratic' style of leadership, and not one where we are deceived, coerced or simply bribed into following the leader's dictats.

3.3.3   Leadership or management?

The resurgence of interest in leadership in the USA in the 1980s arose from its perceived decline. According to Professor Abraham Zaleznik of Harvard University, the term 'professional manager' had assumed a pejorative meaning: managers had become absorbed in what he calls the 'management mystique'.[18] This amounted to a concern with rules, processes and structures, but ignoring people, ideas and emotions as well as direct communication replaced by communication through memorandum or electronic mail. Zaleznik has explained that managers usually disclaim responsibility whereas leaders accept it. In doing so he points to the failure of the 1986 US Challenger space mission due to an overdeveloped hierarchy of management and dilution of responsibility. As early as 1977 *The Harvard Business Review* posed the question whether leaders and managers were different and agreed they are separate entities. It is argued that managers and leaders will have different personalities and experience, and different developmental paths from childhood to adulthood. It is here that consensus, arguably, disappears. Zaleznik says that leaders have mastered painful conflict such as upheaval, pain and the struggle for a sense of identity unique to themselves. On the other hand, managers confront few of the experiences that generally cause people to turn inward and assess themselves. Managers see life as a steady progression of events. Leaders are 'twice-born' because they feel separate from their contextual environment and are, therefore, capable of acting on the drives within themselves; in other words, an inner motivation.

Zaleznik goes on to argue that leadership effectiveness is not pre-ordained, but it can be developed by exposure of the individual to a number of relevant life experiences. For this reason carefully crafted leadership training programmes can be used to develop this potential in individuals. But leadership development takes time; it also requires clear lines to be drawn between leadership and management. John P. Kotter[19] argues that they are distinctive but complementary; management is about successfully addressing organizational complexity, whereas leadership is concerned with successfully handling change. As an example of this interplay Kotter shows how the same tasks require different actions:

Core tasks

(1) Making decisions on what should be done – Action

Action required by the manager:
- Use of planning, budgets, and systems

Action required by the leader:
- Create a vision and determine the direction and strategy of the required action. A 'map' is drawn which can be given to others from which they will understand what has to be done.

(2) Creating networks of relationships to achieve task completion

Action required by the manager:
- The structure of organizations are designed with specific roles for people to fill with a best 'fit'.

Action required by the leader:
- Communicate with all those people who can both deliver the vision and block it – Empower the former and persuade the latter.

(3) Ensuring staff carry out the task as required

Action required by the manager:
- Monitoring, controlling, supervising, solving-problems.

Action required by the leader:
- Inspiring, convincing, motivating, and enthusing.[19]

Finally, we must consider the notion that if we have leaders, then by definition there must exist 'followers'. Arguably, it is no longer helpful to use the term and thereafter we will refer to 'followers' as 'employees' or 'staff' or 'subordinates'. As organizations become 'flatter' and work involves specialist knowledge and competencies, leaders may have to spend large amounts of time acting in response to what their own staff are telling them. Charles Hampden-Turner argues that the complex cultures created in modern workplaces no longer necessarily create 'hierarchial behaviours' based on the authority of the boss as 'leader'. Instead we see the growth of the 'responsibility hierarchy' whereby employees are hired and paid to exercise their own judgement.[20]

Example

A (the boss) is responsible to the shareholders of the company for how well employees B, C and D perform, and this represents a traditional hierarchical behaviour. However, responsibility may be shown through the boss influencing the working environment, terms and conditions including incentives and rewards affecting B, C and D. Hierarchy may take over when it is the job of A to define and decide what will constitute the work and objectives of B, C and D. But responsibility is interwoven into the culture by A seeking B, C and D's help in defining what objectives should be met and the best way to achieve them. The attainment of those objectives can rest with B, C and D while A will enjoy the achievement of creating a high-performance culture. In this way, as Hampden-Turner points out, 'culture stands at the apex of the leader's responsibility hierarchy'.[20]

The informal leader

We must be careful not to assume that all leaders in the organization will be given that role by virtue of their position or resource power (see Section 3.1). 'Informal' leaders may arise because of the respect and trust of others or the affability of the leader, even though they have little or no status within the organization. The task of the formal leader is not to depose the informal one by coercive means, but there are alternatives to dealing with this possible challenge. First, the formal leader must work at developing their own levels of respect and trust with the employees. Second, the support of the informal leader must be gained by respect and trust. The sociability of the formal leader may be high, but he or she must not attempt to usurp the informal leader by trying to be 'one of the boys' or 'girls', to coin a phrase, nor bribe or make promises which cannot be delivered. Only contempt and disrespect will follow quickly.

3.3.4   Style theories of leadership

The essence of this approach is that employees will perform better depending on the adopted style of their leader. This notion developed as a result of the human relation's school of motivation and people management together with democratic values. The leader will be 'followed' because of:

- Fear: Failure to obey will result in punishment. The leader uses physical power.
- Convention: The organizational rules or customs mean the person occupying a certain role is the leader who thus uses position power.
- Respect: Employees acknowledge and accept the person as leader irrespective of any position or formal status; here, the leader is relying on expert power and charismatic power.
- Trust: People will follow this leader because they believe in that person's ability to deliver something that will satisfy their needs, although it may not be exactly what they want. Resource power is the dominant power source here.

These reasons for following and sources of power used are not mutually exclusive. Indeed, the effective leader who is a manager should be able to rely on all of them, but the greater the respect and trust (arising from the relative power sources), the more durable and strong will be the conditions for leadership to flourish.

The originating work on style was carried out by Lewin, Lippitt and White (1939), and despite its shortcoming shows that the same group of people will behave differently depending upon the style the leader adopts. Essentially, style runs along a continuum from autocratic to democratic leadership: shown in Figure 3.5.

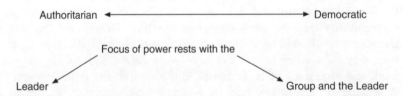

Figure 3.5. The continuum of authoritarian/democratic leadership.

Douglas McGregor's theory X–Y

These extremes are characterized by Douglas McGregor's theory Y and theory X, the former typifying democratic leadership and the latter autocratic leadership.[21] Behind these labels is a set of assumptions about how people behave at work:

- Theory Y: assumes people respond better when treated as intelligent adults who desire responsibility, and will grow into high-performing employees if they are given knowledge, skill and the opportunity to exercise them in the right environment.
- Theory X: assumes that people are naturally indolent and uninterested in their work. They will get away with doing as little as possible unless coerced to do otherwise.

Clearly, this has implications for motivation (discussed in Section 3.4), but for leadership this gives rise to three types of leader:

- **Theory X – Hard:** The leader (if that is what this manager can be called) will use threats and fear as tools to obtain compliance.
- **Theory X – Soft:** The leader will use bribes and attempt to 'sell' ideas or the need for work to the workforce. Both 'soft' and 'hard' attempt to obtain performance by external forces to the individual.
- **Theory Y:** The leader trusts his or her people to work hard and deliver performance at agreed levels. To varying degrees the leader will consult, seek views and be guided by the employees.

Theory X deeply entrenched itself in organizations throughout the twentieth century and will be difficult to eliminate in the twenty-first century. There is a lot of evidence to show that many employees have been conditioned by poor management to conform to the typical theory X worker, and thereby a vicious cycle of low trust and self-fulfilling prophecy has been established.

Fleishman's consideration/task orientation theory

Edwin Fleishman developed the notion of a continuum at the Ohio State University[22] who catagorized leadership by Consideration and Task Orientation:

- **Consideration:** This leader considers the well-being of his or her employees and is constantly engaged in ways to enhance their self-esteem so that morale can be kept high. Typically, this leader would be easy to communicate with face to face, be flexible and adaptable to new ideas from staff, and not use status or authority to characterize their leadership. Strong links to human relations school of management.
- **Task orientation:** This leader is more concerned with the task to be completed and will plan, organize and carry out personal decisions to achieve it. Instructions will be issued to employees to conform with this regime. If necessary this leader will coerce. There is no sharing of ideas. Clearly linked to the theory X and scientific schools of management. Sometimes called 'initiating structure' because it is the leader who initiates ideas and action, not employees.

The continuum model has been further refined by Tannenbaum and Schmidt at the University of California[23] shown in Figure 3.6. At one end of the leadership spectrum the leader not only withdraws but does so in a way that allows complete abrogation of leadership responsibilities so that he or she is subordinate to the collective views and demands of the employee group.

The stages of leadership involvement

- **Tells** – Leader alone tells employees what to do. The leader may or may not consider their feelings, views and sensitivities. Failure to follow instructions will result in 'punishment' (similar to theory X).

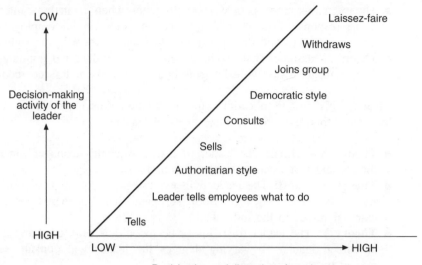

Figure 3.6. The Tannenbaum and Schmidt continuum of leadership. (Based on the diagram from 'How to choose a leadership pattern' by Robert Tannenbaum and Warren H. Schmidt; *Harvard Business Review*, May-June 1973, no. 73311. With permission of Harvard Business Review. Copyright 1991 by the President and Fellows of Harvard College; all rights reserved.)

- **Sells** – The leader will still decide what to do without the involvement of others, but will attempt to 'persuade' employees that what they are being instructed to do is a good thing. There may be a direct or implicit bribe involved.
- **Consults** – The leader remains the sole decision maker, but becomes more open to ideas by explaining the reasons behind the instructions. This may involve the opportunity for the leader to discuss his or her reasoning and the implications of it. From this the leader may formulate a more sophisticated set of instructions.
- **Democratic** – The views of employees will be taken into consideration before the leader takes the final decision.
- **Joins** – Here the leader becomes part of the group of employees for the purpose of reaching a decision. The problem is explained to the group and ideas sought. A range of alternatives may be given to the leader who will then select the most appropriate one.
- **Withdraws** – The leader will define the problem, the constraints and the resources available to solve it, but the group of employees makes the decision on which option to choose.
- **Laissez-faire** – The leader will specify certain limits, but the employee group will assess and define both problem and solutions, as well as making the final decision on what to do. The leader will have made it clear that he or she will abide by whatever the group decides.

The leader–employee relationship may operate on a 1:1 basis as well as with a group of employees.

Blake and Mouton – managerial grid

Extending the principle of different styles a little further beyond 'task orientation' and 'people orientation' brings us to the point where several stages can be identified in both of these styles.[24] You can see from Figure 3.7 that it is possible to occupy one of these stages

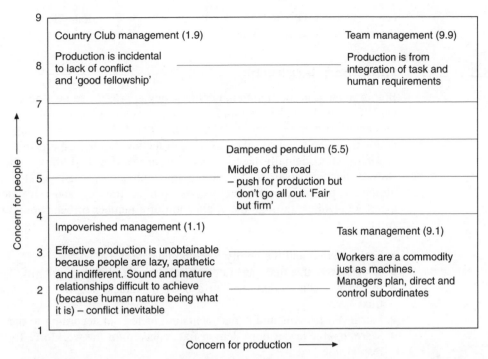

Figure 3.7. Blake and Mouton's managerial grid. (Based on the diagram from 'Breakthrough in Organizational Development', by Robert R. Blake and Jane S. Mouton, Louis B. Barnes and Larry E. Greiner; *Harvard Business Review*, Nov-Dec 1964, no. 64601. With permission of Harvard Business Review. Copyright 1951 by the President and Fellows of Harvard College; all rights reserved.)

that includes both styles by reading the grid horizontally and vertically. For example, reading the grid reference will always begin with the horizontal dimension (concern for the task) followed by the vertical dimension (concern for people). So, the grid reference 5.7 would mean that the leader is only 50 per cent concerned with the task, but more concerned with the feelings of his or her staff. You will note the descriptions used in all four extremes of the grid as well as the 5.5 reading. Although the reference 9.9 indicates the perfect leader who demonstrates a total concern for performance and people this does not mean that all other readings are inadequate. The leader's style may have to be adopted according to the culture of the organization, and this takes us closer to contingency theories. (See also Chapter 4.)

Criticism of style theories

The first difficulty with most of the style theories, except Blake and Mouton, is that they are one-dimensional. Second, the question of task accomplishment or task-centred leaders is not seriously confronted unless in terms of autocracy. Research has shown that democratic or person-centred styles of leadership do not always lead to improvements in productivity and performance. Some work-oriented leaders who are socially distant from their employees and who are directive do achieve increases in performance without being coercive where they give clear instructions and resources to the workforce. However, person-centred leadership does normally result in group cohesiveness and group satisfaction. The lesson seems to be that although leadership styles are helpful to denote a general approach to leading they are unhelpful in allowing us to understand exactly what can produce a satisfied and productive group. Functional leadership and contingency theories may help us to more closely understand how to achieve this.

3.3.5   Functional leadership

Before moving to the traditional contingency approach we need to examine the theory of the UK researcher in leadership, John Adair.[25] Nearly all leadership theorists and exponents of leadership training come from the USA where the topic is of enormous importance in political, business and social terms. One of the few leading experts in the field from the UK is Adair, who originally taught leadership at the Royal Military College, Sandhurst. He stresses that leadership is something that individuals must develop within themselves through experience, self-reflection, as well as training and education. Leadership is, therefore manifest through the application of a number of behavioural traits identified by Adair:

- Enthusiasm – and the ability to communicate it
- Toughness – this may generate respect, but not always popularity
- Integrity – being committed to a body of values, keeping your word and generating trust
- Fairness – rewards and punishments are meted out according to merit only
- Warmth – the leader must demonstrate concern for the workforce for whom he or she is responsible
- Humility – a willingness to listen, take onboard the ideas of others and not believe no one else can ever be right
- Self-confidence – this can become infectious and stimulate others, provided it does not become arrogance.

Bearing these factors in mind, Adair approaches leadership by showing that it is an interrelationship between managing task functions, with group functions and individual

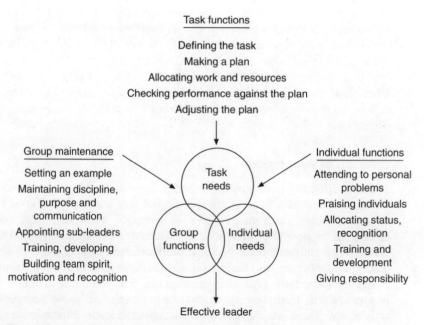

Figure 3.8. John Adair's functional model of leadership.

needs shown in Figure 3.8. Each one exerts an influence on the other two, but the group must be an active one formed for work purposes, not a passive one formed to, say, watch a film. This is a functional approach to leadership – the job of the leader is to ensure that the three needs harmonize as close as possible by managing them effectively through setting objectives, planning, communicating, supporting and nurturing staff, controlling, resourcing, monitoring and evaluating.

- **Task needs:** Employees are there to achieve a number of tasks that must be accomplished.
- **Group needs:** The group must be built and held together as a cohesive body to achieve its tasks.
- **Individual needs:** Individuals within a group will still have their own particular needs, be they social, psychological or physiological.

The functional leader will be aware of all three needs and use his or her skills as a leader to mesh them together to achieve success. The functions are:

- Defining the task(s) to be accomplished
- Planning task accomplishment
- Briefing the group to achieve the task
- Controlling events and the group's activities
- Evaluating progress
- Motivating the group and the individuals that make up the group
- Organizing resources, activities and solutions
- Acting as an example to the group.

Example

Group A must increase sales by 10 per cent in twelve months, but previous managers had set high targets that could not be achieved with the resources available. All the group ever received, therefore, was criticism. Two members of the group are particularly demotivated and their sickness absence record is poor. Moreover, the group is never quite sure what they are trying to achieve and always feel that they do not have the technical knowledge or skills to increase sales significantly. What can the new manager do by demonstrating leadership skills to ensure that this year the group successfully reaches their 10 per cent sales target?

Feedback

Look again at Adair's eight functions of a leader which must be applied to the task, the group and to individuals:

- The leader can redefine the task for the group so that it is SMART (Specific, Measurable, Achievable, Realistic and Time-based).
- Planning can be undertaken using the views and ideas of the group.
- Once the plan is agreed the newly defined task can be briefed.
- The leader should monitor and evaluate progress for the group and for individuals giving support, help and advice where appropriate.
- Resources for the group can be organized. A critical step is to provide training for members of the group. This should help:
- Motivate the group members; also, by having a well-developed and resourced plan the confidence of the group members in their leader should grow.
- Lastly, the leader can demonstrate a willingness to take his or her share of the task.

3.3.6   Contingency theories

Charles Handy's best-fit theory

Handy develops the above approach with four linked influences.

(i)   The leader's own preferred style of leadership (e.g. autocratic)
(ii)   The subordinates' preferred style of leadership (e.g. democratic)
(iii) The task and
(iv)   The environment (resources available, competitive, stable, etc.).

This approaches the problem from the perspective that there is no automatically 'correct' style of leadership, but is only appropriate when all four variables (i) to (iv) 'fit' or overlap. This can be measured on a scale as shown in Figure 3.9.

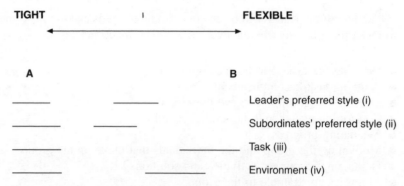

Figure 3.9. Charles Handy's 'best-fit' theory of leadership.

In situation B there is no fit at all and it is probable that disruption, failure and unhappiness will result. In situation A there is a perfect fit. Where it is the leader's own preferred style that does not fit, the leader can alter it to comply with the subordinates' own preferred approach. It is even possible that some alterations can be made to the task and the environment to get a best fit as possible, which would allow for a measure of success. Other well-known theories are those of Fielder and Hersey and Blanchard.

Vroom and Yetton's decision-making model

In this model all leaders are decision makers and their effectiveness can be determined by examining the quality of decisions taken over time. These 'right decisions' depend upon the degree to which the leader has permitted his or her subordinates to participate in the decision-making process.[26] Not all subordinates prefer a democratic leader, and this may also depend upon the situation facing them. The basic notion behind this work is that a leader who understands the subordinates' preferred style of leadership **and** the situation **and** task facing the subordinates can take a conscious decision about the most appropriate style of leadership. It is similar to the Tannenbaum and Schmidt model but goes further in suggesting a specific way of analysing problems by means of eight ordered criterion questions which the leader must ask in order to determine the best course of action.

First, there are five key types of leadership:

● **Autocratic I:** The leader makes the decision using information currently available to the leader. The decision is made without discussing it with anyone, based on personal knowledge or information supplied through documents or a computer.

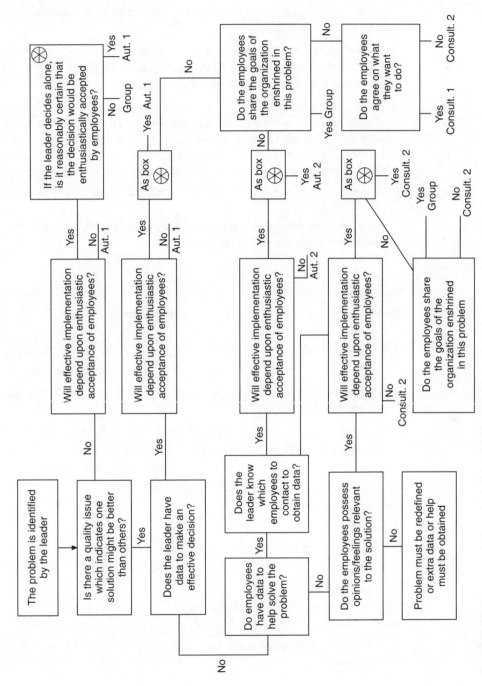

Figure 3.10. Vroom and Yetton's decision-making tree.

- **Autocratic II:** The leader seeks information from one or more subordinates without telling them the purpose. They are not asked for solutions or ideas just information without knowing why.

- **Consultative I:** Subordinates are individually consulted, but the leader will decide alone on the course of action. The problem is shared with the individual employees and their advice is actively sought.

- **Consultative II:** The leader will consult with the whole group of subordinates collectively. The problem is shared with the entire group and the leader actively seeks ideas and solutions, but will still make the decision.

- **Group:** As with the last category, the leader shares the problem with the whole group, alternatives are examined and solutions sought. The subordinates are used as consultants with the leader contributing on an equal footing as the rest without trying to influence the members of the group. Here the group makes the decision that the leader accepts and takes responsibility for, but will describe it by saying: 'We the group took this decision to . . .'

In order to decide on the appropriate style the leader must ask him- or herself seven questions based on the following rules:

Rule	Definition
1 Expertise of the leader	The leader does not have sufficient knowledge to make a qualitative decision
(Styles to consider in order of applicability: Aut. II, Consult. I, Consult. II, Group) (Styles avoidance: Aut. I)	
2 The congruence of organizational goals	The leader does not share or agree with the objectives of the organization
(Styles: Aut. I, Aut. II, Consult. I, Consult II) (Style avoidance: Group)	
3 Definition of the problem	The problem facing the leader is ill defined, poorly structured or lacks information
(Styles: Consult. II, Group) (Style avoidance: Aut.I, Aut. II, Consult. I)	
4 Acceptance and commitment by employees	The employees are likely to reject the leader's decision, and critically without their acceptance of it and commitment it cannot be implemented effectively
(Styles: Consult. I, Consult II, Group) (Style avoidance: Aut. I, Aut II)	

5 The likelihood of conflict over solutions and employees' acceptance of solution

Employees are likely to disagree with the appropriate solution and are likely to reject it, and critically without their acceptance and commitment it cannot be implemented effectively

(Styles: Consult II, Group)
(Style avoidance: Aut. I, Aut. II, Consult. I)

6 Alternative solutions – Commitment

All the possible solutions are as good as each other. Quality is not the issue, but employees may reject the decision and their commitment is necessary for effective implementation

(Styles: Group)
(Style avoidance: Aut. I, Aut. II, Consult. I, Consult. II)

7 Goal compatibility and commitment

The organizational objectives are shared by both leader and employees, but the employees are likely to reject the decision and their commitment is necessary to implement it effectively.

(Styles to adopt and avoid as with number 6.)

In order to address each of these questions in logical order the leader can follow a decision-making 'tree'. This should help the leader decide what style can be adopted with success. You will note from Figure 3.10 that three criteria are built into the decision: the quality or rationality of the decision, the acceptance or commitment of the employees in order to ensure effective implementation of the decision, and the amount of time required to make the decision because a group decision will clearly take longer to reach than if the leader adopted an autocratic I style.

Exercise

Using the case study 'A rush job' decide the most appropriate leadership style. You will have to apply Vroom and Yetton's criteria to the 'decision-making tree' to reach your conclusion.

Case study

'A rush job'

The 'leader' works as a supervisor of a section (comprising twelve employees) in a medium-sized company manufacturing stationery and office supplies. The manager has informed you that another section (which carries out work similar to yours) has a 'rush job on', but has suddenly been afflicted with a lot of sickness absence. The manager requests that the supervisor 'lends three employees to help out in the emergency'.

The work carried out in both sections is fairly routine and the skills level is low. This means that the supervisor can choose any of the twelve employees to work in the short-handed section. There will be no differences in working hours, level of work or in any terms or conditions.

The supervisor has a very good knowledge of all twelve employees and believes there would not be any complaints from the three who are selected.

Feedback

Case Study: 'A rush job'

Solution: Autocratic I style of leadership. There are no quality issues involved, the acceptance and commitment of employees is not an issue and it is unlikely that the three selected employees would object. (Based on study materials for Personnel Decisions Inc.[27])

Do leadership theories work?

Theories should be used as conceptual frameworks for developing personal styles of leadership. Vroom[28] argues that theories can be used for self-reflection and development so that eventually managers at all levels begin to intuitively think as leaders. Only a constant approach to leader development works. For Professor Vroom, this means that personal styles must be compared to theoretical approaches; this helps generate discussion, preferably in groups. Using computer technology, case studies and the results of proposed solutions can be analysed with individual feedback and counselling provided for developing leaders. Vroom says this can produce effective leadership irrespective of size of organization. At General Electric the use of his training approach gave rise to a more democratic style of leadership including the participation of employees in generating ideas and solutions. Over a short period this saved $16 million.

3.3.7   An overview: leadership in organizations

Simplistic one-dimensional theories or a list of traits are unlikely to be of much help to someone wishing to improve or acquire leadership skills. But using more sophisticated approaches can provide the stimulus for reflection and continuing self-development, as Vroom suggests. Organizations can assist this process by recognizing that leadership is not to be developed overnight, but can be a long-term developmental process.

Whichever way leadership is interpreted it must mean that it is about getting people 'to go that extra mile', to be inspired, and to be stimulated into not just doing an average day's work but a better than average day's work. Leaders will achieve this by setting wide parameters in which employees can operate using their own initiative, and if they make mistakes are not 'blamed', but encouraged to do better at the next effort. Everybody in a supervisory position can do this, for example by not amending letters drafted by 'subordinates' unless absolutely necessary or to trusting a team of employees to go ahead with an untried project costing a great deal of money. This type of leader is a 'pathfinder' – laying the groundwork for the success of his or her workers and giving them praise for achieving success. The application of 'soft skills' – emotional intelligence – is critical. Leaders are not just top bosses – the transformational leaders steering organizations through change, but everyone responsible for people at work.

Finally, organizations must support this approach to leadership by supporting leaders, providing them with power and creating a culture conducive to all those positive elements of leadership, which we have explored in this section. Critical to leadership, particularly contingency leadership, is the ability to self-reflect; this requires not a narcissistic self-indulgence, but honesty, resilience and support from within the organization.

Summary

In this section we have looked at the re-emerging importance of leadership theories and ideas. New methods of human resource management require leadership skills which will energize people, invigorate them to put extra effort into what they do. Organizations operating in a highly competitive environment will increasingly find that it is the people factor that will cause success or failure, and to make the difference employers must turn their attention to effective leadership. One of the key elements of leadership is the ability to generate motivation. This is the next subject to examine.

3.4   Motivating people at work

Extract from: Empowering drill

Andrew Rogers, *Personnel Today*, 31 July 1997.

When customers pour into B&Q's new warehouse in Enfield on 22 August, they will be several hours late for one of the most bizarre spectacles in DIY history. Most of the warehouse's 250-strong workforce choose to start the day at 7.30am sharp with a stint of country and western line dancing, American Indian rituals or foot-stomping aerobics – all in the name of customer service.

These five-minute eye-openers, known as 'energizers', are part of the upbeat management style adopted at B&Q's 230 warehouse stores that have been springing up across the UK since 1994. Customer satisfaction levels at warehouses such as Enfield regularly outstrip those for B&Q's established supercentres by 10 per cent, helped by an informal management style, daily team briefings and the all important energizers.

B&Q warehouses are larger than the supercentres and were set up to serve a mixture of trade and domestic customers from a wider catchment area. Part of B&Q's solution to keeping the 250 or so staff who work in these giant stores informed, motivated and feeling like a team are the daily 20-minute briefing sessions held each morning before the store opens. They proved so successful that B&Q introduced them across its supercentre network six months ago.

Each session is opened and closed by the store's general manager, and provides an opportunity to pass on information to the staff. The briefings might also include a training exercise such as a role-play covering areas such as health and safety, loss prevention, merchandising or customer service. Or there might be a trolley dash to help staff develop their product location knowledge.

Such events are offered in a light-hearted manner, says Enfield's general manager Craig Higgins, but are also effective, and learning outcomes are always charted. Then comes the energizer session in which 90–95 per cent of the workforce participate in the physical jerks, even though there is no pressure on them to do so. 'It is about enjoying yourself,' says Higgins.

Linda Chaplin, a customer adviser in the hardware department, has worked at B&Q for several years, joining the Enfield warehouse in June, but the energizer sessions are new to her. 'You cannot help but feel more motivated,' she insists. But she has no plans to take up aerobics as a result. 'Five minutes a day is enough,' she says firmly.

These sessions are only one element of B&Q's empowerment and motivation toolkit. Another has been the development of a 'store within a store' concept.

'The selling space area is easy to get lost in. So we have a general manager who coordinates and a number of store managers responsible for individual areas such as building and hardware, decorative, gardening and showroom,' explains Matthew Brearley, now head office personnel controller but until recently responsible for personnel in the warehouses.

'Having got that organization structure, you have these 250 people and you are faced with how to communicate to them what is going on and how to really motivate them.'

Hence the morning briefings. 'They came out of the reasoning that said if we are going to communicate clearly with people, we need to put in place a mechanism to do so, share success, talk about how the business is performing, and give positive recognition of behaviour.'

The logic is that happy staff equals happy customers. 'If people are having fun at work, there is a much higher chance that they are passing that on to our customers,' claims Brearley. 'If we can get energy going at the start of the day, it is a bit of fun.'

Early morning energizers dovetail with the company's informal, open management style, designed to encourage staff to 'do it themselves'.

'We have a no-status policy. Managers do not wear suits and everyone is on first-name terms right through to the managing director,' explains Higgins. 'It encourages people to take ownership of the business – everyone down to grassroots level.'

Higgins claims that, as a result, employees are more willing to participate and more inclined to make decisions for themselves instead of going to a manager. 'And they have a pride in what they do, which provides higher levels of customer service,' he adds.

With such an apparently relaxed and empowered culture, the question is whether B&Q's corporate policies could get watered down by wayward managers. Higgins himself is clearly a strong personality who is popular with his staff and very much his own man. He admits that the harmony between corporate culture aad his own management style is more down to serendipity – or astute recruitment – than his ability to enforce head office policies. 'What B&Q does is give you the opportunity to manage in your own style.'

For example, B&Q is proud of its policy of employing older staff – a policy designed to anticipate a dip in the available labour force and exploit the likelihood that older people have a better notion of good customer service and more direct DIY experience. As long ago as 1989 B&Q opened a store in Macclesfield staffed entirely by people over the age of 50.

Yet Enfield store manager Higgins bristles slightly at the idea of giving older job candidates priority simply because of their age. 'I have a policy of employing the best person for the job based on their ability to provide service and knowledge,' he says.

Brearley acknowledges that empowerment can cause difficulties with consistency. 'We do not want to cause confusion to our systems,' he says. 'Where there is a way of doing something that it would be crazy to reinvent, we document it and it is in our operations manual.'

Despite the tensions that empowerment sometimes creates, allowing staff to do their own thing can reap huge benefits. Enfield took the advice of one of its customer advisers, a former carpenter who could see a better way of displaying the store's range of 62 screwdrivers. Colin Winterflood, 49, who joined the warehouse in June, argued his case to an audience of senior operations and buying staff and answered a number of tricky questions. 'I know a few managers who would crumble in that situation,' Higgins reflects.

Winterflood himself is impressed with the way B&Q operates but admits his first two days in the job were a real culture shock. 'It is the best time of my life at the moment. I wake up in the morning and really want to get there,' he says, with no trace of irony.

And the aerobics? 'Very good,' he says cautiously. 'First of all it was a shock. You feel daft. Then you realize everyone else is doing it. The more you do, the more you get to know people.'

There seems to be no shortage of anecdotal evidence that the culture and the morning briefings are successful, and B&Q warehouses consistently outperform their supercentre neighbours in the realm of customer service.

'Everyone gets such an exposure to senior line managers that they become comfortable talking to them,' says Higgins, referring to the practice of weekly walkabouts by top managers who stop and ask staff for their opinions on business issues.

Perhaps not surprisingly, B&Q has no figures to prove a direct correlation between tribal dancing and higher customer satisfaction but, clearly, it is doing something right. In 1996–97, the group recorded a 14.1 per cent rise in sales over the previous year and profits leapt 75 per cent from £55.4 m to £97.2 m. Today, B&Q continues to go from strength to strength.

Section objectives

In this section you will:

- Examine all the main theories of motivation and their application to the workplace and
- Study the links between motivation and job design, and rewards and incentives.

Case study

The manager who read too many textbooks

John Willoughby disliked the performance appraisal and performance-related pay (PRP) scheme used at his company, but he tried to make it work as best as he could. It operated simply on the basis of a pool of money determined by profits declared each accounting year, although no employee was to receive more than 5 per cent PRP with average performers getting no PRP at all. As a senior manager John used his discretion to 'bend the rules'; normally he ensured all his staff got something to keep the moans to a minimum. This meant that top performers could get 6–8 per cent, but this hardly rewarded them compared to 'time-wasters' who could get 3–5 per cent.

Month after month John ploughed through personnel management textbooks to give him the answer to his problem. He came to the conclusion that most management theories on employee motivation did not emphasize money as a motivator – indeed, to John it appeared that most positively were against money. The sort of things that motivated most people were:

- Recognition for good work through positive feedback
- Variety and autonomy
- Responsibility
- Sense of accomplishment
- Interesting work
- Personal growth and development
- Good working relationships with others

John decided on a new plan of action. He would emphasize all these factors when giving feedback during the individual appraisal and PRP meetings with employees. He chose not to break the company rules any more and give top performers 5 per cent and average and below performers 2 per cent.

Next day, John had to give Eileen her appraisal. Eileen had only been at the company for one year, but in that time had been a star performer. However, when told she was getting only 5 per cent PRP Eileen got really upset. 'Five per cent?' she said. 'Is that all I am worth after all those fine words you've given me about how I've done a great job?'

John was dumbstruck by this reproach. Surely all the other motivational needs that he was now addressing should have met Eileen's expectations. Eileen spied the great pile of textbooks on John's shelves. 'You read too many textbooks!' she said, and stormed out of the office leaving John with his mouth open.

What assumptions and misinterpretations had John made in respect of human motivation?

Feedback

By reading the various theoretical approaches summarized in this section you should see that although the theorists themselves may have taken different approaches to the subject, the clear message is that human motivation is a complex process. It would be oversimplistic and crude to make sweeping assumptions that everybody will be motivated by the same things. Some people will be motivated by money, and others will value money but will require other motivational needs to be satisfied before money can have any effect. A key factor is that whatever reward is made available, such as PRP it should be felt-fair, and that those rewards that employees expect to receive should they provide the requisite performance should not be snatched away from them at the last moment. These two factors are covered under process theories.

3.4.1   Introduction

The universal task of leaders down through the ages has been to motivate their followers. For managers in the new century the key to success will be the motivation of their workers. As markets become more competitive on a global scale it is increasingly crucial to maximize the performance of the workforce to maintain and grow market position. This can be seen from the opening article for this section. An obsession with an organization's costs is pointless unless people's motivational needs are addressed.

A study of motivation applied theory helps to explain why people work and the amount of effort they will put into it. Armed with this knowledge, the manager of people can construct strategies and apply techniques that will get the best from them. However, you should note that motivation is not something you do to someone, like pouring a motivational balm over them. As we will see, motivation is a psychological process that emanates from within the individual. He or she will come to work with a unique set of motivational needs; the greater the manager can satisfy those needs; the greater will be the person's contribution to their work. The manager cannot induce those needs; neither can the manager guarantee that what motivates one person (i.e. satisfies their needs) will have the same effect with a different person.

A definition of motivation: many abound, but the following one includes many important themes:

'Motivation is the person's unique set of needs in relation to particular situations. These needs explain what drives a person, what his or her reaction will be to various stimuli, the strength of behaviour, its consistency and persistency based on conscious decisions.'

The word motivation derives from the Latin word to 'move'. Of course, we must be careful about associating motivation today with just the movement of someone, e.g. in completing a task. As Frederick Herzberg has pointed out, it can mean anything but motivation if it is caused by coercion, through threats and bullying. This Herzberg calls 'KITA' – 'A Kick in the A—':[29]

Why is KITA not motivation? If I kick my dog (from the front or the back) he will move. And when I want him to move again, what must I do? I must kick him again. Similarly, I can charge a man's battery, and then recharge it, and recharge it again. But it is only when he has his own generator that we can talk about motivation. He then needs no outside stimulation. He wants to do it.

Frederick Herzberg

(Reprinted by kind permission of *Harvard Business Review*, from 'One more time: How do you motivate employees?' by Frederick Herzberg, *Harvard Business Review*, Jan–Feb 1968, no. 68108. Copyright 1991 by the President and Fellows of Harvard College; all rights reserved.)

Most definitions and theories of motivation can be broken down into three common denominators:

- What energizes the behaviour (drive-push)
- What directs or channels the behaviour
- How this behaviour is maintained or sustained (the pull)

Managers need to have accurate information on the drivers of motivation so that they can construct their strategies to direct and sustain it. Simplistic assumptions seldom are successful.

Intrinsic motivation

This type of motivation involves the achievement of personal goals that are not related to physical or external needs such as money, a car, a new holiday. Instead, they are much more closely related to the needs that are an essential part of our psychological make-up such as responsibility, feelings of achievement or freedom to act, and the opportunity to grow in skill, reputation and status. The positive feeling of 'a job well done' would come into this category. These are factors vitally missing in many process jobs discussed in Chapter 2.

Extrinsic motivation

Whereas the satisfaction of intrinsic needs comes from within, these type of needs are satisfied from without. Examples include tangible factors like money, promotion, a bigger office desk, more friends, as well as less tangible factors as praise, thanks, and the esteem of others. Because they are generated from outside that does not mean they are any less important to the individual, but you will have seen from Chapter 2 that a person motivated by financial gain is different from someone who has an instrumental attitude to work who simply wants to obtain money to enjoy life outside work, although there will be a very thin dividing line between the two and, clearly they are often closely linked.

3.4.2   Content theories

F. W. Taylor and scientific management

In Chapter 2 we explored the importance of the work of Taylor[30] on the organization of work and the assumptions made about people which prevailed throughout the twentieth century. (Taylor is also discussed in Section 4.1.) The assumptions can be summarized as follows:

- The primary interest of both management and employees is economic gain.
- Work must be carefully measured and organized to obtain efficient working.
- Each worker should have an individual and specialized task.
- The worker is less efficient working in a group or team, but that work that is passed from one individual to another can be efficient (the continuous workflow).
- The personal ambition of the worker should be stimulated by incentives and other financial gain.

Taylor believed that 'scientific management' would genuinely benefit both workers and management in a form of partnership. However, it has a single focus which underestimates the complexity of human motivation and behaviour. The place of money as a 'motivator' is discussed fully later in this chapter.

McGregor's theory X and Y

We have already examined McGregor's theory in the light of assumptions made by leaders about 'followers' as a determinative of their style.[21] We can also use it for categorizing interrelated views about human motivation.

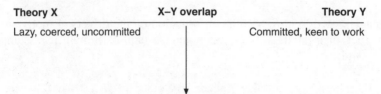

Theory X	X–Y overlap	Theory Y
Lazy, coerced, uncommitted		Committed, keen to work

For example: Needs some coercion, and the risk of punishment to put in optimum effort, but does get some satisfaction from the work, feels a measure of commitment to the work and particularly enjoys problem solving and generating ideas for new products

Figure 3.11. McGregor's theory X–theory Y continuum.

McGregor's theory is often misinterpreted as a perspective that managers fall into one of the two main categories of assumption about people.

X – The so-called 'traditional' view of human behaviour that:

● The average person has an inherent dislike of work and will avoid it if he or she can.
● That because of it they must be coerced, controlled, directed and threatened with punishment to get them to contribute an adequate level of performance.
● The average person, therefore, prefers to be directed, wishes to avoid responsibility, has relatively little ambition, and wants security above all else.

You will notice the distinct similarity between this view and the basis of F. W. Taylor's assumptions. As McGregor pointed out, many organizations have adopted different people management strategies with a multiplicity of techniques and practices which try to mask the central fact that managerial assumptions are closely tied to theory X. Some would argue that the 'hard HRM' strategy of a number of UK, US and Far East companies mirrors this approach. McGregor does not deny that the perspective and behaviour of some workers conforms to the theory X model to varying degrees; the difficult question to answer is whether this type of behaviour is in itself a product of the treatment and assumptions made by management. To what extent is it the product of a self-fulfilling prophecy?

Y: The integrative approach: The assumptions made here are that:

● The expenditure of physical and mental effort in work is as natural as rest or recreation.
● External control and threats are not the only way to maximize performance, but workers will exercise self-direction and self-control to work towards performance objectives provided they are sufficiently committed to them.
● This commitment is a function of the incentives and rewards associated with the achievement of those goals.
● There is a broad distribution among the working population of the capacity and desire to exercise imagination, ingenuity, creativity and innovation in the solution of problems and the birth of new ideas.
● Under the conditions of modern work life, the intellectual potentialities of the average person are only partially utilized.

This optimistic view of human beings is based on the premise that individual's goals can be integrated with those of the employer to bring about optimum work performance. As with theory X it is likely that many possess theory Y attributes to varying degrees. It is also true that some are predominately X or Y in their categorization. But the difficulty for managers is the variable overlap of these two polarized approaches, the extent to which they are the product of managerial treatment or natural behaviour, and most problematic of all, what are the most appropriate motivational strategies to be applied to a group of workers with a mix of these preferences for behaviour?

The human relations school

The first intensive study of human behaviour in an industrial situation was made by researchers led by Elton Mayo at the Hawthorne works of the Western Electric Company, Chicago, USA.[31] In 1924 experiments were begun in the level of illumination in the factory relative to levels of qualitative and quantitative production. The experiments quickly found that, irrespective of the intensity of light each time it was adjusted, production increased. Workers unused to receiving much attention to their needs responded when they became the focus of attention. The conclusions drawn from the experiments included:

- Work is a group activity and the social world of adults centres around their work.
- However, workers' attitudes and effectiveness are influenced by social demands outside work as well as inside it.
- Individuals have a need for recognition, security and a sense of belonging which is more important in determining workers' morale and productivity than the physical conditions under which they work.
- Informal groups at work have a strong influence over their members' work habits and attitudes (see Section 4.1 on the observations of the relay assembly test room).

This work developed partly as a reaction to 'Taylorist' assumptions about people at work. Numerous other studies have supported the importance of social relations at work, i.e. the ability of workers to communicate freely and form companionships and informal groups. Team working too is the preferred method, but has its disadvantages because the informal 'rules' or 'norms' of the group can override those of the employer. Work by Trist and Bamforth[32] shows the importance not only of team work, but of integrating technical systems and satisfying social needs.

With the exception of McGegor's work these theories so far have focused on job context – that is, factors which extrinsically motivate. Those examined next will focus on job content and intrinsic motivation.

Abraham Maslow's hierarchy of needs

In 1943 Maslow described human motivation as a hierarchy of needs whereby the satisfaction of one level of needs triggers the movement to the next higher level of needs.[33] This hierarchy is traditionally shown as a pyramid as in Figure 3.12.

The theory is based on a number of assumptions. First, 'man' is always wanting – a complete state of satisfaction is rare and, even so, of short duration. Second, a satisfied need no longer motivates, and so the next level of needs must be focused on. Third, movement from one level of needs to the next is usually a subconscious one.

The physiological needs represent food and water and the air we breathe; once these have been satisfied our requirements for shelter, 'a roof over our heads', must be met. Once supplies of these vital commodities are met after time we will yearn for the interaction of others, sometimes known as 'affiliation' needs. Self-esteem needs must then be met: job satisfaction, feelings of achievement and responsibility. Lastly, self-fulfilment can also be

Figure 3.12. Maslow's hierarchy of needs.

termed 'self-actualization', meaning reaching a zenith of self-development, sense of purpose and satisfaction. The plight of Robinson Crusoe is often quoted as a fine example of this hierarchy of needs in operation. In recent times many of us will have experienced the anxiety of redundancy or loss of income which immediately threatens our ability to feed, clothe, provide shelter (by paying the mortgage) and educate our family. These needs will subordinate all others.

Maslow's theory has a number of deficiencies despite its apparent relevance. A person may be trying to satisfy a number of needs at any one time, nor will everyone seek satisfaction of the needs in the order suggested; individual and cultural differences will play their part. Also, to suggest that because a manager, for example, made redundant and worried how he or she will cope financially has eliminated all desire for self-esteem seems far-fetched. You should also familiarize yourself with Alderfer's Existence – Relatedness – Growth (ERG) theory.

Herzberg's two-factor theory

Before examining Herzberg's theory complete the following questionnaire:

Here is a list of factors that **may** affect your attitude to your job. Rank them in order of their importance to you personally. Do not rank any factor equal to each other – you must rank them differently.

In ranking these factors, put 1 against the factor that is most important to you, 2 against the next and so on up to 15.

 1 Achievement   . . . .
 2 Advancement   . . . .
 3 Company policy and administration   . . . .
 4 Job possibility of individual growth   . . . .
 5 Job interest   . . . .
 6 Personal relationships – with superiors   . . . .
 7 Personal relationships – with colleagues   . . . .
 8 Personal relationships – with subordinates   . . . .
 9 Personal life (factors outside work)   . . . .
10 Recognition for effective work   . . . .
11 Responsibility   . . . .
12 Salary   . . . .
13 Security   . . . .
14 Status   . . . .
15 Working conditions – physical   . . . .

After reading this description of Herzberg's theory compare your own preferences to those identified by Herzberg as 'motivators'.[29] You will also see from Section 4.1 that his theory is addressed as part of Managing Activities.

The central proposition of Herzberg's theory is that the causes of job satisfaction are qualitatively different from the causes of job dissatisfaction. To reach his original theoretical standpoint he interviewed around 200 'middle-class' male engineers and accountants. His questions were:

- 'Think when you were most happy at work. What made you feel happy?'
- 'Think when you were most unhappy at work. What made you feel unhappy?'

Two lists emerged:

Satisfiers (Motivators)	**Dissatisfiers (Hygiene factors)**
Achievement	Company policy
The job itself – interesting and fulfilling work	Supervision
Promotion	Level of salary
Responsibility	Interpersonal relations
Recognition for good work (achievement)	Working conditions
Opportunity to grow in knowledge and capability.	

The two lists may appear quite distinct, but there are some overlaps; for example, the quality and level of supervision will determine the degree of feedback and recognition for a job well done, and it will also influence the scope of opportunities for growth. The use of the term 'hygiene factors' has a medical analogy because they represent elements of the job which if removed or improved do not bring health but merely prevent bad health. By removing the dissatisfiers the individual does not experience satisfaction. The dissatisfaction merely comes to an end and the individual's feelings about this element move to a mid-point. For example, Herzberg (and others) has shown that a salary rise has a 'motivational' effect for about three weeks, after which it decays in effect.

The elements that have a positive effect on the individual are the satisfiers or motivators. You will note from the list and by comparing it with earlier theories that these are the intrinsic motivators and are related to job content. The dissatisfiers are extrinsic and related to job context. You can attempt to assess your own preferences for these by comparing your motivators with those identified by Herzberg.

It is vital to remember that Herzberg does not suggest that the motivators are any more important than are the dissatisfiers. However, the latter can act as a brake on the former. Unless the dissatisfiers are dealt with the individual will find it difficult to enjoy satisfaction from the motivators. This can be explained by way of a continuum (Figure 3.13).

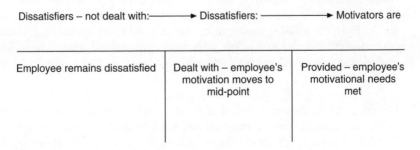

Figure 3.13. Herzberg's continuum of satisfiers–dissatisfiers.

3.4.3   Job enrichment and the quality of work life

The key outcome of Herzberg's work is the concept of job enrichment. This takes us beyond simplistic ways of improving the satisfaction of a job holder by:

- **Job enlargement** – The 'horizontal' growth of the job to encompass more than one activity, but all at the same level of responsibility and complexity. As someone once said, 'Instead of having one boring job to do I've now got seven boring jobs to do'.
- **Job rotation** – The transfer of the individual from one job to another in rotation. There is no implication here of any changes in level of supervision, complexity or responsibility.

Job enrichment, on the other hand, implies 'vertical' growth in the job so that the individual enjoys incremental growth in the level of responsibility, complexity and autonomy. In other words, the job is increasingly loaded with 'motivators' such as:

- Reductions in supervision allowing for greater flexibility, autonomy and discretion in decision making.
- Removing controls while retaining accountability.
- Giving the individual the whole job to complete which may include numerous (and possibly diverse) tasks. At the Saab and Hoover factories they moved away from a 'Fordist' moving production belt to a carousel system whereby individuals could complete a number of interrelated tasks before moving the job on to a colleague.
- Enabling employees to set their own targets (and others with the mutual agreement of a supervisor).
- The creation of natural work units – at Volvo semi-autonomous teams were given responsibility for car production within set parameters. However, you should note that Herzberg warned against the overreliance on the work group, coining the phrase 'the tyranny of the group'. By this he meant that groups will develop their own norms of behaviour that work against the interests of the employer and the individual.

Herzberg's work is very much about the motivation of the individual as can be seen from his original research base.

- The introduction of more difficult and exacting work.
- Improving the amount of direct and individualized feedback from supervisors to the employee. This enhances the sense of achievement and accomplishment.

The concept of growth can be explained by using Herzberg's concept of motivation. In Figure 3.14 you will see that the individual is initially employed to undertake job tasks A, but with a view to carrying out job tasks C, and he or she will be paid a salary commensurate with C, although at a reduced level. With the benefit of training and encouragement the employee will grow into carrying out the full duties associated with C. Providing training and development opportunities helps meets motivational needs at two levels: First, the training itself can be intrinsically motivational. It enables the individual to experience feelings of self-worth, of personal growth and achievement. Second, the training enables the individual to carry out a higher range of tasks, providing in turn feelings of achievement.

Because pay is a dissatisfier according to Herzberg this does not mean it is unimportant. Indeed, it can be the most critical of the dissatisfiers holding back the growth of motivation in the individual. Herzberg believed pay must be fair and related to the quality and level of the work involved, but should not be related simply to output. He exemplified payment-by-results systems as getting employees to run after jelly beans, the employer coaxing

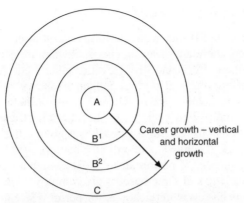

Figure 3.14. Motivation and job growth according to Herzberg. A: Initial tasks on appointment. B^1, B^2: Intermediate career growth – increase in scope and depth of tasks. C: Career growth accomplished in one specific job through training, development and experience.

performance by a series of these incentives only to find that performance will fall back unless another jelly bean is offered. This equates to offering not one but a whole series of carrots to the donkey, each one having to be bigger and juicer than the last one to get the beast to go a few steps further. In employee relations terms a pay rise will be followed shortly afterwards by demands for another one.

In contrast to jelly beans or carrots, Herzberg similarly believed the stick to have disastrous results. Managers should always treat staff fairly. Failure to do so means that employees will remember the pain of unfair treatment as indeed do all human beings from any life experience. Where the pain is intense the individual will possess a 'revenge psychology', the desire to get back at the perpetrator of the original pain.

Herzberg's work has received much criticism over the years, but also a lot of support. Different perspectives can be brought to his essential concepts. It is, however, worth noting key criticisms such as:

● Not all jobs can be enriched. It is impossible for employers to enrich jobs with very specifically defined parameters and those with relatively simple constituent parts. However, lack of imagination on the part of the employer is no excuse for not reassessing the potential of all jobs for a degree of enrichment. For his part, Herzberg did not concern himself with particular jobs, but the process of work and motivation. Job design is fully discussed at Section 3.4.6.
● Not everyone wants their job enriched.
● The diversity of employees means that assumptions about what satisfies and dissatisfies cannot be made.
● Finally, the organizational and employee relations climate is crucial to the theory's successful application.

3.4.4   Process theories of motivation

These theories emphasize the different choices made by people at work and therefore the process of individual motivation. For this reason they are also known as cognitive theories because individuals are making decisions based on their perception of a number of variables, such as their type of work, their desire for rewards and incentives, and their ability to acquire them. They make no assumptions about 'what' motivates only the way in which the individual makes these subconscious or conscious decisions.

Locke – goal setting, Latham and blades

These researchers[34] have concluded that work performance is affected by the goals that people set themselves. Where there are clear, precise goals that are accepted by someone, this helps them to organize their efforts and strive towards attainment. Although employees prefer to be given discretion on goal-setting, evidence shows that they will often overestimate their resources to achieve them, whereas with the help of a supervisor the goals will become more attainable. However, the greater the self-efficacy of the individual (their belief in their own ability to realistically reach the goals), the greater will be the ultimate performance levels. Goal achievement will also be improved where the individual uses a role-model as a 'benchmark' of performance. Goals which are SMART – Specific, Measurable, Achievable, Realistic and Time-based – give employees an exact specification to which they can work. This has clear implications for performance appraisal and review systems. Goals should never be imposed on someone from above without the individual's input, and preferably their agreement after an objective discussion of their realistic achievement. Worryingly, in 2002 a CIPD survey showed employee involvement had declined in recent years.[35]

Jaques' equity theory

This theory has been developed with specific reference to pay, although it can be broadened to encompass other job elements and behaviours.[36] It is based on the premise that there are agreed norms as to what rewards should be available for different jobs or levels of work, and each individual worker is 'intuitively aware' of what forms an 'equitable' payment for their own contribution. The individual seeks a state of balance between what he or she puts into a job and the rewards that derive from it. This state of balance is known as 'psycho-economic equilibrium', and there are two factors which contribute to it:

(i)   A level of work which corresponds to the individual's perception of his or her own work 'capacity' and
(ii) The equitable payment for that work.

If neither condition is met, then disequilibrium occurs. For example, if there is under- or overpayment and/or an imbalance between capacity for work and the work itself, the bigger the gap and the imbalance. As a result, the greater will be the sense of disequilibrium. This will manifest itself through ever-increasing feelings of dissatisfaction. Ultimately the individual may wish to leave the job. This is known as 'psycho-economic negative disequilibrium'. Should the disequilibrium be 'positive' the employee may feel that rewards are in excess of a fair day's work for a fair day's pay, and so concern and even feelings of guilt may result – 'Psycho-economic positive disequilibrium'. Research shows that some will improve their performance where the latter occurs.

These ideas were developed by Adams[37] with reference to personal inputs and outputs. Where there is an imbalance the individual will seek to restore a balance. Rather than emphasizing pay, Adams identifies outputs generally including benefits of different kinds, status, the esteem of others, physical environment, e.g. private office, big desk, etc, as well as pay. Inputs include personal effort, ability, training and age. Furthermore, individuals will compare themselves with others and this too will influence any discrepancy believed to exist between inputs and outputs.

Expectancy theory: Victor Vroom,[38] refined by Porter and Lawler[39]

Essential to this theory is the assumption that individual motivation is determined by two psychological variables:

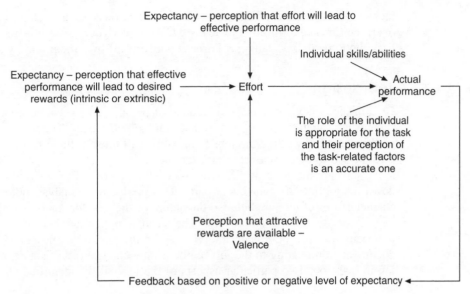

Figure 3.15. Expectancy theory: Vroom Porter and Lawler

- **Valence:** This literally means 'that which stands out' and refers to the preference which an individual has for different possible outcomes of behaviour, e.g. prestige among colleagues **might** be felt to be more important than a higher salary. Valence can be positive or negative, the latter being where the individual would rather something did not happen.
- **Expectancy:** This is a feeling of prediction the individual has about a certain event or outcome which would follow behaviour, e.g. working unpaid overtime is expected to make a good impression with the boss. The individual's expectancy can range from zero to a 100 per cent belief that the outcome will be as predicted.

The theory also assumes that people make conscious decisions about these factors asking themselves two questions:

'What am I most likely to get out of this if I do it?' (Expectancy)
'How much do I want what I am likely to get out of it?' (Valence)

Furthermore, Porter and Lawler have added new dimensions to this equation so that a series of other questions are asked relating to performance and outcomes, and the likelihood of not only achieving the desired outcome but achieving the requisite level of performance to do so. These variables can be shown diagrammatically as in Figure 3.15.

3.4.5   Rewards and incentives

We have already considered the role of money under a number of motivation theories, all of which take slightly different positions. In the absence of positive evidence we can assume that for *some* people money does motivate; as Charles Handy has suggested, salespeople in particular, working for commission, can be financially motivated.[4] For others it will symbolize their own self-worth and the value placed on them by their employer. We have seen from Chapter 1 that an 'instrumental' approach to work will engage the worker seeking as much money as possible to fulfil a meaningful life *outside* work. Wallace and Szilagyi[40] also show that money reinforces motivation because the individual associates its receipt with the accomplishment of other motivational needs such as a project completed, overtime finished or promotion achieved. Whatever your views it is difficult to counter the basic notions of expectancy or fairness put forward by Vroom and by Jacques.

3.4.6   Job design

Organizations have to manage a balance of people factors which often appear to conflict such as job satisfaction, job performance and job efficiency. This balance can be wholly or partly achieved by designing jobs to maximize all three of these factors. First, the job must be analysed to determine its 'characteristics'.

All jobs are made up of different tasks – the process of job analysis results in breaking down the job into its constituent parts. This produces an analysis not only of the specific characteristics of the job, but also the nature of the job. Job analysis can be undertaken by experts or by trained employees. They can adopt a number of techniques including observation of the job holder, interviews with the job holder, peers and with bosses. Also, documentation relating to the job can be examined. The result is a detailed analysis of the job in question. Two particular aspects of the job will be identified:

- The **specific** tasks involved in the job, showing relative importance and frequency and
- The **context** of the job, e.g. the work group, the technology used, the organizational structure and the job fits in and other external relationships and contacts.

Once this analysis is complete steps can be taken (where feasible) to redesign the job to incorporate as many of the characteristics of a well-designed job:

(i)   **Variety:** in both skill application and in using different tools, equipment, machinery, etc.

(ii)   **Autonomy:** and discretion in using skill application, in decision making and making choices.

(iii)   **Interaction** in the job: this involves incorporating a number of interrelated subtasks forming a whole job. This is closely linked with:

(iv)   **Task identity:** giving the whole job a degree of coherence by permitting the individual to see how their own contribution impacts on the construction of a finished product or a delivered service. It is difficult to convince employees of the importance of their own work if they cannot see how it forms any meaningful entity. This is precisely what workers in a 'Fordist-type' work environment are deprived of leading to PIMS – powerlessness, isolation, meaningless work and self-estrangement (see Chapter 2). Isolation in such a workplace means the individual is unable to enjoy:

(v)   **Task interdependence** in the group: the opportunity to work in teams and enjoy a degree of social interaction emphasized in the socio-technical systems approach.

(vi)   **Responsibility:** be allowed to take steps or decisions which will have ramifications. Herzberg has said that it is impossible to convince employees that they are doing responsible work if the tasks are so simplistic and meaningless as to defy any inkling of responsibility.

(vii)   **Task significance:** this means that the product or service has real impact on others – especially customers or members of the public. Examples would include a popular product purchased by customers, a public service which helps the vulnerable members of society or a cooked meal that is enjoyed by restaurant customers.

(viii) To enjoy task significance as well as a sense of achievement it is necessary to have good quality **feedback**.[41]

The job characteristics approach avoids some of the classic pitfalls of 'Taylorized' jobs found in a 'Fordist' work environment, notably:

- Short work cycles
- Continuous pacing of the job (found with conveyor belt continuous production cycles)
- Lack of control over the machinery or technology and
- Loss of individuality.

Summary

Edgar Schein[17] has correctly said that human behaviour is 'complex', based as it is on such a broad range of variables which we have discussed in Chapter 1. Certainly, there is evidence to show that we are 'social animals', that we are 'rational-economic', in other words, consciously seeking material rewards, and that human beings are also seeking self-actualization. In the concluding case study a number of these variables are brought together which apply distinctively to one particular situation with a specific group of employees. Motivation is a very unique process – dynamic and individualized. However, in the case study we are able to apply general principles to solving a company-wide problem. But, underpinning this is the manager's or leader's task of improving workers' motivation by examining personal needs identified in the several theories we have examined here. We should remember that the best performers are normally the easiest to motivate while the poorest performers are the most difficult to motivate. We therefore address that issue next.

3.5 Managing performance

UK sickness absence hits 20-year high point

Official figures released (in April 2002) show that more working days than ever before are being lost because of sickness absence.

Figures from the Office for National Statistics' Labour Force Survey reveal that almost 2.2 million working days were lost to sickness in autumn 2001, compared to 1.9 million days the previous summer.

It is the first time there has been a significant increase in the levels of sickness absence for 20 years. The figure had previously remained static at just under two million days.

The research reveals that women are more likely to be off sick than men, with absence levels among female employees at 3.8 per cent on average compared for male staff.

According to the survey younger staff have the highest levels of absence. Men aged 25 to 29 years old and women in the 20 to 24 age group are most likely to take time off work.

For men the highest absence rates were in customer-facing occupations and the lowest were among managers and senior officials who were absent on average for only 2.4 per cent of working days. Among women the absence rates were among process, plant and machine operatives.

John Knell, director of research at the Work Foundation*, said the ONS findings tie in with the general downturn in employee satisfaction revealed in the organization's Working in Britain Survey.

'The fact that they (sickness absence levels) have increased is significant and it might reflect staff satisfaction levels. The largest increases in dissatisfaction levels between 1992 and 2000 were for workload and working hours,' he said.

'According to our survey the number of people who only work as hard as they have to has doubled and one avenue for dissatisfaction is sick days.'[42]

*Formerly known as the Industrial Society.

**Section
objectives**

In this section you will:

● Examine the possible reasons for poor performance, including substandard work and unsatisfactory attendance
● Assess some of the ways in which poor performance can be managed successfully
● Examine the role of disciplinary action and the skills necessary for carrying it out
● Examine different methods of performance management, including the incorporation of performance appraisal, pay and training and development.

3.5.1   Introduction

Proper application of all the policies and methods discussed so far in this section of the book should help produce effective employees, but poor performance can still manifest itself at any time and in all employees. No one is immune from producing work or having an attendance record which at one time or another is less than satisfactory. The task of the manager or supervisor is to make a judgement between those who are performing at a level less than expected for a justifiable reason such as a bereavement, genuine illness or job induction and those who are not. In all these cases support, albeit of a different nature, should be given to the employee. There will be some who produce substandard work for no discernible reason, and it is here that the manager must take action quickly. (Different aspects of performance management – Target-setting and 'Management by Objectives' – are also discussed in Section 4.2.)

3.5.2   Managing poor performance

In order to prevent poor performance it is critical that employees are clearly aware of the standards required of them for work, conduct and attendance. There are numerous ways in which the necessary behaviour can be communicated to them; these include:

● The job description or job specification (with competency profile)
● The employer's staff handbook or staff code and guidance on standards.
● Disciplinary procedures and rules
● Information provided at induction and during the probationary period
● Day-to-day supervision (both formally and informally)
● Peer group information (both formally and informally)
● Training and development (e.g. personal development plan)
● Management information, e.g. briefs and meetings

Having accepted that there will be legitimate reasons why an employee may fail to come up to standards expected of them, even those with inexplicable or unacceptable reasons should be given help and encouragement to reach them. Standards of performance and conduct must be clearly laid down in unambiguous form, and be SMART – that is, specific, measurable, achievable, realistic and capable of being met and measured within a reasonable time-scale. The role of appraisal, discussed in the next section, has a vital role in this process. Information about unacceptable performance can be observed and/or gathered using a number of methods including:

● Day-to-day supervision
● Performance appraisal/review
● Absenteeism records
● Timesheets or records
● Peer group members

- Quality systems
- Customer complaints, or complaints from other parties such as suppliers.
- Employee surveys, including exit analysis.

Investigation

The first step when unsatisfactory performance is detected is to investigate whether the report is true and if so to monitor it. The reasons must be investigated immediately. Remedial action should also be taken immediately or after a lapse in time depending upon the severity of the poor performance. It may be decided that the performance or conduct is so unacceptable that the organization's disciplinary procedures must be triggered straightaway. Assuming it is not, then the employee must be spoken to as soon as possible to ascertain the reason, and the standards required by the employer explained so that the employee has no doubts about what is expected of him or her. The implications of failing to improve must also be clearly explained, such as disciplinary action or a transfer. One of the main reasons why so many poor performance issues are mismanaged is because of the lack of training or self-confidence in the responsible managers. Another reason is that perhaps managers are too quick to 'blame' the employee without acknowledging that the organization may be partly responsible.

How to handle poor performance

Remedying the defects mentioned in the preceding list could resolve a problem. If not, the temptation may be to rush into disciplinary action. However, there are other solutions, which as ACAS[43] points out, can be more satisfactory for all parties; these include workplace counselling and employee assistance programmes (EAPs), as well as referral to specialists in counselling, advice and addiction. This alternative can help an employee whose poor performance is due in some part to a profound misunderstanding of what is expected of him or her, because of psychological or domestic reasons or addiction to drugs or alcohol. The individual may be sufficiently cured and return as a fully effective member of staff, grateful for the employer's assistance. Other employees too will be vicariously supported by the help given to another employee. Funds spent on disciplinary proceedings and possibly at employment tribunal particularly where there might have been disability discrimination will be saved. (Counselling and Employee Assistance Programmes are discussed in Sections 2.4 and 5.1.)

3.5.3   Disciplinary action

Where these other measures have failed or where the lack of performance or proper conduct is so great, then the employer's disciplinary procedures may then be applied. For example:

- A member of staff has been told three times by her manager that late arrival in the morning is unacceptable and there is no good reason for the persistent lateness.
- An employee secretly drinks during work hours and refuses to accept counselling or external help with his or her addiction.
- A new member of staff with seven months' service continues to fail to meet work standards despite a reorganization of that work, training and coaching.

Definition: Discipline is the regulation and management control of human activity to produce an appropriate level of performance and conduct.

As we have already indicated, discipline at work requires clear, unambiguous rules based on the ACAS Code of Practice on Disciplinary and Grievance Procedures (2000). A new edition of the Code will be available in 2003 as a result of the introduction of the statutory discipline and grievance procedures under the Employment Act 2002. The Employment Rights Act 1996 is amended so that a failure by the employer to follow the statutory procedure when dismissing an employee will bring about an automatic unfair dismissal. A further amendment is made to the 1996 Act so that the statutory procedure must now be expressly referred to in the statement of principal terms and conditions given to any new employee within 2 months of their starting employment. These new rules should come into effect in April 2004. Despite the existence of statutory procedures employers' contractual procedures must also continue to adhere to principles of fairness and reasonableness. It is critical that employees should know exactly of the standards of performance and conduct which they should uphold.

Case study

Detective work

Gerry always seemed to do what was required by the section manager. Last year, apparently unrelated problems started to become noticeable, such as increasingly late arrival for work, sickness absences of one to three days in duration, work having to be carefully checked and colleagues finding that they could not always rely on information passed to them by Gerry. Nothing here, however that would trigger disciplinary proceedings or even great concern in some managers.

But Gerry's new manager was not like most managers. She did notice these things and decided a bit of detective work was necessary to find out what was going on. The manager was well aware that employees' poor performance could be caused by a number of reasons. Some poor performers seem weakest at 'benchmarking' themselves against other employees. In other words, they could not use the performance of colleagues as a standard against which they could compare their own work. Although they have poor self-esteem they are also fiercely defensive of their own performance. This type of employee is often clever at camouflaging their errors. The manager decided that Gerry fitted this description.

If you were Gerry's manager what detective work would you carry out?

Feedback

First, check personal and appraisal records to see if there are any clues as to the reason for the declining performance, and also to get a profile of Gerry's performance.

Second, listen and be aware of all explicit and implicit evidence of the levels of declining performance and its reasons. What are other employees saying about the situation? Begin to collate written information and documentary evidence. Can day-to-day supervision detect the causes? Gerry's senior colleagues will be asked to carefully monitor and record all examples of unsatisfactory or substandard performance.

Third, an informal discussion with Gerry is necessary. The situation can't wait until the next appraisal interview in six months' time. It is necessary to use questioning skills to get behind the reasons for Gerry's performance. The manager will no doubt self-assess the steps that the employer could take to improve leadership, motivation and job design to help Gerry.

Next, the manager may decide to have a more 'formal' meeting with Gerry, but this should be done using questioning skills to probe various possible reasons. Counselling and other forms of support should be offered where necessary.

Gerry may be a lazy person who has no commitment to the employer, but, on the other hand, it is surprising that performance levels have been dropping only recently. This suggests there is a good reason for it, such as her health or the health of a relative at home, financial worries, concerns about something in the workplace, such as bullying, or dissatisfaction or boredom with the job or even workplace stress.

Gerry's manager understands that the problem may lie with the organization and with the employee.

3.5.4   Performance management and appraisal

Performance appraisal and review systems have undergone a lot of change in the last 20 years, but many are still ineffective and costly to run. The growth of performance management has helped improve appraisal effectiveness by incorporating it into a systematic way of managing performance.

According to an Institute of Manpower Studies Report in 1992[44] performance management 'is a management system whereby the organization's objectives are set and met by means of a process of objective setting for individual employees. Performance improvement can be obtained by identifying a 'shared vision' of where the organization wants to be and clarifying the role of each employee in that process. Thus, the achievement of an organization's strategic objectives is assumed to equate with the sum of the achievement of each individual's objectives'.

Why has performance management become popular?

From the mid-1980s onwards there was a big growth in pay systems linked to individual performance, particularly performance-related pay (PRP). Many organizations found it difficult to recruit and retain quality staff in an increasingly competitive labour market. Employers therefore began dismantling their pay structures and systems, such as bureaucratic incremental pay systems, and introducing performance-based pay. The advantages of performance pay are:

- Improved individual performance
- Improved team performance where team-based PRP was introduced (although very few organizations did so)
- Increased flexibility to deal with recruitment/retention problems
- Tangible recognition for employees and
- Reinforced corporate aims and objectives.

However, during the 1990s PRP was criticized for being very costly, unwieldy, and perhaps worst of all for failing to produce improved individual performance. In many cases it was shown that PRP was dysfunctional. In other words, it produced results opposite to those intended and was, therefore, demotivational and cost-inefficient. Partly, this was due to the overemphasis given to the use of pay as a motivational tool.

In the USA greater credence has been given to the use of training and development and effective coaching and objective-setting systems, rather than an overreliance on pay. This idea soon caught on in the UK, and both private and public sector organizations have employed 'mixed' performance management. In local government, for example, the system has been adopted with enthusiasm as a way of breaking away from an old culture of pay increases based on length of service. Research from the IPD in 1992 reflected this movement and showed that personal development plans are now used by the majority of organizations practising performance management. But, in 2002 the CIPD showed that updated performance management and other progressive HR techniques had a poor take-up.[35]

Components of performance management

Ideas about how to improve performance have been informed by a number of sources, including the so-called 'excellence' movement stimulated by such authors as Peters and Waterman (1982) and Rosabeth Moss Kanter (1985). There is no precise agreement of what constitutes performance management, although it seems that there are a number of specific elements:

- Strategy: A clear corporate strategy with defined objectives is necessary on which to base performance management. Objectives must be defined in terms of clear standards, and with individual key skill requirements through competency profiling and succession planning. In addition, a 'mission statement' can outline and communicate to all the organization's core values, and this helps formulate the text of the 'psychological contract' discussed in Chapter 2.
- SMART objective-setting: Corporate objectives must be translated into individual and team objectives, that are agreed by employee and supervisor. This clearly shifts responsibility to workplace level by emphasizing the individual's role in identifying and achieving objectives. The performance plan should look beyond the immediate demands of the job but with a view to having objectives that 'add value' to performance.
- Effective use of performance appraisal: Without an appraisal system it is difficult to see how performance management could function. The very essence of appraisal is the cascading of organizational objectives down to the individual level who is then required to meet their own goals based on these organizational-wide ones.
- However, effective performance can only be achieved using a system that supports and develops individuals. Innovative performance management should celebrate employee diversity. Coaching, counselling, career development and long-term nurturing are necessary to not only aspire to new heights of performance but also to assist those who, for whatever reason, are producing performance levels below those that are satisfactory. Finally and critically, individual performance must be underpinned by appropriate training and development.
- Subsidiarity: This means performance management rests upon the devolution of decision making and objective setting to individuals and their supervisors. The Commander of the USA Tactical Air Force once argued that productivity can be doubled by recognizing human nature as a fact because people will work harder and be more committed if they control their own work.
- Performance-based pay: Most commonly this will include PRP, but other pay systems can include bonuses, shares, profit-related pay and increments based on performance, as well as pay based on productivity. Employee shares can have a double benefit. They can be given to employees or offered at discounted prices as a reward for collective performance. Individually, they can generate interest and commitment in the company because the employee 'owns a little bit' of the company for which he or she works.
- Finally, the organization must conduct regular management reviews to ensure corporate capability is operating at optimum levels. Where necessary, organizational structures, systems and policies must be adapted to ensure that business objectives are achieved through people performance.

In the type of flat matrix organization we have almost anyone could end up taking charge of the project. So the technician, finance person, operations person may end up being the leader. This means our performance management system must be suitably flexible and recognize that whatever role someone is performing everybody must own the issue in-hand . . . Our performance review system will look at the way in which people are committed to driving towards a business or technical solution . . . The recruitment and selection, training, development and reward systems all inter-link to give the organization people who can do exactly that . . .

Senior manager at Goldman-Sachs plc[14]

Three examples of performance review systems

Balanced scorecard: Authors: *Kaplan, R.* and *Norton, D.*: An individual's scorecard should have a balance between performance drivers (lead measures) and lag measures (showing outcomes). These are divided by four elements of organizational performance: financial management, customer service, internal business process efficiency and learning/personal growth.

Human Asset Multiplier: Authors: *Giles, W. J.* and *Robinson, D. F.*: The employee's gross remuneration is allocated points by the application of a multiplier based on a financial formula which reflects the market value of the firm. From this an employee's personal value is determined. A weighting mechanism is also used to reflect their qualifications, skills, attitudes and other attributes including replacement scarcity. Developed in the 1970s by the IPM/ICMA.

Human Resource Accounting: Author: *Flamholz, Prof. E.*: The employee's 'conditional value' and the likelihood that they will not leave the employer are given a score in terms of the current worth of the potential work that could be carried out by that individual if they were to remain with the organization for a specific time period.

Exercise

From your understanding of performance management so far what advantages do you think arise from performance management?

Feedback

- To align corporate and individual goals
- To improve corporate and individual performance (quantitative and qualitative)
- To strategically focus training and development
- To define and communicate corporate objectives and business aims more effectively
- To clarify personal expectations
- To clarify/plan career development
- To provide for both qualitative and quantitive analysis.

The interface of performance management with other HR systems

Throughout this section on performance management and appraisal we have referred to other organizational HR systems. These can be summarized in Figure 3.16.

Summary

In this section we have addressed two closely interlinked processes – the management of poor performance and the management of improving performance. In the former we have examined the manifestations of poor performance (absence, lateness, low productivity, etc.), the causes of poor performance and numerous strategies and skills that can be employed to deal with these situations. At one level there is the use of sound behavioural skills such as discussion, investigation, counselling, and practical help for employees.

Second, performance management was examined. This 'umbrella' term for a coordinated systematic approach to managing and improving people performance relies on three

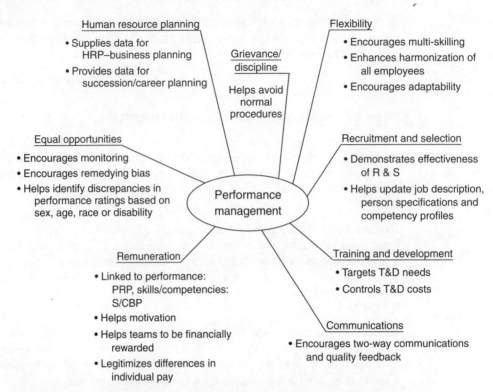

Figure 3.16. Performance management – interaction with other HR systems.

elements: appraisal, training and development and, finally, pay. Increasingly, as organizations attempt to become more competitive and effective, performance management in diverse forms should assume greater relevance to our working lives.

3.6   Learning and development

Section objectives

In this section you will:

● Examine theories of learning and consider their relevance for people management
● Review your own learning processes
● Appraise the concept of the 'learning organization' and assess its value as a model of organizational learning and
● Consider a range of interventions designed to promote continuous learning in organizations.

3.6.1   Introduction

Recent years have seen the subject of learning attracting the attention of both practising managers and researchers in the field. This development is largely attributable to the increasing pace of change and its impact on organizations: as the rate of change accelerates into the new century, organizations and their employees must be able to adapt to ever more turbulent and unpredictable environments. The ability to learn is therefore of paramount importance if organizations are to meet the challenges that lie ahead. Some commentators go so far as to claim that, in the future, the only lasting competitive advantage will be learning.[45]

Case study

The Springboard Housing Association Manager as Developer Programme

Springboard is a registered social landlord providing high quality housing and support services to over 10 000 people, many of whom are classed as vulnerable. In 2003, the Association employed over 800 staff and had a total of over 5500 homes throughout East London, Essex and Hertfordshire. Springboard's mission and values are stated in Section 7.2.

The organization's three-year strategy, drawn up in 2001, was designed to create a platform for future strengthening and growth. The actions planned in pursuit of strategic objectives were underpinned by five key themes: customer focus; developing people; cost effectiveness; developing the organization's capacity for growth; and promoting a positive image of Springboard.

The second theme, developing staff, recognized that skilled and motivated employees are essential to the delivery of high quality services. Specifically, staff should fully understand where the organization was going; be equipped to manage change; be motivated to continuously seek opportunities to improve the business; and have the skills and resources to do their jobs excellently.

The gaining of Investors in People recognition was a specific objective within the overall strategy as the IiP process was seen as a vehicle for attaining the required levels of skill and motivation. A review of the organization against the IiP Standard in 2001, whilst highlighting many examples of effective practice in people management, had identified development needs for those with line management responsibility.

Directors agreed on the need for a learning and development intervention that would not only develop Springboard managers but through them would lead to the more focused development of all staff. The intended outcomes (objectives) were that managers would be able to:

- recognize and support the learning and development needs of both individuals and teams
- explain how learning and development fits in with business strategy and objectives
- develop a supportive, collaborative style of management
- identify and use daily opportunities to coach, rather than direct staff
- develop insights into training and development solutions tailored to individual needs
- evaluate learning and development; and
- conduct effective appraisals, using Springboard's new performance management system.

A competitive tendering exercise resulted in Olympia Executive Ltd, management and human resource consultants, being appointed to design and deliver what came to be known as the Manager as Developer (MAD) programme. The chief executive and the four directors attended the course and participated in all activities along with other delegates.

> The MAD programme ran over four days, one of which involved a review of learning and was held several months after the main course. In the intervening period, managers were asked to complete a coaching project and reflect on their experience with the new performance management system.
>
> (With thanks to Richard Barr, Director of Business Support, Springboard Housing Association)

Exercise

On the basis of the evidence contained in the case study, state with reasons whether or not you think the MAD programme is likely to achieve its stated objectives.

Feedback

The success of any learning and development intervention is to a significant extent dependent on the broader organizational context within which it is commissioned, designed and delivered. Here, the training appears to be taking place within a strategic framework in that it is designed to reinforce core values and support the implementation of corporate objectives. Furthermore, two key features of this programme are the full backing of senior managers and the willingness on their part to participate fully in the training. This will give out strong signals about the perceived value of the experience to other managers, who are then more likely to commit to the process. Also in its favour, the programme was designed and delivered by external consultants, which would tend to enhance its credibility in the eyes of participating managers.[46]

Another determining factor is the establishment of a new performance management system (PMS). Here it should be asked whether or not the new PMS would reinforce the desired behaviours; that is, does it support and promote learning and development? (See the previous section.)

All those involved in the design and delivery of the programme must avoid the pitfalls commonly associated with formal management development programmes.[47] For example, as with any course-based intervention, there is a danger that the learning will not transfer effectively to the workplace. However, it will have been noted that a project has been built into the programme to facilitate the transfer of learning, and that delegates will be expected to report on their progress in implementing the new learning during the follow up day. Also, there is the possibility that managers may respond negatively to the learning and development methods employed on the course. In this regard, the programme designers must be keenly aware of what the prevailing culture will bear; for example, will Springboard managers be prepared fully to participate in the more active – and therefore potentially riskier – exercises?

So it can be seen that there are many variables that can affect the success or otherwise of the learning and development intervention. You probably identified a number of other relevant factors (the quality of the training and the expertise of the trainers, the levels of motivation of the delegates, the venue, and so on). In conclusion, this case gives us an insight into the complex nature of managing individual, team and organizational learning and previews some of the issues we shall be dealing with in this section.

3.6.2   The learning process

In the first part of this section, we investigate what psychology can tell us about the underlying process of learning. Early psychologists noticed the increasing complexity of animal behaviour at each stage of the evolutionary chain. They observed that animals are born with a genetic blueprint for life – like the salmon which is programmed to return to its home river to spawn. The lives of humans, on the other hand, are not predetermined. Although we face the same struggle for survival as animals, we are able to learn many things, and it is this ability to learn that gives us far greater flexibility. Through learning, humans are able to adapt to almost any environment; and it is this adaptability – our ability to learn new behaviours to enable us to cope with constantly changing circumstances – which is perhaps our most distinctive feature. There are a number of theories of learning namely:

- Behaviourist learning theory
- Social learning theory
- Cognitive learning theory
- Experiential learning theory.

Behaviourist theories of learning

The behaviourist school has had a major influence on employee development by introducing key processes such as conditioning, shaping, reinforcement and stimulus – response.

Classical conditioning

The experiments of Ivan Pavlov[48] are probably the most famous in psychology. Pavlov was studying salivary secretion in dogs and had determined that when food was put into a dog's mouth, the dog would salivate. He noticed that when he worked with the same dog repeatedly, the dog salivated in response to certain stimuli that were associated with the food, such as footsteps of the person who brought the food. Pavlov saw that these responses represented a simple form of learning. The basic premise of his work arose from the distinction between salivation in response to food in the mouth and salivation in response to stimuli that had become associated with the food. Pavlov called the salivation in response to food in the mouth an unconditioned response (UCR) because it was not conditional upon the dog's previous experience; it could be accounted for by the dog's reflexes and was therefore an unlearned response. Food in the mouth was called an unconditioned stimulus (UCS), because it always had the effect of making the dog salivate.

Salivation in response to something that was associated with food did not occur automatically, but was conditional on the dog's developing a connection between that 'something' (e.g. the footsteps) associated with the food and the food being in the dog's mouth. This learned response is called the conditioned response (CR), and the new stimulus the conditioned stimulus (CS).

To distinguish between these two kinds of stimuli and responses, remember that:

*un*conditioned = *un*learned; and
conditioned = learned

Pavlov then paired various stimuli with food in the mouth to see if the dog would salivate to the neutral stimuli alone. He found that if a neutral stimulus – something the dog could see and hear – regularly signalled the arrival of food, the dog eventually began salivating to the neutral stimulus alone. His famous experiment, which established the procedure for conditioning, involved sounding a tone just before placing the food in the dog's mouth. After this procedure had been repeated several times, the sound of the tone alone (now a conditioned stimulus) would cause salivation (now a conditioned response). Similarly, if the smell of bread baking makes your mouth water, the smell has become a conditioned stimulus; by association with the taste of bread, the smell triggers a conditioned response.

Pavlov has left a lasting legacy: similar experiments have been carried out on many other organisms, from worms to fish to people, with the same results. These have shown that classical conditioning is the way in which virtually all species adapt to their environments. He also showed how learning, an internal process which takes place in the brain, can be studied objectively.

Operant conditioning

Classical conditioning links simple, involuntary responses with neutral stimuli. But how can we understand more complex voluntary behaviours? It is one thing to teach a dog to salivate at the sound of a bell, but how do we teach a dolphin to jump through a hoop, or a child arithmetic, or an employee to perform a task? Behaviourists would argue that these behaviours can be trained through another type of conditioning. In operant conditioning, the subject becomes more likely to repeat rewarded behaviours and less likely to repeat punished behaviours.

Operant conditioning is associated with the British psychologist, B. F. Skinner,[49] who is the best-known representative of behaviourism. The difference between classical conditioning and operant conditioning is that classical conditioning involves what Skinner describes as respondent behaviour – reflexive behaviour that occurs as an automatic response to a conditioned stimulus (such as Pavlov's tone). Operant conditioning is the learning of a non-reflexive act, called operant behaviour because it 'operates' on the environment to produce rewarding or punishing stimuli. We can therefore distinguish operant from classical conditioning by considering whether the controlling stimulus comes before or after the behaviour:

- **In classical conditioning, the controlling stimulus comes before the behaviour** no matter what the subject is doing (as with the tone eliciting salivation) and
- **In operant conditioning, the controlling stimulus comes after the behaviour**, such as an animal performing a trick to obtain food.

Skinner's starting point was the so-called 'law of effect', i.e. that behaviour that is rewarded is likely to recur. He developed techniques which enabled him to teach pigeons how to play table tennis and rats to press a bar to obtain food. Skinner's achievement was to identify the conditions which result in enduring learning.

In his experiments, Skinner used a procedure known as **shaping** in which rewards are used to guide an animal's natural behaviour to a desired behaviour. Each step the animal makes towards the desired behaviour is rewarded, and all other responses are ignored. In this way, complex behaviours can gradually be shaped.

Skinner argues that we are constantly rewarding and shaping the behaviour of others in everyday life. This is apparent in parenting, where children are taught table manners by using rewards to shape their eating behaviour.

Reinforcement

A reinforcer is any event that strengthens the response that it follows; it is therefore very closely related to the concept of a reward. The distinction is that there are positive and negative reinforcers:

- A positive reinforcer is a stimulus that will strengthen a response (make the response more likely)
- A negative reinforcer is the termination of an unpleasant stimulus (such as turning off an electric shock in an animal experiment)

To illustrate this point, consider a child who throws a tantrum because it wants an ice cream and the parent refuses. If the parent gives in and buys the child an ice cream, then the child's behaviour will be strengthened by positive reinforcement (the parent giving in) and the parent's behaviour will be strengthened by negative reinforcement (the child stops screaming).

The child should gain no request by anger; when he is quiet let him be offered what was refused when he wept.

Seneca, 4 BC–AD 65

Remember, that both positive and negative reinforcers **strengthen** behaviour.

Punishment

Punishment is the opposite of a reinforcer in that it decreases the recurrence of the behaviour that it follows. Punishment is a powerful method of restraining unwanted behaviour, as long as the punishment is strong, immediate and consistent. However, research has shown that the use of punishment to shape behaviour has a number of major drawbacks:

- Skinner argues that what punishment often teaches us is how to avoid punishment. Thus the punished behaviour may appear in settings where punishment is unlikely. For example, the child who is punished by its parents for swearing may do so freely outside the house.
- Punishment can create fear, and the person receiving the punishment may associate it with the person meting it out.
- It can increase aggressiveness, by suggesting that aggression is the way to solve problems.
- Even when punishment suppresses unwanted behaviour, it does not guide the individual towards desired behaviour.

Consequently most psychologists, including Skinner, favour an emphasis on positive reinforcement rather than punishment.

Exercise

How can the principles of operant conditioning be applied in the workplace?

Feedback

- **Managing attendance:** Pedalino and Gamboa[50] showed how reinforcement could reduce absenteeism. They invited workers in one factory who arrived for work on time to pick a playing card from a deck each day. At the end of each week, the worker with the best hand in each department won $20. Immediately absenteeism dropped 20 per cent and remained lowered for as long as the incentive was offered.

Should organizations follow this example and reward employees with a good attendance record?

Attendance is a fundamental part of any job; in fact, it is a contractual obligation. Therefore rewarding attendance may be giving out the wrong signals to employees. In any case, the evidence suggests that such a policy would not solve the problem. In a survey of 327 organizations, 15 per cent provided attendance bonuses in the form of monetary incentives or prizes; however, these companies had a higher absence rate than those who do not reward attendance.[51] Better to shape employees' behaviour by actively managing attendance through interventions such as 'return to work' interviews with line managers when staff have been absent.

- **Rewarding performance:** These principles are discussed in Section 3.4. Research has shown that the positive reinforcement of jobs well done can improve performance. This is especially so when the desired performance is well defined and achievable. It is important to award specific behaviours as opposed to vaguely defined 'merit'. Also, the reinforcement should be immediate. However, rewards need not be material, nor so big that they become political and a source of resentment to those who do not receive them. The effective manager may simply give praise for good work during the normal course of events, or write unexpected notes of appreciation for a completed project.
- **Competencies:** Increasingly, competency frameworks are being used as the basis for employee development and performance management systems (see Chapter 2 and Section 3.2 of this chapter). They are rooted in behavioral learning theory, describing the behaviours and standards required in the performance of work-based tasks.
- **Punishment:** Where organizations are 'blame cultures' (i.e. where managers are looking to punish mistakes), certain activities, such as creativity and risk taking, will be stifled. As stated in Section 3.6.1, punishment creates a climate of fear and breeds resentment towards those handing out the punishments. This will have a very negative effect on employee relations.
- **Computer-based training:** For some tasks, the computer can be more effective than the trainer as operant principles can be applied by shaping learning in small steps and providing immediate reinforcement for correct responses. Through a process known as 'programmed learning', the computer can engage the learner actively, pace material according to the individual's rate of learning, quiz the learner about gaps in understanding and provide immediate feedback.

3.6.3   Social learning theory

Commentators such as Bandura[52] have demonstrated that learning does not occur through experience alone: observational learning, where we observe and imitate the behaviour of others, is also highly significant. The observation and imitation of specific behaviour is often called **modelling**, and the person being observed is the **model**. We learn by observing and imitating models: children learn gender roles from their parents; and in the workplace, co-workers can become role models (modelling is one of the key features of mentoring, for example – see Section 3.6.10). This is known as **social learning theory**.

How is observational learning achieved? Bandura argues that there are four necessary components: attention, retention, production and motivation. Attention indicates that we notice things selectively and choose what to learn; retention means that what we learn does not have any practical effect unless we remember it; and production refers to practice – we learn by doing. Motivation will determine whether observing someone's behaviour will lead us to imitate them, and Bandura holds that we model our behaviour on that of others if we expect to be rewarded for doing so. It is the expectations element in social learning theory that distinguishes it from a behaviourist interpretation because it introduces a cognitive element into learning: we have to make a judgement as to what behaviours to imitate in order to receive a reward.

3.6.4   Cognitive theories

According to Hill,[53] cognitive theories of learning 'are concerned with the cognitions [perceptions or attitudes of beliefs] that individuals have about their environment, and with the ways these cognitions determine behaviour'. The emphasis is on the trying to identify the cognition processes which underlie learning. Cognitive processes include the following:

- Perception
- Memory
- Concept formation
- Language
- Problem solving
- Reasoning

The questions being asked are:

- How do we incorporate information about external events into our minds?
- How do we decide which information either to reject or store?
- How do we retrieve this information to use in our everyday lives?

There are many different aspects of the study of such processes. One of the most important is the work of the gestalt theorists – what came to be known as the Berlin school of psychology.

Gestalt in learning

We noted above that behaviourists are concerned not with conscious thought, but with units of behaviour. The gestalt school of psychology, on the other hand, felt that breaking down consciousness into its parts destroyed its meaning. Wertheimer[54] argued that we see things as a meaningful whole, and that our thoughts are whole meaningful perceptions, not a series of connected images. The German word 'Gestalt' means a 'form' or a 'pattern'. An example of a gestalt is a melody, since it depends on the relation between the notes rather than the notes themselves. The tune is still the same when it is transposed to another key, even though every note is different.

Gestalt learning theory is therefore concerned with the way in which we perceive situations and restructure existing gestalts. The role of insight is key in this process: insightful learning regularly occurs suddenly with a feeling of real understanding; this is sometimes referred to as the 'aha!', or the 'penny-dropping' experience. Such learning is said to be particularly meaningful in that it is likely to be remembered and can relatively easily be transferred to new situations. In such cases the learner sees the whole situation in a new way – a new gestalt has been formed.

The implications for training include the following:

- The learner actively organizes perception by trying to impose pattern and meaning on incoming information, rather than passively receiving the information presented. This means that there is value for learners in discovering meaning for themselves.
- The trainer can help the learner to organize information more meaningfully by helping to isolate the essential material from the background material. Clear headings, subheadings and summaries contribute to this. Novelty, variety and contrast can be used to focus attention and avoid distraction when visual, oral and auditory material is presented.
- There are limits to how much information anyone can take in at once. The trainer must avoid overloading the learner with too much information.
- Learners seek to fit new knowledge into their existing conceptual frameworks. The trainer needs to present, organize and sequence content so as to take this principle into account.

3.6.5 Experiential learning theory

Experiential learning theory, often associated with David Kolb,[55] has been highly influential in the field of human resource development. For Kolb, learning begins with the here-and-now **experience**; is followed by the collection of data and **observations** about that experience; continues with the analysis of that data and the **formulation of concepts and theories**; and reaches the final stage with the **modification of behaviour** and the choice of new experience. The learning process is portrayed as a four-stage cycle (Figure 3.17):

● Concrete experience
● Reflective observation
● Abstract conceptualization
● Planned experimentation.

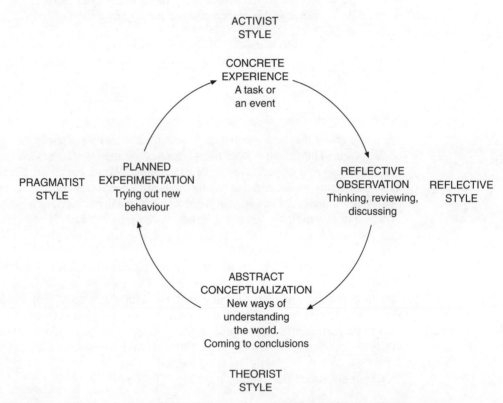

Figure 3.17. Learning as cyclical process (adapted from Kolb, Honey and Mumford).

Experiential learning theory represents a departure from the behaviourist tradition in that it emphasizes analytical and cognitive processes as crucial elements in learning. It therefore overcomes the apparent contradiction between cognitive and behavioural explanations of learning by viewing it as a holistic, integrative process which combines experience, perception, cognition and behaviour – thinking, feeling, perceiving *and* behaving. The crux of experiential learning theory is that by using experience as a touchstone, abstract concepts and ideas created during the learning process can be tested.

For Kolb, learning from experience is the process by which human development itself occurs and is the link between education, work and personal development. Emphasizing the developmental nature of learning, Kolb saw experiential learning not as cyclical process but rather as a spiral, converting feelings and desires into 'higher-order purposeful action' (Figure 3.18) for action to be purposeful, it must be postponed until reflection and judgement have taken place. In practical terms, this means that if we are to develop towards certain 'life goals', we need constantly to reflect on and draw conclusions from our experiences, and apply this new learning to future situations.

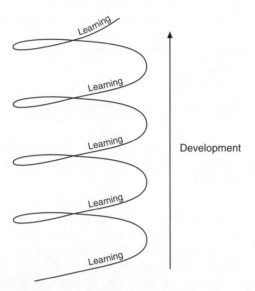

Figure 3.18. A spiral of learning.

Experiential learning emphasizes process whereas behavioural theories stress outcomes. The implications are that focusing on outcomes tends to reproduce existing behaviours which may now be inappropriate. This is one of the potential dangers of a competency-based approach: unless the competencies are regularly reviewed, the organization may be reproducing outmoded behaviours. This suggests that in an organization which is undergoing rapid change, a behavioural approach to employee development may have negative consequences.

One of the key features of the learning organization is that everyday experience is viewed as an important source of learning. Individual employees and work groups must become effective learners from experience in order to cope with change. Individuals must take responsibility for their own learning in that they will be able both to identify their own learning needs in respect of their work roles and know how to meet those needs by learning in a proactive way from their experiences. Learning is therefore self-directed.

The implication of this is that employees directing their own learning need to learn how to learn. Learning is therefore seen as a skill which can be developed. Building on Kolb's analysis, which recognizes different approaches to learning within the learning cycle, Honey and Mumford[56] have identified four **learning styles** (activist, reflector, theorist and pragmatist), each of which is associated with the various stages of the learning cycle. By using Honey and Mumford's 80-point questionnaire, employees can be helped to understand their individual learning styles, thereby becoming more effective learners from experience.

3.6.6   The learning organization

At the beginning of this chapter we stated that through learning, human beings are able to adapt to different environments and that this is one of the most distinctive features of our species. In recent years, a number of commentators have been considering whether organizations can themselves 'learn' and adapt to their external environments. In this connection, the organization has been compared to a living organism which can adapt and evolve in response to changing business conditions. The following quotations from two of the leading authorities in the field illustrate this point:

> (*The learning organization*) *emphasizes adaptability (which is) the first stage in moving towards learning organizations. That is why leading-edge organizations are focusing on generative learning, which is about creating, as well as adaptive learning, which is about copying.*[57]

Probably the best-known definition of the learning organization is that of Pedler *et al.*:[58]

> (*A learning organization is*) *an organization which facilitates the learning of all its members and continuously transforms itself.*

Both of these commentators suggest the possibility of organizations transforming themselves through learning in order to succeed in a turbulent environment. This view of the organization as a living organism is in contrast to the more traditional machine model, popular in the 1960s and 1970s. Here, the organization is seen as a 'machine' with component parts which function in unison. The problem, to continue the metaphor, is that machines become obsolete when technology changes – whereas organisms can evolve to meet the demands of new conditions. This is why, at the turn of the century and at a time of sweeping global change, the idea of the learning organization had such appeal.

What exactly is a learning organization? According to Garratt,[59] a learning organization will have the following features:

- People are helped to learn both regularly and rigorously from their work.
- Robust organizational systems and a positive organizational climate to move the learning to where it is needed.
- Learning is seen to be valued by the organization in achieving its objectives.
- The organization is so designed as to be able to transform itself continuously through its learning to the benefit of its stakeholders.

Pedler *et al.* identify eleven characteristics which signify a learning company, divided into five clusters:[58]

(i) Strategy

- **A learning approach to strategy.** Strategy formulation, implementation and evaluation are structured as a learning process enabling continuous improvement. This implies an opportunistic approach, involving taking risks (albeit 'the right kinds of risks').
- **Participative policy making.** All stakeholders are involved in the development of strategy and policy.
- **Informating.** Using information technology to inform and empower people, providing access to information and more open systems.
- **Formative accounting and control.** The system of accounting, budgeting and control are designed to support learning.

(ii) Looking in

- **Internal exchange.** The treatment of all individuals, departments and sections as being suppliers to and customers of each other. The sharing of information in a collaborative, rather than a competitive, environment.
- **Reward flexibility.** Reward systems that provide an incentive to learn and share information.

(iii) Structures

- **Enabling structures.** Structures which allow and support learning (e.g. appraisal).

(iv) Looking out

- **Boundary workers as environmental scanners.** Using the experience of all employees who interact with external customers to identify and respond to customer needs.
- **Intercompany learning.** Partnerships with both competitors and non-competitors for mutually advantageous learning activities such as joint training and job exchanges.

(v) Learning opportunities

- **Learning climate.** An emphasis on the developmental, nurturing aspect of the manager's job as opposed to the control aspect.
- **Self-development opportunities for all.** Resources and facilities for self-development are made available for all employees and external stakeholders.

An evaluation of the learning organization

The learning organization model has come in for much questioning; some even claim that it is in 'terminal decline'.[60] Specifically, it has been criticized on a number of grounds:

- Do learning organizations actually exist? Burgoyne[61] acknowledges that after a decade of research, there are still no case studies of organizations which accord with the model outlined in the previous section.
- Is the idea just 'old wine in new bottles'? Some commentators, for example Mumford[62] see the learning organization as little more than the recycling of well-established ideas such as Total Quality Management, team work, leadership and personal development.
- How realistic are some of the key features of the learning organization? For example, it is possible to question the practicality of involving all stakeholders, who themselves have conflicting interests, in the development of strategy (see Chapter 7). Furthermore, it has been suggested that the learning organization idea perpetuates a naive view of the organization and how cultural change can be achieved.[63]
- Is the learning organization merely 'trainer-speak'? It is argued that the concept is too closely associated with HRM and has little meaning for managers.

What, then, is the value of the learning organization model? In recent years, it has become closely associated with the idea of **knowledge management**. This is partly in response to concerns about knowledge transmission. In traditional (stable, hierarchical) organizations, knowledge would be communicated to managers by older, more experienced employees on an informal basis. This unrecorded knowledge was an important part of the organization's culture. However, in downsized and outsourced organizations, this 'corporate memory' is in danger of being lost.

Some commentators, such as Nonaka,[64] argue that the ability to create new forms of knowledge and act on them is the source of competitive advantage. He identifies two kinds of knowledge: explicit knowledge, which is easily communicated and quantifiable; and tacit knowledge, discussed in the previous paragraph, which is understood but not described. While data about knowledge is difficult to capture, there is some evidence of accountants trying to develop ways of measuring a company's knowledge assets.[65] The key to organizational success lies in using both explicit and tacit knowledge.

Organizations are using new technology – especially the Internet and intranets – to share information and promote learning among their internal and external stakeholders. So developments in IT have allowed organizations to meet one of the learning company criteria, that of informating.

However, 'knowledge management' is also a problematic concept. Powerful individuals often feel very uneasy about sharing knowledge for fear that it might undermine their power. Furthermore, it is not yet understood how knowledge develops, making its management difficult. There is also the question of intellectual property rights, i.e. who owns the knowledge that is created?

3.6.7   Managing learning in organizations

The manager as developer

Line managers are 'key players' in promoting continuous learning. One of the fundamental tenets of Human Resource Management is that managers should take responsibility for the 'people management', as well as the 'task management' aspects of their role. This is in contrast to the situation where responsibility for employee development is 'hived off' to development specialists, i.e. trainers. There is a very strong rationale for this policy: managers are in day-to-day contact with their reports, they know the job and are aware of the individual's strengths and weaknesses. They are therefore ideally placed to take an active part in development of their staff, whose performance they are, after all, meant to manage.

The problem with this is that managers often tend to be task-driven and do not possess the people management skills necessary to take on a developmental role. Nevertheless, many organizations are now expecting their managers to take a degree of responsibility for employee development, and are putting in place supporting systems to ensure that this happens: continuous, sometimes 360-degree appraisal is being promoted; and staff development responsibilities are being written into job descriptions and appearing in managers' performance objectives. In addition, organizations are trying to provide managers with the skills they need to take on these responsibilities.

Mumford[62] suggests that managers have a number of roles in developing their reports:

- Appraisal of performance
- Appraisal of potential
- Analysis of development needs and goals
- Recognizing and facilitating opportunities
- Giving learning a priority
- Using everyday activities for learning
- Establishing learning goals
- Accepting risks in subordinate performance
- Monitoring learning achievement
- Providing feedback on performance
- Acting as a model of learning behaviour
- Using learning styles
- Offering help
- Direct coaching

It is this last role – the manager as coach – to which we now turn.

3.6.8   Coaching

What is 'coaching'?

The following definitions provide an insight into the nature of coaching:

(Coaching is) improving the performance of somebody who is already competent rather than establishing competence in the first place.[66]

(Coaching is) developing the ability and experience of (people) by giving them systematically planned and progressively more stretching tasks to perform, coupled with continuous appraisal and counselling.[67]

We can see from these definitions that coaching involves the following:

- Stretching potential
- Counselling
- Continuous appraisal
- Integrating learning with work (using everyday experience).

Why do managers coach employees?

Coaching performs several functions:

- To enable the employee to recognize his or her strengths and weaknesses
- To encourage the employee to establish targets for further performance improvement
- To monitor and review the employee's progress in achieving targets
- To identify any problems that might be adversely affecting progress
- To assist the employee in generating alternatives and an action plan for dealing with problems that have been identified
- To improve the employee's understanding of the work environment and
- To assist the employee to realize his or her potential.

It can be seen from these points that coaching involves continuous appraisal; the coach must maintain an ongoing dialogue with staff. Coaching also has several advantages over course-based training:

- Real work is used as a vehicle for learning. This overcomes the problems of transferring learning from the training room to the workplace.
- Feedback is immediate; there is no time-lag between acquiring, applying and seeing the results of new learning.
- Faults can be remedied on the spot through guidance from the coach
- It is a cheaper form of learning than course-based training.

Coaching also has some disadvantages:

- Risks are involved and mistakes may be made
- Learning may be disrupted
- Bad habits can be transmitted

Perhaps the main advantage of coaching, from a continuous learning perspective, is that it is empowering in that it enables the employee to mature and become a better learner: the individual employee becomes more capable and therefore more confident, which leads to a greater sense of control and autonomy. Employees become more independent and less likely to look for hierarchical approval for everything they do.

Furthermore, coaching should give the learner greater insight and understanding into the work environment and how his or her job fits into the organization. This process can be very positive in improving the individual's job satisfaction and motivation.

Also coaching should broaden and deepen employees' use of skills and abilities, enabling them to tackle more difficult problems and to extend their capabilities through new experiences. Related to this, coaching enables the employee to accept greater ambiguity and take risks in their work.

3.6.9   Counselling

Counselling is a process which is very closely related to coaching. In fact, the terms are often paired ('coaching and counselling') or used as synonyms. Counselling is an integral part of the coaching process. The point here is that to be effective coaches, managers have to be able to use some of the techniques and skills associated with counselling. Also, counselling can be used in a range of people management contexts – from mentoring, through career development to change management – so we spend some time examining the process in this section.

What is counselling?

Much workplace counselling is not counselling in the modern definition of the term but relates to situations which require the use of counselling skills. Workplace counselling can be deemed to be any activity in the workplace where one individual uses a set of techniques or skills to help another individual take responsibility for and to manage their own decision making whether it is work-related or personal.[68]

Background and issues

The current theory and practice of counselling owes a good deal to an American, Carl Rogers. Rogers started out from a conventional psychotherapeutic background but abandoned this approach and pinned his faith on the quality of the relationship between the therapist/counsellor and the client. In his view, the relationship should be based principally on the counsellor's warmth, genuineness and empathy operating in an atmosphere of equality and trust. Clients are not seen as 'patients' needing help from a remote expert, but as responsible people who have freely chosen counselling as a means of tackling their difficulties. Thus counselling has often concentrated on helping ordinarily competent people to cope with difficult circumstances.

In recent years, the use of counselling has spread to the point where people sometimes refer, rather disparagingly, to the 'counselling industry'. The workplace has been affected in that the term 'counselling' is regularly used in relation to a number of organizational scenarios (redundancy, career development, discipline, appraisal and coaching, for example). However, 'professional' counsellors would not regard much of this activity as counselling, for the following reasons:

● Much workplace counselling takes place within a power structure and is directed to fulfilling the goals of the organization, not those of the client, even though the latter may gain from the process. It cannot be expected that in the manager–subordinate situation there will be complete openness on either side.

- Counsellors need training and experience. They should also have a high degree of self-awareness, achieved perhaps through undergoing a prolonged period of psycho-analysis. They should also subscribe to a professional code of ethics.

What is workplace counselling?

Essentially, counselling in the workplace takes two distinct forms:

- Helping employees with problems and
- As a means of self-development and personal growth.

It is based on the following values:

- People need to be given special individual attention from time to time, particularly in periods of personal change
- People's feelings have a place at work and
- The importance of showing employees that they are themselves valued.

Are we saying that managers should become counsellors?

No, clearly this is unrealistic and, probably, undesirable. The argument is that managers should acquire and practise some of the skills used in counselling, such as listening and empathizing, so that they can motivate and develop people rather than control and direct them. However, it is important that employees see the process as being genuine and not one of manipulation. The independent counsellor or therapist can handle problems which should not be the subject of counselling by managers who do not have the necessary qualifications.

What are the elements of effective counselling?

The effective counsellor helps the client explore and clarify her problems and find her own solutions. There are five important aspects to successful counselling:

- **Active listening**
- **Recognizing the 'presenting problem'** is rarely a full statement of the real problem.
- **Finding the core problem** which is the heart of the matter that is worrying the client.
- **Recognizing and admitting feelings**
- **Influencing the direction.** Questions should direct the client towards greater self-understanding and an ability to select the course of action which is right for him or her.

3.6.10   Mentoring

Mentoring is another employee development method in which the line manager plays a key role. One of the problems with a term such as mentoring is that people use it in different ways and ascribe different meanings to it. Thus some organizations will appoint a 'mentor' to a new employee as part of the induction process. The 'mentor' will usually be someone who is around the same age as the new employee but who has enough experience of the job to be able to 'show them the ropes'. Other organizations may refer to someone performing this type of role as a 'buddy'; certainly, they are not a mentor in the conventional sense. Still other organizations will use the terms 'coach' and 'mentor' interchangeably.

A more accurate use of the title 'mentor' is that applied to the older, experienced and usually senior employee who takes a younger, junior employee 'under their wing'. This type of mentoring has always gone on informally in organizations, but it is only in recent years that organizations have recognized the value of mentoring as a developmental tool and tried to formalize it. As mentioned earlier, older employees are repositories of both explicit and tacit organizational knowledge; they therefore represent a resource which can be tapped by the organization through mentoring to ensure the transmission of knowledge.

Probably the most common use of formal mentoring systems in organizations is in a management development context. Most graduate training programmes, for example, will incorporate a mentoring scheme. Here, the newly appointed graduate trainee will be allocated a mentor. In this context, the main purpose of mentoring is

- To facilitate the induction of young people (usually management trainees) and
- To identify and develop high-flyers.

How does a mentoring scheme work?

Using the example of a management trainee mentoring programme, the newly appointed trainee will be allocated a mentor on joining the organization. There are, of course, issues around identifying suitable candidates to act as mentors. Because of the nature of the role, it is important to ask for volunteers as someone who grudgingly agrees to become a mentor could cause serious damage. Potential mentors must have a good record for developing people, an in-depth understanding of the organization and sufficient time to devote to the relationship. Mentoring works best if the role of the mentor and the line manager are not confused.

The mentoring process itself needs to be managed, and this responsibility usually falls to personnel and development practitioners. Once mentors have been identified, a matching exercise will take place. Mentors should be provided with guidelines and a clear briefing; ideally, they will receive training to help them succeed in the role. The formal mentoring relationship will be time-bound, its duration normally being determined by the length of the training programme (typically six months to a year). However, this does not mean that the relationship will not continue on an informal basis afterwards.

There will be an initial meeting between the mentor and the mentee (other terms for the individual being mentored are 'protégé' and 'mentoree'). Some organizations give mentors an entertainment budget so that they can take their mentee to lunch. The mentor and the mentee will then agree on a contract, the terms of which will include some ground rules such as the frequency of meetings. It is important that the mentee understands the role of the mentor. According to Bova,[69] a mentor can perform a number of functions:

- A guide and confidant
- A role model
- A tutor or coach
- A listener

One of the key functions of the mentor, therefore, is to act as a sounding board and to use the counselling techniques described above to help trainees solve their own problems. The mentor is definitely not there to listen to complaints about the mentee's boss, and it is important that the mentor does not, or is not perceived to, undermine the trainee's line manager. The mentor–mentee relationship may break down, or may never take off. Under these circumstances, the organization must intervene and reallocate another mentor to the trainee. The scheme should be monitored and evaluated.

Action learning

Action learning is a technique which, some argue, overcomes the drawbacks of more conventional approaches to management development. Mumford[62] states that unsuccessful management development programmes tend to have the following features:

- Their purposes are unclear and unsupported by managers
- There has been poor diagnosis of organization culture and the requirements of the business
- There has been poor analysis of individual managers' learning needs
- The development processes utilized are often unconvincing to managers and unacceptable to individuals
- There is an overemphasis on off-the-job training
- The methods used tend to be 'flavour of the month' and
- Programmes are owned by personnel and development practitioners.

These problems are mainly associated with formal, course-based programmes, sometimes characterized as the 'sheep-dip' approach to management development. Action learning avoids these pitfalls because it uses the actual job of managing as a vehicle for learning. Consequently, it is highly experiential and does not come up against the problems associated with off-the-job training, such as relevance and the transfer of learning from the training room to the workplace.

Action learning is associated with Reg Revans,[70] who holds that learning should begin with the everyday management task of problem-solving. The key features of an action learning programme are the project and the action learning set.

The action learning project

Imagine the following scenario: a training manager needs to learn about marketing the department's services. How can this learning need be met? The temptation might be to recommend that she attends a marketing course. Revans would disagree – he would argue that she should be given a relevant management task to perform. The organization should identify a suitable marketing project through which she can learn the necessary knowledge and skills. This project could be in the HR department, or it could be in another department. She will be supported in this by her membership of an action learning set.

Action learning sets

The action learning set is a group of no more than five managers, each of whom is working on their own action learning project. The set will meet on a regular basis for the duration of the project (usually around six months) and the members will use these meetings to discuss their progress. Revans argues that learning is more likely to be achieved by exchanges with other managers who are themselves anxious to learn. Through the set, managers learn to:

- Give and receive criticism
- Offer support and
- Develop their own capacity for effective action.

The process will be facilitated by a 'set adviser' (normally a trainer) who will help to get the set off the ground and establish cohesion, but will not offer solutions to the managers' problems or attempt to 'teach' (see Figure 3.19).

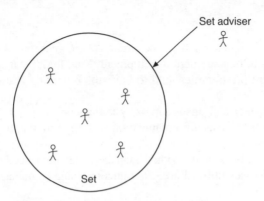

Figure 3.19. The action learning set.

It is important to remember that the project is a live one and that any recommendations the managers make (assuming they are acceptable to the client) will be implemented by the manager. It is at this point, the action stage, where the really useful management learning takes place because the manager is having to use managerial skills such as influencing and negotiating.

It has become quite common for organizations to use action learning sets to develop managers, but without the project element. In this situation, a group of managers will meet on a regular basis to discuss general problems and share experiences. These arrangements are sometimes referred to as self-development groups.

Summary

In this section, we noted the increased interest in both individual and organizational learning as organizations strive to come to terms with rapid and continuous change. We have considered various theories of learning and their application to people management. In considering organizational learning, it was suggested that the learning organization model had certain limitations, although we identified a number of methods which would contribute to fostering a culture of continuous learning in organizations.

Case study

East-Coast plc

East-Coast Building Society became a public limited company (plc) last summer. Since then it has taken over an estate agency and an insurance company. East-Coast now has over fifty branches in the north of London and east of England, along with twenty estate agency offices and several administrative offices. For a number of reasons the customer-base has remained loyal and stable.

Head office, in Norwich, has a small computer that handles records and transactions; it is connected in a network to numerous minicomputers on the desks of staff throughout the fifty branches. The insurance offices and estate agencies are supposed to work in an integrated way with these branches, but the computer and internal e-mail systems have not been installed. This is pending depending upon the outcome of 'a feasibility study'. As a result, the telephone is heavily relied on for immediate intercompany communication, and the postal service for anything non-urgent. As the three arms of the new company become more integrated this is clearly a nuisance to all concerned. The staff in the former building society offices are most affected. In the north London offices employees get very frustrated with delays. All communications must be routed through a supervisor, who has an important role in overseeing staff activities such as cash withdrawals, verifying signatures, dealing with important customers and personally handling their accounts.

East-Coast's managing director, Neil Colbourne, is 40 years old and joined the company from a larger competitor 6 months ago. He is sympathetic to the need to improve communications with and between all branch offices. He wants everyone to have access to e-mail and plans video conferencing as a way of speeding-up management communications. On a tour of several branches to familiarize himself with the company he noted that many managers seemed technologically illiterate, but were surprisingly ambivalent to the problems caused. Several expressed the desire that there was 'nowhere to go for career progression' and 'retirement could not roll on soon enough!' Colbourne decides that most of these managers are 'dead wood' and he will ensure they either improve quickly in attitude and new business generation, or are dismissed. Colbourne's ire was probably made worse by the 'lack of respect' he believes he was shown when visiting the branches – no lunches laid on, few staff addressing him as 'Mr Colbourne' and an 'unenthusiastic climate of welcome' as he described it later.

As a first step to 'bringing the company into the twenty-first century' a deputy has been appointed with whom Colbourne has worked before: Andrew Gregory. The deputy's view of HR management can be summed up as follows: 'the labour market is tight, but the best way to get good performance is to use bribery . . . and fire the worst'. New recruits as well as established employees are trained by having a one-day induction 'experience' (as it is known) followed up by on-the-job training by supervisors and peers. The latter are encouraged to use 'carrots' and 'sticks' (as Colbourne calls them) to ensure employees develop skills and knowledge.

The estate agency arm of South-East is headed by Christine Freeman, who started in the business ten years ago. She has built up the business with great skill and determination. Surprised initially by the approach from South-East she saw the takeover as bringing new capital and prestige to the business. Traditionally, Freeman has been seen by her staff as a great delegator, and managers enjoy the freedom to take decisions without having someone continually checking on them. All senior agents and managers have 'laptops', mobile phones and a networked e-mail system connecting all the estate agency offices. This culture has spread and on a recent tour of the branches Freeman was impressed by the enthusiasm and energy shown by the employees. One senior manager, Baz Drewett, has told Freeman that the main reason for the success is her 'leadership style' and the 'elaborate recruitment process' used. Another manager, Dave Haskins believes the reason is that both quality and quantity are rewarded, not just volume of sales. Freeman says that the key to success is the development of people. She practises coaching and mentoring of all her managers, and encourages them to do so with their own staff. This is done by including plans in their appraisal reviews. In addition, two years ago Freeman introduced 'action learning' whereby different managers meet to form an action learning 'set' for sharing criticism, support, ideas and for generating new projects.

Freeman believes it is time for the three operating arms of the company to merge more than by name only. However, at the recent directors' meeting there were strong disagreements between Freeman and Colbourne on how the company should be run in the future.

Compare the leadership approaches of Colbourne and Freeman. What is your analysis of these styles? What systems are helping the estate agency arm succeed whilst the former building society function seems to be stagnating?

Feedback

Leadership styles: Colbournes' style is based on position power – he demands status and respect based on his authority position. The deputy, Gregory, seems to believe in physical and resource power. Overall, therefore, Colbourne is more likely to be an autocratic leader with certain assumptions about people based on a theory X perspective. He is very task orientated, but has an underdeveloped people dimension, reflecting a 9.1 dimension on the Mouton and Blake grid.

Freeman's style seems based on expert, charismatic and resource power. There is a better mix of concern for task accomplishment, but also the needs of individuals and the group. There seems to be some evidence of greater self-awareness by Freeman than Colbourne. On the Blake and Mouton grid Freeman's style is moving towards 9.9. Also, Freeman is a transformational leader with a developed sense of EQ. Clearly, there is a good sense of trust that exists between her and the staff. People are given autonomy, discretion and the encouragement to work towards goals that are not just volume-driven.

Freeman's approach to building the business has been based on taking care over the recruitment, selection and induction of staff to ensure a 'fit'. The rewards based on quality and quantity imply a performance review system whereby objective results (results-oriented) and behaviour (absolute method) are important. Possibly, this has been consolidated into a competency-driven performance management system.

There are also signs that Freeman has developed a sound socio-technical system of work using technology to enhance job outputs and employee satisfaction. Because of the culture and the way rewards are organized there seems to be a feeling of 'felt-fairness' about them. Some attention has been given to the job design of the employees. Using the 'job characteristics' approach there is autonomy, task significance and variety in the jobs, and possibly all of the characteristics are present. All of this has built to provide a motivational environment in which intrinsic as well as extrinsic motivators are present.

There is little in the case study about poor performance, but it may be safe to assume that as a result of all the other evidence employees are assisted to identify their work difficulties and to take ownership of them and the solutions. There does not seem to be a culture of fear about dismissals, so this should tell us that dismissal is correctly only used as a management tool of last resort.

This overall style of managing people seems in stark contrast to Colbourne's (enhanced by that of his deputy, Gregory). We have already said he is more autocratic than democratic. He has failed to analyse the situation with the branch managers and has made assumption that they are 'dead wood'; this seems to extend to the staff as well. The job of a leader is not to jump to conclusions which may be false, but to assess the situation based on a careful analysis where this is possible. There is no reason why Colbourne has to make a quick decision about the staff.

If Colbourne accepts Gregory's maxim for recruitment and selection a vicious cycle of inappropriate employees with poor motivation and commitment will be aggravated. Colbourne seems not to pay any attention to the job design or the socio-technical systems that prevail in the branches. An oversimplistic view of the benefits of technology dominates. We can safely assume that the recruitment, selection and induction methods used will have poor validity and reliability, and may be ineffective, inefficient and even unfair.

Bribery is the worst possible approach to human motivation, although at a simple level it can help reinforce behavioural change. Even if the assumption that the 'carrot' of money is the prime motivator for these people it should be provided on a basis that takes account of equity and expectancy theories. What of all the other possible motivators? In addition, everyone has been categorized together without any consideration of individual needs that require satisfaction.

From the culture of the branches and the comments of managers it seems that motivation is currently very underdeveloped. Steps as those considered by Colbourne and Gregory could be disastrous. There is clearly no performance management system that is delivering higher expectations from the staff about their own capabilities to improve performance or for personal growth in the job or in another part of the organization. Perhaps no appraisal system exists?

It would appear that Freeman has adopted a coaching and mentoring dimension to her personal leadership style, and encourages other managers to do likewise. However, action learning is also adopted as a principal way of developing staff. It is difficult to argue that Freeman's business is a learning organization, but it is beginning to show characteristics of that approach. There is little in the case study to show that Colbourne is committed to (or understands) more than simple reinforcement learning strategies which will continue to result in under-developed employees.

Let us wish Christine Freeman well in her battle with Colbourne.

In brief

You may ask yourself, 'what can I learn from the broad range of issues in this chapter about managing people effectively?' You may also need to reflect on how they all interrelate to each other. As we have said more than once in this part of the book, managing people is not an easy task, and is probably the hardest of management tasks. This chapter makes no theoretical assumptions about inevitable patterns of relationships, such as perpetual conflict, or the natural order of leaders and 'followers' or one which is based on pluralism or unitarism. However, it has sought to examine different perspectives based on numerous theories and concepts about human relations at work.

What conclusions can we draw? First, that relationships at work are determined by one of power, particularly for managers and leaders who seek to exert influence over others (Section 3.1). These power sources, as identified by French and Raven can be used negatively to coerce, to damage, to subordinate or to feed the status and authority of the few. Alternatively, they can be used positively to give confidence, to reward, to inspire and to lead the many. Combinations of different power sources are likely to give rise to different types of responsive behaviour, as Etzioni has shown.

Second, we have argued that organizations are increasingly recruiting and selecting people to play a productive and collaborative part in organizational life. These people also need, if not demand to be placed in working relationships where power is used in a positive way. Modern organizations require appropriately talented, skilled people with competencies that 'fit' the workplace environment which includes culture, systems, structures, type and activities of the job. This is true whether the job lacks growth and a high 'profile' or it has it in ample proportions. The result is that recruitment and selection is becoming more sophisticated (Section 3.2). By this we mean that instead of relying on a single interview employers will use a range of methods and techniques to successfully obtain the best 'fit'. This range includes tests, questionnaires, assessment centre methods and competency-based interviewing. As a result, the expense of recruiting and selecting is increasing and this in turn leads to greater demands for improved validity and reliability. Critical to this process, and to it being perceived as a 'positive' experience is the necessity for 'fairness' and the application of ethical considerations. This will involve making selection methods free of culture bias and discriminatory practices.

The recruitment and selection process will finish with the introduction of the individual to the organization through induction. One of the first influences an organization can exert is the emphasis it places on motivation (Section 3.4). The motivation of the new employee throughout their life with the organization and the way in which that employee can exert an influence to help motivate others. Despite the surfeit of theories, there are clear lessons we can draw: Human motivation is a complex mixture of the intrinsic and the extrinsic. Managers can and should assess the individual and collective needs of their employees in the context of the organizational environment. Motivation strategies can be applied at this collective and individual level. Of the most important a sense of recognition, achievement and personal growth are key, but tangible rewards, normally in the shape of pay are also critical. As Herzberg once said 'one is not more important than another'. Pay must be felt-fair and equitable. Finally, clear objectives jointly identified by employee/manager must be set against the ability of the individual to achieve them. As Vroom has pointed out this 'expectancy' is dependent on the individual's perception of the attractiveness of the reward and his or her ability to achieve it through the completion of work objectives. To do this the employee must be given the external resources and the internal resources (e.g. training) to do so.

Arguably, motivation of others is the key responsibility of leaders (Section 3.3). If getting things done through people requires building a strong motivational environment then this must be true. We examined the different approaches to leadership including the contingency methods. These involve the leader being able to build a flexible style of leadership which can be applied to different situations. This is not to say the leader has to be a weathervane, constantly shifting in style to confuse and disorientate employees. However, what the leader must do is 'read' the environment. In the Vroom decision-making case studies we saw how a leader in a particular role can assess the strength and weakness of his or her position *vis-à-vis* the employees and the task, and then take a decision on the most appropriate course of action. John Adair's functional model of leadership shows us how the person, task and group can be coordinated to this effect.

The problem with motivation is that it can mean nothing more than a word to many aspiring leaders. It becomes very hard to 'motivate' the poor performer. In Section 3.5 we examined the methods and techniques that can be employed to assist those with performance difficulties to improve. Unfortunately, discipline and dismissal will face those who cannot improve for various reasons. Leadership here is also critical. The application of skill, sensitivity and the ability to take prompt, but fair and effective decisions.

Penultimately, we examined performance management. The leader will know not just how to construct a partnership of ownership with each employee working towards performance achievement, but understand and apply power to construct appropriate appraisal methodologies, to implement them and follow up with the right action. The expectancy theory cycle is, again, very relevant here, as shown in Figure 3.15.

Finally, in this chapter we discussed individual and organizational learning and the direct relationship with people management in Section 3.6. A continuous theme throughout this chapter, and particularly in Sections 3.3–3.5, has been the importance of individual development as a key motivational factor and one of the prime responsibilities of leaders. Despite the difficulties and imperfections of promoting effective learning, organizations are themselves learning that without continuous improvement of human resources they are substantially disadvantaged at all stages and levels of organizational activity, compromising growth and competitive advantage.

There are no guarantees of achievement in people management, but a sensible application of the approaches we have considered in this chapter will certainly help in building success.

Examination questions for this chapter are given in Appendix 2.

References

1 Report available from Roffey Park: £30.00–01293 851644.
2 Butler, G. V. (1986) *Organization and Management: Theory and Practice*. Prentice Hall International/Institute of Personnel and Development. p. 115.
3 Lord Acton (1868) *Historical Essays and Studies*: Appendix.
4 Handy, C. (1993) *Understanding Organizations*. Penguin.

5 Etzioni, A. (1961) A *Comparative Analysis of Complex Organizations – On power, involvement and their correlates*. Macmillan.

6 Pfeffer, J. (1981) *Power in Organizations*. Pitman.

7 French, J. and Raven B. (1958) The bases of social power. In *Studies in Social Power* (ed. Cartwright, D.). Institute of Social Research.

8 Lewis, C. (1985) *Employee Selection*: The Personnel Management Series. Hutchinson.

9 Advisory, Conciliation and Arbitration Service (ACAS) (1997) *Recruitment and Selection*. Advisory Booklet.

10 Analysis of personnel activities and costs. *Personnel Today*, 20 August.

11 Kipling, R. (1902) The elephant's child. In the *'Just-So' Stories*.

12 Employment Review 759, (September 2002) Industrial Relations Services.

13 Cranfield School of Management and Daily Telegraph (10 September 2002). *Personnel Today*.

14 From discussion with the author (June 1999).

15 Bennis, W. and Nanus, B. (1988) *Leaders – The strategies for taking charge*. Harper and Row.

16 Harvey-Jones, J. (1988) *Making it Happen – Reflections on Leadership*. Collins.

17 Schein, E. (1980) *Organizational Psychology*. Prentice Hall.

18 Zaleznik, A. (1990) *The Management Mystique – Restoring Leadership in Business*. Harper and Row.

19 Kotter, J. P. (1990) *Harvard Business Review*, March/April.

20 Hampden-Turner, C. (1991) *Corporate Culture – From vicious to virtuous cycles*. Economist/Hutchinson.

21 McGregor, D. (1960) *The Human Side of Enterprise*. McGraw-Hill.

22 Fleishman, E. A., Harris, E. F. and Burtt, H. E. (1955) *Leadership and Supervision in Industry*. Ohio State University, Bureau of Educational Research.

23 Tannebaum, R. and Schmidt, W. H. (1973) How to choose a leadership pattern. *Harvard Business Review*, May–June, 162–175, 178–180.

24 Blake, R. R. and Mouton, J. S. (1969) *Building a Dynamic Organization through Grid Organization Development*. Gull.

25 Adair, J. (1982) *Action-centred Leadership*. Gower.

26 Vroom, V. and Yetton, P. (1973) *Leadership and Decision-making*. University of Pittsburgh Press.

27 Personnel Decisions Inc. (1991) University of Minnesota.

28 Vroom, V. (1991) In discussion with the author at Yale University, August.

29 Herzberg, F. (1968) One more time: How do you motivate employees? *Harvard Business Review*, January/February.

30 Taylor, F. W. (1911). *The Principles of Scientific Management in Job Satisfaction – Challenge and response in modern Britain* (ed. Weir, M.) (1974). Fontana/Collins.

31 Mayo, E. (1939) *The Hawthorne research studies: Management and the Worker* (eds Roethlisberger and Dickson). Harvard University Press.

32 Trist, E. L. and Bamforth, K. W. (1951) Some social and psychological consequences of the longwall method of coal-getting'. *Human Relations*, **1**, 3–38.

33 Maslow, A. H. (1954) *Motivation and Personality*. Harper.

34 Latham, G. P. and Blades, J. J. (1975) The practical significance of Locke's theory of goal setting. *Journal of Applied Psychology*, **60**, 122–124.

35 Guest, D. and Conway, N. (2002) *Pressure at Work and the Psychological Contract*. CIPD.

36 Jaques, E. (1951) *The Changing Culture of a Factory*. Tavistock.

37 Adams, J. S. (1965) Inequity in social change. In *Advances in Experimental Social Psychology. Vol. 2*. (ed. Berkowitz, L.). Academic Press.

38 Vroom, V. (1964) *Work and Motivation*. Wiley.

39 Porter, L. W. and Lawler, E. E. (1968) *Managerial Attitudes and Performance*. Dorsey Press.

40 Wallace, M. J. Jr. and Szilagyi, A. D. (1990) *Organizational Behaviour and Performance*. Glenview.

41 Hackman, J. R., Oldham, G. R., Janson, R. and Purdy, K. (1975) A new strategy for job enrichment. *California Management Review*, **17**, 57–71.

42 Wigham, P. (2002) *Personnel Today*, April.

43 Advisory, Conciliation and Arbitration Service (ACAS) Code of Practice on Disciplinary and Grievance Procedures (2000).
44 *Institute of Manpower Studies Report into Performance Management* (1992).
45 Senge, P.M. (1990) *The Fifth Discipline: The art and practice of the learning organization.* Doubleday.
46 Mumford, A. (1999) *Management Development: Strategies for Action* (3rd edn). CIPD.
47 From sheep dip to strategic intent. *IRS Employee Development Bulletin 39.*
48 Pavlov, I. P. (1927) *Conditioned Reflexes.* Oxford University Press.
49 Skinner, B. F. (1953) *Science and Human Behaviour.* Macmillan.
50 Pedalino, E. and Gamboa, V. U. (1974) Behavior modification and absenteeism: Intervention in one industrial setting. *Journal of Applied Psychology,* **59.**
51 Industrial Society (1997) Issue 32: *Managing best practice, maximising attendance.* February.
52 Bandura, A. (1977) *Social Learning Theory.* Prentice Hall.
53 Hill, W. F. (1990) *Learning: a Survey of Psychological Interpretations* (5th edn). Harper and Row.
54 Wertheimer, M. (1945) *Productive Thinking.* Harper and Row.
55 Kolb, D. A. (1984) *Experiential Learning – Experience as the Source of Learning and Development.* Prentice Hall.
56 Honey, P. and Mumford, A. (1996) *A Manual of Learning Styles* (3rd edn). Honey.
57 Senge, P. M. (1990) *The Fifth Discipline: The art and practice of the learning organization.* Doubleday.
58 Pedler, M., Burgoyne, J. and Boydell, T. (1991) *The Learning Company: A Strategy for Sustainable Development.* McGraw-Hill.
59 Garratt, B. (1995) An old idea that has come of age. *People Management,* **1,** 19.
60 Sloman, M. (1999) Seize the day. *People Management,* **5,** 10.
61 Burgoyne, J. (1999) Design of the times. *People Management,* **5,** 11.
62 Mumford, A. (1997) *Management Development: Strategies for Action.* Institute of Personnel Development.
63 Guest, D. and Mackenzie Davey, K. (1996) Don't write off the traditional career. *People Management,* 22 February.
64 Nonaka, I (1996) The knowledge creating company. In *How Organizations Learn* (ed. K. Starkey). International Thomson Business Press.
65 *The Economist* (1995) Management Focus. 11 February.
66 Torrington, D. and Weightman, J. and Johns, K. (1994). *Effective Management: People and Organizations.* (2nd edn). Prentice Hall.
67 Buckley and Caple (1990) *One-to-one Training and Coaching Skills.* Kogan Page.
68 *The IPD Statement on Counselling in the Workplace,* Institute of Personnel Development.
69 Bova, B. (1987) A profile of a mentor. In *Learning in the Workplace* (ed. Marsick, V. J.). Croom Helm.
70 Revans, R. (1983) *The ABC of Action Learning.* Chartwell-Bratt.

Further reading

Adair, J. (2003) *The Inspirational Leader.* Kogan Page.
Arthur, D. (2001) *Employee Recruitment and Retention Handbook.* McGraw-Hill.
Bee, F. and Bee, R. (2003) *Learning Needs Analysis and Evaluation.* CIPD.
Belbin, M. (2001) *Managing Without Power.* Butterworth-Heinemann.
Berne, E. (1979) *The Games People Play – The Psychology of Human Relationships (Transactional Analysis).* Penguin.
CIPD (2002). *How do People Learn.* CIPD Research Report.
Conger, J. A. and Kanungo, R. N. (1998) *Charismatic Leadership in Organizations.* Butterworth-Heinemann.
Easterby-Smith, M. and Araujo, L. and Burgoyne, J. (eds) (1999) *Organizational Learning and the Learning Organization.* Sage.

Heron, J. (2002) *Complete Facilitator's Handbook*. Kogan Page.

Hesselbein, F. (2002) *Hesselbein on Leadership*. Jossey-Bass.

Hodges, T. (2002) *Linking Learning and Performance*. Butterworth-Heinemann.

Holbeche, L. (1998) *Motivating People in Lean Organizations*. Butterworth-Heinemann.

Jackson, C. (1996) *Understanding Psychological Testing*. British Psychological Society.

Kirkpatrick, D. L. (2001) *Developing Supervisors and Team Leaders*. Butterworth-Heinemann.

Malone, S. A. (2003) *Learning about Learning – An A–Z of Training and Development Tools and Techniques*. CIPD.

Maund, L. (2001) *An Introduction to HRM*. Palgrave.

Phillips, J. and Stone, R. (2002) *How to Measure Training Success*. McGraw-Hill.

Phillips, J., Stone, D. and Phillips, P. P. (2001) *The Human Resources Scorecard*. Butterworth-Heinemann.

Shipka, B. (1997) *Leadership in a Changing World*. Butterworth-Heinemann.

Web-site addresses

Age Discrimination – Maturity Works: http://www.maturityworks.co.uk

Cabinet Office – Leadership: http://www.idea.gov.uk/prime

Campaign for Leadership: http://www.thecampaignforleadership.co.uk

Chartered Institute of Personnel and Development: http://www.cipd.co.uk

CIPD People Management: http://www.peoplemanagement.co.uk/

Citizens Advice Bureaux: http://www.nacab.org.uk

Confederation of British Industry: http://www.cbi.org.uk

Economic Research Council: http://www.ersc.ac.uk

Hay Pay Net: http://www.haypaynet.com

Health and Safety Executive: http://www.hse.gov.uk

HRnet Web Centre: http://www.the-hrnet.com

Human capital forum (People Management): http://peoplemanagement.co.uk/humancapital

Incomes Data Services: http://www.incomesdata.co.uk

Institution of Occupational Safety and Health: http://www.iosh.co.uk

International Labour Organization: http://www.ilo.org

Investors in People: http://www.investorsinpeople.org.uk

Reward Management: http://www.e-reward.co.uk

Trades Union Congress: http://www.tuc.org.uk

Part Two
Managing Activities

Learning outcomes

To understand and explain:

- The complex nature of managerial work
- The main functions of management and other functions in the organization
- The interrelationship between managers and other organizational functions, including the role of HR management and the special functions of managers
- The importance and methodology of using quality systems in the workplace, as well as customer care systems
- How change management should be applied, the methods and techniques associated with successful change
- The requirements for health, safety and welfare policies and practices.

Introduction to Part Two

An organization's most valuable asset is its people and in order to get the best out of them, managers have to learn how to work with them as individuals or in groups. This involves looking at approaches to interpersonal relations in order to know how to deal with the different types of people and situations managers and other staff meet during their working lives. The study of how people work together in groups and how they respond to a variety of styles of leadership is essential to help develop good working relationships. People need to know how organizations are structured and how that structure is used to focus their efforts to achieve its objectives.

The achievement of these objectives is the responsibility of managers and their staff, but how well managers organize their resources, both human and material, will help contribute to them. Managerial work is not as easy as many believe; it is varied and involves the need to plan, organize and coordinate the efforts of everyone involved. Managers themselves need to be self-motivated, determined and organized. Like their staff, they too have to learn how to follow instructions, work to deadlines and achieve targets. One of the most important activities a manager has to carry out is communicating. Communication is essential for efficient and effective working. Managers need to be able to communicate, not only in written format but verbally too. Managers often have to use committees and meetings to communicate their intentions and deal with problems, consequently they have to learn how to plan and run meetings.

Managers have to educate and train staff and this will involve them in explaining the organization's goals and objectives. They will have to explain to staff the role of the component parts of the organization and the contribution they make to the achievement of objectives. Included in this is an explanation of the various functional departments, their interrelationship and activities.

Managers need to raise staff awareness of quality and its importance to the customer. This will involve empowering staff to take decisions about quality and its improvement. By adopting quality as a focus an organization can find that it needs to change. It is the manager's job to take an active part in ensuring that change is successful, through activities like planning, organizing, coordinating and leading the efforts of others, as well as providing a role model. Resistance to change will need to be overcome and managers have to be able to adopt strategies to deal with resistance and conflict then move the organization and its staff forward.

Managers also have to understand the implications of health, safety and welfare for staff. Health and safety is a key factor that can also present managers with dilemmas. They may be asked to operate safely but within operational constraints that make that difficult. It is into this environment that the manager ventures to operate and use a variety of planning and organizational techniques. Managers need to be able to use information to aid the coordination of their human, physical and financial resources. Having done all of this they need to reflect on the activities they have carried out and decide whether or not they have contributed to the efficient and effective operation of the organization; if not they must change them. With all this in mind the importance of studying managing activities should be evident. Without understanding this dimension people management goals cannot be achieved, irrespective of the manager's expertise in that field.

4   Managerial work

*The most important role of management is to create an environment in which
the distinct and different contributions of individuals can flourish in order to
achieve the organization's overall objectives.*

Mary Bishop[1] C. E., The Shaftesbury Society

**Chapter
objectives**

In this chapter you will:

- Examine management and organization theory from a historical perspective
- Obtain an overview of the variety of work activities managers have to carry-out
- Look at how managers have to balance their time and that of others in order to achieve
  the successful completion of tasks through the efforts of individuals and groups and
- Examine how managers have to use their communication skills both written and oral to
  maximum effect.

**Case
study**

The modern apprentice

Andy is an excellent motor vehicle mechanic who has completed a Modern
Apprenticeship with a main dealership. During his apprenticeship he was voted UK
Apprentice of the year and represented his employers in skills competitions throughout
Europe and the Far East.

Now at the age of twenty-five, with five years' post-apprenticeship experience he was
beginning to long for a challenge. He knew his employers were supportive about
promoting suitable individuals to management positions especially those who had a
detailed knowledge of their products and experience of dealing with customers. Andy
knew it would be a difficult decision but he felt the need to develop his talents further
and for him a managerial position seemed to offer this development.

Should Andy leave the security of the job he knows and move into management and,
furthermore, should his employers encourage him to?

Feedback

Andy is obviously a talented individual who is seeking to develop himself. What he may not
be aware of is just how much a manager is expected to do. He may not be aware of how
different the work of a manager is even in the same organization. Andy's employers will if
they think he is suitable have to carefully plan his transition from being one of their best
mechanics to being one of their managers. They will no doubt be aware that just because
someone is good at a particular job they will not necessarily be good at being a manager.

Andy is undoubtedly enthusiastic and that drive and ambition will serve him well but, as we will see in this chapter, being a manager is not just about having drive and ambition; there are other attributes a manager needs like the ability to control, coordinate, plan and delegate.

Chapter introduction	Management and managers have been around a long time. We may not have called them managers, we may have called them 'generals' or 'mandarins' or the 'master'. However we described them there have always been people who do the work of a manager. What is it that has shaped the work of managers? In order to answer this we need to look at the history of the world and particularly that of Britain. Prior to the Industrial Revolution which began in the mid-1700s relatively few people worked in manufacturing industries, agriculture being the major employer. What happened in the agricultural context was greatly influenced by nature. Farmers and their employees worked when it was light and rested when it was dark. They planted when it was time to plant and reaped when it was time to reap; the rest of the year there was little or no work. The coming of the Industrial Revolution changed the system that had existed virtually unchanged since people settled down to till the land.

Industrialization meant entrepreneurs invested in factories and the means of production and then they needed a return on their investment. This meant maximizing the use of capital and labour with the result that factories and their machinery dictated the times of work, and introduced the possibility of working a 24-hour day. The need to use resources effectively and efficiently has greatly influenced the activities of managers. Indeed, the increase in industrial processes in the nineteenth century gave rise to the 'managerial class'.

According to Drucker,[2] the development of management as a profession has been extremely rapid. The impact of management in terms of its contribution to economic and social development is massive. Managers greatly influence how organizations transform raw materials into goods and services through the efforts of people. The nature of the workforce has changed greatly through the efforts of the education system, according to Drucker.[2] As organizations grew the only model of a large organization they could look to for inspiration was the Army or the Church. These institutions with their ideas of command and control greatly influenced management thinking.

4.1   A brief history of management and organizational theory

Eighty years ago, on the threshold of World War, a few thinkers were just becoming aware of management's existence. But few people even in the most advanced countries had anything to do with 'management'. Now the largest single group in the labour force, more than one third of the total, are people whom the U.S. Bureau of the Census call 'managerial and professional'.

Peter Drucker[2]

Section objectives	In this section you will:

- Examine the history and development of management and
- Examine the nature of managerial work, its fragmentation, its brevity and its diversity.

4.1.1   Classical management views

Henri Fayol (1841–1925),[3] was one of the first people to put his mind to the developing of a set of universal management principles. He used his own experience as the basis of his ideas and developed a list of fourteen principles as follows:

- **Division of work and specialization.**
- **Authority and responsibility.**
- **Discipline.**
- **Unity of command.**
- **Unity of direction.**
- **Subordination of individual interests.**
- **Fair remuneration in relation to effort.**
- **Scalar chain or hierarchical line.**
- **Centralization.**
- **Order.**
- **Equity.**
- **Stability of tenure of manager.**
- **The importance of initiative.**
- **Importance of *esprit de corps*.**

4.1.2   Scientific management

Scientific management is associated with F. W. Taylor (1856–1917),[4] F. Gilbreth (1868–1924) and H. Gantt (1861–1919).

Taylor, like Fayol, based his ideas on his own work experience, and wanted there to be a more systematic approach to management than existed at the time. At the turn of the nineteenth century, as factories were developing, the emphasis was on efficiency. What Taylor wanted was to systematically analyse the work people did. He felt that most workers only made a minimal effort at work because they feared unemployment; their view being that if they worked too hard the work would run out. Other reasons included the unstructured methods that managers allowed to be employed in organizing work. Managers permitted the workforce a lot of flexibility in how jobs would be completed based around their craft skills, a situation which led to similar jobs being done differently.

The final reason for people being reluctant to make more effort was the variation that employees experienced due to the piece rate system in which employees were paid according to the number of units they produced. People felt this system could be abused by management, who, once they discovered how many units employees could produce for a particular rate of pay, would then increase the number required or reduce the pay. Taylor wanted to move away from situations where the workforce decided how the job was to be done. He felt that a method of working could be determined 'scientifically', in other words rationally and logically. The second step was to add to the working method a specified time for actually completing the job. This would mean obtaining all the facts about a task and physically timing with a watch all the various component parts as they were carried out by a skilled worker. This would allow at a later stage the analysis of work step by step and the subsequent removal of inefficient activities.

Taylor also required that workers had only to do the tasks asked of them. Deciding on how the job was to be done was to be the prerogative of management. The workforce would have to be selected and trained 'scientifically'.

Finally, management would have to accept that 'science' would dictate the way jobs were done and how long they took. This would mean managers giving up some of their power over the workforce and having to cooperate with them. There were benefits to be gained

...entific management approach, i.e. improved methods which in turn meant ...productivity. Employees could link effort to reward and were so paid by

...e of the problems associated with scientific management were that it de-skilled work ...reaking it down into its component parts. Scientific management also took away some ...the opportunity for staff to use their initiative and by breaking down work it became ...epetitive and boring. It made management more powerful because they could carefully plan and organize the work without any real reference to the employees. This subsequently contributed to further alienation of the employees from their employers. 'Scientific management' is discussed in the context of managing people in Section 2.1. and, the differences between management and leadership are examined in Section 3.3.

Exercise

The idea of scientific management and its use of methods does not necessarily appeal immediately to everyone. However, it is worth carrying out the following exercise to give yourself a brief insight into its potential. Write down in chronological order everything you have done today from the time your alarm awoke you this morning to the time you arrived at your place of work. Exchange your list with someone else – your partner, a friend or work colleague and critically analyse each other's list. See if you can make some suggestions about how you could improve on what the other person has done so far today. There is an incentive for you here because, depending on how successful you are at improving on that original list, you could end up with extra time in bed!

Feedback

By writing down what you did and comparing it with what the other person has done you should have discovered that people have different routines. Within those routines you can identify which activities are most, least and non essential. If an activity is not necessary you can eliminate it. You can also examine the order in which you do things and learn from others how they do things, then emulate their time-efficient approaches. Scientific management emphasized the need to do things in a logical order. For instance, you might have found that there were things you had to do first and others you could do consecutively. For example, you need to fill the kettle before you boil it but you can prepare your toast in an electric toaster while you are brushing your teeth. The scientific approach would identify these as time savers and should result in a more efficient use of your time. Depending on your circumstances, you will have identified areas where you can do things differently and so plan your actions differently. This will save you time and effort and gives an opportunity to appreciate some of Taylor's thinking.

4.1.3 Management functions

Fayol[3] also suggested that all managers carry out five management functions, namely planning, organizing, commanding, coordinating and controlling. This theme has been supported by others over the years, including Gullick,[5] whose list contained planning, organizing, staffing, directing, coordination, reporting and budgeting.

4.1.4 Human relations approach

Following the classical approaches came the 'human relations' approaches of the 1920s often associated with the work of Elton Mayo (1880–1949) (see Roethlisberger and Dickson[6]). Mayo examined how human attitudes, values and interpersonal relationships affected the workings of organizations.

This approach moved away from the scientific approach of Taylor (based on practising managers) to one based on research carried out by social scientists. Comprehensive studies were carried out at the Hawthorne works which was part of the Western Electric Company in the USA.

In the illumination experiments it was shown that levels of output could not be related to levels of illumination. Sometimes production increased when lighting levels were reduced. The relay assembly test room experiments were carried out on a group of self-selected women whose job it was to assemble relays. The observer worked in the same room as the women and explained what was happening during the experiment.

The results of observations showed a regular increase in output.

Other areas studied

Mayo identified much about people at work, specifically that they are not motivated by money alone, but their sense of belonging and being part of a group is important. The attitudes of those within the group shape an individual's attitude and thus, together with all the other norms, the group can be a powerful motivator that managers ignore at their peril.

4.1.5   The new human relations approach

Following on from the work of Mayo came the new human relations approach from people such as Maslow (1943), Herzberg (1959), Likert (1961) and McGregor (1960). Maslow and Herzberg are well known for their ideas on motivation which is covered in more detail in Section 3.4. Maslow,[7] recognized that individuals have a number of needs they must satisfy. At the lowest level individuals must have food, sleep and shelter, **their basic physiological needs**. At the next level the individual needs to feel safe and so there is a need for a threat-free environment. the so-called **safety needs**. **Love needs**, the next level, it is argued are about relationships with others and how individuals view their positions within the group. Next in the hierarchy we have **esteem needs** where the individual finds the need to be respected by others as well as having respect for themselves. Finally, Maslow argues that people need to find self-fulfilment and this he describes as **self-actualization**.

This work tries to get managers to focus on the higher-level psychological needs of individuals in terms of the need for a challenge, the acceptance of responsibility or growth. From a management perspective Maslow's hierarchy can help identify at what level people are and what motivators might be used on them.

Herzberg,[8] interviewed accountants and engineers to determine what they felt was good or bad about their jobs. These he was able to categorize as being part of one of two groups of factors he called the **satisfiers** and the **dissatisfiers**. The satisfiers like achievement and recognition would motivate but the dissatisfiers such as company policy and salary only acted hygienically and prevented dissatisfaction. This can give management ideas about which areas to focus upon to motivate people and what to concentrate on to prevent people from becoming demotivated, notably the hygiene factors.

X and Y theory (McGregor[9])

McGregor's contribution was to classify the different attitudes a manager might have about their staff, the extremes of these attitudes being X and Y. X is based on the assumption that the average human dislikes work, is lazy and will try to avoid it. He or she will work only if they are compelled to do so. Y-type persons make the assumption that most people do not inherently dislike work. They do not need to be closely monitored or have to be compelled to work, because they will work naturally. This type of person actively seek responsibility, they are self-motivating with a clear idea of what they want.

McGregor argued that managers who operate at the 'X' end of the scale will have to be very specific when they instruct their staff. They will believe their staff need a lot of direct control and need rigid job specifications to keep them under control. At the other end of the scale, that is 'Y', the manager will try to encourage their staff in terms of their own self-development and self-expression.

Likert,[10] analysed managers who appeared to have high productivity levels, low costs and well-motivated staff. Research showed that these managers were using ideas from classical management theory, such as having time-frames allocated to well-defined jobs, but they also took their staff into consideration, staff were encouraged to participate during their work, e.g. in decision making. These managers seemed to be able to create highly motivated, cooperative groups of employees who worked closely together to achieve financial as well as social rewards through their work. These staff were also able to achieve an element of creativity and self-actualization in the way that Maslow's hierarchy suggests. Likert believed that some of the success could be attributed to the relationships between those who managed and those who were managed. These relationships needed to be supportive and staff needed to understand how important it could be to belong to a group and develop personally from belonging to that group. The good managers were those who could relate well to groups and help the group members themselves relate to each other.

Likert's work was extended to a view of organizations where the supportive relationships overlap and link various groups together, an example being where the head of a group may well be a team member of his or her boss's group. This boss in turn is a member of the next boss's group. This gives rise to an organization structure that looks like a functional one but it is actually based on the fact that the teams are interrelated (see Figure 4.1). Motivation and their relationship with improving performance are examined in depth in Section 3.4.

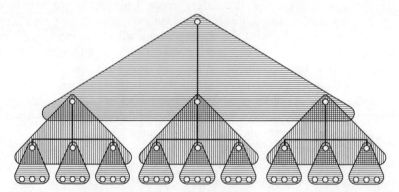

Figure 4.1. Rensis Likert's linking pin model.

Likert[10] developed four different styles of management from his research:

- **Exploitative authoritative**
- **Benevolent authoritative**
- **Consultative**
- **Participative group.**

4.1.6   Systems approach (usually associated with the Tavistock Institute of Human Relations)

In this approach organizations' systems are seen as being complex because they are made up of people, the technology, the organization structure and the environment. In a basic approach they can be viewed as having a number of inputs that pass through the organizational processes and emerge on the other side as a series of outputs. From the outputs data are fed back to the input side. An organization can be made up of a number of systems such as the financial system, the management system and the social system. Some of these systems cross the boundaries between functional divisions and the boundary between the organization and its environment. For instance, a financial system will cross all functional divisions and environmental limits to the customer.

The idea that organizations are systems appeals to some managers, who are attracted to the fact that they are constantly changing. As feedback reaches the input side, the inputs to the organization might change. The subsystems within the organization will have to change depending on the inputs and the requirements of customers or end-users, e.g. line-managers.

For example, we could look at a school and say that its outputs should be teenagers who are numerate and literate. When the headteacher gets feedback from employers that they are unhappy because their recruits are not numerate and literate then the head will have to do something about it. He or she can try to control the inputs and be more selective as a school, recruit more teachers, or reduce the number of pupils. Within the transformation processes within the school the head could change the teaching system or the assessment system and then see how consequently output changes. This process can be repeated until the headteacher is satisfied that the outputs are of the correct quality and standard.

An approach like this also focuses attention on the fact that different subsystems in the organization have different goals that do not necessarily fit in with those of the overall organization. Some teachers may have one goal of academic achievement measured in exam passes, another system of teachers may see it in terms of life skills learned. The financial manager might see it as financial effectiveness and the students might see school as a chore that has to be completed. This then becomes a problem for the head teacher and the management of the school because the three goals are not necessarily all working towards the same ends. The head and the managers will have to concentrate on integration to get the best from the three systems.

Managers will have to focus on the overall view of the organization and not be sidetracked into narrow areas of operation. The reality in the case of the school example is that the variability of inputs from year to year will make managers change their views that the same solution can be used in different situations. School teachers know that what worked for this year's intake will not necessarily work for next year's. Teachers in schools and their managers have to learn to adjust their systems depending on inputs.

Trist and Bamforth,[11] examined the socio-technical systems and realized that if the technology used was changed, so too would the social systems of those who were using the technology. The result of this could be that the benefits of introducing technology may not be maximized. This should make managers think about how they introduce technology and the impact on people affected by its introduction.

4.1.7   Contingency approach

Contingency approaches to organizations draw on the work of Burns and Stalker (1966), Perrow (1967), Lawrence and Lorsch (1968) and Woodward (1980). Different organizations have different ways in which their technology, their methods, their environments and structures are interrelated. This can mean one organization will vary the way it converts its inputs to outputs compared to another. The contingency approach accepts this idea of no single best organization form, concentrating management response instead on the basis that if certain factors exist then certain managerial approaches should be used.

4.1.8   Work activity approach

This is based on the work of Stewart,[12] and Carlson (1951). Rosemary Stewart examined how managers spend their time and what kind of managers there are. She found that, on average, the proportion of a manager's time spent on various activities was as follows:

Discussion	43%
Paperwork	36%
Travelling (not working)	8%
Committees	7%
Inspection	6%

Managers spent their working time in a variety of ways:

Alone	34%
With two or more people	34%
With one or more people	32%

Stewart[12] was able to identify five different types of management jobs which she called **emissaries**, **writers**, **discussers**, **troubleshooters** and **committee men**.

Emissaries

The emissary spent a lot of time away from the company, worked long hours mainly due to the amount of time spent travelling, thus their work was less fragmented.

Writers

The writers spent more time by themselves reading, writing and dictating. They worked the fewest hours but appeared to have more control of their working day due to the smaller number of personal contacts they had and being less involved in day-to-day problems. They included head office specialists.

Discussers

These managers spent most of their time with other people and their colleagues. They were closest to the average for the whole group studied.

Troubleshooters

These managers had the most fragmented work patterns due mainly to their numerous diary commitments and the large number of passing contacts they had. Their work was the most fragmented because they had to deal with day-to-day crises.

Committee men

These had the widest range of internal contacts and spent more time in group discussions, which invariably meant committee work. They concentrated on personnel work and tended to work for larger companies. Many were also production or works managers in process industries.

It was suggested that there are three possible explanations as to what determined how these managers spent their time: the job, the organization and the individual. Groups were distinguishable by the type of job and function.

Stewart[12] went on to pose the question, What do managers do? The main characteristics of their work that she identified were:

- **Fragmentation**
- **Talk**
- **Establish cooperative relationship**
- **Use informal information**
- **Manage on the run.**

Stewart went on to discuss temptations to inefficiency such as not being in control, superficiality and mistaken belief.

4.1.9   The manager's job

Mintzberg[13] assessed the folklore surrounding managerial work and the facts about it. The four myths he identified and the facts (in inverted commas) that are associated with them are as follows:

- **The manager is a reflective systematic planner.** 'Study after study has shown that managers work at an unrelenting pace, that their activities are characterized by brevity, variety and discontinuity and they are strongly oriented to action and dislike reflective activities.'
- **The effective manager has no regular duties to perform.** 'Managerial work involves performing a number of regular duties, including ritual and ceremonial, negotiations and processing of soft information that links the organization with its environment.'
- **The senior manager needs aggregated information, which a formal management system best provides.** 'Managers strongly favour verbal media, telephone calls and meetings, over documents.'
- **Management is, or at least is quickly becoming, a science and a profession.** 'The managers' programs – to schedule time process information, make decisions and so on – remain locked deep inside their brains.'

Mintzberg goes on to describe the manager's job in terms of 'roles or organized sets of behaviours identified with a position'. The roles that Mintzberg identified were **interpersonal**, **informational**, and **decisional**. These three roles were further subdivided into other roles and the following are based on Mintzberg's work:

- **Interpersonal roles** came about because of a manager's formal authority. These involved basic interpersonal relationships:
  - (i)   **Figurehead.** This is largely a ceremonial role such as when the manager represents the organization at official functions.
  - (ii) **The leader role.** Because of their formal authority leaders have a great deal of power and control of the working lives of individuals. They can motivate individuals and have to balance what the individual wants with what the organization requires.
  - (iii) **Liaison role.** This is the role adopted when managers are contacting people outside the vertical chain of command. They may well spend more time with their peers and others than with their own staff.
- **Informational roles** come about because a manager has a range of contacts with and outside their immediate group. The manager will not know everything but will know more than their staff:
  - (i)   **Monitor.** The manager monitors the environment and takes informal information from peers, subordinates and superiors in other departments. This includes gossip and rumour that at times may be useful.

(ii)   **Disseminator.** In this role the manager passes information to staff who would not normally be able to obtain it.

(iii) **Spokesperson.** In this role the manager passes on information to people inside or outside the organization.

- **Decisional roles:** These are so called because of the manager's access to information that is used in decision making. A manager with information is therefore well placed to take decisions concerning their entire department.

    (i)   **Entrepreneur.** Here the manager acts like an entrepreneur working to improve the department and make it more responsive to changing circumstances from the environment.

    (ii) **Disturbance handler.** In this role the manager is more reactive and responding to pressures outside their control.

    (iii) **Resource allocater.** This is the role where the manager decides who gets the resources.

    (iv) **Negotiator.** This role can involve managers in areas as diverse as negotiating the settlement of an industrial relations dispute to a minor grievance with an employee.

We have already mentioned how Mintzberg has dealt with the four myths about management. The ten roles, it would appear, are not easy to separate and general management is really a matter of judgement and intuition, although learned from doing the job. How effective managers are is based on their own insight of the problems, situations and solutions facing them. Managers are often forced to take on a lot more work, handle interruptions, respond rapidly at every chance, make decisions of an incremental nature, do everything at the 'drop of a hat' simply because of the pressures of the job.

4.1.10   The manager as a coach

We have discussed teams and team work in their respective sections but it is worth mentioning here the role of the manager as a coach. The parallels with sport teams should be obvious.

The coach of any sports team can do as much as possible prior to a competition to prepare the team or individual, but once that event begins, the players have to convert all they have been trained to do into action on the sports field. So what is it that a coach does that might be useful for a manager?

Observation

The coach has to be able to see in others skills and knowledge that can be improved and refined to benefit both the individual and the team they represent. Coaching is a time-intensive method, which depends on the attitudes and aspirations of those who are being coached. It has to have a structure, with a clear objective of what the coach is trying to achieve.

Knowledge of people

This will involve knowing something about human nature and how different people have a different approach to life and work. Some make things look easy, others have to work harder at them. Some people read a report and understand its themes the first time, others have to read it several times. Part of the competency of a coach is to recognize this diversity of ability. Coaching is about guiding experience, it is about the more experienced manager or mentor showing the individual what to do and then letting them do it under guidance. The individual may not do it the same way, but then this is not such a bad thing, as it encourages initiative and discovery. Coaching can take many forms, amongst them on-the-job training, where one manager helps a more junior manager develop their talents and avoid the mistakes they made.

If we look at the football coach as an example, we can identify some of the other roles the coach has to play. The coach has to be a **planner**, a **motivator**, a **communicator** and a **visionary**. The football coach sends the team onto the field of play to carry out a plan, that has been developed and rehearsed in training. This plan is the result of often long and painstaking analysis of the opponents' strengths and weakness by other support staff. Once on the field of play, the footballers have to put it into action. This they do well on some occasions and on others they may do it poorly.

This shows the coach as a **forward planner**, who bases the team's actions on all the analysis that has been carried out prior to the game.

That analysis is then developed into an **action plan** to be used during the game, when the coach has to observe and quickly decide what is going right and what is going wrong and then adapt the plan accordingly. These changes have to be clearly **communicated** to the players at half-time, when the coach also spends time **encouraging**, **motivating** or **reassuring** players that they are doing the right things.

Once the game is over, the coach and the team have to reflect on their performance, its strengths and its weaknesses.

The contribution of the coach has to be incorporated into what others think and do, because they have a **vision** of what they want the team to achieve. This vision is much wider than that of the individual player, who is more likely to be involved in the day-to-day work of playing football.

An example, of the successful football coach can be illustrated from an article by Paul Simpson.[14] In the article he states of Arsene Wenger the Arsenal Football club manager, 'Yet he has motivated and inspired a squad to play so far beyond their capabilities, that they romped home to the title, even beating their old rivals away at Old Trafford to clinch the trophy. And he did all this, apparently, without raising his voice – a rarity in a game where coaches habitually confuse volume with eloquence.'

The article goes on to highlight the importance of communication both with players and between players to be more than superficial. Players it is argued want to learn, be understood and develop. He goes on to quote Arsene Wenger as saying 'If they feel deep down that you are only interested in them as a number in the team, or to fit into a tactical system, they won't be as happy and may not play so well. I always tell my players to go out and express themselves.'

This coaching approach can lead to improved motivation. The need to develop a coaching approach in all managers can be illustrated by the fact that companies like Safeway supermarkets who reported[15] that it was 'rolling out a coaching scheme for 900 middle managers after a development programme for top management led to reduced staff turnover and increased profits. The executive coaching programme that was run in 2000 for its 100 most senior managers has helped the company reduce turnover among the firm's 92 000 staff – it has dropped by 15 per cent to 30 per cent a year.'

Exercise

Reflect on your career development so far and identify those managers who have most or least influenced you. Can you explain why they were able to influence you either positively or negatively?

Do you think now with hindsight you would be as easily influenced or would you resist some things you once accepted readily and accept some things you once resisted?

Feedback

The people who influence you may well fall into one of three categories, friends, parents and teachers. Managers in many respects should be like teachers – they need to be able to recognize those who have talent and then encourage that talent through delegation. They also need to know who has less talent and needs more guidance perhaps through a more structured type of work. Managers may well have delegated to you or organized you and structured your work in a way that F. W. Taylor would recognize.

Either way the manager must know how to manage people in different situations. This should be advantageous for the individual, the manager and the organization.

Summary

In this section we have looked at the history and development of management and organizational theory. We have also described the nature of managerial work, its fragmentation, its brevity and its diversity and how in a more democratic age some managers are turning increasingly towards coaching their staff rather than directing them. This has important implications for employees working in teams, and for the ways in which managers actually organize work.

4.2 Prioritization, allocation and organization of work

Time is a scarce resource. It is irreplaceable and irreversible. Few things are more important to us than learning how to save time and how to spend it wisely.

John Adair[16]

Section objectives

In this section you will consider the:

- Prioritization of work
- Delegation and allocation of work
- Organization of work and planning
- Coordination of work
- Implementation of work and the
- Control of work which will include
- How managers set targets and objectives
- What is meant by management by objectives and
- How management of time can be improved.

4.2.1 Introduction

We saw in the previous section that the manager's work is varied, fragmented and limited in timescale. It would seem that managers are forever lurching from one crisis to another as they try to balance the demands of the tasks, the people and the organization. In this section we will see how managers try to put some order into working life by making better use of their staff and planning the use of their time more efficiently.

Exercise

You arrive at work on Monday morning to find the following information at your workstation:

- Your boss wants you to spend two days, Wednesday and Thursday, in Paris with a customer because the boss has a more pressing engagement.
- You have a disciplinary hearing with a member of staff and their union representative arranged for Wednesday afternoon.

- The print shop supervisor wants to talk to you about the excessive amounts of paper usage by two of your members of staff.
- A customer has written a letter of complaint to you personally about some alleged poor-quality goods they have received.
- Your personal assistant has phoned in sick and will be off work for two weeks.
- Your personal computer crashed as soon as you switched it on.
- The garage where you left your company car this morning has phoned to say it needs repairing and the parts will not be available until Thursday morning. In addition, your daughter will be graduating from university on Wednesday afternoon and you had planned to book a day's leave in order to be able to attend.

How will you deal with these conflicting tasks? You should do this giving full details about why you chose your order of priority and what action you will be taking to deal with each situation.

Feedback

Here you are faced with a situation not untypical in many a manager's life. What do I do first? The sort of factors that will influence your decisions are the **importance** of each task, the amount of **control** you have over the situation, whether or not they can be **delegated** and the potential outcomes of **delaying** any single task.

For instance, the disciplinary hearing and the meeting with the print shop supervisor can be rearranged more easily than the meeting with the customer in Paris because you have more control over them. The disciplinary interview might be delegated to a deputy. The meeting with the customer should take highest priority. However, you have the personal pressure of attending your daughter's graduation and so only you can decide between the two. The car is possibly the lowest priority because you may be out of the country anyway and also it is easy to hire a temporary replacement.

4.2.2   Prioritization

Setting priorities is a 'must' for any manager who wants to use his or her time effectively. First, managers must look at the activities involved in their work and list them in terms of where they think they are, between the most important and the least important. The next thing to do is to decide the relative urgency of the activities, again in a range from very urgent to non-urgent. Urgency will include time as a limiting factor both in terms of when it must be done by and also how much time is available. Because managers are often very busy people, priority setting can take a low priority itself but if it can be done in a clear and concise way it is well worth the investment.

Once the priorities have been set then the manager must decide their order. Critical path analysis, as discussed in the section on time management, can be used to plan the sequence in which activities will get done.

The building-site manager who spends time having roads laid while the manager of the site next door gets on with building houses might at first appear to have his or her priorities wrong. However, when the weather worsens and the second site cannot get its supplies delivered easily, the first manager can afford the luxury of a knowing smile.

This shows that in retrospect the first manager is able to see that the timing of activities was correct. Managers need to do this to see if their estimates of what was important are still valid and whether sufficient time was allocated to it. They need to be aware that priorities do change and that communicating them to staff and customers can require tact and diplomacy. It is not easy to explain to someone who has been working on a task for some time that the priorities have changed and it is no longer needed or to a customer that their order is not a priority.

4.2.3   Allocation of tasks

As we have seen from Section 4.1.2, people like Taylor[4] had definite ideas about what work an individual should be allowed to do. Taylor, it will be remembered, thought that individuals should have clear descriptions of what they were and were not allowed to do. His ideas about breaking down work into its component parts and then standardizing the way they were performed heralded the advent of the 'specialist', which still exists to a great extent today although multi-skilling is begining to break down some of these barriers between specialisms.

One approach we can take when allocating tasks is to ask ourselves the following questions, what, why, when, where, how and who; the answers to them will help us to decide how the task is allocated.

- What is the task?
- Why are we doing it?
- When does it have to be done by?
- Where will it be done?
- How will it be done?
- Who will do it?

These six questions can provide a framework for a manager to decide how to allocate work.

We should keep in mind the fact that labour comprising a workforce may still be divided according to a specialist skill. However, as employees become more multi-skilled we should find that we have greater choice of who we allocate work to. We need to clearly define the work that is to be done and look at what skills are required to successfully complete it. Account has to be taken of the legal requirements of the work. We would not expect a junior clerk to authorize the company accounts or a carpenter to service a gas boiler.

This raises issues about the individual's competence to do the job, which in turn will influence its allocation. Not only technical expertise needs to be taken into consideration, the manager must also have to take due regard of the 'politics' of organizations. It is sometimes necessary to allocate on the basis of an individual's position in the hierarchy. Certain tasks may be the exclusive duty of certain grades and to allocate them to a more junior manager would not be acceptable.

If work is important we may well allocate it to our best staff. However, if it is routine we can give it to the less able. If managers have confidence in them and staff have a positive attitude, the allocation of work may be possible. However, if this is not true then they have to think of other ways of allocating the work.

The urgency or lack of urgency will also affect delegation, for much the same reasons as mentioned in the preceding paragraph. However, there is an additional factor the manager can take into consideration here, that of quality. Work can be allocated to a less able person, but it must be pointed out to the customer that, because of the time constraints they have put on it, the task may have to be performed to a lower standard of quality than would otherwise be achieved.

The location where the task is to be carried out will also have a bearing on its allocation. If work is to be undertaken off-site, there will be more difficulty in controlling the staff who do it. For this reason the manager needs to be sure the staff allocated to it can be trusted to do the task as efficiently and effectively as possible without supervision.

The method of doing work will influence how the task is allocated. The manager needs to be able to coordinate and sequence tasks and staff. If work has to be done in a particular way then it may mean that one group of staff or even other resources such as plant or machinery are not available and part of the work then has to be allocated elsewhere. The manager will have to give instructions about how the work is to be done in some cases.

This does not mean the overriding of an individual's technical competence, but merely ensuring that tasks are completed in a satisfactory manner and to an acceptable standard. The manager can take the opportunity here to explain to the individual how work will be monitored and how he or she will decide whether the task has been completed satisfactorily.

The question 'who does the work' is vital and some issues surrounding the individual member of staff have been mentioned earlier, such as their technical expertise. There are other issues to consider and these include an individual's attitude to work itself. Sometimes staff think that a particular type of work is too routine for them or it is of too low a status.

Team work together with approaches such as 'empowerment' can be used as a basis for work allocation. It should also be remembered that the allocation of work can be used as a motivator by making it a reward for good work already accomplished.

4.2.4   Delegation

Delegation is no simple task. In order for managers to be able to delegate they must realize that they have to let go of some of their work. Some managers also do not like the risk it involves making excuses such as, 'I know I get a proper job done if I do it myself'. Managers also need to believe in the abilities and talents of their subordinate staff.

What does to delegate mean? John Adair,[16] suggests that delegation is about 'transferring initiative and authority'. Another way might be to describe it as asking someone to do something on your behalf and in order for them to be able to do so you must give them the power to act. Delegation of duties does not mean that the manager is no longer accountable. All it means is that the subordinate has the authority to act. We have seen in Section 4.2, that managers have precious little time to spare and this is one of the reasons that a manager may use when deciding to delegate. Other reasons might be the level of importance of the work and the ability of subordinates.

Managers must also accept that subordinates are sometimes better technical experts in certain fields than they are. It makes more sense to give work to someone who is professionally more competent. This allows the subordinate's work to fit in with what the manager is doing. Neither should the motivational aspects of delegation be overlooked. The work of managers sometimes becomes routine to the individual manager but it may offer a chance for a subordinate to stretch their abilities and, at the same time, impress the manager. This can give them a great deal of personal satisfaction, as well as make better use of their time and form a foundation for their individual development.

4.2.5   What can be delegated?

What can be delegated will depend on a number of factors such as the importance of the work, the skills required to do it and the time limits set for its completion. Managers need to know what skills and experience their subordinates possess. Careful thought has to be given to the allocation of work. If time is available, then less experienced staff can be coached to the required standard and the delegated work can be used as part of a training plan. Delegation must not be carried out in a cavalier manner. It needs to be thought through and carefully planned.

There are difficulties in delegating and these can be described under the following headings:

- **Who to choose?** The manager has to choose the right person for the type of work they wish to delegate. Similarly, as with an employee seeking promotion, they need to show enthusiasm for the opportunity that is being offered.

- **Individual development.** Throwing individuals in at the deep end is far too risky a strategy. If a manager is going to delegate effectively they need to involve their subordinates and get their views on the delegated task, try them out, find out their strengths and weaknesses. Then they must encourage on-the-job training with routine delegation, increasing to more complex work as their experience grows.
- **Explanation and confirmation.** Communication skills need to be at a peak. The subordinate needs to have a clear understanding of what is expected of them and the implications of their success or failure. They need to know the limits of their task remit and how it fits into the overall departmental or organizational scheme.
- **Letting go.** Despite the parameters laid down by the manager, staff need to have the freedom to operate in their own way. They must be supported, but they need to learn by their mistakes and use their own talents to overcome obstacles.
- **Monitoring and control.** Staff need to know that they have not been left out on a limb with no-one to oversee or support them. They must know that their work will be monitored at regular intervals by their boss to see how they are doing. Delegation is not abdication because they are ultimately accountable for their subordinates' actions.

4.2.6   Time and delegation

Time is always a limiting factor and is not always at a premium. Many managers are reluctant to spend time explaining to a subordinate and checking their understanding. They may consider this to be wasted time and time they could have spent doing the work themselves. This is one of the most common faults of managers.

However, once work has been delegated the subordinate should be allowed to get on with the job. The manager has to accept that the subordinate may do the job differently. As long as it is done to a satisfactory level set by the manager this should be good enough. To ensure this, managers need to have in place a feedback mechanism through which the work can be monitored. Given too much power some individuals can become difficult to control. Once they have delegated work, it is necessary for a manager to ensure that the individual builds the confidence to deal with that work and everyone else knows they have to deal with them and not the manager.

4.2.7   Delegation and its link to management succession

Through the use of delegation internal candidates can be prepared and move smoothly into a vacant position. It is worth mentioning that one of the reasons why some managers do not delegate is because they are trying to make sure they cannot be easily replaced. For a more detailed description of succession see Armstrong.[17]

4.2.8   What are the potential consequences if we do not delegate?

If managers choose not to delegate then staff can become demotivated and leave the organization. If staff do not leave they may lose interest in what they are doing or in the organization as a whole, resulting in poor performance.

4.2.9   What are the potential consequences if we delegate too much?

If managers delegate too much, staff can become resentful because they think that the manager is having an easy time at their expense. Staff can suffer stress due to excessive workload and potential role ambiguity. Am I a manager or a subordinate? is a question often asked. Stress is covered in more detail in Section 2.4. Delegation is a calculated risk that managers take in the belief that their staff have the potential to do some work as effectively and efficiently as they can, albeit after some training. The manager expert in delegation recognizes that time is a limited commodity that has to be used sensibly and in a well-planned manner. From this discussion of delegation you will note that it is different from plain 'dumping' of work; in other words, giving work to a subordinate which the manager does not wish to do him or herself, and without explanation, discussion or any training.

4.2.10   Planning and organizing

Organizing as a management function means taking the work that the manager wants done and subdividing it into various tasks. The manager must make someone responsible for its completion and decide exactly what is to be done and by whom. This will need to be communicated clearly. Good organizing makes work flow freely and smoothly and avoids bottlenecks and other causes of delay. It contributes to the provision of a quality service to the customer, at the right price and when the customer wants it.

4.2.11   Planning

One of the most important activities for a manager is that of planning. Good planning is an essential part of the success of any business. It is often said that proper planning prevents poor performance.

4.2.12   What is planning?

Cole[18] describes planning as 'a major component of management'. Planning is the methodology by which an organization tries to link its objectives, its policies and its results. What it is trying to do is to convert ideas somewhere in the future (objectives) into reality.

4.2.13   Why do people offer resistance to planning?

Managers often resist planning for a variety of reasons, among these are the fact that planning can be very demanding. It is not easy to think ahead and try to predict possible events and outcomes. Planning can also seem to be very vague, with nothing really to show for all the effort that has been made. Plans give managers a certain amount of control, which can be a problem for some because once they have committed themselves to the plan they have to achieve the results they have promised.

4.2.14   The tools used by planners

(1) Forecasting

Forecasting is an attempt by the manager to estimate what will happen in the future. It is a systematic analysis of the available information in order to try to anticipate future opportunities and problems. Forecasting makes managers look beyond the immediate day-to-day operational issues. The criteria that managers often have to forecast against are time (short or long term), direction (what are the trends?) and magnitude (how much of a change is likely to take place?). There are a number of forecasting techniques available where managers can look at historical data and they include time series and regression analysis.

(2) Panels of experts

Some organizations use panels of senior managers who are asked to use their experience and expertise to try to predict the future of the business. Their ideas are then weighted, depending on the probability of them happening. This is not a very accurate approach to forecasting but it can be helpful.

4.2.15   Short-term planning

Brech *et al.*[19] describe short-term plans as covering anything from one day to a year. In these cases the plans can be almost certain to happen with few opportunities for things to go wrong or contingencies that would force a deviation from the plan. This should not lead us to believe that things do not go wrong in short-term planning, because they do. For this reason, even short-term plans need to be flexible.

4.2.16   Long-term planning

Long-term planning can cover anything over one year and, depending on the industry or the government department, planning can be done over decades. The government, for example, might try to plan for 20 or 30 years in advance.

4.2.17   Linking forecasting and planning

Forecasting, as we have identified, is a systematic analysis of available information to help managers estimate what will happen in the future. To this end it is only useful if it is incorporated into plans. The better the forecast, the better the chance that the plans will be realistic and so the greater the probability of achieving our goals. It should be the responsibility of the managers who do the planning to ensure that the goals are achieved. Forecasts can be used in conjunction with a manager's own knowledge of their particular organization and the sector in which it operates.

One area of forecasting that managers do need to address is the 'what if?' scenario. These are situations where things change unexpectedly. For example, what if that old machine breaks down? By anticipating these scenarios, managers can try to ensure that the plans run as smoothly as possible. This is also known as 'contingency planning'.

Forecasting can be used to set benchmarks of performance against which managers can judge the progress of plans.

When using forecasting managers must ensure that they do not let themselves become hostages to circumstances. For instance, when managers begin to look at information they can soon discover that it exists in vast amounts. If managers are not careful this mass of information and data can give them conflicting views, which make plans seem ambiguous. The availability of a large amount of information and data can also encourage planners to be too prescriptive and may restrict the ability of managers to act flexibly as circumstances dictate. This is like the bureaucratic approach, where there are rules for everything and these must be followed even though it may be easier for a manager to decide on another course of action. Part of the art of using forecasts is the ability to determine which information is relevant and has a direct bearing on the planning and which creates confusion and is misleading. By using a combination of experience and objectivity it is possible to use information available and prepare plans that are well written and easily comprehended.

4.2.18   Planning at different levels of the organization

Planning is often described as happening at three different levels: strategic, tactical and operational. However, like most things in organizations, there are overlaps of these three levels of planning.

Strategic planning is covered in Part Three, but it is worth briefly saying something about it. Strategic planning is invariably carried out by the most senior managers, namely the directors. It usually involves the long-term objectives and policies of the organization and is concerned more with what the organization is achieving as a whole rather than how well particular parts of the organization are faring.

Tactical planning is more concerned with answering the question 'How are we going to achieve results with the resources we have available?' For this reason tactical planning appears to take a long-term view, but not over such a long term as that of strategic planning. Tactical planning is often carried out by senior managers.

Operational-level planning is based more around the activities of a department on a day-to-day basis. This is the responsibility of the departmental managers and supervisors who oversee the daily running of the department in the short term, for example based around individual customer orders with clearly defined performance criteria and controls.

4.2.19 General approach to planning

(1) Purpose of the plan

Before we can go very far we need to know what is expected of the plan. In other words, 'what are its objectives?' Objective setting is achieved by using an approach for a manager's operational problems that would be the same, for example, if we were setting the company's objectives. It needs to be approached in a systematic way and if we can, at the outset, involve as many staff from the area concerned, it will be easier to gain their acceptance later. We need to ask:

First	What are our objectives?
Second	What is most important?
Third	What tasks need doing to achieve the objective?
Fourth	How will we know if we have done it properly?
Fifth	Who is confident enough to do the job?
Sixth	How will we know if we are effective and efficient?

These objectives must be easily identifiable, understood, and quantifiable and achievable. It should be noted that there are often a variety of approaches for dealing with a situation and it is important that the alternatives are investigated and assessed and the most appropriate one selected.

(2) Basis of plans

Managerial expertise and experience, as well as good-quality forecasting using clearly defined information, can provide the basis of a plan.

(3) Coordination of plans

It is essential to make sure that plans at different levels of the organization or from different departments do, in fact, contribute to the overall success of the organization. With short-term plans this is much easier. For example, a sales plan can be easily coordinated with a production plan and a human resources plan. As the planning moves from the short term to the long term coordination is hampered by the fact that the decision makers at the strategic level are remote from those at the operational level.

(4) Monitoring for deviation

When plans are set they must be accompanied by a set of objective criteria by which they are to be judged. The progress towards those criteria must be monitored and deviation from them determined for whatever reason.

(5) Flexibility

When deviation from the norm is detected in the monitoring stage, some form of remedial action will need to be taken. This means that the plans need to be flexible enough to cope with those changes.

(6) Communication

When planning is being carried out it is essential that effective communication takes place at all times. For example, during the preparation of plans clear policy guidelines need to be given and the potential impact of plans on all concerned needs to be made clear. There should also be free and open exchange of information about the feasibility of plans and the underlying assumptions about them.

(7) Motivation

Plans must act as motivators for the staff concerned and should not be set too ambitiously so that they cannot be achieved nor be too easily achievable so that staff do not need to try. Perhaps the best way to think about setting them is to make them specific, measurable, achievable, realistic and time constrained, or SMART for short.

4.2.20   Action planning

Action planning is simply the setting of a target or goal for a number of staff to achieve. The staff may vary from the individual to a number working together with their manager. Action planning helps to focus staff on a particular course of action that requires them to be well motivated and committed to its successful completion. From the organization's point of view it helps to control and direct the individuals to achieve their objectives. In this way time is used more effectively and is not wasted through lack of direction. People can be shown clearly, through the plan, what is expected of them.

An action plan should be described fairly simply and made easy to use.

4.2.21   Other methods used to assist time management and planning

(1) Timetables

These are simple to use and easy to keep. Most business people will have a diary to keep track of their appointments and highlight important dates.

(2) Bar charts

Longer-term planning can be illustrated using a bar chart. Figure 4.2 allows the building site engineer to see at a glance what should be happening on-site at any given time of the year.

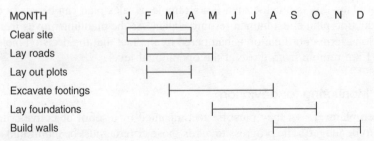

Figure 4.2. Bar chart showing work plan for one year.

It also indicates the relationship between the various tasks and gives an idea of when each begins and should end. It shows how some tasks are dependent on other tasks starting first. For example, the foundations cannot be excavated until the surveyors have laid out the plots.

The simple bar chart can be extended in its usefulness by adding in a measure of time and the amount of work to be done. These are usually described as Gantt charts after their developer (Figure 4.3).

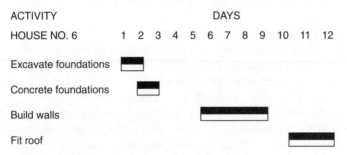

Figure 4.3. Gantt chart showing planned work.

An example of house building can be used from the construction industry to illustrate this type of chart. However, here the times are more specific and there is room below each predicted period for the manager to write the actual period of time the job has taken.

(3) Network analysis

Bar charts are intended to be fairly straightforward ways of scheduling work. There are others that are more complex, such as network analysis, which aims to determine the relationship between the activities in a particular project. To use the example of house building, the activities that we have already identified include excavating the foundations, building the walls, fitting the roof and all the internal work.

Network analysis attempts to determine the sequence of these activities. For example, before we build the walls we have to excavate the foundations. However, we know that life is not as easy as one job following on neatly after the other. We know that jobs can be in progress at the same time and even the seemingly simplest of jobs need to be carefully organized. Network analysis tries to take this into account by asking questions in addition to the one concerning the order of events such questions can be what other tasks can be done at the same time, what needs to be done before a task can begin, and what are the most important tasks that have no margin for error?

4.2.22   Coordination for managers

From Fayol's[3] analysis of management we know that coordinating is the task of harmonizing what individuals and groups do. Managers must then ensure that they get the resources they require at the correct time and that they have an approach that helps to achieve the overall organizational objectives.

Why do managers bother with coordinating? The answer can be found if we remind ourselves that organizations are made up of people, work, resources, etc. As we are aware, people in organizations have their own views about their department, how they fit in and how they contribute towards the overall objectives of the organization. These views must all be harnessed and focused towards the overall objectives. Coordination of the different parts of the organization is essential if the organization is going to meet its objectives. There is a temptation for departments or individuals to take a very insular view and to think only of themselves, not realizing that their actions may well be affecting the actions of others.

The manager's job is to make sure that all the efforts, individual and collective, are timed so that they do not cause delays in another department's work. When priorities are set, they too have to be coordinated because, despite some jobs/tasks having high priority, day-to-day life still goes on. These activities may be the very tasks the organization relies upon. The priority may be to launch a new product but meanwhile someone still has to carry out the routine work.

The resources available to the manager are finite and he or she has to decide who gets them. Everyone may want those resources but the manager's job is to decide where they will best serve the organization's objectives. This serves to achieve the goal of making the organization more effective because the resources are directed to where they are required, and more efficient because the work gets done on time.

Poor coordination can happen because of poor communication. It is not unusual for one department to be duplicating the work of another simply because the communication between them is poor. These misunderstandings can come about because of poor organization structure.

4.2.23   What can managers do about poor coordination?

Managers have to improve communication so that everyone in the organization knows what is expected of them and why interdepartmental rivalries are detrimental to all in the long run. Good planning will aid coordination of work through the use of techniques such as network analysis.

Attention can be given to the organization structure itself in order to ensure that there are clear lines of communication and reporting not only within units but also between them. It may be appropriate to use matrix structures to bring together people from different departments to get them to work together and cooperate more.

Exercise

Think of a group of people you know – they may be friends from outside work, colleagues or a combination of both. Now think of how you would arrange a night out with a group of, say, ten of them.

● What problems might you face in arranging the night out?
● How would you overcome them?
● Do you think your choice of night out affected how difficult or easy it was to arrange?
● What lessons have you learned about organizing and coordination from this exercise?

Feedback

The problems you may encounter trying to arrange a night out will include trying first of all to decide what type of night out people want, when it is to take place and how much people are prepared to pay. Some will want to go to the pub, others the theatre and so on. One way you might overcome the problem is to limit the choice people have or even present them with only one venue. If you choose an unusual venue, for example a Mongolian restaurant but everyone wearing fancy dress, you may find that this is not popular, so you have to take into consideration the range of opinions your guests have. Hopefully, you now realize some of the problems of organizing and coordinating a group, getting people to agree to a venue, determining people's availability and realizing that some people cannot be forced to attend. These are all issues you may face during times when you are trying to organize and coordinate people or events.

4.2.24   Management control

Managers have a duty to the organization of regularly checking the activities they are carrying out. This process has two elements. We need to find out whether the objectives and target have been achieved. Then we need to ask were the objectives and targets we set the right ones in the first place. Managers can do this in a variety of ways.

(1) Direct observation

Walking about on the 'shop-floor' or through an office and talking to staff lets staff know who you are and the fact that you are around, taking an interest in what they are doing. It also gives you an opportunity to see things that are not right. If everyone is standing around chatting, that needs investigating. In some American organizations MBWA or management by walking around is widely practised.

(2) Customer feedback

The term 'customer' now encompasses both internal and external customers. When customers feed back their complaints it says something about your performance. If your customers are not complaining then you could be doing a wonderful job. However, it could be that they cannot be bothered to complain any more because it has not helped in the past.

(3) Financial controls

These consist of internal and external audits of the financial processes used to check whether what you say is happening to your financial resources is the truth. Another financial control is exerted through budgets whereby each part of the work is assessed financially and a limit on spending is set. The exceeding of these limits is not recommended and so it is a method of controlling a manager's financial spending.

(4) The structure of the organization

The structure of the organization affords managers a method of control through the rules, policies and procedures as well as any legitimate position power it bestows on the manager.

(5) Choice of staff

By choosing staff who will fit into the culture of an organization it is possible to introduce an element of control into the management of human resources. It is important to avoid incorrectly allocating people to jobs or methods of working that do not suit their personality, attitudes or competency profile.

(6) Technological control

The use of security swipecards to gain access to buildings is one simple example of how to control the arrival and departure of people. Hours of attendance at work and time spent logged on/off computers are both examples of how technology can be used to control.

(7) People power

Staff themselves can be a form of control. Peer group pressure, as shown by the Hawthorne studies, illustrates how the setting of group norms served to control the group's behaviour.

(8) Feedback

Any information that is gathered must be allowed to feed back into the system to allow improvements to be made or problems to be rectified.

(9) Working from home

Working from home creates a dilemma for managers many of whom like to be able to see their staff and communicate with them face to face. However, there appear to be some advantages to working from home and control is apparently not an issue for some organizations. The article[20] opposite speaks positively of home working.

(10) Corporate governance

Corporate governance, refers to the manner in which a company is directed and controlled by its most senior managers. This form of control is further referred to in Chapter 14, 'Social responsibility and business ethics'.

4.2.25   Targets and objective setting

Managers, as part of their duties, have to give clear guidance to their staff. This is helped by the setting and communicating of clear targets and objectives. It is very difficult for staff to focus their efforts and motivate themselves if they do not know what they are supposed to be doing or how well they are doing it. Consequently the individual benefits through being able to focus and prioritize their efforts, as well as developing on a personal basis. The organization benefits because all staff are working towards one organizational objective.

4.2.26   Practical points

Individuals need to know in detail what their key activities are so that they can make a positive contribution. These key activities can vary from the teaching of pupils to the preparation of financial returns, depending on your occupation.

Individuals should not have too many targets or it becomes a problem about which one(s) to concentrate on, but where they do exist they should be jointly agreed with the manager and remain flexible enough to change with unforeseen circumstances.

Note should be taken of available resources, environmental factors and the ability of the individual. For example, we may be able to improve our sprinting over 100 metres but very few are going to become Olympic champions. In other words, even though resources may be available our own abilities can limit us.

4.2.27   Meeting together

It is important that both parties are clear about what they are supposed to be talking about in terms of the activities they wish to discuss. The individual will need to contribute to the discussions and agree what they both want in terms of objectives and targets. It is important that the individual knows how these targets will be achieved and the time scales involved.

4.2.28   Management by objectives

Management by objectives is a term attributed to Peter Drucker. He believed that by combining the goals of the individual manager with those of the organization both parties would benefit. The idea is that a common sense of purpose can be developed through all

WORK PRACTICES

BT says flexiwork is good for productivity and health

BY QUENTIN READE

Working from home is good for business as well as employees' health and quality of life, a staff survey by BT shows.

Caroline Waters, head of employment at BT, said more than 90 per cent of BT's flexiworkers who responded to the survey said that productivity increased, they had more leisure time and it was easier to help around the home.

The report, *Teleworking at BT – The environmental and social impacts of its workabout scheme*, by the University of Bradford and the UK Centre for Economic and Environmental Development, shows that teleworking also reduces absenteeism.

Seventy-eight per cent of teleworkers said they are now more productive and 22 per cent had worked from home during their last typical working month when they felt too ill to travel.

'BT has been offering flexiwork for years. The survey is a very good affirmation of what we knew,' Waters said. 'It gives people benefits, is good for business, good for society, and good for the local community.'

Reasons workers gave for greater productivity included reduced disruption, reduced commuting time and stress, and greater flexibility about when and where to work.

Ten per cent of those surveyed said they would not be able to undertake their current job unless able to telework, including people with children, carers for ill or disabled people or those with special needs.

The survey shows that teleworking also promotes a better work-life balance – 73 per cent of respondents felt their work-life balance was good or very good, and 85 per cent of teleworkers felt that their quality of life was good or very good.

However, Waters said there are things to watch out for when offering teleworking. Some teleworkers feel isolated, while others find it hard to switch off from work. She said BT hopes to open the scheme up to more people.

quentin.reade@rbi.co.uk

Key survey findings on teleworking

- 22 per cent of teleworkers said they had worked at home during their last working month when they felt too ill to travel to work.
- 73 per cent felt their work-life balance was good or very good
- 74 per cent of new registrants say travel reduction was an important factor in their decision to telework.
- 78 per cent of teleworkers considered themselves to be more productive.
- 82 per cent felt teleworking was important or very important to their quality of life.
- 85 per cent of staff felt their quality of life was good or very good
- 90 per cent were satisfied or very satisfied with teleworking

Source BT

WEBLINK www.btplc.com/betterworld

levels of management in an organization with everyone pulling in the same direction to achieve whatever results the business has set.

Management by objectives is guided by the necessity to achieve results. It is a result of the corporate planning process since corporate objectives and departmental objectives are converted into objectives for each manager. By giving managers a clear, well-defined objective it is hoped that this will act as an incentive to each and every manager and make them work harder.

4.2.29   Job-improvement plans

Once the job description has been agreed between the manager and superior a job-improvement plan needs to be agreed. This is like the action plan discussed earlier. It is a short-term view of the actions to be taken in order to complete key tasks to a satisfactory standard. The key tasks are detailed and any actions that are seen to be a priority are identified with it, with a time frame for completion. Time scales will vary depending on the priority and nature of the situation.

Management by objectives allows managers to compare just how well or poorly they are doing in their jobs against objective criteria. This also gives them the opportunity to raise issues of concern about their progress with their boss because their boss was involved in the setting of the targets. When it comes to appraisal the results should be jointly reviewed. Some managers will never be satisfied while others will be more supportive of their staff and their career ambitions.

Management by objectives can be used to identify other areas of weakness in the organization's approach to its management. If a manager is regularly underperforming in key areas of their job description then it may be necessary to offer them some form of training. Performance appraisal is discussed in Section 3.5.

4.2.30   Managing time

Time, we are told, is money and if you want to make some simple calculations linking time and money you can compare the basic costs incurred for people at a variety of salary levels by doing some calculations based in Table 4.1. If we assume only weekday working, eight bank holidays, a 40-hour week and if we ignore days taken off for annual leave, we arrive at 253 working days. It becomes apparent very quickly how much money an organization is spending when individuals are late for appointments and excuse themselves by saying 'I will be there in 5 minutes' or 'can you hang on for a minute?' If we take account of their cumulative effect during a working day the cost can be enormous. If a telephone call is being made and we are waiting for an answer that never seems to come it would be cheaper to hang up the telephone and redial.

Table 4.1 The cost of time

Salary	1 minute	5 minutes	15 minutes	30 minutes	1 hour	1 day
40 000					19.76	158.10
30 000					14.82	118.58
20 000					9.88	79.05
15 000					7.41	59.29
10 000					4.94	39.53

4.2.31   Time usage

Time usage depends on the individual – some people seem to use it well and others to use it poorly. In order to use time well we need to learn how to organize ourselves, how to be able to set priorities, how to balance a variety of demands on our time and finally, how to schedule our own personal time.

4.2.32   What causes us to waste time?

Exercise

There are many factors that cause people to use time inefficiently. List all the things that you feel cause you to waste time at work. Discuss your responses with someone else in your work or study group. What conclusions can you make about the factors that cause you problems?

Feedback

Your list might include telephone calls, meetings, social conversation. This list is not definitive but serves as an illustration to show how many potential causes there are. Some of the factors causing you problems may be out of your control. Others, though, with a little thought can be more easily dealt with.

Cole[18] identifies three issues affecting the use of time: the job holder, the job holder's role set and the job itself. If we look at Figure 4.4 we can see some of the pressures on a manager's time at work.

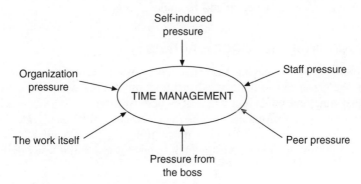

Figure 4.4. Pressures on managerial time.

(1) Organization pressures

Some organizations operate an open-door policy whereby anyone can walk in and talk to their boss. This is good in some circumstances, but it can mean an increase in the number of interruptions the manager has to face.

(2) Individual personality pressures

Some people have the type of personality that makes it difficult for them not to get involved. This can mean they have trouble saying no to requests for help, or to do work resulting in them being overworked. Individuals sometimes have greater aspirations than their talents and they find themselves ending up in jobs where they have difficulty in coping.

The fear of failure is too much for some people to admit and they will not ask for help when they cannot cope, but put themselves under enormous work pressure.

(3) Pressure from staff

A manager's own staff can put pressure on their bosses. This can happen if the manager wants to be psychologically close to their staff and they encourage too much familiarity, which results in staff taking advantage.

(4) Pressure from peers

By demanding priority treatment other managers can put pressure on time usage by trying to achieve their results or work completed first. Managers who cannot cope with a variety of demands from a number of peers may well find themselves overworked and under-performing. Other managers with more forceful personalities or greater talents may be seen as role models and in order to keep up with them, the less able manager puts pressure on their own time.

(5) Pressure from own manager

If a manager has difficulty in saying 'no' to their own manager or if their own manager is very demanding, the resulting pressure on time can be enormous.

(6) The work itself

If the job the manager does is not clearly defined, it is possible that they will be allocated duties that another manager should be undertaking.

4.2.33   How can time management help?

By thinking about managing time we can draw our attention to how time is used and wasted. We can begin to understand just how much time we really have available, who is using that time and when and where it is being wasted.

Some of the main problems of time management can be easily identified. For example, the inability to recognize just how much time we have available is easily dealt with. Figure 4.5 represents a personal timetable you can use while at work, to record what you

TIME	DUTIES	LOCATION	WHO WITH	WHY THAT WORK
8.00				
8.30				
9.00				
9.30				
10.00				
10.30				
11.00				
11.30				
12.00				
12.30				
13.00				
13.30				
14.00				
14.30				
15.00				
15.30				
16.00				
16.30				
17.00				

TIME WASTING

Figure 4.5. An example of how you might fill in the personal timetable.

are doing on a day-to-day basis. You can use this timetable to discover areas where you can improve on the way you spend your working day.

4.2.34   Time wasting

Time wasting is not necessarily a deliberate thing. Sometimes people do not realize they are doing it, in fact they may think what they are doing is being helpful. With this in mind it is important to get people to focus on what they should be doing.

Earlier in this chapter you were asked to keep a personal timetable of your time at work. Once you begin to analyse what you are doing at work you can go on to use that information and ask questions such as 'What am I doing?' 'Why am I doing it?' 'What am I achieving?' This should begin to help you develop an idea of focus.

4.2.35   Planning time

It is not unusual to see people arriving at work and making a list of the things they need to do during the day. This is a basic planning process they are carrying out and although it is simple it is a very powerful tool. It affords an element of control for the individual and gives them targets. Additionally, the list gives structure to the working day.

This can be a good motivator when people look at their list at the end of the day or week and realize that all is completed. If it is not then it can form part of the list for the following day.

All the daily tasks must be allocated a priority.

4.2.36   Failure to delegate

Failure to delegate means a manager is wasting time doing work a subordinate should be doing. Whatever the reason for non-delegation the manager should think very carefully about why they haven't delegated.

4.2.37   Communication failure causing lost time

Communication and communication breakdowns are almost guaranteed to cause time wastage. Even in relatively easy communication situations, for example face to face in a restaurant it is possible to observe incorrect orders being taken and time and effort being wasted in rectifying those orders. Whatever the reason, it is essential to communicate clearly in order to avoid wasting time.

4.2.38   Interruptions

Perhaps the most insidious form of time wasting comes through the inability to control interruptions. The interruptions come in a number of different guises from the telephone call to the little chat. It is surprising that most people think that by dealing with the interruptions they are being customer friendly. However, interruptions distract people from the real work they are supposed to be doing.

4.2.39   Meetings

Meetings of any kind can also be a prime source of time loss. They need to be tightly controlled or otherwise they grow in number and one meeting leads to another follow-up meeting, which may have to have its own pre-meeting. Perhaps the question that should be asked before holding a meeting is 'Is there any other way we can communicate this information?'

Summary

In this section we have examined how managers have to prioritize, delegate and allocate work. We have assessed how work must be organized, planned and coordinated for it to be executed successfully. We have seen how work is implemented and controlled through the setting and achieving of objectives. This has been examined with particular reference to managing by objectives. Finally, we have linked the use and managing of time to all the foregoing in order to emphasize how easy it is to use time inefficiently if we do not learn to plan, prioritize, delegate and coordinate our efforts.

4.3   Communications, written, oral and electronic: working for others

A small boy was asked by his mother to run to the shop and buy some chocolate biscuits. 'But mum' he asked 'What happens if they haven't got any chocolate biscuits?' She replied 'Well just bring anything'. Twenty minutes later the boy returned with an ice cream and a packet of jelly babies.

Anon

Section objectives

In this section you will:

● Examine the effects and symptoms of poor communication
● Consider the process of communication and communication skills and how to carry out report/memoranda writing
● Electronic communication
● Presentations using visual aids, using an overhead projector, and
● Managing your manager and influencing others.

4.3.1   Introduction

The quote at the beginning of this section serves to illustrate how easily communications can be misunderstood, sometimes in innocence, sometimes deliberately. It is with this in mind that we need to examine the importance of good communications in the work environment and examine the particular problems and constraints they can have in the day-to-day operation of organizations.

4.3.2   The effects of poor communication

In order to emphasize the importance of good communication it is worth mentioning at the outset some possible examples of the effects of poor communication. They can include:

● Having drastic effects on production and industrial employee relations
● Continued misunderstandings
● Confusion, mistakes, wastage and even accidents and
● High labour turnover.

4.3.3   Symptoms of poor communications

Poor communication can be evident through the general attitude of staff. If staff seem apathetic or there is a mass of rumours in circulation, you can be fairly sure that the official channels of communication are not working. This can result in staff aggression and their making an increasing number of demands on management for confirmation or denial of what they are hearing on the 'grapevine' (the informal communications network).

Communication can be described as 'an exchange of information, ideas or feelings'. This implies that communication can be a one way-process (imparting of information, ideas or feelings) or a two-way one (exchange of information, ideas or feelings). So why do we want to communicate? It would seem that we wish our communications to have some effect. We may want someone to respond to our communication, as in an exchange process (seeking views) or perhaps take some sort of action as in the one-way process (obeying orders). Of whichever example we think, the recipient has to take a decision and we can link the idea of communication to decision making.

4.3.4   The process of communication

Berlo,[21] suggests that communication is based on 'the transferring of meaning from one person to another'. The process of communication can best be described by reference to Figure 4.6. On one side we have a transmitter of information and on the other we have a receiver of that information. Surrounding the whole process is the environment with all its distractions. The transmitter has to decide what is to be sent. This immediately creates a problem because it means that the information will have to be put into a language that, hopefully, the receiver will easily understand. This language can be written, verbal or diagrammatic. In any format the message can be misrepresented.

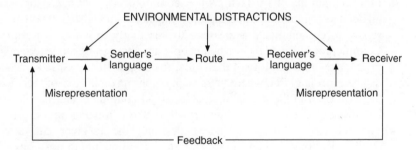

Figure 4.6. The communications model.

The message is now ready for transmission and the route used can be in the form of a conversation or other medium. The receiver now has to make sense of the message they are receiving and so they put it into a language they understand. Again the message can be misrepresented but this time by the receiver. Finally to try to establish that the receiver has got the message some form of check has to be put in place in the form of a feedback loop.

4.3.5   The process examined

In order to understand the process of communication better, we need to appreciate what we mean by the constituent parts of that process:

- We should appreciate the message we are trying to send and the language of that message can be spoken or written, in the form of graphs, tables, diagrams or even via gestures and postures we make. Consider the use of 'sign language' and codes.
- We can send the message by a number of routes. For instance, we can speak face to face, on the telephone, write, use a notice board or a computer. Whichever method we use is

going to be influenced by factors such as the importance of the message, the relationship between the parties and cost.

- Misrepresentation can occur when the meaning of the message is lost as we put it into or take it out of the language of transmission. For example, as transmitters we often find it more difficult to put our ideas in a written form than we do in a verbal form. Similarly, the receiver of a message will find it more difficult to extract our meaning from a written communication compared to a verbal one.
- For the reasons stated above, among others, it is therefore important that we have some form of feedback mechanism to check that the correct message is being received and understood.
- The wider environment has its influence on communication and this can cause problems. The idea of having a telephone conversation or reading a report in a noisy office is one example of this. Others include problems of human fatigue, state of mind and personality.

4.3.6   Barriers to communication

There are many obstacles to good communication – some related to perception, some to status and some to personality. Some of these obstacles are:

- Our own perceptual bias. As humans we can be very selective without realizing it and we only hear what we want to hear or see what we want to see. For example, parents and their children often accuse each other of not listening or only hearing what they want to hear.
- Emotion can also be a factor when communicating. When people are upset it is very difficult to communicate because they may not want to listen. It is also very stressful for the sender to communicate a message that is likely to cause distress to the receiver (for example, for HR managers when people are about to be made redundant or dismissed).
- Problems with the ability of the sender to compile the message can cause confusion. This can be especially true where there is an emphasis on the use of technical jargon. Recently the explosion in the availability of personal computers and their associated technology has resulted in a corresponding growth of the confusing jargon used to describe them.
- The relationship between the sender and the receiver can also be a barrier to communications. Organizations allocate certain people to positions of power and status and those who are subordinate to those positions sometimes find it difficult to communicate with them. People will tell their manager the good news but try to avoid telling them bad. Managers will accept more readily an idea from one of their peers, but may be less enthusiastic about one from a subordinate. This difference in organizational status can inhibit good communications.
- Building on what we said above we can introduce the idea of trust as a barrier or as a lubricant. If we are not confident in the source of our message then we may be reluctant to act on it or feedback to whosoever sent it.
- The sheer mass of information that is sometimes transmitted to the receiver can be a problem. If we use the example of personal computers again, anyone who is thinking about purchasing one is faced with a large volume of information extolling the virtues of one particular model compared to another. Without having the time or skills to assimilate the information (and discriminate between it) the sheer weight and volume of information can dissuade the individual from making a decision about purchasing one.

4.3.7   Formal communication

For managers, communication often means things like the writing of reports, the sending of memos, giving orders or chairing meetings. These can be attributed to the formal communication systems that exist. Most communications in an organization flow vertically. The organization's structure with the senior managers and decision makers at the top lends itself to the situation where orders and plans come from the top down and suggestions and ideas from the bottom upwards. Horizontal communications exist to aid coordination and integration of the various functions. This is especially important in the more organic organizations where functional divisions are not so rigid and there is a need to respond to quickly changing circumstances.

4.3.8   General communication skills

The communication skills demanded of a manager are many and varied, from the oral to the non-verbal. The manager has to use a wide range of skills to assist the transmitting of information. The skills the transmitter of a message may need to concentrate on are language. Invariably when we think of language we think of the spoken language but we should not forget written language. This is especially important now when there is greater pressure on us to use electronic mail to communicate and so we need to use written language skills accurately.

Framing a message

It is important to think about how well or poorly we express ourselves, how we use vocabulary and how clearly we speak. The more careful we are in our choice of words, the less likelihood of misunderstandings occurring.

Receiving a message

We should also put ourselves on the receiving end of a communication and ask how would we react to receiving it. This can prevent negative reactions to the message. There can be tough talking when necessary and at other times a more conciliatory approach can be used. Communication is useless unless it is put to good effect, and with this in mind it is important to recognize the need for feedback. This should be treated as being positive rather than negative.

The receiver of communications also needs to develop their skills and this requires them to have the ability to be able to read and understand what is written. Time should be spent reading text several times if there is any doubt about its meaning. Anyone who has put together self-assembly furniture will appreciate the benefits of reading instructions more than once.

Listening skills

Listening skills are also very important. One sound piece of advice often given to management trainees is that 'You have two ears and one mouth and you should use them in those proportions'. This may mean letting people talk uninterruptedly and concentrating on what they are saying, rather than interrupting with your answer before you have had time to hear all their message.

Written communications

Written communication has to be broken down into its key components and is a very useful skill to develop. With practice and a highlighting pen, it is surprising how quickly the key points can be identified in a lengthy communication.

Knowing what questions to ask when seeking clarification from the transmitter of the message is also worth mentioning here. The transmitter must be given as much opportunity to talk. The receiver should use questions so that the transmitter of the message cannot avoid giving answers that help to clarify the situation. Written communications provide a permanent record of all that has been said and it can be referred to for clarification. This often makes the writer more careful about how it is drafted. Written communications can be lengthy if written by the wrong person and their clarity questionable, especially if they are written by someone who wants to create loopholes that can be exploited at a later date. Written records themselves can become unwieldy and occupy a lot of time and effort in terms of storage and maintenance.

4.3.9   Oral communications

The term 'oral communications' is used to describe face-to-face as well as telephone conversations. Oral communication is often the quickest method of passing on information. It can be formal in meetings or informal in the corridor and perhaps its greatest advantage is that it is a two-way process, where both parties have the chance to speak and give instant feedback. The disadvantage of oral communication can be that the parties do not listen properly, resulting in misunderstandings. This, combined with the fact that often there is no written record of the message, can mean that both parties go away with a completely different view of the situation that can neither be proved nor disproved.

4.3.10   Electronic communications

Electronics has revolutionized communications. In an instant an individual or group of people can be contacted using technologies such as videoconferencing and voice messaging anywhere in the world. The benefits of this can be enormous. Following the events of 11 September 2001 Price Waterhouse reported, 'The company encouraged people not to travel if it was not essential, but decisions were left to individuals. Newton (*global head of HR*) says there has not been a substantial increase in videoconferencing, which was found to be primitive and complicated. Teleconferencing is the preferred choice. New technology such as Internet-based voice messaging was found to have worked effectively. 'That was a bit of a discovery, we now use it widely.'[22]

However, there are problems with having instant access to information. It was reported (that 'Staff Internet abuse tops discipline table' and 'that employers have taken disciplinary action on more occasions in the last year against staff misusing the web than for dishonesty, violence and health and safety breaches combined.'[23]

Dealing with abuse of Internet access is both time consuming and expensive. To try to overcome problems with Internet and e-mail abuse many organizations have been forced to introduce policies. However, these policies are not always effective. It was reported 'that although 86 per cent of organizations have Internet use policies, 40 per cent of HR professionals have received complaints about employees wasting time on the net'.[24]

The CIPD gives guidance to employers about what to include in Internet policies. These include which sites are forbidden, the fact that monitoring of access may take place and what the penalties for misuse are. Further information can be obtained from the CIPD at www.cipd.co.uk.

4.3.11   Report writing

Report writing is one of the most important communications exercises that a manager or their staff have to carry out. Managers are often faced with situations that need investigating and so they either do it themselves or delegate it. The findings from these situations must be reported upon.

4.3.12   General approach

The general approach required of anyone who is asked to write a report can be described in terms of a number of steps that need to be followed:

- The first step is the fact-finding one where the individual is expected to carry out some form of investigation and ascertain the facts of the matter.
- The facts, once obtained, need to be presented in a systematic and clear manner.
- After analysing the facts it is possible to decide what is actually wrong in the particular situation and what can be done about it.
- Suggestions need to be made about what to do about the existing situation.

Additional advice for investigators

- First, the investigator needs to be very clear about the terms of reference and the limitations of the report.
- Second, the investigator needs to know who to contact, what to ask and how to use a range of sources of information.
- Third, writing the report is perhaps the most difficult part of the investigation. This stage is going to depend upon, how good the writer has been at organizing the collected data. The writer needs to remember who the report is for and their level of knowledge. The report will have to be written several times and adjusted accordingly to satisfy the original objectives of the investigation as well as taking into consideration the politics of the situation, something which is often underestimated.

4.3.13   Report format

Written reports can come in a variety of formats: formal and informal. Formal ones are usually associated with being more important and are often likely to be for external organizational use. An informal report is more likely to be used for a relatively minor matter and may remain internal to the organization. Other types of report are the *ad hoc*, routine, non-routine and even verbal. Different organizations have different ideas about how a report should look and the reader has to keep this is in mind and to be aware of their own organization's preferences.

Reports, formal and informal, need to have an easily recognizable structure, and a suggested structure for a formal report could include the following.

4.3.14   Report structure

- **A title page,** which should include an indication of to what the report refers.
- **A page showing the contents,** which should list what the report includes page by page to enable the reader to find things easily.
- **An introduction** that describes the terms of reference covering the background situation, with information about the instigator of the report and the limitations that have been set.
- **A description of the methods used,** which should describe how the writer went about obtaining and recording information.
- **A summary:** this should cover the main sections of the report, its findings, the conclusions and what it recommends.
- **Findings:** this is the section where the facts are detailed, analysed and discussed.

- **Conclusions:** this is the summarizing of what the writer of the report has discovered. This should lead logically to:
- **Recommendations:** these are proposals for action to be taken. This is obviously a very important part of the report and needs to be written very carefully. The reader of the report wants solutions to problems and the writer's recommendations should be a range of solutions.
- **Appendices:** in an appendix, information, evidence or data can be presented that supports arguments of findings in the body of the report. It is important to refer to the appendix by number or letter in the body of the report to avoid confusion and retain consistency.

4.3.15   General guidance

(1) Appearance

It is important to get the maximum impact with a report because first impressions count and all the good work the writer has done during investigation will be wasted if the report does not present an authoritative and well-written impression. Numbering must also be applied to the pages to allow easier accessibility. Other approaches depend on personal preference and an organization's own format.

(2) Use of English

Like any communication where the sender is trying to convey ideas, record details or to impress, it is important to try to hold the reader's attention. This can be achieved by making the report interesting wherever possible, easy to read, brief and to the point.

It is important that the writer acknowledges the strengths and weaknesses of those who are going to read the report. Holding the reader's attention can be more easily achieved if the report is kept short and to the point.

4.3.16   What to include

Business people who are going to read reports have to be convinced that the recommendations are viable. In order to achieve this it is best to take the reader through all the information that has been gathered in a systematic way. Arguments need to be balanced and as objective as possible. Readers are often more impressed where they can easily focus on facts and figures. Therefore, in order to add weight to any argument, if the points being made are quantifiable then it is important that they should be quantified. Also by clearly explaining any financial implications it is possible to convince even the most ardent critic that the argument you are making is valid.

The financial implications are very important and report writers should keep this in mind. Authors of HR reports should remember that references to 'motivation', 'commitment' and 'employee happiness' are laudable, but top management will demand to know the cost–benefits of any new proposals.

4.3.17   Errors that report writers can make

- Lack of clarity in report writing can be disastrous especially where the reader is remote from the writer and the points cannot be easily clarified verbally.
- Writers of reports can become so involved in the report that they lose their focus and fail to address the original issues.

- Writers sometimes leave it to the reader to draw their own conclusions. It is important to remember that the writer has more detailed knowledge and is in a better position than the reader to draw conclusions and make recommendations.
- It should also be remembered that a report can be part of a series of reports in the same subject areas and so they need to be clearly linked through good referencing and numbering.

4.3.18   Formal reports

An example of a formal report might be as follows:

FOR THE ATTENTION OF MRS J. L. HART Personnel Director

FROM   MR. C. PINTON Production Manager 'A' shift
REFERENCE   RB/211/PM
DATE   23/2/03

REPORT ON PRODUCTION STAFF ABSENCE LEVELS AT BLUDELY PLANT.

1.0 Terms of reference
Following complaints from shift supervisors concerning production line staff absenteeism. Mrs Hart requested me, as an experienced shift manager, to investigate absenteeism on all shifts at Bludely Plant and report my findings to her within ten working days.

2.0 Procedure
To determine how serious the problem was a number of views were sought. The following were interviewed:
2.1 The shift supervisors
2.2 The production line staff
2.3 The personnel administrators who keep records of staff absences.

3.0 Summary
Findings
3.1 It was found that the complaints of staff shortages came from only two of the six supervisors concerned who felt that there was a hard core of 'troublemakers' employed on the production line.
3.2 Interviews with production line staff resulted in a number of responses.
3.2.1 Of the fifty production line staff 70 per cent (35 staff) could not understand why they were being asked about their views on absenteeism.
3.2.2 Of the remaining 30 per cent (15 staff) only eight were concerned about absenteeism as an issue and this included the three staff who had been previously identified as having had more than three days' absence each.
3.2.3 Interviews with the eight were most revealing. They all felt they were treated unfavourably by two of their three shift supervisors. (The two supervisors who were complaining most about absenteeism.)
3.3 The results of a comprehensive analysis of absences for the fifty production line staff showed that over the previous three months only five of the staff had any recorded absence. Of these five, only three had more than three days' absence, the other two had only been absent for one day each. Note: a full table of these absences would be placed in an appendix to the report.

4.0 Conclusion
It is obvious from the findings that there is a problem with absenteeism, but this only appears to affect two supervisors and a maximum of eight of the production line staff. Since

there is a problem, but it goes beyond the remit of this report to fully investigate the underlying issues, the following recommendations have been made for your consideration.

5.0 Recommendations
5.1 Absenteeism for the eight line production staff who are most concerned about their supervisors should be monitored over a four-week period by the personnel department commencing on 1 March.
5.2 Each supervisor should be interviewed by the personnel officer to determine what they feel are the wider problems underlying the present situation. This should be completed by 31 March.
5.3 All staff who are under the direct supervision of the supervisors where absenteeism is apparently high should be interviewed again by the personnel department to determine if their views are the same as the eight who have already voiced an opinion. This could be done anonymously using a questionnaire and completed by 10 April.
5.4 Costs. . . .
5.5 Cost–benefit. . . .

4.3.19   Informal report

An informal report can consist of four sections: general headings, introduction, an information section and finally a conclusion.

4.3.20   Memoranda

Although the advent of e-mail has resulted in more electronic communication in organizations the memo is still used. This is employed to instigate action of some form and is usually less formal than a report. Again, employers tend to have their own specific ideas on memo layout but a suggestion is given in Figure 4.7.

COMPANY OR DEPARTMENT NAME

MEMORANDUM

TO   Peter Parrot   Cage supervisor

FROM   Cyril Lyon   Maintenance manager: ext. 1429

Date/Ref.   1/4/03   FLR/1

SUBJECT
It has come to my attention that the floor of one of your cages does not appear to have been cleaned for a number of days. Would you please remedy this situation within the next 48 hours and I shall then inspect the cage.

cc   Head keeper
          Personnel administrator
          Staff file

Figure 4.7. A sample memorandum.

Exercise

On a recent visit to his local shopping centre Mr Beaton purchased a £10 box of chocolates from Smigs the confectioners. The chocolates were a present for his mother's birthday. When she opened them two days later she found that they were mouldy. He has returned the box and contents to you, the marketing manager, at Chunky Chocs Ltd, of Boom Town.

He is demanding recompense for the chocolates, the cost of postage and distress caused to himself and his mother.

In your capacity as marketing manager carry out the following:

● Draft a letter to Mr Beaton explaining what you intend to do.
● Write to the production manager instructing them to carry out a preliminary investigation of how this particular problem might have arisen.
● In detail, draft terms of reference for a report investigating the potential causes of faulty goods reaching the customer.

Feedback

By communicating using a variety of methods to a number of different people you will begin to realize that you have to be more careful with your choice of language and tone. For instance, a letter to a customer cannot include an admission of liability because your legal department will not appreciate it. The fault may be with the retailer for keeping the chocolates too long after the 'sell by' date. However, you do need to assure the customer that the situation is under investigation and that they will be kept informed.

Communication internally can be more direct depending on your position in the organization. A more detailed approach is required for the report when you discuss its terms of reference with the person who will carry it out.

4.3.21   Making presentations

One of the most daunting things most people face is standing up in front of a group of people and giving a presentation. Competent, hard-working people can be seen to be visibly shaken if asked to stand up and present a report. However, presentations need not be as traumatic as we fear if we follow a logical approach. The areas that we need to think about are:

● What we actually want to communicate to our audience.
● In order to do this we will have to list what it is we are going to say and to organize it carefully.
● We have to decide how we are going to physically present the information and then get up and present it.

4.3.22   Organizing what we want to say and saying it

Some people find that at first it is essential to write down everything they want to say. With this done they can begin to highlight what they consider to be the key words or sentences. Once this is done then they can transfer those key words or sentences to prompt cards or overhead projector acetates, to form the basis of the presentation. Keep the cards in the correct order with a clip or tag that cannot easily come undone.

Rehearsal

Before any presentation can take place it is worth rehearsing. Even the most accomplished of public speakers will do some rehearsing. Rehearsing can have a number of advantages especially if you are new to presentations.

First, it gives the presenter an opportunity to familiarize themselves with any equipment they are going to use. It may not be possible to rehearse at the actual venue but at least the equipment will be similar.

Second, the rehearsal can be timed, which in some situations is absolutely essential. Even in routine presentations, if the audience has been told it will last for half an hour and after

45 minutes you are still going strong, the audience may become restless and inattentive. Once you know the time of your rehearsed presentation you can adjust it accordingly.

Third, you can modify your presentation based on how you feel about it. If you do your rehearsal in front of a friend you can get their opinion. It may be that particular words, sentences or even jokes do not seem to work and so now is the time to change them.

Fourth, if you try your presentation in front of a mirror and record the sound it gives you an opportunity to get used to looking at an imaginary audience and to identify if you need to alter the way you use your voice, and even your facial expressions.

Location

Choosing the place we want to present can be a luxury. Most people have little choice about the venue. However, if we do get to choose where the presentation is to take place then we should use this to our advantage. We can choose a time and place that suits us. However, we should not alienate our audience before we start by choosing somewhere they do not like. Presentations in work time are invariably better attended than those outside office hours.

Rooms should be chosen because of their relative comfort. If the audience is uncomfortable they will fidget and distract you and other members of the audience. However, you must remember that when a group of people are put into a room the **temperature** automatically rises due to their body heat. So if you want to avoid your audience falling asleep it is suggested that you make sure there is adequate ventilation. Similarly, **lighting** can raise the temperature quickly as well as dazzling the audience's view of an overhead projector screen. **Noise** is very intrusive so choose somewhere where noise and other interruptions can be kept to a minimum.

As a presenter you should never assume that **equipment** will be available. Like everything in business, good planning is essential and so everything from chairs to overhead projectors have to be booked in advance. If you need the assistance of a technician when using packages like PowerPoint make sure they are available.

Organize your equipment in the room to maximum effect. If you want to feel close to your audience avoid having tables you have to stand behind. If you have to use a table keep it to the side of you because this can create a more informal relaxed feeling. If you have to move between overhead projector and screen make sure there are no obstacles in the way. Watch out for trailing cables – some audiences will take great delight in watching you stumble.

If you are in a large room and using an overhead projector check that you can see it from the back of the room. If you can see the screen so can the majority of your audience.

Any **documentation** that will be handed out needs to be prepared and carefully proofread before it is sent away for mass printing. It is soul destroying to do a wonderful presentation and then find the audience disappointed because the literature to accompany it is incomplete, full of spelling mistakes or not available.

Saying what you want to say

This involves a number of different areas to which you need to pay attention:

- Your own personal appearance (your clothes, hair, etc.) will have an impact. It is worth remembering that some of the basic interpersonal skills can have the greatest influence. Saying 'good morning' or 'hello, my name is . . .' helps you to make contact with your audience. As soon as you stand up, appear or walk on-stage, the audience will form an opinion about you and so it is vital that you make a very positive first impression.
- You need to talk to your audience, and the first minute or two of a presentation can be very stressful. It is worth having some water available if your voice is likely to dry up and you must be aware of the tendency to talk more quickly when you are nervous.

- By rehearsing as discussed earlier you can learn to pace yourself and recognize that you are talking quickly. When you speak you should always try to speak clearly, without appearing to be talking down to your audience, or alternatively patronizing them.
- One aid to clearer verbal delivery is to develop eye contact with the audience. Although this is difficult at first because most people seem to fear their audience you will begin to realize that the majority of audiences are not hostile and they are there to hear what you have to say. By gaining eye contact, you are talking out to your audience, rather than down to your feet or the prompt cards as you read them. The use of the voice is very important and you must learn to vary the way you use it. Stressing some points (e.g. savings made) may need to be done more forcefully.
- Outline to the audience what you plan to talk about, how long it is likely to last and when you will take questions, whether during or at the end of the presentation. Talk to your audience with confidence, but try not to appear to be reading from a script.
- Knowing your audience is one of the keys to a successful presentation. If you cannot find out anything about your audience beforehand, you will have to look for clues during the presentation. Row after row of blank faces speak volumes as do mumbled conversations coming from different parts of the room. It is at this point you must ask your audience if they are following your presentation and adjust or carry on according to their response.
- If you are going to use prompt cards then number each card and, if possible, join them together with string. It can be very embarrassing if you drop them and then cannot put them back in the correct order. Contingency planning also has a role in presentations. Have back-up copies of materials and methods of delivery available. For example, if you leave your prompt cards on the train, instead have pens with you that you can use to write directly on overhead projector acetates.
- In terms of actual delivery one thing that is often underestimated is body language. As humans we instinctively recognize certain types of body language and behaviour. Invariably, if someone smiles we smile back, in certain situations if someone gets too close to us we move away. Fidgeting or moving about too much or constantly crossing the arms are all examples of body language that can distract an audience and should be avoided.
- Depending on the presentation, at some stage you will probably have to answer questions. Whether or not you do this during or after the presentation will depend upon you. Questions taken or asked during a presentation can disrupt the flow of the presentation and cause you to digress. This is very important when your time is limited, because you can soon use up all your allotted time without covering all you wanted.

  Questions can be used to clarify understanding and can also be used to give yourself time to think. They can be used to obtain the widest audience participation possible by asking the same question of a number of people. When audiences ask questions you should not be afraid to admit you do not know the answer although obviously it looks better if you do. Again this can be dealt with through good forward planning and trying to predict the types of questions you may be asked. Some of this comes with experience, but colleagues and superiors may also be able to offer advice. If you do not know an answer, but promise to get back to someone with it, make sure you do so personally, otherwise if they do not get your response your image is tarnished forever.

4.3.23 Using visual aids

The use of visual aids during presentations can be a very effective way of illustrating complex or difficult points. The personal computer now allows easy access to packages such as 'PowerPoint'. Although the personal computer now plays its part in presentations, many are still made using an overhead projector. Visuals when used well can have a major impact on the audience but when used poorly can be equally disastrous. This is equally true of computer-generated visuals or handwritten ones. With a little forethought some of the problems can be avoided. These problems can include:

- Using too many visuals – the audience becomes bored with them.
- Poorly written visuals – even when visuals are printed it is surprising how many people choose a font size that is too small and the people at the back or even the front of a room cannot read the words.
- Information overload – presenters overload the visual with information that takes a long time to read. They continue talking and the audience is trying to read while the presenter is talking and the message fails to get across.

Good practice in the use of visuals is to think carefully about their appearance and design.

A final point on the use of visuals is to remember the KISS principle (keep it simple stupid). Streamline the information you are going to display and make it as easy as possible for your audience to take onboard. This does not mean treating your audience as idiots, but it means focusing on the most important points in your presentation and ensuring that you get them across to the audience.

4.3.24 Using an overhead projector

If you do decide that you definitely want to show visuals and so need to use an overhead projector there are some basic guidelines worth thinking about. As a presenter you want to develop contact and a rapport with your audience. Ask yourself the following questions before you use the overhead projector:

- Will it prevent me from facing my audience and losing eye contact because there can be a temptation to read from the screen?
- Will it be physically between me and the audience, so that they will see it as a barrier I am hiding behind?
- Will the noise and light from it distract my audience and stop them listening to what I am saying?

In order to avoid these problems preplanning and practice can help. For instance, eye contact can be maintained by knowing what is on the screen and only needing to glance at it to prompt your memory. By standing at the side of the projector it no longer acts as a barrier to the audience, and you can look down at the acetate to prompt yourself. The problem raised by noise and light can be reduced by limiting the number of visuals used and turning off the projector when it is not required.

These may sound like easy solutions but they take a long time to perfect. It is easy even for seasoned presenters to develop bad habits and make basic mistakes, so think carefully about whether or not you wish to use visuals.

4.3.25 Working for others and how to influence them

Influencing, it should be remembered, is about using power to get others to change their behaviour in some way. In order to do this people obviously have to possess some power. The way we can use our power to achieve change in behaviour can be done through persuasion. Often we hear people say 'Oh, that was a very persuasive argument' or 'I'm not that convinced'. How do we construct a persuasive argument and what power sources are we using?

What we need to remember are those bases of power we have at our disposal:

- We can use all our expert knowledge to create a good logical argument. As a HR manager if you wanted to persuade someone of the benefits of further education you could use an argument as follows. There have been five vacancies over the last eight years for senior managerial posts. In every case the person who was appointed had an MBA. Therefore, if you want a senior manager's post it would make sense for you to get an MBA and I can provide the funding for it.
- By focusing on what people want or think they want, it is possible to use the power you have to reward and therefore persuade them that if they agree to your plans they will benefit in some way. You can use your resource power to reward people or take something away from them. An example might be if a manager were influential in deciding who did or who did not get a company car. That manager might suggest to someone that if they were to behave in a particular way they might get the car, whereas if they did not, a car would not be available for them.
- Finally there is an approach which is of a more emotive nature whereby the individual can use their referent or charismatic power to persuade people of the merits of an argument. People will be attracted by the individual's personality, rather than the merits of any arguments or rewards.

Assertiveness

Another influencing skill available for managers is the use of assertiveness. Being assertive does not mean being aggressive. Assertiveness merely means that you accept that you also have power and that you are entitled to be treated equally. It means that you are confident enough to comment positively or negatively when asked for an opinion. It also means that you can accept positive and negative comment in return. Assertiveness means being confident about asking for what you believe you are entitled to.

The use of assertiveness for an individual can be very influential on the behaviour of others. For instance, it might be used to influence the behaviour of a manager who keeps trying to overload you with work. Saying 'no' sends out a clear message to the individual, that you are not prepared to take on the extra work. They in turn should change their behaviour and cease trying to give you more work.

The use of persuasion and assertiveness is going to depend on knowing how you want to benefit from their use. You will need to be aware of any potential resistance you might face and develop arguments to counter it.

4.3.26   Managing the manager

When we discuss management of the manager it is in terms of the subordinate managing their own manager. What we need to do in the first instance (and this can be quite difficult) is to put ourselves in their position. How many of us starting in work had the attitude that our boss did not understand the problems we face, they did not listen to us, and they did not care? Then we took our first promotion and suddenly we were in a different situation. Those statements were now being levelled at us and our perspective as the boss was different from the one we had when we were very junior members of staff.

We need to think about the relationship that exists between the manager and the managed. Why are managers there in the first place? What are they trying to do? Where do we fit into the scheme of things? We need to remember that managers are human beings and come in all sorts of differing shapes and sizes. They have all the strengths, frailties and neuroses that are to be found in the human race although thankfully not necessarily in one single individual. It is important that we recognize this because we need to know something about them so that we can learn how to work with them. It must also be pointed out that we need to know ourselves and ask what type of person are we? (Personality is discussed in detail in Section 1.2.)

Obtaining information

We have already looked elsewhere in some detail at what managers do so for the purpose of this section it will be restricted to the achieving of goals. This is done through people, notably 'us', and staff, who need to find out what these goals are. Some managers are better than others at communicating goals – they are more confident than others and are happy to divulge information. One of the talents any member of staff has to develop is to try to elicit as much information from the boss as possible. If you are unsure about what the goal is you must clarify it with your manager. As with any good communication system there has to be some form of feedback. Do not be afraid, you may not believe it but your boss is on the same side as you. If you think about it, part of their goal is to be successful and part of your goal is to be successful. You need them and they need you. It is important therefore that you are both working towards the same ends and only through clarification can you be sure of this. Many managers correctly recognize that they are only as good as their staff.

Power

The relationship between you and your boss is one partly based on power. By virtue of their position in the hierarchy your manager has been given legitimate power that allows them to give you legitimate orders and expect you to carry out those orders. This is an area with which some individuals have difficulty coming to terms. Managers have a right to give us orders and we have to learn how to deal with them quickly and efficiently. In law this is recognized as the 'management prerogative' – managements' right to manage.

Perception

It was mentioned earlier that we also have our own characteristics and our bosses have a perception of us just as we have a perception of them. If they think we are motivated by material gain they will try to use material gain to motivate us. However, if they get those perceptions wrong it is up to us to change them. For instance, they may have the idea that we are not particularly able or perhaps we are lazy. Then they are not likely to delegate challenging or important work to us. If we know something of their perceptions of us we can work to change those perceptions.

Persuasion

Part of what we need to do is to use the power of persuasion to get managers to delegate to us. Managers often will not take the risk of failure because they feel it can reflect badly on them. However, if we can convince them of our ability we can embark on an incremental approach to our own personal development by taking on extra duties a little at a time thus building their confidence in us. From a human resources management view the appraisal process is an opportunity when you can persuade your boss of your merits. In order to do this you must prepare your argument in advance and give your boss enough evidence that they would find it difficult to refuse you. If they do raise objections you should have prepared for them and be able to present a counter-argument.

Diplomacy

You may find yourself in a situation where your boss is not as competent as you in certain areas, for example an area like computers and new technology. Dealing with situations like this can be tricky, but again you need to focus on the fact that your boss is the one with position power and you work for them. This situation might require a great deal of tact, so that it does not appear that you are exercising your expert power at their expense. It may be that you have to suggest some things are better left to you and they take care of the wider issues. However, you must always be aware of the dangers of taking on too much responsibility without the necessary authority.

Managers, their personalities and interpersonal skills vary and we have to learn to deal with both their negative and positive traits. One way that we can deal with a difficult manager is with assertiveness to make them realize that we have rights too.

Environmental pressures on your boss can lead to intolerable amounts of stress. If you can identify those pressures on your boss, you may be able to suggest ways of dealing with them through delegation and improvements in work systems, and hopefully this will result in some positive changes in their behaviour. It is perhaps finally worth reiterating that this relationship is a two-way process and to keep thinking about our own contribution to it, are we being supportive of it or are we causing the strains in it?

Exercise

Think about your present boss or even a former manager and choose any characteristics of them that you feel they would need to improve in order for them to become the perfect boss.

● How do you feel you could help them improve?
● On reflection, do you feel your relationship was good or poor? Justify the reasons for your answer.
● If you had to describe them in 25 words what would you say?
● How would you describe yourself in 25 words?

Feedback

One way you may be able to help managers to improve is by pointing out traits or characteristics they could improve on. You can identify some of these through the descriptions of them and yourself. This will test all your skills of diplomacy and influencing. You should remember that you are part of the relationship and your own characteristics may also need examination. This area links with Section 1.2 on personality.

Case study

Fail to plan, plan to fail

Colin and Jean were approaching their silver wedding anniversary when unbeknown to them their three children decided to stage a surprise party for them. The actual date of the anniversary was Friday, 12 April. Three months before the event the three children Ben aged 25, Carl aged 28 and Kylie aged 21, put forward their individual ideas. They decided that the best idea would be to book a room in a hotel where all the guests could sit down together, eat a meal and then socialize. Guests would be able to book rooms to stay overnight if they so desired and so everyone would be happy, or so they thought.

The three children had very different approaches to life. Carl, the eldest, had a very casual approach, Ben was more serious but not very assertive and Kylie who, although she was very outgoing and confident, was seen by Carl and Ben very much as the baby sister who would have to do as she was told.

Each of them decided what they were going to do and time passed. Carl's job was to find a hotel and send out the invitations. Ben was in charge of the catering and decorating arrangements, something that he would have to coordinate with the hotel. He was quite happy to do this because he had a friend who was a caterer and he would be able to pass on all the work to her. Kylie decided she would organize the entertainment because she had a number of former university friends who were musicians.

One month before the anniversary things started to go wrong. A guest who wanted to stay overnight was told by the hotel that no such event was taking place, in fact its main function room had been booked to the local rugby club for their annual dinner. When the guest asked about room availability he was told there were only three rooms left. The guest then telephoned Carl to ask him what was going on. Carl had apparently made a provisional booking for the function room but when he didn't confirm the booking the hotel let the room go. However, when he contacted the hotel they could only offer him a smaller function room (maximum 50 people) and because of the *close proximity* of the anniversary Carl had to accept it, even though it would mean some guests would have to be told there wasn't enough room for them.

To make matters worse Carl had assured Ben that he didn't need to talk to the hotel manager because it was all under control. Now Ben found out that the hotel didn't allow the use of outside caterers but they would be able to arrange a buffet meal. With much regret Ben had to accept this even though it would mean problems for his friend.

The anniversary party duly went ahead but fate dealt them one more blow. The string quartet that Kylie had arranged to provide background music was virtually drowned out by the volume of the disco music from the rugby club dinner.

Question

Having read the case, what do you think the children should have done?

Feedback

As the title suggests, lack of planning is likely to lead to failure. Good planning is essential to ensure a successful event like this where careful planning and organizing was required.

Time limits should have been set on the work to be done. Progress meetings were required to inform everyone about what was happening and any changes in priorities. The progress should have been regularly monitored by all three of the children acting as a team. The plans needed to be constantly monitored with a contingency plan of action in place in the event of things going wrong so that alternative action could be taken. Someone needed to take charge. An individual with the authority was needed to lead and coordinate the plans.

Their time planning left a lot to be desired and for events such as these where a large number of guests are involved it is essential to manage time effectively.

Summary

In this section you examined communications in the organization and the effects they can have. You have looked at how the process of communications works and how you need to recognize the importance of both verbal and written communication skills. You have also considered how and why we write reports as well as how to carry out presentations using visual aids and overhead projectors. Finally, you have examined the issue of working with others and some of the techniques that have to be used to make those relationships work to the benefit of all parties concerned.

4.4   Working in groups, meetings, committees

A camel is a horse designed by a committee.

Anon.

Section objectives

In this section you will:

- Examine what we mean by groups and why individuals and organizations value them
- Identify aspects of group behaviour and structure
- Examine how groups form their leadership and decision making
- Learn to recognize whether or not a group is effective and how to select group members
- Identify the qualities required to chair committees and
- Identify the purpose of meetings.

4.4.1   Introduction

Mention the word 'group' and immediately a number of images can be conjured up, depending on the individual to whom you are talking. If you are talking to a teenager, it could be used to describe a number of musicians who have a record in the pop charts. Talk to a senior manager and they may have visions of a number of middle managers meeting together and calling themselves a focus group.

This definition does little to illustrate the complexity of purpose or the understanding we automatically attribute through our own experience when we talk of a group. However, it does give us some clues that indicate in the modern working environment what groups are about. It tells us that, first and foremost, groups are about people. So what does our experience tell us about those people who call themselves a group? We know the labels such as committee, working party, steering group but what do these labels mean?

Charles Handy[25] draws the distinction between a number of individuals who randomly find themselves doing the same things but who do not think of themselves as a group (for example, drinkers in a pub). However, once they perceive themselves to be a group then they will become a group (for example, if they are faced with an emergency).

Exercise

Think about all the times you find yourself in the company of others. Then ask yourself 'how often do I think I am a member of a group?' List all the groups to which you belong. What benefit do you think – as an individual – that you get out of working in a group? Would you enjoy your work more or less if you had to work on your own?

Feedback

The idea of being in a group depends very much on individual perception and so whether or not you feel you are in a group will depend upon your individual views. You can, using your own experience, identify what benefits you feel accrue from working in a group. Some people identify social ones such as working with others. Other people like the idea of being able to turn to someone for advice. Some people do not like the idea of working in groups because they dislike having to share decision making or power. From the exercise you can get an idea of whether or not you are the type of person who does or does not like working in groups.

4.4.2   Why should we be interested in groups?

In order to answer this question, we need to ask why individuals join groups and why organizations are so interested in having people working in groups. From our earliest days at school we learn that it is better to be accepted by the majority, the group, rather than be 'the loner or outsider', who then becomes the butt of the group's jokes or, even worse, their combined aggression. This **sense of belonging** gives us the feeling of safety in numbers that later in life can manifest itself in behaviour such as joining clubs for social or work-related reasons.

The group also helps us judge our role in society or at school when we compare ourselves to those group members who show greater sporting or academic prowess. This in turn can give us an idea of our own importance or self-worth. Groups also **represent power** – an individual may have a certain amount of power by virtue of their expertise. However, an individual can be easily replaced. If a number of individuals with a range of expertise or the same type of expertise (for example, dentistry), combine themselves into a group then they can make themselves powerful enough to lobby governments. Finally, groups can often do better in terms of **achieving a goal** compared to an individual. The group is able to call upon a range of expertise, to brainstorm ideas and combine its power and resources to achieve the goal, something the individual would find impossible.

The importance of acceptance by the group should not be underestimated. In the Hawthorne studies[6] it was shown that the group under study had a number of norms of behaviour and those who violated those norms would have social pressure put on them to conform. The groups developed norms of behaviour which can be described in the following ways.

- Do not work too hard, otherwise you will be described as someone who does too much work.
- Do not do too little work or you will be described as someone who does not make a large enough contribution to the group.
- Do not say anything about a colleague to a supervisor if it will be detrimental to that colleague.
- Do not behave in a way that makes you seem socially distant from the group even if you are a supervisor. (Adapted from Roethlisberger and Dickson.[6])

These norms were part of the way in which the group controlled their output. Their perception was that if they increased their output in order to earn bonuses the rate of output required by management would be increased. If fewer workers could produce more, then the group feared some would be laid off. This influenced the group's behaviour and the norms they developed, helped them to control individuals who might have been tempted to work too hard or to be lazy. Individuals who ignored the norms were punished by the group in the form of sanctions – ridicule, name calling, having tools stolen or dropped on their feet.

4.4.3   Why are organizations so interested in having people working in groups?

Handy[25] lists a number of reasons why organizations use groups, these include the distribution and control of work.

4.4.4   Group structure and communication

Group structure describes the pattern of relationships between the different elements in a group and the factors that contribute to the stability of those relationships. The way in which individuals in a group relate to one another is very important and is described as group structure. Individuals are all very different and within groups it is necessary to recognize the various relationships that exist. Individuals can differentiate between themselves in a variety of ways. Buchanan and Huczynski[26] identified those of Status, Power, Liking, Role and Leadership. These five factors all operate simultaneously in group settings.

The main ways in which people differentiate between themselves in a group merits further examination.

Status structure

All positions in a group have a value put on them. This value can be attributed because of the individual's position in an organizational hierarchy and is part of the formal status.

Power structure

The ability to be able to control the behaviour of others in order to allow the group to achieve its goals is absolutely essential. This can be done through a power structure which can be linked to a system of authority and avoid unnecessary power struggles which in turn may mean failure to reach goals. The greater the range of power sources the individual possesses the greater the power that person can use in different situations.

Liking structure

This relates to the way that individuals in groups distinguish between each other, depending on whom they like or dislike. By analysing people's responses to questionnaires it is possible to identify the most and least popular individuals, as well as any subgroups.

Role structure

Everyone in a group carries out certain functions during their interactions with other members. Their behaviour is associated with their position in the group and constitutes the social role of the occupant of that position. For example, a team leader would be expected to be highly motivated and professional, therefore the social role of the team leader would be to motivate others and act in a sensible, mature manner.

Exercise

Think of the job of a head teacher. Who do they work with? How do the relations between the different people interrelate?

Feedback

The headteacher is often the focal person in any meeting. Others who relate to the head are other teachers, the parents, the pupils, administrative staff and maintenance staff. Each of these occupies a role in the school as an organization. When all of them meet they act in different ways and their behaviour gives an indication of the role they play in the meeting.

A parent may demand information about their child. A teacher might support the head's diplomatic answer. These are examples of behaviour and role that we may witness.

Robert Bales[27] found that people adopt specific roles in groups, namely proposing, supporting, building, disagreeing, giving and seeking information. The behaviours can be put into categories and then related to certain roles. For example, the category of information seeking means we need a behaviour that allows us to obtain information such as being persistent in our questioning. This behaviour in turn can be used in the role of information gatherer. In employee relations staff representatives may ask questions on behalf of those staff who are less willing to talk in public.

Leadership

Leadership can affect the way groups work and it is worth referring to the discussion on leadership both in this section and in Section 3.3 on leadership at work.

4.4.5   Group communication structure and leadership

Individuals within a group rely on each other to supply information which invariably comes through a series of people. Whether the information is required for decision making or problem solving, it is essential that people communicate it. Communication chains can distort communications, as we may recognize from personal experience. The person who has control over information can decide how much or little they want to reveal, and this can be a problem where all the information needs to go through one person.

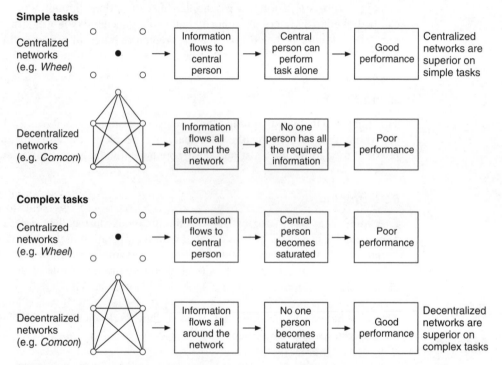

Figure 4.8. Comparing the performance of centralized and decentralized communication networks: The influence of task complexity.

Baron and Greenberg[28] noted that centralized communication networks performed simple tasks quicker and more accurately (see Figure 4.8). In decentralized patterns members were more satisfied because of greater equality of status and involvement in decision making. In centralized patterns those on the edges had less power and were left out of decision making by the more powerful central figures. This resulted in generally lower levels of satisfaction. Centralization and decentralization are discussed further in Section 5.3.

4.4.6   Group formation

According to Homans[29] 'a group is a social system'. He argued that the group exists within the combined physical (layout), cultural (values) and technological (state of knowledge) environment. These environments impose certain activities and interactions on those people who are involved in them. In turn these people develop attitudes and sentiments towards each other and to the environment.

For example, if three people are working together removing rubbish from a sewer, one person must remain on the surface to winch up the rubbish. One person must be at the base of the shaft to attach the rubbish and the third must travel along the sewer to fetch the rubbish.

- The physical environment (layout) dictates that the work must be carried out in a particular way as described.
- The cultural environment (values) dictates that each person must believe that the other group members, though out of sight, can be trusted to work.
- The technological environment (knowledge) means that each person must be able to carry out their duties safely and professionally.

These three environments act upon individuals and influence their attitudes to each other and the overall environment. For example, they may unite in adversity against a potentially hostile physical environment (the sewer). They may develop a system of work rotation as part of their cultural environment and they may refuse to divulge to outsiders their local knowledge of the sewer system. The activities, interactions and sentiments are what Homans described as the 'external system', and are determined by the environment as it is imposed on the individuals. These activities, interactions and sentiments are dependent on one another.

Exercise

Think of someone with whom you work regularly. Do you have a laugh and joke with them? If you do then it is likely that you will have positive sentiments towards them. Then think about someone to whom you feel positive sentiments. It is likely you will interact with them a lot. The two ideas of positive sentiment and level of interaction are interdependent. In other words if we feel comfortable about being with or working with an individual it is likely that we will get on well in our dealings with them.

Homans[29] realized that the external system does not exist in isolation. As the interactions between people increased they developed their own activities and interactions used to influence their working lives. These new ways of doing things were not necessarily the same as those of the formal organization. Homans refers to this as the 'internal system'. We may recognize it as the informal organization.

An example of this might be a health and safety procedure which, although it is technically sound, the group who have to follow it find it cumbersome and the cause of problems. Despite it being the official method the group may develop their own way which they will 'accept' as the correct one even though it is an unofficial method.

The informal and formal systems react with the environment. If the environment changes so do the informal and formal systems. The people involved in the informal system have the capacity to change the formal system because of their ability to change the environment. An example of how this could be done is through staff suggestion schemes whereby those informal/unofficial methods (used on the factory floor) are assessed and, if suitable, turned into formal working practices (acceptable to management). In this way the informal (internal system) can be seen to be changing the physical environment and ways of work.

Homans[29] makes the distinction between required and emergent behaviour. From a management point of view when a job is designed there are certain activities, interactions and sentiments required if the job is to be done successfully. There are those activities, interactions and sentiments that emerge but they are not necessary for the completion of the job.

For example, you may observe on the loading bay of a warehouse that staff help certain lorry drivers by unloading or loading their vehicles while they visit the office and take only a minor part in the loading or unloading. This behaviour is not required by the staff because the driver should be more fully involved. However, because the warehouse staff get on well with them and they are allowed to operate the tailgate, both the drivers and the warehouse staff are content for this system to operate. The driver 'turns round' the delivery faster than he or she would otherwise have done, and the warehouse staff get some variety of work and a break from their routine. However, from a company point of view the warehouse staff could be off loading the lorry more quickly with the driver's help and then return to their own duties. But from the warehouse staff's point of view they get something out of their informal relationship with certain drivers, namely a change in routine that can make life more tolerable for them.

4.4.7 Stages of group development

Tuckman and Jensen[30] believed that groups developed in a standard series consisting of five stages: forming, storming, norming, performing and adjourning (or mourning).

Stage 1: forming

This stage is where group members are trying to find out the purpose of the group, its structure and who will be its leader. Members try to develop formal and informal contacts within the group. They try to determine acceptable patterns of behaviour and identify themselves with the group.

Stage 2: storming

This stage, as its name suggests, is one where conflict manifests itself and individuals resist the limitations the group puts on them. This is often a time where personal aspirations and emotions appear.

Stage 3: norming

This is a time of consolidation for the group, where relationships become stronger, cooperation develops and the boundaries of behaviour, levels of commitment and trust are established.

Stage 4: performing

This is the stage where the group begins to function and carry out its task. The focus has moved away from the group finding out about each other. Now they concentrate on the job, roles become flexible, team work is achieved and solutions to problems are found.

Stage 5: adjourning

If a group are working together on a permanent basis then Stage 4 is the final stage in their development. For temporary groups such as project teams and committees, once the task is completed they have to prepare to disband. This stage can be one of reflection and sadness at parting with co-workers, and so is also called the 'mourning' stage.

Groups do not always move distinctly through the individual stages of this model. It is not unusual to find groups involved in a number of stages at the same time. Work can be carried out at the performing stage while still going through the storming stage. Groups sometimes also return to earlier stages to rethink what they are doing.

4.4.8   Groups and leadership

Groups usually have a formal leader who is known by a title, such as manager, project leader or supervisor. The leader can play an important role in the group's success or failure.

Leadership can be described in terms of styles as suggested by Lewin, Lippett and White (1939). These are often described as being autocratic (policy is decided only by the leader), democratic (where policy is a matter of group discussion plus the leader), or *laissez-faire* (where the group decides with minimum input from the leader) which is not always easily related to high group satisfaction. Although to get high group satisfaction it seems to be necessary to use a more participative style of leadership, it does not necessarily mean that a participative style of management will bring about high levels of performance. In fact sometimes a group led by an autocratic leader will do better than one led by a more participative (democratic) leader.

It is worth looking at some of the theories briefly and how they relate to groups. However, leadership is covered in more detail in Section 3.3.

4.4.9   Fiedler's contingency model

Fiedler *et al.*[31] suggest that effective group performance relies upon the correct balance between the leader's style of interacting with their staff and how much influence and control the situation gives the leader. Fiedler *et al.* wanted to know if an individual leader was more concerned with the task to be completed or with relations between the leader and their staff. They assumed that the leadership styles (task oriented or relations oriented) was innate and could not be changed to fit a changing situation. Fiedler *et al.* developed a method of identifying an individual's style by evaluating how an individual would rate their Least Preferred Co-worker (LPC), that is, someone in their team who they disliked most.

If the leader had a high LPC then they were interested more in relations with staff. If they had a low LPC then they were more interested in getting the job done. Fiedler *et al.* went on to identify three dimensions that they believed define the key situational factors that determine how effective a leader will be as follows:

- Leader – member relations: The degree to which the group supports the leader.
- The task structure: The degree to which the task clearly spells out the goals, procedures and specific guidelines.
- Position power of the leader: The degree to which the position gives the leader authority to reward and punish subordinates.

When trying to match leaders to situations Fiedler *et al.* assessed whether individuals were task or relations oriented. This information was then used with the contingency variables to compare the effectiveness of the leader in a range of situations. Task-oriented leaders did better in situations that were either very favourable or very unfavourable. Relationship leaders did better in moderately favourable situations.

Fiedler *et al.*'s findings can be used to match leaders and situations. Once we know an individual's LPC score we can determine in which situations they would be most effective. We would have to analyse the situations using the three contingency dimensions mentioned earlier. Knowing both the situation and the type of leader we can now decide on a course of action. Fiedler *et al.* assume that the leader's style cannot be changed. We can either identify a situation with the wrong leader type and then change them for another leader of the correct type or a second course of action would be to change the factors that influence the situation. In this way we change the situation from one that is unsuitable for a particular type of leader to one that is suitable for them. The practicality of so doing in a busy workplace is, of course, a very arguable one.

4.4.10 Situational leadership

This is a contingency theory of leadership that concentrates on those who follow the leader. The leadership style required depends upon the readiness of the followers because it is their actions that determine effectiveness. Hersey and Blanchard[32] describe situational leadership as being 'based on an interplay among (1) The amount of guidance and direction (task behaviour) a leader gives, (2) The amount of socio-emotional support (relationship behaviour) a leader provides and (3) The readiness level that followers exhibit in performing a specific task, function or objective'.

Hersey and Blanchard used task and relationship behaviour, but further described them as being high or low and then related them to four leadership styles: Telling, Selling, Participating and Delegating. These can be described as follows:

Telling
: (high task–low relationship)
  The leader defines roles clearly and tells people what to do, how to do it, when to do it and where to do it. This style emphasizes directive behaviour.

Selling
: (high task–high relationship)
  In this case the leader's style shows both directive behaviour and supportive behaviour.

Participating
: (low task–high relationship)
  Here the leader and the followers share in the decision making, with the main role of the leader being to facilitate and communicate.

Delegating
: (low task–low relationship)
  In this case the leader provides very little direction or support.

These styles are used together with four different stages of readiness which can be described as follows:

R1 The people are unable and unwilling to take on the responsibility for doing something. They lack competence and confidence.
R2 The people are unable but want to do the necessary job tasks. They are motivated but at the moment they lack the required skills.
R3 The people are able but unwilling to do what the leader wants.
R4 The people have both the ability and willingness to do what is asked of them.

We now look at Figure 4.9 which combines the variables discussed into the situational leadership model. As the followers move from one level of readiness to another, the leader has to change his or her leadership behaviour. Not only do they change the amount of control over followers, they also change the relationship behaviour. As the followers move from inability and unwillingness (R1) to ability and willingness (R4) the leader also changes. They move from having to be very directive, spelling out clearly what is required and closely supervising the individual (Telling), to a case where the individual is left to get on with what is required without too much interference (Delegating).

4.4.11 Group effectiveness, productivity and satisfaction

In order to examine the idea of group effectiveness we need to consider both group productivity which refers to task completion and group satisfaction which concentrates on the internal elements of the group including its individual members. Group productivity and group satisfaction will be measured in different ways. If we think back to what individuals

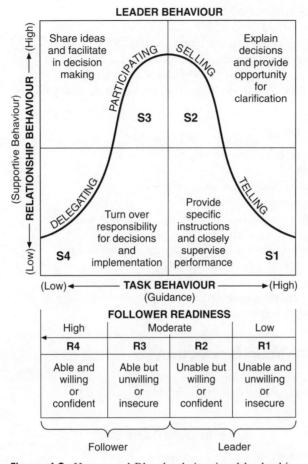

Figure 4.9. Hersey and Blanchard situational leadership.

get from group membership, be it safety or self-worth, then the individual will judge the group's performance on the basis of whether it has satisfied their own need for safety, self-worth, etc. The organization, on the other hand, may judge group success on whether or not the task has been completed. Judging success will depend on your point of view. The goals of management can be different to those of the workforce. Management may be more concerned with getting the task completed at the lowest possible cost in the shortest possible time. The individual may be more concerned with completing a quality piece of work without suffering undue stress.

4.4.12   Effective and ineffective groups

Douglas McGregor[9] listed eleven features which characterized an effective task group from an ineffective one. The following list is adapted from these.

The effective group

- The 'atmosphere' is informal.
- Everyone takes part in discussions.
- Everyone accepts the objective of the group.
- Everyone is allowed to be heard.
- Disagreement exists and the group accepts it.

- Most decisions are reached by consensus.
- Criticism is forthright.
- Ways of working and work are freely discussed.
- Leadership can vary depending on expertise.
- Actions are clearly assigned to individuals and accepted.
- The group will go through self-analysis to determine any problems it has.

The ineffective group

- An indifferent or bored atmosphere.
- A lack of focus.
- Lack of understanding of group objectives.
- People do not listen to each other.
- Conflict is either suppressed or develops into open warfare.
- Actions are agreed by using simple majority voting.
- People are unsure of what they are supposed to be doing.
- The chairperson is the leader at all times.
- Criticism is considered to be embarrassing and personal.
- Personal feelings are suppressed.
- The group's behaviour is not talked about openly.

4.4.13　Influences on group productivity

Kretch *et al.*[33] identified three sets of independent variables that influence group productivity (see Figure 4.10).

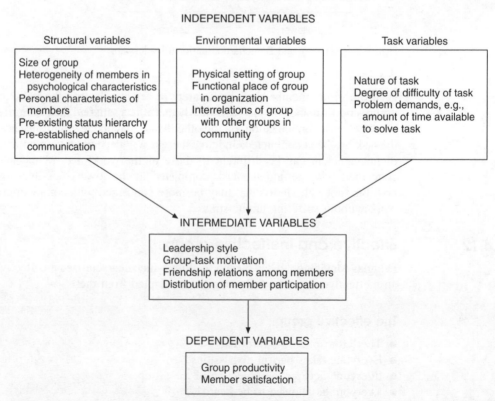

Figure 4.10. The interrelations among the determinants of group effectiveness (from Kretch *et al.*[33]).

If we want to examine the relationship between a number of variables in a situation we need to manipulate one variable in order to see how it impacts on others. If the communication channels are manipulated then this is an independent variable. If we want to know how this affects member satisfaction then this becomes the dependent variable (see Figure 4.11).

In Figure 4.11 the flow of information can directly affect member satisfaction. If that flow of information is dependent on how well people get on, then persons who do not get on so well with others may find themselves starved of information and their satisfaction may fall. If we now look at Figure 4.11 we can identify the links between the independent, intermediate and the dependent variables.

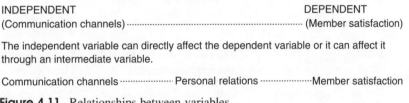

INDEPENDENT   DEPENDENT
(Communication channels) .... (Member satisfaction)

The independent variable can directly affect the dependent variable or it can affect it through an intermediate variable.

Communication channels .... Personal relations ....Member satisfaction

Figure 4.11. Relationships between variables.

Handy[25] highlighted the variables that he considered contributed to group effectiveness namely size, cohesion, member characteristics, individual objectives and roles, clarity of task, the environment, leadership style, process and procedure and finally motivation.

4.4.14 Group decision making and problem solving

Jay Hall[34] examined group decision-making processes and discovered that the effective groups confronted areas where they disagreed as soon as possible in their debate. It would appear that by having a wide range of involvement and opinions in the debate there is a greater opportunity to discover a solution. The ineffective groups looked for areas of agreement as soon as possible by methods such as voting. This meant that they completed the task but did not discover a solution that everyone could agree. This is an opportunity missed because it is likely that by having wider debate other ideas may have been raised that were better than the one on which they agreed. By developing a decision-making process by consensus full use can be made of a much wider range of resources. This can result in original ideas being generated that can be used in areas such as problem solving and resolving conflict. All the parties to the debate can be more likely to support the resulting decision.

4.4.15 Choosing individuals for management teams

Dr Meredith Belbin[35] has been associated with the idea of being able to identify the suitability of certain individuals to play specific roles in management teams. He and his colleagues studied different management teams where they worked in a management college as well as in an industrial environment. The observations they made were used to try to link individual variance with group role behaviour and then relate these to output performance.

The eight major roles, their typical features and the positive qualities are as follows:

Type	Typical features	Positive qualities
Company worker	Conservative, dutiful, predictable	Organizing ability, practical common sense, hard-working, self-discipline
Chairman	Calm, self-confident, controlled	A capacity for treating and welcoming all potential contributors on their merits and without prejudice, a strong sense of objectives
Shaper	Highly strung, dynamic	Drive and a readiness to challenge inertia, ineffectiveness, complacency or self-deception
Plant	Individualistic, serious-minded, unorthodox	Genius, imagination, intellect knowledge
Resource investigator	Extroverted, enthusiastic, curious, communicative	A capacity for contacting people and exploring anything new, an ability to respond to challenge
Monitor evaluator	Sober, unemotional, prudent	Judgement, discretion, hard-headedness
Team worker	Socially orientated, rather mild, sensitive	An ability to respond to people and to situations, and to promote team spirit
Completer/finisher	Painstaking, orderly, conscientious, anxious	A capacity for follow-through, perfectionism

(From Belbin[35] and reproduced with permission.)

Dr Belbin's research[35] identified that:

- It was possible to identify and distinguish eight distinct management styles which were labelled 'team roles'.
- The managers studied tended to adopt one or two of these team roles fairly consistently.
- Which role they became associated with was capable of prediction through the use of psychometric tests.
- When team roles were combined in certain ways, they helped to produce more effective teams.
- Such team roles were not necessarily associated with a person's functional role but the way in which they were combined seemed to affect job success.
- Factors which seemed to contribute to effective management by individuals included correct recognition of own best role, self-awareness of the best contribution they could make to their team or situation and their ability and preparedness to work out their strengths rather than permitting weaknesses to interfere with their performance.

These roles are related to the personality and mental ability of individuals and reflect managerial behaviour in connection with the aims and demands of the manager's job. Since each role contributes to team success a successful balanced team will contain all roles.

It is worth mentioning in more detail each of the eight roles because they can be used to identify potential candidates for team positions, an area of interest for the human resources practitioner.

It is important to note that in order to have regular good results from the team, they should be selected of a mixed nature. However, to select teams like this is very difficult because their equilibrium can be upset easily. Belbin[35] suggests that 'there is a case for forming a group whose members are less specialized in their functions and abilities'. Outgoing, well-disciplined, stable team players with reasonable intelligence can cover all the functions identified and make good teams.

4.4.16   Committees

Committees are formal groups of people who have been set a number of tasks to complete. They have to accept corporate accountability for their actions and vary in function. Some are set up to advise, others to take decisions or investigate past events. Committees need not be formal or even convened on a regular basis. They may meet on a regular or a one-off basis and can be variously described as boards of directors or a planning group.

Committees may be established because it is better to have a range of people with different expertise that can be applied to a problem or task. They can also be used to avoid too much power falling into the hands of one person. On the other hand, they may have to take the decisions collectively due to the reluctance of a single manager to take responsibility.

Committees should consist of enough people for all interested functions to be represented. It also helps if each member is of similar status in order to avoid the more senior member(s) 'pulling rank' and trying to dominate the proceedings.

4.4.17   Composition of committees

It is vitally important to select the right person to chair a committee. The chair or chairperson of a committee must have the confidence and trust of all parties concerned, they must be able to set the tone and introduce the subjects for discussion. It is also important that the chair is familiar with the subject matter and has the eloquence and intellect to be able to integrate ideas. While they are expected to be able to stimulate debate, they must have the ability to keep the discussions on course. This has to be done within the terms of reference that may limit what can or cannot be done by the committee.

The chair needs to be able to encourage discussion and be forceful, but not forceful to the point where they are dominating the proceedings and preventing meaningful discussions taking place. Perhaps one of the most important abilities the chair needs is to sum up clearly and concisely at the end of discussions.

This leads us to think of an agenda for the committee. It is important that before a committee meets all members are issued with an agenda and any supporting written documentation. The issuing of the agenda and documentation should be done early enough to give the individual sufficient time to read and analyse the information.

The recording of committee minutes is a skilled and taxing job and should only be done by competent professional individuals. The minutes need to be used to identify who has agreed to carry out future action and by a specified date. Subsequent follow-up action needs to be itemized for the following meeting.

Committees can succeed or fail, depending on the quality of information they process and so it is essential that they are provided with the most up-to-date accurate information with suggestions or ideas that may help their deliberations.

4.4.18   Procedures

Committees are often accused of being verbose, over-long in their proceedings and too formal. However, they need to have sets of procedures to follow in order to help them run smoothly, to be objective and to treat all people or subjects fairly and equitably. Procedures that often appear bureaucratic to the layperson have a real part to play in committee. One of the most serious is the procedure for voting, because this is where a motion could be won or lost. These rules serve to ensure that everyone gets a fair hearing and that debates are not spoilt by the repressive or aggressive tactics of others. It also prevents criminal activity such as vote rigging.

Committees can be misused by concentrating on relatively unimportant matters that should be the responsibility of managers. Some committee members can see attendance as onerous and make excuses for non-attendance. Most committees must have a minimum number of members attending (a quorum) to proceed with the business.

4.4.19   Advantages of having committees

- They can do more work than individuals working in isolation because they are better organized and have the necessary resources.
- They avoid decisions being taken without full debate because they are able to make a collective assessment based on facts and present a united front against any single powerful figure who may disagree.
- Expertise in committees is wide and varied and brings together people from a variety of backgrounds and results in their collaboration and coordination of effort.
- Committees themselves become a reference point for those working in an organization. They know that information can be obtained from a committee and the same committee can force action where other individuals may be overruled.

4.4.20   Disadvantages of having committees

- The decision making in committees is slower due to the sheer number of interests they may have to take into account. The decisions they do take may be a composite of what different groups or individuals wanted and so the decision itself may not be the best, but it will satisfy most parties.
- The committee can act as a scapegoat for managers who are not prepared to take responsibility. These managers can blame committees when decisions are unpopular.
- Sometimes committees become victims of the 'barrack-room lawyer' mentality and so individuals use the rule book or procedural arrangements to limit the actual amount of time spent on the real subject matter.
- People can easily become committee-types and take over, resulting in the uninitiated leaving it to them with the result that the few can begin to rule the many.
- Committees only exist during their meetings and so if events change between meetings they can find themselves unable to act because it is difficult to get everyone together.

4.4.21   Meetings

Meetings can be a blessing or a curse, depending on your point of view. Some people feel that they distract them from their everyday duties, others just resent the time wasted through attending meetings. On the positive side, though, meetings are an essential element of working life because they enable us to meet with our colleagues to discuss and debate whatever subject we feel is relevant. The fact that in meetings we are sometimes not in control of our own time can make us feel uneasy with others who may seem to have their own hidden agenda for being there. Meetings come in a variety of forms, from those designed to pass on information to those where decisions have to be made.

Meetings can become a way of life for some managers, who seem to thrive on arranging meetings without there being an obvious reason for having them. For this reason we need to think carefully about our reasons for having a meeting in the first place. One thing we should do is to give some thought to the costs of meetings. We should realize that the cost of the meeting is not only its duration but there are other costs such as the time and expense of travelling to and from meetings. We also need to recognize the cost of lost opportunity of managers who attend meetings.

With this in mind we can ask questions such as, 'who needs to be there?' and 'can we sort out the issues in other ways?' This is particularly relevant now, with rapidly developing technology. Could teleconferencing be used? Can substitutes be sent to meetings where the issues are less controversial?

4.4.22 The planning of meetings

Once it has been decided that the meeting is necessary then we need to turn our attention to its planning. The key item we need to concentrate on now is the agenda which should detail what is going to be discussed. The contents of the agenda should be clearly linked to the reason why the meeting has been convened.

The agenda items and their order should be agreed between the chair and the committee clerk in advance. This allows the meeting to follow a clear procedure in an orderly, logical fashion. The agenda should be used to keep control of time, and if the agenda has been circulated before the meeting, then items such as checking the minutes of previous meetings should be done fairly quickly. Less important issues can be used to begin meetings to allow easy resolution and free up more time to debate important items. It is essential that the important items are covered when people are alert and able to concentrate. Time is of the essence in meetings and it cannot be emphasized strongly enough how important it is to set finishing times for meetings. The time management of agenda items is also required to limit discussion and focus debate, although this does not necessarily have to be so rigid that it shortens discussion. There needs to be a flexible approach, but not at the cost of other agenda items.

4.4.23 Chairing meetings

The chair of a meeting needs a clear idea about the reasons for the meeting which should be reflected in the agenda. The chair has a difficult job at times and must ensure there is an equal opportunity for the various parties to discuss and debate their views. Part of the art of chairing the meeting is to keep the debate constructive and prevent it from deteriorating into chaos.

The work of the chair falls into three distinct categories: before, during and after the meeting:

● The pre-meeting work consists of liaison with the administrator or clerk responsible for the distribution of all paperwork, the arranging of agenda items and who will be representing the different parties at the meeting.

● During the meeting. The meeting should be started with a brief statement about why it has been called and how long it should last. The chair needs to keep as far as possible to the agenda items as discussed above. They must ensure that everyone who wants to speak does in fact get a chance to do so. This is easier said than done because people can try to dominate and force through their own agenda. In these situations the chair has to ensure that each person, where possible, gets an equal and fair hearing.

To assist in the understanding of what is happening the chair should also take some time to periodically summarize discussions and clarify the situation at regular intervals. It is the chair's responsibility to decide on a course of action for each item as they are discussed. This needs to be done with the agreement of all parties concerned. Once the discussions are complete it is not unusual (in fact it is probably a good idea), for a chair to confirm who has been agreed the task and when it will be completed. Finally, the chair has to close the meeting and this sometimes has to be done diplomatically because some people try to continue discussions beyond their allotted time.

- After the meeting, the minutes of the current meeting that will need to be agreed at the next meeting need to be checked and agreed by the chair with whoever has taken them. The chair should instruct that they are distributed to the parties concerned prior to the next meeting.

4.4.24   Those who take part in meetings

Meetings are social events, when people get together to discuss issues in which they should all have a common interest. Those who attend meetings should think about the social skills required to contribute to the discussions. Sometimes the ideas that are being discussed may be complex or new. Even if members do not fully understand what is being discussed, they should show some interest even though it may only be out of politeness. To listen to others is an art in itself and it can be most encouraging for the speaker. Good listening means checking with the speaker that what they have said has been understood correctly.

One of the reasons you may have been asked to attend a meeting is for your expertise or advice. You should try to keep your contributions to the meeting as impersonal as possible, always putting views via the chair.

Meetings can be about the use of social skills to build up allegiances, so you need to recognize who is sympathetic to your point of view and who is not. This will allow you to focus your efforts on those who are unsure. It is important to arrive at the meeting well prepared, with all the information you think may be necessary and relevant to support your case. If you have done your preparation and know your facts, your arguments will be so much more persuasive or easier to defend.

Conventional wisdom

Meredith Belbin, *People Management*, 20 November 1997

The Inuit Eskimos are reputed to have 22 different words for snow, while Gaelic speakers can choose between 17 words for mist. If this is true, the general implication is clear: language develops to express the focal interests of its users.

English offers an enormous vocabulary. Its Saxon and Norman origins alone have led to many duplicate words for particular objects or concepts, quite apart from all the terms imported from other languages. This leaves us with vast resources to express almost anything we want to say – or so I always supposed. In fact, the most common response to a request to speak to a named person at work is: 'He/she is in a meeting'.

What sort of meeting? Does this mean that one person is talking to another? Are several people engaged in close conversation in an office? Is a meeting in progress in a boardroom? Is a person listening to a general address, and could they be easily extracted if necessary? 'Meeting' is an indefinite word that could signify a gathering of any number of people, spontaneous or planned, formal or informal, arranged with a specific end in view or for a general exchange of information.

But does this semantic vagueness really matter? Recent evidence suggests that it does, since people who attend meetings rate their usefulness according to a set of recognisable parameters. If managers took account of these, good meetings could be arranged and poor ones avoided.

We developed the Workset scheme to help companies come to grips with the problem. This colour-coded system for describing different types of work was first described in *People Management* earlier this year ('True colours', 6 March).

Workset contains seven categories, each labelled with a different colour. These are used by employees to indicate how their time is being spent. One of the categories is 'pink work', which is used to describe the time that, in the jobholder's opinion, is being wasted through problems such as obsolete procedures, poor planning and interruptions. Among executives, the largest single category of pink work has been found to be time spent in meetings.

For example, during one training seminar for Workset facilitators, a senior administrator in the public sector said that he spent much of his day attending meetings ostensibly, in the words of his job description, 'to report to and advise the chief executive'. The administrator classified this as pink work. He told the chief executive: 'You receive the minutes anyway and you seldom take my advice.'

'Very well,' the chief executive replied. 'Let's cut it out.' Freed from routine meetings, the administrator was able to spend more time on other duties, increasing the volume of useful work he accomplished by one-third.

It would of course be too simple to dismiss the general value of meetings. But the overriding issues should be: what principles should underlie the formation of meetings and who should attend them?

One person's useful meeting is another's waste of time. Typically, the people who classified their meetings as pink work were those who did not speak or who were not consulted. If there is a general pattern, it is that the larger the meeting, the more pink work figures. This is to some extent inevitable, since larger meetings give less scope for individual contributions.

Although size seems to be the most important factor governing the usefulness of meetings, other factors also affect behaviour, such as differences in seniority, how far functional roles determine and define the part an individual plays, and whether there are established structures for conducting the meeting.

But many of these factors operate as dependent, rather than independent, variables. For example, in large meetings seniority seems to have a major effect on the roles that

OVERVIEW OF MEETINGS AND BEHAVIOUR

Code Description	Likely size	Predominant behaviour	Opportunities	Risks
SM1 Sub-meeting	<4	green	white	
TM1 Informal teams	selected 4–5	orange	white	
TM2 Semi-formal teams	selected 5–6		orange	
GM1 Semi-structured groups	6–8	green/orange, yellow		
GM2 Structured group	8–10	yellow		pink
FM1 Formal and structured	10–12	blue		pink
FM2 Formal and seniority driven	12–20	yellow	white	pink
MM Mass address	>20	yellow		pink
UM1 Unstructured and new	uncertain			pink, yellow versus yellow
UM2 Collapsed structures	uncertain		orange	pink

individuals adopt. But when a small number of people get together, seniority becomes less important and personal relationships become the governing factor.

Taking into account the variety of meetings and the distinctive types of behaviour that they generate, there is clearly a case for developing a standard working vocabulary. Size is a good starting point for grouping meetings. It acts as a hub to which other features attach themselves. But unstructured meetings can prove the exception, because their lack of constant elements puts them in a class of their own. I have come up with the following groupings.

Sub-meetings (SMs)

When two or three people meet, their discussion often takes the form of a chat. There is seldom a fixed agenda and there are few constraints on how business is conducted. Calling it a meeting seems almost grandiose. So the term 'sub-meeting' is preferred. SMs are intensive and depend heavily on interpersonal relationships. While they allow a great deal of green work (tasks that vary according to the response of others), the conditions also encourage white work (new and creative undertakings).

Team meetings (TMs)

The term 'team' has its roots in sport. This is significant, because members of sports teams have a fixed position and have to be selected – professional footballers, for instance, cannot count on being selected for every match. Similarly, in business there is an important difference in effectiveness between smaller groups consisting of selected 'players' and larger unplanned groups. A large team is virtually an oxymoron: additional members add nothing to performance and get in the way of real progress.

The smaller the team, the more likely it is that selection has played a part in getting the desired balance. In the classical, perfectly balanced TM1, there are individual and shared roles, but no leaders. Members choose informally the roles they will adopt, are versatile and are often interchangeable.

In the slightly larger TM2, some structure guarantees ordered working. For instance, a chairperson may be appointed from the outside or elected by the team. In either case, the effect is to limit the roles available to others. Despite this, most TMs give opportunities for interaction and so encourage interactive tasks (green work) and shared responsibility (orange work).

Group meetings (GMs)

Unlike team meetings, these occur where membership of a group confers automatic membership of the team. In other words, the meeting is synonymous with the collective gathering of the group. Departmental meetings fall into this category, as do committee and other meetings where representatives have an automatic right to be present.

By their nature, group meetings are larger than team meetings. The more intimate GM1 leaves some room for members to choose their own roles, whereas roles in the larger GM2 are determined by occupation and seniority. Invariably, the manager takes the lead and maintains a strong grip on all yellow work (personal responsibility for meeting an objective).

Formal meetings (FMs)

Meetings that extend beyond the working group may contain members who rarely see each other. These raise issues of status relationships, as seniority may not be clear cut.

In FM1s, the appointment of officers facilitates progress and reduces conflict. They perform set duties with plenty of blue work (tasks carried out to a prescribed standard), while rules govern the way that the meeting is conducted.

The problem is that proceedings can be slow. That risk grows with even larger meetings, but is averted by the form of an FM2. Here, progress is accelerated by the presence of a senior manager who can overrule others, if necessary. The enhanced role of the chairperson offsets the need for officers and reduces opportunities for other contributions. Although this can increase the amount of pink work, an enterprising member who succeeds in catching the leader's eye can achieve creative white work, which could also put them in line for promotion.

Mass meetings (MMs)

Some meetings are too large for interpersonal relationships. These are seldom about people conferring or exchanging information. They tend to be assemblies where someone is addressing an audience. Even if the MM fails to reach its ideal size, it does not change things, since the address is not designed to invite comment.

Unstructured meetings (UMs)

If FMs are at one end of a spectrum, UMs are at other meetings, because their form does not have a significant size dimension. UMs are assemblies without a structure and they fall into two types.

With the UM1, the subject is new, which is why the meeting is being convened. As a consequence, attendance remains uncertain and a structure has not had time to form. Here, pink work is at its pinkest.

Such a meeting needs to be distinguished from the UM2, which commonly grows out of the ashes of an FM1 and therefore contains a ghost of a structure. This happens when previous officers have resigned or organisations have lapsed, yet a body of rules, traditions and, perhaps, assets still exist. They present an opportunity for ambitious people to operate in cabals and give scope for orange work.

Meetings have disadvantages. They consume time and money and can become sources of boundless frustration. But they also have advantages. Specific types of meetings serve particular purposes and the world cannot do without them.

SMs are suited for acts of spontaneous creation. For instance, prime examples of intrapreneurial enterprise have resulted from a fortuitous meeting between three people in a canteen. TM1s have more to do with organised creativity, while TM2s are the standard models for effective project work. GM1s are about shared planning and are well suited to handling important issues of detail. GM2s are concerned with direction and are the recognised vehicle for leadership in the working group.

FM1s focus on co-ordination across functional boundaries, while FM2s can project central goals and the need to counter fragmented effort. MMs typically contain an announcement of unusual importance, but otherwise they are intended to be inspirational. Finally, UMs are spontaneous gatherings to establish or restore a form of organisation.

In an ideal world, each type of meeting would comprise an ideal number of people meeting for the ideal period. Realistically, other factors always distort the situation. Attending a meeting may allow escape from the dull office routine, open up social connections and enhance personal status in the organisation. People are attracted to meetings like bees to honey. But where the numbers invited, or self-invited, exceed the desired figure, effectiveness is compromised.

The ideal model is worth considering. Size should be seen as critical to purpose and outcomes. It should be controlled wherever possible. Another lesson is to avoid mixing types of meeting as far as possible. All too often, laziness or expediency results in meetings becoming heterogeneous and too long. Loss of focus increases pink work and lowers morale.

If managers treat meetings as a subject that can add to corporate learning, they will do away forever with the image of 'meetings, bloody meetings'.

Reproduced with permission of Dr Meredith Belbin of Belbin Associates, 3–4 Bennell Court, West St., Comberton, Cambs., CB3 7DS.

4.4.25   Participants feeding back

Once meetings are over you will need to report back to your manager or staff about what has happened and you must have a clear understanding about what has been agreed because any action they take will depend on your advice.

Summary

To briefly summarize this section you can now appreciate why individuals and organizations have an interest in belonging to and having groups. Groups are not simple but are dependent on a wide number of variables for their successful operation. You have examined how they form and how we need to be aware of their design if we are going to have a successful team.

You have also looked at committees and meetings, how they operate and how they need to be planned and carefully directed by a chairperson.

Case study

Blue skies

Franz Bugler was a man with a mission. He had worked successfuly as a senior manager at Disneyworld for ten years and now at the age of 35 he wanted to branch out on his own. Together with his wife Claudia and with financial backing from a group of European banks they had purchased a poorly performing holiday complex on the south coast of Malta.

Claudia had been an international skier who also worked for a number of French skiing companies setting up self-catering ski resorts in the French Alps. Franz's big idea was to use the popularity of football following the success of the 2002 World Cup and create a family holiday with a sports theme. The sports would be provided at differing levels of ability from the keen amateur to the complete novice. Not all sports would be offered, only rugby, football, swimming, water skiing and tennis. Franz decided to call his venture, Blue Skies to reflect his vision of sport being enjoyed under a beautiful Mediterranean sky. Franz believed that by offering sports coaching for all ages and abilities together with access to a large beach area would mean that there was something for all members of the family to do.

Franz and Claudia together planned their venture in the finest detail. They recruited coaching and managerial staff from their native Austria and France where they chose people who she had worked with in the ski resorts. Local Maltese staff were recruited to provide catering and domestic support although the chefs in charge were either Austrian or French. Franz was the kind of manager who gave orders and expected them to be carried out to the letter while Claudia's experience in France meant she had a more mellow approach.

After extensive refurbishment Blue Skies opened to holidaymakers and during its first year things went relatively smoothly. The majority of guests were drawn from Austria and France.

As part of their meticulous approach Franz and Claudia put in place strict procedures for managers to follow. They then left the managers to carry out the day-to-day work of running the complex while they attended to their other business interests in the USA, Austria and France.

Staff were organized into groups based around the sports instruction they were delivering or the duties they were performing. The sports instructors saw themselves as the most important group. Groups often consisted of just one nationality, Austrian, French or Maltese, although there was some mixing of the various nationalities. However, when this happened, subgroups seemed to form within the main group. Group membership tended to be of a transient nature because they often consisted of young people who would work for a few weeks and then move on, leaving behind a nucleus of workers who knew each other well. Despite having some considerable experience, group members were not encouraged to voice their opinions; they were told that their targets were all-important and that is what they should concentrate on and follow their written procedures.

This led staff to become bored, have low motivation and caused conflict to arise among group members who had different views of what was expected of them.

It was in year two, during a period when Franz and Claudia were absent in Austria, that problems began to arise. Two groups of holidaymakers clashed over the availability of some of the sports facilities, caused by a series of staff misunderstandings. Both groups claimed they had booked the facilities and staff were unable to deal with the situation and a scuffle broke out. The situation wasn't helped by the fact that the staff themselves began to argue about whose fault it was. The situation escalated, people were injured, property was damaged and the police were called. They restored order and threatened the complex with closure if the situation reoccurred.

Some staff felt the situation had been inevitable and said they had been surprised that something as serious as this hadn't happened before. They got together in their various national groupings and agreed that they weren't prepared to risk physical injury because of what they saw as management failings. Many agreed to go on strike and despite the pleading of their managers they refused to work until Franz and Claudia returned to sort things out. Franz and Claudia were notified and returned to a hastily convened meeting of their senior managers to try to determine what had gone wrong.

Question

In a group of two or three people examine this case and suggest why you think this situation might have occurred and what can be done to prevent its recurrence.

Feedback

There are a number of areas we could use to suggest reasons for the events outlined in the case. We could look at the leadership of Franz and Claudia. Suggested roles by Mintzberg, include Leadership, Monitor and Disturbance handler.

Their leadership leaves something to be desired because they seem to want to carry it out by writing instructions for others to follow plus they do not seem to be totally focused on Blue Skies as an organization. This reflects on what they see as a priority. It staff think that this organization isn't a priority for the boss then why should it be a priority for them?

In the monitor role they should have their finger on the pulse of the organization and be aware of what is happening even if it means listening to what is being said on the grapevine.

This would give them an idea of what staff are thinking and the problems they are facing. They don't seem to be doing this because staff seem to be saying they can see these situations coming but the managers can't.

When they were needed in the disturbance handler role they were absent and the managers they had delegated to were not able to deal with the situation. Again this is an indication of their leadership styles. When they write everything down for the managers then if anything falls outside of those procedures the managers don't seem to have the confidence to act on their own and use their initiative.

This leads us to the subject of delegation. If we choose to delegate then we must choose the right person and that person must have the opportunity to develop in the role. Their activities must be monitored and controlled just in case too much has been delegated and the individual is unable to cope. In this case it seems that there has been a great deal of delegation very quickly but in this particular crisis the managers were unable to cope.

Management control is also an important issue that may have played a part. Direct observation can be very important and by walking about the complex managers will learn a great deal about what is going on. However, if management control is carried out solely through written procedures then individuals can grow to resent them and become rigid in how they approach their work.

There appears to have been a breakdown in communications in this organization. This is not surprising given the different nationalities and cultures that are being brought together in one organization as well as the reliance on written instructions and a formal approach to communication.

This can also be seen in the approach to group work. The groups seem to be too temporary and because of this they don't seem to be able to go through the full process of forming, storming, norming and adjourning. These groups may well be ineffective especially if they feel they can't speak out, they lack focus and they have low motivation.

Suggested approaches for the future would be for Franz and Claudia to examine their leadership roles and where their priorities lie. There are a range of approaches to leadership and they might want to consider a number of options before deciding which is best for them and an organization like Blue Skies. They need also to consider carefully their policy of delegation. They must choose carefully who to delegate to and then make sure they receive the correct support, are monitored carefully and that the communications between them are excellent.

Communications need to be extended from the formal written format to the informal. There is a range of ways to communicate from team briefings to reports. As many forms of communication as possible should be used especially in organizations where there is the possibility that the message may be distorted and misunderstood, something that has evidently happened at Blue Skies.

Groups at Blue Skies need attention and in order to make them effective it is important to try to keep the groups together so that they have time to bond and go through the whole process of development. This may mean looking at what training is being given and examining why people are leaving after a few weeks. We may also need to consider whether the groups are actually working by asking if group productivity and member satisfaction are acceptable. This may take us back to questions about group leadership, motivation and personal relationships within the groups themselves.

In brief

At the beginning of this chapter we looked at how management has been viewed over the years. Now we can begin to appreciate how complex is the work of a manager. We know that managers have a variety of activities they must carry out and that in order to do them they need to use their staff effectively and efficiently. This involves the management of the time which the staff have at their disposal through the prioritization and organization of work. Managers have to understand the behaviour of their staff as individuals and in groups. They need to be able to communicate effectively and also to work as part of group. In this chapter we have examined the interrelationships between all these factors.

Examination questions for this chapter are given in Appendix 2.

References

1 Bishop, M. (2003) Chief Executive, The Shaftesbury Society.
2 Drucker, P. (1989) *The New Realities*. Mandarin.
3 Fayol, H. (1949) *General and Industrial Administration* (ed. Storrs, C.). Pitman.
4 Taylor, F. W. (1947) *Scientific Management*. Harper and Row.
5 Gullick, L. (1937) *Notes on the Theory of Organisations. Papers on the Science of Administration*. Columbia University Press.
6 Roethlisberger, F. J. and Dickson, W. J. (1964) *Management and the Worker*. Wiley.
7 Maslow, A. (1943) A theory of human motivation. *Psychological Review*.
8 Herzberg, F. (1959) *The Motivation to Work*. Chapman & Hall.
9 McGregor, D. (1985) *The Human Side of Enterprise* (25th anniversary edition). McGraw-Hill.
10 Likert, R. (1961) *New Patterns of Management*. McGraw-Hill.
11 Trist, E. L. and Bamforth, K. W. (1963) *Organisational Choice*. Tavistock.
12 Stewart, R. (1988) *Managers and their Jobs*. Macmillan.
13 Mintzberg, H. (1973) *The Nature of Managerial Work*. Prentice Hall.
14 Simpson, P. (2002) *Personnel Today*, Sept 02.
15 Safeway article (2002) *Personnel Today*, Aug 02.
16 Adair, J. (1982) *Effective Time Management*. Pan Books.
17 Armstrong, M. (1998) *Personnel Management Practice*. Kogan Page.
18 Cole, G. A. (1993) *Management Theory and Practice*. DP Publications.
19 Brech, E. F. L. *et al.* (1975) *The Principles and Practices of Management*. Longman.
20 Reade, Q. (2002) *Personnel Today*, Nov 02.
21 Berlo, D. K. (1960) *The Process of Communication*. Holt, Rinehart and Winston.
22 Price Waterhouse Coopers (2002) Case study. *Personnel Today*, Sept 02.
23 Reade, Q. (2002) *Personnel Today*, Sept 02.
24 Reade, Q. (2002) *Personnel Today*, July 02.
25 Handy, C. (1985) *Understanding Organisations* (3rd edn). Penguin Books.
26 Buchanan, D. and Huczynski, A. (1985) *Organisational Behaviour*. Prentice Hall.
27 Bales, R. (1950) *Interaction Process Analysis*. Addison-Wesley.
28 Baron, R. A. and Greenburg, J. (1990) *Behaviour in Organisations*. Allyn and Bacon.
29 Homans, G. (1951) *The Human Group*. Routledge and Kegan Paul.
30 Tuckman, B. and Jensen, N. (1977) Stages of small group development revisited. *Group Organisational Studies*, **2**.
31 Fiedler, F., Chalmers, M. and Mahar, L. (1977) *Improving Leadership Effectiveness: The Leadership Match Concept*. Wiley.
32 Hersey, P. and Blanchard, K. (1988) *Management of Organisational Behaviour* (5th edn). Prentice Hall.
33 Kretch, D., Crutchfield, R. S. and Balachey, C. L. (1962) *The Individual in Society*. McGraw-Hill.
34 Hall, J. (1971) Decisions, decisions, decisions. *Psychology Today*.
35 Belbin, M. (1981) *Management Teams: Why they succeed or fail*. Butterworth-Heinemann.

Further reading

Cole, G. A. (2000) *Management: Theory and Practice* (5th edition). Continuum.
Cope, M. (2003) *Personal Networking – How to Make Your Connections Count*. Financial Times/ Prentice Hall.
Dawson, A. G. (1991) *The Art of Practical Management*. Allen Accountancy.

Dobson, P. and Starkey, K. (1993) *The Strategic Management Blueprint*. Blackwell.

Drucker, P. (1999) *Management Challenges for the 21st Century*. Butterworth-Heinemann.

Evenden, R. and Anderson, G. (1992) *Management Skills. Making the most of people*. Addison-Wesley.

Gillespie, R. (1991) *Manufacturing Knowledge: A History of the Hawthorne Experiments*. Cambridge University Press.

Goodworth, C. T. (1986) *Effective Delegation*. Random House Business Books.

Johnson, G. and Scholes, K. (2001) *Exploring Corporate Strategy*. Financial Times/Prentice Hall.

Mitchell Stewart, A. (1994) *Empowering People*. Financial Times/Prentice Hall.

Mullins, L. J. (2001) *Management and Organizational Behaviour* (6th edition). Prentice Hall.

Robbins, S. P. (2001) *Management* (7th edition). Prentice Hall.

Stanton, N. (1986) *What Do You Mean 'Communication'?* Pan Breakthrough Books.

Web-site addresses

Confederation of British Industry: http://www.cbi.org.uk
Department of Trade and Industry: http://www.dti.gov.uk
Institute for Learning and Research Technology – University of Bristol: http://www.bized.ac.uk/
Institute of Management: http://www.inst-mgt.org.uk

5　The work organization

Organizations are not islands that can live unto themselves, ignoring the world around them. They are shaped by their environment and also help to shape it.

Rosemary Stewart[1]

Chapter objectives

In this chapter you will:

- Examine what is meant by health and safety at work and the role that Human Resources Management plays in ensuring that it is carried out.
- Discover what is meant by functional departments and what they do and
- Develop an understanding of how organizations are structured

Case study

Leon is a qualified baker (and football fan) who noticed five years ago how popular pies and Cornish pasties were as snacks for football fans. Leon thought 'would it be possible to also sell the patties and other delicacies that he enjoyed making?' to fans. This he felt was a great business opportunity. He would bake and retail these delicacies and create for himself a niche market. Like many small businesses initially the going was tough but through hard work and support from family and friends the business grew. Its success was so great that from fairly humble beginnings of cooking in the kitchen at home and selling outside football grounds from a van the business boomed to the point where he was employing around 40 people mostly in non-managerial roles. He also moved the business to larger premises.

Leon was the driving force behind the success and was active in all aspects of the business from cooking to sales and distribution. He took it upon himself to take the roles of financial controller, marketing manager and played a part in overseeing production.

Recently he has made a breakthrough by winning a contract with a major supermarket, which will mean extra work for everyone. He knows this will mean changing his approach and has come to you for advice.

Feedback

This is a problem many small businesses face as they expand. Among other things, Leon needs to consider how to structure his organization. In the past he has taken responsibility for all the main functions, finance and production and now he needs to recruit/promote individuals to take charge of these roles. He could consider a structure based on having functional departments like marketing and production or he could structure the organization along product lines. In either case he will need to employ others to head these departments but retain overall control by taking the role of managing director.

Leon also needs to be aware of other dangers his employees may encounter due to increased workloads, namely the temptation to cut corners and breach health and safety legislation. These and other issues will be discussed in this chapter.

Chapter introduction

As Rosemary Stewart implies in her quote at the start of this chapter, organizations are not immune from the environment that surrounds them. This includes not only the people who work in them but also their customers, those who live in the same vicinity as the organization and any other member of society whom it affects. This means that organizations have to respond to the changing mood and norms of society. When the populace has concerns about environmental issues, health and safety, methods of work or employment levels this will impact on the organization. In this chapter we will look at some of those issues through an examination of the health and safety responsibilities of organizations. We will also examine the work of the functional departments and the structures of the organizations themselves to see how the wider environment has an effect on them.

5.1   The role of human resources management and health and safety law

Protecting people from the hazards of their work is an unremitting task for all active trade unionists. It requires dedication, patience, skill, determination – as well as detailed knowledge of workplace hazards and how to overcome them. But it is also one of the most worthwhile tasks that any trade union member can undertake. For no one should ever forget the sense of anger, frustration and despair that follows a futile accident or disease at work which could have been prevented by taking simple precautions.

Norman Willis, former TUC General Secretary[2]

Section objectives

In this section you will:

● Examine the role human resources management has to play in health and safety at work
● Examine some of the European and UK health and safety legislation and
● Look at how we can introduce health and safety policies.

5.1.1   Introduction

Both managers and employees need to be aware of the necessity of a safe working environment for all. Managers especially have a responsibility as part of their management function to promote safe working methods. However, like so many issues in business, health and safety is also affected by external pressures such as social, political, economic and technological factors. Employees and trades unions are aware of how dangerous a workplace can be and they and society as a whole can put pressure on organizations and government to do something about unsafe working practices. Sometimes this can be as a result of the outcry following disasters like the Potters Bar Railway Station crash on 10th May 2002 where seven lives were last and many were injured. The public put pressure on governments to introduce legislation to protect people at work and to protect the public generally when they use the services or products supplied by employers. Economic factors

Figure 5.1. How human resource management can influence health and safety.

influence health and safety when precautions are not taken because they are deemed to be too expensive or economies are made to save time and allow employers to make more profit or reduce expenditure. Finally, the issue of technology and its rapid development is critical. As technology advances, more pressure is put on workers to change their working methods without any real understanding of the impact these might have on their physical and mental well-being. The current debate about the lack of safety of mobile phones is a case in point. It is in this arena that the manager has to come to terms with their obligation to health and safety issues.

How does the human resource management impact on health and safety as an issue? It can be seen from Figure 5.1 that human resource management has a number of different ways that it can impact on health and safety issues. The following is a brief outline of each area of impact.

Recruitment

By paying close attention to the people who are recruited organizations can reduce the risk of health and safety being compromised. It may be possible to identify individuals who are less likely to break rules or, in particular, take unnecessary risks. It may also be that an organization develops a reputation for being a good, safe employer and this in turn will attract the type of candidate who is more attuned to working in such an environment. For example, the construction industry pays close attention to its safety record insisting that all employees (except Sikhs who are exempt by statute) wear hard hats in areas where it is clearly indicated that they must do so. The advice being no hats, no boots, no job. In this way some construction companies develop a reputation for providing a safe working environment.

Philosophy of human resource management

Having a philosophy that puts the person at the centre of the organization's operational focus will mean that issues such as individual employee health, safety and welfare become a central part of management philosophy. This should help to convey the message throughout the organization that the organization cares for its employees in this way.

Human resource planning

The planning of work is an ideal opportunity to critically examine existing working methods. It is then possible and, indeed, advisable for the employer at the time they design new working methods to build in safe working practices. This will (hopefully) focus attention on and encourage safe working practices to be adopted.

Employee relations

The HR manager has a dual role to play: on the one hand, it can help foster good industrial relations by emphasizing to the workforce the positive contribution health and safety makes. However, on the other, it may have to represent the employer at employment tribunals or in court when issues of health and safety are pursued to seek a legal remedy. The HR manager must also be aware of the need to develop a good working relationship with any recognized trade unions who represent employees in order to get their full support.

Appraisal

Knowledge of current health and safety issues and practice can be built into the appraisal process. If a gap in the appraisees' knowledge is detected then managers can recommend an appropriate course of training.

Legislation

Due to the fact that there is a great deal of health and safety legislation it is necessary for the HR manager to keep abreast of the legislation. The key reason for this is that invariably other managers will expect the HR manager to advise on health and safety issues that affect the organization as well as represent the organization when dealing with external agencies. However, you will note that under the Management of Health and Safety at Work Regulations 1992 the organization must appoint a 'competent person'.

Training

It is the role of the HR manager to raise awareness of health and safety issues for all staff. Because of their unique position (access to senior management, legal documents, new data and training) the HR manager can ensure that health and safety is taken seriously and with the support of senior management ensure that everyone knows his or her responsibilities.

5.1.2   Health and safety law in the United Kingdom

It is not the intention of this book to try to cover every aspect of health and safety legislation for it is very extensive, but to give the reader an idea of its origins and its breadth and depth.

Health and safety law in the UK is a mixture of statutory and common law, which may give rise to both criminal and civil actions. Statutory law has been enlarged very considerably over the past 20 years and more recently through the influence of the European Union and its directives. Several statutory regulations such as the offshore installations (Safety Representatives and Safety Committees) Regulations 1989 have been introduced because of widely publicized national disasters, like when the *Piper Alpha* oil-drilling platform was ravaged by fire in 1987 with the loss of 167 lives. The first health and safety laws in the UK were introduced in the early Victorian era to combat safety risks in factories which employed children as young as 5 years. Together with the common law these two sources provided the mainstay of the country's health and safety law until the 1960s. The biggest development of the twentieth century was undoubtedly the introduction of the Health and Safety at Work Act 1974 and Regulations made under it.

5.1.3   Common law duty

Under common law there are obligations both for employer and employee. The following are a brief résumé of them:

- An employer is obliged to take such steps as are **reasonably** necessary to ensure the safety of their employees. This can be done in a number of different ways:
  (i)   By providing a safe place of work, safely constructed and maintained.
  (ii)   Providing a safe means of access to a place of work, for example a footpath.
  (iii)   Providing safe systems of work – this includes staffing, equipment and supervision.
  (iv)   Providing adequate and safe equipment and materials including clothing.
  (v)   Employing competent fellow-workers.
  (vi)   Protecting employees from injury including injury from criminals.
- Employees' duties: Every employee while at work has the duty:
  (i)   To take reasonable care for the health and safety of 'himself' and of other persons who may be affected by 'his' acts or omissions at work and
  (ii)   To cooperate with his employer, in respect of compliance with the law.
- In addition, the employer must:
  (i)   Provide compulsory insurance against liability. The Employers' Liability (Compulsory Insurance) Act 1969 (as amended by the 1998 Regulations) obliges every employer carrying on a business in Great Britain to maintain insurance against liability for bodily injury or disease sustained by employees in the course of their employment.
  (ii)   Take care of employees and visitors under the Occupiers Liability Acts 1957/1984.
  (iii)   Have a vicarious liability for acts of employees. An employer is vicariously liable for the acts of their employee if they are committed in the course of the employee's employment. Thus, if a van delivery driver drives negligently while in the normal course of his duties and causes an accident his employer is held liable for the damage or injury resulting.

5.1.4   Health and safety statutes

- The Factories Act 1961
- The Offices, Shops and Railway Premises Act 1963

These are two examples of health and safety statutes but have largely been superseded by the regulations made under the Health and Safety at Work Act 1974 (particularly regulations emanating from directives of the European Union).

5.1.5   The Health and Safety at Work Act 1974 (HSWA)

The original HSWA itself does not specify details of prescribed behaviour or penalties but does lay down a framework on which detailed regulations are built. The legislation permits the Secretary of State to introduce regulations concerning specific health and safety issues quickly. An example is the Control of Substances Hazardous to Health (COSHH) Regulations in 1988 (as amended in 1999). Because the HSWA is an 'enabling' statute, it enables the government to introduce secondary legislation where health and safety matters must be legislated for quickly.

5.1.6   The Health and Safety Commission

The Commission is made up of both employer and employee representatives and third parties who are experts in their field (see Figure 5.2). The Executive comprises three of the

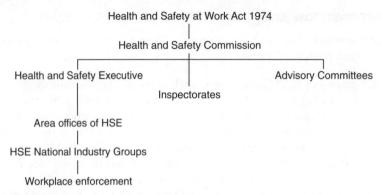

Figure 5.2. The structure of the Health and Safety Commission.

Commission's appointees approved by the Secretary of State for Education and Employment. The Commission's chief function is to advise and make suggestions for the implementation of the provisions of the HSWA.

The H&S Executive

The Executive enforces the HSAW and consists of a number of departments, for example the Factories Inspectorate and the Agriculture Health and Safety Inspectorate.

Powers of the Executive

The Commission working through the Executive tries to operate on the basis of using powers of persuasion first. However, it has the power to act to ensure adherence to health and safety law. The following detail some of the powers of the Commission and the Executive:

- Inquiries: The Commission can authorize investigation on any accident, occurrence, situation or other matter that it thinks is necessary to investigate.
- Codes of Practice: The Commission is empowered by the HSWA to approve and issue Codes of Practice under the Act or to complement regulations introduced under the Act (for example, an employer giving a reasonable amount of paid time off for the training of safety representatives).
- Enforcement: The Executive and local authorities are responsible for the enforcement of the Act.

5.1.7   Powers of inspectors

Every enforcing authority has the power to appoint inspectors. An inspector has many powers to enforce the statutory provisions for which their enforcing authority has responsibility. These include:

- The issuing of Improvement Notices to require an individual to remedy a situation.
- The issuing of Prohibition Notices (for example, to prevent persons using dangerous machinery). An appeal against these can be made to the County Court.
- In more serious cases the inspector can begin criminal proceedings against an offender.

5.1.8   Examples of regulations made under the HSWA

- Reporting/recording accidents: The Reporting of Injuries, Diseases and Dangerous Occurrences Regulations, 1995 (replaces the 1985 Regulations).
- First-Aid Regulations 1981.
- Control of Substances Hazardous to Health Regulations 1988 (COSHH) (as amended in 1999).
- The Fire Precautions Act (1971) (FPA) and the Fire Safety and Safety of Places of Sport Act (1987) (as amended in 1995).
- The Health and Safety (Consultation with Employees) Regulations 1996.

5.1.9   Health and safety legislation derived from European directives

Twenty-two original directives were proposed in 1992 and more have been proposed under the Social Chapter.

Nearly all European health and safety law is brought into effect in the UK through Regulations made under the HSWA. EU legislation establishes an approach to health and safety that covers the creation of 'systems' to carry out risk assessment and give high priority to safety as well as communication and consultation with trade unions and employee representatives (Health and Safety (Consultation with Employees) Regulations 1996). The aim is to improve safety, not simply to maintain the status quo.

5.1.10   European strategy for health and safety

Recently the European Commission has set out its latest strategy for health and safety. The following article[3] is reprinted with permission from the *Health and Safety Bulletin*.

Commission unveils safety strategy

The European Commission has finally published its 'strategy' for improving health and safety in the Union over the next five years.[1] Despite claiming three 'novel features' (see box), the plan is similar to its safety work programme for 1996–2000 (*Eurosafety* 10, p.2) and social action programme for 1998–2000 (HSB 269 p.11). The new strategy is long on description, short on firm or new ideas for action, and often impenetrable in presentation and language. Nevertheless, it is an important document, coming, as it does, from the body that has reshaped the legislative infrastructure of all member states over the past decade.

European injury rates, claims the Commission, indicate 'that the preventive approach set out in Community Directives has not yet been fully understood and taken on board by the various players, nor applied effectively on the ground'. The strategy therefore sets out eight objectives:

- A reduction in occupational accidents and illnesses: this would involve quantified objectives – something the UK is already pursuing with its 10-year *Revitalising health and safety* targets (HSB 290 p.17).
- Ensuring that gender is in the 'mainstream' of risk evaluation, preventive measures and compensation arrangements.
- Prevention of social risks: the Commission feels that stress, harassment, depression, anxiety, and alcohol and drug dependence should be the subject both of specific measures and part of a holistic approach to healthcare.
- Enhanced prevention of occupational illness, with priority given to asbestos, hearing loss and musculoskeletal problems.

- Taking account of demographic changes.
- Taking account of changes in the form of employment, work organisation and working time: the Commission reports increased risks for workers who are on temporary contracts, have been with an employer for only a short time, and who work part-time or at non-standard working times.
- Taking account of the size of firms: the Commission wants to see information, awareness and risk prevention measures for small businesses, the self-employed and unpaid family helpers.
- Analysis of new and emerging risks: notably the interaction between chemical, physical and biological agents, as well as ergonomic, psychological and social risks.

The strategy contains few concrete legislative proposals. The Commission will continue to adapt existing Directives to reflect scientific and technological progress and changes in the world of work. Specifically, it will: propose extending the scope of the carcinogens Directive, submit a communication on musculoskeletal complaints that looks at their causes in the light of existing EC legislation; amend the display screen equipment Directive; and propose provisions in 'fields in which coverage is still incomplete', such as workplace ergonomics. Despite claiming that psychological harassment and violence at work require legislative action, the Commission merely restricts its commitment to an examination of "the appropriateness and the scope of a Community instrument'.

Finally, the Commission acknowledges that its legal framework is complex and unclear. It promises simplification and rationalisation through consolidation of Directives and a single report on their implementation. At the same time, it will try to improve the application of existing law, notably by the EU Senior Labour Inspectors Committee.   **HF**

The 'novel' aspects

The 'novel' aspects of the strategy – which have, in fact, featured in previous Commission communications – are that it:

- adopts a 'global approach to wellbeing at work' that takes account of changes in work and new – especially psychosocial – risks, and is geared to enhancing the quality of work (global is used in a holistic, rather than worldwide sense);
- is based on consolidating a culture of risk prevention, partnerships and combining legislation, economic incentives, best practice and corporate social responsibility. The strategy is disappointing on economic incentives, noting merely their longstanding application and that 'these kind of practices would seem to warrant more systematic application,' and
- emphasises that 'an ambitious social policy is a factor in the competitiveness equation' (and that not having a policy will 'weigh heavily on economies and societies').

---

[1] *Adapting to change in work and society: a new Community strategy on health and safety at work 2002–2006'.*
Commission of the European Communities, 11 March 2002. COM(2002) 118 final.

5.1.11   Work-related upper limb disorders

Current health and safety issues are many and varied. For many groups of workers arm pain is an issue. The following article[4] highlights the groups of workers affected by upper limb disorders and suggests a framework for the management of upper limb disorder risk.

Tackling work-related upper-limb disorders

Musculoskeletal disorders are the most common work-related ailment afflicting the population in Britain, accounting for more than half of all self-reported occupational ill health. A 1995 household survey (HSB 270 p.9) estimated that 44% of this group – approximately 506 000 cases – were suffering from 'upper-limb disorders' (ULDs). The HSE estimates that work-related ULDs caused the loss of 4.2 million working days that year, with each employee affected taking an average of 13 days off work, at an overall cost to employers of at least £200 million.

   The HSE defines 'upper limbs' as the part of the body, from the tips of the fingers to the shoulder, extending into the neck and including the tissues involved, the soft tissues, muscles, tendons and ligaments, the bony structures, skin, circulatory and nerve supply to the limb. 'Disorder' refers to the clinical effects produced by underlying changes in the tissues. These include symptoms, such as pain, and signs of abnormalities. Clinical effects are accompanied by functional changes, such as a reduction in use of the affected part of the limb and an associated restriction in speed or movement. Clinical and functional effects are confined to the limb itself, but their presence often makes the sufferer feel less healthy in general, leading to a reduction in the quality of their life. The phrase 'repetitive strain injury' is sometimes used to describe the same conditions, but is misleading because of the many factors that can contribute to the onset of the conditions.

Management cycle

As part of its strategy to cut the incidence of work-related ULDs, the HSE has revised its 10-year-old guidance on their prevention and management.[1] The guidance uses a framework for managing ULDs that is based on a seven-stage management cycle:

- understand the issues and commit to action;
- create the right organisational environment;
- assess the risks of ULDs in the workplace;
- reduce the risk of ULDs;
- educate and inform the workforce;
- manage any episodes of ULDs; and
- carry out regular checks on programme effectiveness.

Each stage of the framework (see below) is considered in a separate section of the guidance. There are four appendices that:

- provide real-life examples where the risks of ULDs have been managed;
- offer practical advice on risk assessment, a risk assessment filter and worksheets and suggestions for reducing the risk;
- give background information on medical aspects of ULDs; and
- set out the legal duties on the prevention of ULDs.

Risk factors

ULDs are not confined to any one particular group of workers or industrial activity and are widespread in the workforce. High levels of arm pain have been reported, however, in some jobs that share recognised risk factors. These risk factors are task-related, environment-related and worker-related.

Task-related factors include:

- repetition, where the same muscle groups are used over and over again during the working day, or frequent movements are performed for a long period;
- working postures that are awkward or static;
- force, which if excessive can lead to fatigue and, if sustained, to injury. The need to grip raw materials, product or tools is particularly significant; and
- duration of exposure – many types of ULD are cumulative in nature, with the risk of injury decreasing with duration time.

Environment-related factors include:

- vibration, particularly resulting from hand-held or guided power tools or the need to hold the item being worked when using fixed equipment;
- cold, which decreases blood-flow, dexterity, sensation and maximum grip strength, as well as increasing muscle activity;
- lighting, since workers' posture can be largely dictated by what they need to see; and
- psychosocial factors, such as the design, organisation and management of work.

Worker-related factors arise from the fact that all individuals are different and that there may be some people who are more, and some less, likely to develop a ULD.

Adopting an ergonomic approach should ensure that tasks are within the capabilities of the entire workforce. Ergonomics is concerned with ensuring work is designed to take account of people, their capabilities and limitations.

Risk assessment and management

Employers can use two approaches to identify ULD problems in the workforce, by seeking signs of problems and symptoms, or by examining the work tasks themselves to see if risk factors for ULDs are present.

A detailed assessment of every job could be a major undertaking and might be an unnecessary effort. To help identify situations where a detailed assessment is necessary, the HSE has devised, and included in the guidance, a filter to screen tasks. Where the filter identifies several risk factors in combination, the risk of ULDs is likely to be greater. (The TUC has recently urged union safety representatives to use the filter in their workplace.)

Once an employer has identified tasks that create a risk of ULDs, it should conduct a more detailed risk assessment, involving managers and workers, in order to ascertain the likelihood and severity of risk. Where it identifies risks, it should adopt a hierarchical approach to reduction, with priority given to eliminating risks at source. Worker participation is particularly important here.

Adequate control of risk factors will go a long way to prevent the occurrence of ULDs. But individual differences in the body's response to stresses mean it is not possible to prevent all ULDs. Employers therefore need a system to manage any reports or cases of ULDs, and to maintain a climate that encourages early

FRAMEWORK FOR THE MANAGEMENT OF ULD RISKS

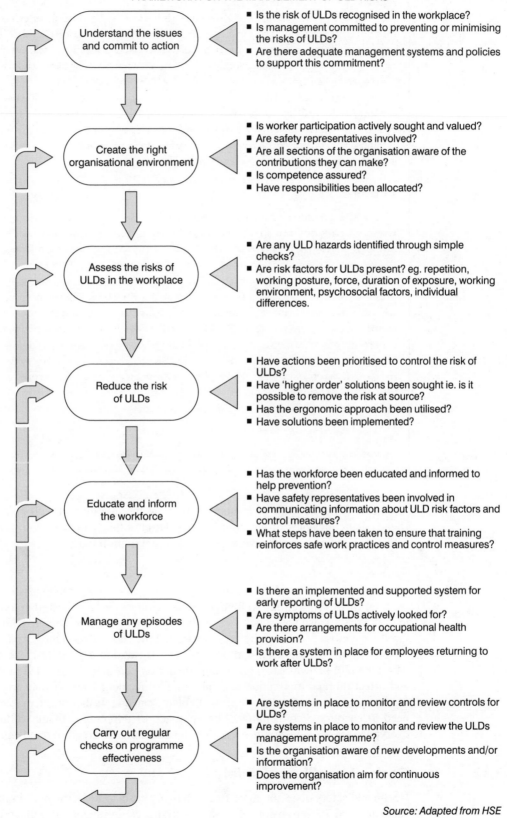

Understand the issues and commit to action
- Is the risk of ULDs recognised in the workplace?
- Is management committed to preventing or minimising the risks of ULDs?
- Are there adequate management systems and policies to support this commitment?

Create the right organisational environment
- Is worker participation actively sought and valued?
- Are safety representatives involved?
- Are all sections of the organisation aware of the contributions they can make?
- Is competence assured?
- Have responsibilities been allocated?

Assess the risks of ULDs in the workplace
- Are any ULD hazards identified through simple checks?
- Are risk factors for ULDs present? eg. repetition, working posture, force, duration of exposure, working environment, psychosocial factors, individual differences.

Reduce the risk of ULDs
- Have actions been prioritised to control the risk of ULDs?
- Have 'higher order' solutions been sought ie. is it possible to remove the risk at source?
- Has the ergonomic approach been utilised?
- Have solutions been implemented?

Educate and inform the workforce
- Has the workforce been educated and informed to help prevention?
- Have safety representatives been involved in communicating information about ULD risk factors and control measures?
- What steps have been taken to ensure that training reinforces safe work practices and control measures?

Manage any episodes of ULDs
- Is there an implemented and supported system for early reporting of ULDs?
- Are symptoms of ULDs actively looked for?
- Are there arrangements for occupational health provision?
- Is there a system in place for employees returning to work after ULDs?

Carry out regular checks on programme effectiveness
- Are systems in place to monitor and review controls for ULDs?
- Are systems in place to monitor and review the ULDs management programme?
- Is the organisation aware of new developments and/or information?
- Does the organisation aim for continuous improvement?

Source: Adapted from HSE

reporting. Where symptoms are such that continuing work does not make them worse, it may be enough to provide the worker with reassurance, advice on risk factors and to review the individual's work tasks with them. Where continuing to work exacerbates the symptoms, further advice should be sought from a health professional. Access to an occupational health service will allow the worker and the manager to obtain appropriate advice with minimal delay.

Confirmation of a ULD case should prompt consideration of the adequacy of existing risk assessments and controls. Where individuals have to take time off work, the exact timing of any return will depend on medical advice. It is often possible for an individual to return to work before symptoms have been cleared up – in some cases, this may be advantageous.

Targets

The HSC's strategy for reducing musculoskeletal disorders, including ULDs, adopts the principles set out in *Securing health together: a long-term occupational health strategy for England and Wales* (HSB 291 pp.13–18), which is an integral part of the Government's *Revitalising health and safety* initiative (HSB 290 pp.17–21). Musculoskeletal disorders, including ULDs, are one of eight priority areas where most improvement is needed to enable the targets for occupational health and safety to be met: the HSC has set a target to cut musculoskeletal disorders by 20% and to reduce working days lost by 30% by 2010. The priority programme aims to improve compliance with the law, to promote continuous improvement, and to develop the necessary knowledge, skills and support systems to achieve the MSD targets. The new guidance forms one strand of the support for employers, employees and those who advise them. It should ensure that they have the right information and advice to prevent and manage ULDs in the workplace.

1 *'Upper-limb disorders in the workplace'*, HSG60 (rev), HSE Books.

Reproduced with kind permission of Employee Health Bulletin.

Exercise

Accidents either at work or at home can affect the morale and well-being of the family, friends and colleagues of the injured party. Discuss this statement with one or two fellow students drawing on your own experience where appropriate.

Feedback

When someone is involved in an accident our immediate feelings should be for their welfare. However, we may well begin to feel vulnerable ourselves (it could have happened to me). We will also feel shock especially if we see the injured person. Almost certainly the family and close friends of the person will feel the shock over a longer period of time. The effect on work colleagues might be anger and frustration especially if the potential danger was generally known. This anger and frustration can then be directed at the organization and affect morale, motivation and output. The accident in itself may trigger thoughts of recrimination as people seek someone to blame causing further problems for morale and the need to encourage cooperation. The approach of adopting a blame culture may lead to everyone playing safe in whatever they do and so stifle creativity and initiative.

5.1.12   Costs of health and safety

Health and safety does not come free. There are costs to be borne both in the prevention of accidents and the provision of a safe working environment as well as the cost of any accident. The range of costs we can identify following an accident are listed below. This is not a comprehensive list and does not include costs such as medical expenses or the human suffering that may result, but nevertheless it gives a good idea of the different costs incurred.

Damaged materials, tools, buildings
Repurchase of any of the above
Clean-up costs
Delays to production
Costs of catching up on lost production
Cost of additional workers and their training
Managerial time carrying out investigations
Administrative work
Legal expenses and possible fines and/or compensation (damages)
Reputation of the company
Lowered morale of other workers
Industrial unrest.

5.1.13   Human resource management and health and safety

Human resource management has an important role to play in management of health and safety. Michael Armstrong,[5] identifies five basic principles to fashion the management of health and safety. He suggests they are: tracing the causes of industrial disease and accidents, identifying the potential hazards, the commitment of top management, management accountability and employee training. The causes of disease and accidents can be dealt with if health and safety is made a central tenet of managerial effort and are dealt with systematically.

The identification of hazards forms part of the EU's approach to health and safety where by reporting all accidents and injuries at the workplace and investigating their causes risk situations can be identified (see the Reporting of Injuries, Diseases and Dangerous Occurrences Regulations 1995) (as amended).

Management support and accountability at all levels is required to ensure full implementation of health and safety procedures. They have to be at the forefront of everyone's mind.

As things change and old machines or processes are abandoned it is always good practice to use the opportunity to build in newer safer methods that may have been learned from past mistakes.

5.1.14   Workforce health

HR managers can take an active role in the health and well-being of the workforce. Everyone at some time in their working life has felt ill at work but decided to carry on working. With this in mind, it should be realized that people's health needs to be monitored. Organizations sometimes employ their own trained medical staff and it would make a great deal of sense to use these staff to keep others healthy and at work. The organization can be proactive in trying to get its staff to identify behaviours that make them unhealthy and unwell.

Some organizations offer free medical insurance as part of their benefits package but this can be expensive. It would be just as sensible to spend time performing an audit of staff health before there was a need to take remedial medical action. This may mean organizations getting actively involved in the well-being of their staff by educating them about the problems associated with poor diet, smoking, stress and alcohol abuse, to name but a few. Some organizations have begun this approach and later in this section we will consider their attitudes on violence at work and alcohol use. By taking an active part in the prevention of disease the organization retains its workforce in employment and any costs associated with prevention can be offset against potential absenteeism.

5.1.15   Human resource management and safety representatives

Human resource management should support the use of employee health and safety representatives and safety officers. Advice can be sought from a range of organizations such as the St John's Ambulance Brigade, the Fire Service and HM Inspectorates as well as obvious sources such as the HSE.

The employees themselves will have first-hand experience of the problems they face on a daily basis and will be able to inform managers of potential problems. HR managers can play an active role in developing procedures for safety representatives to use during regular safety checks. These should be done on a formal basis with clear guidance about what is to be checked, whether the checks will be routine or random. Some mechanism for reporting back needs to be used to alert management of divergence from acceptable standards.

5.1.16   Producing a health and safety policy

Health and safety policy and policy formulation is greatly influenced by the HSWA and is applicable to all organizations with five or more employees. The Act states that every employer must prepare and revise as necessary a written statement of general policy towards the health and safety of their employees.

The Health and Safety Executive[6] suggest that the policy statement should indicate responsibility for health and safety. The HSE advice also includes the necessity to either include in or attach to the policy statement details about risk assessment and how protective and preventative health and safety measures are planned, controlled, organized, monitored and reviewed.

Determining the policy statement

The policy statement should include the organization's approach to the issues and details of the manager's and employees' responsibilities to health and safety. Health and safety policy should cover everything from people to plant and machinery, as well as working methods and product design.

It is important that the policy is regularly communicated to employees, understood and acted upon. Everyone needs to know the key players in health and safety issues and their responsibilities for the identification of problems, analysis of the risks involved and then dealing with them.

Staff involvement

It is essential that staff are fully involved in health and safety to the point where it becomes a way of life to them. Staff all need to be competent at their work and have all the requisite skills that allow them to carry out their work safely. This may mean the organization makes the effort to assess them and, where necessary, train them.

Managing staff

Staff need to have a role model when it comes to health and safety and so all managers should be dedicated to the idea of good health and safety practice. They should be able to give a clear indication to staff about what is and is not acceptable practice. Where people have a particular expertise they should be identified to all staff so that they become a point of reference when questions are raised about their particular specialisms. All staff, including supervisors, should know what is expected of them and what their responsibilities are.

Consulting with staff

It is essential that staff and their representatives, trade unions or other associations are fully involved as much as possible in the development and reassessing of health and safety policy. Staff have a vast amount of practical knowledge and experience that they can bring to any discussions. Furthermore they are the people who will be carrying out the procedures and ironing out any problems, so their insight will prove invaluable. By involving them as early as possible in the process it is possible to get them to accept ownership of the policy and work extremely hard to ensure its success. If they are not involved they may view it as being imposed and so either resist its implementation or reject it outright.

Communicating with staff

Good communications are of paramount importance. If people are ignorant of dangers it is not surprising that they have accidents. Health and safety issues need to be debated regularly and details about hazards and the risks that people are taking need to be pointed out. If preventative actions are available then staff should be made aware of them and how to use them.

Plans and specifications

It is often said that good planning prevents poor performance and in the case of health and safety this is no different. Planning for health and safety issues needs to be carried out in a logical pattern, first deciding what the organization is trying to achieve, locating any hazards, evaluating risks and then introducing acceptable levels of performance to an agreed specification. Once organizations have located a hazard and evaluated the risk it presents then they can develop a method of either controlling or removing it. However, organizations can only do this within the legal framework. For instance, if the organization can identify a toxic waste byproduct of its processes they cannot just decide to dump it on the street but will have to find a safe disposal or storage method.

Organizations can also take preventative measures and plan to eliminate the toxic waste before it enters operational processes.

All these approaches need to be judged against a specification so that organizations can see how well or poorly they are doing.

Health and safety specifications for organizations to aspire to can prove to be motivating and positive. For health and safety purposes the specifications can cover anything from the products and services we provide to the raw materials purchased and stored.

An example of the types of specifications required are those used by organizations to check electrical equipment. A named and trained individual is given the responsibility for carrying out a number of tests on electrical equipment *in situ* for example in offices. Managers know the individual, they know what they do, they know they carry out the tests at regular intervals and if the electrical equipment does not meet their agreed specification it is not passed as being fit for use and is withdrawn from service. Wherever possible organizations should try to make the specifications measurable, achievable and realistic.

Exercise

You work in a factory where one of the processes is considered dangerous as it involves the use of caustic fluids. Your manager acting independently has discovered a way of carrying out the process more cheaply and wants you to begin using the new process. You are not sure where you stand because you think this might carry an increased health and safety risk.

Feedback

Legislation exists that makes it a legal requirement for employees to be consulted with regard to health and safety issues. This can be done either by a trades union safety representative or for non-union employees by a representative they select. Examples of legislation covering this issue are The Safety Representatives and Safety Committees (SRSC) Regulations 1977 and the Health and Safety (Consultation with Employees) Regulations 1996. It also makes good practical sense to have employees involved because this will help encourage a culture of good health and safety at work since they are the people who are carrying out the work and both they and the employer have a duty to encourage safe working practice.

Assessing performance

In business when thinking about performance, organizations often think they could do better. With this in mind they ask the questions 'where are we now, and where would we like to be?' Once they have done this and recognized they are not the best, then they ask, what is the difference between the standard set by the best and our performance? They need to know why they are not achieving that standard. They can approach this situation by using two different ways of monitoring on a proactive or a reactive basis.

Proactive monitoring means taking action before accidents happen. Organizations must have regular inspections and checks to ensure that the specifications set are in fact being put into action and that management controls are functioning properly.

Reactive monitoring is a response after the event. In this situation organizations have to analyse what has happened and why it happened. This can cover anything from two aeroplanes involved in a near-miss to the investigation of an outbreak of food poisoning. Like the findings from any other form of analysis, the information gathered is only useful if it is acted upon. For this reason, it is necessary to get the information to those decision makers who have the power to introduce the necessary changes. It is important when this information is presented to have already carried out some form of risk assessment and given priority to those areas of greatest risk. Organizations need not only to recognize the immediate reasons why a situation has arisen but also to check to see if there are deeper hidden reasons.

For example, if the driver of a vehicle falls asleep while driving, fatigue can be identified as the cause and with more rest breaks the accident would not have happened. However, if the situation is investigated further it might show that the delivery schedules are so tight and wages so low that in order to earn an acceptable wage the drivers are driving too many hours, and so breaking EU–UK law. Remedies for this situation will be more complex, involving careful examination of how routes are organized, how drivers are paid and how hours are controlled. Some of these remedies will need the authority of senior managers in order to implement them.

It is important in the monitoring stage that the organization has some way of knowing how it is performing. It needs to build in some form of checking so that it knows if it is actually carrying out work to its own specifications as well as adhering to the requirements of the law. These checks can be fairly simple ones where notices are posted reminding staff to carry out duties and then physically checking to see if they have. Managers can keep records of accidents in an accident book and use this to try to quantify their cost. Some organizations monitor how long staff have been logged on to computers and then at regular intervals flash messages on the screen to encourage them to take a break. These approaches can reinforce the message to staff that the organization is committed to health and safety and they too should take it seriously.

Reviewing performance

It is often said that in hindsight we have perfect vision. By recording how well the organization is doing at health and safety activities it can reflect on how well or poorly it performed. This can be done either internally or by using external advisers. Having someone to audit health and safety activities can greatly improve performance. External auditors can bring their experience of other organizations and compare performance with that of the industry's best. This benchmarking against other organizations can be motivating as well as bringing the idea of best practice from other organizations. League tables or progress charts can be used to convey the message to staff.

Reviews can highlight areas where we need to take immediate action because specifications either do not exist or are not good enough. Once deficiencies have been highlighted then action must be taken. It is very difficult to deny knowledge of a potential hazard if someone has pointed out that hazard. Insurance companies are reluctant to compensate people who have been warned about dangers, have ignored those warnings and then have suffered injury. For example, holiday medical insurance is an absolute essential if you are travelling to some parts of the world. If you underinsure then you do so at your own risk. The same principle applies with health and safety issues. If you have been alerted to a potential danger and have not taken any action to remedy it, but when someone is injured and takes a legal suit for damages, you cannot expect the courts or the insurance companies to look on you favourably.

5.1.17   Work-related health problems

Working with visual display units (VDUs) and keyboards

Problems that are said to come from the use of VDUs are usually associated with the eyes, headaches, neck aches and back aches. These types of problems are not unique to VDU work, supermarket checkout operators have problems with back ache associated with the design of cash tills. The use of laptop computers can be less comfortable than a desk-based one because of their design characteristics. The problems that can result from prolonged use of such machines as personal computers and checkout tills are described as work-related upper limb disorders (WRULD). For more details see article in Section 5.1.11 Some of the causes are excessive workload, repetitive movements, poor working position and lack of job variation.[7]

Many of the problems associated with VDU use can be eased by better design of workstation layout using sound ergonomic principles.

The following are some of the basic principles of workstation layout adapted from those suggested by Willis:[2]

- The feet should touch the floor or a footrest.
- There should be adequate leg room to enable comfortable working and stretching.
- There should be adequate support for the back.
- The VDU should be at a height which permits it to be viewed with the head at a comfortable angle.
- The viewing distance should be comfortable.
- The height of the desk and keyboard should prevent significant flexing of the wrist.

- The document holder should be positioned to minimize neck movement.
- Wrist or palm rests should be provided where necessary.

Other areas of interest concerning work-related health problems include the ongoing debate about the prolonged use of mobile phones especially in confined spaces such as cars. Further information on this issue can be found on the web-sites at the end of this chapter.

Violence at work

The following article[8] is reprinted with permission from the Employee Health Bulletin.

Violence against NHS staff on the rise

The action plan to reduce violence in the social care sector was launched as a new survey suggested that the incidence of attacks on staff in the NHS is rising.

The number of violent incidents against NHS staff rose by more than a fifth in the year to April 2000, according to a survey in *Health Service Report*, also published by Industrial Relations Services*. Employees in the average trust were subjected to 511 incidents last year, giving an average rate of 1200 incidents per 10000 employees. The rise in violence in the NHS has occurred against a background of initiatives to tackle the issue from government, NHS and trade unions.

Other highlights from the survey include:

- more than 90% of employers have violence at work policies;
- trade unions have been involved in negotiating violence policies;
- the vast majority of NHS trusts undertake risk assessments in relation to violence;
- although most trusts provide training to staff in post, relatively fewer (57%) include how to handle violent situations in induction training;
- more than two-thirds of employers provide at least some staff with mobile telephones; and
- only a fifth of respondents said they expected to achieve a 20% cut in the incidence of violence by 2001, and only a third expect to achieve the 30% target set by the Government for April 2003.

* *'Getting to grips with workplace violence: a snapshot survey', Health Service Report, winter 2000/01, tel: 020 7354 6742. Violence against social workers: http://www.doh.gov.uk/violencetaskforce/report.htm*

Many organizations are aware of the increase in violence at the workplace, whether it is in an A&E unit or in a school. Employers are aware that they have to protect their staff from violent behaviour, which can range from verbal abuse to physical attack. Perhaps the first thing that needs to be dealt with is recognizing the problem and who is in fact at risk. It is worth considering the types of jobs people do and where they work.

Someone who is working alone with violent people, for example a psychiatric nurse, must face a higher risk of attack than someone who works in a team and never has contact with the public (e.g. some civil servants). Risk can increase when the factors that contribute to violence appear at the same time, for example working alone at unsociable times or in a position to be able to enforce legislation against the public. An example of this might be a police officer walking alone through a city centre at night when the public houses are closing. A group leaves a public house and begins to sing loudly. The officer is responsible for keeping the peace and is confronted by people who do not want to do so. The combination of a lone officer trying to enforce the law could easily deteriorate into a violent situation.

The way we prevent violence is by examining where the risk is and why it happens. In another example, if we know that violence occurs at a customer help desk, then we can think about redesigning the desk and its immediate environment. If we then investigate why the violence happens and find it is because of frustration caused by long waiting times we can change our working practices and perhaps introduce an appointments system. These are just two approaches, but they serve to illustrate that with the right diagnosis followed by a preventative strategy we can begin to deal with the problem. We can also train staff to recognize potentially violent situations and to use the requisite interpersonal skills to deal with aggressive people.

The following articles highlight the seriousness of the issue and how organizations are responding. They are reprinted with permission from the Employee Health Bulletin.[9,10]

Head teachers call for action against violent parents[9]

Staff in another area of the public sector – education – are calling for action on the growing problem of assaults committed by parents. The National Association of Head Teachers (NAHT) dealt with 140 cases of physical assaults or threats of violence against its members in the 12 months to June 2001, and is calling on the Government to intervene. The NAHT wants the removal of uncertainty surrounding the powers of head teachers to exclude pupils because of the violent behaviour of their parents. Local authorities should also operate a zero tolerance policy in relation to parental violence, NAHT believes.

Doctors' insurers call for security at A&E[10]

Security guards should be employed to patrol the accident and emergency departments of Britain's hospitals and GPs should be provided with personal attack alarms, according to a report on violence in the NHS from the doctors' insurers, the Medical Defence Union (MDU)*.

A nationwide survey conducted by the MDU found that 75% of the 1,044 doctors questioned thought they were seen as 'fair game' in an increasingly violent workplace. The threat of violence is increasing, even though only a small minority of patients or relatives actually commits an assault, the MDU adds.

The conclusions of the MDU survey are that:

■ almost two-thirds (65%) of doctors believe that the actual threat of violence against them is a growing concern in their professional lives:
■ around a quarter (23%) of doctors have been physically assaulted in the workplace on at least one occasion in the past five years; and

- in three-quarters of incidents, an assault was provoked by a cause unrelated to a medical condition; for example, lengthy waits for treatment or drunkenness.

Violent patients to face withdrawal of treatment

Meanwhile, the Secretary of State for Health, Alan Milburn, has announced yet another initiative to tackle violence and the threat of violence in the NHS as part of a longer-term commitment to reduce incidents against health service staff by 30% by 2003.

New guidance will be published later this year to help employing trusts develop policies that could include the withdrawal or withholding of NHS treatment from violent patients as a last resort. Patients with severe mental health problems or with a life-threatening condition will not be denied treatment under the terms of the guidance.

The guidance will encourage trusts to develop local solutions to the problem of violent patients and relatives. However, the yellow and red 'carding' system operated by Barts and the Royal London Hospital – among others – has been cited as an example of the kind of solution that might be developed.

* Contact the Medical Defence Union, www.the-mdu.com

Alcohol and drug abuse

The following report was published in the Employee Health Bulletin,[11] and is reprinted here with permission.

European employers get tough on alcohol at work

Pilots in the former Soviet Union state of Georgia are tested daily for the presence of alcohol in their blood stream, while Latvian employers can legally break a worker's employment contract if alcohol is consumed at work, according to a new study from the World Health Organisation (WHO)*.

The study finds that workplace health programmes covering alcohol and drugs play an important part in reducing the social cost of alcohol misuse in European countries. For example, the development of formal alcohol policies in Austria has resulted in two-thirds of workplaces adopting what the study describes as a 'negative' stance on alcohol, with employees in such workplaces drinking less than colleagues in more 'alcohol-friendly' organisations.

The vast majority of countries covered in the WHO study (33 out of 39) have some form of restriction on alcohol consumption in the workplace, with just under half of these banning its consumption completely (see table below). A number of eastern European and Baltic States have very tight, blanket restrictions on alcohol at work. Like airline pilots, Georgian government security officers are subject to daily workplace testing for the presence of alcohol in their blood. In other countries alcohol is restricted at work according to the nature of the job and workplace – usually on the grounds of safety.

Educational and healthcare buildings, governments offices and public transport systems in many countries are also alcohol-free zones. Variations exist between areas of Europe – for example, the newly independent states of the former Soviet Union are more likely to ban alcohol in the workplace than are western European countries.

Alcohol policies

Over 2,000 employers in Germany operate alcohol policies and programmes, while in Switzerland, programmes are only operated by the largest employers. Workplace policies are most widespread in western Europe compared with central and Eastern Europe, where only half of countries reported that employers have policies and the newly independent states of the former Soviet Union, where only one-third reported the existence of workplace alcohol policies.

These policies and restrictions are operated against a background of growing evidence of the social cost of alcohol in the work setting. According to the study around 6% of the Belgian workforce may have a drink problem and alcohol may be a factor in 30% of accidents at work. In France, between 10% and 20% of accidents at work are accounted for by alcohol, the WHO study suggests.

Alcohol restrictions in different settings

Setting	Countries with restrictions	Countries with bans
Workplace	33	16
Healthcare buildings	31	21
Government offices	27	12
Educational buildings	32	24

n = 39 countries. Source: WHO report.

* *'Alcohol in the European region: consumption, harm and policies'. Nina Rehn. Robin Room and Griffith Edwards, World Health Organisation. February 2001.*

It is possible that a member of staff at work could be injured or injure someone else if they were under the influence of drink or drugs. The employer therefore needs to be aware they have a duty of care in respect of their staff's health and safety at work. If they know of an individual who has a problem with alcohol they should do something about it. The employee also needs to realize that they have a responsibility to take reasonable care in their work. Organizations should have a policy on how to deal with alcohol and drug abuse. The abuse **can** be recognized, some of the indicators being sudden changes in behaviour, a tendency to become confused, and poor timekeeping.

Staff also need to be educated about organizational policy on drinking or drugs. Staff who have a problem could be offered counselling and, after counselling, treatment and rehabilitation. There may be a case for offering dismissed staff re-engagement subject to satisfactory performance.

5.1.18　Further contributions of human resource management

Human resources management can offer a number of different strategies to assist with health and safety.

Planning work

Critical examination of the way employees work and the workplace can help managers to build into new methods or workplaces improved ways of dealing with health and safety. This can be done in conjunction with a work study department or with the production designers or engineers. By using ergonomics[12] to design workplaces with staff as the focus, organizations can go some way to reducing stress and discomfort as well as minimizing their exposure to hazards.

Showing commitment

It is essential that senior management shows commitment to health and safety and does not pay 'lip service' to it. Staff get to know whether senior management are committed to health and safety and respond when they see action being taken, whether this is due to the intervention of a safety committee or to an individual manager. If these actions do not receive senior management support then it is more difficult for staff to accept them.

Checking the place of work

If you walk into the kitchen of a restaurant you can get an idea whether or not the staff are concerned about health and safety on first impressions. This idea of management by walking about (MBWA) is not new, but it can be used by HR managers positively by involving trade unions and safety officials. The approach can be linked to staff 'wellness' schemes, used by some companies to regularly check the health of employees.

Installation of agreed methods

The methods that are introduced need to be within the remit of the designated manager. Managers need to be aware of what they are and are not allowed to do. They must not be faced with the dilemma where they are expected to put safe working methods into practice but at the same time are denied the funds to do so. Neither should they be told to work safely but be put under pressure to meet targets, forcing them to compromise safety.

Train everyone

The organization should try to involve everyone in health and safety training. By doing so they can develop the necessary skills and knowhow to maximize staff output. By enforcing the rules the organization can change the behaviour of staff and get them to internalize the positive aspects of health and safety. For example, when the no-smoking rule was first introduced on public transport it faced opposition. However, now smokers automatically extinguish their cigarettes before boarding and the environment on-board is much more pleasant. Everyone benefits from the internalization of the 'no-smoking rule' and the same idea can be applied in work situations.

Involve staff

There is an obligation under the HSWA for organizations when requested by safety representatives to set up a safety committee. This is an ideal opportunity to focus the energies of staff, help solve organizational problems, develop solutions and put them into practice. Staff can do this on the same basis as a quality circle (see Chapter 6) and they can be involved in solving health and safety problems.

Oversee methods

Unless methods are supervised they can easily fall into disuse and disrepute. It is important for the health and safety of all, that legislation and health and safety arrangements are **made** to work in practical situations. Human resources management can take an active part in ensuring that this is done by training employees and monitoring their knowledge through appraisal interviews.

Document

There needs to be some documentation of what the organization is doing. In the same way that quality assurance (Chapter 6) seeks to monitor quality, organizations need to be checked to determine if they are doing what they say they are doing in terms of health and safety. For this to happen a set of criteria needs to be developed such as staff knowledge of health and safety issues.

Summary

In this section you have looked at the main legislation concerning health and safety at work. You have seen how EU-driven legislation has found its way into UK law through directives being transposed into regulations under the Health and Safety at Work Act 1974. You have looked at the contribution HR managers can make to the development of health and safety policy, as well as examining some workplace health and safety issues in more detail. HR managers also have a role to play in terms of the education and training of staff to raise awareness of the costs of health and safety in terms of the human as well as financial costs.

5.2 The functional departments

Section objectives

In this section you will:

- examine the different functional departments
- gain an insight into what they do and
- learn how they differ and how they interrelate.

5.2.1 Introduction

Grouping activities in an organization is commonly carried out on the basis of function. Functional grouping draws together specialist knowledge that is required for its activities. For example, an engineering department would bring together electrical, electronic and mechanical engineers. This allows the function to focus on engineering activities. Typical functions are: research and development, finance and human resources management.

Exercise

List all the activities you think your department is involved in. How many links do you think your department has with other departments?

Feedback

The list you will make depends on your own personal circumstances and knowledge of your department. The activities will vary from one department to another depending on which specialist function you are thinking about, from invoicing in a finance department to sending out job application forms by HR management. The links that any one department has with another is often something of a mystery to staff. Employees seldom have much contact with other departments and so have little idea what they do. It is with this in mind that the following section seeks to clarify some of the work of other departments.

5.2.2 Research and development

Research and development, as its name suggests, consists of two different types of work.[13] Research in its purest form is a scientific investigation to discover new knowledge or applied research is where there is a practical link between the research and the production of a particular product. Development follows the research and is normally used on a small scale to develop the research knowledge through the design of a manufacturing process that can be used eventually for large-scale production. Development work can also be used to describe the work done to improve an existing product.

5.2.3 What is a Research and Development department required to do?

The Research and Development department has an important part to play in the corporate planning of any organization. Research and Development is involved in the analysis of the products and services supplied by the organization and the processes used to make them. By looking at the organization's products Research and Development can identify whether there are opportunities to develop them further and extend their life cycle. Threats that products face from superior products can be identified and remedial steps taken to make them competitive.

In terms of production processes, Research and Development can identify areas for improvement and provide the ideas that make this possible. This can be linked to knowing the current state of scientific knowledge, since research and development staff should know what equipment and technology is available and at what cost. This can allow organizations to be more competitive in terms of price particularly if they can use that technology to improve efficiency and reduce costs.

The development part of Research and Development should be involved in the conversion of scientific research into products and services that can be sold to make profits. This means that they have to be involved in all stages of product development from the writing of the specific product's technical specifications to prototype production, field testing and finally to its eventual launch onto the market.

5.2.4 Objectives of a Research and Development department

The objectives of a Research and Development department can vary because of the long time spans of some of the projects they undertake. Generally some of the following could be included in the objectives of a Research and Development department:

- Trying to keep ahead of competitors in terms of technology. If an organization cannot keep ahead of them, it should at least be trying to keep up with them.
- Introducing new products within agreed timescales and budgets so that as some products become obsolete there are others to take their place.

5.2.5 Managing in a Research and Development environment

Research and Development and the marketing function have to work closely together. Where organizations are committed to a customer-focused approach they also need to concentrate on quality as an issue. With this in mind they have to ensure that despite its technical excellence, the product is one that the customer wants. Sometimes when technology appears to be 'too complicated' potential customers can be dissuaded from its purchase. Similarly, Research and Development need to know what plans senior management have for the product. For example, is it to be a long-term investment or a short-term one? These can cause tensions to develop between those who develop the products and those who have to market and sell them.

Associated problems

Research and development can cause major financial pressures for an organization. In some industries, pharmaceuticals for instance, it can be up to 20 years before a piece of research can be introduced as a product into the marketplace. For this reason research and development managers are faced with the problem of financial control and how to fund long-term, complex assignments that may or may not turn out to be profitable.

People who work in research and development can often be single-minded individuals who are 'not the easiest staff to control',[13] and may only be interested in the pursuit of knowledge without any real concern about the commercial viability of the work.

It is important that the researchers have a great deal of freedom to encourage innovation and creativity. This means relatively narrow spans of control, and greater amounts of delegation and decisions being taken at the level of the scientist carrying out the work. Management style is likely to be very much 'hands off', although to balance this, staff are under pressure to provide results.

Motivation is also an issue because these staff are very innovative and that alone can be the motivation to work together with the respect of one's peers. However, this does not ignore the fact that salaries are important. If the organization wants to recruit and retain the best candidates, then they need to think very carefully and consider any financial package offered (see Section 3.4).

5.2.6   Finance department

Organizations need money to pay their staff and staff need money to pay for goods and services in the wider economy. It is important from the organization's view that the Finance department has an input into how money is spent and how it is earned to ensure that they can control income and expenditure. According to Mullins,[14] 'The stewardship of financial resources is of vital concern to the majority of organizations'. This puts the Finance department at the heart of organizations. It will be involved at all levels of the organization. In planning terms it will be involved in the long-term strategic decisions, at a departmental level it will decide budget allocation, on an operational level it will decide control procedures.

5.2.7   Companies and sources of finance

When companies need finance they have a number of sources to which they can turn. The banks are an obvious source of finance and so is the government, who will offer grants and tax-exempt status in some circumstances to organizations. The Stock Exchange can provide a source of finance through either the capital markets or the issuing of shares. Share ownership can be with the individual investor, the corporate investor or increasingly through schemes where employees buy or are given shares.

The management of all financial matters is the ultimate responsibility of the Finance department. They are responsible for the documentation of financial transactions, cash handling and the keeping of accounts.

5.2.8   Activities of the Finance department

Financial accounting

Financial accounting involves the documenting of financial transactions in a particular way, usually laid down by the accountancy profession. It is a legal necessity and has to be carried out on a regular basis.

Treasury management

This concentrates on how the monies that are borrowed by the organization are sourced, used efficiently and repaid as required. It involves a degree of financial planning, in close cooperation with other managers, about cash budgeting.

Working capital management

The capital available to an organization can take a variety of forms: cash, debts, credit and stocks. The debts due to the organization need careful management and control. Debtors need to be pursued as soon as possible before debts become impossible to collect and force the organization to borrow even more money.

Creditors should be paid within agreed deadlines but some companies do delay paying their creditors in the mistaken belief that they are saving money.

Cost and management accounting

Cost and management accounting is heavily involved in the planning, control and decision-making processes. It seeks to provide management with information that can be used as the basis for decision making.

5.2.9   The management of the finance function

Since finance is such a crucial part of the organization it is vital that it runs effectively and efficiently. It is important to realize that the Finance department relies upon quality information being communicated from other departments. These relationships between different departments are essential. For instance, it is important for the Marketing and Sales department to supply up-to-date sales figures to the Finance department to facilitate good credit control. Similarly, the Research and Development department needs to pass on details of material requirements that can then be given to the cost and management accountant who can then estimate the potential impact of using those materials on future projects.

5.2.10   Planning and the Finance department

The Finance department can be used to make sure that other departments adhere to their financial responsibilities and meet their objectives. The fact that departments have a quantitative measure with which they can identify can be a motivational factor by providing a performance measure by which they can be judged.

Exercise

Think about an aspect of your personal finances, for example when you wanted to make a large purchase, maybe a piece of furniture, carpet or a car.

● How did you approach that purchase?
● Did you look at a range of products?
● Did you think about how you would pay for it?
● Did anything happen to make you think that perhaps you would delay its purchase?

Feedback

An approach that might be taken by a Finance department could include an in-depth analysis of the costs of purchase. An appraisal of the investment required would include taking into account the depreciation of the purchase over its expected life. Alternative sources of finance would be examined to determine the most favourable interest rates as well as taking into account such issues as whether to buy, hire or lease. Finance departments have to be very careful when spending company money because they have to set an example to the rest of the organization for balanced use of finance.

5.2.11   Purchasing

Muhlemann *et al.*[12] describe the Purchasing department in terms of having to procure goods and services of a suitable quality, in the right numbers, at the agreed time, transported to the correct location, from the right supplier, for the right price. In order for the organization to begin this process it needs to know clearly what it wants to purchase. This means that the organization needs to have detailed product specifications from the production department or end user. Communications is very important at this point because the supplier has to be properly briefed by the Purchasing department about what the end user wants. This is why the specification is so important and should be fully understood by the supplier.

It is the Purchasing department's responsibility to buy at the right price for the most suitable quality. Sometimes price and quality issues conflict and what the Purchasing department has to do is to balance the two. For instance, we can buy extremely fast but expensive personal computers for use at work but does it matter to the average user of computers if their machine is 10 nanoseconds slower? The slower version could cost considerably less and do the job just as well, but to convince staff of its quality is going to take time.

In order for Purchasing to control the quality of its inputs we can use a basic four-stage approach:

- Specify clearly the quality required.
- Choose the suppliers who can meet the quality requirements. Here the organization can use its knowledge of quality assurance and only use suppliers who have been certified to the required standard.
- Ensure that the supplier knows exactly what is required.
- Check the purchases when delivered and seek remedies if standards are not met. Where we deal with a quality supplier this check should not be necessary.

5.2.12   Selecting a suitable supplier

Rather than immediately seeking a source of supply outside the organization, management should look inside first. Many an organization duplicates its purchases of services or purchases them more expensively outside. Training is a good example of this. In all organizations there are many managers who spend hours developing skills in their staff and training them on a variety of processes. The same organizations will pay premium prices to bring in an outside provider to train others in different departments the very same skills and processes.

If no internal provider is available then the organization must look outside. The factors the organization should be aware of are:

- Quality Assurance – whether the supplier has an accredited quality assurance certificate and/or
- Whether the supplier has a good reputation for performance of the same type of contract

Purchasing should build up a list of preferred suppliers with whom they can negotiate on prices and possible discounts. This list should provide as many alternative sources of supply so that the business does not become reliant on too few suppliers.

5.2.13   The purchasing mix

As we have already stated, purchasing is, among other things, about the procurement of goods. To this extent we can link the purchasing mix through four related areas, quantity, quality, price and delivery (see Figure 5.3).

- Quantity will be dependent on how fast the organization is using stock and whether the cost of production delays can be offset by holding less stock. The reason for this is that holding too much stock ties up capital and is very expensive. Organizations try to limit stock holding, but, if production stops this costs money. Organizations try to balance this by reordering when stocks falls to a particular level or by using a Just-in-time method of stock control, where stock is only reordered when required.
- Quality – we have looked at quality issues in the drafting of a specification for the supplier and the use of quality suppliers.
- Price – the monitoring of price over time is essential to try to get the best deal for monies spent. This can be achieved by buying ahead or bulk purchases.
- Delivery – if stock is running low then it is essential it is replaced or production will stop. With this in mind it is important to note the importance of good stock control, but the importance of delivery dates and times to the production process should also be emphasized to suppliers.

Quantity	Quality
Price	Delivery

Figure 5.3. The purchasing mix.

5.2.14   Purchasing planning

This forms a very important part of the purchasing function. As we have mentioned earlier, the idea of keeping stock costs to a minimum and reordering just in time is a very attractive proposition but it requires a lot of careful planning and control. Hence the need for close liaison with the production manager and the Finance department.

Purchasing impacts on areas such as warehousing, security and production, among many others, and it is for these reasons that purchasing requires good planning. Purchasing managers have to take part in all aspects of decision making in the organization, sometimes decisions about the import of raw materials or part-manufactured goods.

Purchasing managers affect the organization's expenditure and if they get it wrong it can be very expensive. The arrival of total quality management (TQM) has meant purchasing managers having a wider company role where they can insist on changes being made if the company is to achieve its quality goals. A good purchasing approach will try to get the best value for money, reduce stockholding and thus contribute to profit.

Purchasing managers need to be in touch with the business environment and fellow-managers, especially line managers, to advise on market changes in terms of products, designs and materials. They are not confined to the manufacturing industry but can be very influential in the service industry in areas as diverse as computer purchasing to the negotiation of hotel prices for staff who have to spend time away from home.

5.2.15   Production and operations management

In manufacturing the Production department is responsible for the transformation of raw materials into finished products through the various production processes. This requires a great deal of planning and organization.

The Production department needs to work very closely with the other functional departments – Purchasing, Research and Development, Finance, Human Resources and especially Marketing. This close liaison with Marketing is necessary because it is they who research the market to determine exactly what the customer wants and this information becomes an input to the Production department who take over and create the product or service required. The distribution of the product or service is then within the remit of Marketing and so the links should be evident.

Production management can be said to consist of five separate areas, according to Muhlemann *et al.*,[12] product, plant, processes, programmes and people.

The production manager needs to be able to liaise with a wide range of managers from the other functional groupings. The production function needs to be fully involved in corporate planning because they personify the function that will convert the inputs into the outputs required by the customer. This is done through the coordination of product, plant, processes, programmes and people. The Production department, therefore, needs to know what is expected of it and whether it has the capacity to match those expectations.

5.2.16   Human Resources Management (HRM) department

The following is a brief overview of the work of the HRM department. More detailed approaches to some of the issues raised are covered in Chapters 2 and 3. HRM is responsible for the people in an organization and their interrelationships in the work situation. The department seeks to involve people in all aspects of the organization and get them to fully support the organization's goals and to use them as effectively and efficiently as possible. HRM finds itself involved in areas as diverse as the corporate planning process, the motivation of staff as well as the smooth running of relationships within the organization and the organization's social responsibility. One of the main areas with which HRM is involved is the planning of how much labour is required. Human Resource Planning (HRP) looks at the demand for labour on one side and the supply of labour on the other. The amount of labour that is required will be influenced by the organization's corporate objectives. HRM denotes a new approach to the management of people. Personnel management, is according to Guest (1993) and others, a traditionally reactive approach. This covers a number of approaches such as 'firefighting' problems, carrying out administrative tasks, attempting to fulfil all the HR functions instead of devolving some to functional departments and 'policing' policy and adherence to rules and procedures. HRM, on the other hand is, arguably, a strategic approach to managing people, whereby it is much more closely tied into the corporate objectives of the organization. People are recognized as the most important resource of the organization, and, therefore must be closely allied with corporate aims, while day-to-day operational matters are devolved to line management who are more competent than a 'remote' personnel department to handle immediate activities such as recruitment and selection.

5.2.17   HRM activities

Corporate planning

A simplified view of this can be seen in Figure 5.4. The organization is influenced by its environment and is represented by political, economic, social and technological, legal and

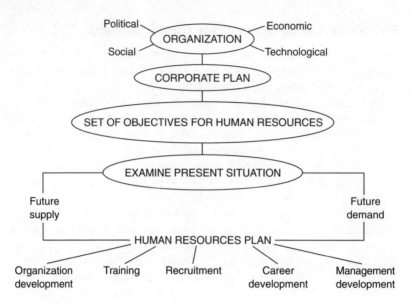

Figure 5.4. HRM and the corporate planning process.

environmental (PESTEL) pressures on it. Out of this, the organization has to decide what it wants to do and this can be anything from entering new markets to launching new products. These form part of the corporate plan and will have implications for the human resources required. The requirement needs to be assessed by looking at the present levels of staffing, taking into account the future supply of labour and the organization's future demand for labour. These then lead us to the idea of an 'internal market' and an 'external market' for labour: The dual labour market concept. Organizations can promote employees internally by carrying out career planning for them or they can recruit externally and bring in fresh ideas from outside. The use of internal labour can be good for motivation but by bringing in outsiders we can get a different approach which also can be beneficial. Many organizations often combine the two approaches.

Motivation (see also Section 3.4)

Another major area where HRM is involved is the motivation of staff. HRM can have a considerable impact on the motivation of staff by closely analysing their conditions of service and the type of work they do. By looking at the ways people are rewarded for their work can improve motivation. In the same way, paying attention to staff welfare will also motivate some people. One further way people can be motivated is by analysing the type of work they do and the degree to which it is repetitive. Job design techniques can be applied to achieve this, preferably with the involvement of staff on how their work is controlled. By redesigning work and involving staff, organizations can get their support for any changes to be made. We can then vary the type of work and the degree of responsibility they have to take. (Job design is discussed in Section 3.3.)

5.2.18   HR managers and internal relationships

Employee relations within any organization need careful handling and it is important for HRM to open clear and easily accessible channels of communication for all employees. These can vary from drop-in sessions of an informal nature for individuals to more formal approaches through joint staff and management committees. The use of training can also help communications by reinforcing what is expected of employees and letting them know what issues are contemporary as well as the obvious outcomes such as developing their skills. Employers can use also planned change by close involvement of staff in organization development to improve communications.

Having clear, fair and well-written grievance and disciplinary procedures can also help internal relations. In both procedures the rules should be set out so that both parties get a chance to speak and present their case. It is a relatively simple procedure with a number of identifiable stages. The use of the procedure can ensure relatively prompt but fair decision making. At least both parties know they have been treated fairly and that they have had a chance to put their case forward. While the outcomes might not be to everyone's liking at least the problem has been dealt with fairly and reasonably. In instances like these HRM can play a major advisory role in guiding managers and staff alike. (The handling of discipline is discussed in Section 3.5.)

HRM needs to meet an organization's social and legal responsibilities and this can be done through a number of HR activities such as recruitment, employment, health and safety and pay, to name but a few. In terms of recruitment this is where Human Resource management has to become involved in the labour market and create interest and communicate any details of jobs the organization may have to offer. This means that they must act fairly and be honest when giving details of any job in terms of pay, prospects and duties. Details about the job should be made as widely available as possible in the labour market so that there is no discrimination in favour of one group against another. Organizations also need to be aware of their local environments and support them accordingly. Wherever possible they should try to recruit locally rather than bringing people in from long distances. (See recruitment and selection in Section 3.2.)

In managing health and safety at work the employer must strive to provide the employee with a safe working environment (see Section 5.1).

In terms of payment of wages and salaries the employer has both a social and legal responsibility. First, there is a contractual obligation for an employer to pay wages in full and at the agreed time provided the employee has met their side of the contractual bargain. Second, the employer has a social responsibility to the dependants of the employee who also rely on monies being paid in full and on time. It is evident from the four activities summarized here that HRM has a wide and varied role to play.

5.2.19   Marketing and sales

Kotler[15] describes the marketing concept thus: 'the marketing concept holds that the key to achieving organizational goals consists in determining the needs and wants of target markets and delivering the desired satisfactions more effectively and efficiently than competitors.' Marketing should not be confused with selling. Selling is the process by which a salesperson gets the consumer to take part in an exchange process for their goods or services; usually this is in the form of money. Salespeople concentrate on the product or service they are selling on behalf of the producer or seller. Marketing focuses on the customer and attempts to find out the customer's needs and in what ways those customer needs can be satisfied.

5.2.20   Marketing activities

Segmentation

The marketplace is made up of a diverse number of customers who want a wide variety of products. In marketing terms these can be described as market segments which can allow organizations to focus on particular groups of consumers. These segments can be further divided based on a number of criteria, for example on age, gender or income. If we think of the music market, a young customer may buy 'pop music' regularly, but on a small scale whereas an older customer may buy more on an irregular basis and of a different type of music.

<table>
<tr><td>

Exercise

</td><td>

Do you have a supermarket loyalty card? Have you ever wondered why the supermarkets don't just reduce prices instead of giving points that add up to cash reward? Have you asked 'Why do they invest in all the technology and administration?'

</td></tr>
<tr><td>

Feedback

</td><td>

Every time you make a purchase using your card the supermarket adds details of your purchases to its database and can use that data to build a profile of an individual or group of customer's buying habits.

   This information can be used by the supermarkets to target individual customers or groups of customers when they wish to launch a new product, or a range of products. The information can be used to tailor certain products to certain customers, for example low-fat foods to those customers whose database shows a history of purchasing 'healthy' products. For a very small reward the customer gives the supermarket a great deal of information that would be very expensive for it to collect by other means (for example, through market research surveys) and the supermarket can then use that information to influence buyer behaviour.

</td></tr>
</table>

Segment identification

Perhaps the most important part of marketing is the carrying out of research into markets or marketing research. Marketing research consists of identifying, obtaining and analysing any information relating to the marketing activities. This can cover anything from the product or service to the way it is packaged. Marketing information is used to aid decision making.

Gathering marketing information

Primary research is sometimes called field research, and is carried out using sales staff, specialist agencies or contacts with professional bodies. This research can be done through direct observation, questionnaire completion or even experimentation (the tasting of foods). Secondary research relies on the analysis of existing data that is available from sources such as books, magazines, trade journals and government statistics.

5.2.21   The marketing mix

Once data are collated the organization can turn to the marketing mix. The 'marketing mix' is usually described as the four p's: product, place, promotion and price. If we consider an organization that is marketing orientated, what it is trying to do is make a profit by satisfying the wants of the customer. In order to do this there needs to be a balance between what the organization can do and what the customer requires. The 'marketing mix' tries to balance how the organization promotes its products in certain markets (places) and how the customer obtains the satisfaction of their wants by buying (price) the product:

- Product: covers the item being sold in terms of its size, weight, colour, packaging and quality.
- Place: covers how the product is transported to the customer, i.e. the type of sales outlet, warehousing and distribution network.

- Price – will be partly determined by factors such as what competitors are charging and any discounts offered. For example, in the motor industry companies can offer a minimum trade-in discount off the price of a new or used car.
- Promotion – covers the totality of communications used to inform the customer about the product. This can vary according to the product. If it is a new one the company must ensure the customer gets to know about it. If it is an existing product the aim has to be to keep it in the customer's mind. There are different approaches to promotion, the main ones being advertising, exhibitions and direct mailing.

5.2.22 Marketing planning

Marketing planning will influence the strategy used to try to make the organization's marketing effective. Predicted sales values and the number of customers the organization hopes to attract will influence the strategy. For example, if a large number of customers are targeted, the company can adopt a growth strategy. Where there are a limited number of customers a strategy of focusing only on a single group can be adopted.

We also have to take into account the fact that products can have a limit to their usefulness. This can be best described by thinking of a product as having a lifecycle (see Figure 5.5). When a product is new to a market it may not sell in large numbers and make profits. In fact, because of the initial investment required it may even make a loss. As time goes by the sales increase and so do profits. When the market is saturated and the product is at its peak so are the profits. When, for whatever reason, the product is no longer purchased, then sales naturally decrease and so do profits.

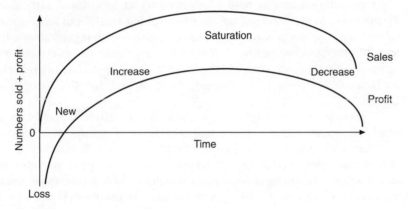

Figure 5.5. Product life cycle.

Depending on where a product is in its lifecycle will influence the marketing approach. In the 'new' phase the organization will have to concentrate on making the customer realize it exists, making sure it can supply it in sufficient quantities. As sales increase the organization may be able to do less direct advertising and concentrate more on distribution and production issues. At the saturation stage the organization may need to remind the customer it still exists by looking to our Research and Development department for potential modifications that may extend its life. Finally, as sales decrease, marketing may have to be reduced and concentrated in other areas.

5.2.23 Sales

A sales department is tasked with creating direct communications with the customer on a day-to-day basis. Salespeople are expected to win new business and retain and increase existing business. They also serve as sounding boards between customers and providers, and are the staff to whom customers complain and therefore are expected, to resolve any problems that are raised between customer and provider. This is good in terms of feedback because organizations receive it from the customer while giving them a feeling of being cared for when it is done well.

5.2.24   Information Technology (IT) department

IT departments are often associated only with computers without really appreciating fully what they do, and play a major role in supporting other departments. The IT department is often tasked with providing management with information. With this in mind, IT have to work closely with functional managers to decide just what information they want, in what form they want it and how often do they want it. These are just some of the criteria they need to take into consideration as well as the question of how much it costs to provide.

Information is a very powerful resource and it can aid decision making as well as allowing individuals and groups to exert control within the organization. IT departments often have a responsibility for providing managers with information, which can be anything from how much profit a supermarket makes per square metre of floor space to how many units of production are made by each production worker. This information can assist decision making greatly because the organization can predict what profit levels will need to be made to make the planned supermarket viable. If predictions mean having an exceptionally high turnover which cannot be sustained by the local market, then the organization may have to revise its plans.

By providing managers with information on an operational, tactical and strategic level, IT can begin to take some of the decision making away from local managers. An example of this might be the credit rating systems used by some organizations. If an individual fits a set of criteria developed by headquarters, they score a certain number of points and can automatically be given credit. If they do not, then the decision is referred to headquarters. In both examples the local manager, more or less, has the decision taken out of their hands.

IT provides different types of information to different people for different reasons. Decision-support systems give managers a range of options and courses of action. If data are changed in one part of the system then IT can see how it affects the rest. For example, if mortgage interest rates were to increase then mortgage repayments would rise and this might reduce the demand for houses which, in turn, might cause unemployment in the construction industry. By using a range of different interest rate rises, it is possible to predict a variety of unemployment rates in the construction industry. It can be a great advantage to the manager who has to make the final decision because they are able to see the range of effects their actions will have. It can have major implications for human resource management who can use the information to plan for redundancies or recruitment, whichever is required.

IT departments can also provide expert information by linking experts in a particular field from any part of the world to non-experts who need their advice. Recent experiments have been performed where using this method heart surgeons in one part of the world have directed surgeons in another part.

For business this means the manager can have access to a phenomenal amount of expertise. Senior managers can use information technology to keep control or monitor any part of their business operation. This can mean they could have easy access to information on anything, from profits per business subdivision to how much each office costs to heat and light.

People working in IT departments can often need the same type of management as those associated with research and development, namely to allow creativity and innovation to flourish but at the same time to retain control by ensuring targets are met and quality is ensured.

It should be apparent that IT needs to liaise very closely with all departments. Production will need IT for its processes and control of quality; Finance need IT for anything from financial reporting to payroll payments; Marketing need IT for their research analysis and consumer behaviour modelling; and Human Resources need IT for staff planning and record keeping. This gives IT a crucial role to play and it is under constant pressure to keep ahead of all developments in technology, whether it is voice-activated word processing or video conferencing. This demand for the latest in technology cannot always be met and IT departments have to decide who gets the latest technology and who gets second-user equipment. This can lead them into conflict situations with end-users who are asking for the impossible in terms of technical support or instant maintenance. It is a further dilemma for the managers of IT departments: the high expectations of end-users who may not know what they really want and the limitations of what the technology can actually do.

5.2.25   The Administration department

Central administration often exists in large organizations where it is necessary for one department to control and administer the routine work of all the other functions. The work that the central administration department carries out can vary from one organization to another, but the following are some of their areas of work.

Keeping a database

A database of sources of information can be retained and maintained by central administration for items such as small *ad hoc* purchases and details of service providers such as machine repairers or telephone engineers.

Providing a customer/organization interface

Enquiries from the public either in person or by telephone can be dealt with by central administration. Indeed they can act as a filtering mechanism by preventing key personnel from being interrupted by enquiries of a routine nature. They can also act as diary keepers for staff who have to go off-site, but with whom there needs to be contact.

Organizing staff support requirements

By having a contact person in administration it is possible that a degree of consistency is maintained when dealing with the making of travel arrangements, hotels and other forms of support requirements for staff travelling on company business.

Providing clerical and word processing support

Central administration can provide an efficient, effective and professional service in terms of word processing, photocopying and collation of all written materials. They can also provide a professional to record the minutes of meetings accurately, followed by their speedy accurate typing. One of the least appreciated of their services is that of training functional administrative and management staff in the use of organizational standard procedures (for example, the standardized layout of correspondence, use of report formats and any other company-wide printed documentation). As software packages for word processing are updated it is often left to central administration to train managers in their use. Where there is no purchasing function in an organization the responsibility for purchasing office equipment and stationery can rest with central administration.

Filing

Central administration often collate and maintain routine computer files containing items such as standardized letters of response to general enquiries.

Conference planning

Central administration can play a key role in room allocation for on-site conferencing or meetings, including refreshment provision. They can arrange for the provision and duplication of any literature required and also be available to organize off-site conferences and guest speakers.

5.2.26   Central administration as a focal point

Often Central administration is used as a place where mail enters and leaves the organization. Because of this it becomes a meeting place for other staff as they collect such mail. This makes it one of the main channels for communication in the organization, where people meet and exchange information of a business as well as a social nature. This can be good for worker morale as well as giving feedback to people on what is happening in other parts of the organization and it also forms a critical part of the informal organization.

Exercise

'HRM is an additional cost that we can do without.' Together with one or two other students discuss this statement.

Feedback

You should be able to construct an argument in defence of the HR function along the following lines. Obviously there are costs to running an HRM department. However, the contribution that HRM makes to the smooth and efficient running of an organization through its involvement in activities from recruitment and selection to giving legal advice make it an invaluable asset. Without HR organizations would probably not have the consistency of dealing with their human resources that they get with HR. This in turn might mean a less efficient and effective organization.

Summary

In this section you have examined the different functional departments and the variety of activities they are involved in, from research and development to administration. This has given you an insight into how different their specialist functions are. Now you should be able to recognize not only how they differ but also how they interrelate. You have looked at how some of those functions have wide-ranging contacts and influence in the organization, functions such as the finance department felt to be at the heart of the organization, or Information Technology, which has to provide all functions with information.

5.3   Organization structures

An organization is the rational co-ordination of the activities of a number of people for the achievement of some explicit purpose or goal, through division of labour and function, and through a hierarchy of authority and responsibility.

E.H. Schein[16]

Section objectives

In this section you will:

● Examine organization structure, culture, power, politics and conflict
● Look at the component parts of a structure and their relationship

- Study different types of structure bureaucracy, matrix
- Consider different types of culture
- Look at different sources of power and organization politics
- Examine views of conflict and conflict management.

Exercise

Ask your HR department for a copy of your organization chart, making sure that it includes your department.

Feedback

An organization chart can provide you with a lot of information, for example a career path you might want to follow or how to locate certain individuals. Other areas include, it should be relatively clear from the chart on what basis it has been drawn (functions, departments). You should be able to easily follow the chain of command from your own position through that of your bosses right to the top of the organization. You should also be able to see how many levels of management there are in the organization and then determine whether or not it is a tall, narrow organization with many levels or a short, flatter organization with few levels. This will give you an additional opportunity to identify problems with these two types of structure such as slower communications and lack of promotion opportunities.

5.3.1   Introduction

We all spend time in our organizations without sometimes really appreciating what goes on or how complex they really are. It is with this in mind that the study of organization structures can begin to give us an idea of the rational coordination that is referred to by Schein. We know from our own experience that there is a hierarchy in organizations but we may not be aware of other issues such as organizational politics or power distribution with which it interrelates. By looking more closely at organizations we can obtain a critical perspective of some of these activities.

5.3.2   Structuring organizations

Before we begin to examine the structure of organizations we need to think about what organizations are, what they do and how they do it.

Organizations come in many different forms and sizes. Some are charities in the voluntary sector, some exist to make profits and some to provide services. Some organizations are privately owned by families, others owned by their shareholders and a few controlled by the government.

So what are they? Organizations can be viewed as merely collections of people who have to work together to successfully achieve some goal that has been set for them. How do they achieve this? The answer is by using all the resources available to them – plant, machinery, money, people and time – and converting them into a product or service that customers want. This means that there has to be some way of organizing what is being done in order to achieve the outcomes required, namely goods or service production. We can further add that someone needs to be directing the efforts of those who are working in the organization, who need to have power and authority in order to get others to obey them and hence get things done. With this in mind we can see that organizations include not only the way we organize efforts but also how we apportion authority and power and, furthermore, how we might delegate.

5.3.3   Organizations can be both formal and informal

Chester Barnard[17] believed that people needed to have a group purpose to coordinate what they do and a formal organization would appear when:

- People were willing to work to a common purpose and
- They communicated with one another.

The informal organization depends more on what the people 'want' rather than what the formal organization 'says'. For example, management may set out a formal way of dealing with some aspect of work. However, those doing the work may decide upon their way of doing it which satisfies their social desires. It is important to recognize that there is an informal organization. It can be the case that if you are not accepted by those people who have worked together for some time and developed their own way of doing things and social groupings then you will be ostracized and even forced out. As a long-term investment or survival strategy it is worth learning who are the important players in the informal organization and what are the most important of their rules and ways of doing things. These organizations can get things done without going through the normal channels, and at times this can be useful. Informal organizations have their own channels of communication and they can, if not carefully monitored, work against the best interests of the organization. However, if they are directed positively and valued for the way they can unite people they can be very hard working in the interests of the organization. An example of a formal structure is the bureaucracy which we will discuss later.

Now that we know that organizations exist to provide a product or a service this idea that it has a purpose needs to be put into action and organized. As we have already mentioned, it is necessary for some people to have more power and authority than others so that they can get things done. However, this is not the only aspect that will affect structure. Other things such as what it does, where it operates, its size, its customers, its complexity and its technology are all examples of influences on its structure. For example, you can imagine a multinational petrochemical organization being structured differently from that of a firm comprising father and daughter operating as market traders.

The idea that some people have more power than others within an organization leads us to the view that within organizations there needs to be different levels of power and authority. Since people look to their leader to give them permission and if we accept that organizations are made up of groups of people with different skills and power, it then follows that the different group leaders will look to their leaders and so on. This brings us to the ideal that there is a logic to having a number of levels or a hierarchy of power and authority within an organization. As decisions become more important there are fewer people who can take those decisions and effectively a pyramid of authority develops (Figure 5.6).

The staff at level 1 look to their leader from level 2 to give them 'permission' to act. At level 2 all the team leaders could together decide on a course of action. However, without the 'permission' from their leader at level 3 this cannot happen and so we realize that the organization has a pyramid-like structure with the greatest authority vested at the top.

Staff level 4 – Senior manager

Staff level 3 – Administrative manager

Staff level 2 – Junior manager (team leader)

Staff level 1 – Supervisor

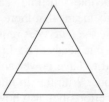

Figure 5.6. The pyramid of authority.

This authority and how it is delegated helps to create the relationships that exist between groups of people. Remembering, of course, that management gets things done through people it is important to know who should be given responsibility and how to coordinate the different groups of specialists who do the work. In organizations three types of relationship exist: line, staff and functional. However, before doing so it is worth mentioning the term 'span of control'. This refers to the number of staff who report directly to a particular manager and that manager is responsible for the work they do. The more staff a manager controls, the broader their span of control, the fewer staff controlled, the narrower their span.

5.3.4 Line relationships

In a line relationship there is a direct line of authority between the most senior person (the finance director) and the most junior (the accounts clerk) (see Figure 5.7).

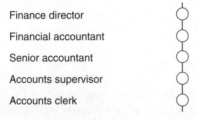

Finance director

Financial accountant

Senior accountant

Accounts supervisor

Accounts clerk

Figure 5.7. Line relationships.

5.3.5 Staff relationships

Staff relationships involve other groups who provide support to a department. For instance, the IT department can give advice to the administration department. But the administration department does not have to accept the advice because although they may not be specialists in information technology they are specialists in administration and they may not see any sense in accepting the advice from the IT department.

5.3.6 Functional relationships

A functional relationship is one where a department does have the right to determine how another department operates in certain circumstances. For example, a Finance department can insist that all departments accept a standardized approach to accounting or budgeting practice.

5.3.7 Designing an organization structure

When it comes to the design of an organization structure Handy[18] suggests that an appropriate structure would be determined by a number of forces, the technology, the market, size and staff.

5.3.8 Departments

We can further divide an organization into departments and these departments can be chosen based on a variety of criteria. Organizations can be divided according to the following.

Function

This is where there is a concentration on specialization. For instance, the organization can subdivide the Finance department into areas such as financial accounting, management accounts and audit. This can result in a very narrow view of the organization and it is not unusual for departments to be inward looking and suspicious of other departments and so failing to work together. The coordination of their efforts is not an easy task and to break down the barriers and obstacles such as departmental self-interest can be a difficult task (see Figure 5.8).

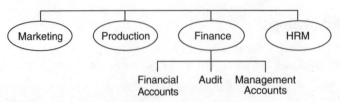

Figure 5.8. Function division.

Product

In this situation each departmental manager has the responsibility for a particular product such as cat food, dog biscuits or any other type of product. Product-specific departments may also have functional departments within them such as finance or production. This can allow greater integration of the various functions into the activities of producing a particular product and staff and management can be judged by the performance of the product. Concentration on one particular product can focus the development of expertise in that area and can be used to differentiate the organization from the competition. However, the coordination of all these efforts and the potential for duplication of functional overheads can result in cost escalation (see Figure 5.9).

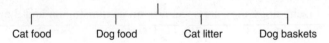

Figure 5.9. Product division.

Geography

Some organizations choose to subdivide based on which particular part of the country or world they are operating in. This can move the organization closer to local markets and move decision making to the regions. This autonomy can be beneficial because it means decisions are made by the people who are going to carry them out closer to the market. It can also raise the issue of control as local efforts or ideas may not fit in with those of head office.

Customers

Where a customer is important enough or large enough to dictate it, departments can be created to deal with them and them alone. For example, in the gas supply industry a sales department may be divided along the lines of industrial and domestic customers.

Process

Where products pass through a variety of processes before completion it is possible to form departments based on those processes. For example, during manufacture a car might go through an assembly department, a painting department and a finishing department before it is completed and so might a tractor. This allows us to bring together in those departments plant, machinery and people with the necessary expertise to work on both. This can be advantageous in terms of efficient use of machinery and labour.

It is worth noting that although a number of criteria; function, product, geography, customers and process have been used this is not necessarily a definitive list. What is important to remember is not to be too rigid in terms of structure because each method has its advantages and disadvantages. Some departments are combinations of approaches.

5.3.9   Bureaucracy

Max Weber[19] is the writer most often associated with the term 'bureaucracy'. Weber studied power and authority and concluded that power was the ability to get things done by threats of force. Authority, on the other hand, was managing to get things done because the manager's orders were seen by others as justified or legitimate. This led Weber to identify three types of authority, which can be described as traditional by right of birth, charismatic from some perceived special quality, and legal–rational which comes by way of the laws of the land or an organization's rules.

Weber stressed that administration needed to be founded on the rules of experts and officials and bureaucracy had the following characteristics which have been based on his work:

- Specialization: Each job requires its own particular expertise.
- Hierarchy: The bureaucracy has a structure with a clear demarcation between those who rule and those who are ruled.
- Rules: There has to be a set of rules which are virtually unchanging and can be learned by staff. The rules cover virtually everything and management must follow the rules.
- Impersonality: In a bureaucracy everyone is treated fairly and objectively.
- Appointed officials: Staff are appointed based on their technical qualifications.
- Full-time officials: Officials should occupy the one job in the bureaucracy which should occupy them full time.
- Career officials: The jobs should be based on a system of progression that is determined by seniority or achievement.
- Private/public: Any official duties/money/property must not be mixed with personal/private duties/money/property.

5.3.10   Matrix organizations

An alternative to structuring an organization by specialist department is the matrix structure, which is used when there is a need to deal with complex projects. The principle behind the idea of matrix structures is that while retaining an element of functional specialization the staff of each function, and indeed the function itself, must be flexible to work on a range of projects or even products.

In a typical matrix structure (see Figure 5.10) the three functions – Finance, Production and Marketing – would be expected to supply resources, including people, to the three projects A, B and C. The people would be under the control of the functional head as well as the project leader. Although this can cause some confusion the matrix structure has its advantages in terms of the following:

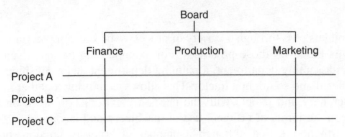

Figure 5.10. A typical matrix structure.

- Flexibility: People have the opportunity to work on a number of projects with new challenges.
- Communications: Project working will mean greater opportunities to network with other individuals and departments and improve formal and informal communications.
- Responsibility: Responsibilities for results are allocated to individual project managers who then know what is expected of them.
- Skills development: By bringing together people from different functional disciplines skills can be transferred between individuals and best practice can be exported to functional departments.
- Motivation: Employees can take control over some of the decision making and this in turn can give them ownership of their project with a vested interest in its success.

There are, however, disadvantages associated with matrix organizations and these can include:

- Conflict: Conflict can arise between functional and project managers. It is necessary when using this approach to clearly define who has authority and in what areas of the project.
- Role conflict: The traditional approach to management is that each person should only have one boss. In matrix management an individual can have two and this can result in the individual having divided loyalties and being confused about to whom they are answerable.
- Managerial costs: Management costs can increase because a functional as well as a project manager are required to carry out the management of the project and the functional department.
- Management resistance: The self-interest of either the functional or project manager can create resistance if either or both feel that their authority or position is threatened.

5.3.11   Centralization and decentralization

This refers to the degree to which authority is delegated in an organization. In other words, where and at what level in the organization decisions are made. It is impossible to have an organization that is totally centralized or decentralized. There must come a point where individuals have some decision-making capability. Similarly, with decentralization there must come a point where there must be some centralized control.

There is an emphasis toward centralization where managers want to:

- Exercise a greater degree of control over the organization's activities
- Enforce standard practices and procedures throughout the organization and
- Try to guarantee improved or greater coordination of subunits.

There is an emphasis toward decentralization when we need to delegate authority:

- To fully utilize local knowledge and expertise
- To keep spans of control narrow enough to be practical
- To reduce centralized structures that are costly and duplicated and
- To empower staff through involvement and consequently motivate them.

Why does decentralization happen?

- As an organization grows and develops, specialization is also likely to increase as will the number of levels in the hierarchy. The chain linking the very top with the bottom will also lengthen. This means that in order to deal with the more remote parts of the organization delegation and hence decentralization is more likely to take place.
- The advent of cheaper technology has meant that it is possible to decentralize more but still retain strong central control. This is through a linked technology system that can ensure that managers have easy access to control information and is achieved through management information systems and executive information systems that can allow senior managers access to performance data.
- Decentralization can also occur where organizations want to set up individual cost centres to make units responsible for their own costs and revenue generation.

5.3.12   Organization design and structure

The following article[20] by Keith Rodgers outlines how organization design can improve performance.

What is it?

The concept of 'organisational design' is pretty much self-explanatory, although the word 'design' gives it a far more creative feel than it often merits. Most companies have evolved along traditional departmental lines, driven from the top down in a classic management hierarchy with little novel thought applied to the way that employees interact with each other, or with the outside world. Not surprisingly, this approach rarely proves to be the best way to meet customer demand, and it is certainly not the best way to leverage human capital. Organisational design addresses these issues – it is all about shaping the company to maximise its effectiveness.

The story so far

Organisational design has occupied the minds of the great and the good for decades. In 1937, for example, British economist Ronald Coase published The Theory of the Firm, arguing that organisations should stick with rigid hierarchical structures even in agile markets, because that was the most cost-effective way of carrying out transactions.

Coase's work, which won him a somewhat belated Nobel Prize in 1991, shot back into prominence in the late 1990s. That, you'll recall, was when the internet was supposed to change everything. Cyber-gurus such as Don Tapscott, whose long list of admirers included Bill Clinton, argued that the internet finally provided a platform for cheap transactions between organisations, freeing companies to experiment with new, more fluid structures. Suddenly, rigid hierarchies were out and flexibility was everything. The concept of collaboration moved into mainstream business thinking, describing the way in which highly-agile organisations come together at will to form mutually beneficial relationships – sometimes long-term, sometimes to tackle one-off projects.

This approach turns organisational design theory on its head. When Henry Ford's motorcar business came to dominance, he owned his supply chain. Everything from the rubber plantations that supplied material for his tyres, to the mahogany forest that supplied the wood. By contrast, when Cisco became the most valuable company in the world at the height of the dot com boom, it only owned a handful of the different plants that make its products. They were primarily built and assembled by others, and in some instances they were shipped directly to customers without even going through Cisco itself. The reason? The internet made this kind of approach cost-effective.

The advent of the internet also accelerated another trend – towards empowering the customer. Historically, organisations have been structured from a supply perspective – what they sold was primarily driven by what their manufacturing plants were geared up to make. Today, globalisation and internet-based communications give the customer far more flexibility to shop around, and the emphasis is now on supplying what the customer wants, when they want it. This too has enormous implications for organisational structure. To understand all the facets of customer need and provide comprehensive customer service, all the different units within companies need to work together far more coherently. That means departmental 'silos' are history.

The promise

One of the great things about flexible and agile business environments is that they continually challenge the status quo. In practice, that means the largest, most established organisations dominating today won't automatically dominate tomorrow – in fact in many cases, their sheer size and traditional structures will play against them. Theoretically, therefore, organisations designed for maximum flexibility can make their mark with a speed that historically hasn't been possible. But the flipside, of course, is that they can also lose it all even faster.

Effective organisational design holds out the promise for companies to transform their ability to do business. By breaking down the barriers between internal departments, they can maximise their human capital through better team-work, improving customer management and retention, and maximising their supply efficiencies by building truly collaborative relationships.

One thing to bear in mind about organisational design, however, is that the promise doesn't always match the reality. Take Cisco – for all its organisational flexibility, it hardly proved immune to the high-tech collapse. And look at the whole business process re-engineering movement, started off in the late 1980s by Dr Michael Hammer, and responsible in the 1990s for some hugely regrettable corporate cock-ups.

Pros and cons

The good news is that the renewed corporate focus on organisational design reflects business reality. Agility and collaborative capability are essential, and the only question is the degree of change required in different sectors and the speed with which it has to happen. From HR's perspective, a further upside is that today's organisational design theory places a high emphasis on unleashing employee value, and as such, it is a key plank of Human Capital Management strategy.

The cons, however, are both cultural and practical. Quite simply, building an agile business is a momentous task. An organisation structured around product sets, for example, will need to be fundamentally reorganised to become truly customer-centric – instead of business processes designed to build and supply individual products, it will require processes designed to fulfil individual customer need from any combination of product. This kind of change management programme is extensive.

Likewise, for all their faults, hierarchical structures are comfortable for employees, particularly in terms of management reporting, career structure and perceived status. Agile structures that encourage cross-departmental activity, team-working and project-based assignments present a whole host of new challenges, which are likely to encounter resistance.

In addition, new ways of working require new infrastructures. Business agility has much to do with the way that information flows across an organisation, so information technology plays a critical role. While vendors have been re-architecting their product sets for years to meet the challenge of business agility, in practice users will still face challenges, particularly in terms of integration between systems.

Who is on board?

Pretty much everyone, from management theorists to the technology vendors that provide much of the supporting infrastructure. Bear in mind that the key players may not be visible under the guise of organisational design per se, but proponents of business philosophies such as customer relationship management view organisational design as a key plank of their thinking.

Dissenting voices are most likely to be found within the ranks of organisations. They won't just be those of trade unionists anxious about the implications of increased flexibility and fluidity in job roles. They will also include line managers jealous of their power bases, and even senior executives.

Verdict

There is huge momentum behind organisational design change to create agile, collaborative enterprises, but the practical hurdles are significant. Ultimately, organisations will be well advised to take a pragmatic approach, seeking to gain benefits from a series of small change projects which improve their business responsiveness while building towards a longer-term collaborative goal.

The HR contribution

Absolutely crucial. Organisation design is an area where HR can exert great influence, demonstrating both its strategic vision and its tactical prowess. Fundamentally, organisational design is about processes and people – that's HR's game.

5.3.13 Culture

If we think about our own organization and what happens each day when we arrive at work, we are expected to behave in a particular way. Some of the norms or unwritten rules for behaviour are that we say 'good morning' and are usually polite to people. This behaviour is part of the socialization process of work and life generally and it is behaviour like this that contributes to organizational culture. We are also aware of what is and is not acceptable practice. We know that we must attend a certain number of hours, we know that we will be consulted in certain situations. These also contribute to culture and when we change jobs and work for another organization we know that its culture may well be different. It may have some similarities but it will also have some pronounced differences.

An organization's buildings can also make a statement about its culture. Walk around the City of London and the power, wealth and stability of the financial sector becomes obvious and this reflects in the behaviour, hopes and attitudes of the employees. Contrast this with a small advertising agency in the West End where accommodation is limited and the approach to work is frenetic and you can begin to appreciate the differences in culture. In other words, organizational culture is the collective set of values that inform individual and collective behaviour – it is the way things are done.

Handy[18] developed the idea of four different types of culture – Power, Role, Task and Person.

Exercise

Examine two different departments in your organization. What do you notice?

Feedback

Each department should exhibit signs of its own culture. This may be recognized through the actions of those who work in each department. One department might appear to be casual, sociable and flexible with a democratic approach to work. The other might appear serious, quiet, structured and less flexible. Each of these departments has its own culture (or sub-culture) and there should be a dominant overriding organizational culture that bonds the whole organization together. From the dominant culture we can get an idea about how the organization wants us to behave but within this there is scope for individual departments to develop their own codes of behaviour (as in the examples above) as long as they don't conflict with the organization's norms. The ability to recognize the culture of an organization or department is very important because it tells you how they operate and if you don't like the way they operate you can avoid working in those organizations or departments. Likewise, if you recognize the culture and like it then you may want to join the organization or department because they operate in a way you find attractive.

The influences on culture

Handy[18] goes on to discuss various influences on the choice of culture for an organization. The following are based on Handy's choice of six influences: history and ownership, size, technology, goals and objectives, the environment and the people.

Other views on culture

Tom Peters and Robert Waterman[21] noted that 'in an organizational sense, these stories, myths and legends appear to be very important, because they convey the organization's shared values or culture' and that 'If companies do not have strong notions of themselves as reflected in their values, stories, myths and legends, people's only security comes from where they live on the organization chart'.

Edgar Schein[22] suggests that all organizations have three levels of culture and these are described as artifacts, values and basic underlying assumptions:

● **Level 1 Artifacts and creations:** The visible level is what Schein calls visible artifacts which includes the technology an organization uses, its buildings, dress codes and behaviour patterns between managers and their staff.

- **Level 2 Values:** At this level, Schein identified values that led to a greater awareness of culture which can be used by the organization and its staff to condition the basic underlying assumptions. These included ideas such as company mottos and stories and myths about past events and people that might have been successful or even failures but in some way united people. Organizations could encourage this by rewarding those who support the official culture.
- **Level 3 Basic assumptions:** The basic underlying assumptions are invisible and taken for granted. They vary very little within the culture and members and if people were to act differently other than in ways governed by the assumptions others would find it strange. Basic assumptions covered areas such as the nature of human relationships and human nature. Examples of this might be how people viewed others' attitude to work or manager/staff relationships.

What do cultures do?

Robbins[23] argues that culture has a number of functions:

- It ensures differences between organizations by defining what is acceptable and what is not. What is acceptable in one organization may not be in another and so the limits of acceptable behaviour are set.
- Culture makes a statement about the individuals who work in a particular organization and gives them something of which they can feel proud.
- Culture encourages the subordination of an individual's goals to those of the organization.
- The culture is a framework of behaviour that unites all members of staff.
- Culture is a method of control whereby the values and attitudes of staff are moulded.

Robbins[23] suggests that once owner–founders have decided upon what they want to do with the organization those values live on. From the values of the founder, organizations then reinforce the culture by only selecting individuals to join the company who will fit in with the culture. This means that Human Resource management can contribute to cultural reinforcement.

Human Resource management is party to the recruitment of the individual who must fit in with the values of the organization. This is done by careful attention to the selection process and how the person specification is written. Once in the organization HRM can monitor their progress through the appraisal system where adoption of the culture can be rewarded. Senior management have their part to play by leading by example. Staff take their lead from role models such as their managers and will copy their approaches, good or bad.

Finally, because staff must fit into the culture they have to learn the company's way of doing things. For example, when we went to our first infants' school we had to adapt to a set of rules which were more rigid perhaps than those of our parents at home. As we grew older and changed schools we had to learn ways of doing things at our new school. We already knew some ways we had learned at our infants' school and we took those with us. We learned some new things when we arrived, but after a short period of time we began to do things automatically according to the new rules and so we entered into its culture.

5.3.14   Politics, power and conflict

Power allows us to get things done so power is what we have to influence others. It is also worth mentioning the idea of authority at this point. To have authority means that the individual is allowed to make certain decisions because of where they are positioned in the hierarchy. The higher the person is, the greater their authority and power. The relationship between power and authority within the structure will detail what each individual is meant to do and what their relationship is with others.

Authority and power move from the top of the organization to the bottom and gives managers the right to make certain decisions, to allocate work to staff and to expect their legitimate orders to be carried out.

Power can be used to influence people and those who may not have the authority can still have power to make people act. This is how informal leaders are able to operate. They may not have the position of authority but if they have the power then they can influence their followers.

The way people use influence will vary depending on the power used. For example, if physical power is used then this will usually mean the method of influence is force. People's behaviour will also be influenced by the implementation of rules by those with position and resource power. The use of bargaining and negotiation will depend on the strength or weakness of each party and whether alternatives are available. In this case expert or resource power can be used. Referent or personal power can be used to persuade people to change.

French and Raven[24] suggested five bases of power: coercive, reward, expert, legitimate and referent power.

- **Coercive power** depends on fear. The idea behind the use of coercive power is that we fear something unfavourable will happen to us if we do not do as we are told.
- **Reward power** depends upon whether or not an individual can give or withhold something that is held to be valuable by others.
- **Expert power** exists if people believe an individual has some superior intelligence and expertise that will help to complete particular types of work.
- **Legitimate power** is usually conferred by the position that an individual occupies within an organization's hierarchy. Their legitimacy is based on the formal role that an individual has within the organization.
- **Referent power** is sometimes referred to as charisma in the belief that the leader has traits and qualities that people like and will admire.

Use of power by managers

A manager may be called upon to use any of these bases of power depending on the situation. The bases can be complementary and are useful when a manager needs to use them to influence staff. For instance, a manager may use expert power that impresses employees. This, in turn, may enhance the manager's referent power.

It should be remembered that managers need to use power carefully because it is part of a dependency relationship. Dependency relies very much on how much more power one person has over the other and how much the second person desires whatever it is the first can offer. If this dependency relationship is compromised then problems can occur.

Power distribution

Power is not distributed evenly in an organization's hierarchy and it may be that senior managers have a great deal of position power but they depend upon their staff to support them by inputting into their decision making.

5.3.15   The political dimension

Organizations are made up of people who have their own personal agendas. Organizational politics will involve individual petty jealousies, they will consist of those who wish to win at the expense of the organization and dominate either through coalitions with others or by the force of their own personalities.

Mintzberg[25] has identified the political 'games' that are played in organizations and how they can be both stimulating for the organization and also detrimental to it. He has highlighted what he called the 'games people' play, namely:

- Games to resist authority
- Games to deal with this resistance
- Games to build power bases
- Games to defeat rivals and
- Games to change the organization.

It is obvious from the list that some of these are going to be detrimental. For example, if people are having personal vendettas within the organization, then their efforts are not being directed to the aims of the organization.

How can managers operate in difficult political circumstances?

One way is for managers to develop their own power base so that others are dependent on them. It can also be advisable to improve network peer support and develop social and informal contacts to pre-empt problems.

5.3.16   Conflict

Conflict can come in many forms and from many sources and can be between individuals between groups or between management and organized labour. These types of conflict may seem to be about dividing loyalties between a trade union and the organization but it is possible to reconcile the goals of the organization and the goals of the trade union.

The sources of conflict are many and varied and they include employment relationships, competition for resources, ambiguity over responsibility, interdependence and differentiation, to name a few. These are covered in more detail in Chapter 6.

Conflict can manifest itself in many forms

The Marxist view is that conflict is about a struggle between classes: those who own and control the means of production and the workforce who provide labour. As a result of their differences in power, conflict occurs. The only way is to balance the power of the owners with that of organized labour. Organizations are therefore seen as places where conflict is inevitable because of the imbalance of power.

A traditional view of conflict sees it as a failure of management, because it is management's job to get everyone working towards the common goal of the organization. If this is not happening, as in conflict situations it must be the fault of management. This is sometimes referred to as a unitary perspective of organizations. By accepting that organizations are made up of many and varied individuals all of whom have self-interest as well as an interest in the organization a pluralist view develops that conflict is natural due to competition between individuals and groups. The parties in the conflict can vary. Conflict can involve a large number of people with a rational plan with clearly defined objectives or individuals who feel aggrieved.

Tactics used in conflict

Handy[18] identifies a number of tactics used in conflict situations including information control and distortion.

When using these tactics the parties must be aware that they can have a negative effect on the conflict including:

An escalation of the conflict.
An increase in mistrust brought about because of suspicion about available information.
A lot of wasted time and effort and
The total breakdown of a once cooperative situation.

Management strategies for dealing with conflict

The strategies managers can use for dealing with conflict can also vary. Thomas[26] has shown that managers could adopt five differing styles or approaches to deal with conflict, competition, collaboration, avoidance, accommodation and compromise. These approaches depended upon the degree of assertiveness each party to the conflict displayed and the amount of cooperation each party felt was necessary to placate the other. They can be briefly described as follows.

- **Competition** (one party assertive and uncooperative): In the language of the negotiator this is an 'I win, you lose' situation. This is not necessarily good in the long run because the parties may still have to work together in the future.
- **Collaboration** (both parties assertive and cooperative): A negotiator would see this as an 'I win, you win' situation with a good chance that cooperation will continue into the future.
- **Avoidance** (one party unassertive and uncooperative): This is an approach taken by one of the parties which is very much like burying one's head in the sand and pretending the problem does not exist. The conflict is, in fact, suppressed but not necessarily dealt with.
- **Accommodation** (one party unassertive and cooperative): In this situation one party allows the other's concerns to take precedence and so maintain a working relationship.
- **Compromise** (both parties are mid-range on both dimensions): Here both sides have moved some way to compromise and give and take. This is usually described as an 'I win, you win' situation.

Exercise

It is said that 'fight or flight are the only two choices when it comes to conflict'. Discuss this statement with one or two of your fellow students. Do you think it is true?

Feedback

In extreme survival situations this may be true. However, we know that conflict comes in differing degrees. We do not need to resort to war to deal with minor conflicts. An approach we might want to take is to ask ourselves, How did we get into this situation in the first place? The causes of conflict are many and varied. There are also a number of different ways in which we can deal with conflict. We have to find a way of dealing with conflict that is acceptable to all parties involved, therefore we should try to avoid behaviour that inflames the situation. By finding a mutually acceptable solution we avoid the situation where one party feels they have lost and goes away only to seek revenge at some time in the future, resulting in ongoing disruption to the efficient and effective operation of our organization.

Summary

In this section you have examined organizational structure, culture, power, politics and conflict. You have looked at the component parts of a structure and different types of structure such as bureaucracy and matrix.

- You have spent some time comparing different theories of culture and types of culture.
- You have briefly looked at sources of power and organizational politics as well as a range of views of conflict and conflict management.

Case study

Pine Construction

Pine Construction are a large privately owned French company who have recently been acquiring more small building-related firms in the UK over the last two years to help them expand.

These acquisitions seem to have been happening rather too quickly and the managing director has decided that they need to take stock of the whole of their portfolio. In order to do this he has decided to ask a number of people to look at different parts of the portfolio and to suggest way forward. One of these people is his youngest son Jean Michel, aged 28, who despite his youth has ten years of experience in the construction industry. He is often described as a natural communicator. As well as being a qualified construction engineer he speaks four European languages and those who have worked with him are said to be impressed by his professionalism.

The task his father has given him is not an easy one. The company relies upon eight rather small joinery workshops to provide all their timber requirements for UK projects. This includes doors, window frames and flooring.

Four of the workshops were acquired from the same parent company two years ago and are now causing some concern because of their low productivity, high accident rates and increased absenteeism. These four workshops are managed by an autocratic general manager, Norman Oaks (known by his staff as 'Nasty Norman'). Each workshop has a manager who Norman appointed and who are referred to as 'Norman's Gnomes'. The workshops serve particular geographic areas and do not really cooperate with the other four individual workshops whose work area often overlaps. Within the workshops work is carried out on a production line basis with strict demarcation between workers. This is at the insistence of the managers and a constant source of irritation to the employees who would like a greater variety of work.

What sort of problems do you think Jean Michel will face? What sort of solutions do you think he might suggest?

Feedback

From the case study it should be possible to identify some areas that are likely to cause concern. The four workshops that are managed by Norman Oaks no doubt have their own individual cultures as well as a collective culture from their previous parent company. It is possible that there is a clash of cultures that could lead to conflict situations arising that will need immediate attention.

From the case it is obvious another area that will need to be addressed is that of health and safety. High accident rates cannot be tolerated and Jean Michel will have to investigate very carefully.

A further area worthy of investigation is that of organization structure. It would appear that there are four workshops operating as a group and four others operating on an individual basis.

Possible solutions that Jean Michel might suggest are to:

- Create a new structure and merge some of the workshops
- Try to develop a new culture in the merged workshops

- Involve the staff more in the operation of the workshops by working in a matrix structure within the workshops in order to allow more varied project type work
- Ask the staff to take ownership of the high accident rate and use them to solve the problem and at the same time use that to develop a culture of safe working as part of a new workshop culture
- Carry out an analysis of leadership styles in use and train and retrain managers and staff to encourage closer team working.

Jean Michel will have to use all the power available to him whether it is his charismatic power or expertise. He will also have to have systems in place to deal with the inevitable conflict situations that arise in times of change like this.

In brief

The subject matter in this chapter has been varied. We began by looking at health and safety legislation and the part human resources management can play in its successful implementation. We next examined a wide range of functional departments and discovered the range of activities that is carried out in them. Finally, we turned our attention to the issue of organizational structures, culture and conflict. We looked at a number of approaches to organizations and a wide range of views of culture and its importance to organizations. We ended by looking at conflict and conflict management issues.

Examination questions for this chapter are given in Appendix 2.

References

1 Stewart, R. (1970) *The Reality of Organizations*. Pan Books.
2 Willis, N. (1988) *Hazards at Work*. TUC.
3 European Strategy, Health and Safety Bulletin, May 2000.
4 W. RULD
5 Armstrong, M. (1998) *Personnel Management Practice*. Kogan Page.
6 Health and Safety Executive Leaflet (1992) *Five Steps to successful H&S management*.
7 *Employment Health Bulletin*, (2), April 1998 p. 6.
8 Violence-NHS, *Employee Health Bulletin*, April 2001, p.6.
9 Head Teachers article, *Employee Health Bulletin*, August 2001, p.3.
10 Doctors' insurers article, *Employee Health Bulletin*, August 2001, p.3.
11 European employers article, *Employee Health Bulletin*, April 2001, p.4.
12 Mulhemann, A. *et al.* (1992) *Production and Operations Management*. Pitman.
13 Eyre, E. C. (1987) *Mastering Basic Management*. Macmillan.
14 Mullins, L. (1992) *Management and Organizational Behaviour*. Pitman.
15 Kotler, P. (1983) *Principles of Marketing*. Prentice Hall.
16 Schein, E. (1970) *Organizational Psychology*. Prentice Hall.
17 Barnard, C. (1938) *The Functions of an Executive*. Harvard University Press.
18 Handy, C. (1985) *Understanding Organizations* (3rd edn). Penguin Books.
19 Weber, M. (1947) *The Theory of Social and Economic Organization*. Collier Macmillan.
20 Rodgers. K. (2002) *Personnel Today*, Nov 2002.
21 Peters, T. J. and Waterman, R. H. (1982) *In Search of Excellence*. Harper and Row.
22 Schein, E. (1991) *Organizational Culture and Leadership*. Jossey Bass.
23 Robbins, S. (1993) *Organizational Behaviour*. Prentice Hall.
24 French, J. R. P. and Raven, B. (1968) The bases of social power: In *Group Dynamics Research and Theory*. (eds Cartwright, D. and Zander, A.). Harper and Row.
25 Mintzberg, H. (1983) *Power in and around the Organization*. Prentice Hall.
26 Thomas, K. (1976) Conflict and conflict management. In *Handbook of Industrial and Organizational Psychology*. (ed. Dunnette, M.). Rand McNally.

Further reading

Bratton, J. and Gold, J. (2003) *Human Resource Management*. Palgrave Macmillan.

Brown, A. D. (1998) *Organizational Culture*. Financial Times/Pitman.

Caulkin, S. (2002) *The change agenda: People management and business performance*. CIPD.

Christopher, M., Payne, A. and Ballantyne, D. (2002) *Relationship Marketing: Creating Stakeholder Value*. Butterworth-Heinemann.

Hammonds (2002) *Health and Safety at Work*. CIPD.

Handy, C. (1998) *Understanding Organizations*. Penguin Books.

Storey, J. (1993) *New perspectives on HRM*. Routledge.

Ward, A. (2003) *The Leadership Cycle – Matching Leaders to Evolving Organizations*. Palgrave.

Zeithaml, V. A. and Britner, M. J. (1996) *Services Marketing*. McGraw-Hill.

Table of statutes

1 Health and Safety at Work Act 1974
2 Employer Liability (Compulsory Insurance) Act 1969
3 Occupiers Liability Acts 1957/1984
4 Reporting of Injuries, Diseases and Dangerous Occurrences Regulations 1995
5 First Aid Regulations 1981
6 Control of Substances Hazardous to Health Regulations 1988 (as amended 1999)
7 Fire Precautions Act 1971
8 Fire Safety and Safety of Places of Sport Act 1987 (as amended 1995)
9 Health and Safety (Consultation with Employees) Regulations 1996
10 (Framework Directive) Management of Health and Safety at Work Regulations 1992 (as amended 1999)
11 Manual Handling Operatives Regulations 1992

Web-site addresses

British Safety Council: http://www.bsc.org.uk
Chartered Institute of Marketing: http://www.cim.co.uk
Department of Health: http://www.doh.gov.uk
Health and Safety Executive: http://www.hse.gov.uk
National Radio Protection Board: http://www.nrph.org.uk
Royal Society for the Prevention of Accidents: http://www.rospa.com
Trades Union Congress: http://www.tuc.org.uk

6   The issue of quality

Quality management is a systematic way of guaranteeing that organised activities happen the way they are planned. It is a management discipline concerned with preventing problems from occurring by creating the attitudes and controls that make prevention possible.

Philip Crosby[1]

Chapter objectives

In this chapter you will:

- Obtain an overview of the issues involved in quality by looking at the implications for organizations for ignoring quality
- Gain an insight into the subject of customer relations and the customer's importance to the organization and
- Look at the issue of change and how it affects organizations and the people who work in them.

Case study

Food for thought

Bob and Betty enjoyed visiting historic towns and this weekend was going to be especially important because the visit coincided with their birthdays. The day passed pleasantly enough and they set out in the evening for a local restaurant.

The restaurant had been recommended and booked by the receptionist at their hotel. The meal started well enough, the waiting staff were attentive and their starter arrived promptly. It was then that things started to deteriorate. There was a long delay before the main course arrived, the waiter realized the delay was occurring and apologized making polite conversation to help keep them happy.

However, when the food arrived Bob cut into a piece of chicken only to find that the centre was still frozen. Bob angrily confronted the waiter who apologized and offered to change the meal. Reluctantly Bob agreed to this, especially when the waiter told him that the sweets and coffees would be free of charge.

When the bill was delivered (by a different waiter), it was apparent that they had been charged for the sweets and coffees. Bob confronted the manager who angrily told him that 'The waiter had no right to do this and there was nothing wrong with the food in his restaurant'. The waiter was called and the argument continued with the waiter arguing with the manager and the manager arguing with Bob. This seemed to cause both amusement and consternation to the other diners. Eventually the manager agreed they could have one sweet and one coffee free. They reluctantly agreed and left promising the manager they would take further action.

On their return to the hotel Bob recounted their story to the hotel receptionist who apologized and said he wouldn't recommend the restaurant in the future. This conversation was heard by a number of other guests in the hotel lobby. On arriving home Bob wrote a letter of complaint to the Environmental Health Department responsible for the restaurants in the town. Some months later he discovered that the restaurant had been fined for a number of infringements of hygiene regulations.

Why do you think this situation occurred? What could the restaurant have done to avoid the situation?

Feedback

This case shows the importance of quality issues and attention to customer relations. When customers enter a restaurant they expect a particular level of quality (quality of design). It is for the restaurant to have in place the systems that can deliver that quality (quality of conformance). There needs to be a system in place to deal with this. There also needs to be a system to deal with customers when things go wrong. In this example the waiter and manager are sending conflicting messages to the customer. The dissatisfied customer in turn tells many others (the hotel receptionist, the other hotel guests, the other diners) and no doubt friends and colleagues about his experience. This then reflects on the restaurant's reputation and other potential customers stop visiting.

A simple relatively cheap gesture (free sweets and coffees as part of a complaints procedure all staff know about) on the manager's part would have avoided the more expensive visit from the Environmental Officer together with its accompanying bad publicity.

Chapter introduction

Like any discerning customer we all look for value for money. However, we are often unsure what we mean by the term. The subjects of this chapter draw our attention to two main areas, those of quality and change. The common link between the two is the customers who have their own ideas about what they think is value for money, and they are becoming more and more discerning about how they spend their money. Organizations through their marketing efforts are realizing the need to retain customers and so they are beginning to put the customer at the centre of the organization's efforts. But the customer, like the organizations that seek to serve them, exist in a world that is dynamic and changing. Not only are organizations subject to change, but so are customers who are having to cope with changing patterns and methods of work, shopping and socializing.

6.1   Quality assurance and other quality issues

Section objectives

In this section you will look at the issue of quality and learn:

- What is meant by quality and how to achieve it
- What is meant by quality circles
- What the implications of quality are for management
- What costs are associated with quality and
- What is meant by quality assurance.

6.1.1   Introduction

All organizations have a reputation and this reputation can be built on a number of factors, including quality, reliability, delivery and price. These are competitive factors and if we can learn to use them well, we can enhance our reputation. Quality is perhaps the most important of these factors and so its management needs to be learned and used well because if we develop a reputation for poor quality, it can take a long time to lose it. So how do we define quality? A description of quality might include ideas about the standards of excellence a product or service enjoys. Other ideas can include quality as a way of satisfying the needs of the customer.

Quality obviously means different things to different people. Someone at an opera might refer to the music they were listening to as being of the highest quality. They may also consider pop music to be of an inferior quality. However, if we were to ask a teenager what they considered to be quality music we might get an answer that makes pop music superior and opera inferior. For both, the view of quality is based on the idea that one particular type of music is somehow superior to the other.

From a provider's point of view, we need to think of what exactly the customer requires. This is just as true for an internal customer as an external one.

6.1.2   Views on quality

Two features of quality highlighted by Juran[2] are those of quality of design and quality of conformance to design.

Quality of design

Quality of design tells us to what extent the product or service has been designed to the requirements of the customer. If the quality of design is poor, the customer will not be satisfied. Good design and quality can only be achieved by having a very good specification that includes quality of materials input into production as well as the processes through which those materials go.

In terms of service sector industries an example of this could be the recruitment of the right people, who then have to go through a standardized training programme. This together with ongoing career development contributes to what the customer needs in terms of customer-focused service providers with the requisite social and technical skills.

Quality of conformance to design

Here managers are comparing how closely the organization is getting to providing customers with what has been agreed in the quality of design. By checking conformance they are attempting to build in quality and make sure that things go according to what was planned in the quality of design. Managers cannot expect to achieve this by constantly inspecting at various stages of production because this can become prohibitively expensive. What they must seek to do is to be concerned with the processes that convert raw materials into the products or services customers require. Due to the complexity of organizations and the number of functional departments that exist there are a multitude of processes being carried out and these processes are often interlinked. In the earlier example of people being recruited and then trained, those people may be recruited by one department, to be trained by another and to work in a third. Managers must be aware that each of these processes, whether it be recruitment or training, must have a clearly defined system of management and these will need to be controlled, monitored and analysed. Managers will need to ask questions such as, 'How do we carry out our recruitment and selection?' 'What sort of training do we give our staff?'

6.1.3   How do we achieve quality?

In the past quality control often consisted of a number of individuals whose only job was to inspect work at different points during the work process. The problem with this approach is that it passes responsibility for quality from the worker who is actually doing the job to someone else. This means that even those who carried out the inspections could allow errors to continue, in the belief that they would be discovered in final inspection and then rectified before being forwarded to the customer. Once the idea of total quality management (TQM) was conceived this changed and the idea of making everyone responsible for quality began.

6.1.4   The internal customer

In all organizations there are those who provide goods and services to other departments and those who use those goods and services. This relationship between those who provide and those who use the goods and services can eventually have an impact on customers from outside the organization. For example, if managers ignore the quality of product or service provided internally then this will reflect in the quality or service provided to external customers. It is therefore critical for managers to emphasize to all staff that they are in some way the customers of and providers to other departments. This can be described as a provider-customer chain of quality and, like any chain, it is only as strong as its weakest link. If one individual employee or piece of machinery fails to meet the requirements of customers it results in the breakdown of the chain. The results of this breakdown invariably impact on the external customer and those who have to deal with them on a personal basis. Managers need to encourage staff to realize that what they are required to do is to think holistically and add value to the product or service whenever possible.

6.1.5   Adding value

An example of adding value can be illustrated by the production of potato crisps. Once organizations know what the customer wants in terms of potato crisps a specification is written in order to achieve it. The potatoes must pass through a number of processes before they reach the customer as crisps. Finally, the organization needs some way of knowing whether they have satisfied the customer's needs in terms of specification. In a simplified version of what might happen we might find that the potatoes are purchased unwashed from the farmer. They are then washed, peeled, sliced thinly, deep fried, flavoured and finally packaged. Through each process in their transformation – purchasing, washing, peeling, slicing, frying, flavouring and packaging – we add value because at each stage they are worth more.

To take a non-manufacturing example, a college might recruit its students, educate and train them academically as well as vocationally with the end result an individual who is valued more by society, the employment market and, perhaps most importantly, by the individual themselves.

Exercise

Examine the situations vacant in any newspaper and compare salaries/wages for unskilled, semi-skilled, skilled and professional jobs.

Feedback

From your comparison you should notice that the greater the skills and qualifications people have, the greater their chances of employment at a reasonable salary. This will give you an idea of how the college has added value to people by enhancing their skills and knowledge through the various academic and vocational education processes.

6.1.6   Define total quality

In order to achieve total quality, managers have to understand that the whole organization needs to be involved. In order for them to achieve quality they need to look at the management of people, planning, customer relationships, communications and team work, strategy and costs.

6.1.7   Managing people and quality

It is through people that organizations get things done and without their full cooperation it is almost impossible to achieve quality output. People help organizations to compete in ever more demanding markets. Organizations can lose their competitive edge because they ignore their human resources, adopting a 'top-down' approach of 'we know what is best for you' rather than involving more junior staff. Other areas can include problems with research and development (e.g. not exploiting discoveries and turning them into viable products).

It is generally accepted that a modern workforce needs to be multi-skilled and flexible. It is necessary therefore to understand that those workers need to be managed in a different way if we are going to maximize their potential. In order to understand which management approach is needed to achieve quality goals we need to look at the work of the writers on Total Quality Management such as Deming (1930), Crosby (1979), and Juran (1951).

Deming[3] has been a major influence in raising the awareness of organizations to the issue of quality. After the Second World War, Deming advised the Japanese about statistical quality control and the need to reduce uncertainty and variability in the design and manufacturing process. Deming's view emphasizes that quality improvement must be driven by senior management and that with improved quality we get higher productivity, which in turn provides long-term competitiveness.

6.1.8   Management approaches to quality

Deming[3] suggested a fourteen-point plan for managers who wanted to adopt a quality approach that is briefly summarized below:

● Organizations need a clear mission and management should be committed to it.
● The organization needs to focus on the customer and this can only be done by removing the 'them and us' attitude that often exists.
● If we think someone else is going to inspect our work then we often let them do just that. This passes the responsibility onto someone else.
● We need to avoid basing purchasing decisions on price alone and to look at quality as well.
● Constant incremental improvement, even though those improvements may be small, should be made based on what the customer feeds back to us.
● Constant training is required so that all employees have skills and knowledge that are not limited to their own job.
● Managers should encourage employees in how to do the job, rather than spend time constantly supervising them.
● If some form of punishment happens because workers fail to meet targets, then the fear this engenders will make those same workers focus only on short-term targets and not on long-term results.
● Interdepartmental feuding needs to be reduced and the efforts of all focused on the customer.
● Workers are not fooled by the use of 'buzz-words' to persuade them to improve quality.

- If targets seem difficult to achieve then workers may cut corners and quality may suffer. If targets are easily achieved then workers may take it easy. By setting quotas managers can encourage short-term thinking whereas they really want long-term continuous improvements.
- Managers and the workforce need to cooperate.
- People need to be educated in the fullest meaning of the word not just in a job-specific sense.
- Total quality management must be fully supported by senior management, who should make the greatest efforts possible to include all the workforce in it.

Crosby[1] developed what he called the 'absolutes of quality management'; these are quality through conformance to requirements, quality through prevention, zero defects and measuring quality through the price of non-conformance. It is worth making some comment on each of the four absolutes in order to aid understanding.

- It is necessary to clearly define what is required. Once something is done we can test to see whether it conforms to requirements. If it does not then it means that some quality is missing.
- Problems with quality occur in the functional departments and they should be made aware of them and then learn how to deal with them.
- Zero defects should mean doing things right first time and not accepting the view that it is acceptable to make mistakes.
- If we do not conform to our requirements then it will cost us in some way (reworking). This cost needs to be made public to highlight the problem, which can then be addressed.

Crosby also produced a fourteen-point quality improvement programme to assist the introduction of total quality management. This like Deming's approach included the need for management commitment, team working, quality awareness, quality measurement, quality evaluation, education, goal setting, costing and error cause removal. The others related to training, use of committees and celebration of success.

6.1.9   Planning and quality

By careful analysis of the costs of poor quality (reworking, visiting customers' premises for repair and investigation) we can identify areas of costs and their interrelationships. By using methods such as process charts, we can identify those areas and plan what needs to be done before certain events take place. These can enable managers to avoid some of the pitfalls that may lead to poor quality, as well as plan alternative courses of action where necessary.

6.1.10   Customer relations and quality

Customer relations, both internal and external, has been allocated its own separate Section 6.2 later in this chapter.

6.1.11   Organization structure and quality

Traditionally organizations have been arranged on a functional basis allowing a logical division of work into specialist areas, for example Finance, Marketing and Administration. These are usually arranged in a hierarchical format as in Figure 6.1.

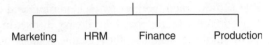

Figure 6.1. A simple functional structure.

The functional structure has its problems, namely those linked to coordination, because work is organized by specialization and not because of customer requirements. This can lead to increased managerial complexity, without really focusing on the needs of the customer because the people within those specialist functions have become insular and parochial.

In order to encourage the idea of quality, organizations have to make their employees understand that potentially everyone is a customer or provider of goods and services, especially in the sense of internal customers. This means making people realize that if someone in the organization needs them to do or make something, before a piece of work can be progressed further then that person is an internal customer and they are providing them with a product or service. This encourages staff to think about the whole process of what they do and its impact on external customers.

The 1990s saw many organizations reduce the number of levels in their hierarchies. The delayering of organizations led to a different focus in terms of what is required of the more junior levels. They were given an increased amount of power to investigate problems and provide the solutions to them. This new focus on problem solving in turn had implications for quality, since the junior levels are more likely to have contact with customers and have day-to-day experience of the problems. They are in a better position to deal with them because of that experience.

Delayering meant improved communications and this too can contribute to improved quality by making it easier for people to get access to key decision makers and dealing with problems while they are still in the development stage.

Some organizations (for example, education establishments), form committees of senior managers to plan for academic quality. These committees are intended to highlight an organizational commitment to quality. Part of their task is to regularly set quality objectives for the organization and to draw together the work and quality approaches of the different departments/faculties. This may include the incorporation of best practice that might exist in one department to the whole organization.

6.1.12 Team work and quality

Team work and quality are closely linked through issues such as empowerment, communications and leadership which are dealt with in other sections of this book. However, at this point it is worth mentioning a particular type of team work and its contribution to quality – the quality circle.

6.1.13 Quality circles

Quality circles have long been used by Japanese companies as part of their focus of on-going quality improvement. They consist of a number of employees who volunteer to meet on a regular basis and discuss any problems concerning the work they are doing. Their day-to-day knowledge of the work is considered to be of paramount importance. This allows them to identify the problems and their causes and ultimately to suggest a solution which may or may not be accepted by management.

Being part of a quality circle can be a great motivator because people are allowed to take some control over the decision-making process and influence their day-to-day working lives. Some people gain personally through being part of a quality circle because it gives them the opportunity to develop skills in communication and problem solving. If group members are weak in some of the skills required, then management will often provide training to deal with this.

The skills development should also include how to understand the potential company-wide implications of their ideas, suggestions and problems. This can be especially important if management has to reject a suggestion because the group will have a better understanding of the reasoning behind that rejection.

Everyone who wants to be involved in a quality circle should be encouraged to do so but, like any group, there are problems with this in terms of personality clashes and limitations on group size. Full participation in idea generation should be encouraged no matter how obscure those ideas might seem. The success or failure of a quality circle is closely linked to management attitude. If management is fully committed to the ideas then teams will be encouraged. However, lack of commitment from management may be demoralizing.

6.1.14   Quality circles and problem solving

Problems can be solved by the use of a number of different techniques and teams need to be trained in their use.

Brainstorming

Brainstorming is probably the best known of the techniques associated with problem solving. It is used to produce as many ideas as possible in the knowledge that one person's idea may act as a catalyst and produce an idea from another. All ideas are recorded and then analysed at a later date by the whole team.

Pareto analysis

Pareto analysis or the 80/20 rule can help a team to prioritize its problems. If 80 per cent of complaints are coming from 20 per cent of customers then we need to deal with their complaints first.

Cause and effect or Ishikawa diagrams

These diagrams (see Figure 6.2) are used to link problems with their causes and help to identify where action needs to be taken in other processes. It should be obvious we can trace back along the figure and identify all the contributing factors to the poor paint finish we have on the door. This allows management to take action to make sure they do not happen again.

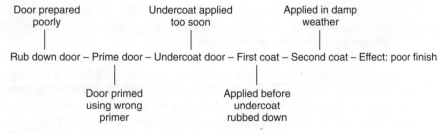

Figure 6.2. An example of a cause and effect diagram.

Critical examination

After the team has all the information it needs to analyse problems, critical examination allows it to use the basic questions what, why, when, how and who. These in turn help make the following links to purpose (what is achieved?), means (how is it achieved?), sequence (when is it achieved?), place (where is it achieved?) and finally person (who achieves it?). We can now create a matrix as in Table 6.1 to aid problem solving.

Table 6.1 Critical examination matrix

Present method	Questions	Alternatives	Choices
What is achieved?	Why is it necessary?	What else could we do?	What should we do?
How is it achieved?	Why do we do it that way?	How else can it be done?	How should it be done?
When is it achieved?	Why do we do it then?	When else could it be done?	When should it be done?
Where is it achieved?	Why do we do it there?	Where else could it be done?	Where should it be done?
Who achieves it?	Why do they do it?	Who else might do it?	Who should do it?

Exercise

In groups of three or four choose a problem that you have faced or have experience of at work. Use the critical examination matrix and apply it to the problem and then report on your results.

- Did they surprise you?
- Did the use of the chart make you think differently?

Feedback

Using the matrix should help to develop a systematic approach to dealing with problems and avoid situations where possible solutions are missed.

6.1.15   Continuous improvement

Continuous improvement has been successfully used by the Japanese for a number of years and the Japanese word 'kaizen' is used to describe it. The idea of kaizen is not to sit back once improvements have been made to a product, but to be almost like bees working away at a hive. Each does a little at a time, but by adding on an incremental basis they can eventually produce something that is much larger and better. The issue of quality can be approached in the same way, so that very minor changes over time can result in a considerable improvement in performance. For example, the levels of fuel efficiency in the average saloon car have improved dramatically over recent years. This has been made possible due to the cumulative effects of continual minor changes in car body shape, fuel delivery systems and engine design.

This idea of continuous improvement can be linked to Deming's[3] idea of Plan, Do, Study and Act, where a problem is examined, information gathered and a plan to improve it is suggested. The 'Do' part is when the plan is tested on a small scale, followed by the 'Study' stage where evaluation of the trial takes place to see if any other issues have arisen. The 'Act' stage is where the plan becomes standard and is carried out continuously. This leads back into the 'Plan' stage for further analysis.

6.1.16 Strategy and quality

Organization strategy is discussed at length in Part Three, but it is worth briefly mentioning here how strategy and a quality approach are linked. Porter[4] suggests that there are a number of strategies for competitive advantage that organizations pursue – cost leadership, differentiation and focus.

Cost leadership

If an organization adopts the idea of cost leadership then it is saying that it wants to be the lowest-cost producer. A quality approach can impact on this because as part of that approach it focuses on getting things done right the first time, therefore avoiding rework costs. This example very simply links the idea of how, by concentrating on quality, organizations can reduce costs.

Differentiation

If an organization adopts differentiation as a strategy then it recognizes the need to focus on a particular characteristic of the product or service. Here a quality approach can contribute by focusing on the quality of the design of the product or service and positioning the product at the luxury end of the market.

Focus

By adopting a focus strategy the organization concentrates on certain niche markets within a wider market and focuses on particular customers. In this type of niche, organizations find that the customer is prepared to pay premium prices for goods or services. However, in return they expect, among other things, high levels of quality. An example of this might be the Morgan Car Company, whose customers are prepared to wait several years for a car but they know that Morgan focus on quality craftsmanship and they obviously feel this is something for which it is worth waiting.

6.1.17 Costs associated with quality

- Costs incurred in the prevention of rejected work, including the maintenance of equipment used in inspection or quality control.
- The costs of administering a system of quality control and any training required.
- Costs incurred finding out whether something is of the correct quality. These can include costs incurred when the quality of inputs such as raw materials are checked.
- The cost of having someone check quality during the production process as well as the costs of final inspection check.
- There are also costs incurred when there is failure to achieve the required quality and these can include finding what has caused the failure, costs of rechecking the reworked product and also the cost of waste in the form of effort, time and materials.
- Customer reaction to poor quality can also create costs for organizations. These include the repair or replacement of products and administration costs associated with the need for a customer complaints department. Perhaps the most underestimated cost is the loss of goodwill, where customers take their business elsewhere and at the same time speak poorly of the organization that has treated them badly.

It is possible that by adopting a Total Quality Management approach organizations can address many of these costs and take action to reduce them.

6.1.18   Quality assurance

Quality assurance means having in place a quality management system that will allow a more standardized approach. The system uses a variety of statistical quality control tools such as cause and effect diagrams and statistical process control. Organizations are expected to record and analyse quality costs.

The organization that adopts this approach would be moving from a situation where it reacts to non-conformance to quality to one where it actively tries to prevent non-conformance. This means that it has to involve people more and spend more time on the design and planning of products and services.

Quality assurance can be extended to where the organization guarantees the quality of the goods and services supplied to a customer.

This allows customers to be involved in any problem solving or adjustments to the product before it is introduced into their production process. It also allows them to eliminate pre-delivery inspections because the products are made to their standards when they leave the factory.

6.1.19   Quality standards

This type of quality assurance scheme is often certified under the relevant British Standards or internationally accepted standard. Organizations are awarded the standard only after an independent assessor has verified through an audit and inspection process that its quality systems meet the required standard. This does not ensure the quality of a particular good or service, but it does mean that quality management systems of a suitable standard are in place at the organization.

It is beyond the remit of this book to detail the contents of the relevant British Standards but it does include the necessity for management responsibility and document control.

6.1.20   The quality manual

The quality manual is a written record of current good practice to show an assessor the existence of a quality system. It gives an opportunity to examine current practices and improve on them as well as using them to develop consistent practice throughout the organization. The manual should include items such as an explanation of any changes that have taken place, details of the mission statement and policy on quality, company details and organization chart, together with the responsibilities of senior managers. Details of paperwork used as part of company procedures such as order forms, training records and customer questionnaires should also be included.

6.1.21   Quality monitoring

A basic feedback system is required for an organization to determine whether it is reaching its own targets for quality. One method of doing this is through feedback from customers and complaints, although these responses can be misleading.

Feedback from internal sources helps as well, especially those who are involved in quality circles. They and other forums such as team meetings should be used to highlight problems of quality in production or service provision. The issue of people management and quality was examined in Chapter 2.

Summary

In this section you have looked at the issue of quality and should know what is meant by quality and how it can be achieved. You should understand that there are many implications of taking a quality approach. You should appreciate the costs associated with quality. It should be evident that quality as an issue is of the utmost importance. For this reason we should be aware of how failure to focus on quality can have serious consequences for organizations and how quality assurance gives management an opportunity to document its quality procedures.

6.2 Customer relations

It is a policy which, once introduced, can never be allowed to lapse. It has to be practised every day that the company continues in business.

Andrew Brown[5]

Section objectives

In this section you will:

● Examine why we need to develop our customer relations
● Learn how to recognize the importance of good communications in customer relations
● Look at customer relations problems and how to deal with them and
● Study the contribution made by staff to good customer relations.

6.2.1 Introduction

Who are our customers? This is perhaps the most important question an organization has to answer. One thing organizations know is that it is often only after a number of years of effort that they are able to build up a consistent number of customers. Their next problem is to keep them and this is where customer relations plays a major part. Organizations do not have an automatic right to customers who are free to do business with whomever serves them best. Managers know from their reading on quality that they need to try to satisfy customers' expectations. This can only be done by working closely with customers, both internal and external, in order to determine what exactly their requirements are. Working to develop these relationships is done for sound business reasons.

If managers ask what are they trying to get from their customers the answers include:

● Repeat orders and therefore keeping ourselves in business
● Their recommendations to other customers and the enlargement of the customer base and
● Their knowledge and expertise so that it can be used to improve products and services.

6.2.2 Customer communications

It is absolutely vital for good customer relations to be able to communicate well with customers. For example, by examining organizational communication managers soon realize that there are many varied ways to communicate, from notice boards to e-mail.

Exercise

Think of organizations and how they communicate with you as a customer.

Feedback

One of the main sources of communication is advertising and it is used not only to attract but also to retain customers. Customers need to be reassured that they have chosen the right company to provide a product or service. Companies use advertising to reassure us that we have chosen correctly by using terms in their communications like 'privileged customer, special discount, priority application. These terms are used to make us feel special and help to develop a loyalty between us and the company so that we will return to the company for any future purchases.

6.2.3   Contacting the customer

The customer, especially the external one will be getting communications not only from the systems of the organization but also from competitors. It is therefore essential that managers seize the initiative and make communications count.

One of the best ways of doing this is to ensure that organizations target the right people. Customers may well have a number of different contact points depending on with whom they are dealing. Managers must get to know contacts by name and if they leave, find out (preferably before they leave) the name of the person who will be taking over as quickly as possible.

6.2.4   Communication plans

Communication plans should be considered very carefully and organizations need to be as honest and open as possible if they are going to develop long-term mutually advantageous relationships. The following is some outline guidance for making communications effective:

- Managers need to know from the customer how often and how much contact they want.
- As mentioned earlier, both the organization and they as customers need to provide the name, address, telephone number, fax, and e-mail details of the relevant contact person dealing with the business at hand.
- Specifications should be written in a clear unambiguous way in order to avoid misunderstandings.
- If problems occur, then by contacting the customer immediately it is possible to find an interim way to deal with the problem before it escalates.
- Always check that things have happened as agreed.
- Questionnaires and feedback forms give customers the chance to let the organization know what they feel.
- Always respond to enquiries.
- Learn about the customer's business and discuss regularly your business relationship, hopes, expectations and the future.

6.2.5   Ways to communicate with customers

Offer privileged status

Certain customers can be given privileged status allowing them first options on products or services. This obviously will depend upon their relative importance but if the organization is getting the majority of its business from a few customers then they need the most attention.

Visits

There are many ways we can communicate with customers, for instance through sales visits and presentations.

Telephone contact

The initial contact with a customer may be by telephone and it is important that staff remember to be polite and clearly spoken. Eyre[6] notes 'an unhelpful telephone operator can mar the organization's public image'. It is also worth planning calls by making a list of questions to be asked and then tick them off as they are answered.

Meetings

Meetings are dealt with in Chapter 4, but because meetings with customers can also involve having to negotiate, they are a good way of building customer relations. The idea of negotiations is that both parties benefit from them. The aim of negotiations is to pave the way and set out the ground rules of business relations with the customer.

Exercise

'Parents are in charge, they tell their children what to do and children obey.' In a group of three or four students think about this statement and the topic of negotiation. Is the statement true, or is it more complex than it first appears to be?

Feedback

We are involved in negotiation sometimes without thinking about it. Children do not necessarily blindly do what their parents tell them and nor do employees. Most parents find themselves negotiating with their children especially as they get older and become more independent. Parents will say 'I want you home by 9 o'clock' their children may well reply, 'All my friends stay out until midnight'. Then a period of negotiation may ensue and an agreement will be reached whereby the children agree to be home by 10.30 pm or face some sort of penalty. Both parties get something out of the negotiation (for the parents it is the child returning before midnight and for the child it is an extra one and a half hours with their friends), and as long as both parties stick to the agreement all goes well. However, if the child doesn't return home at 10.30 then there is likely to be some penalty to be incurred. If the parents do not stick to the agreement they may face an even more rebellious child. In business life similar types of negotiation take place and it is better to have both parties feeling they have gained something from the negotiations rather than having one who appears to have won and the other to have lost. The party who loses may seek revenge at some later date or decide just never to do business with 'the winner' ever again.

6.2.6   Customer relations problems and complaints

If business relations ran smoothly all the time the world would be a perfect place. Sadly, they do not and so we need to think about relations when times are tough as well as when they are good.

Many complaints never reach the ears of managers for a variety of reasons:

- Often people do not complain but merely stop doing business with an organization.
- Complaining customers are dealt with by the public-facing staff who, often to their credit, do an outstanding job. However, they often do not feel the need or are afraid to report complaints because of the fear of criticism from senior managers. This can be a major cause for concern, because the underlying cause for customer complaint may not have been dealt with. It is not only complaints that fail to get through to staff. Often

customers who communicate their gratitude fail to get that message to the right person and a chance of motivating or rewarding an individual is lost.

6.2.7 Overcoming obstacles to complaining

The obstacles to customers voicing their concerns need to be overcome and the value of customer input needs to be stressed. We can do this in a number of ways:

- We can set up a system by which all comments, both positive and negative, are recorded and forwarded to managers.
- We need to make it easy and convenient for customers to take part in feedback. They can be invited to face-to-face sessions such as focus groups by using questionnaires or by telephone surveys. Whatever the method we use, by making it more convenient for the customer we have a greater chance of getting them to take part.
- We also need to emphasize to managers and staff that they will not be disciplined for mistakes unless they continue to happen. We need to reassure them that they can learn from their mistakes and training can prevent them from happening again.

6.2.8 Customer relations and dealing with problems

There are advantages to having good customer relations when things go wrong because organizations learn about mistakes very quickly. Methods that might be used in this case could be in-house communications. If organizations have a well-developed financial reporting system and can identify that customers are becoming slower at paying bills then they need to contact them as quickly as possible to find a solution. It is not impossible for organizations to defer payments when a long-term customer is facing difficulties. There can also be situations where the organization may need to rely on the goodwill of customers because of internal problems.

6.2.9 Customer relations staff

Good customer relations are only developed through people and it is important to recognize the contribution they make. We should always try to ensure that the people who are critical to customer relations have the necessary social, interpersonal and technical skills. These staff should have the characteristics that are most helpful in a given situation. For example, if we know we have a customer who is prone to outbursts of aggressive behaviour, it may well be better to have someone who is diplomatic to deal with them, instead of an equally aggressive person who might further inflame the situation.

The relationship that develops between the organization and the customer may take many years to develop. In that time people get used to dealing with particular individuals. It is therefore important that if individuals are to be moved from their role, then we need to give our customers plenty of notice. We should, whenever possible, ensure that the person taking over does so before the existing incumbent leaves.

6.2.10 Training

It important to note that good customer-facing employees do not suddenly just appear out of the blue. There has to be a conscious effort on the part of the managers involved (human resources, sales and marketing, operations) to commit themselves to the recruitment, training and retention of suitably qualified and trained customer services staff. It is essential that the staff dealing with customers get good-quality training.

6.2.11   Company knowledge

Staff should know about as much of the company as possible. Too often they become isolated in their departments and know little of the rest of the company. With the right effort managers can train these staff so that customers who are trying to contact the organization, get a positive impression of the company. This can be as simple as ensuring that everyone has a copy of the organization structure and an up-to-date internal telephone directory.

6.2.12   Empowerment

People who deal directly with the customer need to be able to take action. Customers want to know that their problem or request is being dealt with and who is dealing with it. They do not want to be passed from one person to another within the organization because no one has the authority to take action. It is therefore important for customer-facing staff to have the authority to take action. British Airways, for example, have empowered their staff who deal with customer complaints to use a range of solutions at their discretion.

6.2.13   Organizational flexibility

Flexibility of approach is a benefit to customers who often feel frustrated when they are faced with a bureaucratic approach from staff. The person who adopts the approach of 'I couldn't possibly do that, it's more than my job's worth' may soon find that there is no job because all the customers have gone elsewhere. Staff need to be aware that customers need helping, not hindering.

6.2.14   Managing customer relations

People involved in managing customer relations need to know how to motivate their staff, and how to be aware of their objectives in relation to customer satisfaction. They need to have the skills (leadership, communications) to carry out their job and to be aware of their contribution to overall company success.

6.2.15   Customer retention

The retaining of customers should now be a key part of an oranization's activity because the costs of retaining a customer are much lower than the costs of acquiring a new one. HR can make a contribution to customer retention by looking at how customers are dealt with by employees. If our own employees are unhappy and not committed to our customers then this will no doubt reflect on the customer relationship. HR must ensure all employees are well trained, motivated and dedicated to providing a long-term service to customers and so encouraging their satisfaction.

Case
study

Clones Ices

Charley Farley is the marketing and sales manager of Clones Ices and considers himself to be an excellent networker. Every year he sends his major customers a Christmas card and at the end of the financial year a copy of the company's annual report. Charley thinks he is a good communicator and that by keeping in touch, his customers appreciate his efforts at good customer relations. With his sales staff, Charley can be a bit of a tyrant and although he usually manages to achieve his targets, if he does not, then his sales staff get what he calls 'a good old fashioned talking to'. Consequently Charley does not really talk *to* his staff but *at* them and as for listening to them, he believes that management's job is to manage and the staff's job is to do as they are told. Unsurprisingly they do not often voice their opinions but merely tell him what they think he wants to hear.

Clones recently introduced a new ice cream into their range, the raspberry double, a larger than average portion of ice cream with a crushed nut topping. This introduction was executed rather hurriedly, despite the reservations of the production staff who felt they were not able to guarantee quality. Similarly, the sales staff were worried because they knew that many of the small shopkeepers to whom they sold ice cream were reluctant to have fewer but larger ice creams in their fridges at a time of year when turnover is high. Charley dismissed these reservations complaining that it was these small shopkeepers who made his life a misery with their complaints and he preferred dealing with the supermarkets any day.

Eight weeks after the launch of the new ice cream Charley was summoned to the director's office to explain why a major customer's complaint about the new product had not been dealt with for six weeks and why so many small shopkeepers were telephoning her to complain. The major customer was threatening to take his business elsewhere and the director was understandably irate. Charley was speechless because this was the first he had heard about the complaint.

- Using your knowledge of customer relations explain why you think this situation has arisen.
- What steps do you think Charley can take to ensure that it does not happen again?
- Why do you think it is important for organizations to have good customer relations?

Feedback

The situation has arisen because Charley does not really understand what comprises good customer relations. Moreover, he does not really know his own staff, he does not understand his customers. He manages his staff by fear and thinks his larger customers are most important. This is a mistake. He needs to develop a clear communications system both with his staff and his customers. He also needs to examine his own interpersonal skills. Good customer relations will bring repeat business and closer cooperation with the customer, a bonus for all parties concerned.

Summary

In this section you have assessed why we need to develop our customer relations and how to communicate with customers. You have examined the importance of good communications in customer relations and how to deal with their problems. You should now be aware of the role people play in this customer relationship, both in the contribution they make to service provision behind the scenes as well as the contribution made by the customer-facing staff.

6.3   Introducing change

Section objectives

In this section you will:

- Identify the pressures for change
- Examine why people resist change and how to deal with it
- Study the causes of conflict and conflict handling
- Determine how to make successful change and
- Investigate what is meant by organization development.

6.3.1   Introduction

As stated earlier, organizations do not exist in splendid isolation, they are expected to interact with the wider environment. The wider environment in turn experiences a multitude of pressures that affect it. With this in mind we can begin to understand that for organizations, change in some form or other is inevitable and on-going. Some of the pressures to change can be listed as below. This is not a definitive list but it should give the reader an idea of the diversity of pressures that can cause change.

6.3.2   Pressures for change

These can include:

- Economic conditions
- Competition
- Government intervention
- Technology
- Resource availability
- People

Economic conditions

Following the bursting of the dot.com bubble in 2001 when many investors lost their savings together with the collapse of global operators like Enron in 2002 (where corporate fraud is suspected), many organizations were forced to examine their businesses. Organizations began to look at how they were operating and some began to divest parts of their businesses and concentrate on their core activities. Economic conditions like these either on a global scale or a regional scale put pressure on organizations to change or take the risk that they might fail.

Competition

All organizations face competition and as markets have globalized, organizations have found they are competing with competitors in all parts of the world. Dyson vacuum cleaners announced in 2002 that they were moving their production facilities from the UK to a low-labour cost area simply because they felt they would no longer be able to compete otherwise.

Political intervention

One aspect of national government involvement was mentioned under the heading of competition. It should also be realized that government policy can be included on a local, national and international basis. The impact that politics has on organizations by way of local or European legislation is well known. The introduction of further legislation under the Working Time Directive in 2003 (loss of 48-hour opt out) will affect organizations and their employees.

Technology

Technological change, and especially the rate at which it has changed, has greatly affected organizations over recent years. Technology has affected the way organizations operate and communicate. The developments that have ensued from this such as working from home and the virtual office, have meant that organizations have had to change their structure, the way they employ people and the work they are expected to carry out. Contracts for people are no longer based around attendance on a full-time basis at an office but can vary from part-time to self-employment at home.

Resource availability

As resources become more scarce then organizations have to change and adapt to business without them. If financial resources are not available to organizations or even governments they need to be innovative and seek finance elsewhere. An example of this is the government and the private sector cooperating through the Private Finance Initiative to build hospitals and infrastructure such as railways.

As skilled human resources have also become scarce organizations have changed their policies to recruit, train and retain them. This has even meant organizations employing people throughout the world and using advanced telecommunications to link them and allowing them to operate in areas of customer service such as call centres. Some of these are located in places like Scotland and Northern Ireland but actually dealing with people throughout the whole of the UK. Recent changes (2002) have seen call centres moving to India but still dealing with UK customers. (See *Personnel Today*, 17 September 2002 for further details.)

People

As people are improving their education and becoming more aware of their power they are influencing governments to introduce more legislation to protect them at work. This awareness of not only employment legislation but also the greater choice offered through advertising and other information channels, latterly the Internet, has meant that consumers are altering their buying habits. The change is potentially so important that organizations are having to become increasingly customer focused in order to survive.

6.3.3   Strategic thinking

One of the goals of strategic thinking is to look ahead and try to determine the way forward for the organization. This can be based around a number of apparently simple questions such as 'Where are we now?' 'Where do we want to be?' 'How do we get there?' Despite the apparent simplicity of these questions, this is in fact a very complex problem that usually means a significant amount of change throughout the organization.

Major transformations of organizations do not happen very often, but organizations change regularly on an incremental basis. Incremental change gives an organization time to be more adaptive and allow them to be managed more easily on an on-going basis. However, when the environment does change rapidly organizations need to be able to deal with the changes. This transformational change is often precipitated by a crisis, such as the need to introduce new technology and become more competitive.

Exercise

Think of your own employment. Is your job safe? Do you have a long-term future with the company?

Feedback

Organizations face a number of pressures that force them to change. How well or badly they react to those pressures will impact on job/career prospects for employees. It is important that you are aware of how your company and indeed how you yourself are planning ahead and evaluating the possible success or failure of changes the company may make. Proper planning will help prevent poor performance or in the case of your own employment by having a contingency plan in place will help you deal with the shock both financial and emotional that will occur if you are made redundant.

6.3.4   Planning for change

It is possible to use a similar approach to that of problem solving when planning for change as follows:

- Decide whether a change is required
- Prepare an outline plan for change
- Determine possible support/opposition to the change
- Decide on which option you want to accept
- Decide on a time frame for implementation
- Communicate the plan
- Put the change into practice

6.3.5   Individual resistance to change

Robbins[7] identified five reasons why individuals resist change: habit, security, economic factors, fear of the unknown and selective information processing. The following are based on those headings. The individual and organizations, which after all are collections of individuals, both resist change. Some elements of this resistance are similar and some are quite different.

If we begin by looking at the individual and change it may be easy for us to relate to them.

Routine

Each and everyone of us is a creature of habit. Despite having a wide variety of choice, invariably we confine ourselves to a narrow band of options. Whether it is which train to catch to work in the morning or which sandwich filling to have for lunch, we will mostly limit our selection.

Our work patterns are ordered in a very similar way. These routines give us order in our lives and that order helps us to deal with day-to-day living.

This is all well and good until something happens that requires us to change our routines, then we resist.

Safety

Our habits give us order in life and changing them can threaten our security too. We like to believe we will have a job for life, we will not be the person made redundant, after all there are plenty of other people in the organization. The thought of lost security and the subsequent vulnerability makes us resistant to change.

Loss of income

Loss of income is a very emotive issue in the workplace because of its link to status, lifestyle and the provision of support for family. When people think that change is going to mean a fall in income because of their inability, for example, to keep up with the new technology, then this will encourage them to resist change.

Attitudes to new experiences

Travelling to work should run like clockwork. For example, we know how long it takes us to get to the station, what time the train leaves, how long the train journey takes and how long it takes us to walk to the office. This is a routine we can grow comfortable with because it is a structured timetable of events and is predictable. However, once we hear rumours of station closures or timetable changes then our first reaction is one of anxiety. How will I get to work? What other forms of transport are there? Will I have to drive? All these potential changes create resistance in us and resentment toward those who have changed the timetable or are thinking of closing the station.

Perception

Many a parent talking to their teenage son or daughter about what is an acceptable time for coming home at night will say one thing and their son or daughter will hear another. Teenagers will hear only what they want to hear. In the same way when changes are being suggested we are very selective about what we take on-board. Sometimes we only remember the negative side of things and completely ignore the positive.

Exercise

Think of an instance at work over the last year where you have been asked to do something different but you refused. How many of the above headings were involved in your decision to refuse?

Feedback

Often we think we are supportive of change but when we look objectively at our response to a change very often we can find some of the factors listed affecting us.

6.3.6 Organizational resistance to change

Katz and Khan[8] identified a number of reasons for organizational resistance to change: structural inertia, limited focus of change, group pressure and loss of power. The following is a brief description of each based on those ideas.

Structural inertia

Organizations have processes that encourage stability, rules and regulations about behaviour, incremental pay scales to encourage long-term loyalty and internalization of organization culture. All these militate against any change which faces the organizations, for example 'we have always done it this way and it works so why change it?'

Limited focus of change

As a result of the complexity and interdependence of the various processes and systems within organizations, when we try to change part of a smaller system this will have an impact on the workings of the whole system. For example, we may change the way people work in one area and this means that we need fewer people in that area. If we do not change the work of other people who do similar or the same jobs in other parts of the organization then we have limited the amount of change, and people may perceive those changes only by the fact that they had a limited impact.

Group pressure

As you will have seen from your studies of motivation (Section 3.4) and the Hawthorne experiments, groups can exert pressure on individuals within them. Some individuals may want to accept the change but they know the rest of the group will ostracize them or punish them in some way if they do. This pressure is likely to make sure that the individual goes along with the group view of opposition.

Loss of power/expertise/resources

This can take a number of forms, from the greater availability of knowledge to the loss of contacts or importance to more senior managers. For example, as change is introduced in the education system, individuals have greater access to knowledge. This can change power relationships in several ways. In the education system teachers have to be more aware of the fact that they are not the only source of information for students and can be challenged about their knowledge. Similarly, when these students join organizations they are just as likely to challenge the power of managers with their more up-to-date knowledge.

Probably one of the most important sources of power and the one that provokes the most resistance when we try to change is that of the control of resources, whether they be people, finance or machinery. Anyone who has attended a budget allocation meeting will have witnessed how managers are prepared to fight very aggressively to protect their budgets.

6.3.7   Dealing with resistance to change

Kotter and Schlesinger[9] suggest there are a number of ways that we can use to deal with the resistance to change: education and communication, participation and involvement, facilitation and support, negotiation and agreement, manipulation and co-optation and explicit and implicit coercion. The following is a brief description of them.

Education and communication

If we assume that the people affected by the change have not been fully informed about it because of poor communications then by arranging to meet them and discuss or explain the changes in any way possible, we can go some way to overcoming resistance.

Participation and involvement

When people are involved in decisions that concern them from the earliest possible opportunity, they are likely to be more supportive of those decisions.

Facilitation and support

By offering training and guidance during the change process we can overcome some of the worries that people may have about not being able to cope with change.

Negotiation and agreement

Negotiation can be used where the resistance to change needs to be overcome by offering a reward to individuals in return for their support. This may mean having to deal with the key figures in the area under change, for example the offering of lucrative redundancy packages to key workers or golden handshakes to departing chief executives.

Manipulation and co-optation

This occurs where influence is achieved by presenting information in such a way that it appears to be attractive but it is not in reality.

Explicit and implicit coercion

In this situation managers essentially force people to change by explicitly or implicitly threatening them. This may be a risky approach because people inevitably strongly resist forced change.

It is suggested that organizations should use a range of these approaches to introduce change successfully, often by combining them and recognizing their strengths and limitations.

6.3.8   Conflict

There are many opportunities for conflict to occur during times of change. Conflict can be over anything from resources to status and can be between individuals, individuals and groups or between groups. What we do know is that we have to learn how to deal with conflict and prevent it from becoming destructive.

6.3.9   How can we tell if we have a conflict situation?

Conflict is not always that obvious but if you notice individuals or departments not cooperating, or problems being passed from one department to another without anyone taking responsibility, then these can be indications of potential conflict situations.

Handy[10] identified the following causes of conflict: formal objectives diverge, role definitions diverge, the contractual relationship is unclear, roles are simultaneous and there are concealed objectives.

Although conflict may seem to be negative this is not always the case. Conflict does have some positive aspects that are worth noting:

- Conflict can reveal problems that have been hidden, which means that managers get the opportunity to deal with them.
- Conflict can unite a group of workers against an outsider, which can mean longer-term consolidation of group identity.
- Conflict can bring out the best in people too. Many people are united in adversity and by necessity can become very inventive and creative. An example of this is how civilian populations are drawn together in wartime and still survive despite the harshest of circumstances.
- Conflict can improve communications because people find themselves in position where they feel they have to voice their opinions. This can result in the setting up of formal communication channels to deal with future conflict before it escalates. In the 1960s the Cuban missile crisis resulted in improved communications between the USA and the former Soviet Union.

6.3.10   Dealing with conflict

Robbins[7] suggests a number of approaches for dealing with conflict and the following are based on them.

Conflict-resolution techniques

- **Problem solving.** Face-to-face meeting of conflicting parties for the purpose of identifying the problem and resolving it through open discussion. This can be done with the aid of a third-party arbitrator if necessary.
- **Super-ordinate.** Creating a shared goal that cannot be attained without the cooperation of each of the conflicting parties.
- **Expansion of resources.** When a conflict is caused by the scarcity of a resource (for example, financial promotion opportunity), office space expansion of the resource can create a win–win solution.
- **Avoidance.** Withdrawal from or suppression of the conflict and where conflict is avoided at all costs. This has the disadvantage of appearing to sweep the problem under the carpet.
- **Smoothing.** Playing down the differences but stressing the areas of common interest.
- **Compromise.** Each party to the conflict has to give up something of value.
- **Authoritative command.** Management uses its formal authority to resolve the conflict then communicates its desires to the parties involved.
- **Altering the human variable.** Using behavioural change techniques such as human relations training to alter attitudes and behaviour that causes conflict.
- **Altering the structural variables.** Changing the formal organizational structure and the interaction patterns of conflicting parties through job redesign, transfers, creation of coordinating positions and the like.

Robbins also suggests the following conflict-stimulation techniques:

- **Communication.** Using ambiguous or threatening messages to increase conflict levels.
- **Bringing in outsiders.** Adding employees to a group whose backgrounds, values, attitudes or management styles differ from those of present members.
- **Restructuring the organization.** Realigning work groups, altering rules and regulations increasing interdependence and making similar structural change to disrupt the status quo.
- **Appointing a devil's advocate.** Designating a critic to purposely argue against the majority positions held by the group.

6.3.11 ACAS

At this point in our discussions on conflict resolution it is worth mentioning the work of the Advisory, Conciliation and Arbitration Service (ACAS). ACAS was formed in 1974 and since then it has been instrumental in strengthening and at times repairing the employer/employee relationship. ACAS employs experts who deal with employment relations to help foster good working practices. This includes not only the major strikes (witness the recent Fire Brigades Union dispute in November 2002) but also in the encouragement of preventative measures such as the introduction of codes of practice (see Chapter 3 in the section on disciplinary action).

ACAS will advise on a range of issues surrounding an individual's working life by giving objective information, for example, the rights of employees and employers. This helps prevent disputes from escalating to the point where there is a need to perhaps involve employment tribunals.

ACAS by informing employers and employees alike can encourage both parties to work more harmoniously for their mutual benefit. As ACAS's full title states they are there to advise (give information), conciliate (bring the different factions together with a view to develop a consensual solution) and arbitrate (make a decision that sometimes may be legally binding about the result of a conflict situation).

ACAS play a very positive role in the field of conflict resolution and are an invaluable source of help that both employers and employees should be encouraged to seek.

6.3.12   Lewin's force field analysis

Lewin[11] devised the technique of force field analysis which can be used to deal with potential change situations. His idea is based around the thinking that within any organization there are forces both for and against any changes. These forces work against each other to maintain an equilibrium or status quo. The argument is that there are forces for change to a new situation (the driving forces) and forces that want to keep things as they are (the restraining forces). He suggested that change went through three stages: Unfreezing, Movement and Refreezing. The forces can be shown as in Figure 6.3.

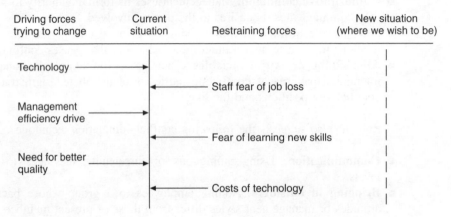

Figure 6.3. The force field.

Equilibrium of the relationship between people and their environment is an important part of force field analysis. People like to have a known and accepted way of dealing with their jobs and their colleagues. They feel at ease when their working behaviour and that of others has been internalized and things are in equilibrium. When this equilibrium is disturbed people move to restore the balance. The driving forces for change could include fear of job loss, monetary rewards, fear of loss of company perks.

The restraining forces for change could include personal dislike of those attempting to introduce the change, personal dislike of the organization and fear that once output has been increased on one occasion it will be increased again and again.

Exercise

Think of any change that has happened at your company or in your life over the last five years. Compile a force field analysis showing who or what started it and what resistance was offered. Did the change happen? If not, why not?

Feedback

This gives an opportunity to identify the forces for change in a situation that the student may or may not have recognized. It also helps to show the resistance that may have developed and that resistance may have come from a variety of sources.

When analysing the force field diagram it should be noted that the number of forces on either side of the equilibrium does not have to be the same but their total strength on each side does in order for us to have equilibrium.

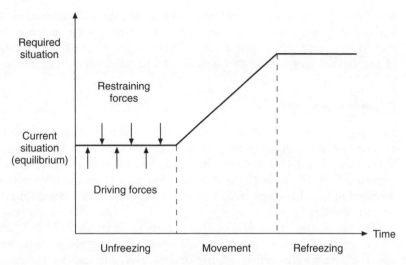

Figure 6.4. The stages of change (adapted from the Lewin model).

The force field can also be shown graphically (see Figure 6.4) against a time scale which helps to illustrate Lewin's three-stage change model, namely Unfreezing, Movement and Refreezing.

We can see from Figure 6.4 that what we are trying to do is to move from our current situation to a required situation over a period of time. We can relate this to the three-stage model.

Unfreezing

We can see that when the driving forces and the restraining forces are equal and opposite we are in a state of equilibrium. It is this stage that we have to unfreeze. We have to overcome or reduce the restraining forces if we are going to move to our required situation. This means we have to gain acceptance for the need to change by, among other things, explaining the benefits of the change and allaying people's fears. Practically we can offer the resisting staff financial inducements to change or redundancy packages if they want to leave. We can guarantee employment if staff are fearful of job losses. We can offer retraining or staff development if there are fears of skill deficiencies. These approaches are based on the idea of either reducing the restraining forces or increasing the driving forces or a combination of the two.

Movement is when behaviour is changed

Now we can see that this change of forces results in movement toward our required situation. It is important that during this stage we actively encourage communication, participation and education to help change behaviour. We can use external change agents to help with this.

Refreezing

In this final stage it is important for management to reinforce the new behaviour and to get people to internalize it. Managers should ensure that activities become standard company practice. This can be achieved through the establishment of joint agreements, training, quality controls and absorbing the activities into the organization's culture. It should be noted that it is not always possible to reach the required situation in one go. The reason for this is that as the change begins to happen resistance can be decreased in some areas but it may increase or newly appear in others. It is not always worth it to the organization in terms of lost flexibility, goodwill or financial cost to continue.

6.3.13   Change agents

Before going much further we need to discuss the role of change agents. It is argued that anyone can be a change agent – a manager, a production worker or an outside consultant. The change agent should be at the centre of any change process and one of the most important jobs for them to do is to develop a good relationship between all the parties involved in the change process. This is vital to ensure that commitment, trust and mutual respect develop.

The change agent must also be able to carry out a number of roles during the process. At times they need to direct and tell people what to do. At other times they will need to be less directive and merely reflect on the options available and let the other people involved decide. The range of skills, abilities and talents required of the change agent is also wide, from interviewing and listening skills to rational problem solving and intellectual skills.

6.3.14   Successful change

Greiner[12] found two key factors that distinguished between successful and unsuccessful change:

- Successful change was accompanied by the redistribution of power within the organization so that traditional decision-making practices moved towards greater use of shared power.
- Such a power redistribution occurred in one organization through a developmental change process. Successful changes did not take place in one dramatic step but involved a series of momentum-building phases.

6.3.15   Organizational development

Organizational development is about trying to make the organization more effective by changing its structure and the people within it. This is often attempted by a combined approach from internal management and external advisers.

Managers are interested in organizational development because of its relationship with change. Organization development is concerned with the process of change rather than change itself as well as with change that affects the whole organization.

For example, a college has a number of inputs to it and a number of outputs from it. Those inputs go through a series of processes within the college and then emerge as outputs. However, the college does not exist in a vacuum, it is surrounded by a general environment that affects its way of operating. There are pressures from this environment that we can describe under the headings of political, economic, social, technological, legal and environmental. If we consider Figure 6.5, we can see how it is possible for these pressures to impact on the organization's processes, thus precipitating the need for change. The changes will obviously have an impact on people, and organization development tries to show individuals and groups who are part of those processes how to develop personally in their work and cope with change.

Organization development consists of a number of aspects. These are shown in Figure 6.6.

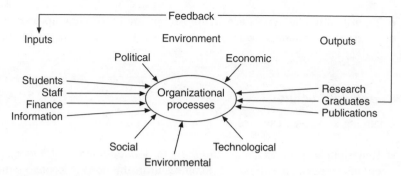

Figure 6.5. The organization as a system.

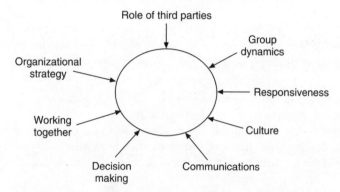

Figure 6.6. The various aspects of organizational development.

6.3.16 The stages in an organizational development programme

● Establish the need for organization-wide change, this usually comes from senior management who should select a change agent.
● Analysis and diagnosis is carried out to determine the current situation within the organization.
● The next task is to draft a set of aims for the programme and these can vary from the introduction of new technology to the total change of the organization's structure in order to streamline communications.
● Organizational development must be planned carefully.

6.3.17 What to change

Usually these activities can be targeted at individual behaviour, organizational structures, problem solving, organizational culture and technology.

Changing behaviour

Changing behaviour can be attempted in a number of ways including:

● Sensitivity training is where interpersonal feelings, attitudes and relationships are examined.
● Coaching and counselling are where subordinates can look at the particular aspects of their working relationships with their boss.

- Team-building activities are where groups are shown how to operate more cohesively.
- Leadership training is where managers can be shown how to develop their leadership skills.

Changing structures

Changing structures can also be approached in a number of ways:

- Redesigning jobs to take into account job enrichment (reducing control) and job enlargement (increasing duties) can result in the need to change structures.
- Role analysis looks at the role people perform to see if they have changed.
- Organizational analysis can involve managers in the whole structure of the organization. In this way they can focus on the way they organize people, plant and machinery.

Problem solving

This can be dealt with in a number of ways:

- We can develop questionnaires to assist people to identify areas of concern to them. We can even use quality circles to identify the problems.
- We can use people from outside the organization to advise us about which behaviour to use when dealing with different situations such as conflict.
- Training in the prioritization of work and decision making is discussed further under the heading 'Time management'.

Culture change

Change of an organization can often be caused by a crisis of some kind that disturbs the equilibrium. Changes in culture can happen at the same time and has been dealt with elsewhere in this book.

Hampden-Turner[13] suggests that managers must first know about the culture before they can try to change it and states that there are a number of ways in which a manager can discover how culture works. These are: find the dangers, bring conflict into the open, play out corporate dramas, reinterpret the corporate myths, look at symbols and create a new learning system.

Exercise

On an individual basis consider your own organization and ask yourself what sort of culture do you think it has.

- Are you encouraged to speak out?
- Do you have separate dining facilities for managers and other staff?

Now compare your answers with those of the person sitting next to you. What do you think any differences tell you about your organization's culture?

Feedback

Obvious signs as we have seen from the section on culture include how an organization and its managers interrelate. These are not always obvious at first, but things such as separate dining facilities speak volumes about those relationships. Other indicators of culture should appear as you compare your own organization with someone else. Then you can ask why it was that one organization has adopted its particular culture.

6.3.18   Approaching culture change

Robbins[7] suggests that a change of culture is most likely to happen when there is a dramatic crisis, a turnover of leadership, a young and small organization and a weak culture. He goes on to identify a number of aspects to consider during change and the following is based upon these:

- The positive use of senior managers is essential.
- Challenge existing ideas. For example, was school the best time of your life?
- Only employ people who have the right values.
- Ensure that the socialization processes are compatible with the beliefs and ideas you are seeking to introduce.
- Use financial incentives to promote support of your desired approach.
- Enforce rules and regulations in place of informal approaches.
- Use job rotation to make people think and act differently through different work experiences.
- Encourage a high degree of staff participation to build trust and achieve agreement by consensus.

6.3.19   Changing technology

Technology is used to describe computers, word processors, production machinery and armaments such as missiles. This gives an idea of the range of technology available.

The advent of the microchip and smaller more powerful personal computers together with cheaper and faster telecommunications has begun to influence the ways organizations use their technology and human resources. The talk now is of homeworkers, virtual offices, automated production systems and video conferencing, among other impacts of new technology. What the result of these will be for organizations is not fully understood, but some things that they may have to take into consideration are as follows:

- How do we organize our technology and our human resources?
- Do we centralize or decentralize?
- How do we motivate our employees?
- How do we reward our employees?
- On what basis do we employ our employees?
- What control do we have over our employees?
- How much training or development should we give to our employees?

Some of these issues have begun to be addressed through ideas about flexible working, zero-hours based contracts, short-term contracts and the contracting out of some work, and are dealt with in more detail in Section 2.3. Also your attention is drawn to the following article.[14]

Steps to successful home working

When the concept of home working is introduced into an organisation, it is often said that the least suitable people instantly volunteer. To overcome any potential problems, you need to outline from the start not only the type and level of the role that may be suitable, but also deal with each application on its own merits, in accordance with pre-specified criteria.

Not everyone wants to work from home. Those who are most suitable tend to be:

– Self-motivated
– Responsible and reliable
– Results-orientated
– Goal setters
– Effective time managers
– Effective communicators
– Highly skilled

Home working is often offered by organisations on an informal basis, with a handful of people working one day a week out of the office, perhaps when they feel they have a need for some quiet time away from interruptions.

But one financial organisation is now actively encouraging more formalised home working. Rapid expansion has meant that the company is running out of office and car parking space.

It believes it is important to recognise teams have very different requirements and that some are growing out of space faster than others. Keen not to introduce a 'one hat fits all' solution, it has chosen to look at each case on its own merit. Through a series of practical workshops, line managers have been helped to identify from the offset some of the pros and cons of home working.

When considering home working, roles need to be considered on an individual basis through a structured process. It should be the responsibility of the individual to approach his or her line manager with a request to work from home.

Reviewing the home working is also important. Both sides need to have a way back if the arrangement isn't working. It has to be remembered that it is the job that is given the home-working label and not the employee. If the person takes on a new position it doesn't necessarily follow that his/her new role can be undertaken from home.

Many home workers may feel guilty when using their 'prescribed' work time to hang out the washing or put the dinner on. Whether or not it is acceptable depends entirely on the role and the contract that has been agreed. If the job is more project-based, such rigidity probably isn't required. In no circumstances should home working be used as an alternative method of childcare.

By Carol Savage, Managing director, Flexecutive

6.3.20 Leadership and change

In change situations the leadership of senior management is vital. During change senior managers will find that they may have to draw deeply on the force of their own personality in order to get things done. They may also find themselves having to adopt the role of the transformational leader. Leaders have to develop a clear sense of direction and to keep the organization on track towards the agreed goal and have to use their interpersonal skills to motivate people with their own enthusiasm for change. They have to take on-board the organization's values whether it be trust in people, respecting others or customer care. Leaders need to be able to get things done through people. This can be achieved through encouraging team work, empowerment and accepting that on occasions people will get things wrong.

6.3.21   Use of managerial power and influence during change situations

Again we can use French and Raven's[15] five bases of power: coercive, reward, expert, legitimate and referent power to discuss its use during change.

During times of change a manager may be called upon to use any of these bases of power depending on the situation. The bases can be complementary and are useful during change. For instance, a manager may use expert power that impresses employees. This in turn may enhance the manager's referent power because staff see the manager as self-confident and knowledgeable.

Power is used to influence behaviour and during change it is important to note that those whom managers are seeking to change may also have power and can resist what they are trying to do. Managers also need to realize that they as leaders are also dependent on others for their power, hence the need for change agents to have the full support of senior management. Managers can increase their ability to influence people by increasing their power base. If they can use referent power to influence a number of employees and get them 'on our side' then they may well bring the rest of the employees along with them. By using referent power they have widened their ability to influence more people. Managers should remember that they need to use power carefully because it is part of a dependency relationship. For example, the change agent is dependent on the power of senior management and the employees are dependent on the referent power of the change agent. However, the employees have the power to influence their friends whom the agent may seek to influence. Dependency particularly relies on how much more power one person has over the other and how much the second person desires whatever it is the first can offer.

6.3.22   Strategy

The following article[16] appeared in *Personnel Today* as part of a series on developing HR Strategy.

Developing HR strategy: building up resources

In the sixth part of our series on developing HR strategy, Keith Rodgers examines the key issues HR will encounter when dealing with organisational development

A much-loved subject among academics and management consultants alike, organisational development spans a huge range of HR skills and activities. From the theory of leadership and the concept of the Learning Organisation at one end of the scale, to the mechanics of electronic training infrastructures at the other, it is a subject that can rapidly spiral out of control.

But, as with other aspects of HR strategy, the overriding priority in building organisational development initiatives is to define the business impact. Most of the components are intuitively beneficial in terms of good management practice – but that alone is not enough. If HR wants organisational development to be taken seriously in the boardroom, it must be able to show how it leads to tangible improvements to the bottom line.

In our sixth article examining the central planks of HR strategy, Personnel Today examines the key issues HR practitioners face.

1. Defining the boundaries

Although there are significant areas of crossover between organisational design and organisational development, the two are distinct areas of HR strategy. Design is primarily about building a structure that meets business needs, particularly in terms of effective cross-departmental working practices and flexibility. Development is about building the resource to take the organisation forward.

The crossover occurs because both management philosophies require organisations to understand where they are starting from – what skills and knowledge they have – and where they want the business to go.

There are numerous ways that organisational development can be defined, but at an individual employee level, it can be usefully broken down into four constituent parts: experience, knowledge, competencies and behaviour.

Competencies are the hardest to define as the terminology is applied to a wide range of components including skills, abilities and characteristics, such as 'openness' or 'flexibility'.

Although much development theory has been focused on behaviour, an effective programme will address all four of these areas at both an individual and departmental level.

Ultimately, development is also about the kind of company values that an organisation strives to adhere to. Turning value statements from lip service to reality is a major endeavour because it frequently requires a shift in corporate mindset. That will only occur when it is driven from the top down.

2. Leadership development

The age-old argument about whether leaders are born or nurtured is great for the theorists – but pretty much academic for the HR function. While it is possible to buy in leadership qualities for specific strategic roles, the issue can't be tackled by recruitment alone. In reality, leadership is a quality that needs to permeate the entire organisation, from CEO down to shop-floor supervisors. That means most of the individuals filling leadership positions will require training.

Developing leadership skills requires a blended approach combining business theory and practice. To begin with, the difference between leadership and management must be understood. In a seminal article published by Harvard Business Review in 1990, John P Kotter argued that management is about coping with complexity, while leadership is about coping with change. To put it another way, management is essentially a control process that uses tools such as budgeting to tackle complexity; leadership is about having a vision and the strategies to turn it into reality.

Once putative leaders have grasped this distinction, pragmatism becomes the watchword in leadership development. That means focusing individuals on leadership challenges where they can easily understand which qualities are required, and have faith that those qualities are within reach.

Most organisations start leadership development at the top, which can be the hardest area to tackle – senior executives tend to assume they are already effective leaders, and often find it hard to acknowledge that they are lacking in an area so fundamental to their role.

These barriers can sometimes be tackled with change management programmes, where the emphasis is not on tackling leadership qualities per se, but on building specific skills for new business environments.

Executive coaching, or mentoring, is also an increasingly popular route. Ultimately, however, corporate culture is the critical factor – if the CEO and the board encourage openness in tackling the perceived 'weaknesses' of individuals, then half the battle is won.

It is less common for companies to make a concerted effort to tackle leadership development further down in the organisation, but those that do tend to focus on frontline staff first. While this is a logical approach, it can lead to problems if the leadership development requirements of middle managers are bypassed.

3. Succession planning

Another area where lip service is more prevalent than practical results, succession planning is a perennial irritant for HR. However carefully a strategy is mapped out to nurture the next generation of leaders and key employees, it is inevitable that people will leave and business needs will change before the plans come to fruition. That is not, however, any reason to avoid doing it. As well as providing a framework for continuity (however flawed it may be), succession planning also helps to identify key employees and is a central plank of staff retention.

It is important to bear in mind that succession planning isn't a tool just for senior roles. In highly-specialist areas, it can take years to build skills and knowledge for specific roles and the loss of key individuals can have a significant impact on business performance. Demonstrating that knock-on impact on the business is one way of justifying the need to invest in effective retention strategies.

4. Training and learning

It is a truism that in tough times, training budgets are one of the first items to be cut. But as Cheryl Fields Tyler, vice-president of consulting at the Concours Group, points out, in many cases, it is actually the training strategy that gets hit the hardest. In other words, companies will continue to spend, but they invest less in training planning and management and as a result, have less effective programmes.

There has been some progress on this front. As the concept of the Learning Organisation evolved in the 1990s, corporate education began to be seen as a strategic tool rather than an interruption to day-to-day activities. At an operational level, companies began experimenting with new types of educational processes, such as computer-based training. At a strategic level, there was also a shift in corporate mindset which manifested itself in a growing willingness to learn for the future, rather than to apportion blame for the past.

Yet, despite those changes, few organisations today take a co-ordinated approach to learning. In fact, many would struggle simply to put a figure on how much they spend on training and development. As Tom Raftery, a senior consultant at Watson Wyatt points out, training is typically seen as a one-off event, not a process that is integrated with the business. To be effective, all learning programmes – from on-the-job ad hoc training to classroom-based courses – need to be structured as part of an overall development strategy.

5. E-learning and the broader business case

E-learning systems provide some answers to this problem. Designed to provide the platform for new training techniques, these systems allow organisations to supplement traditional classroom-based training with a range of internet-based learning options, from live instructor-led sessions to self-paced training courses.

The core infrastructure, a Learning Management System, co-ordinates the process and helps organisations to keep track of which courses participants have taken, a major benefit for both budgetary control and employee assessment.

Although e-learning is often lauded primarily for the cost-savings it generates, it is most effective when integrated into a broader HR picture. Linking training information to appraisal, competency management and other HR systems is fundamental to building a long-term organisational development strategy. By putting development in the context of performance management, expenditure can be justified to senior management on a basis they really understand – business impact.

Case study: Kendle International

When Sherry Gevedon, director of global training and development at clinical research firm Kendle International, was approached with a training request at 8pm on a Monday evening, she could have been forgiven for dismissing it out of hand. Her IT director for global business systems had an urgent requirement to train 120 people in three different time zones by noon on Wednesday. That gave her just 40 hours.

In the event, the company was able to get 110 people up to speed by the deadline – and the remaining 10 received the information that evening.

The delivery tool was a learning management system within the group's corporate university, which offers both structured and unstructured educational facilities over the web 24 hours a day.

For Kendle, which provides project-based clinical research services for the pharmaceutical and biotechnology industries, the ability to react in this way is an essential component of business flexibility. Its e-learning applications, based on Saba's Learning Management System, provide cost savings in terms of reduced travel expenses, lower presenter costs and opportunity cost. But in a business that needs to respond quickly to changing market and customer demand, the just-in-time training capability is just as important to Gevedon.

Kendle's technology platforms are a core part of its organisational development strategy, which embraces a wide range of HR activities. The basic framework is a series of competency profiles, which were initially developed on the basis of job type and then personalised by line managers for individual employees. These form part of an employee's personal workbook, which features a job description, skill requirements, relevant courses (such as project-specific training), standard operating procedures for the clinical environments in which that person operates, and external training.

Gevedon acknowledges that building this information database was 'a long, arduous process', but one that has been adopted by the executive leadership as a way of delivering quality to customers. The next phase of the programme is linking employee development to performance management, primarily through the performance appraisal system.

The company's organisational development strategy primarily covers three areas: leadership development, succession planning, and training in the context of recruitment and employee retention.

The first component, leadership development, is the focus of a programme that will kick off during the first quarter of 2003 using a series of web-based courses aimed at entry-level managers, middle managers and the senior executive leadership. When each module is completed, managers will be assigned a mentor from their business unit to help them build case-specific scenarios. This mixture of people led and technology led training is specifically designed to stimulate learners' interest.

Succession planning will also be a core focus for 2003. As Gevedon points out, e-learning is a critical component here – not just because it provides the infrastructure for training programmes to help develop the next generation of managers, but also because Learning Management Systems provides an archive of the training that has been carried out by their predecessors.

'We have the opportunity for people to come in and bring themselves up to speed on things that would no longer be available with live training,' she says.

This learning infrastructure also underpins Kendle's retention and recruitment strategies.

'When we're recruiting, we can say "we invest a significant amount of money in your career". For example, we have 300 courses for professional development – such as project management and leadership development – and they help prepare people for promotion within Kendle. From a retention perspective, it's the same thing. We're a learning organisation, and we're in a position to support people's careers.'

Take-home points . . .

1 Always define the business impact when building organisational developments
2 Corporate culture is critical
3 Invest in effective retention strategies
4 Co-ordinate learning in line with organisational goals
5 Link training to appraisal, competency and other HR systems

Summary

In this section you have examined the pressures for change and why people resist it. You have also looked at ways of making change successful by identifying people's resistance and learning how to overcome them. You have also considered organization development in detail and the role it has to play in organizational change.

Case study

St Cuthbert's

St. Cuthbert's is a lively, reasonably successful, secondary school that operates a selective recruitment policy for their pupils. Gwen Ardmore was recently appointed head teacher at St Cuthberts. Gwen has extensive experience both as teacher and manager in secondary education. Most recently she worked as deputy head teacher at a similar school and this promotion she sees as a natural career progression. St. Cuthbert's isn't by any means a failing school but its governors wanted it to improve and the imminent retirement of the old head teacher was an opportunity to recruit a new head teacher. It was hoped the new head would take the school forward in its quest to be a school with a reputation for the excellence of its staff, pupils and examination results. The school has a number of staff who are within 5 years of retiring and others who only have 2 years' experience with no real career path for them to follow.

If Gwen came to you for advice what would you suggest?

Feedback

Responding in general terms, it is important for Gwen to think strategically and ask, 'Where do we want to be in ten years' time?' This then becomes the strategic focus for everyone. Since the governors have a vision of it having excellent staff, pupils and examination results these will be the areas she needs to focus on.

She will need to think about planning the various changes and the resistance she will meet. She will have to get to know who shares her vision (other than the governors) and try to work with as many of the different groups who will be affected by the changes. This will involve those who may be on the point of retiring and may not see the point of changing. However their experience may be invaluable.

Gwen will also have to be aware of the other stakeholders in the school (pupils, parents, governors, staff) who also have an interest. These groups will have to be convinced of the viability of her plans because it is these people she will have to recruit and retain. For example, the less experienced teachers will have to be reassured there is a future for them at the school and they will need to see a clear career path and evidence of succession planning. Gwen's plans will take her into many different areas of HR activity but she must not forget the issue of the quality of education provided and the need to constantly improve this. She will need to be aware of the importance parents and pupils put on quality and how they monitor it through league tables of examination results.

In brief

In this chapter you have examined the issues involved in quality and how organizations need to concentrate on quality provision and quality processes. The costs of ignoring quality can be devastating for organizations, as the UK motor industry has found to its cost. Quality and issues such as value for money are key influences on customers. Customers also want to be treated well and kept informed. They do not necessarily want to remain passive but want to input into the organization. For these reasons and more practical ones such as customer retention it is important for organizations to pay special attention to customer relations. In today's world of work things are changing at a very fast rate and managers need to know how to deal with change and the conflict it can bring. You have looked at resistance to change and how it should be dealt with. However, it should be remembered that change is not always bad and that good can come from change.

Examination questions for this chapter are given in Appendix 2.

References

1 Crosby, P. (1980) *Quality is Free*. McGraw-Hill.
2 Juran, J. M. (1989) *Juran on Leadership for Quality Progress*. Free Press.
3 Deming, W. (1986) *Out of the Crisis*. MIT.
4 Porter, M. E. (1980) *Competitive Strategy*. Free Press.
5 Brown, A. (1989) *Customer Care Management*. Heinemann.
6 Eyre, E. C. (1987) *Mastering Basic Management*, Macmillan.
7 Robbins, S. (1993) *Organizational Behaviour*. Prentice Hall.
8 Katz, D. and Khan, R. L. (1966) *The Social Psychology of Organizations*. Wiley.
9 Kotter, J. P. and Schlesinger, L. A. (1979) Choosing strategies for change. *Harvard Business Review*, **27**, No. 2.
10 Handy, C. (1985) *Understanding Organizations* (3rd edn). Penguin Books.
11 Lewin, K. (1951) *Field Theory in Social Science*. Harper and Row.
12 Greiner, L. (1967) Patterns of organization. *Harvard Business Review*, **45**, No. 3.
13 Hampden-Turner, C. (1991) *Corporate Culture, From vicious to virtuous cycles*. Economist/ Hutchinson.
14 Savage, C. (2001) *Personnel Today*, July 2001.
15 French, J. R. P. and Raven, B. 'The Bases of Social Power' in Cartwright, D. and Zander, A. (eds), *Group Dynamics Research and Theory*. Harper and Row, 1968.
16 Rodgers, K. (2002) *Personnel Today*, December 2002.

Further reading

Bank, J. (2000) *The Essence of Total Quality Management*. Financial Times/Prentice Hall.
Burnes, B. (1992) *Managing Change – A Strategic Approach to Organizational Development*. Pitman.

Burnes, B. (2000) *Managing Change*. Financial Times/Prentice Hall.
Bruhn, M. (2003) *Relationship Marketing*. Financial Times/Prentice Hall.
Dale, B. G. (1999) *Managing Quality*. Blackwell Business.
Senior, B. (2002) *Organizational Change*. Financial Times/Prentice Hall.

Web-site addresses

Accounting for People leadership campaign: http://www.accountingforpeople.gov.uk
Arbitration, Conciliation and Advisory Service, The: http://www.acas.org.uk
Chartered Institute of Marketing: http://www.cim.co.uk
Chartered Institute of Personnel and Development: http://www.cipd.co.uk
Personnel Today magazine: http://www.personneltoday.co.uk

Part Three
Managing in a Business Context

Learning outcomes

To understand and explain:

- The main features of the business environment within which organizations operate
- The nature of corporate strategy and the key elements within the strategy process
- The application of analytical management techniques, such as PESTLE and SWOT analyses
- The economic setting for organizational activity, including the operation of the market and the role of the state in the economy
- Global markets and their implications for management
- The interplay between the economic and political systems, including the European dimension
- The social structure of the UK and the impact of social change
- The legal framework, including the nature and impact of both UK and EU law
- Technological change and its implications for management
- The concepts of business ethics and corporate social responsibility.

Introduction to Part Three

Few commentators would deny that continuous change has always been a feature of corporate existence although many argue that today's organizations are subject to unprecedented levels of turbulence and uncertainty. Whatever the pace and nature of change, organizational survival depends on managing its consequences. Therefore, in formulating and implementing strategy, managers need to understand, anticipate and respond to the changing demands of the business environment.

The theme of this part of the book is the way in which the external environment impacts on corporate strategy. As we shall see, environmental analysis is a key stage in the process of strategy formulation. We therefore start with an assessment of corporate strategy, focusing on the environmental analysis aspect of strategy development.

We begin our overview of the business environment with an examination of the economic context of management. Here, key issues such as the operation of the market and the management of the economy are discussed in some detail. A feature of this chapter is a section devoted to the phenomenon of globalization, one of the major forces shaping the business environment.

We continue with an assessment of the political context, noting the constitutional and other relevant changes. This is followed by an analysis of a critical issue facing the UK in the new century, that of European integration.

Next discussion of significant social and cultural issues takes into account factors such as class, education, equal opportunities and social attitudes. We also examine the far-reaching implications of demographic change.

Our analysis of the legal framework includes an overview of the legal system and a focus on employment and business law. In the following chapter we assess the impact of technological change, both in the workplace and on wider society.

We conclude this part of the book with a discussion of social responsibility and business ethics in relation to the behaviour of managers.

7 The strategic framework of management

In this chapter you will:

- Examine the meaning of corporate strategy
- Consider the main stages in the strategy process
- Appraise the role of stakeholders in the development of strategy
- Apply key analytical management techniques, such as PESTLE and, SWOT analyses
- Evaluate approaches to creating an organization which is able to deliver business strategy

Chapter introduction

This chapter provides a context for the third part of the book. The theme is the purpose, scope and long-term direction of the organization – in short, corporate strategy. The chapter itself is divided into four sections. The first provides an overview of the strategy process and examines how organizations define their purpose. The second section sets the scene for the following chapters, in that it considers environmental analysis as a key aspect of strategy formulation and implementation. It is here that a number of important analytical management techniques, such as PESTLE and SWOT analysis, are introduced. The third section deals with choice of strategy and the fourth considers alternative views of how strategy is formulated.

7.1 Corporate strategy

7.1.1 What is strategy?

At its most basic, strategy is the **long-term direction** of an organization. In defining - strategy, some writers stress its **planning** and **integrating** functions. For example:

*A strategy is the pattern or **plan** that **integrates** the organization's major goals, policies and action sequences (or operational activities) into a cohesive whole.*[1]
*Strategy is a unified, comprehensive and **integrated plan** . . . designed to ensure that the basic objectives of the enterprise are achieved.*[2]

These definitions portray strategy as a kind of master plan which both directs and coordinates the activities of an organization. They therefore go some way to helping us understand why some organizations produce strategic plans.

Other commentators emphasize the **business planning** aspects of strategy. Thus for Kay[3] '[corporate strategy] is concerned with the organization's choice of business, markets and activities'. Still others focus on the processes and issues involved in strategy formulation and implementation:

*Strategy is the **direction** and **scope** of an organization over the **long-term**: which achieves **advantage** for the organization through its configuration of **resources** within a changing **environment**, to meet the needs of **markets** and to fulfil **stakeholder** expectations.[4]*

Exercise

Consider the following case in the light of these definitions of corporate strategy.

Case study

Ikea

The Swedish furniture-retailing phenomenon Ikea had by the turn of the century grown from a tiny mail order business to a $5.8 billion multinational concern.[5] In 2003 and in uncertain economic times, the company was still opening new stores. The effect that Ikea's 1986 UK arrival had on the furniture market is illustrated by the following anecdote. A Habitat employee, interviewed by the BBC, described how before Ikea's arrival, Habitat employees were ushered into a darkened training room. Suddenly, the slide projector clicked on and the sales manager described in solemn tones how 'this blue and yellow monster' was going to arrive from Sweden and take their business.[6] Ikea subsequently acquired Habitat, probably its closest UK competitor.

How can we account for Ikea's success? Consider the typical furniture store. It has showrooms that display samples of merchandise (sofas, dining tables, etc.), but those items represent only a fraction of the choices available to customers. Salespeople often escort customers through the store, answering questions and helping them choose from the thousands of product varieties available. Once the customer makes a selection, the order is relayed to a third-party manufacturer and the furniture will be delivered to the customer's home in around six to eight weeks.

In contrast, Ikea uses a self-service model based on clear in-store displays. Rather than rely solely on third-party manufacturers, Ikea designs its own low-cost, modular, ready-to-use furniture. In huge stores, Ikea displays every product it sells in room-like settings, so customers don't need a decorator to advise them on how to put the pieces together. Adjacent to the furnished showrooms is a warehouse with the products in boxes on pallets. Customers are expected to do their own pick-up and delivery.

Although much of its low-cost position comes from having customers 'do it themselves', Ikea offers some extra services that its customers do not (e.g. in-store childcare and extended hours). Those services are uniquely aligned with the needs of its customers, who are young, not wealthy, likely to have children and, because they work for a living, need to shop at odd hours.

So Ikea targets young people who want stylish design at affordable prices. The brand is driven by the philosophies of its founder, Ingvar Kamprad. The 'Ikea way' enshrines a set of values that govern the company's relationship with its customers. Its mission statement is reproduced on page 337.

Ikea permits no status symbols and refers to all employees as co-workers. The philosophy is reinforced by the company's president who is famous for flying economy class and refuses to take taxis when public transport is available. In 2000, Ikea shared one day's takings from a sale at Ikea stores with its entire staff.

What appear to be the key features of Ikea's strategy? To what extent is the company's strategy reflected in its approach to people management?

Feedback

The company has a clear purpose (expressed in its mission statement) and values which shape both its business goals and its relationship with customers and employees (**stakeholders**). While there is no direct evidence to suggest that the organization has a strategic **plan**, it is possible to infer that it almost certainly does, although what form the plan takes (a detailed written document or a broad framework) is impossible to discern.

The **business planning** aspects of Ikea's strategy are more obvious from the case study and its choice of business, markets and activities are clear: it is very firmly positioned within the furniture market. Thus according to Michael Porter: 'Ikea . . . has a clear strategic positioning. [It] targets young furniture buyers who want style at low cost. What turns this marketing concept into a strategic positioning is the tailored set of activities that make it work . . . Ikea has chosen to perform activities differently from its rivals.'[7] Not only has Ikea positioned itself very differently from the more traditional furniture retailers, but also the activities of the company, centred around the ideas of limited customer service, self selection by customers, modular design and low manufacturing cost, are key to its strategic position.

So in Porter's terms, business strategy is about a company differentiating itself from its competitors and 'deliberately choosing a different set of activities to deliver a unique mix of value'. This idea of 'positioning strategy' to achieve competitive **advantage** is referred to later in the chapter when we discuss strategic choice.

Ikea's idea of 'democratizing' design appears to be reflected in its approach to people management. 'Single status' is actively promoted, with the most senior managers living by these 'democratic' principles. The suggestion is that this non-hierarchical approach to management reinforces a culture that is closely aligned with, and therefore supports, business strategy.

So how does strategy come about? The strategy process can be viewed from both a **prescriptive** and a **descriptive** perspective.

7.1.2   The prescriptive (or 'planning') view of strategy

This view seeks to explain how management *should* make strategy. Based on rational decision-making models developed by writers such as Herbert Simon,[8] this perspective is particularly associated with Ansoff.[9] In the middle part of the twentieth century, strategy was seen as a highly systematized process which

- Involved **prescribed sequences of steps** and
- Made extensive use of **analytical tools** and **techniques**.

Following this method of strategy development would, it was believed, greatly increase an organization's chances of corporate success. Although these approaches are now criticized as being too rigid, strategy is still represented in the same broad sequence by contemporary writers. However, these models of the strategy process are now intended to provide a framework for analysing real processes, rather than as policy prescriptions.

The elements of strategy

Table 7.1 identifies six key stages in the strategy process. Each stage links to one of a series of basic questions that are crucial to strategic decision making. The process begins with an expression of the organization's purpose; management often articulates this as a mission or aim. The next stage is to analyse the business environment, which covers a range of internal and external factors. Environmental analysis allows management to develop its broad aim into more detailed objectives, which specify more clearly what they want the organization to achieve.

The production of clear objectives is followed by the formulation of strategies which specify how the organization will achieve the objectives. Options must be analysed as it is often necessary to make a choice between different strategies. Management then puts the chosen strategies into action (the implementation stage). Finally, to ensure that the organization remains on target, management needs to put systems in place to monitor and control performance and progress.

As Table 7.1 suggests, in its broadest sense the process can be viewed as just two phases: strategy formulation and strategy implementation. Each stage in the process may result in the production of a written document. Many organizations produce separate mission statements and statements of aims, objectives and strategies. Sometimes a single document, the strategic plan, will contain all of these. Furthermore, there may be a set of complementary plans for different parts of the organization, in line with the cascading principle.

Table 7.1 The strategy process

Stage of the strategy process	Description
STRATEGY FORMULATION	
Mission/vision statement Statement of aims Statement of values	A definition of the business that the organization is in or should be in, i.e. the organization's purpose
Environmental analysis	Monitoring and analysing the forces at work in the organization's business environment
Objectives	A precise statement of what is to be achieved and when the results are to be accomplished. They represent a more detailed expressions of aims
Strategic choice	Deciding, from a range of strategic options, how objectives are going to be achieved
STRATEGY IMPLEMENTATION	
Plans	The specific actions, in terms of operational activities and tasks, that follow from strategies
Monitoring and control	The process of monitoring the proposed plans as they proceed and adjusting where necessary. Strategies may well be modified as a result

Exercise

Why do you think organizations produce strategic plans?

Feedback

● **To give a sense of direction.** In order to be successful, an organization must have a clear and well-understood purpose, supported by clear objectives.
● **To secure a united approach.** A well-designed and effectively communicated corporate strategy will ensure that individuals, teams, departments and divisions work towards the same objectives.
● **To provide a context for operational (i.e. day-to-day) decisions.** Strategies must provide a guide to action and form a basis for monitoring progress.

Defining organizational purpose

The initial stages of strategy development involve defining organizational purpose or choice of business. This is likely to be a more significant component of the strategy process for private sector organizations: as a rule, private companies have freedom to choose which business they want to be in; whereas public sector organizations such as local authorities and government agencies are obliged by law to perform certain functions.

Missions, visions, aims and objectives

An expression of an organization's overall purpose may take the form of:

● A mission statement
● A vision statement
● A short statement setting out a single overall aim or
● A set of strategic (or corporate) objectives.

Mission and vision statements usually express organizational purpose in very general terms, and it is management's task to develop them into more specific objectives. Vision statements tend to set out the desired end states. They then describe what the management of the organization would wish the future to be like and are sometimes characterized as 'an aspiration towards something which does not yet exist'. The following are some of the ways in which organizations express their purpose:

Ikea
To contribute to a better everyday working life for the majority of people, by offering a wide range of home furnishing items of good design and function, at prices so low that the majority of people can afford to buy them.

Barclays Bank plc
Barclays' objective is to be one of the best financial services groups in the eyes of customers, staff and shareholders.

Springboard Housing Association
Springboard is a customer focused, substantial provider of quality housing and support services. We aim to be progressive, open and dynamic, enabling individuals and their local communities to realize their full potential.

Organizational values

An organization's values are often expressed through their statements of purpose. A key goal of planning is the creation of clarity and unity of purpose within an organization. One way of achieving this is to identify a set of values to which organizational stakeholders (those involved with the organization) can subscribe, and which defines what the organization represents. Values often relate to promoting success in businesses but many also seek to convey the organization's image and its reputation as an employer. Public service organizations often stress values relating to fairness and community involvement. Here are some examples of organizational values:

Springboard Housing Association values
Being a sound social business
Offering value for money
Treating people as individuals and with respect
Embracing diversity

Ikea values include 'innovation', 'simplicity' and 'democratizing design'.

Stakeholder expectations

Statements of organizational purpose and values will reflect the expectations of stake-holders, both internal and external to the organization. The degree to which those outside the organization (individuals, groups or society at large) can actually influence its actions will depend on their relative power (see Section 7.2).

The values, attitudes and beliefs of employees are at least of equal importance. Groups or individuals can either promote or block change in organizations and it is crucial that this is recognized. Cultural and political tensions will exert influence at all stages of the strategy process, in all organizations.

Many organizations have mission statements; however, it is possible to question their value. Kay[3] holds that visions or missions are symptoms of a '**wish-driven strategy**' which fails to recognize the limits to what might be possible gives finite organizational resources. He refers to the case of Groupe Bull.

In practice

Groupe Bull, the government-backed French computer company, tried for many years to challenge the global market supremacy of IBM. After a period of success in the 1960s, the company's performance began to falter and it became apparent that it would never alone be able to tackle the technical supremacy of IBM; consequently, it would be unable to make significant inroads into the world's largest market, the USA.

The company formed alliances with GEC and Honeywell in the USA in an attempt to penetrate the market, but this strategy was unsuccessful. In 1989, Bull reformulated its objectives, shifting the emphasis from the USA to Europe ('to become the major European supplier of global information systems'). By this time the computer market had moved away from mainframes towards personal computers. In 1992, Groupe Bull announced an alliance with IBM.

Throughout the period described, the company was driven by an unrealistic vision which it did not have the resources to realize. According to Kay, Bull 'epitomises a wish-driven strategy, based on aspiration, not capability'.

Source: adapted from Kay[3]

Having defined organizational purpose, management must translate this into specific objectives that specify what the organization wishes to achieve. This involves 'cascading' the corporate-level objectives down to the levels of business units or departments and, often, to individuals (see Chapter 3 for a discussion of performance management systems). Corporate objectives often include targets which quantify what an organization seeks to achieve within a time frame. Before management can establish these detailed objectives, however, it needs to undertake the next stage in the strategy process – environmental analysis.

Organizations operate within the context of a business environment that creates both opportunities and constraints. Management must take these into account in formulating objectives and strategies. Knowledge of the business environment will inform the specification of corporate (sometimes called 'core') objectives that flow from the broad statement of organizational purpose. It will also help to identify objectives that reflect what management wants to do differently or better (i.e. those objectives related to 'change').

7.2 Analysing the business environment

This section has three main themes:

- The nature of the environmental factors which impact on organizations
- How managers cope with changes in the business environment and
- The way in which strategies are adjusted in response to environmental change.

Organizations are part of an open system in which they are constantly interacting with other organizations and individuals – including their customers, suppliers, financiers and competitors. Furthermore, they are exposed to continuous change and uncertainty in the wider external environment.

Environmental analysis, or developing an understanding of the business environment, is a critical early stage in the strategy process. The analysis stage can be broken down into three main elements – management has to decide how each of the following affects strategy:

- What stakeholders expect of the organization
- The forces at work outside the organization
- The organization's internal resource capabilities.

7.2.1 Stakeholder analysis

Lynch[10] defines stakeholders as 'the individuals and groups who have an interest in the organization and, therefore, may wish to influence aspects of its mission, objectives and strategies'. He notes that, in relation to strategy, there are two sets of interests:

- Those who have to formulate and implement strategy – the managers and employees, or **internal stakeholders** and
- Those who will be interested in its outcome – shareholders, customers, suppliers, creditors, the community and the government, or **external stakeholders**.

All organizations have a range of internal and external stakeholders, whose interests can often conflict. This is because stakeholders are themselves subject to a wide range of influences which will affect their views and expectations of organizations. The expectations of internal stakeholders will to a significant extent be shaped by the dominant culture of the organization.

External stakeholders – including suppliers, financiers, central and local government, shareholders and customers – also have expectations of organizations and will seek to influence strategy in various ways. They may be able to influence staff or board members directly through personal contact, or they may seek to exert influence indirectly, for instance by the use of the press and other media.

Different stakeholders will have different expectations, some of which are outlined below:

Shareholders – growth in dividend payments
Customers – competitive prices
Suppliers – timely payment of debt
Employees – fair remuneration
Government – adherence to the country's laws
Lenders – timely payment of debt

Exercise

Can you identify any other stakeholder expectations?

Feedback

- Shareholders – growth in share price
- Customers – quality, reliability, return and replacement policies
- Suppliers – liquidity
- Employees – good terms and conditions, job security, job satisfaction, opportunities for career/personal development
- Government – efficient use of energy and natural resources, paying taxes, provision of employment, value for money in the use of public funds
- Lenders – assets available for security, potential to pay interest and capital.

Stakeholder power

An analysis of the business environment must include an assessment of the strategic importance of these expectations. This can be achieved through stakeholder mapping, which aims to assess:

- The likelihood of each stakeholder group seeking to impress its expectations on the organization
- Whether each group has the capability or means to do so
- The likely effect of these expectations on future strategies.

Stakeholder mapping attempts to identify the relative power of each stakeholder group, as this will determine its ability to influence organizational strategy.

Stakeholder mapping

Once a list of stakeholders has been identified, the company needs to be able to establish which groups have priority. A framework helps determine the levels of power and influence of various stakeholders (see Figure 7.1).

Figure 7.1. A framework for identifying stakeholder expectations (adapted from Johnson and Scholes[4]).

- Stakeholders with a low level of both interest and power require 'minimal effort' from the company.
- Groups who have a high level of both power and interest are known as 'key players'; it is vital that the organization takes this group into account when making decisions.
- Those groups who have a high level of power but low interest levels need to be 'kept satisfied'. Institutional shareholders may fall into this category, although under some circumstances they can join the 'key players' group if those who represent them (e.g. pension fund managers) feel that the company is not acting in their best interests.
- Those stakeholders with a low level of power but a high level of interest need to be 'kept informed' as they can influence the attitudes of more powerful stakeholders, for example through lobbying.

Stakeholder mapping is of value for the following reasons:

- To ensure that the interests of significant stakeholders are taken into account when strategy and decisions are being made
- To determine whether the organization needs to pursue strategies to 'reposition' certain groups of stakeholders. This might be a desirable course of action if it was necessary to lessen the influence of a key player or to create more key players to champion a course of action. This latter option is crucial in the public sector
- To identify who are the 'blockers' and 'facilitators' of change
- To determine which stakeholders will need to be helped to maintain their level of interest or power.

Exercise

Produce a stakeholder map for a primary school and analyse it using the principles discussed in the previous section.

Feedback

The stakeholders would be:

Parents
Pupils

Staff
The community
The local education authority
The governing body
Ofsted
Her Majesty's Inspectors of Schools
Other bodies (e.g. churches).

The levels of power and interest of these groups will vary over time and depending on the circumstances. For example, the power of parents (formally expressed through the governing body) has increased greatly in the last twenty or so years, as has their interest. Therefore schools now tend to 'prioritize' this group, whereas at one time they may have thought it sufficient to 'communicate' with them. To take another example, the local community may for most of the time be classed as having low power and low interest, but this may well change dramatically if the school wishes to expand its premises and needs the agreement of its neighbours to obtain planning permission.

Should companies aim to achieve a balance of stakeholder interests or should they give priority to the interests of certain groups? Some argue that the 'success' of a company depends on certain key stakeholders – shareholders, customers, employees and suppliers – who should receive equal priority because companies compete in each of the relevant markets, for labour, capital and goods.

Other writers observe that firms typically put the interests of their customers before those of employees because profits depend on the former. They would argue that, since it is impossible to satisfy all stakeholders, in a capitalist economy shareholders should come first.

Overall, it is probably true to say that the long-run success of organizations depends on taking stakeholder expectations into account, although the relative importance of each group's interests will change over time and from situation to situation. The ethical issues associated with stakeholder interests are discussed in Chapter 14.

7.2.2   Analysing the external environment

There are many other forces at work outside the organization in addition to external stakeholders. These forces interact with each other, producing complex cause and effect relationships where the direction of causality is often unclear (see Figure 7.2). Consequently, it is difficult to pinpoint precisely how these forces affect the organization and its markets, and almost impossible to make predictions about how they will continue to do so in the future. Strategists charged with analysing the external environment are therefore confronted with the twin problems of complexity and uncertainty. Nevertheless, efforts must be made to develop an understanding of the external environment, in order that strategy can be adjusted to reflect changes and developments in the outside world.

The task involves the collection, analysis and interpretation of information from a wide range of sources, which will include published statistics and various forms of externally or internally commissioned surveys or market research studies. Essentially, there are two levels of information:

- Information relating to the 'macroenvironment', that is, the wider environmental factors over which the organization may have little or no control but which impact on the organization's activities.
- Information relating to the organization's 'microenvironment', that is, the immediate operating environment involving its own customers, suppliers and competitors.

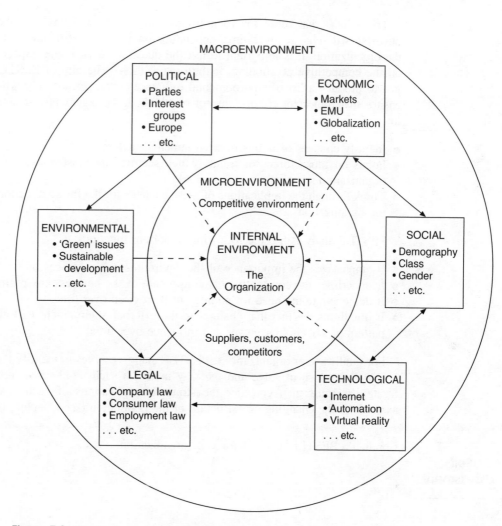

Figure 7.2. The business environment.

Organizations are more likely to be able to exert some control over the factors operating at this level.

At both levels the aim is to use the information to answer the following questions:

● How is the external environment changing?
● What impact will these changes have on the organization, its customers and markets?
● How should strategy be adjusted to take account of the opportunities and threats posed by the changing environment?

PESTLE analysis

A common approach to trying to make sense of what is happening in the **macroenvironment** is to undertake a PESTLE (political, economic, socio-cultural, technological, legal and environmental) analysis. The technique aims to identify the main external sources of influence on organizations.

The effects that these macroenvironmental factors will have on the strategy of the business will change over time depending on the size, structure and growth stage of the organization. It is important to ask the question 'what is the impact of these changes on the competitive positioning of the organization? The aim of PESTLE analysis is not just to produce a list of environmental influences although, as a checklist, it does help to ensure that important factors are not overlooked. Management also uses the framework to:

- Identify changes or trends in environmental factors
- Focus on those forces or trends which seem to be most relevant and critical to the organization's business
- Think through the implications of these changes for the future direction and strategies of the organization

PESTLE analysis has the following important functions:

- It emphasizes the importance of the environmental influences on strategy.
- It underlines the constantly changing nature of the business environment.
- It demonstrate the need for strategy to be revised over time.
- It highlights the fact that changes in the external environment will affect and alter the pattern of stakeholder power and influence over time.

For public sector organizations, PESTLE analysis serves to identify the problems which society may wish to solve and the way in which such problems or needs are changing. Strategists must then consider the strategic implications of such change. An obvious example is the changing age structure of the population (see Chapter 10).

Self-assessment

Conduct a PESTLE analysis for your organization.

Forecasting scenarios

It is important to recognize the dynamic nature of environmental forces. Strategists can apply statistical techniques to identify rates of change which might help in predicting future courses of action. But it must be recognized that past trends cannot be assumed to continue and that analysis must extend to some consideration of the future. The planning model of strategy has been criticized for over-emphasizing the value of forecasting, which can often result in highly inaccurate, and therefore misleading, predictions of the future.

Another possible approach is to build up a number of possible scenarios of what the future may look like. Scenarios will typically be developed for:

- Best-case outcomes
- Worst-case outcomes
- Intermediate outcomes.

Strategists and managers would evaluate these alternative scenarios with the intention of identifying the most likely outcome. The main benefits of scenario-building are that it discourages reliance on a single view of the future, and alerts the organization to the importance of adapting strategy to an ever-changing environment.

The competitive environment

Those factors which shape the immediate competitive environment and affect the organization's ability to compete effectively in its chosen markets are a major concern of environmental analysis. Examination of the forces at work in this competitive environment – the microenvironment – forms a basis for the development of an organization's competitive strategy.

The definitive aim of competitive strategy is to increase profitability which, according to Porter,[11] depends on the following:

● The structure of the industry in which the organization operates
● The organization's own position, or relative performance, within that industry.

By analysing these variables, a firm will be able to identify areas where it enjoys or where it has the scope to create competitive advantage relative to its competitors. Porter himself developed a series of techniques for analysing the competitive environment. The first of these, the **five forces model**, provides a useful starting point for the analysis of industry structure. The five forces are:

● **The threat of potential new entrants.** New entrants pose a threat when they are easily able to enter a market in pursuit of profits. The strategic issue here is that of barriers to market entry. One of the main barriers to entry is economies of scale, discussed in Chapter 8. The lower unit costs afforded by large-scale production mean that new entrants to the industry have themselves to come in and produce on a large scale; the risk associated with such a strategy is a major deterrent to firms entering the industry. Other barriers include strong product or service differentiation; branding, special levels of service and customer knowledge create barriers by forcing firms to spend extra funds or take longer to become established in the market.
● **Bargaining power of buyers.** Buyers (or customers) are strong when
  (i)   They have substantial bargaining power. For example, national governments can (in theory) drive a hard bargain on defence contracts because they are the only buyers.
  (ii) The product is undifferentiated and the buyer can switch from one to another without any problems.
  (iii) If backward integration is impossible (in other words, the organization cannot produce the product or service itself).
  (iv) The selling price from the organization is unimportant to the total costs of the buyer.
● **Bargaining power of suppliers.** All organizations have suppliers of raw materials or services which are used to produce the final goods or services. Suppliers are particularly strong where they can command a price premium for their products, as is the case when there are only a few suppliers or if there are no substitutes for the supplies they offer.
● **Threat of substitute products or services.** Substitutes usually pose a threat as a result of a technological or low-cost breakthrough. For example, product developments in the pharmaceutical industry have rendered certain drugs largely redundant, e.g. Zantac (produced by Glaxo-Wellcome) largely replaced Tagamet (produced by SmithKline Beecham) as the major treatment for ulcers.
● **Degree of rivalry between existing firms in the market.** Some markets are more competitive than others. In highly competitive markets, companies engage in extensive monitoring of key competitor companies whereas in other markets, companies compete but not with the same degree of intensity. There are some conditions in the industry that may lead specifically to higher competitive rivalry. In some markets (the European steel market, for example) competitors are of roughly equal size and no one company

dominates the market. Under these circumstances, when one competitor decides to gain share over the others, rivalry will intensify as profits fall.

Porter's five forces model has been criticized on a number of counts:

- It assumes that an organization's own interests come first; this is not the case for many public sector and non-profit organizations.
- It assumes that buyers have no greater importance than any other aspect of the micro-environment. Commentators such as Harvey-Jones,[12] who proclaim the primacy of the customer, would fundamentally disagree with this proposition.
- The model's starting point is that the environment poses a threat to the organization, leading to the consideration of suppliers and buyers as 'threats' which have to be tackled. In some industries, firms have found it useful to engage in cooperation with suppliers.
- Porter's analysis ignores the human resources aspect of strategy; for example, it does not take into account the management skills or cultural aspect of corporate strategy.
- It assumes that, once the analysis has been conducted, a corporate strategy can be formulated to handle the results. Those who subscribe to the emergent view of strategy discussed in Section 7.5 would question the predictive nature of this assumption.

These critical comments do not detract from the fact that Porter's model provides a very useful starting point in the analysis of the business environment. By identifying the nature and direction of key forces in the competitive environment, organizations will be able to develop strategies which are appropriate to the environment in which they are operating. For instance, can the organization do anything to increase its power over suppliers and buyers? Industry analysis will also enable strategists and managers to judge the profitability of different industries, considered by Porter to be a key determinant of company profitability. Analysis will therefore influence strategic choice, including the possibilities of withdrawal from some markets or development of new markets. The application of PESTLE and five forces analysis will allow organizations to identify the major influences in the external environment and to gauge their impact on strategy.

Before taking any decisions about strategy, organizations must also review their own competitive position relative to others within the industry.

Analysis of consumer needs and demands

It could be argued with Harvey-Jones and others that buyers, i.e. customers, are the most important force in the competitive environment. It is therefore crucial to recognize the role of external analysis in identifying consumer needs and demands. Organizations need to know what factors determine demand for their products or services as well as understand how individual consumers value their products or services. Since demand is a function of several factors (see Chapter 8), this means that organizations have to consider, among other things, demographic trends, changes in incomes, tastes and preferences and the role of price in determining appropriate future strategy.

Many of these factors will have been identified in the course of the PESTLE analysis, but a much more detailed market research is necessary. This might highlight individual shopping patterns, attitudes towards particular firms or brand names, or satisfaction with existing products or services. In addition, there are several valuable sources of information held internally, including rates of customer enquiries and sales, which can be used to determine changing patterns of demand.

7.2.3 Internal analysis

Environmental analysis also requires an examination of the organization's internal environment. Internal analysis is concerned with the **resources** and **capabilities** which an organization must seek to understand before it can pursue any form of strategy. Assessment of capability must, therefore, take account of the following:

- The overall balance of resources in the organization
- Its mix of activities
- The quantity or quality of the different resource inputs (e.g. buildings, machines, people) and
- The way in which the separate activities involved in designing, producing, marketing, delivering and supporting the organization's products or services are performed and the linkages between them.

In order to develop an understanding of its capabilities, an organization needs to

- Assess its resource base
- Examine the way in which resources are used and linked together in the different activities which create each output or service
- Assess whether its range of products or services are appropriately balanced

The principle of competitive advantage then dictates that some form of comparative analysis be undertaken. Hamel and Prahalad[13] note that although organizations may have many attributes, which distinguish them from their competitors, management needs to focus on those which are critical for long-term success. Such distinguishing factors that create competitive advantage are often referred to as **core competencies**.

Internal analysis is therefore concerned with identifying the organization's core competencies, with a focus on performance relative to competitors. A number of tools have been developed to help organizations assess organizational capability; some of these will now be discussed.

Assessing the resource base

An understanding of core competencies could be achieved by conducting a resource audit, which 'identifies and classifies the resources that an organization owns or can access to support its strategies'. The audit would cover the organization's physical, human, financial and other resources. This should include resources which are not owned by the organization, but to which it has access. The audit would address the following types of questions:

- Is the organization's plant, machinery and other equipment up to date?
- Do staff have the necessary skills and qualifications?
- Does the organization have an appropriate financial structure (debt/equity mix)?
- Are financial control systems (such as credit and debt control) effective?
- Does the organization have important intangible resources (such as goodwill)?
- Are there important resources outside the organization (such as good relationships with key customers or suppliers)?
- Can any unique resources be identified? An example would be a patented product.

Analysis must then proceed to develop a deeper understanding of the way in which these resources are deployed in the various activities of the organization. A widely adopted method is value chain analysis.

Value chain analysis

Value chain analysis is a technique which is designed to provide an in-depth understanding of the way in which resources are deployed to achieve competitive advantage. Porter[7] applied the established accounting practice of calculating the value added of a product by individual stages in a manufacturing process to the activities of an organization as a whole. The rationale for this approach is that activities must be examined separately in order to identify sources of competitive advantage.

As shown in Figure 7.3, activities are divided into two categories.

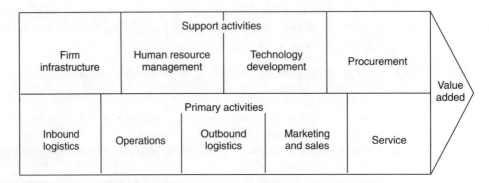

Figure 7.3.   The components of the value chain (adapted from Porter[11]).

Primary activities relate directly to service delivery or production. These include:

● 'Inbound logistics' (activities such as materials handling, warehousing and inventory control)
● Operations (activities which create the product, such as machining and packaging)
● 'Outbound logistics' (such as storing finished products, order processing and distribution)
● 'Marketing and sales' (the activities which create consumer awareness of the product)
● 'Service' (including activities such as installation, training support and repairs service).

Each of these activities will add value to the organization in its own way. They may undertake this task better or worse than competitors (for example, lower production costs, higher standards of service, etc.). In this way they provide the areas of competitive advantage of the organization.

Support activities include:

● 'Procurement' (the processes for acquiring the various inputs to the primary activities)
● 'Technology development' (research and development, process development)
● 'Human resource management' (recruiting, managing, training, developing and rewarding people in the organization)
● 'Infrastructure' (systems of planning, finance, quality control, information management, and the structures which sustain the culture of the organization).

These support activities also add value, but in a way that is more difficult to link with one particular part of the organization.

Value chain analysis is usually undertaken without detailed quantification of the value added and makes broad comparisons with competitors. Its significance is that it recognizes that individual activities in the overall production process play a part in determining the cost, quality, image and so on of the end product or service. That is 'each can contribute to a firm's relative cost position and create a basis for differentiation'.[11] These are the two main sources for competitive advantage identified by Porter. Analysing the separate activities in the value chain helps organizations to identify what underpins competitive advantage by addressing the following issues.

- Which activities are the most critical in reducing cost and adding value?
- What are the key cost or value drivers in the value chain?
- What are the most important linkages in the value chain, which either reduce cost or enhance value, and which discourage imitation, and how do these linkages relate to the cost and value drivers?

The importance of value chain analysis is its role in understanding competitive advantage, which cannot be understood by looking at an organization as a whole. According to Porter, competitive advantage can be gained by:

- Controlling costs (e.g. through economies of scale or efficient capacity utilization)
- Enhancing value (e.g. through improved customer care) and/or
- Reconfiguring the value chain, that is, finding a more efficient or different way of designing, producing, distributing or marketing a product or service.

Lynch[10] argues that the problem with the value chain in strategic management is that it is designed to explore existing value-added areas of the business; it works within the existing structure. Real competitive strategy may require a 'revolution' that moves outside the existing structure. This view is shared by Hamel and Prahalad.[13] They argue that in the quest for competitiveness, much management effort in the 1980s and 1990s was devoted to restructuring (especially downsizing) and re-engineering of business processes but that these processes are focused on preserving the past rather than on creating the future. 'It is entirely possible for a company to downsize and reengineer without ever confronting the need to regenerate its core strategy, without ever being forced to rethink the boundaries of its industry, without ever having to imagine what customers might want in ten years' time and without ever having to fundamentally redefine its "served market".'

7.2.4   Portfolio models

The majority of companies offer more than one product or service and many serve more than one customer. Decisions on strategy usually involve a range of products in a range of markets, and this is the subject of portfolio analysis. A useful model, developed by the Boston Consulting Group (BCG), is the growth/share matrix which examines the market share of individual products or services in relation to the growth rate in their particular markets (see Figure 7.4).

When an organization has a number of products in its portfolio, they are likely to be in different stages of development; some will be relatively new and some much older. Many organizations will not wish to risk having all their products in the same markets at the same stages of development. It is useful to have some products with limited growth but producing profits steadily, as well as having others with great potential but in the early stages of growth. Indeed the products that are growing steadily may be used to fund the development of those that will provide growth in the future. The strategy implications of this model are that organizations should produce a balanced portfolio of products.

Competitive position (market share)

Market growth		High	Low
	High	Stars (develop)	Question marks (investigate)
	Low	Cash cows (milk)	Dogs (divest)

Figure 7.4. The growth/share matrix.

The model's assumptions are that higher profitability and competitive advantage are associated with high market share and that growing markets are more attractive than static or declining markets.

The matrix categories are explained as follows:

- **Cash cows.** Characterized by high market share in a mature market; probably 'stars' of the past now in maturity. They occupy a leading position, and have little need for investment in production capacity. They are likely to be cash generators which can be 'milked', contributing to the development of future stars.
- **Stars.** Have a high market share within a growing market but expenditure on capacity and marketing may be high so that the product or service both generates and uses cash. They are likely to be the cash cows of the future.
- **Question marks.** Also found in growing markets, but have a low market share. They are typically products or services that are at an early stage in life requiring substantial amounts of cash to be spent in an effort to increase market share; however, the payback from high spending is uncertain.
- **Dogs.** Experience low market share in low-growth markets and are likely to be draining the organization of amounts of cash and using a disproportionate amount of management time.

7.2.5   Analysing organizational performance

Assessing whether strategies designed to meet particular objectives are proving effective is an important part of the strategy process. It is also necessary to establish how these performance levels compare with others within the industry and perhaps also beyond; as mentioned in the above examination of value chain analysis, competitive advantage can be defined only in these relative terms.

A term now often used to describe performance assessment is **benchmarking** which, according to Johnson and Scholes,[4] 'seeks to assess the competences of an organization against "best in class" wherever that is to be found'. Often this is taken to mean only measures of output performance which can be defined in quantitative terms (e.g. comparisons of financial performance, key financial ratios and other measures of output such as market share, production throughput). However, there are also more qualitative, less tangible features of performance which result in quality or satisfaction, such as attitudes towards customers, and are particularly important in service sector organizations. Assessment of these features is more difficult and it can often only be done by direct observation or by surveying users. Benchmarking should include quantitative and qualitative measures of performance, and its emphasis should be on continuous quality improvement.

Internal benchmarking

Most organizations monitor their own performance in order to identify changes in key business activities over time. This may mean looking at the performance of the organization as a whole, or comparing the performance of different individuals, teams or business units with each other. Performance monitoring is a continual process. Those with an interest in an organization's business (e.g. shareholders, analysts, management, etc.) will wish to compare results over time in order to reveal trends in business performance. This is the only way to discern whether performance is in line with expectations. Management will be interested in far more than overall organizational performance. In line with the concept of value chain, managers will assess the performance of the individual activities involved, not just of business units. Part of this process will involve regular analysis of performance against targets, e.g. financial performance against budget, sales and production achievements against target.

Performance assessment is also a common feature of public sector management. This is a result of central government's desire to increase competition and/or value for money in the provision of public services.

External benchmarking

This involves comparing performance with that of other organizations. Organizations need to decide:

- What activities or other dimensions of the organization should be compared with others
- Who the other organizations should be
- How information on other organizations can be obtained.

In reality, external benchmarking can be time consuming and be hampered by the difficulty of obtaining relevant information. There are also problems of finding comparable organizations to benchmark against, especially in the public sector – one of the criticisms of the publication of school league tables is that they do not compare 'like with like'.

Nevertheless, most organizations will wish to assess their own performance relative to industry norms. They could do this with reference to industry averages or to the performance of the best-performing organizations. However, a danger in relying solely on industry norm analysis is that the industry may itself be performing badly. Obviously the scope for cross-industry comparison will be more limited but could relate, for example, to employee costs or to research and development expenditure.

7.2.6   Matching the internal organization to external demands

Once an analysis of environmental influences, including the nature of the competitive environment and of internal resources and competences, has been conducted, a framework is required to bring the results together and identify the implications for strategy. This is often described as a process in which the 'fit' between the organization's internal capabilities and its external environment is assessed (the concept of 'strategic fit' was mentioned at the beginning of this chapter). A technique often used to assist managers in this process is SWOT analysis.

SWOT analysis

SWOT stands for strengths, weaknesses, opportunities and threats, and is perhaps the most well known of all analytical management techniques. Strengths and weaknesses are usually pinpointed in the course of internal analysis so that the results of the value chain and portfolio analyses would be pertinent. Opportunities and threats relate to trends and the likely developments in the external environment and would be identified in the PESTLE and five forces exercise. Thus a strength may be a highly skilled workforce and a weakness out-of-date plant and machinery; while a new product line might constitute an opportunity, but competition from cheaper imports could pose a threat.

Lynch[10] identifies several factors which will enhance the quality of a SWOT analysis (see Table 7.2):

Table 7.2 Checklist of some possible headings in a SWOT analysis

Strengths	Weaknesses
● Market dominance	● Share weakness
● Core strengths	● Old plant
● Economies of scale	● Poor record of innovation
● Low-cost position	● Weak organization
● Leadership and management skills	● Poor reputation
● Strong financial position	● Dependent on a few products
● Differentiated products	
● Product quality	
Opportunities	**Threats**
● New markets and segments	● New market entrants
● New products	● Increased competition
● Diversification opportunities	● Substitutes
● Market growth	● Low market growth
● Competitor weakness	● Economic downturn
● Demographic and social change	● Technological developments
● Change in political environment	● New international barriers to trade
● Change in economic environment	

- Keep it brief; long lists suggest a lack of strategic judgement
- Wherever possible, relate strengths and weaknesses to key factors for success
- Strengths and weaknesses should be stated in competitive terms
- Statements should be specific; avoid 'motherhood and apple pie' statements
- Be realistic about strengths and weaknesses
- Be able to back each point up with argument and evidence

Resource-based theory of strategy

Some writers hold that too much emphasis has been placed on the influence of external environmental factors on strategy, arguing that strategies based on an organization's internal resources or capabilities form a stronger foundation for future success. Thus the basis of competitive advantage is the organization's resources.

Hamel and Prahalad[13] believe that distinctive core competencies internal to the organization are the foundation of successful strategies, rather than the external comparisons. Kay[3] has developed the argument further by suggesting that there are three possible areas of core competence: innovation, reputation and 'architecture', which he describes as 'the system of relationships within a firm between the firm and its suppliers and customers, or both'. All are products of organizational resources. Through the use of examples, Kay demonstrates how the success of many well known firms is based on one or more of such distinctive capabilities.

Resource-based theories of strategy do not deny the importance of competition but they lay greater emphasis on the internal resources of the organization. As Lynch[10] notes, they are relatively new areas which have not been as thoroughly researched as other areas of strategy discussed here.

7.3   Strategic choice

Strategic choice refers to making decisions about the organization's future response to factors identified in the environmental analysis. Choice exists at two main levels:

- **Level 1 – choice of objectives.** As discussed earlier, this involves answering the basic question: what business are we or should we be in? Should the organization, for example, provide a wider range of goods or services or concentrate on a narrower range? These first-order choices, concerned primarily with the organization's scope, will be reflected in its statements of organizational purpose. Decisions on organizational scope, in turn, define organizational boundaries and shape decisions on organizational structure and ownership. These are typically corporate-level choices.
- **Level 2 – choices between strategies** or means to achieve organizational objectives. Alternative strategies will require detailed analysis and appraisal before a choice can be made. The final selection should reflect whatever the organization believes is necessary to create and sustain competitive advantage in its chosen markets. Organizations that operate in more than one market will typically conduct the identification and evaluation of options at the level of individual business units or departments.

7.3.1   Identifying strategic options

In considering possible strategies to achieve its objectives, management faces a further three choices:

- On what basis do they wish to compete with or differentiate themselves from their competitors? This is sometimes referred to as deciding a positioning or generic strategy.
- Should they develop new products or services, new markets, or a combination of the two? Should they drop certain activities? This concerns choosing strategic direction.
- Having made the first two sets of decisions, how should they develop the new services, products or markets? This concerns choosing the means of developing strategy.

7.3.2   Generic strategies

Porter[11] claims that what really matters in the marketplace is sustainable competitive advantage in relation to competitors; this, he argues, is the only basis for a successful strategy. Applying the analytical techniques common to industrial economics (see Chapter 8), Porter said that a firm's primary task is to find market niches it can defend from competitors; it should do this by way of the two basic types of competitive advantage that a firm can possess: low cost or differentiation. From this he developed the idea that there are three generic strategies or means by which companies could position themselves to develop and maintain competitive advantage:

- First, **cost leadership** is a strategy whereby a firm aims to produce its product or service at a lower cost than its competitors can. This could mean developing a large market share to bring economies of scale in production costs, so that cost leadership does not necessarily mean low price. Of course, a low-cost base will not in itself bring competitive advantage. What matters is the value perceived by the customers or users of the product or service.
- The second generic strategy is **differentiation**, whereby a company aims to offer a product or service that is distinctive – and valued as such by customers – from those of its competitors. Porter claimed that differentiation is 'something unique beyond simply offering a low price' that allows firms to command a premium price or to retain buyer loyalty during cyclical or seasonal downturns in the market. Firms that develop a reputation for reliability, for example, may be able to enhance their market share or to achieve higher margins by charging slightly higher prices which consumers are willing to pay.

Exercise

Consider the ways in which the following companies differentiate themselves from the competition: Coca-Cola; Marks & Spencer; BMW.

Feedback

All three companies have very strong brand images through which they are able to differentiate themselves. Probably the most distinctive brand is Coca-Cola, which is regarded as an American icon. This ensures that the company retains customer loyalty, even though there is (arguably) very little other than the brand to distinguish it from its competitors.

The image of BMW stems from its reputation for quality, style and reliability. The BMW marque is also viewed as something of a status symbol, which means that the company is able to charge premium prices.

Marks & Spencer also has a reputation for value, as well as for quality and reliability, although by the turn of the century this had begun to slip as its profits fell drastically. Its competitors were threatening its seemingly unassailable market lead and its clothing products were criticized for being drab and overpriced. Perhaps M&S was losing its distinctive image? However, by 2003 and after much upheaval, its profits were beginning to recover.

- The third variant, **focus** strategy, occurs when management applies either cost leadership or differentiation to a narrow market segment rather than to a whole market. Porter refers to two variants, cost focus and differentiation focus.

A firm has to choose between the two basic strategies of cost leadership and differentiation, although many commentators argue that companies follow both policies simultaneously. For example, by controlling costs better than competitors, companies can reinvest the savings in unique features that will differentiate their products or services. Some of these ideas will be developed in Chapter 8 on the economic context.

Choice of the basis for competitive advantage is complex and requires that environmental analysis provides a clear understanding of who the competitors are and of consumer demands, needs and values. Ultimately, user value (the worth placed on the good or service by the consumer) will determine the organization's ability to sustain competitive advantage. In the public and not-for-profit sectors, however, the idea of user value is more complicated. Often it is not the ultimate service users but the government that pays for the goods or services. This means that public and non-profit organizations may pay as much attention to the interests of their sponsors (i.e. those who provide the funding) as to those of their end-users. A common problem is that the main interests of government or its agents is in the concept of value for money, which tends to emphasize cost efficiency over product or service effectiveness.

Kay[3] notes that 'there can be no greater competitive advantage than the absence of competitors'. By this, he means that competitive advantage derives not just from the capabilities of firms themselves but from the structure of the industry. In a very competitive market even where firms have obvious competitive advantage this may not yield substantial profit. Yet mediocre, or even poor service can bring large profits where the competition is weak or absent – as in many of Europe's remaining public utilities. Competition provides the incentive to control costs or to provide a better service to gain custom, and this is one of the basic tenets of market economics (see Chapter 8). For example, in the run-up to deregulation of the market for domestic gas supply in the UK British Gas was forced to review its strategy. Other companies are now competing for business largely by offering lower prices, and British Gas has had to respond to these new market conditions.

7.3.3 Strategic directions

The second set of choices facing organizations concern the direction of strategy development. Options can be set out in a product/market matrix as shown in Table 7.3. This type of matrix, originally developed by Ansoff,[9] tends to assume the existence of growth opportunities, which may not always be available. Instead, decisions may be about altering the service mix to use existing resources more efficiently and effectively.

7.3.4 Existing markets, same product/service

An organizations's choice of whether to focus on their current product/service and markets will depend among other things on whether the market is growing, in decline or has reached maturity.

- **Consolidation.** This choice would aim to increase business in a growing market in order to retain market share. In mature markets, firms might focus on improving cost efficiency and customer service. In declining markets, one option is to acquire companies. Alternatively, managers may decide to withdraw from the market or to streamline operations.

Table 7.3 Strategic directions – the product/market matrix

	Existing products/services	New products/services
Existing markets	Consolidation Market penetration Withdrawal	Product/service development
New markets	Market development	Diversification: ● Horizontal ● Vertical ● Unrelated

Source: Adapted from Ansoff[9]

- **Market penetration.** Market penetration is designed to increase market share, which is more likely to be a successful strategy in a growing than in a mature market. Strategies may involve price competition, increasing advertising expenditure, or improving productivity.
- **Withdrawal.** Under certain circumstances, complete or partial withdrawal from a market is a legitimate strategy option.

7.3.5   Existing market, new product–product development

The advantage of product (or service) development as a strategy is that it allows a company to retain the security of its present markets while developing new products or altering existing ones. The recent shift by several retail supermarkets into petrol sales is an example of product development. Similarly, privatized utilities in the UK are seeking to develop new product lines on the basis of the strength of their existing customer base; for example, we now see electricity companies selling gas. New product development as a strategy can be risky; furthermore, it is likely to require the development of new organizational skills, which was certainly the case when retailers such as Marks & Spencer, along with several supermarket chains, developed into financial services.

7.3.6   New markets, present product/service – market development

Here, the company is seeking new markets for existing products or services. This could mean new groups of customers or new purchasing markets, for example selling over the Internet. Business can also extend geographically.

7.3.7   Diversification

Diversification takes three basic forms:

- **Vertical integration** – occurs when a firm expands backwards towards its sources of supply or forwards towards its markets. For example, an oil company which bought oil wells would be practising backwards integration, while if it purchased filling stations this would be forwards integration. The advantage for the company would be assured supplies of the product and control over its outlets.
- **Horizontal integration** – occurs when a company takes over firms at a similar stage of production. An example would be an oil company which already owned a string of petrol stations taking over a competing chain.
- **Unrelated diversification** – involves developing into new products or markets outside the industry. This strategy is illustrated by the operations of conglomerate companies, which have interests in many different industries. Unrelated diversification may be undertaken as a means of spreading risk or to achieve further growth where existing markets have reached saturation.

Case study

Xfm write-off hits profits at Capital Radio

Capital Radio's investment for the future has hit the company's immediate short-term profits badly. The country's largest commercial radio operator yesterday reported that first-half pre-tax profits had fallen from £16.9 million to £13.7 million.

The bulk of the downturn stems from a £4.5 million write-off of goodwill in its recently acquired Xfm radio station and its Café Radio and Havana music-related restaurant chains. The company, which also owns Capital FM and Capital Gold, has also had to invest heavily in Xfm, which it bought for £15 million nine months ago.

Peter Harris, Capital's finance director, said 'We have been investing money to turn Xfm around . . . We put in £1 million during the first half and expect to invest a similar amount during the second half'. He said goodwill write-offs for the recently acquired Xfm and Red Dragon radio stations would continue for up to five years.

Despite the costs of expansion, Capital remains on the acquisitions trail. It said its key strategic objective was to grow its British radio business. It would apply for new analogue licences and 'seek out acquisition opportunities'.

The group is also hoping to build Xfm into a near national digital radio station by acquiring licences in larger urban areas. Capital, which did not apply for a national digital multiplex because of its high cost, said: 'Local digital gives us the opportunity of extending our brands, building national coverage across major conurbations and rolling out our licences, at much lower costs'.

The group has decided to ring fence its restaurant business from its radio operations. Mr Green said that shareholders were not happy with the idea of cash generated by the radio business being pumped into the restaurant chains. The non-music related restaurants were being sold, and the remaining chains would have to fund themselves, he said.

Capital is continuing to invest in Capital Interactive, an Internet web page and e-commerce business launched three years ago.

The Radio Advertising Bureau said yesterday that the advertising revenue of UK commercial radio stations rose 18% to £434 million in the year to the end of March.

The Guardian, 15 May 1999

Exercise

Using the product/market matrix, how would you classify Capital Radio's strategic direction?

Feedback

- Existing markets, existing products – market penetration (increasing its market share in a growing market for commercial radio)
- New markets, existing products – market development (Capital Radio's plans to achieve national coverage)
- New markets, new products/services – unrelated diversification (developing into new products outside the commercial radio industry, namely restaurants).

7.3.8   Alternative means of developing strategy

This relates to how organizations can pursue chosen strategies.

7.3.9   Internal development

The advantage of this method is that all aspects of the development of new products or services are totally within the organization's control. Where the product involves a highly technical design and manufacturing process, the organization's internal management and production expertise can be utilized.

7.3.10   Acquisition and merger

Acquisition allows rapid entry into new product and/or market areas, and is a central feature of Capital Radio's strategy (see above case study). It may also be adopted as a strategy to take advantage of new market opportunities where the acquiring company lacks the necessary resources. Mergers give companies the opportunity to tap into new markets and to save costs; indeed, this was the motivation behind the merger of many banks and building societies in Britain.

7.3.11   Joint developments and alliances

Organizations may turn to partners to cooperate in developing products or services, often in order to minimize risk. Examples of joint developments or joint ventures are common in large construction or civil engineering projects such as the Channel Tunnel. Forms of joint development include franchising, licensing and subcontracting. Franchising is a common form of development in many retailing activities.

7.3.12   Screening and appraising options

Management is likely to identify or generate alternative options in the process of developing strategy. Since most options will be mutually exclusive, options must be evaluated in terms of their suitability, feasibility and acceptability. There are several techniques available to assist these decisions, e.g. decision trees and cost benefit analysis.

7.4   Strategy implementation

Formulating and implementing strategy are closely related. The implementation stage relates to moving from strategy to action. It is a mistake to assume that plans will be implemented once they have been developed. Indeed, some writers refer to an 'implementation deficit', which relates to the fact that strategies are sometimes only partially implemented, or are not implemented at all. There could be several reasons for this, including lack of resources or resistance to the strategy from within the organization.

Managing implementation is complex. Johnson and Scholes[4] consider there are three main tasks:

● **Planning and allocating resources.** This involves asking the following questions:
  (i)   What resources (physical, financial, human, etc.) are required to implement the strategy?
  (ii) How will these resources be allocated among different divisions or departments?
  (iii) How are new production facilities to be financed?
● **Organization structure and design.** This involves asking the following questions:
  (i)   What are the responsibilities of different departments?
  (ii) What operational and control systems need to be put in place?
  (iii) What are staff training and development needs?
● **Managing strategic change.** This involves asking the following questions:
  (i)   What will the existing culture bear? Will it need to be changed?
  (ii) Is there likely to be resistance to change? How can it be overcome?

7.4.1   Aligning the organization to the business direction – the role of HR

There is an ongoing debate about the role of the HR function in the strategy process. Ulrich[14] argues that it is not for HR practitioners to formulate strategy; rather, HR should 'impel and guide serious discussion about how the company should be organized to carry out its strategy'. One framework that can be used to assess the extent to which all parts of the organization are working in unison to achieve business objectives is the McKinsey 'Seven S' model (Figure 7.5). The argument is that all the seven Ss need to be addressed; for example, creating new organizational structures is not enough, people need to acquire the skills and motivation to work in the new structures and, typically, managers need to adopt new styles of operating. A distinction is sometimes made between the 'hard triangle' of strategy, structure and systems and the 'soft square' of staff, style, skills and shared values. The tendency is for managers to focus on the former and neglect the latter, which may explain why change programmes so often falter.[15]

7.4.2   The relationship between strategic planning and strategic management

As we have seen, strategic planning is the process of formulating objectives, priorities and strategies. Strategic management includes the further development of strategy and managing its implementation.

7.4.3   Monitoring progress

Monitoring the implementation of the strategy is the last stage in the strategy process. Information systems which allow management to monitor progress must be in place.

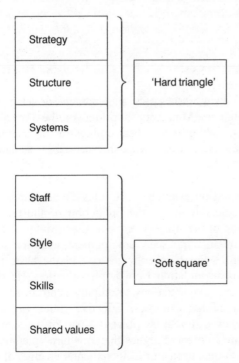

Figure 7.5. The McKinsey 'Seven S' model.

Organizations will normally assess achievements in relation to their own objectives and targets, using measures such as turnover, operating costs and other financial information against budget. They will also compare their performance with their competitors. Performance can be judged in both quantitative and qualitative terms, perhaps by using quality measures. Monitoring progress is the last stage in the strategy *model*, but not of the strategy *process*; strategy is a continuous process, with organizations constantly adapting and adjusting to the changes in the business environment. Monitoring and review is just one element in the process providing new information that feeds back into the reformulation of strategy.

7.5   Alternative approaches to strategy – 'descriptive' views

The planning view of strategy assumes that human beings always behave rationally and that the world can be viewed and interpreted in purely objective terms. Two alternative perspectives highlight the weaknesses of the traditional planning view and illustrate further the 'formulation/implementation dichotomy', i.e. difficulty in separating formulation and implementation.

7.5.1   Emergent strategy

When I was younger I always conceived of a room where all these strategic concepts were worked out for the whole company. Later, I didn't find such a room . . . The strategy of the company may not even exist in the mind of one man (sic). I certainly don't know where it is written down. It is simply transmitted in the series of decisions made.

The *Financial Times*, 16 February 1996

Writers such as Mintzberg[16] view strategy as an emergent or adaptive process rather than as a planned, top-down one. Mintzberg's critique of the formalized approach to strategy discussed up to now highlights the shortcomings of the planning model. In his opinion, strategic planning suffers from what he describes as three 'fundamental fallacies':

● **The fallacy of predetermination.** Mintzberg disputes the assumption that the strategy process develops in a predictable way: 'the prediction of the environment through forecasting . . . the unfolding of the strategy process on schedule . . . and the imposition of the resulting strategies on an acquiescent environment, again on schedule'.
● **The fallacy of detachment.** Mintzberg criticizes one of the basic tenets of strategic planning, that of separating formulation from implementation. He also questions the tendency on the part of some organizations to employ centralized teams of strategic thinkers isolated from operational activities. Effective strategy-making requires that implementation and formulation should be viewed as part of the same process.
● **The fallacy of formulation.** Mintzberg argues that structured planning tends to inhibit innovation by introducing 'a bias in favour of incremental change, of generic strategies and of goals that can be quantified'.

The conclusion of Mintzberg's critique of the planning model is that there is no one best way to develop strategy. He regards the structured analytical approach advanced by writers such as Ansoff[9] as wholly unsuitable for many (although not all) of today's organizations, especially those operating in turbulent environments. This style of planning, he argues, may be appropriate for certain types of organization but not for others. Mintzberg therefore advocates a flexible approach to strategy.

Other writers are in broad agreement with Mintzberg; Kay[3] writes that there are 'no recipes and generic strategies for corporate success . . . there cannot be, because if there were, their general adoption would eliminate any competitive advantage . . . the foundations of corporate success are unique to each successful company'.

Case study

The Honda story

Honda's takeover of the US motorcycle market in the 1960s is an illustration of successful strategy.

In 1975, an analysis of strategy alternatives for the UK motorcycle industry focused on what consultants assumed was Honda's deliberate strategy to dominate the world market.

According to this view, later echoed by strategy academics, Honda deliberately built a cost advantage and targeted the bottom end of the US market to exploit this advantage and outmanoeuvre established competition.

On the face of it, this is a classic example of the successful application of textbook 'planning' view of strategy using analytical techniques. But subsequent research in 1982 by Richard Pascale, a professor from Stanford, uncovered a quite different account of events.

According to Pascale, Honda executives said that the low price of the Honda 50 cc in 1959 derived from its engine design, not from production economies of scale. At that stage production was relatively inefficient and the company only invested in a large, modern plant in response to events rather than as part of a prior deliberate strategy.

The Honda executives' account of what happened when they went to the USA in 1959 differs even more dramatically from the earlier version in that they claimed to have actually played down their smaller bikes. In reality 'the dramatic success of the Honda 50 cc came about through accident, good luck and Honda US executives' willingness to respond to events and learn from the market. They did not even try to sell their small bikes until their larger ones started breaking down badly as a result of being driven longer and harder than in Japan.'

Originally, Honda had felt that the 50 cc bikes were wholly unsuitable for the US market, where large bikes dominated. However, Honda executives used the Honda 50s themselves to ride around Los Angeles. They attracted a lot of attention and, according to the Honda executives they had a call from a Sears buyer . . . 'but we still hesitated to push the 50 cc bikes out of fear that they might harm our image in the heavier, more macho market. But when the larger bikes started breaking, we had no choice. We let the 50 cc bikes move.'

The strategy which gradually moved Honda towards a market dominance began from this muddled start, but the actual strategy process that led to this success was contrary to the textbook model.

Source: Reported in the *Financial Times*, 16 February 1996

Kay[3] argues that 'we shall never know the extent to which Honda's success was truly the result of chance or rational calculation [but] like all successful strategies, it was based on a mixture of calculation and opportunism, of vision and experiment'. The key point is that managers should see departure from 'the plan' as an inevitable response to unforeseen circumstances and as necessary to take advantage of new opportunities.

Mintzberg emphasizes this point by making a distinction between underlying and emergent strategies (see Figure 7.6).

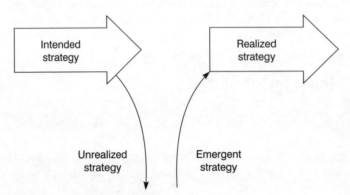

Figure 7.6. Types of Strategies.

He accepts that planning is a necessary part of the strategy process, and recognizes that elements of the plan (deliberate strategy) may in fact be realized. But he argues that realized strategies often bear little resemblance to the original plan. Indeed, it is likely that some plans failed to be implemented at all (unrealized strategies) and that others, which he describes as 'emergent strategies', were not expressly intended. Lynch[10] notes that emergent corporate strategy 'can best be considered as a process whereby the organization's strategy is derived as a result of trial, repeated experimentation and small steps forward: in this sense, corporate strategy is *emergent* rather than *planned*'. The process moves forward as economic conditions change, the market develops, individuals and teams in the organization change, etc. Clearly, the process is difficult to predict in a clear and structured way. According to Mintzberg, a flexible approach to strategy is one which recognizes that the 'real world inevitably involves some thinking ahead of time as well as some adaptation en route'. Writers such as Senge[17] have emphasized this *learning* approach to strategy, which encourages managers to undertake a process of trial and error to devise the optimal strategy (see Chapter 3, Section 3.6).

7.5.2   Strategy as logical incrementalism

The essence of this view of strategy is that, far from being an objective and value-free process, strategy formulation and implementation is pervaded by value judgements. Furthermore, there is a distinct political dimension at work in that the conflicting interests of various stakeholders must be taken into account. Strategy is therefore an incremental process characterized not by objective analysis, but rather by bargaining between stakeholders. The outcome is marginal adjustments to existing strategy. Johnson and Scholes[4] describe this view of strategy as logical incrementalism which 'can be thought of as the deliberate development of strategy by "learning by doing" '.

Public sector organizations are restricted in their choice of strategy which is often largely imposed upon them from outside and is heavily influenced by political bargaining.

There are three important points to note about these different views of strategy:

- Both the emergent and the incrementalist models oppose the rigid planning view of strategy, but nevertheless accept that a structured approach to strategy has its place: 'Too much planning may lead us to chaos, but so would too little, more directly.'[16]
- Approaches to strategy adapt to the changing environment and are influenced by changing socioeconomic conditions. Thus the planning model better fitted the stable conditions of the 1960s, whereas the adaptive, learning approach associated with the emergent strategy model is better suited to the twenty-first century. Similarly, different planning styles emerge in response to different social and economic conditions. The planning style of the 1960s seemed to suit the relative stability which characterized the period. Today's highly competitive, increasingly global and fast-moving markets may be better matched by a learning, adaptive strategy.
- These different approaches can be combined, and this is the reality of the strategy-making process today. As Lynch[10] observes, the perceived drawbacks of the planning view are '*limitations* on the prescriptive approach rather than issue which cannot be overcome'.

In brief

In the first part of this chapter we appraised various definitions of corporate strategy and saw that whereas some commentators emphasize the long-term planning and integrating functions of strategy, others focus on positioning in the marketplace or on the strategy process itself. A consideration of 'planned strategy' followed and we introduced a six-stage model of the strategy process.

We then went on to examine each of these six stages in turn, beginning with decisions about organizational purpose. The second section, on environmental analysis, introduced some important analytical management techniques, each of which is designed to assess either the internal or external environments of organizations. The framework provided by one of these techniques – PESTLE analysis – is used as the basis for our examination of the business context of management in this part of the book.

The third section covers strategic choice and discusses how organizations make choices between possible strategies, based on the results of an environmental analysis. The fourth section examines the implementation of strategy, focusing in particular on how the organization and people management interventions can be aligned to business strategy.

Finally, we saw that there are alternative views of corporate strategy, which suggest that the rigid planning view does not accord with reality. However, we can conclude that organizations nevertheless need to take a structured approach to strategy and in this sense, the stages of the planning model provide a set of guidelines for managers.

Examination questions for this chapter are given in Appendix 2.

References

1 Mintzberg, H., Quinn, J. B. and Ghoshal, S. (1998) *The Strategy Process*. Prentice Hall.
2 Glueck, W. F. (1980) *Business Policy and Strategic Management*. McGraw-Hill.
3 Kay, J. (1996) *The Business of Economics*. Oxford University Press.
4 Johnson, G. and Scholes, K. (1999) *Exploring Corporate Strategy*. (5th edn). Prentice Hall.
5 *Personnel Today* (2000) 15 February.
6 BBC1 (2002) *Habitat and Me*, 4 December.
7 Porter, M. E. (1996) What is strategy? *Harvard Business Review*.
8 Simon, H. A. (1947) *Administrative Behaviour*. Macmillan.

 9 Ansoff, H. I. (1965) *Corporate Strategy*. Penguin.
10 Lynch, R. (1997) *Corporate Strategy*. Pitman.
11 Porter, M. E. (1985) *Competitive Advantage: Creating and Sustaining a Superior Performance*. Free Press.
12 Harvey-Jones, J. (1991) *Getting it Together*. Heinemann.
13 Hamel, G. and Prahalad, C. K. (1994) *Competing for the Future*. Harvard Business School Press.
14 Ulrich, D. (1998) A new mandate for human resources. *Harvard Business Review*, Jan./Feb.
15 Holbeche, L. (2001) *Aligning Human Resources and Business Strategy*. Butterworth-Heinemann.
16 Mintzberg, H. (1994) *The Rise and Fall of Strategic Planning*. Prentice Hall International.
17 Senge, P. M. (1990) *The Fifth Discipline: The art and practice of the learning organization*. Doubleday.

Further reading

Johnson, G. and Scholes, K. (2002) *Exploring Corporate Strategy* (6th edn). Prentice Hall.
Lynch, R. (2002) *Corporate Strategy*. Pitman.

Web-site addresses

Official Government Statistics: http://www.statistics.gov.uk

8 The economic and global context of management

Chapter objectives

In this chapter you will:

- Examine the operation of the market
- Review approaches to market regulation
- Consider the relationship between growth, unemployment and inflation
- Examine the role of the state in economic management
- Examine the rationale for and structure of international trade
- Review the framework of international institutions which oversee trade
- Consider the forces driving globalization
- Analyse the effects of globalization on managers and organizations
- Examine the role of multinational enterprises in the process of globalization

Chapter introduction

Responsibility for the production of goods and services falls to managers, who are constantly making choices about the effective and efficient deployment of available resources. Because managers play such a fundamental role in economic activity, it is vital that they are able to identify the opportunities and threats posed by a continually changing economic environment. This is true for all managers, whether they are dealing with day-to-day activities or developing business strategy.

A feature of this chapter is a section examining the profound and pervasive effects of globalization on nations, individual citizens and businesses alike. Indeed, globalization has become the economic issue of the age; and moreover, expert opinion suggests that, for the foreseeable future, the pace of global economic change is likely to accelerate. Therefore managers must understand what globalization is, what drives it and how it impacts on them.

This chapter begins with a case study designed to demonstrate how management decisions are affected by economic factors. The themes highlighted here are developed throughout the chapter.

Case study

Train crush

What a grand idea for a day out: London to Brighton and back, by train, for only £1. And on a Bank Holiday weekend too. To cap it all, the railway company, Thameslink, donated the fares to charity. Many people thought this was too good an opportunity to miss. Too many. On Sunday night, May 24, there was a queue ten deep and 200 yards long for trains back to London.

This is an extreme example, the result of a daft (if well-intentioned) pricing decision. That said, train travellers in the south-east of England are more than used to overcrowding. There is standing room only on peak-hour journeys to and from London's mainline stations, and on the Underground. Since the railways were privatized in 1996–7, grumble many commuters, overcrowding (not to mention the frequency and punctuality of services) has got worse. But should not some commuters, with their noses pressed against the windows or their neighbours' armpits, whisper a prayer of thanks? For the growth in commuter travel is largely a byproduct of economic activity: overcrowding is a sign that the economy is doing well.

In fact, the annual growth rate of the number of rail commuters into central London during the early-morning rush is pretty closely correlated with the growth rate of the Gross Domestic Product (GDP) (see Figure 8.1). Commuting boomed with the economy in the mid-1980s, plunged as recession took hold and is now surging again.

This is bringing money into rail operators' coffers. But the strength of the economy is also pushing up their costs. One transport boss says that his firm is having to pay wage increases above the inflation rate in order to keep fare-collecting staff. He adds that his problem is beginning to creep northwards and is now affecting subsidiary firms in the Midlands. This suggests that the obvious solution to the problem of overcrowding – running more trains – might not be as profitable as it looks. More workers would have to be hired to operate them. Especially in the south-east, where unemployment is 4.5 per cent, compared with the national average of 6.4 per cent, they may be hard to come by. But if the economy is slowing down, as many economists believe, the trains may be less crowded anyway.

The Economist, London (1998)

- Why was the £1 return fare to Brighton a 'daft' pricing decision?
- If the decision was so obviously 'daft', why did Thameslink take it in the first place?
- Why should commuters have to pay peak fares for the privilege of travelling on overcrowded trains, when those who travel off-peak pay considerably less and have a more comfortable journey?
- What factors must Thameslink managers take into account when making pricing decisions?
- What are the issues facing rail operators when deciding whether to invest in extra capacity (trains, track, etc.)?

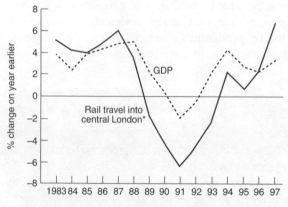

*Surface rail plus Underground, 7am–10am

Figure 8.1. All aboard – percentage change on previous years (*The Economist*, 30 May 1998).

This case introduces some key economic principles and concepts.

- The £1 return fare created massive *excess demand* because it was set far below the *market clearing price* at which *supply* is brought in line with *demand*. This demonstrates the role played by *prices* in *rationing scarce resources*.
- This was clearly a public relations gimmick designed to attract custom and show the company in a 'socially caring' light. It seems that it may have backfired!
- *Prices* must reflect the *costs of production*. Production costs include *capital investment* in trains, track, stations, etc. The size of the system is determined by the extra capacity required to cope with peak demand; therefore those who use the railways at peak times should bear the additional cost. The same principle applies to peak pricing for electricity, telephone calls, air flights, etc.
- Apart from peak pricing, managers need to be aware of the *competition*. Although the rail operators do not face competition from other operators (they are *local monopolies*), they do compete with other forms of transport, such as cars and buses. Therefore, they must consider the effects that their pricing decisions will have on the demand for alternative forms of transport; and similarly, how changes in the prices of alternative forms of transport will affect demand for rail travel (for example, what would happen to the demand for rail travel if the price of petrol fell?).
- Until the point at which the system reaches capacity, the cost of an extra passenger is zero. However, once capacity has been reached, the cost of an extra passenger is a new train (and possibly new track, signalling equipment, etc.)! This, coupled with the fact that demand for rail travel follows the *economic cycle*, complicates investment decisions.

Other economic issues highlighted by this case include: the relationship between the market for goods and services and the labour market; the appearance of labour shortages as the economy grows; and the concept of 'market failure'. These issues will be examined in this chapter.

8.1   Economic systems

8.1.1   What is 'economics'?

Essentially, economics is concerned with the **production and consumption of goods and services**. It involves examining the following issues:
Regarding production:

- How much the economy produces
- What combination of goods and services is produced
- How much each firm produces
- What methods of production firms use
- How many people firms employ.

Regarding consumption:

- How much people spend and save
- The pattern of consumption
- How much people buy of any particular good or service
- What specific individuals choose to buy
- How consumption is affected by prices and other factors, such as advertising.

While it is true to say that economics is about the production and consumption of goods and services, this does not really answer the question: what, exactly, makes a problem an *economic* one?

The economic problem

The central problem faced by all individuals and societies, regardless of wealth, is that of **scarcity**. This term has a very specific meaning for economists, who assume that human wants for goods and services are unlimited; that is, people, whether rich or poor, have an almost infinite capacity for desiring material things. However, the means of meeting these wants are limited. It is therefore impossible to meet everyone's wants because the world only has a limited amount of resources with which to produce goods and services. These resources, or **factors of production** as economists call them, fall into the following categories:

- **Labour** – the **human resource**. The labour force is limited not only in numbers but also in terms of skills. This explains why labour shortages can exist during periods of unemployment.
- **Land** – the **natural resource**. This refers to 'land' in the literal sense of the word, and all raw materials.
- **Capital** – the **manufactured resource**. This consists of all the inputs (factories, machines and other equipment) that themselves had to be made in the first place.

So the reason for scarcity is that human wants are unlimited, but the resources available to meet those wants are limited. The fact that people, whether rich or poor, want more than they can have will cause them to behave in certain ways in their roles as producers and consumers. It is this behaviour that is the subject matter of economics.

Demand and supply

Another way of looking at consumption and production is in terms of demand and supply.

Supply and demand are central to economics and the subject is sometimes characterized as being wholly about studying the interaction of these two 'forces'. It is therefore important to understand these terms and their relationship to scarcity.

Demand is related to wants. If goods and services were free, wants would be unlimited. **Supply**, on the other hand, is limited by scarce resources. Potential demand will always, therefore, exceed potential supply. The problem for society is how to match demand and supply. This applies at the level of individual goods and services; it also applies to the economy as a whole, where total spending will need to match total production.

If potential demand exceeds potential supply, how are actual demand and actual supply to be made equal? Either demand needs to be stemmed, or supply increased, or there needs to be a combination of the two. It is this process, the interaction of the forces of supply and demand, that is the subject matter of economics. It studies how demand adjusts to available supplies, and how supply adjusts to consumer demand.

8.1.2   Two branches of economics

Economics naturally divides into two branches of study. **Macroeconomics** is concerned with the study of the economy as a whole ('macro' means 'big'). It is therefore concerned with **aggregate demand** and **aggregate supply**. 'Aggregate' is the word economists use to denote 'total'. Aggregate demand means total spending in the economy. There are several categories of spending: consumer spending on goods and services; government spending; spending by firms on investment goods such as machinery, factories and offices; and spending by overseas customers on a country's exports. Aggregate supply means the total national production of goods and services.

Scarcity means societies want to ensure that available resources should be used as efficiently as possible and that, over time, national output should grow. Macroeconomics, then, studies how national output is determined and its growth over time. It also studies the problems societies face in trying to secure steadily growing national output (inflation, unemployment and achieving a balance in international payments) and the policy choices facing governments in dealing with these problems.

Microeconomics is concerned with the individual parts of the economy. It focuses on the demand and supply for:

- Particular goods and services (e.g. for cars, clothes or holidays) and
- Resources (e.g. oil, computers and managers)

Scarce resources mean that choices have to be made. Thus society has to answer the following questions:

- **What to produce?** What goods and services are going to be produced with the scarce resources available, and in what quantity?
- **How to produce?** How are goods and services going to be produced? What resources are going to be used in production? What technology is going to be used?
- **For whom to produce?** How is the nation's output going to be distributed? What will be the incomes of the various occupational groups?

All societies have to make these choices, although they can be made by different groups – essentially, individuals or the government. These are microeconomic choices as they are concerned about individual products.

8.1.3   Opportunity cost

All choices involve sacrifice. At an individual level, if you choose to buy one particular product, the less money you will have to buy others. At a national level, if a society chooses to produce more of one particular good, it will be able to produce less of others. This is brought into sharp focus if we consider some of the actual choices facing society: a decision to produce more arms means fewer hospitals; a policy of building more homes means fewer schools . . . and so on. So the production or consumption of one thing involves the sacrifice of alternatives. This is the concept of opportunity cost, which is defined as follows:

Opportunity cost is the cost of any activity measured in terms of the best alternative forgone.

Rational choices

Another important concept in economics is that of rational choices. Economists assume that the economic actors – consumers and firms – will make rational choices when deciding what to buy or produce, i.e. they will weigh up the *costs* and *benefits*. Rational decision making for consumers involves choosing items that give the best value for money, i.e. the greatest benefit relative to cost.

For firms, managers will weigh up the benefits of an investment – in a new production line, for example – against its cost. The benefits of such an investment would be the revenues that the firm received as a result of the extra production; and the costs would be the extra labour, raw materials, etc. required. The investment will only be justified if benefits (in terms of revenues) exceed the costs; that is, if it earns a **profit**.

8.1.4   The circular flow of income – a thumbnail sketch of how the economy works

Because the economy is a highly complex system involving countless transactions between people, economists have found it useful to produce models which capture the essence of how the economy works. The circular flow of income is one such model.

The satisfaction of human wants involves people in their dual roles as producers and consumers. The relationship between these two roles is represented in Figure 8.2. In this model, consumers are conventionally labelled 'households' and producers are described as 'firms'. Each of these 'players' is in a 'demand and supply' relationship with the other.

- Households demand goods and services, which are supplied by firms. In the absence of money, people would exchange goods and services directly and workers would be paid in bundles of goods. This situation is described as a *barter economy*. In a money economy, firms exchange goods and services for money, which flows from households to firms in the form of consumer expenditure. Goods and services flow in the opposite direction, from firms to households. The coming together of buyers and sellers is known as a **market**, which could take several forms – from a street market to the housing market.
- Firms demand the use of **factors of production**, owned by households (i.e. individuals), which they need in order to produce goods and services. Households, as the owners of factors of production (land, labour and capital), supply *factor services* to firms. In return, they receive from firms *factor incomes* – rent for land, wages for labour and interest and dividends for the financial capital which they have lent to companies. Just as there is a market for goods and services, as discussed above, there is also a market for the factors of production – so we can talk of the labour market and the capital markets.

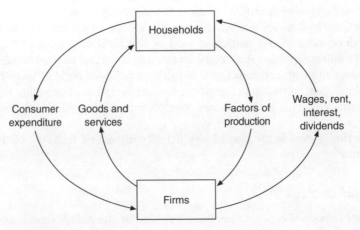

Figure 8.2. The circular flow of income and goods.

It can be seen that there is a **circular flow of incomes**: households earn incomes from firms and firms earn incomes from households. Also, in the opposite direction, there is a circular flow of goods and services. This model helps to distinguish between micro-economics and macroeconomics:

- **Microeconomics** is concerned with the composition of the circular flow in terms of what combination of goods make up the goods flow, how resources are combined to produce these goods and how factor incomes are distributed.
- **Macroeconomics** is concerned with the total flow of goods and services and what causes it to expand and contract.

8.1.5   Defining economic systems

An economic system is the way in which society organizes itself in order to answer the 'economic problem'. Although in reality each country appears to have a unique economic system they are **all** essentially just different versions of the following three basic types:

- **Market economies** – also commonly referred to as 'free enterprise', '*laissez-faire*' or 'capitalist' systems. In a market system, the basic economic problem is solved by **market forces**. There are six essential features of such a system:
  - (i)   **Private property.** Individuals have the right to own land, buildings, machinery etc., and to accumulate private wealth.
  - (ii) **Freedom of choice.** Thus consumers are free to decide what to buy with their incomes; workers are free to choose where and how much to work; and firms are free to decide what to sell and what production methods to use.
  - (iii) **Self-interest.** Supporters of 'market economies' argue that the pursuit of individual self-interest leads to the benefit of all. Thus the following assumptions are made: (a) Firms seek to maximize profits; (b) consumers seek to get the best value for money from their purchases; (c) workers seek to maximize their wages relative to the human cost of working in a particular job.
  - (iv) **Competition.** All consumers and firms are relatively small and cannot exploit the market, so that competition improves efficiency.
  - (v)   **Markets and prices.** The most basic feature of market economies is their use of the 'price mechanism' in allocating scarce resources to various uses; in other words, the way prices (determined by the forces of supply and demand) act as indicators to producers (firms) thereby ensuring that what is produced is what consumers have demanded.
- **Command economies** – often referred to as planned economies. Problems of 'what', 'how' and 'for whom' to produce are worked out by state or government planners who produce economic plans for the whole country. In order to do this, however, the state must own and control the country's economic resources. For example, in communist countries all land, houses, factories etc. are owned by the state and labour is 'directed' to work in the occupation and geographical location decided by the state. The absence of an efficient method (such as the market mechanism) of matching supply to demand presents state planners with a number of problems:
  - (i)   **Production.** In a modern industrial society each product normally involves many stages of production and so the production of one thing depends on the production of other things. This makes the task of planning extremely complicated; it is impossible to plan the production of each individual factory, farm, etc., so planners usually have to set targets for each whole industry. This can result in the under- or overproduction of certain goods, leading to shortages or surpluses.

(ii)   **Distribution.** If production is planned, the pattern and volume of consumption is only likely to match it if distribution ('who gets what') is also planned. However, this is not feasible, since even in communist countries, consumers expect to have some choice about how they spend their incomes. In the absence of the price mechanism to indicate consumer preferences, planners have to use movements in the level of stock as an indicator of consumer demand.

(iii)   **Labour.** If it is considered unacceptable for planners to dictate to people what work they do, they may have to use 'prices', in the form of wage differentials.

- **Mixed economies.** Most economies of the Western world fall into this category. Although basically 'market economies', they incorporate a significant state sector and some regulation of market forces. In practice, all economies are a mixture of planned and free-market systems. It is therefore the degree of government intervention which distinguishes different economic systems. The communist regimes of Eastern Europe were centrally planned economies, but many goods and services were allocated through the market. For example, the produce of collective farms was sold in street markets, where prices were determined by supply and demand rather than by the state. Workers were free to purchase what they wanted, even though production was planned and choice severely limited. People also had considerable choice about where they worked. Such economies could therefore be described as *mixed planned economies*. In mixed *market* economies, the government may control the following:

(i)   The relative prices of goods and factors of production, by taxing them or by subsidies, or through direct price controls.

(ii)   Relative incomes, through income taxes and welfare payments.

(iii)   The pattern of production and consumption by outlawing some products (e.g. unsafe goods, recreational drugs) and itself providing some goods and services (e.g. education), by taxes and subsidies, and by nationalization.

(iv)   Macroeconomic problems such as unemployment and inflation, as well as exchange rates, etc.

The worth (or otherwise) of the various combinations of market and government provision depend on the nation's economic objectives (such as economic growth, efficiency in production and full employment) and political goals (liberty, equality, etc.).

Perfect competition

It is important to realize that in this context the word 'perfect' does not mean 'best'. It refers to the idea of 'total' competition, in that there is a total absence of market power, entry barriers and product differentiation, plus total information for producers and consumers in the market.

Economists study highly competitive markets because the model provides an approximation of how the real world works and gives a useful insight into the workings of the market economy. Both producers and consumers are *price takers*. This means that they have to accept the prices set by market forces. This is very close to reality for consumers because there are few occasions on which we can haggle about the prices of products. For producers, perfect competition means that firms are too small and have to compete with too many other firms to be able to raise prices. This is the case for some producers in some markets, but in many cases firms do have the power to determine prices (although they do have to take into account consumer demand in doing this).

A problem of trying to classify economic systems is that countries also differ in the type of government intervention as well as the level (see Figure 8.3). For example, governments intervene in the following ways:

Figure 8.3. A classification of economic systems.

- Through planning
- Through nationalization
- Through regulation
- Through taxes and subsidies
- Through partnership schemes with private industry.

There has been a general movement towards the free-market end of the continuum since the late 1970s. In Western economies, this has been the result of the deregulation of markets and large-scale privatization (the selling of nationalized industries to the private sector and in the UK, the compulsory competitive tendering of state-run services, thus opening them up to private sector provision). In East European economies, central planning has been abandoned and a large measure of private enterprise adopted, especially since the late 1980s. However, as the following extract shows, the transition to the free market has been far from smooth.

The former communist states of Eastern Europe face difficulties in converting from a planned to a market economy

Ten years ago, there was much optimism about the economic prospects of the former communist states of Eastern Europe. After a difficult but brief transition period, they would be transformed into dynamic market economies through a combination of foreign investment and a well educated and trained workforce. However, the statistics show that the transition has been more difficult and more prolonged than expected. According to a report by the European Bank of Reconstruction and Development (EBRD), between 1989 and 1997, the Czech economy shrank by 2 per cent, the Hungarian economy shrank by 10 per cent, and the Bulgarian economy shrank by 37 per cent. Further east, things are even worse: the Russian economy shrank every year apart from 1997; and the economy of the Ukraine is now only one third of the size it was under communism. Only Poland has been relatively successful – its economy has grown by 12 per cent since 1989. In contrast, the economies of Western Europe have experienced steady economic growth, widening the gap between east and west.

According to Joe Hellman, an economist at the EBRD, 'The depth of restructuring of the economies that was required was underestimated. The centralised communist state economies which weren't based on economic incentives but on political orders led to such a distorted system'. Approximately 70 per cent of industry had to be dismantled and reorganized and millions of people were in the wrong jobs. For Russia and the Ukraine, the situation was made worse by the fact that some one third of industry was involved in the production of defence goods, and this sector of their economy completely disappeared.

The market reforms also had knock-on effects. For example, once the massive state subsidies to the state-owned farms were removed, they could no longer afford tractors and ploughs. This had a devastating effect on manufacturing output, as around one quarter of all investment in some states was accounted for by agricultural machinery.

The EBRD claims that the economic reforms have not been radical enough. Hellman argues that 'The countries which have reformed the fastest have made the strongest output recovery, while those which have made only partial reforms have made a slower recovery'. It has been difficult to overcome the political blockages – often governments have been too weak and the forces of reaction have managed to stave off the reforms.

Reported in *The Observer*, 6 December 1998

8.2   Markets and firms – a closer look at the free-market economy

8.2.1   Demand

When the price of a good rises, the quantity demanded will fall. We know this intuitively, just as we know that when the price of a good falls, the quantity demanded will rise. Demand is also affected by other factors, such as tastes and fashion, the price and availability of substitute goods (for example, the demand for coffee depends on the price of tea), complementary goods (those goods which are consumed together, such as cars and petrol), and income (as people's incomes rise, their demand for most goods will rise but they will tend to buy more better-quality products).

Exercise

Consider the following:

- What will happen to the demand for coffee if it is heavily advertised?
- What will happen to the demand for coffee if it is seen to be drunk by the stars of popular American TV situation comedy programmes?
- What will happen to the demand for coffee if the price of tea falls?
- What will happen to the demand for coffee if incomes rise?

Remember that there are different types of coffee (instant, filter and cafetière, 'designer coffees' sold in fashionable cafés).

Feedback

- Demand will rise
- Demand for designer coffee will rise
- Demand will fall
- Demand for the more up-market brands will rise

8.2.2   Supply

When the price of a good rises, the quantity supplied will also rise. This is because the higher the price of the good, the more profitable it becomes to produce. As with demand, there are determinants of supply other than price, such as costs of production (as costs rise, firms cut back on production and supply falls), and the profitability of producing other alternative products.

Supply and demand decisions of firms and households are transmitted to each other through the **price mechanism**. Prices play a crucial role in a market economy as they act as *signals* and *incentives* to producers and consumers. Prices respond to shortages (which cause prices to rise), and surpluses (which cause prices to fall). If consumers decide they want more of a particular good or service, or if producers cut supply, demand will exceed supply. The resulting shortage will cause the price of the good to rise. This provides an **incentive** for firms to shift resources into producing goods and services whose relative price has risen. At the same time, higher prices will discourage consumers from buying so much – price will continue rising until the shortage has been eliminated.

If consumers decide they want less of a good (or if producers decide to produce more), supply will exceed demand. The resulting surplus will cause the price of the good to fall. This will act as a disincentive to producers, who will shift resources out of the production of the good, since it will now be less profitable to make it. At the same time, lower prices will encourage consumers to buy more. Price will continue falling until the surplus has been eliminated. The same analysis can be applied to factor markets. If the demand for a particular type of labour exceeds its supply, the resulting shortage would drive up the wage rate (i.e. the price of labour), thus reducing the firm's demand for that type of labour and encouraging more workers to take up that type of job. Wages would continue rising until demand equalled supply, and the shortage was eliminated. Similarly, a surplus of a particular type of labour would lead to a fall in wages until demand equalled supply.

The effect of changes in demand and supply

The pattern of consumer demand changes in response to changes in taste – particularly changing fashions. Similarly, the pattern of supply changes, for example as a result of technological developments.

Changes in demand

A rise in demand is signalled by a rise in price, which in turn acts as an incentive for supply to rise. Firms looking to maximize their profits are diverting resources from goods with lower prices relative to costs of production (and hence lower profits) to those goods which are more profitable. A fall in demand is signalled by a fall in price, which in turn acts as an incentive for supply to fall as the goods are now less profitable to produce.

Changes in supply

A rise in supply is signalled by a fall in price, which represents an incentive for demand to rise. Conversely, a fall in supply will cause prices to rise and will be signalled as such, resulting in falling demand.

8.2.3   Elasticity

It is possible to measure the responsiveness of the demand and supply of a particular good in relation to changes in price. This concept is known as elasticity of demand and supply.

Elasticity of demand

We have already noted that the quantity of a good or service demanded depends on price; but, from a practical point of view, it is useful to know by exactly how much quantity demanded will fall if prices rise. A moment's thought will show that this is vital information for firms making marketing decisions, for example. The factors affecting the elasticity of demand are as follows:

- **The availability of substitutes.** If no substitute for a product is available, consumers will be obliged to keep buying it even after a price rise. In this case, demand is said to be inelastic. However, products for which there are plenty of substitutes available can be expected to have a high elasticity of demand, i.e. demand is relatively responsive to changes in price.
- **Price of a product relative to total expenditure.** A doubling of the price of, say, a box of matches is unlikely to affect the quantity demanded very much as this product represents too small a proportion of an individual's spending for households to react.
- **Income.** The demand for high quality or luxury goods tends to be responsive to changes in income.

A knowledge of the value of elasticity of demand is important to managers for a number of reasons:

- Businesses wish to know the effects that changes in price will have upon their sales. Raising price when demand is inelastic will increase the firm's revenues; but doing so when demand is price elastic may be disastrous.
- Governments wish to estimate the yield of indirect taxes, such as VAT and petrol tax.
- Elasticity of demand matters when assessing the effect of a fall in the international value of the pound sterling. Such a drop may be good for exporters as it reduces the price of UK exports; but will this fall in the price of exports persuade foreigners to buy enough British exports to pay for imports from abroad?

Elasticity of supply

It is useful to know how much supply will increase in response to higher prices, or by how much it will decline if prices fall. The supply of most goods and services tends to be more price elastic (responsive to changes in price) in the long run because the scale of production can be stepped up in response to what would be perceived by producers as a sustained increase in demand. (The long run here is defined as the time it takes to invest in new production capacity (plant, machinery and factories).) In the short term, however, supply is limited by the existing scale of production, i.e. once full capacity is reached, output cannot be increased.

8.2.4   The interdependence of goods and factor markets

A rise in the demand for a good will raise its price and therefore its profitability and firms will respond by supplying more. Consequently, there will be an increase in demand for the inputs required to produce that good, i.e. for the necessary factors of production. The demand for the inputs will rise, causing a rise in the price of those inputs. This will result in the owners of those inputs (resources) supplying more. **The market for goods and services therefore affects factor markets.** This process can be illustrated through a consideration of the labour market. The price of labour (wages) will rise in response to an increase in demand for particular occupational skills, which is in turn a result of higher demand for certain products. As wages rise, more workers will join the market, i.e. the supply of labour increases.

8.2.5   The advantages of a free-market economy

One of the major advantages of a free market economy is that it functions automatically without the government or any other body having to coordinate economic decisions. The market is able to respond quickly to changes in the conditions of supply and demand.

Highly competitive markets mean that no one producer or consumer has any great power. Competition between profit-maximizing firms keeps prices and costs of production down. Each firm has to use the most efficient combination of resources to stay in business, otherwise its costs would be above those of its competitors and wipe out any profits – and it would go out of business as a result. On the demand side, customers are looking to get the best value for money from products.

So the agents operating in a free market are pursuing their own self-interest but, paradoxically, in doing so, they are encouraging the efficient use of a nation's resources in line with consumer wishes, therefore addressing the economic problem of scarcity.

If this is true, then it is a very persuasive argument in favour of the free market. The problem is that markets do not, in reality, achieve the optimum allocation of scarce resources and governments to a greater or lesser extent intervene to solve the practical problems of the free market. These problems take the following forms:

- It is often the case that competition between firms is limited and that markets are dominated by a few large firms. These firms can charge high prices and therefore make large profits. Far from responding to consumer wishes, they may wish to try and create demand for a product through advertising.
- High profits and lack of competition may lead firms to become inefficient.
- Power and property may become unequally distributed.
- The practices of some firms may become socially undesirable (see our discussion in Chapter 14 on corporate social responsibility).
- Some socially desirable goods and services would not be produced by private enterprise.
- A free-market economy may lead to macroeconomic instability.
- The self-interest ethos associated with a market economy may encourage selfishness, greed and materialism.

8.2.6   Monopoly

A monopoly exists when there is only one firm in the industry. However, whether an industry can be classed as a monopoly is not always clear. For example, a pharmaceutical company may have a monopoly on a certain type of drug, but there are usually alternative drugs to treat a particular illness – see the example in Chapter 7.

The boundaries of an industry are often ill-defined. More important for a firm is the degree of its monopoly power, and that depends on the closeness of the substitutes produced by its competitors. For example, the Post Office has a monopoly over the delivery of letters, but it faces competition from faxes and e-mail.

Because there is only one firm in the industry, the monopolist can raise its price and consumers have no alternative but to pay the higher price or go without the product. The demand for the product will depend on whether there are any reasonably close substitutes available.

An effective monopoly must be able to exclude competitors from the market through barriers to entry. These barriers take various forms:

- **Economies of scale.** There are many industries where larger firms can operate at lower costs than smaller ones. The main categories of economies of scale are:
  - (i)   **Technical economies.** These occur when costs fall for technical and engineering reasons. Large firms can use large, efficient machines and utilize the division of labour (the specialization of workers in particular parts or operations of the production process) more fully.

(ii) **Managerial economies.** These result from the way in which large firms can deploy specialized managers.

(iii) **Financial economies.** Large enterprises find it easier to raise funds than do smaller ones.

(iv) **Marketing economies.** These arise from the lower costs of buying inputs (e.g. through bulk buying) and selling outputs.

(v) **Risk-spreading economies.** A larger firm can produce a broad spread of products and supply a wide range of markets, thereby avoiding the risk associated with having to rely on one or a few products.

Economies of scale form a barrier to the entry of new firms because companies wishing to enter the industry would be unable to start up on a very large scale. Thus it would be difficult for any firm to start up from scratch the production of cars for the mass vehicle market on account of the enormous investment costs of doing so.

- **Natural monopolies.** 'Utilities' such as the water, gas, electricity and telephone industries produce a service which is delivered through a distribution grid or network of pipes and cables into millions of separate homes and businesses. It is often argued that these businesses are natural monopolies; competition would be wasteful because it requires the duplication of these highly costly distribution grids. Given the likelihood of monopoly in these industries, a public policy choice exists between the option of private monopoly subject to public regulation and the public ownership of monopoly.

- **Product differentiation and brand loyalty.** If a firm produces a clearly differentiated product, where the consumer associates the product with the brand, firms will find it very difficult to break into that market. Note that Michael Porter[1] identifies product differentiation as one of the sources of competitive advantage, along with price competition (see Chapter 7).

- **Control of raw materials and market outlets.** Firms may try to establish exclusive control over the source of raw materials for their products in order to deny access to competitors (for example, the South African diamond company De Beers' ownership of the Kimberley diamond mine). In a similar way, British breweries have bought up public houses in order to establish exclusive market outlets for the beer they produce.

- **Legal protection.** One way to maintain a monopoly is to hold the patent or copyright to it, which prevents other people legally making the same product. Another is through tariffs (i.e. customs duties) and other trade restrictions to keep out foreign competitors.

- **Mergers and takeovers.** Where economies of scale exist, large firms can be more efficient than smaller ones. These efficient large units can emerge in two ways: through internal growth, as the firm expands its share of the market; or through takeover and merger, as the firm joins with rivals to form a single unit. The threat of takeovers may discourage new entrants.

- **Aggressive tactics.** An established monopolist is able to bear losses for longer than a new entrant. Thus it can undercut its competitors (start a 'price war'), mount large-scale advertising campaigns, introduce new brands to compete with new entrants, and so on. The monopolist may also resort to illegal means to force a new entrant out of business.

The disadvantages of monopoly

Monopolies may be against the public interest for a number of reasons:

- **Higher prices and costs than under perfect competition.** Under perfect competition, firms are forced to produce at the lowest cost possible, taking into account the current state of technology and available resources, which keeps prices down while allowing them to make a reasonable profit. However, barriers to entry allow the monopolists to charge higher prices and make large profits, even if it is not producing in the most efficient way. While there is less incentive to be efficient, if it can lower its costs by developing more efficient methods, it can gain large profits which will not be competed away.

● **Power and wealth.** The high profits, wealth and power of monopolists may seem unfair and socially undesirable. Large monopolies (often multinational corporations – see Section 8.2.6) are often able to exert pressure on national governments.

The advantages of monopoly

Despite these drawbacks, monopolies have some distinct advantages:

● **Economies of scale.** Monopolies can produce at lower costs, for the reasons discussed above. Thus in producing some products, they are more efficient than smaller firms could ever be. For example, it is argued that there are, potentially, almost unlimited economies of scale available in the production of aircraft; no small company could hope to produce such a product efficiently, bearing in mind the vast research and development and other investment costs.
● **Competition for corporate control.** Monopolists are subject to the discipline of the financial markets. If a monopoly, with potentially low costs, fails to perform, then it may be subject to a takeover bid.

8.2.7   Imperfect competition

Very few markets are either perfectly competitive or a pure monopoly; nearly all firms compete with other firms, but have a degree of market power. Therefore most markets lie between the two extremes of monopoly and perfect competition, in the sphere of *imperfect competition*.

There are two types of imperfect competition: monopolistic and oligopoly.

Monopolistic competition

This is a situation in which there are many firms competing, but each firm has a degree of market power in that it has some discretion over what price to charge for its product. The assumptions of monopolistic competition are as follows:

● There is a large number of firms in the market. No firm has a big enough share of the market to influence the behaviour of its rivals.
● There is freedom of entry into the industry, where any new firm is able to set up business.
● Each firm produces a product which is in some way different from those of its rivals. Consequently, it can raise prices without losing its customers. This assumption of **product differentiation** distinguishes imperfect from perfect competition.

Some examples of imperfect competition are restaurants and petrol stations. Retailers are typical examples of firms operating under conditions of monopolistic competition in that although there are many firms in the industry, there is only one in a particular location. In this sense, they are local monopolies. A firm facing little competition whose product is sufficiently differentiated from its rivals may be able to earn relatively high profits. An example might be an Indian restaurant which sets up in an area where there is only a fish and chip shop. In the longer term, however, new firms will enter the industry, attracted by the potential profits. Thus the following year may see the establishment of a Thai restaurant, followed by a kebab shop. The relatively high profits of the Indian restaurant will fall as some of their customers take advantage of the choices of cuisine now available.

Monopolistic competition also involves **non-price competition**. Non-price competition has two major elements: product development and advertising. Product development involves providing a product or service which is better than, or different from, its rivals. Thus in the case of the Indian restaurant, this may involve a free home-delivery service. The aim of advertising is to sell the product by informing the consumer of the product's existence and persuading them to buy the good. Thus the restaurant may deliver 'flyers' around the locality to advertise its products. The effects of product development and advertising are to increase the demand for the product, at the same time raising its cost.

Oligopoly

Oligopoly occurs when just a few firms share a large part of the industry. Oligopolies have two key features: barriers to entry, similar to those under monopoly but which vary in size from industry to industry; and interdependence, in the sense that, because there are only a few firms in the industry, each will be affected by the other's actions. Rivals are likely to respond to actions such as increases in advertising or price changes. Therefore no firm can ignore the actions of other firms in the industry. Oligopolists have therefore to predict the actions and reactions of their rivals.

Oligopolists are subject to two opposing forces: on the one hand, they are drawn to collude with each other to act collectively as a monopoly and maximize industry profits; but on the other, they are tempted to compete to gain for themselves a bigger share of the available profits. The problem for oligopolists if they compete on the basis of price or advertising, their profits are bound to fall as industry prices drop and costs rise.

Sometimes firms will *collude* by agreeing on prices, market share or advertising expenditure. This collusion reduces the uncertainty faced by these firms. Formal collusive agreements are known as **cartels**, which are prohibited in Britain under restrictive trade practices legislation, unless the firms involved can prove to the Restrictive Practices Court that their agreement is in the public interest.

8.2.8 The 'public interest' and competition policies

The real world is characterized by imperfect markets, with firms having different degrees of *market power*. Governments consider the extent to which this market power will be in the public interest when they develop legislation to deal with monopolies and oligopolies. Market power, from the consumer's point of view, seems inevitably to be undesirable because firms are able to exploit the powerless consumer. The greater the firm's power, the higher will be its prices relative to its costs of production. However, this is not necessarily the case as firms may still charge a relatively low price because of their economies of scale; furthermore, they may use their profits for investment and research and development, with the consumer benefiting from better products at lower prices.

Consequently, competition policy does not ban potentially anti-competitive behaviour such as mergers or price fixing arrangements between oligopolists. Rather, governments tend to adopt an approach whereby each case is examined on its merits.

There are three categories of competition policy:

● **Monopoly policy** targets the existing power of monopolies and oligopolies and aims to prevent firms from abusing their monopoly power. The problem for the government is to calculate whether, if it insisted on the firm reducing its price, it would cut investment and research and development, with the consumer losing out in the long run.

- **Merger policy** aims to monitor mergers and prevent those considered to be against the public interest (see Chapter 7 for an explanation of different types of merger). The costs and benefits of the merger for the public must be evaluated before the government can make a decision on whether the merger can proceed. One of the main advantages of mergers is that the merged firms may be able to rationalize. With any merger, savings can be made as head offices are closed down and combined profits allow for greater investment in research and development. Horizontal mergers may result in economies of scale as production is concentrated on fewer sites and labour and capital used more intensively. Other savings may arise from more efficient distribution and warehousing. Vertical mergers may result in the stages of the production process being concentrated on one site.

The disadvantages of mergers are that they result in a greater concentration of economic power, which can be used against the interests of consumers. Horizontal mergers, in particular, lead to fewer firms for the consumer to choose from. Even in conglomerate mergers, profits gained in one market where the company has market power can be used to cross-subsidize prices in competitive markets, to the detriment of competitors. Furthermore, rationalization is likely to lead to redundancies.

In framing its policies on mergers, governments must consider the effects that a threat of a merger will have on firms' behaviour. Competition for corporate control may lead to the consumer benefiting through lower costs. Thus managers can prevent the threat of a takeover if they secure the economic strength of the business and ensure that shareholders see them as better able to make profits than alternative ownership or control. However, competition for corporate control could result in the firm exploiting its monopoly power in takeover battles against the interests of the consumer. Government policy towards mergers and the threat of mergers will need to ensure that they encourage, rather than reduce competition.

- **Restrictive practice policy.** Normally governments legislate to restrict oligopolistic collusion because it involves using their combined power to make bigger profits and exploit the consumer. However, it is very difficult to prevent tacit collusion, or informal agreements made in secret.

The legislation relating to competition policy is discussed in detail in Chapter 12.

The Department of Trade and Industry is responsible for monopoly and mergers policy. The two main bodies involved with operating the policy are:

- **The Office of Fair Trading** (OFT) which, under its Director General (DGFT), is responsible for monitoring firms which appear to be behaving uncompetitively or against consumers' interests. The DGFT is also responsible for advising the government on the operation of monopolies and mergers policy and for recommending cases to be referred to the Competition Commission.
- **The Competition Commission** (CC – formerly the Monopolies and Mergers Commission). The CC is an advisory body whose role is to investigate possible abuses of monopoly power and proposed mergers. The CC makes recommendations to the minister, who then decides what action should be taken. The following cases could be referred to the CC:
  (i) Any firm whose market share is 25 per cent or more of the national or local market, or any two or more firms whose joint share is 25 per cent or more, if it is suspected that they are informally colluding to restrict competition.
  (ii) Any proposed merger that would result in a firm with assets of over £30 million or in a firm with a market share of 25 per cent or more.

The CC and the OFT are concerned with how market power is used by firms rather than with the fact of its possession. Some commentators argue that because each case is judged on its own merits, this can make decisions seem arbitrary.[1] Furthermore, the government can reject the CC's recommendations, and has done so on numerous occasions. Others, particularly those on the right of politics, argue that there is little need for any intervention as even the largest and most powerful firms face competition, particularly in a global market. Regarding mergers, the great majority – 97 per cent – have not been referred to the CC, and most cases that have been referred have been abandoned or ruled against by the CC.[2] This suggests that policy is too weak; studies have shown that mergers have resulted in a greater degree of market concentration in the UK, yet the benefits to the consumer have been few.

Policy towards restrictive practices

A restrictive practice is 'where two or more firms agree to adopt common practices to restrict competition'.[2] The UK government bans all open collusion unless it can be proved to be in the public interest. All agreements between firm over prices, quantity and other aspects that limit competition must be registered with the OFT. If the OFT considers that there has been collusion, the firms will be required to appear before the **Restrictive Practices Court** to justify the agreement. This agreement will automatically be terminated if the firms cannot prove that they are serving the public interest.

European Union competition policy

Article 85 of the Treaty of Rome covers restrictive practices and Article 86 is concerned with monopolies and mergers. These articles focus on the specific practices that are against the public interest, and firms can be banned form committing such anti-competitive practices. In effect, the European Union has much greater powers to ban collusive behaviour.

8.2.9   Alternative theories of the firm

One of the basic tenets of the economic theory of the firm is the assumption that businesses will always try to maximize profits. This assumption has been called into question by those who argue that firms have aims other than profit maximization. The issue here is the motives of those who *control* the enterprise. The traditional theory of the firm assumes that it is the owners of the firm who will make the pricing and output decisions that determine profit levels. It is reasonable to assume that *owners* will wish to maximize profits; however, what is open to question is whether in reality, the owners make such decisions.

In public limited companies, the shareholders are the owners and it is reasonable to assume that they will want the firm to maximize its profits. However, shareholders elect directors, who in turn employ professional managers who are given a good deal of latitude in making decisions. There is therefore a separation of ownership from control of the firm as discussed in Chapter 14. This begs the question: what are the objectives of managers? Do they have other aims than to maximize profits?

Managers are assumed to maximize their own interests, which in essence entails pursuing a range of discretionary policies that would bolster their salary, job security, status and power. This behaviour may well involve pursuing goals which do not necessarily result in profit maximization. Once sufficient profits have been made to keep shareholders happy, managers may seek higher salaries, greater power or better working conditions. Thus alternative theories of the firm tend to assume that large companies are **profit satisficers**, with managers aiming for a minimum level of profits but not attempting to maximize profits.

See the web site for a more detailed discussion of alternative theories of the firm.

8.2.10   Reasons for government intervention

Markets in the real world fail to achieve an efficient allocation of resources. This is because very few markets are perfectly competitive; and the existence of **externalities**, which are the side-effects of economic activity. Whenever the actions of producers or consumers affect people other than themselves in a beneficial way, we speak of **external benefits**. When people are affected adversely, there are said to be **external costs**.

Externalities

- **External costs of production.** Whenever there are external costs, the market will lead to a level of production and consumption above the socially desirable level. When a company pollutes the environment, the community bears the cost – they are forced to 'consume' the side-effects of production. This is because no one has legal ownership of the environment (the air, rivers, etc.) and can prevent or charge for their use as a waste dump. The control of pollution therefore falls to the government.
- **External benefits of production.** Company A may spend money training its employees, a number of whom are subsequently 'poached' by company B, a competitor who does not train (see Chapter 11, Section 11.5). The result is that company B's costs are reduced. Company A has no incentive to train because it is not able to internalize all the benefits of its investment. However, society loses out because the result is a lower level of training than is socially desirable. This is an argument for government intervention in the labour market to ensure that companies undertake the training required by the economy.
- **External costs of consumption.** When people consume goods and services, others suffer from the side-effects of that consumption. Examples are driving (the side-effects of which are fumes and congestion), noise from hi-fis and radios, cigarette smoke and litter. In many cases the government will intervene to limit external costs of consumption.
- **External benefits of consumption.** When people are vaccinated, it is society as well as the individual who benefits. In such cases, there is a strong argument for the government to intervene to maximize the external benefits.

Public goods

The free market will not produce some socially desirable goods. These are known as 'public goods' and represent another argument for government intervention. Public goods have two key characteristics: non-rivalry and non-excludability:

- **Non-rivalry.** This is where the consumption of a good by one person will not affect another's enjoyment of it. If an individual eats a sandwich, it cannot be consumed by someone else. However, if that same individual drives safely along the street at night with the benefit of street lighting, it does not prevent anyone else doing the same. However, there is no incentive for private individuals to provide street lighting because it would be difficult to charge consumers for its use. Such a good is therefore socially desirable, but privately unprofitable – an argument for government provision of goods such as lighthouses, pavements and public services such as law and order and even national defence.

- **Non-excludability.** This is where it is not possible to provide a good or service to one person without it being available for others to enjoy. Imagine a situation where people living in a private road jointly decide to have it resurfaced and divide up the cost equally between them. However, one household refuses to pay its share. What would the other residents do? They would probably be reluctant to go ahead with the project because one of their number would be enjoying the benefits of the newly surfaced road without having to bear the cost. This is known as the *free-rider problem*.

When goods have both these features, i.e. non-rivalry and non-excludability, the market will not provide them. Thus these public goods can either be provided by the government, or by private firms subsidized by the government. Examples of the former are law and order (the police, courts, etc.); examples of the latter are private prisons.

Merit goods

Sometimes people make poor economic decisions in a free market and the government may feel that they need to be 'protected from themselves'. This is the justification for outlawing certain goods and services, such as prostitution and recreational drugs, but also for discouraging the consumption of other goods (such as alcohol and tobacco) by imposing taxes on them. These products are known as 'demerit goods'.

By the same token, the government may feel that people consume too little of products that are good for them, such as education and health care. These products could be provided by the market, and indeed are. However, the government takes a paternalistic view and provides them free or subsidizes their production to avoid their underconsumption. This category of good is known as a 'merit good'.

Other reasons for government intervention

As discussed above, monopolies and forms of imperfect competition can result in firms abusing their market power and exploiting the consumer. This is seen to be socially undesirable and governments intervene to regulate the activities of such firms.

Another criticism of the free market is that it is not able to achieve certain social goals which society sets itself. Take the problem of **inequality**: those on the political right see inequality as the inevitable price to be paid for an efficient, growing economy. High incomes act as an incentive for people to work, invest (including investing in themselves through education and training) and take risks. While many in favour of the free market would wish to see some action to alleviate poverty, they would object to the large-scale redistribution on the grounds that it is likely to remove incentives and thereby reduce growth.

Those on the left would argue that the distribution of income should be based on need rather than on the workings of the market. A truly socialist society would be a much more equal society, although many socialists accept that a minimum level of inequality has to be tolerated to provide the incentives for the functioning of the economy. Thus if one of the goals of society is greater equality, this will not be achieved by the free market.

The free market is unlikely to achieve simultaneously the macroeconomic objectives society sets for itself, namely sustainable economic growth, full employment, stable prices and a balance of international payments.

Exercise

Compare and contrast the following quotations. What do they tell us about the ability of the free market to solve society's problems?

Every individual endeavours to employ his capital so that its produce may be of the greatest value. He generally neither intends to promote the public interest, nor knows how much he is promoting it. He intends only his own gain. And he is in this led by an invisible hand to promote an end which was no part of his intention. By pursuing his own interest he frequently promotes the interests of society more effectually than when he really intends to promote it.[3]

I know of no example in time or place of a society that has been marked by a large measure of political freedom, and that has not used something comparable to a free market to organise the bulk of economic activity.[4]

(Advocates of the free market) never faced up to the fact that, whereas their idea of political democracy rested on the principle of 'one man, one vote' and was thus very equalitarian in its foundations, their so-called economic liberalism rested on a very different and most unequal weighting of men according to their business drive, their efficiency as producers, their possession of property as a starting advantage, their unscrupulousness, or ruthlessness, or sheer luck.[5]

Feedback

The famous 'invisible hand' quote from Adam Smith's *Wealth of Nations* suggests that the free market is the most effective way of organizing economic activity: the economic agents (producers, consumers, investors, workers) try to maximize their returns (profit, interest and wages) with the result that consumer needs and wants are met at the lowest cost (in terms of resources used for production). The suggestion is that when the government intervenes in the economy, the efficiency of the market is undermined.

In the second quote, Milton Friedman argues that alternatives to a market economy, such as command economies, militate against political and personal freedom because they entail a high degree of control over people's lives.

Lastly, Cole[6] argues that the market system is fundamentally unfair because the economic actors all start from different points in terms of skills, intelligence, wealth, etc.

8.2.11   Forms of government intervention

The government has a number of policy instruments available to correct the failings of the free market.

Taxes and subsidies

These can be used for two purposes: to alter the composition of consumption and production; and to redistribute incomes. If taxes are to be used as a means of achieving greater equality, the rich must be taxed proportionately more than the poor. The extent of distribution will depend on the degree of 'progressiveness' of the tax. With **progressive** taxes, as people's incomes rise, the percentage of their income paid in tax also rises. The more progressive the tax, the more equal will be the population's post-tax income.

Taxes and subsidies can also be used to correct market imperfections where these occur:

- **Taxes to correct externalities.** If a factory emits smoke and pollutes the atmosphere, thus imposing costs on society, then the government could impose a tax on that company equal to the cost imposed on society as a result of the pollution for which it is responsible. Similarly, if a firm produced an external benefit, then it should receive a subsidy equal to the value of that benefit to society. For example, if a firm trains labour and that represents a benefit to society, the firm should receive a subsidy for each person trained.
- **Taxes to correct monopoly.** The government can impose a tax on monopolies and oligopolies to tackle excessive monopoly profits.

The **advantages** of taxes and subsidies are that they force firms to internalize the full costs and benefits of their actions while allowing the market to operate. Furthermore, if firms are taxed for polluting, they are encouraged to find cleaner ways of producing; and if firms are subsidized for following good practices, then they will be likely to adopt more good practices. The main **disadvantages** are that they would be very difficult to administer, given that each firm produces a different type of pollution at different levels.

Laws regulating undesirable structures or behaviour

Market imperfections are frequently corrected by laws, such as the following:

- **Laws to prevent or regulate monopolies or oligopolies.** These were examined in Section 8.2.8.
- **Laws to prevent firms from making false or misleading claims.** Firms could sometimes take advantage of the fact that consumers have imperfect information by making false claims for their products or by producing poor-quality goods. Consumer protection laws (discussed in detail in Chapter 12) make it illegal for firms to do this. However, it is difficult to make legislation watertight and firms can often get around it.

Regulatory bodies

These have the following functions:

- To identify potential cases for investigation (e.g. potential cases of pollution or abuse of monopoly power)
- To conduct investigations and make decisions, against predetermined criteria, about whether certain activities should be permitted or modified
- To take action to enforce decisions, or report to another body that will do so.

Examples of such bodies are the Competition Commission (see Section 8.2.8) and the various bodies set up to regulate the privatized utilities, e.g. OFWAT, the Office of Water Supply.

The advantage of this approach is that the bodies use a case-by-case approach, resulting in the most appropriate solution being adopted. However, investigations tend to be costly and time-consuming, with only a few cases being examined. Also, the bodies sometimes neglect to follow up cases, allowing firms to continue with the offending behaviour.

Price controls

Price controls can be used to prevent abuses of market power by oligopolies and monopolies. Thus the privatized utilities are not allowed to raise their prices by more than a certain percentage below the rate of inflation.

Price controls can also be used as a vehicle for redistributing income. In the case of production, minimum farm prices can be used to protect the income of farmers (see Chapter 10) and minimum wage legislation can help people on low incomes. In the case of consumption, low rents can help those on low incomes afford housing, and price ceilings on food and other items during a national emergency can allow poor people to afford the basic essentials. The problem with price controls is that they cause surpluses in the case of high prices (e.g. the CAP) and shortages in the case of low prices.

The direct provision of goods and services

In the case of pure public goods (e.g. defence, street lighting, law and order) the market fails to provide and the government must therefore take over this role. However, this does not necessarily entail direct government provision – they could pay private firms to do so.

The government could also provide goods which are not public goods directly, for the following reasons:

- **Merit goods** – services such as health and education should be provided free of charge, as a matter of social justice.
- **External benefits** – people other than the consumer may benefit substantially from provision as in the case of health care (everyone benefits from measures to halt the spread of disease).
- **Dependants** – the government may choose to provide education and health care free to protect children from 'uncaring' parents. If parents had to buy their children's education through the market, they may choose not to do so.
- **Ignorance** – consumers may not know how much they benefit from services such as health care; if they had to pay, they may choose to go without, against their own best interests.

Public ownership

Goods and services can be produced by publicly owned (nationalized) industries and sold in the market.

8.3   The macroeconomy

As we saw earlier, *microeconomics* focuses on the interaction of the forces of demand and supply in individual markets; whereas macroeconomics is concerned with the total level of spending in the economy, and the total level of production. Thus macroeconomics involves the examination of *aggregate* demand and *aggregate* supply.

8.3.1   The major macroeconomic issues

Economic growth

If the economy is growing, this means that there are more goods and services to consume. The UK economy has for many years experienced relatively poor rates of economic growth, compared to other competitor nations. This raises the question of why countries grow at different rates. There is also a problem with short-term growth rates, which fluctuate considerably. Output may grow by as much as 3 per cent in some years, whereas in other years the economy may slide into recession with negative economic growth. ('Negative economic growth' refers to a fall in output. In the UK the official definition of a recession is where output falls for more than two quarters.) Governments would ideally like to achieve both high long-run rates of growth and stable growth to avoid recessions.

In practice, growth tends to fluctuate: in some years, economies experience high rates of growth and the country experiences a boom; in other years, economic growth will be low, or possibly negative, and the country experiences a recession. This cycle of changes in the

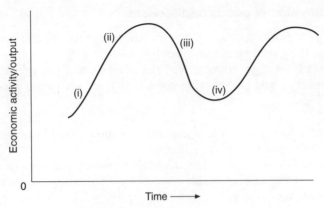

Figure 8.4. The economic cycle.

level of economic activity over time is known as the *economic cycle, trade cycle or business cycle*. There are four phases in the economic cycle, as illustrated in Figure 8.4:

(i) **The recovery phase.** During this phase there is rapid economic growth and fuller use is made of resources (raw materials, labour and capital).

(ii) **The boom phase.** During this phase, growth slows down as output peaks.

(iii) **The recession phase.** During this phase there is little or no growth, or even a decline in output.

(iv) **The upturn phase.** During this phase, growth rates begin to rise after output reaches a low point.

The economic cycle illustrated in Figure 8.4 is a stylized version that allows us to distinguish between the various phases. In reality, however, the cycle is very irregular as the length of the phases vary (sometimes recessions and booms are short, and sometimes they are long), as do rates of economic growth. This irregularity can be seen in Figure 8.5,

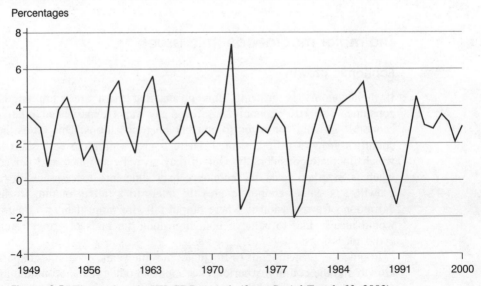

Figure 8.5. Fluctuations in UK GDP growth (from *Social Trends 32*, 2002).

although note that cycles are still clearly discernible (especially if growth rates, rather than the level of output, are plotted on the vertical axis).

The causes of growth

In the short run, growth rates are determined by variations in aggregate demand. **Aggregate demand**, or total spending, comprises four elements:

- **Consumer spending**
- **Investment spending** (by firms)
- **Government spending**
- **Spending by foreign nationals on UK exports** (the spending of UK citizens on imports from abroad must be subtracted from this figure, as this expenditure 'leaks' out of the UK economy).

A sharp rise in aggregate demand will create shortages, stimulating firms to increase output. A fall in aggregate demand will result in stocks building up and remaining unsold; producers will therefore cut output. A boom is associated with a sharp rise in aggregate demand, while a recession is associated with a fall in aggregate demand.

A rapid rise in aggregate demand is not enough to ensure high growth rates over a number of years. There must be an expansion in *potential* output or actual rises in output will cease. Once there is full employment of labour and capital and the economy reaches capacity, the rate of growth will be restricted.

Causes of potential growth

This involves an examination of the *supply* side of the equation and what determines the productive capacity of the economy. The two determinants of potential capacity are the amount of resources available, and their productivity.

Increases in the quantity of resources

- **Capital.** The output of the nation depends on its stock of capital. Therefore, investment will increase output. It is therefore important to consider what determines investment: factors such as business confidence about the future demand for their products, the profitability of businesses, the tax regime and the rate of interest. In the long term, investment is dependent on savings – people must be willing to forgo some of their consumption to provide the resources to invest in productive capacity.
- **Labour.** An increase in the working population will result in a potential increase in output. If this results in a higher participation rate, the productive capacity of the economy will increase. However, an increase in the working population can be offset by a proportionately greater increase in the number of dependants (as in the case of economies with an ageing population). In this situation, potential output per head will fall (see Chapter 11, Section 11.1).
- **Land and raw materials.** Essentially, land is fixed in quantity. Occasionally, nations discover new sources of raw materials, as was the case with North Sea oil for the UK. However, these windfalls are usually one-off benefits, providing short-term growth until the source is exhausted.

Increases in the productivity of resources

One of the prime concerns of classical economists, exemplified by Thomas Malthus (1766–1834), was that an increase in one factor of production while others remain fixed would represent a serious limitation on growth. Malthus famously postulated that economic growth would have positively harmful effects on society as the resulting population growth would be unsustainable: land is fixed in supply and the rate of growth of the population would outstrip the supply of food. The population would be brought back into line with the available food supply through famine and disease. This pessimistic scenario for the human race led to economics being dubbed 'the dismal science'.

However, it is clear today that the productivity of factors can be increased in various ways, for example by technological improvements making capital more productive. Modern computer-numerically controlled machines can do the work of many people and have replaced their less efficient forerunners. Before that, more productive electronic equipment had replaced steam-powered machines. Improved methods of transportation and communications have had similar effects on the productivity of capital. Similarly, the productivity of labour has increased over time with new skills and improved education and training.

Policies to achieve growth

Governments are naturally keen to implement policies which will bring about growth. These may focus on managing the level of aggregate demand to ensure that firms wish to invest for production; or they may give priority to increasing aggregate supply through encouraging research and development and education and training.

Alternatively, policies may focus on encouraging enterprise by allowing free markets to flourish, or concentrate on active intervention, possibly advocating a degree of state planning to ensure that the levels of investment necessary for high growth are achieved and maintained.

8.3.2   Unemployment

What is 'unemployment'?

Unemployment can be expressed as a number (e.g. 1.9 million) or as a percentage (e.g. 2 per cent). The economist's definition of the number unemployed is: those of working age who are without work, but who are available for work at current wage rates. The figure is often expressed as a percentage of the total labour force. The labour force is defined as: those in employment plus those unemployed. If 23 million people were employed and 2 million were unemployed, the unemployment rate would be:

$$\frac{2}{23 + 2} \times 100 = 8\%$$

However, official measures of unemployment are more problematic because politicians disagree as to who should be classified as unemployed. The two most common official measures of unemployment are claimant unemployment, which is a measure of all those in receipt of unemployment benefit, and standardized unemployment rates, which are measures used by the International Labour Organization and the Organization for Economic Cooperation and Development. These bodies define the unemployed as persons of working age who are without work, available for work and actively seeking employment. Using a 'standardized' definition for all countries makes international comparisons possible. The figures are compiled from surveys of the labour force.

The standardized rate tends to be higher than the claimant rate as it includes people seeking work yet not entitled to claim benefits (e.g. those seeking part-time work). However, there will also be those who are claiming benefits but not seeking work; economists would not regard these people as being genuinely unemployed, but they will have the effect of lowering the standardized rate in comparison to the claimant rate. The tougher the eligibility conditions for benefits, the lower will be the rate of claimant unemployment compared to the standardized rate.

The most obvious **costs of unemployment** are borne by the unemployed themselves. These consist of financial costs in terms of loss of earnings, and personal costs, consisting of low self-esteem, stress and the consequent strain on personal relationships. There are also costs to the economy and to society:

- Loss of output
- Loss of tax revenues (the unemployed pay no income tax and spend less, thereby paying less VAT and excise duties)
- Firms lose the profit they could have made if there had been full employment
- The long-term unemployed become deskilled
- Higher levels of crime.

The causes of unemployment

- **Excessive wages.** The 'classical' economists of the 1920s and 1930s blamed the mass unemployment of the age on wages being too high. Excessive wages were also blamed for unemployment by the Conservative governments of 1979–97. According to this theory, the solution to unemployment is, of course, lower average wages. However, what the economists of the 1920s and 1930s did not recognize was that even if the government does succeed in cutting average wages, the result will be a fall in consumer spending and a consequent drop in aggregate demand.
- **Cyclical unemployment.** This type of unemployment is associated with economic recessions. Demand falls as the economy moves into recession. Finding that they are unable to sell their output as stocks build up, firms cut back on production. This involves cutting the amount of labour they employ. This results in further falls in demand as people who lose their jobs also lose their spending power. Consequently, the recession deepens.

  As the economy begins to recover, unemployment will start to fall again and it is these fluctuations in unemployment in line with the business cycle which account for the label 'cyclical unemployment'. Cyclical unemployment is also referred to as 'Keynesian unemployment' after John Maynard Keynes, who saw a deficiency in aggregate demand as being responsible for the high unemployment of the interwar years. Many economists are known as 'Keynesian' because they see aggregate demand as the key determinant of a nation's output and employment.[7]

  The low level of aggregate demand causes the goods market to settle at a point where output is too low to generate full employment. Firms' output (supply) is low because aggregate demand is low. There is no incentive for firms to produce more and take on more workers because business confidence is low and they believe the recession will continue. The difference between aggregate demand and aggregate supply is known as a **deflationary gap** (see Figure 8.6). In this situation, a fall in average wages would exacerbate rather than cure unemployment. This is because the incomes of those in work would fall, leading to a further drop in output and a consequent increase in unemployment. In an attempt to reduce cyclical unemployment, governments have tried to manage the level of aggregate demand to ensure that it is high enough to ensure full employment.

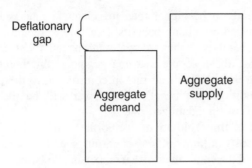

Figure 8.6. A deflationary gap.

- **Natural unemployment.** Even when there are as many job vacancies as there are people unemployed, there will still be some unemployment. The problem is one of mismatching and is due to problems such as skills shortages in certain occupations. There are various categories of 'natural' unemployment:

  (i)   **Frictional unemployment.** This occurs when people leave their jobs, either compulsorily or voluntarily, and are unemployed for a time while they are looking for a job. The problem arising here is one of imperfect information. Workers do not know what work is available, and employers are not fully informed about what labour is available. Therefore, both employers and employees have to **search** for workers and jobs respectively. There are two ways of alleviating frictional unemployment: by improving job market information (e.g. through job centres and newspapers); and, more controversially, by reducing unemployment benefit to make the unemployed more desperate to get a job.

  (ii) **Structural unemployment.** This is where there is a change in the structure of the economy as some industries contract and others expand. This may be a result of the **pattern of demand**: for example, a shift of consumer demand away from coal to other fuels will lead to structural unemployment in mining areas. Another type of structural unemployment is **technological unemployment**, where technological advances allow the same amount of production with fewer workers. Structural unemployment also occurs in particular regions of a country. This is known as **regional unemployment** and is a result of certain industries being concentrated in particular areas. One of the main factors affecting the level of structural unemployment is the **mobility of labour**. A distinction can be made between geographical and occupational mobility: geographical mobility is the ability or willingness of people to move to jobs in other parts of the country; whereas occupational mobility is the ability or willingness of people to move to other jobs, regardless of location. Thus unemployment occurs when labour is unable or unwilling to move to new jobs, i.e. it is immobile. It is possible to tackle structural unemployment by encouraging people to search more actively for work, if necessary in other parts of the country. (Norman Tebbit, employment minister under Margaret Thatcher in the early 1980s, famously exhorted the unemployed to 'get on their bikes' and look for work.) Another possible solution is government-funded training schemes to help workers acquire new skills.

  (iii) **Seasonal unemployment.** This occurs where the demand for particular types of labour fluctuates according to the seasons of the year. In some parts of the West Country, for example, unemployment can reach high levels in the winter (i.e. out of the holiday season).

8.3.3   Inflation

The rate of inflation is measured by the annual percentage increase in prices. It is usually measured by reference to retail prices and the government publishes an index of these each month (the Retail Price Index (RPI)).

Although it is possible to see why both a lack of economic growth and unemployment are undesirable, it is less clear why inflation is a problem; provided wages keep pace with inflation, there will be no fall in living standards. The problem with inflation arises from the difficulties that both individuals and firms have in predicting its rate and adjusting to its effects. Specifically, the costs of inflation are as follows:

- **Redistribution.** Inflation redistributes income away from those on fixed incomes (such as pensioners and the unemployed) to those with assets (e.g. property) which rise in value over time, but particularly during periods of inflation.
- **Uncertainty.** Inflation tends to cause uncertainty among the business community because it makes it difficult for them to predict their costs and revenues; consequently, they may be reluctant to invest.
- **Danger of 'hyperinflation'.** Relatively low (single-figure) levels of inflation are relatively harmless to the economy. However, if this develops into 'hyperinflation', with prices rising by hundreds or perhaps thousands of percentage points per year, it can destabilize the economy and, in the worst cases, lead to economic collapse. Here firms constantly raise prices in order to cover their rapidly rising costs, and workers respond by demanding massive pay increases to maintain their standards of living. The wage increases feed into firms' costs, resulting in firms' raising prices again. Thus prices spiral out of control. There have been a number of cases of hyperinflation this century, the most notable being Germany between 1921 and 1923.

There are two categories of inflation: demand-pull and cost-push.

Demand-pull inflation

Also known as 'demand-side' inflation, this is caused by rises in aggregate demand. These rises in total spending may be a result of an increase in any one, or a combination of all, the components of aggregate demand (consumer demand, investment, government spending or foreign demand for UK exports).

What causes aggregate demand to rise? This is a highly controversial question in economics: some commentators, known as **monetarists**, argue that an increase in aggregate demand is entirely due to increases in the money supply; whereas others argue that total spending can rise with no increase in the money supply.

Whatever the cause of rising aggregate demand, where it exceeds the value of aggregate supply (i.e. the total output of the economy), inflation will occur. This is because the excess

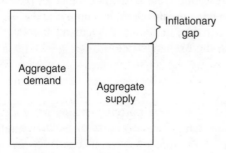

Figure 8.7. An inflationary gap.

demand for goods and services cannot be met by the economy (which is operating at full production capacity) and is therefore met by rises in the price of goods. This is illustrated in Figure 8.7. This figure depicts total spending in the economy exceeding total output. 'UK plc', working at full capacity, is unable to meet the extra demand; there is an **inflationary gap**. As with markets for goods and services, if supply is fixed, an increase in demand will be translated into price increases as excess demand 'pulls' up price levels.

Demand-pull inflation is associated with a booming economy. During a recession, demand-pull inflation will be low; in fact, there will be a *deficiency* of demand, resulting in unemployment.

Cost-push inflation

Also known as 'supply-side inflation', this arises when costs of production rise independently of aggregate demand. The response of firms to rising costs will be a desire to pass them on to the consumer in the form of higher prices. Just how much prices can be passed on to the consumer will depend on the *elasticity of demand* for products: the less elastic this demand is, the less sales will fall. If demand is relatively elastic, then output will be cut.

The rise in costs may have a number of different origins:

- **Wage increases.** Under some circumstances, depending on their industrial power, trade unions are able to push up wages independently of the demand for labour.
- **Import prices.** This is where rises in the prices of imports add to firms' costs, e.g. the oil price increases of 1973–4.
- **Profits.** Firms can use their monopoly power to make bigger profits by pushing up prices independently of consumer demand.

Demand-pull and cost-push inflation can interact, since wage and price rises can be caused by increases in aggregate demand and by these other causes independently pushing up costs. This is illustrated by the **wage–price spiral**: unions demand increasing wages to cover higher costs of living; firms raise their prices to cover higher and higher costs of production; the government prints more and more money; and wages and prices accelerate in a vicious circle.

8.3.4   The balance of payments

A country's balance of payments account records the flows of money between residents of that country and the rest of the world. The **balance of payments accounts** are divided into two parts: the **current account**, which records transactions arising from trade in goods and services; and the **capital account**, which records international transactions in company shares, government securities or bank loans. The accounts show the total receipts and payments of foreign exchange resulting from trade. A balance of payments surplus means that the demand for sterling has been greater than the supply; and a deficit means that the supply of sterling has been greater than the demand. Demand and supply are brought into balance by means of changes in the exchange rate.

Exchange rates

An exchange rate is the rate at which one currency trades for another on the foreign exchange market. People are familiar with the notion of exchange rates from travelling abroad: if we wish to holiday in France, we have to exchange our pounds for euros. Similarly, if a UK firm wants to import goods from France, it will need to purchase euros to pay the French supplier. Likewise, if Americans wish to come on holiday to the UK, they will need to buy pounds for dollars at a particular *rate of exchange*, say £1 = $1.60. By the same token, if US nationals want to import products from the UK, they will need to exchange their dollars for pounds to pay UK suppliers.

Exchange rates are quoted between each of the major currencies of the world, and they are constantly changing as a result of supply and demand. When UK importers wish to buy goods from abroad, they will use pounds to buy foreign currency on the exchange markets, thus *supplying* pounds. The higher the exchange rate for the pound, the more foreign currency they will be able to buy. If foreign nationals wish to buy goods from the UK, they must buy pounds to do so; the lower the price of the pound, the more sterling will be *demanded*, because the cheaper it will be for them to purchase UK products.

What are the implications for the economy?

It is useful to consider an example: During a boom period, aggregate demand is expanding rapidly and consumers are buying more goods and services, including more imports. The supply of sterling on the foreign exchange market would increase, and the exchange rate would fall. The lower exchange rate would make UK exports cheaper for foreigners; demand for sterling will consequently increase. The lower exchange rate will also make imports into the UK more expensive and therefore less will be bought. If the government does not intervene in the foreign exchange market, the exchange rate will rise or fall according to demand and supply. This is known as a system of **floating exchange rates**.

However, frequent changes in the demand and supply of sterling would cause the exchange rates to fluctuate. This leads to uncertainty for businesses as those who import and export products are unable to predict their future costs and revenues accurately. Therefore the government may not be willing to let the pound float freely. A consequence may be **government intervention in the foreign exchange market**, involving: the Bank of England either buying or selling sterling with its foreign currency reserves; borrowing foreign currency from abroad to buy sterling; or raising interest rates to encourage foreigners to deposit money in the UK and UK residents to keep their money in the country.

The relationship between growth, unemployment, inflation and the balance of payments

During the recovery period of the economic cycle, aggregate demand grows rapidly and the 'slack' in the economy will be taken up. There will be a faster growth in output and unemployment will fall. However, the growing shortages lead to inflation and balance of payments problems arise as the UK 'sucks in' imports from abroad. The result is the exchange rate falls which raises the price of imports, thus stoking up inflation.

At the peak of the boom, unemployment is low and output high, but growth has already slowed down or ceased; inflation and balance of payments problems are acute. In short, the economy is *overheating*.

As the economy moves into recession, falling aggregate demand will make growth negative and unemployment higher, but inflation slows down and the balance of payments problem is alleviated, although there may be a time lag before this happens.

This sequence of events has for many years characterized the UK economy. The dilemma facing the government is that if they reflate the economy, this will have a positive impact on unemployment and growth but make inflation and the balance of payments worse; but if they deflate, it will have the opposite effect. This sequence of events has come to be known as the 'boom–bust cycle'. Another dimension to this problem has been described as the political business cycle. Here, governments engineer booms to coincide with elections.

By careful economic management, the government can get all four objectives to look good at the same time. Once they have regained power on the back of the 'feel-good factor' generated by the favourable economic conditions, they can deflate the economy to remove inflationary pressures and improve the balance of payments. Although an unpopular recession is likely to follow, the government can reflate the economy in time for the next election. However, the responsibility for setting interest rates in the UK has now (since 1997) passed to the Bank of England, giving the government less scope to manipulate economic events as described above.

8.3.5   The national income

The four macroeconomic objectives, as we have seen, are interrelated. The foremost of these objectives is sustainable economic growth, for it is growth in output that results in increased standards of living for individuals; after all, the very reason for economic activity is to produce goods and services to meet unlimited human wants. Therefore, the more the economy produces, the better! However, if this growth is to be *sustainable*, it must take place in an economic climate where prices are stable, unemployment is low and the balance of payments is under control. Because growth is such a key economic indicator, governments go to significant lengths to measure national income and output, as a measure of the economy's performance. The questions we are interested in are as follows:

- How does the UK national income compare with that of other countries?
- How much has the economy grown over the last so many years?
- Which countries in the world have the highest standards of living?

The measure used to assess the value of the nation's output is known as the **gross domestic product** (GDP). The GDP is the value of the output of the economy over a twelve-month period. There are three different ways of measuring the GDP:

- **The product method.** This involves adding up the value of all the goods and services produced in the country. The government measures the 'value added' in each part of the economy; so for a manufactured product such as a car, it will calculate the value added at each stage of the production process (raw materials, components, assembly, etc.) right up to the point where the completed good is sold to the consumer. If it does this calculation for all goods and services that the economy produces, then it will have a measure of its total output.
- **The income method.** This involves adding up all the incomes in the country. This is the same as the sum of all values added is the difference between a firm's sales revenue and the costs of its purchases from other firms. Another way of looking at this is to consider a barter economy. In the absence of money, what individuals *produce* is also their *income*, which they then exchange for (*spend* on) the goods and services produced by others. So output, income and expenditure are the same thing from different angles. Value added is distributed as factor incomes (wages, rent, interest and profits) to reward the owners of the factors of production for their part in the productive process.
- **The expenditure method.** The expenditure method involves estimating the total spending on the output of the economy. This involves adding up total expenditure, which, as we have seen, comprises consumer expenditure, government expenditure, investment and the balance of spending on imports and exports.

Because of the way the GDP is calculated, national product, national income and national expenditure calculations will all give the same result.

One of the problems of measuring the national income is that the government has to use money values. However, as we have seen, the value of money can change independently of the *real* value of output. Thus the *money* value of national income could double in a year; does this mean that the economy has doubled its production of goods and services over that period? No, the *real economy* may even have contracted. If, in this imaginary scenario, the growth rate of the *real economy* was 0 per cent, then the doubling of *money* national income would be accounted for by a doubling of prices. Therefore *real* national income is measured using a base year (say, 1990) and calculating national income in that year's prices in order to iron out the effects of inflation.

The government collects data on the national income every year through surveys and other methods, and the resulting statistics are included in the government publication *UK National Income and Expenditure* (Office for National Statistics).

8.3.6   Keynesian economics

John Maynard Keynes has been described as the most influential economist since Adam Smith. Certainly, it is common to hear the term 'the Keynesian revolution' used to describe the changes ushered in by the ideas contained in his most influential work, *The General Theory of Employment, Interest and Money.*[7] The theme of *The General Theory* was a rejection of a key tenet of so-called 'classical' economics, that unemployment is a short-term problem and the economy will recover if markets are allowed to operate freely. The economic orthodoxy of the day was that mass unemployment which characterized much of the 1920s and 1930s was caused by what we now call inflexible labour markets, i.e. workers pricing themselves out of jobs. The classical argument was that if workers could be persuaded to accept wage cuts, producers' costs would fall, resulting in a corresponding decrease in the prices of goods and services. This in turn would stimulate domestic demand and demand for the country's exports. The economy would recover, and unemployment would fall.

The government of the day, in pursuing this policy, did in fact impose pay cuts on its own employees (e.g. civil servants) in an attempt to reduce the general level of wages in the economy. However, the economy stubbornly remained in recession, even though wages and the general level of prices were falling. Keynes argued that, far from solving the problem of unemployment, this policy would exacerbate it as it would result in further falls in consumer spending. Aggregate demand would fall, followed by output, and the economy would move further into recession.

Keynes also rejected the classical idea that increased savings, and a consequent fall in interest rates as the supply of loanable funds increases, would stimulate investment and growth. 'Savings' and 'investment' are two sides of the same coin: the money that individuals save in financial institutions such as banks is loaned to the business sector at a 'price', i.e. a rate of interest. The more people save, the greater the supply of loanable funds and the lower the rate of interest. Keynes showed that investment depends more on business confidence than it does on the rate of interest. Even if interest rates were low, a slide into recession could destroy such confidence.

Classical economists had also argued that an increase in the money supply would merely lead to an increase in prices. Keynes said that if there is a lot of slack in the economy, with high unemployment, idle machines and idle resources, increased spending (and therefore higher aggregate demand) could result in substantial increases in output and leave prices unaffected.

Keynes argued that if aggregate demand rose, firms would respond by producing more and employing more people. Conversely, if aggregate demand fell, the result would be less output and rising unemployment. The crux of Keynes' analysis was that **an unregulated market economy could not ensure sufficient demand** to avoid lengthy recessions. It was true that, in the long run, the economy would recover in the absence of government intervention but, as Keynes famously observed, 'in the long run we are all dead'. In other words, unemployment causes human misery and destabilizes society; the government *can* do something about it and should not be deterred from intervening in the economy by a doctrinaire adherence to the principles of *laissez-faire*.

8.4   Economic management

8.4.1   Keynesian demand management

Here it is necessary to consider withdrawals from and injections into the circular flow of income. The basic model of the circular flow was introduced in Section 8.1.4. Only part of the incomes received by households will be spent on the goods and services produced by domestic firms. Similarly, only part of the incomes generated by firms will be paid to UK households. The remainder will be withdrawn from the circular flow. These **withdrawals** (W) take three forms:

- **Savings** (S). As mentioned above, households choose not to spend all their income; they put some aside for the future, which will be deposited in financial institutions.
- **Taxes** (T). Taxes also represent a withdrawal from the circular flow, but in this case people have no choice.
- **Imports** (M). Not all consumer expenditure is on domestically produced goods. Some household incomes are spent on imported goods and services.

Total withdrawals are the sum of savings, taxes and expenditure on imports:

$$W = S + T + M$$

Only part of the demand for firm's output is accounted for by consumer expenditure. The remainder comes from other sources, known as **injections** (J). Injections into the circular flow take the following forms:

- **Investment** (I). This is the money firms obtain from financial institutions which they spend on new plant and equipment or on building up stocks.
- **Government expenditure** (G). Government spending on goods and services produced by firms counts as an injection into the circular flow.
- **Export expenditure** (X). When foreign residents buy our exports, money flows into the circular flow.

Total injections are the sum of investment, government expenditure and exports:

$$J = I + G + X$$

When withdrawals are greater than injections, aggregate demand will fall; and when injections exceed withdrawals, aggregate demand will rise (remember, I, G and X are components of aggregate demand) (see Figure 8.8).

Keynes' analysis of employment and inflation

A rise in injections – possibly from firms investing more – will result in an increase in aggregate demand. Firms will respond by using more labour and other resources, thus paying more incomes to households. Household consumption will rise and firms will sell

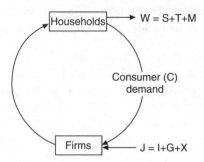

Figure 8.8. The circular flow of income showing injections and withdrawals.

more. Firms will respond by producing more, and using more labour to do so. Household incomes rise again, and consumption and production will follow suit. Thus there will be a 'ripple effect' of multiplied rises in incomes and production. This is called the **multiplier effect**. However, at each stage the 'ripples' get smaller – each time household incomes rise, households save more, pay more taxes and buy more imports. In other words, withdrawals rise. When withdrawals have risen to match increased injections, national income will stop rising. In the same way, a fall in injections, or a rise in withdrawals, will result in a multiplied fall in national income and employment. The principle here is that one household's spending represents another's income.

If aggregate demand is too low, there will be a recession and unemployment will rise. Keynes argued that governments should, under these circumstances, intervene to boost aggregate demand by the use of two policy levers:

- **Fiscal policy** – which involves using taxation, government borrowing and public spending to manage the level of demand in the economy. In a recession, a government should raise G and lower T. This will involve running a budget deficit, which was anathema to pre-war governments who put great store by a 'balanced budget' (government revenues matching government expenditure). The government borrows from the public by issuing government stock. Public debt was seen as a 'bad thing' because it accumulates over the years (the 'national debt') and the interest payments on the debt are a drain on the nation's reserves. Keynes argued that borrowing to finance public expenditure was justified because savings were lying idle as a result of the lack of business confidence; the government was putting these savings to productive use.
- **Monetary policy** – which is where the government uses interest rates to alter the supply of money in the economy. Increasing the money supply would mean that there is more available for spending, interest rates would fall and aggregate demand would rise.

If aggregate demand rises too much, inflation begins to set in as the economy reaches full capacity. Keynes argued that under these circumstances, governments should use *contractionary* fiscal and monetary policies to reduce demand: by raising taxes and/or reducing government expenditure, and raising interest rates.

After 1945, the UK government adopted Keynesian demand management policies to counter fluctuations in the economic cycle. When the economy began to grow too fast, the government adopted *deflationary* fiscal and monetary policies; and when a recession appeared imminent, it adopted *expansionary* fiscal and monetary policies.

Across the post-war industrialized world, Keynesian demand management policies were followed. Until the mid-1960s, inflation and unemployment remained low (averaging

3.8 per cent and 1.7 per cent respectively in the UK). However, from this point on, there was growing criticism of what came to be known as *stop–go policies*. In the UK, this criticism took the following forms:

● **Hitting a moving target.** Policy makers are faced with the problem of time lags. It is impossible to know how the economy is performing at the present moment; the economic statistics are always several months out of date. Therefore, the policy levers may be thrown at the wrong phase of the economic cycle. So, for example, a reflationary policy may start to impact on the economy when inflationary pressures had already set in, further fuelling inflation.
● Governments often had to pursue deflationary policies to cope with persistent balance of payments problems, even though unemployment was rising.
● The UK growth rate was running well below that of its competitors. Some attributed this to an overemphasis on demand management and a failure to deal with the underlying structural problems of the country.
● The economy was experiencing **stagflation** (a combination of low growth and inflation), with inflation and unemployment rising simultaneously.

8.4.2   Supply-side policies

Powerful criticisms of Keynesian demand management were emanating from **Monetarists**, the most influential and best known of whom is Milton Friedman.[8] The policy implications of Keynesian demand management were that governments could lower the rate of unemployment if they were prepared to accept more inflation; in other words, there is a 'trade-off' between inflation and unemployment. Monetarists, on the other hand, argue that a policy of increasing aggregate demand would in the long run merely lead to inflation. Unemployment would be dip only briefly in the short run, and would then return to its 'natural' rate – a rate determined not by the amount of demand in the economy, but by the structure of the labour market. According to Friedman, the way to reduce unemployment is through the unfettered operation of market forces. The labour market must be freed up – in other words, flexible labour markets are advocated.

Flexible labour markets – the 'supply-side' solution to unemployment

If labour markets worked in the same way as markets for goods and services, all those workers who wanted jobs would be able to find employment because they would offer to work for wages below those of people already in work. Employers, striving to minimize their costs of production and therefore preferring a cheaper labour force, would hire them; those in work would have to accept lower wages or lose their jobs. Under these conditions, everybody who wanted to work would be able to do so and the only unemployment would be of a temporary nature. However, in the real world full employment is difficult to achieve because the wage rate (price of labour) can get stuck above the level at which supply equals demand. Indeed, many economists and politicians argue that the cause of unemployment in the UK and in other industrialized countries is **inflexible** (over-rigid, over-regulated and overpriced) labour markets – in other words, workers have priced themselves out of jobs. The term 'labour market flexibility' invariably refers to downward wage flexibility, or the ease with which wages fall in response to changes in demand. This should not be confused with the notion of the 'flexible firm' (see Chapter 2).

Labour markets tend to be inflexible for the following reasons:

● **Trades unions.** Unions, it is argued, are monopoly suppliers of labour who, through collective bargaining, raise wages above the competitive level discussed above. At the higher wage rate, firms want to hire fewer workers. They are prevented from hiring non-union labour, and thereby cutting their wage costs, by closed-shop deals and strike threats.

- **Insiders against outsiders.** The labour force can be divided up into two groups: 'insiders', or employed workers, and 'outsiders', the unemployed. In employment, insiders acquire the skills that firms need. This makes it costly for firms to replace insiders with outsiders, who would need expensive training. Thus insiders have market power in that they can command a higher wage than outsiders can. Outsiders would be prepared to work for less than insiders do, but firms do not want to hire them because training them would add to their costs. The insiders prefer to secure higher wages for themselves, rather than have a higher number of people employed but with everyone on lower wages.
- **Minimum wages.** Many countries set minimum wages in order to protect low-paid workers' living standards. Some would argue that minimum wages eliminate the jobs of those that they are supposed to help. There is some evidence to suggest that this may indeed be the case with the worst effects being felt by the young, who start in low-paid jobs.
- **Taxation.** Governments raise most of their revenues from taxes (income tax and national insurance contributions in the UK) which result in the labour costs that firms pay being higher than the cash that workers take home. These taxes may make people less eager to work and firms less willing to hire them.
- **Welfare benefits.** This argument states that the level of welfare benefits has a major effect on unemployment. If the unemployed can get as much on the dole as they can in employment, then the incentive to work disappears.

Alongside labour market reforms, other 'supply-side' measures were advocated:

- **Market deregulation** (of the transport and finance markets, for example)
- **Privatization** (of nationalized industries and public utilities, as well as the contracting out of state-run services)
- **Lowering taxes** (to provide incentives for businesses to invest and individuals to work)
- **Promoting enterprise**
- **Cutting public spending** to reduce the size of the public sector and free up funds for private investment and
- **Reforming the public sector** by introducing market reforms, for example the 'internal market' in the National Health Service.

Keynesian demand management was rejected and monetary policy was to be used to control the money supply and inflation. This range of policies came to be associated with **'Thatcherism'** (or its American equivalent, 'Reaganomics').

Exercise

How have supply-side policies affected organizations and their managers?

Feedback

Supply-side policies have had a profound impact on organizations; indeed, it could be argued that they have made possible a 'revolution' in management. Certainly, the balance of power has shifted in management's favour with the changing role of the trades unions. But some of the most far-reaching changes have occurred in the public sector as a result of privatization: managers are now expected to behave commercially and respond to market forces, in the same way as their private sector equivalents.

8.4.3   Changes in the structure of the economy

The last twenty years of the twentieth century saw a number of structural changes:

- An acceleration in the process of 'deindustrialization', with the further decline of manufacturing and staple industries (such as coal and steel)
- The corresponding growth of the service sector
- The automation of manufacturing
- A highly competitive global economy (see the next section) and
- Organizations in both the private and public sectors responding to competitive pressures by cutting back staff numbers.

The late 1990s witnessed a period of relative economic stability in the UK, with the economy growing steadily, falling unemployment and relatively low interest and inflation rates. However, the trends mentioned above continued, particularly the decline of manufacturing and the corresponding growth of the service sector.

8.5   The global economy

In this section we shall be examining the impact of globalization on organizations and on management decisions. An understanding of the complexities of the global economy is possible only if we have an appreciation of the principles of international trade and a familiarity with the framework of associated international institutions.

8.5.1   International trade and protectionism

Background to the debate

The principle of free international trade has over time and to varying degrees been under threat from protectionist measures. **Protectionism** can be defined as any departure from free trade designed to give some protection to domestic industries from foreign competition.[8] As long ago as the sixteenth century, English foreign policy was dominated by the debate over trade and protectionism; the Anglo-Dutch wars of the late seventeenth century and the eighteenth century wars with France were fought over these very issues.

It was against the background of protectionist measures that Adam Smith wrote *The Wealth of Nations* in 1776, mentioned above in the context of free markets. Here he argued that a nation's wealth was determined by the annual output of goods and services available to its citizens; and that this wealth can be increased by countries **specializing** in forms of production to which they are most suited. By then trading with other nations, world output would increase to the benefit of all.

Comparative advantage

The advantages of trade are best understood by reference to the principle of **comparative advantage**, which states that a country should specialize in what it is *relatively* best at. Thus although country A might produce most products more efficiently than country B, country A should still specialize, allow country B to produce the products which it produces most efficiently and engage in trade. In this way, both countries will be better off.

To take an example: it is sometimes argued that buying goods from countries that pay low wages amounts to exploitation. However, if countries like India export textiles to the

West, this will help increase the wages of Indian workers. If India has a comparative advantage in labour-intensive goods (such as textiles), these goods will earn a better price than being sold entirely in the domestic Indian market. Providing some of the extra revenues go to the workers, they will gain from trade.

The years following the publication of *The Wealth of Nations* saw the gradual dismantling of protectionist structures until, by 1860, free trade could proceed more or less unfettered. This coincided with a period of expansion and economic growth which led the Victorians to associate free trade with prosperity.

The UK has adhered to the principle of free trade ever since, with the notable exception of the 1930s when the world slump led to the adoption by the government of a protectionist policy. As a trading nation, Britain consequently suffered.

What form does protectionism take?

We can distinguish between traditional and new protectionism. **Traditional protectionism** includes:

- **Tariffs** which are taxes on imports. These do not prohibit imports but discourage them by raising their price. The effect of import duties will depend on how responsive demand for the imported product is to changes in its price.
- **Subsidies** are given to home producers to enable them to compete in both home and overseas markets. Subsidies artificially reduce the price of exports below cost price, a practice known as 'dumping'. This measure was used by some governments in the 1930s as a way of ridding the country of surplus goods. Dumping is seen to be particularly harmful because it results in the export of unemployment.
- **Quotas** are quantitative limits places on the import of specified products.
- **Exchange controls** can be used to deny residents access to foreign currencies. Governments can thereby control the quantity of imports.

New protectionism – or non-tariff barriers – is a feature of the late twentieth century and has been used as a way of imposing import controls while adhering to the letter of international obligations such as GATT (see below). It tends to be used to discriminate against particular countries and specific commodities and includes:

- **Administrative restrictions,** such as product safety laws and other bureaucratic measures. An example is France famously processing all imports of Japanese video recorders at a small customs post at Poitiers.
- **Voluntary export restraints,** such as those imposed by EU countries on Japanese car imports. In fact this example was not a 'voluntary' agreement at all as failure to agree would have resulted in even more damaging non-tariff action to limit imports. In 1991 it was agreed to phase out this arrangement by the year 2000. The passages below provide an account of the US experience with voluntary restraint arrangements.

The USA and 'voluntary restraint arrangements'

The early 1980s saw the US economy experiencing severe structural problems. The strength of the dollar made competition in overseas markets difficult; and fierce competition from Europe, Japan and Korea was eroding US companies' share of the home market. The resulting massive balance of trade deficit prompted Presidents Reagan and Bush (who, ironically, were strong advocates of free trade) to take action to limit foreign imports, particularly in key industries such as automobiles, steel and silicon chips. One of the most widely used instruments to limit imports was the voluntary restraint arrangement (VRA), where an importing country agrees to limit its exports to a set amount, or quota.

In the case of the US automobile industry, VRAs were first 'negotiated' with Japan in 1981 and imports were subsequently cut. This measure allowed the automobile industry to survive a difficult period of restructuring and to emerge in the 1990s as a more efficient producer of higher-quality products. However, a high price was paid by the US consumer. Studies have estimated that VRAs have increased the price of Japanese cars by up to $3000 per car, and US cars by up to $1000 per car as a result of reduced competition.

- **Agricultural protection** achieved by the farming industry in developed countries and taking the form of state intervention in markets. The EU's Common Agricultural Policy is the prime example.
- **Government contracts.** There is an incentive for governments to discriminate against foreign producers in the awarding of such contracts, which tend to be extremely lucrative and account for a high proportion of public expenditure.

The case against protection

This is based on the case for free trade and the costs of protection. Many of these issues will be discussed in more detail below in the section on 'Globalization'. The benefits of free trade include:

- **Specialization** by countries in forms of production to which they are best suited
- **Efficient production.** Firms which compete in world markets need to keep their production costs to a minimum
- **Access to the cheapest source of supply** of factors of production – raw materials, capital and labour
- **Greater choice** for consumers
- **Global markets.** Firms operating in global markets can take advantage of economies of scale
- **Gains from increased competition.**

The harmful effects of import controls are:

- **Acting as export controls** as other countries retaliate
- **Protecting inefficient producers**
- **Reducing specialization**
- **Raising prices to consumers**
- **Protecting monopolists** who are free, in the absence of competition, to use their monopoly power to exploit the consumer
- **Reducing living standards** as inhabitants are unable to benefit from the advantages of specialization and competition and must therefore tolerate slower economic growth
- **Encourage resistancing to structural change.** For example, firms have less incentive to adopt up-to-date management and working practices or the latest, most technologically advanced production methods.

The case for protectionism

This is based on the contention that, in the real world, free trade is subject to market imperfections. It does not, therefore, operate to the benefit of all, as suggested by the economic principles discussed above. The arguments for protection include the following:

- To retain foreign currency reserves and thereby improve the balance of payments
- To prevent dumping
- To promote the development of infant industries
- To cushion the decline of major industries
- To retaliate against import controls imposed against the country
- To combat so-called 'unfair' competition.

8.5.2   The institutional architecture of international trade

The fragility of international trade has persuaded the international community to put in place a framework of institutions to oversee the effective working of the system.

The General Agreement on Tariffs and Trade (GATT)

GATT was a result of the desire to avoid a return to the protectionist environment of the 1930s, which precipitated the world slump. Twenty-three countries signed a tariff reduction agreement in 1947, which became the General Agreement on Tariffs and Trade.

GATT states that members enter into 'reciprocal and mutually advantageous arrangements directed to the sustantial reduction of tariffs and barriers to trade and to the elimination of discriminatory treatment in international commerce'. This statement implies a number of principles for the conduct of trading relations:

- **Non-discrimination.** Each member state is required to grant 'most favoured nation' treatment to all other members. The European Union contradicts this principle as EU member states do practise discrimination in favour of fellow members and against non-members. However, the GATT agreement allows for regional groupings such as the EU.
- **National treatment.** Imports must receive equal treatment with domestically produced goods once they have entered the country.
- **Import quotas or quantitative controls.** These are prohibited, with the following exceptions: to alleviate a balance of payments crisis; or if a competing domestic industry is injured by a sudden surge in imports.
- **Export subsidies.** These are generally prohibited as they result in 'dumping', as mentioned above. The exception is agricultural products.

The World Trade Organization

As well as being a treaty, GATT is also an international organization. In 1995, it became the World Trade Organization (WTO). Based in Geneva with a staff of around 400, the WTO performs the following tasks:

- Monitoring trade arrangements
- Watching out for policies which conflict with GATT agreements
- Arbitrating in trade disputes between members
- Providing the secretariat for meetings/talks on trade liberalization.

By the late-1990s membership had risen to 120 states, accounting for over 90 per cent of world trade. There have been eight 'rounds' of negotiations since GATT's inception in 1947, the three major ones being: The Kennedy round (1964–7); the Tokyo round (1973–9); and the Uruguay round (1986–93). The Uruguay round took place against the backdrop of increased protectionism, particularly of the non-tariff variety (as discussed above). The main concerns of the Uruguay round were:

- To bring trade in agriculture and textiles fully within the GATT system
- To achieve further reductions in tariff and non-tariff barriers
- To extend GATT to new areas such as intellectual property, investment and services and
- To strengthen the GATT system so that it can deal more effectively with trade distortions and disputes.

At more than one time during these talks it seemed that agreement would never be reached, but negotiations were eventually completed in 1994. The Uruguay round was a qualified success, with the above concerns being either fully or partly addressed.

How did the UK benefit from the Uruguay round?

One outcome, the liberalization of trade in services, was of particular concern to the UK. Rules were adopted to limit the power of countries to restrict the provision of services (e.g. banking and insurance) by foreign companies, and to restrict multinational investment (e.g. by forcing them to use a proportion of local inputs). Also, voluntary codes were to be adopted by member states to limit the practice of government procurement favouring domestic suppliers. This means that UK banks and insurance companies can operate freely across national boundaries; national telecommunications monopolies will be dismantled; shipping and civil aviation will be liberalized; and UK multinationals will have greater freedom of operation. These are all areas in which the UK is strong, so an agreement including such provisions is particularly beneficial to Britain.

The Organization for Economic Cooperation and Development (OECD)

The OECD came into being in 1961. Its aims are:

- To encourage economic growth and high employment with financial stability among member countries and
- To contribute to the economic development of less advanced member and non-member countries and the expansion of world trade.

The OECD publishes regular statistical bulletins covering the main economic statistics of member countries and regular reviews of the economic prospects of individual members as well as *ad hoc* reports of special studies covering a wide range of subjects, e.g. world population growth. It has been particularly important as a forum for the industrial countries to discuss international monetary problems and in promoting aid and technical assistance for developing countries. The term 'the OECD countries' is often used as shorthand for 'the countries of the developed world' or 'the industrialized countries'.

The International Monetary Fund (IMF)

The objectives of the IMF are to achieve the free convertibilty of all currencies and to promote the stability of international money markets. Each of the members of the IMF is required to contribute a **quota** to the fund. The size of the quota will depend on the national income of the country and upon its share in world trade. In this way it was hoped that there would be enough of any currency in the pool for any member to draw on should they get into balance of payments difficulties.

The IMF consists of around 150 member countries including all the industrialized and developing nations of the world. The former socialist bloc countries joined in the early 1990s.

The role of the IMF declined significantly during the 1980s. Many developing nations were thought uncreditworthy by the IMF; and in addition, some countries were unwilling to borrow from the IMF because of the strict austerity programme which it imposed when making loans. The UK suffered a bout of deflation in the mid-1970s as a result of its borrowing from the IMF to stave off a severe balance of payments problem.

The World Bank

The World Bank, otherwise known as the International Bank for Reconstruction and Development, was set up as a sister organization to the IMF. Its original purpose was to make loans for the economic redevelopment of post-war Europe. The membership of the World Bank is the same as that of the IMF; it is also financed on the same basis, i.e. through quotas. As it developed the World Bank began to focus on the poorer countries of the world, and today it is almost wholly concerned with helping these nations.

Although there is a great need for the services of the IMF and the World Bank, their roles are limited by a lack of funds and political disagreements.

The North American Free Trade Association (NAFTA)

NAFTA is an example of a **free trade area**, where member countries remove tariffs and quotas between themselves, but retain whatever restriction each member chooses with non-member countries. A free trade area is similar to a **customs union**, such as the European Union, the difference being that members of a customs union must adopt common external tariffs and quotas with non-member countries.

NAFTA was formed in 1993 and consists of the USA, Canada and Mexico. These countries have agreed to abolish tariffs between themselves in the hope that increased trade and cooperation will follow. While new non-tariff restrictions will not be permitted, many existing ones can remain in force thereby preventing the development of true free trade between the members. The NAFTA countries hope that, with a market similar in size to the EU, they will be able to rival the EU's economic power in world trade.

Having examined the principles and structure of international trade, we can now turn to examine the major issue in this field: globalization.

8.5.3 Globalization

What is globalization?

Essentially, globalization refers to the growing integration of national economies, evidenced by an **increase in cross-border flows** of trade, investment and financial capital. What this means in practical terms is that:

- Consumers are buying more foreign goods
- More firms operate across national borders and
- People are investing more abroad.

What are its origins?

The increasing international economic integration we are witnessing today is by no means unprecedented. As we saw earlier, the years between the mid-nineteenth century and the First World War witnessed a period of globalization which was driven by reductions in trade barriers and falls in transport costs made possible by technological developments associated with steam power. This phase ended with the First World War, after which the world moved into a period of trade protectionism and restrictions on capital flows which precipitated the Great Depression of the 1930s.

Capital controls were maintained after the Second World War, but the reduction of trade barriers was seen as vital to economic recovery. This led to the establishment of the General Agreement on Tariffs and Trade (GATT), discussed earlier. Then, from the mid-1970s, restrictions on the international flow of capital were gradually abolished, thus preparing the ground for a resumption of the process of globalization.

What is driving globalization today?

Globalization occurs when managers in certain companies make decisions which lead to an increase in these cross-border flows. It has become more attractive for managers to make such decisions for the following reasons:

- **More and more countries are embracing the free market.** The global trend away from economic planning and towards a free-market ideology on the part of economic policy makers has been discussed earlier in this chapter.
- **The growing economic importance of developing countries.** The adoption of free-market principles by developing countries has promoted new capital investment and faster economic growth, with the consequence that the focus of economic activity is shifting away from the developed world.
- **Technological advances have resulted in improving communications.** Costs of transportation, telecommunications and computers have fallen sharply in the last forty years.

These declining costs have had two main effects:

(i) The cost of shipping goods has fallen
(ii) The more effective and reliable management of geographically distant operations via technologies such as electronic mail, video conferencing and the internet.

What form does globalization take?

Globalization has a number of dimensions:

- **The globalization of markets for goods and services.** We are seeing the emergence of global products as tastes become universal. An example here would be designer footwear in the form of Adidas or Nike trainers, which are seen in every major city across the world.
- **The globalization of firms.** The growth of multinational corporations is one of the most distinctive features of the age and will be discussed below.
- **The globalization of labour markets** as technological advances allow product components to be manufactured all over the world. This phenomenon is discussed below under the heading 'The new international division of labour'.
- **The globalization of investment** as corporations seek a physical presence in many countries. In the 1950s and 1960s, the great majority of foreign investment was made by American firms. Now most developed countries, including America, see significant flows of both outward and inward investment. As a consequence, many US citizens work for Japanese, French, German or British companies, just as many citizens of these other countries work for US firms.

What does the future hold?

If the rate of globalization is increasing, companies must adapt quickly in order to gain a competitive advantage. The following changes in the global economy look extremely likely:

- **The economic importance of the developing countries will increase** to the point where, within 20 years, they will be pre-eminent. Thus China is predicted to become the new economic superpower.
- **Global competition will intensify** as rapidly growing companies from emerging economies such as China, India, Brazil and Mexico begin to dominate the corporate landscape.
- **The costs of computing, telecommunications and transportation are likely to continue falling.** This will intensify the search for the most cost-effective production locations.

Multinational enterprises (MNEs) as vehicles for globalization

Multinational enterprises, sometimes called 'transnational corporations', are firms that produce or distribute in two or more countries. These organizations are often extremely large and dominate production in major industries such as automobiles, electronics, petroleum and pharmaceuticals. Glaxo Wellcome PLC is an example of a MNE as it has subsidiaries in 23 different countries and sells its products in many more. In 1990 there were about 37 000 MNEs, compared to 7000 in 1969. Today, the largest 500 MNEs conduct over 80 per cent of the world's stock of foreign direct investment (FDI) and more than half its trade. Foreign direct investment has been the primary means for MNEs to develop foreign operations. (FDI is the acquisition of the controlling interest in foreign production facilities either by purchasing existing facilities or building new ones.)

Why would a company wish to transfer some of its production abroad?

There are several answers to this question:

- **In response to local market conditions.** Today's advanced and differentiated products require flexible responses to local needs; these cannot be achieved by centralized production at the organization's home base.
- **To overcome non-tariff barriers.** Location of production in large foreign markets avoids the risk of exports from the home base being disadvantaged by 'protectionist' measures. For example, it is argued that a major reason for Asian MNEs investing in the UK is to overcome trade barriers erected by the European Union.
- **Many MNEs are in service industries.** In the rapidly expanding global market for accounting, management consultancy, marketing and financial services, a physical presence is needed to produce a service in a particular country.
- **Advances in technology have allowed production to be organized on a global basis.** Product components are typically manufactured in many locations, with production being directed to the lowest cost locations.

This last point introduces a key issue in the debate surrounding globalization: the New International Division of Labour (NIDL).

The New International Division of Labour

Since the 1970s it has for the first time become possible to manufacture products not only in the industrialized countries but also in the developing ones. Production is being increasingly subdivided into parts which can be assigned to whichever area of the world can provide the most profitable combination of capital and labour. The NIDL came about because of technological developments which revolutionized manufacturing processes, as well as transport and communications techniques mentioned above. These developments meant that MNEs were able to take advantage of the huge reserve of labour in developing countries, which could be employed at low wages and under poor terms of employment.

How will globalization impact on managers?

Global competition will have the effect of depressing prices of goods and services. To compete in the global economy, it is argued, will require greater flexibility and innovation, which imply new organizational forms. These entail the breakdown of job demarcation and pyramidal bureaucracies. Multiskilled, flexible workers are seen as the key to these changes wherein, as demands change, workers are able to drop old tasks and take up new ones. There is a premium on knowledge and organizations need to ensure the continuous learning of their workforce. The role of the manager in this type of organization is not to supervise subordinates, but to coach associates; the manager is an enabler, rather than a controller.

An alternative view of globalization

For many commentators, globalization is a far from positive development.[9] They point to the following issues:

- Globalization is likely to lead to lower wages and widespread unemployment in the developed world as industrial capitalism, in its drive to maximize profits and minimize costs, searches out the cheapest labour it can find.
- Cheap labour means lower production costs, which result in more being produced; but, ironically, lower wages and unemployment in the developed world means that we are less likely to be able to afford them.
- Transnational corporations are, logically, the main advocates of free trade, market forces and globalization. However, TNCs rely very heavily on the state. When a TNC wishes to set up a plant, it holds an auction with competitive bids from nation states offering tax breaks, grants, power supplies and a compliant 'flexible' labour force. They are, therefore, very heavily subsidized.
- Unregulated world financial markets are inherently unstable and the world financial system subject to regular crashes – witness the 'Asian crisis'. These crashes result in great suffering for the people of those countries affected.
- The threat that jobs will go abroad is a major cause of the job insecurity, erosion of non-wage benefits and the weakening of trade unions which characterize developed economies today.
- With globalization, workers and businesses become more mobile and therefore more difficult to tax. It will therefore become harder for governments to raise the taxes to finance the public spending which has offset the worst effects of free trade, such as unemployment.

From this perspective, globalization is a malevolent force wherein unregulated market forces destabilize and diminish the lives of millions.

In brief

We began this chapter by considering the nature of economics and continued with an examination of the market. We argued that the market system, as a way of organizing economic activity, has distinct advantages over its alternatives. However, it was noted that there are certain circumstances under which the market fails to bring about an optimal allocation of resources; when this is the case, government intervention in the economy is justified. When evaluating the theory of the firm, we saw that some of the assumptions made about the way in which companies operating in a competitive market behave are open to question. Alternative theories of the firm stress the importance of managerial behaviour in this context.

In our discussion of the macroeconomy we examined the relationship between economic growth, employment and inflation. We also compared Keynesian and supply side approaches to economic management and concluded with an overview of the changes in the structure of the UK economy that have taken place in the 1980s and 1990s.

The final section focuses on the challenges facing managers and organizations arising from the formation of a global economy. At the outset we traced the origins of international trade and discussed the rationale for free trade. We then went on to examine the framework of international institutions which oversee trade. This led us to an analysis of the phenomenon of globalization. What has become clear from our study is that globalization offers opportunities for organizations, but also poses significant threats. Operating in global markets could well lead to a redefinition of the role of the manager.

Examination questions for this chapter are given in Appendix 2.

References

1 Porter, M. E. (1985) *Competitive Advantage: Creating and Sustaining a Superior Performance.* Free Press.
2 Sloman, J. (1999) *Economics* (4th edition). Prentice Hall.
3 Cyert, R. and March, J. (1963) *Behavioural Theory of the Firm.* Prentice Hall.
4 Smith, A. (1974) *The Wealth of Nations.* Pelican Classics.
5 Friedman, M. (1962) *Capitalism and Freedom.* Chicago University Press.
6 Cole, G. D. H (1950) *Socialist Economics.*
7 Keynes, J. M. (1936) *The General Theory of Employment, Interest and Money.* Macmillan.
8 Friedman, M. (1970) *The Counter Revolution in Monetary Theory.* Institute of Economic Affairs.
9 Stiglitz, J. (2002) *Globalization and its discontents.* Penguin Books.

Further reading

Chrystal, K. A. and Lipsey, R. G. (1997) *Economics for Business and Management.* Oxford University Press.
Thompson, G. (ed.) (2001) *Governing the European Economy.* Open University/Sage.

Web-site addresses

Centre for Economic Performance: http://www.cep.ise.ac.uk
Financial Times: http://www.ft.com
Institute of Economic Research: http://www.warwick.ac.uk/ier
London Stock Exchange: http://www.londonstockexchange.com
Organization for Economic Co-operation and Development http://www.oecd.org

9 The political context of management

Chapter objectives

In this chapter you will:

- Examine the nature of politics
- Consider the democratic process and the roles of elections
- Review the roles of political parties and interest groups in public policy formation
- Examine the machinery of government and the legislative process and
- Evaluate the notion of citizenship.

Chapter introduction

The last years of the twentieth century witnessed the ongoing 'modernization' of the British constitution: the House of Lords is to be reformed; devolution to Scotland and Wales is a reality; and electoral reform is on the political agenda. Meanwhile, European integration continues to have profound effects on the UK political system. The political landscape has also changed in that the old divisions between 'left' and 'right' have largely disappeared. The argument is no longer 'socialism or capitalism?' rather it is 'which kind of capitalism?' In practical terms, this means that we see a Labour government promoting free-market policies and fostering links with business.

It is important for managers to come to terms with the workings of the UK political system because government decisions and the actions of other players in the political arena help shape the environment within which businesses operate.

9.1 Politics and the democratic process

9.1.1 What is 'politics'?

Politics is both a reflection and a consequence of certain aspects of human existence: it is a reflection of human nature in that we are not all alike (the presence of *diversity*); and it is a consequence of the human condition because of the problem of *scarcity* (there is never enough to go round – see Chapter 8). 'Politics', therefore, is closely bound up with the phenomena of conflict and cooperation. The existence of rival opinions, competing needs and diverse interests will result in disagreement about the 'rules' under which people live. On the other hand, people recognize that there needs to be a degree of cooperation for the rules to be upheld. Politics is therefore often depicted as a process of conflict resolution, where competing interests are in some way reconciled with one another. However, it is probably more accurately portrayed as a *search* for conflict resolution, as not all conflicts can be resolved.

Politics is difficult to define because of the word's plethora of meanings. We talk of 'politics' in everyday speech in a number of contexts: for example, in an organizational setting, the term 'office politics' is in common usage, and we expect managers to possess 'political sensitivity' (indeed, this is seen to be a core competency for middle and senior managers). Furthermore, politics is often thought of as a 'dirty' word associated with double dealing, disruption and even violence.

Another problem with defining politics is that there is disagreement about its meaning even among authorities on the subject. It is defined in contrasting ways: as the exercise of power, the exercise of authority, the making of collective decisions, manipulating and deceiving people, the allocation of scarce resources, and so on. Essentially, however, the different views of politics can be categorized into four areas:

- Politics as the art of government
- Politics as public affairs
- Politics as compromise and consensus
- Politics as power and the distribution of resources.

Politics as the art of government

This is classical definition of politics, developed from the original Greek meaning. The modern form of this definition is 'what concerns the state', so to study politics is essentially to study government. However, this is a restrictive conception of politics in that it implies that all politics is exercised within and through the machinery of the state, i.e. official government institutions such as parliament, the cabinet and the civil service. This means that most social institutions – for example, businesses, universities, families, etc. – are outside politics and are therefore 'non-political'. This definition ignores factors such as the global forces which are increasingly influencing our lives and the impact of multinational organizations (see Chapter 8).

Politics is also associated in the public's mind with the activities of politicians, who are often perceived as power-hungry, hypocritical and corrupt. This perception is more common today as politicians are subject to intense media attention, bringing to light examples of dishonesty which may have remained hidden from public scrutiny in the past. Nevertheless, even those who have such a negative view of politics would accept that it is an inevitable feature of social existence. Without some way of deciding on rules, allocating values and reconciling conflicting interests, society would break down. For the consequences, we only have to look as far as Northern Ireland, where the attempt to find a 'political solution' to the troubles implies that the alternative to politics is civil war.

Politics as public affairs

In this conception of politics, the distinction between the 'political' and 'the non-political' reflects the distinction between the *public* and *private* spheres of life. This begs the question of where the distinction between public and private life should be drawn. Traditionally, the distinction between the public and private realms equates to the division between the state and civil society. The institutions of the state (essentially, those institutions which are funded out of taxation) can be regarded as public, whereas other institutions such as businesses, trade unions, community groups and so on comprise 'civil society'. These latter groups are 'private' in the sense that they are set up and funded by private citizens to satisfy their own interests. On the basis of this division, politics is the preserve of the state.

Another way of looking at the distinction between 'public' and 'private' is in relation to a division between 'the political' and 'the personal'. Civil society contains institutions which can be thought of as 'public' in the sense that they are open institutions operating in public and affecting society by their actions. In this perspective, therefore, businesses and trades unions are seen as part of the public realm and the economy becomes 'political'. However, politics does not impinge on the 'personal' realm of the family and domestic life, and it is with reference to this concept of 'political' matters that politicians can claim that certain types of behaviour in their personal lives do not affect their conduct in the public arena.

Politics as compromise and consensus

This is politics as 'the art of the possible', that is, a way of solving conflict through compromise and negotiation. This interpretation is often associated with Bernard Crick, who defined politics as 'the activity by which differing interests within a given unit of rule are conciliated by giving them a share in power proportionate to their importance to the welfare and the survival of the whole community'.[1]

This implies that politics involves the dispersal of power throughout society and the resolution of conflict by debate and discussion. However, this definition presupposes a liberal democracy where individuals and groups have the opportunity to voice their views and pursue their interests; it tells us very little about dictatorships and one-party states.

Politics as power and the distribution of resources

This is a broad definition which does not restrict politics to one sphere ('public' or 'private'). Rather, it sees politics as a feature of every aspect of human existence: the family, the relationship between men and women, groups of friends, as well as taking place on the national and international stage. Politics is distinguished from other forms of social activity in that it is at base about the allocation of scarce resources – who gets what, when and how. Politics is a struggle over scarce resources, and power (the ability to achieve a desired outcome) is the means through which this struggle is conducted.

Feminists and Marxists advocate this view of politics. Feminists argue that women have traditionally been confined to the 'private' sphere of life, revolving around the family and domesticity, whereas men have dominated the 'public' arena. They view relationships within the family, between husbands and wives and parents and children as highly political, and on the same level as the relationship between the government and its citizens. Marxists believe that political power is rooted in the class system (see Chapter 11) and that 'civil society' is at the heart of politics.

Exercise

Using the above definitions, consider the ways in which a manager's job can be described as 'political'.

Feedback

Managers usually control resources and have a degree of authority, both of which confer power on individuals. Often managers find themselves in competition with other managers for resources, and this can result in 'power struggles'. Sometimes wider political issues can be played out in an organizational setting, for example 'gender politics'. As mentioned earlier, senior management roles can be highly political, and in large companies managers can find themselves negotiating with government ministers (over a decision to relocate a production facility, for example).

9.1.2   Democracy

The popularity of democracy has threatened to undermine its value as a political term to the point where it is in danger of becoming meaningless; there is no political regime and few political groupings which would not claim to be democratic. However, with the collapse of communism in Eastern Europe, the diminished attraction of socialism and concerns about global capitalism, 'democracy has emerged as perhaps the only enduring principle in the postmodern political landscape'.[2] It is therefore important to examine the nature of democracy and its significance for the UK political system.

Like so many political terms and concepts, 'democracy' has its origins in ancient Greece. The Athenians practised a form of government by mass meeting which is known as **direct democracy**. This is based on the direct and continuous participation of citizens in the task of government. It is therefore a system of popular self-government, whose modern equivalent is the use of the referendum. While only being achievable in small communities, direct democracy has certain key merits:

● It gives citizens control over their own destinies.
● It creates a better-informed and more sophisticated citizenry.
● It enables people to express their own views without having to rely on politicians.
● It legitimizes government as people are more likely to accept decisions they have made themselves.

Western-style democracies are characterized by a limited and indirect form of democracy known as **representative democracy**. It is limited in that popular participation in government is infrequent, being limited to the act of voting every few years. It is indirect in the sense that the public selects those who will exercise power on their behalf, rather than exercising power themselves. The strengths of representative democracy are:

● It is a practicable form of democracy in a mass society.
● It relieves ordinary citizens of the burden of decision making.
● It allows political power to be placed in the hands of those who are best qualified to govern.

Although there are several possible models of democracy, in practice there is broad acceptance of the liberal democratic model. The features of a **liberal democracy** are its indirect and representative nature and the fact that it is based on regular elections. It operates through party competition and electoral choice. These are achieved through political pluralism, tolerance of a wide range of contending beliefs and the existence of rival political movements and parties. Furthermore, in a liberal democracy there is a clear distinction between the state and civil society; in effect, this means that the market is allowed to operate with a minimum of state intervention and economic activity is organized along capitalist lines.

The UK is a **parliamentary democracy**. This is a form of democratic rule which operates through a democratically elected assembly which establishes an indirect link between the government and 'the people' (those who are governed). In this sense, democracy means a responsible and representative government – government of the people, by the people and for the people. Government is accountable not directly to the public but to the public's elected representatives. The representatives are, by virtue of their education and experience, better able to define what is in the people's interests than the people themselves.

There is considerable controversy about how liberal-democratic systems work in practice. The **pluralist** perspective is that power is dispersed widely and evenly throughout society rather than concentrated in the hands of an **elite**, or ruling class. Individuals are largely represented through their membership of groups and such groups have access to the policy process. The main feature of a system of pluralist democracy is competition between political parties and the ability of pressure groups and interest groups to state their views freely establishes a link between the government and the governed. The **corporatist view** is one where government officials, organized labour (the trades unions) and business interests are allowed to deal directly with one another. This tendency to integrate economic interests into government was particularly strong in post-war Sweden and Norway, for example. It was also evident in the UK until 1979, when the Thatcher government, representing the 'new right', made a concerted effort to reduce state intervention and pursue a policy of promoting free market economics.

9.2   The electoral system and political parties

9.2.1   The electoral system

Elections are often seen as democracy in action and therefore at the core of the political process. They are a means by which people can exercise some control over the government. While direct democracy is not achievable, representation is perhaps the closest we can come to government by the people. However, representation is itself a controversial issue.

Representation is a relationship through which an individual or group stands for a larger body of people. Representative democracy constitutes a limited form of democratic rule only if it links the government and the people in a way that their views and interests are reflected. But what form should representation take? The model proposed in the eighteenth century by the famous parliamentarian, Edmund Burke, is that representation is the moral duty of those who possess education and experience; this political elite acts in the best interests of the electorate. An alternative interpretation is the delegate model, where the individual conveys the views of others but does not exercise his or her own judgement.

Both these models were formulated before the advent of modern political parties. Now, individual candidates are elected on the basis of their representing a particular political party, rather than on the basis of their personal qualities. The concept of representation which emerged alongside the development of political parties is the mandate model, based on the principle that a party gains a popular mandate in winning an election. This allows it to carry out when in government the policies and programmes it outlined in its election campaign. Because people voted for the party rather than for an individual, the politicians serve their constituents by staying loyal to the party line. This guarantees responsible government because the party in power can act only within the mandate it has received. However, this model has been criticized on the grounds that it is not at all certain that voters select parties on the basis of policies and issues; they can be influenced by a range of irrational factors, such as the personality of the leader. Also, from the government's point of view, the mandate can limit its ability to respond to changing circumstances by an obligation to carry out election pledges.

Elections

Representation is umbilically linked to elections and voting. However, elections can take a number of different forms:

● Which offices are subject to election? The general principle is that it should be those offices whose holders have policy-making responsibilities. However, there are exceptions such as the House of Lords in the UK.
● Who is entitled to vote? In some US states, electoral registration is voluntary, whereas in Australia, voting is compulsory.

- How are votes cast? Modern political elections are usually held on the basis of a secret ballot, thus guaranteeing a 'fair' election (voters are not subject to intimidation and there is less scope for corruption).
- Are elections competitive? Only about half the countries which use elections give the electorate a real choice in terms of both candidates and parties.
- How is the election conducted? There is a wide range of possible systems.

Functions of elections

Liberal democratic electoral systems are characterized by universal suffrage, the secret ballot and competition between candidates. One view is that through elections, politicians are held to account and pressed into adopting policies which reflect public opinion; and alternative perspective is that elections are a method by which the ruling elite manipulate public opinion and legitimize and perpetuate their own positions. In reality, elections may have both characteristics. Nevertheless, the basic functions of elections are as follows:

- **Recruiting politicians.** Parties select candidates to stand for election to political office.
- **Making governments.** In parliamentary systems, elections influence the formation of governments, particularly when the electoral system delivers an overall majority for one party.
- **Providing representation.** Fair and competitive elections are the means by which the wishes of the people are transmitted to the government.
- **Influencing policy.** Elections can deter governments from pursuing unpopular policies, but they only really influence policy when a single issue dominates the election campaign.
- **Educating voters.** Campaigning provides the electorate with information about policies and the political process. However, this information is often incomplete and distorted.
- **Establishing legitimacy.** Elections provide justification for a system of rule and encourages citizens to participate in politics. Low turn-outs of voters at elections are a cause for concern because they are seen to undermine the legitimacy of the political system; an example is the very low turn-out in the elections to the European Parliament in 1999.

Types of electoral system

An electoral system is a set of rules that governs the conduct of elections. These vary throughout the world but can nevertheless be classified into two types: *majoritarian* systems in which the larger parties typically win a higher proportion of seats than the proportion of votes they gain in an election. Labour's landslide victory in the 1997 general election, when they won 64 per cent of seats, was achieved with only 44.4 per cent of the vote. On the other hand, there are proportional systems, which ensure an equal relationship between the seats won by a party and the votes gained in an election. The principle is that a party which gains 45 per cent of the vote in a proportional system will win 45 per cent of the seats.

The debate about electoral reform centres around what constitutes 'good government'. For example, is a system that promotes compromise and consensus preferable to one which favours conviction? What is more important, effective or representative government? Each system will have strengths and weaknesses based on these criteria.

The 'first past the post' system

The majoritarian 'first past the post' system which is used in the UK for general and local government elections (and also in the USA and India) has the following features:

- The country is divided into single-member constituencies of equal size
- Voters select a single candidate
- The winning candidate needs only to achieve a 'plurality' of votes (more votes than any other candidate does on a single count).

The system has a number of strengths: it establishes a clear link between representatives and constituents; it offers the electorate a clear choice of potential parties of government; it makes it more difficult for small extremist parties to gain seats; and it makes for strong, effective and stable government as a single party usually has majority control of the assembly.

The disadvantages of the 'first past the post' system are that it underrepresents small parties and 'third' parties such as the Liberal Democrats; it offers only limited choice because of its dominance by two major parties; it undermines the legitimacy of government in that governments tend only to enjoy minority support; and it creates instability because a change of government can result in a radical shift of policies.

The major criticism of majoritarian systems is that they distort popular preferences. This point is illustrated by the 1997 election results:

- Labour won 44 per cent of the vote (an increase of 9 per cent on 1992). This translated into 418 seats, which is 63 per cent of the total.
- The Conservative Party won 31 per cent of the vote, (a decrease of 12 per cent on the 1992 total). This translated into 165 seats, which is 25 per cent of the total.
- The Liberal Democrats won 17 per cent of the vote (a decrease of 1 per cent on 1992). This translated into 46 seats, which is 7 per cent of the total.

In representative terms, these biases cannot be justified, especially in view of the fact that third parties, like the Liberal Democrats in the UK, tend to be centrist, not extremist. Furthermore, such distortions bring the legitimacy of the political system into question. The Conservative Party remained in government between 1979 and 1997, implementing a raft of radical reforms, without ever gaining more than 43 per cent of support in elections. This represents a very strong argument in favour of proportional representation systems, which are clearly more representative.

Proportional representation (PR)

The principle of proportional representation is that parties should be represented in an assembly or parliament in direct proportion to their overall electoral strength; so, if the party receives x per cent of total votes cast, it should get the same percentage of seats. The term 'proportional representation' is used to refer to a variety of electoral mechanisms which achieve a high degree of proportionality. The best-known PR systems are the party list system, the single transferable vote system and the additional member system.

Probably the main criticism of proportional representation is that it produces coalition governments, whose policies are usually hammered out at post-election negotiations; consequently, any electors do not endorse them. Furthermore, small parties sometimes hold the balance of power and can dictate to larger parties.

Electoral reform in the UK – the Jenkins Report

The incoming Labour government commissioned a report on electoral reform in November 1997 (the Jenkins Report). The committee, chaired by the late Lord Roy Jenkins, reported in October 1998. It recommended the abolition of the first past the post system while preserving the fundamental elements of the British electoral system, particularly the constituency link.

The favoured system to replace FPTP would be the alternative vote, with top-up members (called Alternative Vote Top-Up) to ensure the number of each party's MPs more accurately reflects the votes cast. The system would work as follows:

- Constituency boundaries would be completely redrawn, reducing the existing 659 constituencies to between 530 and 560.
- Every voter gets two votes, one of which goes to a constituency candidate. The other goes to a top-up MP. Electors would number constituency candidates in order of preference.
- Any candidate getting 50 per cent of the vote would automatically be elected. If no one reached the halfway mark, the least popular candidate would be eliminated and their supporters' second preference votes would then be taken into account. This means, for example, that a Conservative candidate in second place to Labour after the initial count could win the seat, once Liberal democrat second preferences are redistributed. (Note how this differs from the 'plurality' principle in the FPTP system.)
- The remaining 15–20 per cent of MPs would be top-up MPs, chosen on a city-wide or county basis. Parties that do not poll so strongly in the first constituency ballot will be helped by the top-up system.

The new system ensures that the proportion of votes cast for parties is more accurately reflected in the final result at Westminster. The report received a generally positive, if not enthusiastic reception. The prime minister Tony Blair declared that 'it makes a well-argued and powerful case for the system it recommends' (*The Guardian*, 30 October 1998).

9.2.2   Political parties

Political parties exist in the majority of countries and in most political systems. They are a feature of mass politics, originating in the nineteenth century with the establishment of representative government and the extension of the franchise. The Conservative and Liberal parties started out as legislative factions in Parliament, and went on to develop a party machinery with constituency branches to appeal to a growing electorate. In contrast, the Labour Party has its origins outside government, beginning as a coalition of socialist groups and trades unions and developing into a parliamentary party to shape public policy.

A political party is a group of people that is organized for the purpose of winning power, by electoral or other means. Four characteristics distinguish them from other groups:

- Parties seek to exercise governmental power by winning political office.
- Parties are organized bodies with formal, 'card-carrying' members.
- Parties typically adopt a broad issue focus, addressing each of the main areas of government policy. Small parties, however, may have a single-issue focus which makes them more like interest groups. An example would be the late Sir James Goldsmith's Referendum Party, which campaigned solely on the issue of Europe at the 1997 General Election.
- To a greater or lesser extent, common political preferences and an ideological identity unite parties.

Broadly speaking, political parties can be distinguished on the basis of their ideological orientation. Parties seen as 'left-wing' are characterized by a commitment to change in the form of social reform or complete economic transformation. They draw their support from the poor and disadvantaged, or in urban societies, from the working classes. 'Right-wing' parties usually uphold the existing social order and their supporters include business interests and the economically secure middle classes. However, as Heywood[2] observes: '. . . this notion of a left–right party divide is at best simplistic and at worst deeply misleading . . . electoral competition has the effect of blurring ideological identities, once-cherished principles commonly being discarded in the search for votes. [Furthermore] the shift away from old class polarities and the emergence of issues such as the environment, animal rights and feminism has perhaps rendered the old ideas of left and right redundant'. (Social class is discussed in Chapter 11.)

Most modern parties therefore dilute their ideological identity to appeal to the greatest number of voters. This has certainly been true of the UK Labour Party, which began life as a socialist movement but has gradually transformed itself into a centrist party.

Political parties have a number of functions:

- **Representation.** This concept was discussed in Section 9.2.1 and in this context refers to the ability of parties to respond to and voice the views of the electorate.
- **Providing political leaders.** Political parties provide a training ground for politicians. In the UK, cabinet and other ministerial posts are usually filled by senior party figures.
- **Goal formulation.** Parties are vehicles for setting the collective goals of society. They formulate programmes of government and initiate policy.
- **Articulating interests.** Parties help to articulate the various interests in society. They draw these competing interests together in a coherent whole.
- **Political socialization.** Parties encourage groups to play by the rules of the political game. For example, the emergence of the Labour Party in the early twentieth century was an important way of integrating working-class interests into the political process.
- **The organization of government.** Parties help with the formation of governments and provide them with an element of stability, especially if members are drawn from a single party as in the UK.

The two-party system

The UK has a two-party system that is, the two 'major' parties have a roughly equal prospect of winning government power. Such systems have the following features:

- Only two parties have sufficient electoral support and legislative strength to have a prospect of gaining political power (this does not preclude the existence of other minor parties).
- The larger party can rule alone, while the other provides an opposition.
- Power alternates between these parties.

The UK is often held up as the model of a two-party system (the other main example is the USA). However, although power alternated between the Labour and Conservative Parties four times between 1945 and 1970, the latter part of the twentieth century was characterized by sixteen years of uninterrupted Conservative rule (1979–97).

The main advantages of a two-party system are that it that delivers strong and stable government; furthermore, the two parties are able to offer the electorate a clear choice between policies and alternative governments. It also promotes moderation, as the two parties have to battle for the 'floating votes' of the centre ground.

However, the early 1980s in the UK saw the system take on an adversarial quality as the Conservative Party pursued Thatcherite policies and the Labour Party lurched to the left. It has also been argued that a choice between just two systems of government is inadequate in the individualistic and diverse society, which has developed at the beginning of the twenty-first century.

Are parties in decline?

Some commentators have spoken of a 'crisis of party politics', evidenced in the UK by the decline in party membership (the Labour Party lost approximately two-thirds of its members between 1950 and the mid-1990s, while the Conservatives lost a half).

This decline has been attributed to the fact that modern societies are increasingly difficult to govern. There is disillusionment with parties failing to deliver on their election promises once in power, combined with a cynicism arising from the perception of politicians representing them as corrupt and self-serving. The growing power of interests groups and the demands of a globalized economy have confronted governments with major difficulties. As class loyalties have subsided with the changing occupational structure of society, new priorities have emerged in the form of environmentalism, gender politics, gay rights and animal rights. These social movements, and the interest groups which represent them, may be replacing parties in providing the link between the government and the governed.

9.3   Interest groups

An interest group (or pressure group) is an organized association, with shared interests or common concerns, which aims to influence the policies or action of government. Interest groups differ from political parties in that they seek to exert influence from outside government, rather than to form a government. They are usually concerned with a specific cause or the interests of a particular group and are distinguished from broader social movements by their greater degree of formal organization. The two most common classifications of interest groups are sectional and promotional groups.

Sectional groups

Sectional groups exist to advance or protect the (usually economic) interests of their members. They have existed for many years, in one form or another. Norton[3] observes that the growth of government activity after the Second World War resulted in the development of a large body of well-organized sectional groups to ensure that their members could influence the distribution of public spending. Government, on the other hand, benefited from the advice and information gained from these groups, and from their cooperation.

The principal examples are trades unions, business corporations and professional bodies. Their 'sectional' nature reflects the fact that they represent a section of society: employees, businesses, consumers, and so on.

Business

Business is, of course, profoundly affected by government economic policies and its representatives naturally wish to exert influence. Many firms depend on government subsidies and contracts; others will be interested in broader issues of economic policy such as interest and exchange rates.

Large organizations can act as 'pressure groups' in their own right. Multinational corporations can and often do influence the economic policies of countries. For example, BMW threatened to relocate its Rover subsidiary to Hungary unless the UK government agreed to contribute to the development of new production facilities. Particular industries often form federations like the Society of Motor Manufacturers or the Engineering Employers' Federation to present a united front for the industry. The Confederation of British Industry (CBI) was formed in 1965 and provides a 'peak' organization to represent the views of its members to the government and provide a forum for discussion (it holds an annual conference). The CBI has around 15 000 members and is dominated by big companies. The CBI famously confronted the Conservative government in the early 1980s over its interest rate policy and campaigned against the European Social Charter (see Chapter 10). More recently, however, it has been keen to open a dialogue with the TUC.

The Institute of Directors is a more right-wing and political campaigning body. It vigorously supported the free market policies of the Conservative government between 1979 and 1997. Other organizations such as Aims of Industry are used to raise support and, indirectly, revenue for the Conservative Party.

See the website for a further discussion of the various groups representing UK businesses.

Trades unions

Traditionally, trades unions have had two distinct roles: to fund the Labour Party and help formulate its policies; and to represent the interests of their members on pay and working conditions negotiations with employers. Some three quarters of unions are affiliated to the Trades Union Congress (TUC), which speaks for the trades union movement as a whole.

The 1970s probably saw the height of trade union power: they successfully opposed the 1971 Industrial Relations Act, which sought to control union activities such as unofficial strikes, and played a key role in bringing down Edward Heath's Conservative government in 1974. Under Mrs Thatcher, however, the economic and political influence of trade unions declined. There were a number of reasons for this: membership fell (see passages below); industrial action was defeated, notably the print workers at Wapping and the miners' strike of 1984–5; legislation hostile to trade unions was effective; the government refused to consult with the trade unions; and the trade union movement was itself divided over issues such as single-union agreements.

Trade union membership

When Mrs Thatcher came to power in 1979, 53 per cent of workers belonged to trade unions. By 1993 the proportion was 38 per cent, and in 1999 it stood at 30 per cent. This fall has been a consequence of the decline in manufacturing employment and an expansion in employment of part-timers and women, two groups that are weakly organized. However, trade union membership rose in 1998 for the first time in nineteen years, according to the 1999 Labour Force Survey (LFS). Also, union membership among women had risen by 60 000 since the 1997 LFS.

The TUC general secretary, John Monks, said the figures showed that the unions' recruitment efforts were starting to pay off. There is also an expectation that legislation, which creates the legal right to union recognition where more than half the workplace wants it, will help create the conditions for union growth. In 1979, over two-thirds of the workforce were employed in organizations where trade unions were recognized, whereas in 1999 the figure was 44 per cent.

Reported in *The Guardian*, 7 May 1999

Promotional groups

Sometimes called cause or attitude groups, promotional groups are set up to advance shared values or principles. They have no exclusive membership – anyone who is sympathetic to their cause is free to join them. Their causes are many and varied, including pro- and anti-abortion, smoking, censorship, and so on.

The arguments for interest groups centre on the view that they strengthen representation by voicing interests that are ignored by the political parties. Against this, it is argued that they are divisive in that they advance minority interests against those of society as a whole.

How do interest groups exert influence?

The methods that groups use vary according to the issue with which the group is concerned, how policy in that area is shaped and the resources at its disposal. These resources include:

- Public sympathy for the group and its goals
- The size of its membership base
- Its financial strength
- Its organizational capabilities
- Its ability to use sanctions which impact on government
- Personal or institutional links it may have to political parties or government bodies.

For example, business groups are more likely to mount expensive public relations campaigns or use professional lobbyists than trades unions, simply because they can afford to do so. The main points of access are:

- The civil service
- Parliament
- The mass media
- The European Union.

Interest group activity tends to centre on government officials as the civil service is seen as the focus of policy formulation. Access via this channel is limited to the major sectional groups such as employers' associations, trades unions, farming interests and the key professions (particularly law and medicine). The consultative process is informal, taking place through meetings and regular contacts that tend not to be publicized. Business groups tend to have ready access to government officials:

The crucial relationship here is usually between senior bureaucrats and leading business or industrial interests. The advantage that business groups enjoy in this respect include the role they play in the economy as producers, investors and employers, the overlap in social background and political outlets between business leaders and ministers and senior officials, and the widely-held belief that business interests coincide with the national interest ('what is good for General Motors is good for America'). The relationship is often consolidated by a 'revolving door' through which bureaucrats, on retirement, move to well-paid jobs in private business.[2]

Influence exerted through parliament is often called lobbying. The US Congress is subject to intense and extensive lobbying, whereas lobbying activities are less important in the UK, where party discipline is strong and Parliament is subject to executive control (see the next section). A lobbyist is a person hired to represent the arguments of interest group clients. Professional lobbying has been criticized as effectively 'buying political influence'. A lobbying industry developed in the UK in the 1980s, when there was a trebling of the amount of money spent on professional lobbying.

Interest group pressure is also exerted through political parties, the main method of influencing parties being through donations to fund campaigns. The Conservative Party is funded by business contributions and, as we have already mentioned, trades unions are closely tied to the Labour Party. However, their influence has diminished as the Labour Party has tried to shed the image of being 'controlled' by the unions.

Very different methods are used to influence the government indirectly, through the mass media and public opinion campaigns. Here methods could include petitions, protests, demonstrations, civil disobedience and violence. Some of these tactics may reflect the group's outsider status and its inability to obtain access to government decision makers. A new form of activist politics emerged in the last thirty years of the twentieth century, with groups such as Friends of the Earth attracting media attention, and thereby public support, for various causes.

Sectional interest groups have also come to terms with the fact that ranges of policy decisions are now made at a European level. This is particularly true of agriculture, trade, competition and workers' rights. Business groups operating at an EU level exert influence in various ways: through direct lobbying by large corporations and trade bodies; and through a range of associations such as the European Round Table of Industrialists and the Union of Industrial and Employers' Confederations of Europe (UNICE). To some extent, the TUC has compensated for its marginalization by the UK government by conducting its campaign for workers' rights through the EU.

Exercise

In what ways can business organizations influence the political process?

Feedback

You probably identified some of the following methods:

- Donations to party funds. There is no doubt that some organizations and individuals contribute to political party funds in the expectation that their respective causes will be looked upon favourably in the future. This is a controversial area and there have been several cases where governments have been accused of allowing political donations to influence policy.
- Through employers' bodies such as the various employers' federations, the CBI and at a local level, chambers of commerce.
- Through the mass media. Large organizations tend to have their own public relations machinery and will sometimes use the media to influence government policy. Local traders' associations can do a similar thing: an example might be persuading a local paper to report an unpopular decision by the local authority, such as placing parking restrictions in a busy shopping area.
- Direct campaigning. Organizations will sometimes conduct their own campaigns, as some DIY stores did in the case of Sunday trading when they asked customers to sign a petition in favour of the measure.
- Appointing former ministers or retired senior civil servants to the board of a company.
- Large companies who are vital to the success of 'UK plc' will often have direct access to government decision makers.
- Through professional bodies such as the Law Society, the British Medical Association and the Chartered Institute of Personnel and Development.

9.4   The machinery of government

Government can be divided into three distinct branches:

- **Legislatures** make law; they enact legislation
- **Executives** implement law; they execute the law
- **Judiciaries** interpret law; they adjudicate on the meaning of law.

This division of government institutions, known as the *separation of powers*, is the traditional basis on which to analyse government. The principle is that each of the three functions of government (legislation, execution and adjudication) should be entrusted to a separate branch of the government in order to fragment government power and defend liberty.

9.4.1   Parliament

Parliament is the legislative arm of government. Most liberal democracies have adopted some form of parliamentary government, often based on the model of the UK Parliament. Often depicted as the 'mother of parliaments', the Westminster Parliament dates back to the thirteenth century. The central feature of a parliamentary system of government is the fusion of legislative and executive power: the government is drawn from and accountable to Parliament. Contrast this arrangement with the American system, where the executive (the president) and the legislature (Congress) are separate institutions. What this means is that the president is not a member of and is therefore not drawn from Congress, whereas the prime minister is a Member of Parliament.

The strength of a parliamentary system, according to constitutional theory, is that it results in effective but responsible government (a government that is answerable to an elected assembly and therefore to the people). While a parliamentary system violates the principle of the separation of powers, government is effective because the ruling party from which it is formed holds a majority of seats in the assembly; it can therefore ensure that the legislative programme is passed. However, responsible government is maintained because the government can only govern as long as it retains the confidence of parliament. Parliament has ultimate power because it can always remove the government.

However, the political reality is rather different. Parliamentary government is often associated with the problem of executive domination, as is the case in the UK: a combination of strict party discipline and an electoral system which is not based on proportional representation normally allows the government to control parliament through a reliable majority in the House of Commons. Many would argue that Parliament is little more than a 'talking shop' and its members 'lobby fodder'.

Functions of Parliament

The main functions of Parliament are:

- **Legislation.** Parliament is vested with legislative power to ensure that the laws it makes are seen to be binding. This is because legislation is openly debated and the impression is given that the people make the laws themselves. As already mentioned, this is a misleading picture. With the exception of private member's bills, legislative programmes originate with the executive.
- **Representation.** As discussed earlier, Parliament plays an important representative role in providing the link between the government and the people.

● **Scrutiny and oversight.** While the legislative and executive roles of assemblies have diminished, the emphasis has shifted to the ability of assemblies to constrain and check executive power. Parliament subjects ministers to written and oral questioning. Question Time, for example, allows the prime minister to be cross-examined twice a week, and subjects other ministers to scrutiny about once a fortnight.
● **Recruitment and training.** Parliament provides a pool of talent from which future ministers can emerge.
● **Legitimacy.** Parliament promotes the legitimacy of the government by encouraging the public to see them as 'rightful'.

The structure of Parliament

Parliament is a **bicameral**, or two-chamber, legislature. The House of Lords (the upper house) is constitutionally and politically subordinate to the House of Commons (the lower house). This is because the government is responsible to and largely drawn from, the lower house. The House of Lords has powers to delay non-financial legislation for a year, although it can veto the sacking of judges. The majority of the members of the Lords are still hereditary peers, although the Labour government is pledged to reform the upper house by altering the balance between hereditary and life peers. The main function of the second chamber is to check the power of the Commons and the government.

Committees are an increasingly common part of government. There are two types of committee: standing committees, which carry out detailed consideration of legislative matters; and select committees, which scrutinize government administration and oversee the exercise of executive power.

9.4.2   The legislative process

Legislation is subject to a clearly defined procedure once it has been submitted for parliamentary approval (see Table 9.1). The first reading represents the formal introduction of the bill, which is not debated at this stage and does not even exist as a printed document. Once the bill is formally introduced, it is printed and set down for a second reading when the principle of the bill is debated and approved. It is then referred to a standing committee for consideration of its specific provisions. Each committee has a membership of between

Table 9.1 Legislative stages in Parliament

Stage	Where taken
First reading	On the floor of the house (formal introduction – no debate)
Second reading	On the floor of the house (debate on the principle)
Committee	In standing committee (considered clause by clause; amendments may be made)
Report	On the floor of the house (bill reported back to house – amendments may be made)
Third reading	On the floor of the house (final approval – no amendments possible)
Lords	On the floor of the house (consideration of the amendments made by the other house)

Source: adapted from Norton.[4]

16 and 50 members (usually about 18 members) and they meet to discuss bills clause by clause. Standing committees are not able to make amendments that run counter to the principle approved by the house.

Once the standing committee has completed its deliberations, the bill is then returned to the house for the report stage, during which further amendments may be made. At the third reading, the house gives its final approval to the measure; no amendments can be made at this stage. Once the house has approved the third reading, the bill is then sent to the House of Lords. If the Lords make any amendments, these are sent to the Commons. If the house disagrees with these amendments, it will inform the House of Lords which will not usually press its amendment. Once the bill has passed both houses, it receives Royal assent and is passed into law. It should be noted that there are also limited opportunities for private members to introduce bills of their own.

9.4.3   The executive

In constitutional theory, the executive is the branch of government responsible for implementing the laws and policies made by the legislature. It extends from the head of government to the police and the military, and includes ministers and civil servants. However, the term is now used in a narrower sense to describe 'the government of the day', that small group of decision makers who take responsibility for government policy. These can be distinguished from the civil service, which is the bureaucratic, as opposed to the political, executive.

The **political executive** comprises elected politicians drawn from Parliament. Their job is to make policy, according to their party's political priorities, and oversee its implementation. The **bureaucratic executive** comprises appointed and professional civil servants who offer advice and administer policy. In reality, this distinction is blurred because senior civil servants make a major contribution to policy making – as viewers of the television series *Yes, Minister/Prime Minister* will know – and because much use is now made of political advisers.

The executive has a hierarchical structure, with the monarch as the head of state and the prime minister as the chief executive. The monarch, although a symbolic figure without real political power, is the personal embodiment of the state's power and authority. In the USA, the president is both the chief executive and the head of state. Beneath the chief executive is a range of ministers or secretaries who have responsibility for developing and implementing policy in specific areas. There is a pecking order among ministers, which is a reflection of the importance of their policy areas and departments (with the Treasury and the Foreign Office being the most prestigious), or by their entitlement to sit in the cabinet. At a lower level are the bureaucrats and administrators, and below this are the police and armed forces.

The prime minister

The prime minister's power, as head of government, is derived from his or her leadership of the majority party in Parliament. The most important formal power possessed by the prime minister is the power of patronage – the ability to hire and fire, and promote and demote, ministers. The support of the cabinet is very important to the prime minister, who is designated *primus inter pares* (first among equals). This means that he or she has to operate through a system of collective cabinet government. The power of prime ministers is therefore dependent upon the degree to which, through patronage and cabinet management, they can ensure that the cabinet serves *under* them. There is agreement that prime-ministerial power has grown in recent years. This results from the tendency of the media to focus on personalities, resulting in prime ministers coming almost to personify their parties. Margaret Thatcher and Tony Blair are examples of strong, charismatic leaders who have brought a 'presidential' quality to the office of prime minister. However, unlike John Major, they both enjoy(ed) large parliamentary majorities.

The cabinet

The cabinet is the principal link between the legislative and the executive branches of government. Its members are drawn from Parliament, but also serve as the political heads of the various government departments. In constitutional theory, policy-making responsibility is shared within the cabinet, with the prime minister being the 'first' in name only. The system is usually underpinned by collective responsibility – the cabinet ministers are required to 'sing to the same hymn sheet' and support official government policy. The political reality, however, is that the growth of prime-ministerial power has undermined the collective nature of cabinet government. Furthermore, most decisions are made elsewhere, in the government departments and cabinet committees.

However, prime ministers have paid the price for ignoring the cabinet: Margaret Thatcher's resignation in 1990 was to a significant extent a result of her losing the support of her cabinet colleagues.

9.4.4 Local government

Many public services, such as housing, education and public health, are delivered at a local level, by elected authorities. Local government is government that is specific to a particular locality, for example a village, district, town, city or county. It is entirely subordinate to central government, which can reform and restructure it at will. However, this does not mean that it is politically irrelevant; indeed, it is administratively necessary and the fact that they are elected means that local politicians have a degree of democratic legitimacy.

Traditionally the UK possessed a relatively decentralized system of local government, with local authorities exercising significant discretion within a legal framework laid down by Parliament. The expansion of the state's economic and social role after 1945 ushered in a partnership approach, where local authorities were increasingly given responsibility for delivering services on behalf of central government. This approach was abandoned by the Conservative governments of the 1980s and 1990s, which saw local government as an obstacle to implementing their radical free-market policies.

The most decisive step in ending the central–local partnership was the introduction in 1984 of 'rate capping', which took away local government's most important power: the ability to set local tax levels and thereby determine its own spending policies. Local authorities that challenged central government, such as the Greater London Council and the metropolitan county councils, were abolished. The responsibilities of local government were also restricted through measures such as the introduction of a national curriculum for schools and legislation that permitted schools to opt out from local authority control. The aim of these policies was to remodel local government by creating 'enabling' councils whose role is to supervise the delivery of services by private bodies through a system of contracting out and privatization, rather providing the services themselves. Alongside these developments, local authorities have been subjected to intensified pressure from the local community in their new roles as 'customers' and 'clients'.

The Labour government's agenda for local government includes reversing several of these initiatives. New policies and their implications for local government are as follows:

● Devolution to Scotland and Wales (discussed below) and the decentralization of power to the English regions (including the creation of a London-wide strategic body, the Greater London Authority, under an elected mayor) have created new focal points of subnational government.

- The opportunity to reduce the extent of unaccountable governing bodies (popularly known as quasi-autonomous non-governmental organizations ('quangos')) by transferring them to control by elected local or regional authorities. In recent years, these ministerially appointed bodies have become responsible for more public expenditure than local authorities without being required effectively to account for it in any elected body.
- The relaxation of the local tax-capping regime, while central government retains the ultimate power to restrain the spending of local authorities.
- The ending of compulsory competitive tendering (the requirement to put out certain services to private tender). The way local services are provided should be a matter for local decisions, not something to be determined by the national government. Local authorities retain a discretion to put out services to competitive tender, but should not be compelled to do so, thus making this once more a matter for local choice.

9.4.5   Devolution

In referenda held in September 1997, Scotland voted convincingly for a devolved Scottish Parliament and Wales narrowly supported the establishment of a Welsh Assembly. Further devolution to the English regions is also on the political horizon. The combined impact of these events will involve the redrawing of the British constitution through the establishment of new political institutions and practices. Specifically, devolution will bring about the following political changes:

- A movement away from the first past the post (FPTP) electoral system. The 129-member Scottish Parliament has 73 members elected by FPTP and 56 additional members elected using proportional representation. There is a similar pattern for the Welsh Assembly.
- The likelihood of coalitions and power sharing, particularly in the Scottish Parliament. This represents a break with two-party politics and one-party government.

The Scottish Parliament has responsibility for education, health, housing, local government, law and order and the judicial system, agriculture, fishing, the environment, sports and the arts. Westminster, however, retains responsibility for foreign policy and defence, national security, employment law, economic policy and social security.

The Scottish Parliament also has limited powers of taxation and substantial powers to determine its own priorities and frame legislation that may be substantially different from Westminster. For example, the Scottish Parliament has abolished university tuition fees. This sort of tension suggests that relations between Edinburgh and London are bound to be tested.

9.4.6   Citizenship

The notion of 'citizenship' is bound up with the so-called 'third way' in politics and the idea of a 'stakeholder society', both closely associated with New Labour (although the term 'stakeholding' was rarely heard once the party was in power). Here we examine its relevance for policy making.

A citizen is a member of a state, endowed with a set of rights and obligations. The idea of 'citizenship' is that individuals are able to participate in the life of their communities to the extent that they possess entitlements and responsibilities. Marshall[5] argued that citizens have civil rights (such as freedom of speech and freedom of assembly) and political rights (such as the right to vote); but they also have social rights, which guarantee them a minimum social status, and thereby a 'stake' in society. These social rights are controversial in that they imply a degree of redistribution which free-market liberals regard as economically damaging: it is argued that the provision of welfare tends to lead to a 'dependency culture' and undermines incentives to work and invest.

Etzioni,[6] whose views influenced the Clinton administration in the USA as well as the UK Labour Party, argued that social fragmentation and breakdown has largely been a result of individuals' obsession with rights and their refusal to acknowledge reciprocal responsibilities. Therefore, citizens must be made to recognize that they do have social and moral responsibilities, as well as rights. In policy terms, this is reflected in the UK in measures designed to ensure that individuals honour their parenting responsibilities, and active labour market policies such as 'welfare to work' and the 'New Deal' to tackle long-term unemployment.

In brief

We began this chapter by considering the nature of politics and the concept of democracy. It was noted that, with the demise of socialism and the rise of globalization, democracy has emerged as an enduring political principle. A discussion of the UK electoral system and the case for its reform was followed by a critique of the political party system. An examination of interest groups focused on the ways in which business and employee groups can influence the political process. We then moved on to consider the machinery of government, highlighting constitutional reforms such as devolution. We concluded with an evaluation of the concept of citizenship and its relation to the policies and beliefs of New Labour.

Examination questions for this chapter are given in Appendix 2.

References

1 Crick, B. (1993) *In Defence of Politics*. Penguin.
2 Heywood, A. (1997) *Politics*. Macmillan.
3 Norton, P. (1994) *The British Polity* (3rd edn). Longman.
4 Norton, P. (1993) *Does Parliament Matter?* Harvester Wheatsheaf.
5 Marshall, T. H. (1950) Citizenship and social class. In *Sociology at the Crossroads* (ed. Marshall, T.). Heinemann.
6 Etzioni, A (1995) *The Spirit of Community: Rights, Responsibilities and the Communitarian Agenda*. Fontana.

Further reading

Jones, B. (2001) *Politics UK* (4th edn). Harvester Wheatsheaf.
Webb, P. (2000) *The Modern British Party System*. Sage.

Web-site addresses

UK Parliament: http://www.parliament.uk
CBI: http://www.cbi.org.uk
TUC: http://www.tuc.org.uk

10 The European context of management

Chapter objectives

In this chapter you will:

- Review the origins and development of the European Union (EU)
- Examine the economic, political and social dimensions of European integration
- Consider the costs and benefits of monetary union
- Obtain an overview of the framework of EU political institutions.

Chapter introduction

Alongside the 'war against terror,' Europe is arguably the major issue facing the UK at the beginning of the century. The controversy over European integration shows no signs of abating and there can be no doubt that European union has had, and will continue to have, far-reaching implications for UK organizations.

We begin this chapter with an overview of the origins of Britain's membership of the European Union. This is followed by an examination of the various dimensions of European integration and their significance for business and management. We then proceed to consider the institutional framework of EU decision making.

The following case study highlights some of the problems organizations face in employing people from other EU member states. Note that some of the economic concepts discussed in this piece are examined in Chapter 8.

Case study

Managers on the move

Senior management have to be able to work and manage teams across European borders if they are to succeed in an open market, writes Leah Larkin.

Long gone are the days when you went to college, came home, got a job at a local company and worked there until retirement. Now you are likely to work for several companies, in different cities, different countries, and on different continents.

Mobility is the name of the game. 'It's very important with the development of the European market,' notes Patrice André, vice-president of HR at UPS Europe. 'We see the European market quickly developing into a single market. We need to develop senior management that has the ability to work and manage teams and be successful across European borders.'

A British citizen is in charge of the engineering and technical aspects of UPS's operation in France, a German manages the company's Spanish unit, and the company's country manager in Italy has German and US citizenship. The ball really got rolling within Europe when borders started to come down in the early 1990s, says Maury Peiperl, a professor at the London Business School (LBS), who studies the career paths of European executives. Researchers at LBS did a study of more than 200 chief executives in 15 countries. They found that international experience among the group was substantial, with the average CEO, who speaks 2.8 languages, having worked in four countries, half of these outside of Europe.

Peiperl spoke of a European zeitgeist 'of actually needing to spend time in a foreign country as part of one's development as a human being'. Individuals want to be global citizens who can successfully move in different cultures and spheres, he said, 'as if that is something that is essential to function in our age'.

It seems essential if one wants to move up the corporate ladder. 'People who have international experience make more effective managers. They have a better feeling for the organisation,' says Elaine Hughes, head of international assignment services for UBS, a financial services company . . .

In addition to the difficulties posed by a lack of language skills and keeping the family content, there are other significant barriers to global mobility. Diploma recognition is one. Firms in the UK, for example, may find it difficult to evaluate the skills and credentials of a candidate from another European country, and vice versa. Although the EU has pledged to create more flexible labour markets within Europe, progress has been slow. Numerous obstacles still exist, including differential tax burdens, a lack of pension portability, differences in social security systems, differences in employment law and inconsistent immigration policies.

UPS's André sees the development of a common pension system among European countries as the major challenge of the future. 'We need a pension that will work across borders. We are still relying on country-specific pension systems,' he says.

The EU has developed a 'European CV' to help mobility:

The European CV

What is it?

A two-page standardized format for the presentation of information. The EU CV can be downloaded from Cedefop's website www.cedefop.eu.int/transparency/CV.asp

What is included:

A work experience, education and training section, and a language section. Also sections on social, organizational, technical and artistic skills and competencies.

The CV is to be used voluntarily – so how useful is it?

globalhr put the CV to two HR professionals: Marco Campiglia, director of HR at BMW, and Roberto Ferrata, head of HR at Kellogg. Both liked it, although neither gave a firm commitment to use it. No businesses were involved in the drawing up of the CV – although a spokesman from the EU assures globalhr that businesses had been consulted. It still leaves room for cultural misunderstanding. For example, in Italy, students may study law at university because it is a qualification prized by businesses, not necessarily because they wish to become lawyers. But a business seeing a law degree on a CV might see it as a sign of failure and ask: What stopped you from becoming a lawyer?

Kellogg's Ferrata says that effectively Microsoft has done the job before the EU. The most common CV he receives is in a standard Microsoft format. This format has the potential to become a world-standard, not just an EU-standard CV.

What is left out?

The form is politically correct, with no mention of marital status, disability or ethnic origin. There is also no section for free time.

The Certificate Supplement: can be downloaded from Cedefop's European Training Village's website at www.trainingvillage.gr/etv/transparency/index.asp. To be used with the CV, explaining qualifications in detail. This should make it easier to compare non-formal qualifications.

What remains to be done?

Language is still a major barrier. HR is hindered by bureaucracy when taking on workers from other European countries. There are major issues on the transferability of pensions and social security contributions, which mean that without careful management, workers may miss out. Campiglia says the complicated administration is a dissuasive factor in taking on European workers. Ferrata says that workers coming from other countries still have to offer something extra.

Why the European CV will be an effective recruitment tool

If a graduate with a three-year degree from the UK applies for a job in Italy, the chances are that degree will not be recognized because it is too short. On the other hand, a UK employer probably will not recognize that a first degree in Italy, which may take six or seven years to complete, is the equivalent of a UK Masters. Clearly, a classic lose–lose situation.

A promise to workers from the European Union is the possibility of movement in the member states, and a key promise to business is the prospect of the free movement of capital and resources. Europe already has a single currency and most Europeans believe in an eventual convergence in taxes and welfare – whatever the politicians may say. Laws have been enacted to protect the European workforce from discrimination.

But in practice, the enormous variance between education systems and professional qualifications throughout states is a major hindrance to workforce mobility in the EU. How can HR departments compare the worth of a degree from another country, and the value of professional qualifications? It is difficult choosing the right person for the job if you don't know what their diploma or degree means. To understand all the ins and outs, European-based multinationals need an exhaustive knowledge of European training and educational systems.

'The European policy of mutual recognition of qualifications was not a great success in the 1980s,' says Philippe Tissot, who is in charge of co-ordinating transparency at Cedefop, the EU's centre for professional training and development. 'Much time was spent but we only got recognition on some diplomas in the medical sectors and nursing. We needed a way of explaining differences in a clear manner.'

The more the CV is used, Brussels thinks, the more transparent job applications will become. Tissot says the Union is encouraging individuals to use the CV, both in their mother tongue and in other languages if applying abroad. But it is also going to be up to big companies. If they start asking for the European CV it will soon become the standard model. 'While European citizens are, in theory, entitled to undertake training and to work anywhere in the Union, there are still a large number of obstacles. The CV, which presents skills and experience clearly and comparably, is a step in the right direction,' says Viviane Reding, member of the European Commission responsible for education and culture.

Personnel Today, 1st July 2002

Question	What are the main obstacles faced by organizations when employing people from other EU member states?

Feedback	There are still significant barriers to labour mobility in the EU, arguably the greatest of which is qualifications. Recognition of other states' qualifications tends to be on an *ad hoc*, bilateral (i.e. between two member states) basis and is easier in technical subjects like engineering than in culturally shaped professions like the law. Another major difficulty is, of course, language but there are also other serious obstacles in the form of differential tax, pension and social security arrangements. In addition, there are differences in employment law across the Community and HR departments need to be aware of measures such as the Posting of Workers Directive, which forces employers to respect local agreed collective agreements. Clearly, the European CV is an attempt to help organizations (and potential employees) come to terms with the complexities of employing staff from other member states.

10.1   The European Union

What we now know as the European Union has its origins in the end of the Second World War in 1945. The twentieth century had already seen two catastrophic global conflicts originating in Europe, and the post-war governments of the founder states were committed to take action to ensure that war would never again break out in Western Europe. They realized that the only way of securing peace, security and prosperity was by uniting many of the countries of that region. Furthermore, they felt that by acting together, these countries could be an effective political and economic force in a world dominated by the USA and the USSR.

The first substantive moves towards European union came with the signing of the Treaty of Paris in 1951, the aim of which was to ensure that the economic reconstruction of the signatory states (France, Germany, Italy, Belgium, Holland and Luxembourg) could proceed in harmony. France and Germany produced a plan for a coal and steel 'pool', which was the basis of the European Coal and Steel Community (ECSC).

The European Economic Community (EEC) came into being on 1 January 1958, the original six member countries having signed the Treaty of Rome in 1957. Although the emphasis at this time was on economic unity, the longer-term vision of the founders was a politically united Europe, and it is this aspect of European union which is now so controversial in the UK.

Britain declined involvement with these early bodies. The economic and political arguments for joining did not carry great weight with British politicians for the following reasons: Britain was still seen as a world power and was enjoying a period of prosperity; it had strong trading links with the Commonwealth; it had a 'special relationship' with the USA, and it had stood alone successfully in the Second World War. Furthermore, Britain had not had the experience of German occupation and was politically stable, so the psychological appeal of a united Europe was not as strong as it was on the continental mainland.

However, in the 1960s the attitude of the British government to the EEC underwent a significant change. Britain's economic performance was faltering and compared poorly with the six EEC member states. The Commonwealth was not proving to be the source of trade and materials that had been expected and even the special relationship with the USA had proved not to be as 'special' as the British had thought, with the American administration paying more attention to the EEC.

The British political establishment began to see the EEC as a vehicle through which the UK could once again play a leading role on the world stage. Economically, it would provide a tariff-free market of 180 million people. British companies would be able to take advantage of the consequent economies of scale and industry would become more efficient through more vigorous competition. The political benefits were tied up with the economic advantages: a united and economically strong Europe would be better able to resist the USSR (remember that this was the height of the cold war). In 1972, the Treaty of Accession was signed and the UK, along with Ireland and Denmark, joined the EEC. Greece joined in 1981 and Spain and Portugal in 1986. In 1995, Sweden, Austria and Finland joined.

Another flurry of measures to tighten the bonds of European union came in the period 1985–91. In 1985 the Commission proposed that 1992 should achieve full economic union. This was embodied in the Single European Act (SEA), which came into force in 1987. The SEA was designed to add fresh impetus to the creation of a Single European Market (SEM), a process which had become bogged down in bureaucracy during the 1970s and early 1980s. The prime function of the Act is to provide the legal framework for common economic procedures and regulation and complete freedom of movement of people, goods and money throughout the Community.

Before the terms of the SEA were finally implemented two further sets of agreements were reached at a summit meeting in the Dutch border town of Maastricht. This occurred in 1991 in order to make progress on both European Monetary Union (EMU) and European Political Union (EPU). Following the collapse of communism in Eastern Europe and the reunification of Germany, the governments of the EC member states (especially of France and Germany) thought it essential to accelerate the process of economic and political integration. The UK government was a dissenting voice at the Maastricht summit, disagreeing on a number of issues, notably monetary union. Nevertheless, a number of momentous decisions were made:

- The introduction of a single currency by 1999 at the latest was agreed. The currency would be managed by the European Central Bank. An opt-out clause was devised especially for Britain (technically, the UK was given the right to join the single currency when the economic conditions were 'right', i.e. the prime minister, John Major, did not agree a complete opt-out).
- Closer coordination of members' foreign and defence policies.
- The development of a common security policy (to encourage greater cooperation between the police).
- A common social policy. Note that, in the language of European integration, the term 'social' in the sense of 'social policy' and 'social regulation', refers to employment matters.
- All EU nationals became 'citizens of the Union', granting them freedom to live and work wherever they choose in the EU.

The Maastricht Treaty (officially the Treaty on European Union) was therefore a major step towards full economic, political and social union. However, on the matter of the 'deepening' of the Union (i.e. further integration), the word 'federalism' was dropped (on Britain's insistence) as the community's objective in favour of the phrase 'ever closer union'. Even so, decision making by majority voting was extended to education, public health, the environment and energy.

The Copenhagen summit of 2002 saw the existing member states agreeing to a large-scale expansion of the EU. The following ten countries expected to join by 2004: Estonia; Latvia; Lithuania; Poland; Czech Republic; Slovakia; Hungary; Slovenia; Cyprus and Malta. The accession treaties are due to be ratified in 2003, when nine of the ten states will hold referendums.

The overall effect of this enlargement will be to bring Europe's cold war divisions to an end and close the gap in living standards between the existing and the new member states. However, it also creates a number of problems for the EU, not least of which is how the existing decision-making machinery will cope with the expansion. Also, there are other countries, namely Romania, Bulgaria and Turkey, whose applications to join, originally rejected at Copenhagen, are due to be reconsidered.

10.2   European integration

The process of creating a unified Europe is known as European integration, which essentially means an ever-closer union of member states. There are a number of dimensions to European integration: economic, political and social. We shall be looking at each in turn.

10.2.1   The economic dimension

The remit of the EEC was to harmonize the economic and social regulations of the member states, with a wider objective of laying 'the foundations of an ever closer union amongst the peoples of Europe' (Preamble to the Treaty of Rome). In the first nine years of membership, British exports to EC countries increased by 27 per cent a year compared with a 19 per cent average annual growth in exports with the rest of the world. In 1973, 36 per cent of British exports went to EC countries; twenty years later, it was 57 per cent, with exports to Germany alone equalling the total of exports to the USA and Japan combined. Britain also attracts significant EC inward investment from countries such as South Korea, as well as the USA and Japan.

Britain also receives money from the Union's 'structural funds' – the European Social Fund (ESF), the European Regional Development Fund, and the European Agricultural Guidance and Guarantee Fund. The ESF was established to assist with the training and retraining of workers and between 1983 and 1993, Britain received either the highest or the second-highest allocation from the fund. The Regional Development Fund came into being in 1975 to promote economic activity and the development of the infrastructure of the poorer regions of the Union. The UK receives a substantial part of the fund, particularly for building the infrastructure in the north of England, Scotland, Wales and Northern Ireland.

The Agricultural Fund has caused much controversy in the UK. The guarantee part of the fund supports the Common Agricultural Policy (CAP), which was designed to create a guaranteed food supply for the people of the Community. However, the payment of guaranteed prices to farmers has been extremely costly, inefficient and the cause of much complaint from producers outside the EU.

The EU also administers a number of other funds and programmes, such as one to provide assistance with energy research and development. It also operates the European Investment Bank, which grants loans and guarantees that support the financing of new investment projects concerned with modernization.

The SEA involved a commitment to a barrier-free Europe by the end of 1992, removing the remaining non-tariff barriers to trade (see Chapter 8 for a discussion of non-tariff barriers to trade). Despite clear terms set out in the Treaty of Rome, many of the original barriers remained obstacles to the free movement of people, goods and capital; member states had consistently failed to agree on a common overall approach for the removal of these barriers. Under the terms of the SEA, by 1992 the following barriers were to be removed.

Physical barriers

- **Free movement of people.** All controls for travellers were to be removed by 1992. The complete removal of all controls at the internal frontiers of the Union involving the introduction of the European passport. Individuals also have the right to live and work in any other member states, and vocational qualifications obtained in one member state must be recognized by other member states. This means that engineers, accountants, medical practitioners, teachers and other professionals are able to practise throughout Europe. However, in reality mobility of labour has been difficult to achieve (see opening case study).
- **Free movement of goods.** Cross-border documentation was a real barrier to trade. At one time, as many as 70 different forms were used in the Community. These have now been replaced by a single form called the Single Administrative Document, a development which has rationalized the paperwork involved, saving time and money for companies.

Technical barriers

- **Free movement of goods.** Different product standards and regulations operate from one member state to another. In itself, the development of national standards and regulations has been valuable in guaranteeing that products provide a minimum level of safety for the consumer and that they protect the environment. However, they could be used as a disguised form of national protection against similar goods imported from other states. For many years, the community attempted to remove these barriers by *harmonization* – the adjustment of national regulations to an agreed standard. Harmonization proved difficult and complex and years were spent trying to reach agreement on the technical nature of products. However, the EU has now adopted the principle of *mutual recognition* – which any goods legally manufactured and marketed in one state should be able to be sold in another. Nevertheless, seven years on from the 1992 deadline technical barriers remained, as the following extract illustrates:

Cadbury kept sweet in EU chocolate war

The Observer, 20 June 1999

One of the most ludicrous of European battles is over – with victory for Britain and a seven-nation alliance of chocolate soldiers.

After a quarter-century of hostilities, peace will break out tomorrow when warring members of the European Union sign up to the new 'chocolate directive'.

The deal, to be agreed in Luxembourg by ministers responsible for the internal market, will be good news for Cadbury Schweppes.

Since 1973 several EU countries, led by Belgium and egged on by the Swiss, have objected to Whole Nut, Milk Tray and Cadbury's Creme Eggs being called chocolate.

Brussels joined the chocopurists in trying to outlaw Britain's use of vegetable fat and high milk content instead of cocoa butter, pure and simple. Austria, Denmark, Finland, Ireland, Portugal and Sweden have joined Britain in the dock – forced to resort to an opt-out from a 1973 directive banning cocoa-butter substitutes.

After years of wrangling, however, a sweet compromise has now been reached. Six fats can now be officially added: palm oil, mango kernel, kokum gurgi, sal, shea and ilipe.

Woe betide anyone stooping to coconut oil, though: it can be used only in ice cream choco-coatings.

And as for Cadbury's Dairy Milk – in Europe it now becomes 'family milk chocolate' to keep the Belgians happy.

'It looks as though they'll finally reach agreement on Monday,' one top chocolate source said. 'The bureaucrats are fruit and nuts, but it'll be a very satisfying outcome for Cadbury and other rebels.'

Fiscal barriers

Goods moving from one country to another are documented so that VAT and excise duties can be collected. The Community has always intended to harmonize indirect taxes as they distort competition and create artificial price differences between member states.

Other barriers to free trade

- **State procurement.** Governments (national and local) tend to buy from their own national industries. Public contracts to supply equipment and services to state organizations are now open to tenders across the EU. In view of the fact that member state governments spend on average 20 per cent of the countries' GDP, this represents significant opportunities for companies.
- **Financial barriers.** There were barriers to financial dealing in other member states, such as exchange controls, limited entry to stock markets, licensing of financial dealers, restrictions on the right to sell financial services across EC borders, restrictions on cross-country mergers and takeovers.

The benefits and costs of the SEM

When the SEM was created it was difficult to estimate the costs and benefits. This is because removing barriers merely creates an opportunity – it is impossible to predict how the firms of the various member states would exploit the opportunities of an open market. However, several studies, which have been undertaken since then have identified the following benefits:

- Costs and prices are likely to fall as a result of greater specialization. Member states can specialize further in those goods and services that they produce most efficiently (in terms of comparative advantage – see Chapter 8).
- There has been a savings arising from fewer border delays, lower administrative costs and a reduction in technical regulations.
- Greater economies of scale can be exploited by Europe-wide countries.
- Greater competition which will bring prices down and, in the long run, stimulate greater innovation.

The costs of the SEM are:

- Unemployment resulting from the economic change necessary to achieve the full economies of scale.
- The development of monopoly power with the establishment of giant 'Euro-firms'. This could lead to higher prices and less choice for the consumer.
- Governments are less able to intervene at a microeconomic level.

The main economic advantage of EU membership is in relation to trade. The free flow of goods and services associated with the SEM is providing major benefits: There has been a narrowing of price differentials for manufactured products between member states, especially for cars; the elimination of border controls for goods has reduced costs and shortened delivery times; several national government contracts have been won by firms from other member states; and many of Europe's larger retailers, such as Tesco and Carrefour, are expanding across Europe and looking to take advantage of economies of scale. The financial services sector is also facing greater competition from other member states.

The biggest barrier to the future development of the SEM was the existence of national currencies and the costs of changing money, coupled with the uncertainties associated with currency fluctuations. Some argued that the SEM would never be complete without a single European currency.

European Monetary Union (EMU)

The initials 'EMU' are sometimes used to refer to *Economic* and Monetary Union. It was mentioned earlier that the Maastricht Treaty set in train the move towards full economic and monetary union, laying out a detailed programme to achieve this goal. Economic and monetary union involves the complete economic and financial integration of the EU countries. This entails not only a single market, but also a single currency, a single monetary policy and a single bank.

It was to be achieved in three stages, the first of which required the achievement of certain 'convergence' criteria. Convergence of economies is where countries achieve similar levels of growth, inflation, balance of payments, government borrowing as a percentage of GDP, etc. At the second stage, a European Monetary Institute (EMI – to become the European Central Bank) would be set up, and the third stage would involve complete monetary union and a single currency by 1999 at the latest. There are certain costs and benefits associated with EMU:

The advantages of EMU:

- **The elimination of the costs of converting currencies**
- **Increased competition and efficiency.** More transparency in pricing would put pressure on high-cost firms and countries to reduce their costs and prices.
- **The elimination of exchange rate uncertainty (between members).** Removal of this uncertainty would help to encourage trade between member countries.
- **Increased inward investment.** Countries outside the EU would see the attractions of investing in a single market where there would be no fears about internal currency fluctuations.
- **Low inflation and interest rates.** An independent central bank will give priority to stable prices and 'sound money', resulting in less need to manipulate short-term interest rates to defend the currency and lower long-term interest rates.

The disadvantages of EMU:

- **The surrender of national economic and political sovereignty.** National governments would lose control over a major lever of power, monetary and exchange rate policy. The UK, with higher rates of inflation, would be unable to make its goods competitive with the rest of the Union because it would be unable to devalue or run a deflationary monetary policy. Britain may then become a depressed 'region' of Europe, with rising unemployment.
- **Different economic cycles.** The UK's economic cycle is out of line with those of the majority of the other member states. This could mean that a monetary policy, which is appropriate for the rest of Europe at any one time, may be positively harmful to the UK economy.

Because EMU is such an emotive political issue, it is difficult to conduct an objective assessment of these arguments – the economic and the political are inextricably linked.

EMU was achieved and the Euro came into existence in January 1999, replacing the national currencies of the 12 'Eurozone' countries in January 2002. All in all, monetary union has been problematic. The Euro's first appearance in 1999 was followed by a collapse in its international value and the arrival of notes and coins in 2002 coincided with a sharp reduction in economic growth and rising unemployment (growth in Germany, traditionally seen as the economic locomotive of Europe, slowed sharply in 2002). Furthermore, polls show that many EU citizens remain sceptical about the project fearing that the overall effect has been to cause price inflation.[1] These developments have served to undermine the Euro's reputation.

But what of the UK's position? By 2003 both popular and governmental support for the Euro had fallen and one-time plans for a referendum that year on Britain's membership had been dropped. Moreover, the Treasury's five economic tests that the UK has to pass before the government will consider membership of the single currency had yet to be met. These 'five tests' are as follows:

- **Test one**   Would joining economic and monetary union create better conditions for firms making long-term decisions to invest in the United Kingdom? Pro-Europeans argue that staying out of the Euro will deter foreign companies from investing in the UK. Sceptics claim that investors want well-trained employees and free-markets, not a single currency.
- **Test two**   How would adopting the single currency affect our financial services? Pro-Europeans say that staying out of the Euro will undermine the pre-eminent position of the City of London. Sceptics argue the opposite, claiming that the financial markets value the dollar more than the Euro.
- **Test three**   Are business cycles and economic structures compatible so that member states could live comfortably with Euro interest rates on a permanent basis? Economists say the merging of economic cycles is the key test of Britain's readiness. Sceptics argue that the UK economy follows the US economic cycle, not the European one and that consequently this condition will never be met.
- **Test four**   Is there sufficient flexibility within the Eurozone's economic structures to cope with economic change? For example, the Stability and Growth Pact determines member states' levels of government borrowing. Sceptics argue that this arrangement is not flexible enough to allow them to use deficit financing to counter downturns in economic activity and therefore that joining the Euro will unnecessarily prolong recessions.
- **Test five**   Will joining the Euro help to promote higher growth, stability and a lasting increase in jobs? Pro-Europeans argue that joining will remove the final barrier to trade within the SEM and consequently promote growth. Sceptics counter that since its launch in 2001, the Euro has exacerbated the economic downturn in the Eurozone.

10.2.2   The political dimension

The debate over political integration revolves around the concept of **federation**. The UK is a unitary state in the sense that sovereignty (or the right to self-determination) is concentrated in Parliament and not shared with other centres of power (see Chapter 9). This principle has been weakened by the creation in 1999 of a Scottish Parliament and a Welsh assembly, although the UK parliament still remains the sovereign body.

In a federal system, sovereignty is shared between the central (or federal) parliament and government and those of the constituent states. Examples of federal states are the USA, Germany, Australia and India. Economic, defence and foreign policy are normally determined at the centre while law and order, health care and education are dealt with at a state level. One of the main problems faced by federal countries is the division of power between the centre and the states, and this is the issue that concerns those who are against further integration. In federal states, there is a tendency for the centre to acquire more power as was the case in the USA, which started in 1776 as a loose confederation but gradually became more centralized. The 'Eurosceptics' fear that this will happen in Europe.

Those in favour of a deepening of ties with Europe – the 'Europhiles', 'Euro-enthusiasts' or 'Euro-fanatics', depending on one's viewpoint – envisage the creation of a federal Europe. The term 'United States of Europe' is sometimes used to highlight the similarities such an entity would have with the USA. This might be seen as an inevitable outcome of the Maastricht Treaty and EMU. There are a number of arguments against further political integration:

- Maastricht and EMU are moving Europe inexorably towards a federal Europe. Pro-Europeans would argue that federalism does not necessarily mean centralization. The principle of 'subsidiarity' (that decisions should be made at a national level wherever possible) is enshrined in the Maastricht Treaty.
- With the end of the cold war, the old tensions in Europe have disappeared, making a political union unnecessary. The counter-argument is that American withdrawal from Europe, coupled with instability in Eastern Europe and in the Balkans, makes a political union necessary.
- The deepening of European ties should not be at the expense of widening (i.e. the enlargement of the Union). The opposing stance is that deepening is necessary to create the stability which makes enlargement possible.
- There is a 'democratic deficit' in the EU. This refers to the fact that the democratically elected body has relatively little power in comparison to the Commission.

10.2.3   The social dimension

Articles 117–28 of the Treaty of Rome refer to social policy and call for collaboration between member states on laws relating to employment, health and safety at work and collective bargaining rights, and equal pay for men and women doing the same work. Very little was done in the 1970s and 1980s to harmonize Community social policy, but in 1989 the European Commission produced a Social Charter to address the social dimension of the single market. The aim of the Social Charter was to create a floor of employment rights across the community, thereby ensuring a 'level playing field' where no member state could distort the market by offering different conditions of employment, a practice known as 'social dumping' (see Chapter 8, Section 8.5). However, the Charter was only a recommendation and therefore had no force in law.

The Conservative government of the day found the Social Charter abhorrent, referring to it as 'socialism through the back door'. The feeling was that the measures would add to the costs of UK producers; and that they had not spent the last ten years trying to liberalize the UK labour market, only to have an even greater degree of regulation imposed on it by Europe. However, the Social Charter emerged again in 1991 with the Maastricht Treaty, which included a social chapter designed to commit the community to implementing the details of the Social Charter. The UK government refused to sign this part of the Treaty; the Social Chapter was therefore removed and signed by the other member states as a separate agreement (or 'protocol'). The new Labour government in 1997 eventually signed the Social Chapter, and the UK is now subject to any directives based on that part of the Treaty (see the website for a detailed account of the provisions of the Social Charter).

Since the signing of the Maastricht Treaty, there has been slow progress in putting the principles of the Social Charter into practice. Some of the principles are rather vague (what is 'fair' remuneration?). This is to be expected as wage rates and terms and conditions of employment vary greatly across the EU. However, progress has been made with the following measures:

- The right for EU citizens to live and work in another EU country for the same wages and under the same terms and conditions as workers for that country
- The passing of various categories of equal opportunities legislation
- The working-time directive: a maximum 48-hour working week; a minimum daily rest period of 11 hours; at least one day per week off; four weeks' minimum annual holiday
- The establishment of works councils
- Employment rights for part-time workers
- Requiring employers to inform workers of their conditions of employment
- Enhanced maternity rights
- The right to parental leave.

Exercise

How have the single market and the social dimension of Europe affected people management?

Feedback

Clearly, issues for particular companies will depend on their current or future involvement in Europe. However, all companies will be affected in some way, as follows:

- The opportunities for expansion and the threats posed by greater competition have meant large-scale reorganization for some companies. Mergers and takeovers have greatly increased, resulting in significant job losses. Other countries have changed the location of their manufacturing sites to low-cost regions, or have established a central manufacturing plant to serve the whole of the EU market.
- Employers may recruit throughout the EU area and employees may work in any EU state. Free movement means employers can look further afield to fill their vacancies, resulting in increased competition for staff. Employers wishing to recruit from other member states have had to learn new techniques, e.g. familiarization with other member states' labour markets, assessing qualifications and experience gained in other member states, how to approach induction training to overcome cultural differences (see opening case study).
- The social dimension has had major implications for HR practitioners. The various social policy directives emanating from Europe and being passed into UK law have to be implemented, and their administration is often a complex process (e.g. the maximum 48-hour working week).

10.3   The EU institutions

The EU has five key institutions:

- The European Commission
- The Council of Ministers
- The European Council
- The European Parliament
- The European Court of Justice

The European Commission

The Commission acts as the civil service of the EU. It is headed by nineteen commissioners (two from each of the large states and one from each small one) and a president (Romano Prodi was appointed in 1999). It proposes legislation, ensures that EU treaties are respected and is responsible for policy implementation. It is the 'conscience of the EU' and is supposed to develop ideas that transcend national interests. Since 1995, commissioners appointed have been subject to approval by the European Parliament.

The Council of Ministers

This is the legislature of the EU, and comprises ministers from the fifteen states who are accountable to their own assemblies and governments. The presidency of the Council of Ministers rotates around the member states every six months. Decisions are made by unanimous agreement, and others are reached through qualified majority voting or by a simple majority. Qualified majority voting means that the British government may be overruled but it still has to implement the legislation agreed by the majority. Thus the importance of majority voting is that it is a way in which national sovereignty may be lost.

The European Council

This is the forum in which heads of government, accompanied by foreign ministers and two commissioners, meet to discuss the overall direction of the Union's work. The council usually meets twice a year. It has initiated some of the key EU developments, such as the SEA and the Maastricht Treaty.

The European Parliament

The European Parliament is composed of 626 Members of the European Parliament (MEPs) who are directly elected every five years. The EP has been a scrutinizing assembly rather than a legislature. Its major powers, to reject the EU's budget and dismiss the European Commission, were thought to be too far-reaching to exercise. However, it flexed its collective muscles in 1999 by playing a key role in the resignation of the Commission after a damning report into the mismanagement of EU funds.

It has also secured legislative powers in nearly all fields of policy: the Amsterdam Treaty has given MEPs the role of co-legislators with the Council of Ministers in fifteen policy fields, including transport, consumer protection, employment, social policy and the free movement of citizens. Furthermore, MEPs have gained rights to monitor appointments to the Commission and the European Central Bank. However, the European Parliament is still a remote body to most Europeans, a fact brought home by the very low turnout at the 1999 elections to the Parliament.

The European Court of Justice

The ECJ interprets, and adjudicates on, European Union law. There are fifteen judges, one from each member state, and six advocates general who advise the court. As EU law has primacy over the law of the EU member states, the court can 'disapply' domestic laws. This demonstrates that the UK Parliament is no longer sovereign (see Figure 10.1).

Proposals normally originate from the Commission, which will usually have consulted with interested parties beforehand. The proposals are then sent to the Council of Ministers, and simultaneously to the EP and the Economic and Social Committee. The EP scrutinizes

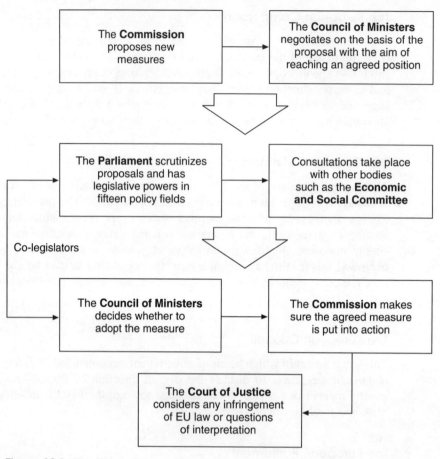

Figure 10.1. The EU decision-making process (adapted from *The Guardian Education*, 28 February 1995).

proposals and has the right to put forward amendments. The final stage of the process is when the Council reaches its decision, taking into account the advice received. As noted above, the EP now has a role as joint legislators with the Council of Ministers.

It should also be noted that there is a vast array of interest groups lobbying the EU institutions. There are over 500 such groups, which bring together interest groups from the member states. It is not usually effective or feasible to lobby the Commission as an UK interest group. The commission has limited staffing resources and prefers only to consult with groups representative of the EU as a whole.

In brief

In this chapter, we have considered a range of issues around the UK's membership of the European Union. We noted the highly controversial nature of European integration, particularly in relation to monetary union and the creation of a federal Europe. The focus of our discussion has been the implications of economic and social integration for business strategy and people management. The conclusion is that the effects have been, and will be, profound.

Examination questions for this chapter are given in Appendix 2.

References

1 The Euro one year on. (2002) *The Guardian*, 27/28 December.

Further reading

Bromley, S. (ed.) (2001) *Governing the European Union*. Open University Press/Sage.
Dinan, D. (1999) *Ever Closer Union? An Introduction to the European Community* (2nd edn).
  Macmillan.
Goodman, S. F. (1996) *The European Union*. Macmillan.

Web-site addresses

European Union Foundation Publications: http://www.eurofound.eu.int/publications
European Union Information: http://www.europa.eu.int
UK Euro information site: http://www.euro.gov.uk
TUC: http://www.tuc.org.uk
CBI: http://www.cbi.org.uk

11 The social context of management

Chapter objectives

In this chapter you will:

- Consider how demographic change affects management decisions
- Evaluate the impact of social class on the workplace
- Review the influence of social trends on corporate strategy
- Assess the social significance and business benefits of fair treatment at work and
- Examine the relationship between education, training and economic performance.

Chapter introduction

In this chapter we review a range of external environmental factors associated with social and cultural change. The issues and developments highlighted have major implications for corporate strategy. We begin by discussing the crucial importance of demographic change and continue with an assessment of the debate around social class. We then examine how changing attitudes impact on organizations and proceed to consider the key issue of equal opportunities. The chapter is concluded with an overview of the relationship between education, training and economic growth.

Case study

Single households set to soar

Felicity Lawrence Consumer affairs correspondent

The number of people living on their own will soar over the next five years, transforming the consumer landscape, according to a report published by market analysts Datamonitor yesterday.

By 2005 Britain will have 1.7 million fewer people living as part of a family, and 1 million more people over 50, than there were in 2000. In Europe the figures are 11 million fewer people living in families, and an additional 1.4 million couples without children.

Social and demographic change means that the nuclear family is likely to continue its decline. In 2000 37% of the population of Europe lived as part of a nuclear family, but this will decrease to 34%, or 133 million people, by 2005.

As couples delay marriage and childbirth, the youth market is shrinking. The number of children aged between three and nine years old in Europe will fall from 2000 levels by 2.6 million.

At the same time the number of under-18s will shrink by nearly 3.5 million, while the number of retired people will increase by 6 million. The effect will be to create a new market of people who live alone and whose purchases will reflect different values.

Those living on their own are more likely to buy services to avoid chores, choose convenience foods, and look for products with health benefits or 'added value'.

Datamonitor's analysis of purchasing trends shows that these growing sectors spend more on 'personal care' – particularly new products such as 'cosmeceuticals, which combine beauty products with active vitamin or drug ingredients' according to Piers Berezai, Datamonitor's consumer analyst and the report's author.

'They also have a strong interest in organic food, and labour-saving goods. The number of people cutting down on their meat consumption will continue to grow, but becoming vegetarian is a trend on the wane. In 2000 there were 11.3 million vegetarians across Europe, a figure forecast to increase to 12.1 million in 2005, but to slow down thereafter.

'These massive demographic changes will force marketing people to reassess their priorities. Youth marketing may remain cool, but there may be cooler money to be made elsewhere.'

The Guardian, 27 November 2002

Exercise

What are the key social and cultural changes highlighted in this case study? How are these changes likely to impact on business organizations?

Feedback

The article focuses on the forthcoming changes in the size and structure of Europe's population – that is, demographic change. Specifically, the number of single households in Europe is set to grow substantially; and the region's population is ageing. From a marketing and product development perspective, the youth market is in relative decline, but there are also implications for people management as fewer young people come onto the labour market. The discussion of the social and cultural dimension centres on changing patterns of consumer demand caused by these developments. Thus people who live alone and are 'child free' tend to consume certain types of products and services. Furthermore, their overall lifestyle differs from people with families and organizations would need to take single people's specific needs into account when designing reward strategies; for example, this group would not value help with childcare (crèche facilities, childcare vouchers, etc.) as part of a benefits package.

Generally, the implications of an ageing population are profound and will be considered in some detail in this chapter.

11.1   Demographic change

11.1.1   What is 'demography'?

Demography is the study of the characteristics of populations, in terms of their size and structure. As the above case study suggests, when the size and the structure of the population shifts, the prospects of entire industries can be transformed.

The UK is currently experiencing a whole series of major demographic changes, which will have far-reaching implications for organizations, as employers, and producers of goods and services. It is important that managers come to terms with the effects of these changes in the opening years of the new millennium, as it is then that the full impact of these demographic trends will be felt.

11.1.2   The size and structure of the population

The size of the population

Changes in the size of the population are caused by:

● Changes in the relationship between birth and death rates
● Migration (i.e. population movement into and out of the country)

The birth rate

The birth rate is the number of live births per thousand of the population in a given period, usually a year. It is calculated as follows:

$$\frac{\text{Total births} \times 1000}{\text{Total population}}$$

The death rate

The death rate is the number of deaths per thousand of the population in a given period, and is calculated in a similar way:

$$\frac{\text{Total deaths} \times 1000}{\text{Total population}}$$

The birth rate in Western Europe is about 12 at the moment; the death rate is about 11, which represents a rough balance between births and deaths (see Figure 11.1).

Self-assessment

The UK population was 58,836,700 in 2001, compared with 38.2 million in 1901. In 1801, the population was less than 12 million. Why do you think the population trebled during the course of the nineteenth century, but grew by less than half in the twentieth century?

Demographic transition

The UK has undergone a process known as **demographic transition**, which began with the onset of the Industrial Revolution. During the first stages of economic development, the balance between births and deaths is very different from that witnessed today in the industrialized world. In developing countries, birth and death rates are high and, although the infant mortality rate (the number of deaths of infants under the age of one, expressed as a ratio of 1000 live births) is high, the population remains stable.

One of the first effects of economic advance is a decline in the death rate, which is attributable to:

● Higher incomes, leading to better nutrition and housing
● Improved public health services, especially water and sewage and
● Scientific and medical advances.

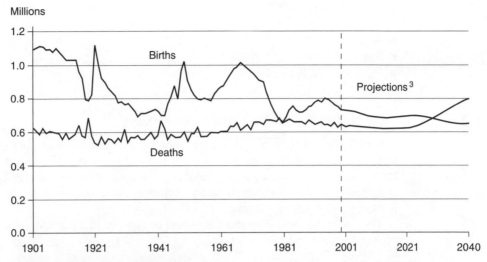

Figure 11.1. Births and deaths in the UK (from *Social Trends* 32, 2002).

There follows a period when the sharp fall in the death rate is not matched by any fall in the birth rate, resulting in a fast growth in the size of the population. Next, birth rates fall, due to:

● The spread of contraceptive knowledge
● The realization that children will survive into adulthood
● The changing role of women and
● The increasing cost of raising children in a society where years of education are expected (i.e. children can no longer be viewed as economic assets).

Ultimately, society arrives at a point where both birth and death rates are low and the population size is once again stable. However, as is borne out by the UK example, the population is now far larger than at the start of the process.

Demographic transition is the long-term hope for world population size, which is projected to reach 8.5 billion by the year 2025 (compared with 3 billion in 1962). Population growth has significant environmental effects, because if the population is growing very fast, the economy has to grow quickly if income per head is not to fall. The resultant increased output will cause raw materials to be consumed more quickly, more pressure on food supplies and more pollution as production expands.

The structure of the population

This refers to how the population is distributed in terms of age, sex and occupation.

Self-assessment

What kinds of demographic data are most likely to be of use to your organization? What do you need to know about the characteristics of:

● Your staff and
● Your customers.

in terms of their

- Age
- Sex and
- Occupational background?

11.1.3   Demographic data about customers

It is important to be aware of the demographic characteristics of your customers, as these will affect the pattern of demand for products and services. For example, in recent years there has been an increase in the number of women in the workforce. This has resulted in the growth of the childcare industry (nannies, nurseries, etc.) and an expansion in the market for convenience foods.

The following cases illustrate the impact of changes in the age structure of the population on organizations' customer bases.

Case study

Trainers

Nike, the leading sports wear manufacturer, experienced rapid growth in the 1990s, largely on the back of sales of its fashionable sports shoes. However, by 1997, this growth began to slow, allowing rivals such as Adidas and Reebok to take a bigger share of the multi-billion dollar market. Smaller brands, such as Airwalk and Vans, have also benefited.

One of the marketing problems facing Nike was that the brand was in danger of losing its credibility as a teenage fashion item when older people began wearing Nike sports clothes. The demographics show that the number of teenagers in America is projected to grow from 25 million in 1997 to 31 million in 2010; and alongside this, their purchasing power is growing. Rather than advertise the product through sports stars as did Nike, Vans has used the Californian teenager as its marketing role model. Vans believe that the teenage style leaders are no longer the inner-city youngsters targeted by Nike, but the California teenager. Whereas Nike focused on the established team sports such as basketball, Vans aims at individual sports such as skateboarding and mountain biking. Vans goes to great lengths to stay close to its customers, to the extent of hiring teenagers to work for them and test designs.

Reported in *The Economist*, 7 June 1997

Case study

Care homes

A practice rather cruelly known as 'granny farming' is on the increase. The UK's ageing population means that the care homes market will grow rapidly in the early part of the next century. Private healthcare providers such as BUPA are looking to consolidate their positions in the market to take advantage of this growth.

Reported in *The Economist*, 29 November 1997

It can be seen from these cases that firms base a whole range of business decisions, such as production planning and marketing, on demographic factors.

Effects of an ageing population on the demand for public services – the 'demographic timebomb'

The UK population is approximately 59 million, but only some 26 million are in the workforce. The relation between the number of workers in a country and the total number of people is the **dependency ratio**. Its main use is to show the number of children and old people supported by the workforce. In the UK and in other developed countries, an ageing population is creating:

- A higher dependency ratio (i.e. a rise in the dependent population) and
- An increased call on welfare services.

The last two factors combine to increase the tax burden on the population; whether this will markedly affect their living standards depends on the growth of incomes and productivity.

The cost of an ageing population

A report by the personal social services research unit at Kent University has claimed that spending on the long-term care of the elderly must rise by more than 150 per cent over the next 30 years. The resulting increase in the bill – £14 billion – is considered 'not unaffordable' (even though it outstrips economic growth), although it could climb steeply if there is a fall in the contribution now made by informal carers.

The researchers assessed the demand for long-term care and its likely costs from 1995–2031, when the number of over-65s is projected to rise by 57 per cent, and over-85s by 79 per cent. The result was an estimated 61 per cent expansion of care provision.

The study predicted a 153 per cent overall increase in care spending by 2031, made up of a 174 per cent increase in health expenditure, a 124 per cent rise in social services spending and a 173 per cent jump in private payments. This is compared to a forecast rise of 123 per cent in gross domestic product.

The research team emphasize that these are projections which could fluctuate with certain variables. However, on the basis of these projections, the number of elderly people in residential or nursing care will rise from 407 000 to 666 000; numbers receiving domiciliary or home care services will go up from 517 000 to 804 000; and those receiving community nursing will increase from 444 000 to 717 000.

Reported in *The Economist*, 19 December 1998

Exercise

What would be the effects of a fall in the average age of the population?

Feedback

The effects are associated with more children and young people in the population. They include: a need for more school places and maternity wards; changing patterns of consumption (an increase in the demand for toys and family homes); and the growth of the working population.

11.1.4   Demographic data about staff

Labour market information

Demographic data can be used for workforce planning, where it is important to know:

- Levels of skills and knowledge in the labour market
- The sex, age and ethnic make-up of the labour market and
- Unemployment rates.

The impact on recruitment – The demographic dip

In the early 1990s, fewer young people were coming onto the labour market. Between 1979 and 1983, an average of 900 000 16-year-olds were joining the labour market per year. By 1993, the number had fallen to 620 000. This came to be known as the 'demographic dip' and it meant that organizations had to consider recruiting individuals from other groups which were often underrepresented in the workplace, such as:

- Women
- Older workers
- People from ethnic minorities and
- The disabled.

In the event, the fall in the number of young people entering the workforce in the early 1990s was offset by rising unemployment and a looser labour market than had been expected. However, organizations still need to take account of demographic changes such as more women in the workforce and changes in the ethnic make-up of the population.

Recruiting and retaining women

Until recently, many organizations had done very little to encourage women to join them. Indeed, the way work was organized often positively discouraged women from working. Women with childcare responsibilities found it difficult to respond to the inflexible full-time, nine-to-five working regime expected by most employers.

However, with many more women than men entering the workforce, organizations have been left with little choice but to make work more attractive to women by introducing what are sometimes termed 'family-friendly' employment policies, such as:

- Introducing more flexible working hours
- Providing support for childcare (e.g. nursery vouchers or childcare facilities)
- Offering career breaks, often combined with 'keep-in-touch' measures such as refresher courses and training during the break period
- 'Home working' (employing home-based staff)
- Increasing the number of part-time and temporary posts
- Offering contracts which are more attractive to some women (e.g. school term-time only working and job sharing)
- Enhanced maternity leave arrangements.

How family-friendly is your organization?

Self-assessment

- Does your organization have a policy to attract and retain women staff?
- Does your organization offer any of the above incentives to attract and retain women staff?

Recruiting and attracting older people

Some organizations, particularly in the retail sector (e.g. Sainsbury's supermarket), have a policy of recruiting older workers to offset the effects of the demographic dip and to benefit from the advantages of employing older people. However, many organizations discriminate against older people in employment (see Section 11.4).

Self-assessment

What are the advantages and disadvantages of employing older workers?

The costs and benefits of an older workforce

- **Greater commitment and reliability.** Employers often perceive older workers to be more committed. This greater commitment is sometimes attributed to insecurity (older workers tend to be targeted in redundancy programmes) and the absence of childcare responsibilities.
- **Customer care.** In some industries, for example the DIY segment of the retail sector, customers prefer to deal with older, more experienced workers.
- **Pay and benefits.** In most firms, pay, holidays and pension contributions rise with age and seniority.
- **Workplace safety.** People over 65 have half as many accidents at work as their younger colleagues, but take longer to recover and are more likely to die from job-related injuries. Some jobs may therefore have to be redesigned if they are to be done by older people.
- **Employee mobility.** As workers get older, they put down firmer roots and are less willing to move to other locations.
- **Career paths.** As employees from the 'baby boom' generation age, they will create increasingly top-heavy structures in organizations, blocking the career paths of younger workers. Some organizations, such as Hewlett-Packard in the USA, have persuaded older workers to take on roles which do not involve managing others in order to address this problem.

Recruiting and attracting people from minority ethnic groups

Minority ethnic groups are underrepresented in the workplace, particularly in managerial positions. Not only does this imply discrimination, it also represents a waste of resources. These issues are discussed in more detail in Section 11.4.

Self-assessment

What measures can organizations adopt to recruit and retain people from minority ethnic groups?

- Priority hiring from ethnic groups
- Advertising jobs in publications read by members of minority ethnic groups
- Auditing the ethnic mix of the local community and trying to ensure that the ethnic make-up of the organization more closely matches its ethnic mix
- Equal opportunities training for recruitment staff

Many companies formally recognize the implications of these changes:

Extract from the City of Bradford Metropolitan Council's statement on equal opportunities

For all local authorities it should be important that the organization broadly reflects at all levels and in all occupations, the community it serves. Thus in

Bradford, the Council should aim to reflect in its workforce profile the make-up of the district we serve, particularly bearing in mind our specific labour market demographics.

Source: the IPD Statement on Managing Diversity

Recruiting and retaining people with disabilities

People with disabilities are also discriminated against in employment. This is often a result of organizations equating 'disability' with 'inability'. Again, this represents a waste of resources.

Self-assessment

What measures can organizations adopt to recruit and retain people with disabilities?

● Make it easier for disabled people to enter and move around inside buildings
● Modify equipment for use by disabled people
● Review communications within the organization and adapt these to the needs of disabled people.

Summary

In this section we have seen how changes in the size and structure of the population impact on organizations as employers and producers of goods and services. These factors must be taken into account by managers both when developing business strategy and in human resource planning.

11.2   Social structure and social stratification

11.2.1   Social structure

'Social structure' can be explained in terms of the various institutions in society, their relationship and how the individual fits in to the general framework (see Figure 11.2).

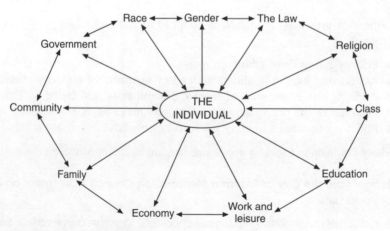

Figure 11.2. Social structure.

Exercise	What connections can you make between the various institutions which make up society?

Feedback	Family, class, education and work are very closely linked. The family background of individuals will dictate their social class, which will determine the form of their education, which in turn will have a very significant influence on the sort of work they obtain and how they are viewed in the community.

In certain societies (Northern Ireland or the former Yugoslavia, for example), an individual's religion will be a reflection of his or her race and will determine their relationship with both legal and governmental institutions.

Institutions regulate human behaviour in the same way as instincts channel animal behaviour. Indeed, society can be said to control individuals in a number of ways:

- Political and legal control – involving the (tacit) threat of violence
- Economic pressures
- The desire on the part of individuals to conform to group norms
- Persuasion, i.e. trying to convince us that what society wants us to do is actually in our best interests
- Fear of ridicule, ostracism and gossip if we do not conform
- Morality, customs and manners.

Exercise	Mrs Thatcher once famously said that 'there is no such thing as society. There are individual men and women, and there are families.' What do you think she meant by this?

Feedback	It is difficult to believe that Mrs Thatcher actually meant that society does not exist as we are all, to a greater or lesser extent, aware of belonging to some form of collective entity which is known by that name. However, society, and indeed the institutions which make up society, do not have a material form but exist only in our minds – that is, they are social constructs which have been invented by humans for the purpose of social control. In this sense, there is indeed 'no such thing as society' (however, note that the family is also a social construct!).

We can get a clearer picture of what the former prime minister actually meant if we put the above extract from one of her speeches into its wider context:

Too many people have been given to understand that if they have a problem it's the government's job to cope with it . . . They're casting their problem on society. And you know, there is no such thing as society. There are individual men and women, and there are families. And no government can do anything except through people, and people must look to themselves first. It's our duty to look to ourselves and then, also, to look after our neighbour. People have got the entitlements too much in mind, without the obligations. There is no such thing as entitlement, unless someone has first met an obligation.

The message here seems to be not that people are isolated economic actors; rather, it appears as a call for individual responsibility and a warning against a 'dependency culture'. Indeed, talk of 'entitlements' and 'obligations' corresponds closely with the 'rights and responsibilities' associated with stakeholder theory and the so-called 'Third Way' favoured by New Labour (see Section 9.4.6).

11.2.2   Social stratification

Every society has a system of ranking, relating to superordination, subordination, privilege, power and prestige. The criteria by which individuals are assigned to their different levels vary from society to society. They range from social class through to caste, the latter of which is a formal system based on heredity and occupation; status is set at birth and is almost impossible to change. The system of social stratification in the UK is based on class.

What is 'social class'?

Britain is often described as 'a class-ridden society' and British people as 'obsessed by class', but what exactly is social class? The following definitions give us an insight into the notion:

Classes – for example, professional people or factory workers – are formed socially out of the division of labour. They make up more or less cohesive and socially conscious groups from those occupational groups and their families which share similar work and market situations.[1]
(class is) a force that unites into groups people who differ from one another, by overriding the differences between them.[2]

These definitions suggest that class has the following characteristics:

● It has an economic basis
● It is related to people's occupations
● It reflects social cohesion
● It involves social consciousness
● It is about having certain things in common with others.

Karl Marx has had by far the greatest influence on our conception of class. Indeed, the work of Marx had a profound effect on the history of the twentieth century, as it was Marxist ideology which inspired the establishment of Communist regimes around the world, as well as the creation of socialist political parties such as the UK Labour Party.

Marx and social class

Marx was writing in the middle of the nineteenth century at the height of the Industrial Revolution. He saw how British society was changing with a mass movement of people from the land to the cities and towns, to take up jobs in the factories, mills and mines. He also observed how the old ruling elite, the aristocracy, was being usurped by a new group, the capitalists or the 'bourgeoisie'. The capitalists were the owners of factories, mills and offices (what he called 'the means of production') who had become 'newly rich' as a result of the country's rapid industrialization. The capitalists, who were often owner–managers of their enterprises, ruthlessly exploited their workers by driving down their wages in the relentless pursuit of profit.

Marx argued that social institutions such as religion and education were all designed to suppress the working classes, or the 'proletariat' as he called them, and maintain the dominance of the capitalists. Marx predicted that the working class would eventually overthrow the capitalist class, the people who were oppressing them and forcing them to live such miserable lives.

So, for Marx, class reflected ownership – the 'haves' and the 'have nots' – and was the dominant characteristic of society. Conflict between classes was endemic and would eventually result in the establishment of a society, where property would no longer exist (i.e. everything would be owned by the state on behalf of the people) and production would be equally distributed. However, not only has capitalism survived, but it is now the dominant force in a global economic system. So was Marx wrong?

The language of class is based on Marxist terminology.

- **The class struggle:** the fight for supremacy between the classes.
- **Class consciousness:** an awareness of belonging to a particular social class, and all that entails.
- **False consciousness:** a state of not knowing where one's true interests lie. It is argued that working class people who vote Conservative are victims of false consciousness.
- **Class traitor:** someone who has betrayed their working-class roots. An example would be Ramsay McDonald, the first Labour prime minister, who was accused of betraying the party by forming a coalition government.
- **Class enemy:** someone who acts against the interests of the working class. Arthur Scargill referred to Margaret Thatcher as a class enemy during the miners' strike of the early 1980s.
- **Class solidarity:** a feeling of unity between people from a particular class.
- **Class war:** open conflict between the classes.

Social class in modern industrial societies

In the early part of the twentieth century, UK society clearly exhibited the characteristics of a 'class society'; there were substantial differences in wealth and power which had some degree of intergenerational stability. Furthermore, there were feelings of solidarity promoting economic and political action which reflected class interests. However, this situation has been altered by the social and economic changes of the post-war period:

- **Ownership is now more widely spread** – very few businesses are now owned by just one person. In the 1980s and 1990s, we saw the growth of 'popular capitalism' as public utilities were privatized and building societies demutualized (see Chapter 8).
- **Changes in occupational structure** resulting from deindustrialization, i.e. the decline of the manufacturing sector and the growth of services. This has resulted in the expansion of non-manual occupations relative to manual occupations, which gives rise to upward social mobility as the number of white-collar and managerial jobs grows.
- **An overall increase in living standards** resulting from sustained economic growth.
- **Changing patterns of residence.** Many more people are now owner–occupiers. Fifty years ago, it was unheard of for a member of the working classes to own their own home.
- **The expansion of education.** In particular, the huge growth of higher education since the 1960s has opened the way for social mobility (see Section 11.5).

Class and occupation

Another way of ranking people is by their occupation, which was first claimed as the basis for class by Max Weber. The government now uses an occupational model, called the Registrar General's Social Class Groups classification, to categorize people into classes. A version of this, the ABC classification, is used by market research companies and public opinion pollsters (Figure 11.3).

A **Upper middle class:** Higher managerial, administrative or professional

B **Middle class:** Intermediate managerial, administrative or professional

C1 **Lower middle class:** Supervisory or clerical and junior managerial, administrative or professional

C2 **Skilled working class:** Skilled manual workers

D **Working class:** Semi and unskilled manual workers

E **Lowest subsistence level:** State pensioners or widows (no other earner), casual or lowest grade workers

Figure 11.3. The ABC classification of social class.

A middle class revolution?

In 1999, Tony Blair heralded a radical shift of power in Britain away from the 'old establishment' towards a new middle-class majority who have achieved their status on merit rather than by birth. Similar aspirations had already been voiced by the former prime minister, John Major, who talked of a 'classless society'. But is there any evidence for an expanding, meritocratic middle class?

According to a study by the market research company, National Readership Survey, between 1975 and 1998 the middle class grew in size while the working class shrank (see Figure 11.4). However, if we look at people's own perception of class, we can see that between 1966 and 1997 the number of people categorizing themselves as middle class rose by only 5.5 per cent, and the majority (60 per cent) still see themselves as working class (Figure 11.5).

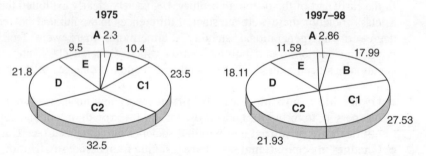

Figure 11.4. Change in social class by occupation, 1975–98 (from *National Readership Survey 1998*).

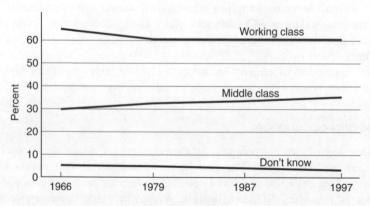

Figure 11.5. People's own perception of class (from a British election survey).

Table 11.1 The new classification of social class

Class 1:	The new elite of professionals, for example: doctors, lawyers, teachers, professors, editors and employers, administrators and managers in large organizations with 25 or more staff.
Class 2:	'Associate professionals': nurses, laboratory technicians, estate agents, journalists, actors, social workers and employers, administrators and managers in small organizations and supervisors of intermediate staff.
Class 3:	Intermediate occupations in administrative, clerical, sales and service work: secretaries, nursery nurses and computer operators.
Class 4:	Self-employed non-professionals: driving instructors and builders.
Class 5:	Other supervisors and craft related workers: plumbers and telephone fitters.
Class 6:	Workers employed in routine occupations in manufacturing and services: lorry drivers and assembly line workers.
Class 7:	Workers in elementary occupations in manufacturing and services: labourers, waiters and cleaners.
Class 8:	The underclass of the long-term unemployed and those who have never worked.

Whatever the real picture, the government's Office of National Statistics produced a new classification of social class to reflect what it sees as fundamental changes in modern British society. It can be seen that 'middle-class' occupations dominate, while the unemployed 'underclass' is recognized for the first time (see Table 11.1).

Class in organizations

There is a strong case for arguing that in some industries and occupations, people are discriminated against on the basis of their social origins. But class is an issue for UK organizations in other ways:

- **The blue collar–white collar divide.** Traditionally, managers and administrators (white-collar, or office workers) enjoyed better pay and terms and conditions than did shopfloor (blue-collar) workers. An example would be that office workers would be able to join the organization's occupational pension scheme, whereas shopfloor workers would be excluded. This was clearly divisive and a recipe for poor industrial relations, so many organizations are now moving towards 'single status', where all employees have access to similar terms and conditions.
- **Trade unionism.** Trade unionism has its roots in the class conflict of the nineteenth century, and this was reflected in the militancy of the 1960s and 1970s. After they were sidelined in the 1980s by the last Conservative government, a number of trade unions have tried to lose the militant reputation and adopt a more cooperative (some would say diluted) approach to industrial relations.

Summary

In this section we have depicted society as a framework of interconnected social institutions. We examined one of these institutions, social class, in some detail and concluded that UK society is still divided along class lines. We also noted that social class manifests itself in the workplace in ways which can have a negative effect on the management of human resources.

11.3 Social attitudes, values and beliefs

Changes in people's attitudes, values and beliefs are important because managers need to know:

● What concerns the organization's customers
● How staff think and
● How the organization is viewed by the wider society.

Values, attitudes and beliefs are interrelated:

Beliefs are the specific thoughts of individuals, which may be based on fact or opinion.
Values are feelings about what is good or bad, based on beliefs.
Attitudes are ways of behaving which reflect opinion.

Beliefs, values and behaviour are therefore the components of attitudes (see Figure 11.6).

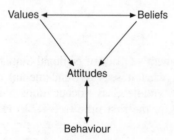

Figure 11.6. The components of attitudes.

11.3.1 Measuring attitudes

The government attempts to measure people's attitudes and the results are reproduced in publications such as *Social Trends*.

See the website for a case study focusing on a survey designed to measure people's attitudes.

11.3.2 Attitudes and behaviour

The important issue here is how attitudes influence behaviour, and vice versa. To take two examples:

● **Attitudes, behaviour and customers.** People are now more aware and less tolerant of unethical business practices. This has led to some financial institutions making a marketing virtue of the fact that they follow 'ethical investment' policies (see Chapter 14).
● **Attitudes, behaviour and employees.** Organizations positively promoting equal opportunities make it clear that they will not tolerate, and indeed will punish, discriminatory behaviour. Such a policy will influence attitudes, albeit not immediately and not for all employees.

11.3.3 Social trends

Social trends are changes in people's attitudes and behaviour. The main social trends are related to economic, cultural and demographic factors. We have examined the last of these influences on social trends in Section 11.1; for example, we considered changing attitudes towards women and work. It is important to realize that each of the above factors which influence social trends is related to the other – for example, economic factors influence social factors, as will be seen.

Economic factors, attitudes and behaviour

Economic change has a profound effect on people's attitudes and behaviour. For example, increased wealth affects people's attitudes to social class.

Self-assessment

Can you think of any other ways in which economic factors influence people's attitudes and behaviour?
    Increased wealth will also affect people's attitudes towards consuming certain goods and services, such as housing and education.

Cultural factors, attitudes and behaviour

The post-industrial societies of the West are characterized by individualism, increased wealth and more leisure time. In many countries, the notion of 'lifestyle' has become central and we see the development of what has been described as a 'consumer society'. Thus the 'cultural industries', such as entertainment and the media, have become more influential in contemporary society, bringing with them the 'cult of celebrity'. Choices about the food we eat, the clothes we wear and how we decorate our homes – i.e. lifestyle choices – are profoundly influenced by the media and the advertising industry. Those who lack the economic and cultural means to make such lifestyle choices increasingly find themselves a marginalized group in society (an 'underclass').
    Cultural change in this sense results in an acute emphasis on the individual as a consumer of products and services. People as consumers now have a great deal more choice than they did 50 years ago. Spending patterns have reflected that growing discretion over how they spend their income, and that part spent on basic physiological necessities has correspondingly fallen.

Self-assessment

What are the implications for organizations of these cultural changes?

● More discerning customers who expect more choice and higher-quality products and service
● An increase in the importance of leisure and the accompanying growth of the leisure industry.

Other social trends relate to people's growing concern for:

● The environment and
● Ethical business practices.

Summary

In this section, we have examined the relationship between social attitudes, values and beliefs, focusing on how attitudes influence behaviour in organizations. We then considered social and cultural trends and their implications for managers, particularly in relation to socially responsible business practices.

11.4 Equality of opportunity

In recent years, UK society has become increasingly aware of the need to treat different groups of people fairly and equally. Legislation has been passed to ensure that people are not discriminated against on the basis of gender, race or disability. Many organizations actively promote equal opportunities by encouraging people from disadvantaged groups to join and progress through the organization.

The climate of opportunity in an organization will have a profound influence on the management of the employment relationship. Equality of opportunity is therefore of particular relevance to personnel and development managers because it impacts on key human resourcing interventions such as recruitment and selection and training and development.

See the website for a detailed discussion of the relevant areas of anti-discrimination law.

11.4.1 What are equal opportunities?

Equal opportunities are about equality of access and fair treatment irrespective of gender, race, ethnic origin, religion, nationality, age and disability. It involves treating people within a framework of human rights and eliminating discrimination in the workplace. Organizations which practise equal opportunities maximize the use of their human resources.

Equal opportunities and discrimination

Discrimination is a legal term. It is unfair behaviour towards someone based on sex, marital status, race, ethnicity, national origin and disability which is unlawful. Discrimination amounts to 'less favourable treatment' of someone because of these reasons. It may be caused consciously or unconsciously by the perpetrator. The law probably protects people on the basis of their sexual orientation and their religion. There is no law which directly protects people on the basis of their age, but discrimination on these grounds can be unlawful in certain circumstances.

What causes discrimination?

Discrimination is based on an individual's prejudice. Prejudice is what someone negatively thinks and feels towards someone else because of apparent differences between themselves and that other person. It is based on preconceived (mostly irrational) ideas about them. Prejudice can be based on the colour of another person's skin, their age, accent or dress appearance – it is a negative attitude towards someone for these and other reasons (see Section 11.3 for a discussion of attitudes). When these attitudes influence an individual's behaviour it becomes discrimination. The more power people have to translate that prejudice into behaviour, the more effective becomes the discrimination. Sometimes, in order to overcome discrimination, it may be necessary to treat some people differently. This type of treatment is known as 'positive action' and is discussed in Section 11.4.3.

What is 'stereotyping'?

This is where people are grouped into 'pigeon holes' or mental compartments because it is the easiest thing for us to do when faced with people who are different from us. It involves having preconceptions about other people based on their shared characteristics. Some common stereotypes are:

- All black people are lazy
- All young women will eventually leave or want to work part-time because of child bearing and childcare
- All Jewish people are obsessed with money
- All Muslims are militants and
- All people in wheelchairs are incompetent or stupid.

Where these stereotypes are based on prejudice they are likely to lead to discrimination. Stereotyping means that people are not treated as individuals. Furthermore, it is unfair and can be unlawful.

Because we have held certain prejudiced views about other people since childhood, it is often very uncomfortable and difficult to have these challenged by others; and it is at least as difficult to question our own prejudices. Consequently, we will mostly reject information which challenges our own stereotypical view of others.

11.4.2 Equal opportunities and diversity

In recent years, the notion of 'diversity' has come to the fore. Diversity goes much further than equal opportunities, and organizations wishing to practise it must be operating in a culture which embraces equal opportunities in word and in spirit.

'Managing diversity' is a strategy which accepts that the workforce consists of a diverse population. There are visible and non-visible differences. As well as the differences identified above under the heading of 'equal opportunities' it will include:

- Personality
- Economic class
- Workstyle
- Military experience
- Religious affiliation
- Culture.

Managing diversity means harnessing these differences to create a productive environment in which all employees feel valued, and where their talents are being fully used. This will subsequently lead to the achievement of organizational objectives. An organization which is following a policy of managing diversity will put less emphasis on fulfilling legal requirements and taking steps to redress imbalances of opportunity. Rather, it will take account of the less obvious differences between people.

Disadvantaged groups

Inequality in the workplace particularly affects the following people:

- Women
- Minority ethnic groups
- The disabled
- Older members of the workforce.

11.4.3 Gender issues

Self-assessment

What conclusions abut the position of women in society can be drawn from the following data?

- Women employees working full-time earn on average only 80 per cent of the average hourly earnings of men full-time employees.

- In 1998, there were 121 women Members in a parliament of 659 – 18 per cent of the total.
- In 1997, women accounted for 32 per cent of all public appointments (from a total of 28 083 appointments to the boards of public corporations, such as the BBC, and non-governmental public bodies, such as Learning and Skills Councils).
- Forty-three per cent of women employees of working age and 8 per cent of men employees work part-time.
- A quarter of the working population now works part-time, and the figure is set to rise by a third by 2006.
- Nearly 4 million women care for elderly dependants compared to 2.5 million men.
- In 1997, women accounted for one-third of managers and 40 per cent of all professional occupations. However, 83 per cent of checkout operators and 82 per cent of catering assistants were women.

Source: *Facts about Women and Men in Great Britain 1998,* Equal Opportunities Commission

You probably came to the following conclusions:

- Women are paid less than men.
- Many more women than men work part-time; part-time work has worse pay and conditions than full-time work.
- There are many more men in powerful positions than there are women.
- Women are more likely to be carers than are men.
- Men dominate the better-paid occupations.

Why do women earn less than men?

There are several reasons for this, including the following:

- Women's careers are often interrupted by maternity leave and breaks for childcare; this allows men to progress more rapidly.
- The lack of subsidized childcare provision in the UK makes it difficult for women with childcare responsibilities to continue with their careers.
- Women tend to work in low-status, poorly paid jobs.
- Relatively few managers are women.
- Women face stereotyping and discrimination at work.

11.4.4   Ethnic groups

Ethnic minorities in Britain

Britain has always had ethnic minorities; people with diverse languages, beliefs and cultures have settled in the UK for thousands of years. Some, like the Huguenots who arrived in the seventeenth century, gradually became assimilated. Others, such as the Irish and Jews, who came at various periods, have to some extent retained separate identities. People from South Asia, Africa and the Caribbean arrived in substantial numbers after the Second World War to help meet labour shortages. The most recent arrivals in Britain include refugees and asylum seekers from Vietnam, Somalia, Turkey, the Middle East and the former Yugoslavia.

At the 1991 census, just over 3 million (5.5 per cent) of the 55 million people in Britain did not classify themselves as white. Half of these groups are South Asian (i.e. of Indian, Pakistani and Bangladeshi descent) and 30 per cent are black.

Inequalities faced by ethnic groups

- In 1996, the unemployment rate for people from ethnic minorities (18 per cent) was more than double the rate for white people (8 per cent).
- In 1996, unemployment levels were highest for both men and women in the Pakistani and Bangladeshi groups, at 27 per cent and 28 per cent respectively.
- Nearly 40 per cent of black women aged 16–24 were unemployed in 1996, compared to just over 10 per cent of white women in the same age group.
- In 1995, average hourly earnings of full-time employees from ethnic minorities were about 92 per cent of those of white employees.
- Nearly half of all Pakistani and Bangladeshi workers in the West Midlands earned less than £4.50 per hour in 1995, compared with 32 per cent of Indian workers, 31 per cent of white workers and 21 per cent of black workers.
- There is a higher proportion of white non-manual workers than is the case for non-white groups

Source: Commission for Racial Equality Fact Sheet, *Employment and Unemployment*, 1997.

We can conclude from these data that:

- White people on average occupy better jobs than other ethnic groups.
- Black people experience much higher rates of unemployment than do white people.

Many organizations have sought to improve their recruitment rates among the ethnic minority populations.

11.4.5   Disability issues

- Two-thirds of disabled people do not work.
- Disabled women have lower rates of sickness, absence and accidents at work than do non-disabled employees.

Disabled people face a particular set of problems at work and there are certain steps that employers can take to address these issues, as discussed in Section 11.1.4.

Ageism

- One-third of the workforce was over 45 by the year 2000.
- Forty per cent of the 9.3 million people aged 50 to 64 are now not working.
- Age discrimination is costing Britain £26 billion a year in lost potential output by older workers forced out of the labour market.

Source: *The Employers' Forum for Age*, 1998.

These figures tell us that older workers are discriminated against in the following ways:

- Older workers are often targeted in redundancy programmes.
- Many organizations favour recruiting younger workers for certain jobs.
- Age discrimination represents a waste of resources.

The employment of older people was discussed in Section 11.1.4. You should also read references to these subjects at Section 1.4.7 and in Chapter 2.

Summary

In this section we have examined the related concepts of equal opportunities and diversity. We proceeded to assess the way in which inequality manifests itself in the workplace. A detailed overview of the relevant areas of anti-discrimination law can be found on the website.

11.5 Education, training and economic performance

11.5.1 Education and economic performance

It is a widely held belief that educational achievement and economic success are closely linked. In recent years, the intensity of global competition has highlighted the importance of education as a means of improving economic performance. Among the emerging economies of Asia, Latin America and Eastern Europe, the most successful are the ones that have educated most of their workers up to, and typically beyond, levels achieved in the West.

In the developed countries, deindustrialization has resulted in an expanding service sector. The jobs being created, in both the manufacturing and the service sectors, are to an increasing extent based on information and will require literate, numerate and adaptable – in other words, educated – workers. But is there a demonstrable link between education and economic performance?

Human capital theory – investing in people

For over 200 years, economists have assumed a link between education and economic performance. It was Adam Smith, writing in 1776, who first suggested that education constitutes an investment in individuals which is comparable to investment in machinery. He argued that the higher wages commanded by educated individuals reflected the rewards necessary to compensate those individuals for the costs of acquiring skills.

Human capital theory assumes that there is a direct link between education systems and economic productivity; and that some countries are more successful than others in organizing and delivering education in a way that enhances productivity.

In human capital theory, human capital is an accumulation of capabilities that can be acquired by individuals through education. Individuals and organizations benefit from education: individuals, in the form of higher wages; and organizations, in the form of higher revenues. However, there are costs (time, resources and loss of income for individuals and organizations), as well as benefits, associated with education. If the benefits realized outweigh the costs, then it is possible to say that a worker has become more productive through education (in accounting terms, that there has been a positive return on the investment in human capital). Increased productivity leads to improved competitiveness, which in turn leads to economic growth.

In human capital theory, the relationship between education and technological change has two dimensions: first, as discussed above, technological change requires the increased use of more highly educated labour; and second, education leads to the development of new technology.

Calls by governments to improve education systems are based on the idea that education leads to economic growth but that, in the absence of state provision, the market will fail to produce enough education to meet the needs of the economy.

Alternative views of the role of education

● **The screening hypothesis.** Critics of human capital theory question whether the enhanced productivity of an educated worker is a result of education that he or she has received.[3] They would say, rather, that higher levels of productivity are, in fact, a result of innate ability and that certain individuals would be more productive regardless of any additional education and training they may undertake; higher education, in particular, contributes very little in the way of economic 'value added'. However, this theory does acknowledge a useful role for education in 'screening' potential employees by identifying levels of ability, if not in contributing to economic performance. However, if 'screening' is the only role achieved by higher education, should governments subsidize it?

What are the benefits of higher education?

In developed countries, the average proportion of those aged 18–21 in higher education rose from 14.4 per cent in 1985 to 22.4 per cent in 1995. It is clear that individuals benefit from higher education – OECD research shows that British graduates earn 80 per cent more than people with only secondary education and are far less likely to be unemployed – but it is much more difficult to measure the benefits that accrue to society.

There is some evidence to support the screening hypothesis: a cursory glance at job advertisements tells us that there is strong demand for graduates in the labour market; and many countries have rigid academic requirements for particular professions.

If screening is the only purpose performed by higher education, there are persuasive arguments against its public funding, namely:

● *The wage premium associated with higher education means that many people would be willing to pay to study*
● *There are cheaper ways to screen than through universities and*
● *As more people enter higher education, its efficiency as a system of screening is undermined.*

The difficulty of demonstrating that an investment in education, particularly higher education, results in economic growth, has certain policy implications, the most important of which is that more of the cost of higher education should be borne by individual students. The government has been persuaded by this argument, forcing students to contribute £1000 per annum to the cost of their education from 1998.

Reported in *The Economist*, 13 December 1997

● **Correspondence theory.** From a Marxist perspective, education reflects and supports the existing economic and social order.[3] The role of education is to transmit the attitudes and values required to maintain the capitalist system. For example, in an economy characterized by Fordist production methods and Taylorist scientific management, submissiveness, passivity and loyalty will be rewarded by the education system while creativity, aggressiveness and independence will be penalized.

Education policy

'**Education, education, education.**' The Labour government was elected in 1997 partly on the basis of a commitment to reform education in the UK. Education is a highly contentious issue and different groups have strongly held opinions about the direction that education policy should take. Ball[4] has identified a number of perspectives on educational provision in the UK, which have influenced educational policy development:

Modernizers

This group sees educational provision as being too academic and anti-industrial. As a consequence, national economic performance is under threat. Education should cater for the needs of industry and the economy, emphasizing applied knowledge, flexible skills and 'correct' attitudes. The consumers of education (employers and parents) should have control and influence over education, to ensure that education is responsive to the market. In terms of delivery, there should be a shift of emphasis from teaching to learning. Cooperation, group work and social skills should be promoted

Traditionalists

This group sees educational provision as being too permissive, resulting in a threat to national culture and academic standards. Education should focus on the academic, emphasizing the reproduction of culture.

There should be stronger state control over the curriculum and institutions. Delivery should be characterized by formal relationships between tutors and students. Formal examinations and selection should predominate. Competitive individualism should be encouraged and there should be an emphasis on cognitive skills.

Progressives

Educational provision is too staid, reinforcing the dominant interests in society and threatening rights and equity. The focus should be the needs of citizens, who should be helped to acquire critical skills and the knowledge and understanding to function in society. Learners should control what is learnt, and educational provision responsive to the needs of the local community. Provision should be learner-centred and the curriculum negotiated. Cooperation and group work are advocated, with an emphasis on 'empowerment'.

Exercise	Which of the above groups (the 'modernizers', the 'traditionalists' or the 'progressives') do you think has had the most influence on education policy since the Second World War?

Feedback	**1945–1960** The post-war period saw the establishment of grammar, secondary modern and technical schools. This was known as the tripartite system and was firmly rooted in 'traditionalist' principles. By the 1960s, this system was coming under severe criticism from those who saw it as failing the majority of the population. The critics' argument was that it was élitist, with very few children from working-class backgrounds achieving places at grammar schools. Moreover, the standards at the secondary modern schools were very low and few emerged from these with any qualifications at all. Only a very small number of technical schools were established.

1960–1980

By the late-1960s, most local authorities had established comprehensive systems of education in their areas of jurisdiction. Comprehensive schooling was based on principles of equality of educational opportunity and equal treatment of individuals, regardless of ability. At this time, 'progressive' views about education were in the ascendancy, a reflection of the prevailing 'radical' culture of the time. Progressive methods were also practised in primary schools.

1980 to the present day

The comprehensive system was in turn criticized by the traditionalists for not allowing the intellectually more able pupils to achieve their potential and for tolerating low standards. By the 1980s, the modernizers were in control. The modernizers' main argument was that schooling in the UK was overly academic and was not producing enough young people with the skills and attitudes required to meet the needs of a rapidly changing economy.

One of the main problems was seen to be the influence of the teaching profession and educationalists over education policy. The modernizers saw these as responsible for promoting progressive practices and philosophy and, in an attempt to place education under the control of 'consumers' (i.e. parents) allowed schools to opt out of local authority control and gave more power to parent governors. In addition, a new National Curriculum was established and tighter systems of quality control put in place.

They argued for a curriculum which contained a greater vocational element and for 'parity of esteem' between vocational and academic qualifications. The consequence of this is measures such as the General National Vocational Qualifications, which were being promoted as 'vocational A levels'.

The influence of the 'modernizers' was also felt in post-compulsory education, with the establishment of the competency-based National Vocational Qualifications (NVQs) and the creation of the Training and Enterprise Councils, which were employer-led bodies delivering the government's vocational education and training programmes (succeeded in 2001 by the Learning and Skills Councils).

The Labour government have continued on this 'modernizing' track and by 2000 had introduced performance-related pay for teachers in an attempt to raise classroom standards and attract well-qualified graduates into teaching.

11.5.2   Training and economic performance

It is common to place at least part of the blame for the UK's relatively poor post-war economic performance on the comparatively low skill levels of the country's workforce. The implication here is that if skill levels can be raised through vocational education and training, this will lead to an improvement in economic performance.

It is worth considering the evidence underpinning the contention that economic performance can be improved by upgrading the skill base. In the case of the UK, comparative research into the relationship between training and productivity in Britain, France and Germany was carried out by the National Institute for Social and Economic Research (NIESR) during the 1980s.[5] Part of the research programme involved a study of manufacturing plants in Britain and Germany which were compared on the basis of 'matched samples' (i.e. similar samples in terms of type of industry and size of firm), in an attempt to hold constant other variables which may affect productivity. The research found significantly higher levels of productivity in the German plants than in their British equivalents and suggested that the variations in training provision were the main causal factor. Their conclusion was that:

. . . in today's world of international competition, efficient production even of technically unsophisticated products, benefits from technically advanced

machinery operated by a workforce with a high level of skills. Moreover, high levels of skills were in fact a pre-condition for the successful selection of appropriate machinery and its efficient utilization.

These results, then, appeared to provide convincing evidence that it was national systems of training which accounted for differing levels of labour productivity; indeed, the results of the NIESR programme have taken on a doctrinal status in that they are frequently quoted by those who wish to blame the UK's training system for its relative economic under performance.

A discussion of the relationship between economic performance and training is informed by reference to the concept of a 'skills equilibrium'. Ashton *et al.*[6] note that it is possible to identify two kinds of skills shortages facing industry: the disequilibrium kind, and the equilibrium kind.

Disequilibrium skills shortages – the pro-cyclical nature of training

Figure 11.7 shows that disequilibrium skills shortages depend on the economic cycle:

- Point A – training spend/volume peaks at the height of the economic cycle
- Point B – the economy moves into recession; training spend/volume falls steeply
- Point C – the level of economic activity is at its lowest point; training spend/volume falls further; training departments are disbanded
- Point D – the economy is recovering, but the volume of training is much slower to recover; skills shortages appear, driving up wages
- Point E – the economy begins to overheat as inflationary pressures build up, fed by higher wages.

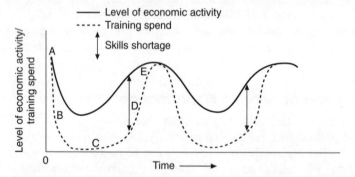

Figure 11.7. Disequilibrium skills shortages and the economic cycle.

Training in the UK is said to be 'pro-cyclical'. Disequilibrium skills shortages are associated with an upturn in the economic cycle, where firms compete to attract skills in short supply, usually by offering higher wages. As can be seen in Figure 11.7, when the economy moves into recession, organizations cut back on training spend and the volume of training falls.

Equilibrium skills shortages

It is argued that the UK economy is stuck in a 'low-skills equilibrium'.[7] The process of deindustrialization has resulted in a restructuring of the labour market, where firms specialize in lines of production which are relatively low-skilled when viewed in relation to international competitors. Much of industry perceives training needs in terms of immediate shortages, an attitude which tends to preclude the adoption of a systematic, long-term strategy towards training. Finegold argues that there are factors militating against training:

- **Short-termism.** A short-termist perspective therefore results in the UK being locked in a low-skills equilibrium. Organizations who are under pressure to achieve short-term profitability are unlikely to invest in human capital because of the long payback period associated with investments in training. Shareholders expect immediate returns on investment.
- **The returns to training.** Earlier we spoke of investing in human capital as being analogous to investing in physical capital (i.e. plant and machinery). However, there are two essential differences between these types of investment:
  - (i) **The free rider problem.** Plant and machinery are fixed – 'bolted to the floor' – whereas people are mobile. It is possible, therefore, for a firm to invest in human capital but be unable to realize the returns on that investment. This manifests itself in the problem of poaching – trained staffs are employed by competitor firms who offer a higher wage. These competitor firms do not themselves train and therefore do not incur the costs of training – they are 'free riders'. This means that many firms in the industry, acting rationally in their own self-interest, will decide not to train because they are unable to internalize the benefits of that training. In economic terms, this is a case of market failure (see Chapter 8). It is argued that without government intervention, the labour market will fail to generate enough training to meet the skills needs of the nation. This is a justification for policies such as a training levy (or tax) to force firms to contribute to the cost of training in their industries and to alleviate the free rider problem.
  - (ii) **Measuring the payback to training.** It is notoriously difficult to capture the returns to training, and even harder to quantify them. When firms invest in fixed capital, e.g. a machine producing a particular product, they can apply accounting techniques which will calculate, relatively accurately, the financial return on that investment throughout the lifetime of that machine. Not so for investing in people – the returns to training, particularly of the 'hearts and minds' rather than the job skills variety, tend to accrue into the future and consequently the benefits of training are difficult to extricate from other organizational variables which may have impacted on performance, e.g. rewards.

Exercise

If there are such strong disincentives for organizations to train, why do you think that many do?

Feedback

Many organizations like to 'grow their own timber' and see training as a tool for transmitting organizational culture as well as for teaching work-related skills. Nevertheless, it is true that a number of organizations have a problem with training which involves generic (or transferrable) skills which are marketable outside the organization. In countries with a strong pro-training culture, such as Germany, companies like Volkswagen tend to train more apprentices than they are likely to need. The rationale for this is that they can then take on the best performers and the rest can join the labour market armed with their experience and qualifications. Generally speaking, the more short-termist the attitude of the organization, the less training it is likely to undertake.

11.5.3 Lifelong learning

The UK's approach to education and training has been described as 'front-loaded'. This is evidenced by the fact that, until the late 1980s, the majority of young people left school at sixteen and relatively few progressed to higher education. Many of those who left school at sixteen never received any more education or any training for the rest of their lives. Furthermore, when people did enter the labour market, they received initial job training which stopped either when they were 'qualified' or once they were seen to be performing competently. It is argued that the level of education and training provision delivered by this approach is inadequate to meet the skills needs of a nation operating in competitive global markets. As we have seen (in Chapter 2), the popular wisdom is that, in the future, jobs will be far less secure and people will need to change their careers several times during their working lives. If this is the case, then people will require re-education and retraining throughout their careers, i.e. people need to learn continuously throughout their lives. Professional bodies such as the Chartered Institute of Personnel and Development have recognized this and require from their qualified members evidence that they have taken steps to further their professional development on a continuous basis. Furthermore, the government has made some legislative proposals to support the creation of a 'learning society', where lifelong learning is the norm.[8]

This section will be concluded with a quotation from Will Hutton,[9] who identifies a clear link between economic performance and education and training and, in doing so, makes a strong case for investing in human capital.

There are strong positive returns to training and education if the proper levels of skill are attained. Vocational training provides a significant return for those who undertake it relative to those who have no qualifications at all. Men and women who succeed in getting at least one A level have higher lifetime earnings than if they had worked during that extra period of study and invested their surplus earnings in the stock market . . . If returns for individuals can be high, then the wider social returns on good education can be high too, even if they are notoriously difficult to measure. If it has more skills available to it, the economy can grow more rapidly without reaching inflationary bottlenecks. With lower unemployment and a skilled labour force, social security spending is reduced, thus allowing a compensating increase in investment spending for any given level of public expenditure. Above all, productivity levels are raised as the human capital stock improves.

Summary

We began this section by considering the link between education and economic performance. We discussed the debate around the value of higher education and went on to examine a number of perspectives on education policy. In assessing the economic arguments surrounding training, we concluded that organizations are more likely to see training as an investment if they take a long-term view of business planning.

Examination questions for this chapter are given in Appendix 2.

References

1 Halsey, A. M. (1995) *Change in British Society*.
2 Marshall, T. H. (1950) Citizenship and Social Class. In *Sociology at the Crossroads* (ed. Marshall, T.). Heinemann.
3 Elliott, R. F. (1991) *Labour Economics: a Comparative Text*. McGraw-Hill.

4 Ball, S. (1990) *Politics and Policy Making in Education: Explorations in policy sociology.* Routledge.
5 Steedman, H. and Wagner, K. (1989) *Productivity, Machinery and Skills: Clothing manufacture in Britain and Germany.* NIESR, May.
6 Ashton, D., Green, F. and Hoskins, M. (1989) The training system of British capitalism: changes and prospects. In The *Restructuring of the UK Economy* (ed. Green, F.). Harvester Wheatsheaf.
7 Finegold, D. and Soskice, D. (1988) The failure of training in Britain: analysis and prescription. *Oxford Review of Economic Policy*, **4**, No. 3.
8 DfEE (1998) The Learning Age (green paper).
9 Hutton, W. (1995) *The State We're In*, Jonathan Cape, London.

Web-site addresses

Chartered Institute for Personnel and Development: http://www.cipd.co.uk
Commission for Racial Equality: http://www.cre.gov.uk
Department for Education and Skills: http://www.dfes.gov.uk
Disability Rights Commission: http://www.drc.org.uk
Equal Opportunities Commission: http://www.eoc.org.uk
Learning and Skills Council: http://www.lsc.gov.uk
Office for National Statistics: http://www.ons.gov.uk
Official Government Statistics: http://www.statistics.gov.uk
University for Industry: http://www.ufiltd.co.uk

12 The legal context of management

By tradition the conduct of civil litigation in England and Wales, as in other common law jurisdictions, is adversarial. Within a framework of substantive and procedural law established by the state for the resolution of civil disputes, the main responsibility for the initiation and conduct of proceedings rests with the parties to each individual case, and it is normally the plaintiff who sets the pace. The role of the judge is to adjudicate on issues selected by the parties when they choose to present them to the court.

From the Interim Report on the Civil Justice System in England and Wales, 1995, page 7, by Lord Woolf, Master of the Rolls

Chapter objectives

In this chapter you will:

- Examine the sources, structure and administration of the legal system, with particular reference to England and Wales and
- Review the operation of key branches of the law relevant to employment organizations.

Exercise

Suppose an employee of seven years' service has a three months' mutual notice period incorporated into his contract of employment through a collective agreement made between his union (of which he is a member) and his employer. Also assume that this employee suffers a serious accident at work which requires him to be away for several weeks, and he blames his employer for the accident. The employer decides to dismiss the employee because of his absence, but with only one month's notice.

What legal action can the employee take? Which branches of the law are likely to be involved in such a case?

Feedback

As improbable as it may seem, this type of case is quite common. The different types of law involved are several:

- The Employment Rights Act 1996 entitles the employee to one weeks' notice for every year of service up to 12 weeks. The Act also entitles the employee to claim unfair dismissal and to claim breach of contract on termination of contract. The employee could take these complaints under civil law (that is, **employment law**) to the employment tribunal.
- There might also have been a breach of the regulations under the Health and Safety at Work Act 1974. Although the employee cannot take a claim to the employment tribunal under this statute the Health and Safety at Work Executive could prosecute the employer in the **criminal courts** (that is, the magistrates' court or the crown court).

● **The law of contract under the common law** is also relevant: By failing to look after the employee's health and safety the employer is in breach of one of the implied terms of the contract of employment. If the employee can also show there was negligence by the employer he could sue for damages for the **tort of negligence**. This action would be taken in the civil courts, such as the county court. The employer's breach of contract of the express term to give the employee three months' notice and the **implied term** to look after his health and safety could be added to the actions in the employment tribunal and the latter give rise to a claim for constructive dismissal as well as unfair dismissal.

This scenario informs us that there are a number of complex but interlocking legal rights, duties and means of redress using different parts of the legal system. Some of the main ones will now be examined.

Chapter introduction	Today, the law has an unprecedented influence on work organizations and the employment relationship. The interrelationship between the law and the other contextual influences on organizations discussed in this book is a complex one. In the UK it is the product of our unique history, political, social and economic development. The exact influence, role and importance of the law remains contentious depending on individual perspectives; some, for example, believe that the law should play a direct regulatory part in organizational activities, others that a balance should be struck between 'interference' and 'freedom of behaviour'. There is also a strong body of opinion that believes the law should take a minimal role by providing a framework of standards allowing much of the day-to-day behaviour of organizations and individuals to be determined by freedom of choice. You will see these preferences reflected in the chapters on the political, social and economic contexts.

12.1   What is 'law'?

Law is a 'way of regulating behaviour, of deciding what can be done and what cannot be done'.[1] It is a set of rules which prescribe behaviour of citizens, rather than describing behaviour as would be the case in the laws of science. In other words, the law is 'normative' so that it lays down a required pattern of behaviour.

12.2   The rule of law

The standards which should 'fix' the application of the law irrespective of the desire of individual or collective rulers is known as the 'rule of law'. According to F. A. Hayek,[2] it provides 'that government in all its actions is bound by the rules fixed and announced beforehand – rules which make it possible to foresee with fair certainty how the authority will use its coercive powers in given circumstances, and to plan one's individual affairs on the basis of this knowledge'.

The degree of certainty encapsulated and enforced by the law permits employers and government to plan for economic growth in an environment of social stability. The rule of law can be a buttress against authoritarianism. This relates directly to the 'fair and just' rules that we see exercised in employee relations, such as in disciplinary procedures.

12.3   The nature and development of English law

In contrast to continental Europe the English legal system is based on the common law of the land rather than the influence of Roman, and later Napoleonic, law (*circa* 1805). The principles of the English system were laid down by the Saxons and augmented during the Middle Ages, then developed gradually throughout the period 1600–1900.

During the late nineteenth century numerous changes were made to the courts and key laws that provide the basis for today's legal system.

12.3.1   The common law

The decisions of the courts established in the medieval period quickly formed a body of legal principles known as **precedents**, often based on traditional customs of the country. Because of the country-wide jurisdiction of these courts this case law became known as the common law and was applicable in criminal as well as civil matters. Despite the growth of statute law (legislation) which is superior to the common law, today the latter is still a major source of employment and other legal rights.

Equity

The early common law could not always provide full remedies for the parties involved and a second arm of the administration of justice developed – the law of equity. It was originally administered by the Lord Chancellor in the court of Chancery, who acted as a 'go-between' God and the monarch. Equity is not the rival of the common law, but is there to supplement it. The ecclesiastical origins of equity mean that it will emphasize the performance of the morally right; one of the maxims of equity is that it acts '*in personam*', that is, upon the conscience of the defendant. So, for example, the plaintiff may have an equitable (that is, a fair and reasonable) right to something even though that right cannot be enforced in contract only. Decisions were based on the 'facts stated' – there was no recourse to precedent; the case was decided by the judge according to what was fair and reasonable, in a way, trying to dispense justice like the biblical Solomon. The law of equity attracted much criticism because of its uncertainty; one critic said that 'equity varied with the length of the Chancellor's foot'.

12.3.2   The development of collective rights

In 1871, 1875 and 1906 three pieces of legislation were passed; these have been termed 'the golden formula' by Lord Wedderburn because they have enabled trades unions to operate without automatic risk of being outside the law. The legislative formula remained virtually unaltered until the 1971 Industrial Relations Act. The growth of industrial society in the nineteenth century led to the concentration of large numbers of working people in metropolitan centres. By changing the law when they did Parliament was responding not only to a tangible pressure for change, but in so doing adapting to evolving social trends. Any analysis of the laws applicable to unions and collective relations in the UK will find that they have changed, but only when strong economic forces have been at work alongside public acceptance of change. The decline of trades unions from a membership of 13.0 million in 1979 to 7.8 million in 2002 is not because of the so-called 'anti-union' legislation of the Thatcher and Major governments (1979–1997), but because of economic and social changes discussed in Chapters 8 and 11.

12.3.3   The development of the individual employee–employer relationship

An employer . . . may refuse to employ (a workman) from the most mistaken, capricious, malicious, or morally reprehensible motives that can be conceived, but the workman has no right of action against him.

Lord Davey in *Allen* v. *Flood* (1898)

The industrialized waged worker became legally bound to the employer through a contract of service (i.e. a contract of employment), a legally binding agreement that primarily gave rights to the employer. However, the common law also developed to provide mutual rights and duties which today form part of the implied terms of the contract of employment. These include the employer's duty to pay wages where the employee is ready and willing to work, to take reasonable care of the employee's safety and not to ask the employee to do something which would be unlawful. Similarly, the employee must provide faithful and loyal service to the employer, to work in a way that does not endanger the safety of fellow workers, and obey reasonable orders given by the employer. Until the 1960s the employment relationship primarily rested on the common law rules (exemplified in *Allen* v. *Flood*) implied into contracts while very little state regulation existed.

12.3.4   Development of state involvement in the employment relationship

The difficulty for the individual prior to the 1960s was that the common law notion of the employment relationship based on contract was one of equality between the parties. The ideas of market capitalism meant that both parties were free to enter as well as terminate the contract on terms agreed by them. This fiction meant that the only significant bargaining protection workers possessed was to organize collectively and place pressure on employers through membership of trades unions. Before the 1960s state intervention in the employment relationship had been limited, with some minor exceptions, to health and safety. Throughout the nineteenth century a series of Acts of Parliament had been passed to secure higher standards of health and safety in factories and in other workplaces. In the early twentieth century extensive legislation was enacted to lay down the hours and circumstances under which children and young persons (i.e. 16- to 18-year-olds) could be employed.

The Second World War was in many respects a watershed for the role of the state. During the war the government had intervened in the economy of the UK in an unprecedented way. With increasing technological, economic and globally competitive pressures governments, not only in the UK, sought to influence the efficacy of the employment relationship, at both the collective level to prevent disputes and strikes and at the individual level. During the 1960s it became increasingly accepted that a stable, motivated and committed workforce was more likely to exist if individuals were given a sound level of basic employment rights enshrined in statute, rather than the slowly evolving common law.

A further emphasis was given to this trend in 1972 when the UK joined the European Economic Community (now the European Union: EU). From the 1970s onwards the European Community has developed legislation under its Social Policy objectives to improve the working lives of the citizens of the Community in the light of volatile labour markets and transnational flows of capital. The full impact of the legislation of the EU is discussed in Chapter 10. But it should be remembered that intertwined with these institutional and structual changes is the changing norms of society. After 1945 the populations of Western democracies demanded new legal rights and means of redress to accompany improved economic status brought about by the consumer age. Working people were no longer prepared to accept notions of an employment relationship that was reflected in master and servant, but looked for one with both legal and normative rights attached to it. The flexibility of the rule of law is exemplified by remembering that it was legally as well as socially acceptable (if not accepted by all) that in the 1940s and early 1950s working women would keep their marriage a secret from their employer for fear of being dismissed. The assumption of many employers was that a married woman would naturally want to have children and leave work at an inconvenient time or take time-off to look after their children. Several employers had a 'single-female' only recruitment policy.

12.3.5   The development of state involvement in commercial bodies and transactions

With the growth of commercial enterprises in the eighteenth and nineteenth centuries, so there grew up laws to regulate and define the activities of these bodies. Law has had to be developed to apply to large, multinational corporations with diverse financial interests which are not always easily identifiable. Sometimes the law is designed to lift the 'corporate veil' or to penetrate the obscure detail that accompanies the rules of many large corporations. The basic reason for state intervention in this area is to provide a counterbalance to the financial power and market position of commercial organizations. The key beneficiaries are consumers, shareholders, suppliers and competitors.

12.4   Sources of law

We have already seen in Section 12.1 that English law has two branches: **civil** and **criminal**, and these, in turn, each have two main sources: **common law** and **statute**.

12.4.1   Common law

We have already seen how the common law has developed over the centuries. Some common law in the employment field can be traced back to the thirteenth century, although most principles were developed in the nineteenth and twentieth centuries, particularly concerning the contract of employment. One senior judge has summed up the common law as the 'common sense of the community . . . crystallised and formulated by our forefathers'. However, it would be wrong to suppose that common law is of relevance only in the past; the decisions of the judges today contribute to the dynamic nature of the common law.

It is important to note that one of the key tasks of the judiciary is to interpret the statute. An example is the decision of the House of Lords in *Polkey* v. *AE Dayton Services Ltd* (1988) (a). The interpretation of Section 98 of the Employment Rights Act 1996 gave rise to the House of Lords declaring that the employment tribunal, when hearing an unfair dismissal complaint, should ask itself the question: 'Did the employer act reasonably at the time of dismissal?'

The decisions of the judges in higher (or superior) courts binds lower (or inferior) courts. The core of the judgment which lays down a binding precedent is called the *ratio decidendi*. In some cases where there is no binding precedent lower courts look for guidance by examining similar cases decided by the higher courts; even though something said may not form part of the ratio it may, however, be a persuasive precedent. Where judges make statements not forming part of the ratio, but which may be relevant for cases in the future, these statements are known as being *obiter dicta* (literally, something said by the way). Decisions of the courts and the employment tribunals are reported and recorded by a number of sources.

12.4.2   Statute

Today, statute is the most important source of law. Legislation passed by the UK Parliament takes precedent over all other sources of law except relevant EU law. Since the 1960s there has been a significant movement away from the *laissez-faire* principles to a significantly more interventionist and regulatory environment.

The Labour governments from 1964 to 1979 were responsible for the introduction of legislation aimed at addressing discrimination in the workplace (see Chapter 11) and providing protection for workers, mainly through extending the concept of fair and unfair dismissal. Before this the main source of individual redress was by initiating potentially expensive and time-consuming civil litigation. From 1979 to 1997 the Conservative government was concerned with redressing the perceived imbalance of law in favour of trades unions and consequently passed seven pieces of legislation to curtail collective power, particularly in the arena of industrial action.

Parliamentary sovereignty means that all legislative-making power is vested in Parliament and that there is no theoretical legal limit to its powers. However, there are various checks and balances referred to in Chapter 9. With the growth of delegated legislation to other bodies such as local authorities and public services the courts have an important role in ensuring that the government as well as these other bodies have not acted *ultra vires*, that is, beyond the limits of its powers defined in law.

The purpose of statute law is to amend and update existing law and create new law. An example of the former is the Equal Pay (Amendment) Regulations 1983 which amended and brought up to date the Equal Pay Act 1970. You will note that a lot of updating is done by secondary legislation. An example of new law is the Employment Act 2002. Statute can also be introduced to consolidate the law. A good example is the Trade Union and Labour Relations (Consolidation) Act 1992 which brought together several pieces of collective statute together into one act of Parliament, but did not introduce any new law.

12.4.3   Equity

This body of rules to correct defects and unfairness in the workings of the common law was discussed in Section 12.3.1.

12.4.4   Custom and practice

This source of law is less important now than it was before the turn of the twentieth century. However, it continues to exert an influence in both employment and commercial laws. For example:

- Employment law – The establishment of the employee's right to receive an annual bonus is because it became customary practice to pay one.
- Commercial law – The payment of a fee becomes customary when particular services are rendered.

- Land law – The legal 'right of way' across a tract of land is established over several years by persistent usage.

For custom and practice to establish a legal right or duty it must be notorious (well known), certain (firmly established without ambiguity), reasonable (subject to the test of reasonableness in the courts) **and** have a history (be established over a period of time).

12.4.5   Codes of Practice

These have become increasingly important and may derive from the Secretary of State or from agencies charged by the government to issue them. In the employment field four are of particular importance:

- Advisory, Conciliation and Arbitration Service (ACAS): Codes on disciplinary and grievance procedures (no. 1), also: time off from work (no. 2), and information for collective bargaining (no. 3).
- Commission for Racial Equality (CRE): Code for the elimination of racial discrimination and the promotion of equality of opportunity in employment.
- Equal Opportunities Commission (EOC): Code for the elimination of discrimination on the grounds of sex and marriage and the promotion of equal opportunities in employment.
- Disability Rights Commission (DRC): The reissuing of the Code originally published by the Department for Education and Employment; its principal purpose is for the elimination of discrimination on the ground of disability.

12.4.6   The European Union

In 1972 the UK joined the European Economic Community (after 1992: the European Union). Since then the EU has had a significant impact on the UK law through the incorporation of EU binding legislation (directives). Where matters of EU law are concerned UK law is subordinate to it. The supremacy of EU law has caused a number of legal and political tensions. In the 1970s the (then) EEC developed a Social Policy with the aim to improve the lives of all the citizens of the Community. Thereafter, a series of Social Policy Action Programmes were issued to contain legislation to achieve this objective. Some of the directives issued under this Policy are:

- The Equal Treatment Directive 1976, and Amendment Directive 2002
- The Equal Pay Directive 1975
- The Collective Redundancies Directive 1976
- The Acquired Rights Directive 1977
- Several Health and Safety Directives since 1992, including the Working Time Directive
- The Pregnant Workers Directive 1992
- The European Works Council Directive 1994
- The Part-Time Workers Directive 1996
- The Fixed-Term Work Directive 1999

The source of all EU law is the founding treaty – The Treaty of Rome 1957, as amended by subsequent treaties, e.g. 1997 Treaty of Amsterdam.

The European Commission brings forward proposals for legislation; it is the executive body of the EU with a civil service supporting the Commissioners who are appointed by the Member States. Draft legislation is presented to the Parliament for consultation, but this body does not have any veto or initiating powers for legislation. The Social Partners (EU-wide unions and employers' bodies) can agree special implementation of draft directives and be consulted on drafts. The final approval of directives remains with the Council of Ministers which is the forum for the elected politicians of the Member States of the EU.

12.4.7   Books of authority

Written by eminent jurists and academics, these have received relatively little attention in the UK compared to continental Europe. They may carry weight almost equal to that of judicial precedents and be cited for an authoriative view in courts or tribunals. Modern examples include *Salmond's Law of Torts* and *Croner's Employment Law.*

12.5   The legislative process

The process whereby a Bill becomes an Act of Parliament (primary legislation), shown in Figure 12.1, can be lengthy and will depend on the degree of government support and/ or the urgency of the proposed law. It is not always possible or appropriate for such primary legislation to contain detailed sections on implementation or practical operation. The Act may be drafted so as to provide a broad framework allowing ministers to 'fill in' the details by means of regulatory secondary legislation. Such legislation is known as a Parent Act or an Enabling Act, a fine example being the Health and Safety at Work Act 1974.

An Enabling Act 'enables' the minister to introduce further regulations under the auspices of the original legislation when further periods of consultation or research have been completed. The Parent Act permits the principles of the new law to be established but detailed operational measures to be introduced, sometimes over a long period of time. The secondary legislation is usually passed in the form of a Statutory Instrument, of which there are many examples in the employment field:

- Regulations made under the Health and Safety at Work Act 1974. The statutory instruments are the 'teeth' of the legislation, such as the Control of Substances Hazardous to Health Regulations 1999. Most health and safety regulations now emanate from the European Union.
- Regulations made under the Sex Discrimination Act 1975. Normally, these will add to or clarify areas of regulatory responsibility, e.g. the Sex Discrimination and Equal Pay (Remedies) Regulations 1993 were introduced to give effect to the decision of the European Court of Justice that the UK's ceiling on compensation in sex discrimination cases was unlawful and contrary to the EC Equal Treatment Directive. Subsequently, the compensation limit was lifted and there is now no ceiling.

The minister who is given the power to make delegated legislation may only make Regulations within the limits defined in the Parent Act otherwise he or she will be acting *ultra vires*, and subsequently may be challenged in the courts.[3]

New primary statute law must begin as a Bill introduced into either the House of Commons or the House of Lords, although it is more likely to be the former (see Chapter 9). The process of how a Bill becomes an Act of Parliament can be summarized as shown in Figure 12.1.

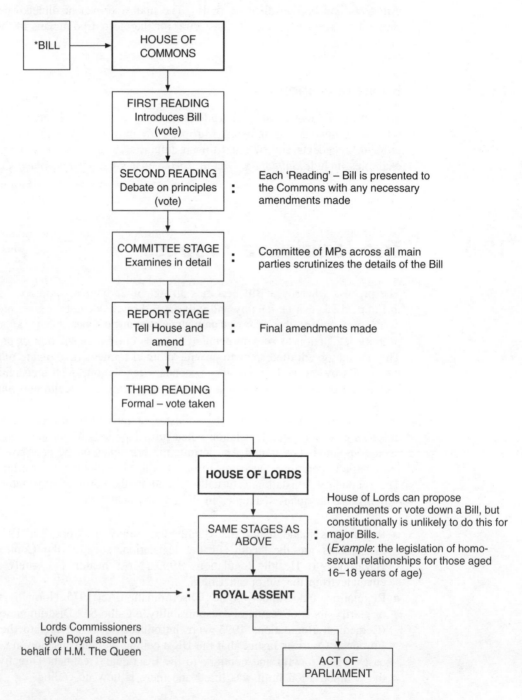

* May be a Private Member's Bill or introduced as part of the Government's legislative programme announced in the Queen's speech.

Figure 12.1. How a Bill becomes an Act of Parliament.

12.6 The administration of the law: the system of courts

Although the system of courts in England and Wales dates back to medieval days they have undergone reform over time, particularly in the 1870s and 1970s. The system of courts can be divided into three categories (see Figure 12.2):

- Inferior courts (e.g. the county court)
- Courts of special jurisdiction (e.g. employment tribunal) and
- Superior courts (e.g. court of appeal), including the European Court of Justice.

12.6.1 Inferior courts

The role of the inferior courts is twofold: To act as courts of first instance (i.e. where cases will first be heard) and to settle minor cases that need not be referred to superior courts.

- **The county courts**, of which there are about 300, hear cases under civil law. These are not based on the old shire system of courts nor related to any specific geographical area of the country. The courts' jurisdictions are known as 'districts', divided into judges' circuits. The County Courts Act 1984 gives these courts wide jurisdiction to

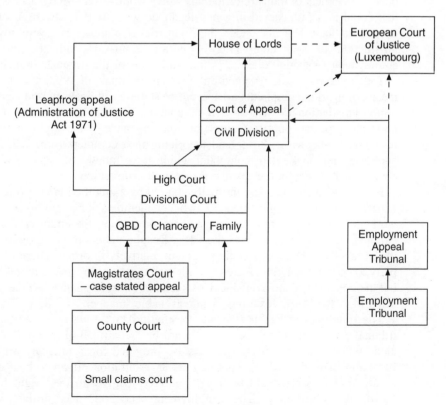

The civil courts of England and Wales

Figure 12.2. The civil courts in England and Wales.

cover actions in contract, tort, recovery of land, equity, probate and monies recoverable under statute. Legal procedure is simpler and litigation costs less in the county court where solicitors and barristers have right of audience. There are no jury trials, the case being heard by one judge.

The financial limitations on the value of damages sought in the county court is generally £50 000. Small claims, that is, those not exceeding £1000 (at the time of writing) will be heard by a district judge, who is a solicitor (previously known as a Registrar). The losing party does not pay legal costs. There is also a new small claims arbitration procedure for claims not exceeding £8000 (at the time of writing). This is an informal method of dealing with claims that are too large to go through the small claims procedure.

- **The magistrates' courts:** The key role of these courts is to hear criminal cases; there are special juvenile courts to hear cases involving children under seventeen years of age.

(Note: At the time of writing reforms have been planned for the civil judicial system.)

12.6.2   Courts of special jurisdiction

There are several tribunals and minor courts that exercise power over specialized jurisdictions. Of particular interest to the HR practitioner is the employment tribunal.

Employment tribunal

In 1968 the Donovan Commission Report on Industrial Relations in the UK recommended the establishment of industrial tribunals which would offer speedy, accessible, cheap justice that could be administered in a non-legalistic way. In 1971 the tribunals (which already existed to hear appeals under the Industrial Training Act) were given an increased jurisdiction to hear complaints of unfair dismissal. With the growth of statutory employment protection after 1971 the workloads of the tribunals dramatically increased.

Today, the tribunals, renamed employment tribunals in 1998, are the principal judicial means of hearing complaints arising out of statutory obligations and rights. There is some minor jurisdiction to hear breach of contract claims, but these must arise out of the termination of the contract. Complaints must be made by the applicant on a form IT1. The respondent who wishes to defend the claim must complete form IT3. In most cases the applicant must make their complaint within three months of the date of the unlawful act complained of, e.g. unfair dismissal or sex discrimination.

Employment tribunals are normally chaired by a qualified lawyer (either a solicitor or a barrister) who is accompanied by two lay members, one traditionally drawn from the workers' side (e.g. a trade union), and the other from the employers' side (e.g. from an employer's association such as the CBI). Despite the enormous growth in the complexity of the law the tribunal proceedings remain relatively informal. There is no need for either party to be represented by a lawyer (although most employers are represented in this way), but there is no legal aid available. Costs are not awarded against one party unless they have acted in a 'frivolous, vexatious or unreasonable' manner.

The Employment Rights (Dispute Resolution) Act 1998 reformed the workings of the tribunals, allowing more cases to be heard by a chairman of tribunal to hear cases sitting alone without lay members. The Act also provided for a voluntary arbitration system to be administered by ACAS. This permits an arbitration officer to hear and decide a case of unfair dismissal should both parties agree to give up their right for the case to be heard by the tribunal. The Employment Act 2002 has further reformed tribunal procedures. The means of redress are identical to those that can be awarded by a tribunal.

However, there is no appeal from arbitration once the parties have agreed to be bound by the arbitrator's decision.

The Employment Appeal Tribunal (EAT)

Appeals from the tribunal are allowed on a point of law only to the EAT. The chairman is usually a lawyer or judge who normally sits with two or four lay members. Where the tribunal decision is made by a chairman sitting alone the EAT chairman may also hear the case sitting alone. Appeals must be made within 42 days of the decision of the employment tribunal.

Besides some special courts there are also domestic tribunals which govern the conduct of certain professions:

- Solicitors' Disciplinary Tribunal
- Disciplinary Tribunals of the Bar
- Professional Conduct and Health Committees of the General Medical Council

12.6.3 Superior Courts

The Supreme Court of Judicature comprises the Crown Court (Criminal) and the High Court of Justice (Civil).

The Crown Court

This is the main court to hear criminal cases, although it does have some minor civil jurisdiction. England and Wales is divided into 94 'circuits' like those for the county courts, with a permanent administration. The Crown Court circuits are presided over by a High Court judge or a presiding judge, specially appointed by the Lord Chancellor.

The High Court of Justice

Any legal matter may be heard in any division of the High Court throughout the country, although the three divisions of the Court will usually hear matters relevant to their own special jurisdictions:

- **Chancery Division:** This is headed by the Lord Chancellor and the Vice-Chancellor. It will hear cases on appeal or at first instance concerning trusts, the administration of estates, company law, partnership, patents and non-contentious probate matters.
- **Queen's Bench Division:** This has mainly a first-instance jurisdiction in respect of breaches of contract, tort, land and property claims and breaches of statutory duty. There is no theoretical ceiling on the value of claims that can be heard or on damages awarded. A key duty exercised by the Queen's Bench Division is to hear cases of judicial review, for example writs of a public body acting *ultra vires*. It will also hear applications for injunctions. There are also special courts for hearing commercial and admiralty matters.
- **Family Division:** This hears cases of first instance and on appeal concerning family, matrimonial and probate matters.

Court of Appeal

Twenty-nine Lords Justices of Appeal sit in the Court of Appeal; they should not be confused with the Lords of Appeal in Ordinary sitting in the House of Lords. The Court is divided into two divisions:

- **Civil Division:** The Master of the Rolls is the President of the Court. It may hear appeals on a question of law from all three divisions of the High Court and the county courts. Appeals are heard by rehearing the case, and 'leave of appeal' must be granted by the Court before a case can be heard. This does not mean that all the witnesses are recalled, but the Court will examine all the written evidence and records, will hear legal argument from the parties' barristers, but not accept new evidence.
- **Criminal Division:** The Lord Chief Justice is the President of the Court. Appeal on a question of law is by right, but those that are a mixture of law and fact must be given leave of appeal unless the trial judge recommends appeal. Appeals can be heard on sentence, but the Court can increase a sentence as well as reduce or 'quash' it.

The House of Lords

More properly called the Appeal Committee of the House of Lords, this was created in 1876 and comprises a number of Lords of Appeal in Ordinary who are past and present senior judges who are also members of the House of Lords. The Committee may hear civil and criminal appeals. In matters of purely UK law (i.e. not emanating from the EU) the Committee is the highest court in the land, including Scotland and Northern Ireland. Its decisions are absolutely binding on all lower courts, although it may now depart from its own previous decisions.

The Judicial Committee of the Privy Council

This body is based on the Monarch's Council, but after 1833 senior judges constituted the appellate function. The Privy Council heard appeals from the superior courts of the British Empire and later the Commonwealth, but nowadays very few countries exercise this option.

12.6.4   European Court of Justice (ECJ)

The ECJ is one of the EU's four institutions; its role is to interpret and enforce EU law. The judgments of the Court have had significant impact in the field of employment rights and commercial law. The Court consists of fifteen judges, one appointed by each of the Member States and a sixteenth judge appointed by the larger States in rotation. They are assisted by six Advocate-Generals (senior legal officers) who investigate a case and give reasoned opinions to the court on the issues of EU law raised in each case. The judges do not have to accept the opinion of the Advocate-General, but usually do so. Because of the number of cases it normally takes eighteen months for a case to be heard.

Under different articles of the 1957 Treaty of Rome the jurisdiction of the ECJ varies:

- Article 169 – Actions against Member States for failure to comply with EU legislation.
- Articles 173 and 175 – Actions against EU institutions for failure to comply with EU law.
- Article 177 – Preliminary rulings on matters referred to the Court by a court or tribunal of a Member State for interpretation or meaning of some aspect of EU law. For example, in 1997 the House of Lords referred the case of *R* v. *Secretary of State for Employment, ex-parte Seymour-Smith & Perez* (b) to the Court concerning whether the UK's two-year qualifying period for claiming unfair dismissal was contrary to the EU's Equal Treatment Directive.

12.6.5 **The European Court of Human Rights and the European Convention on Human Rights and Fundamental Freedoms**

The Convention is an international treaty of the Council of Europe adopted in November 1950 and brought into force in 1953. By 1997 forty countries had signed the Convention. The UK was the first state to ratify the Convention, but failed to fully implement it into domestic law. There has been no obligation on states to incorporate it into domestic law, but Article 1 required that the state 'secure' Convention rights to everyone within their jurisdiction, and Article 13 requires an 'effective remedy' to be provided for those whose rights have been violated. Eventually, in 1998 the UK government enacted the **Human Rights Act**, which came into effect in 2000.

The Act specifically applies to public bodies and rights can be directly enforceable in the UK courts and tribunals, which themselves must uphold the statutory provisions. All legislation, even that enacted before the Act came into effect, will be subject to its provisions. The Convention permits appeals to the European Court of Human Rights in Strasbourg (not to be confused with the EU's European Court of Justice in Luxembourg).

Some of the provisions of the Act prohibit torture, degrading treatment, slavery, forced labour and unlawful imprisonment and provide a right to liberty, security, privacy in private and family life, freedom of thought, conscience and religion, freedom of expression, freedom of assembly and association and freedom from discrimination.

The Act has head a clear impact on issues of privacy, but in other areas such as picketing, collective matters and discrimination its effect has been minimal.

12.7   The law of contract

12.7.1   Introduction

Contract is based in common law, that is, common law rather than legislation. The simple definition of a contract is: 'An agreement enforceable in law made by two or more persons (the offeror and offeree) for one or both parties to perform some act(s).'

However, there are a number of requirements for a contract to be lawful: First, there must be an **offer** and **acceptance** of the offer. A contract is more than just the exchange of mutual promises; there must be some **consideration**, i.e. money or monies for the performance of the contract, such as the payment of a fee for work carried out. This is sometimes known as 'the price of the bargain'. **Privacy of contract** means that only that contract and no others will bind the parties to the contract, even though they may be affected by it. Finally, there must be the intent (on the part of the parties) for the contract to be legally binding; for example, an agreement between a husband and wife would not (without further evidence) be legally binding.

A further factor that is key is the **legal capacity to contract**. Two special categories exist: minors (those under eighteen years of age) and those suffering from mental illness or intoxication of alcohol; in both cases special rules apply.

In relation to offer and acceptance there are a number of interesting principles which must be present: There needs to be **more than a mere interest to make a contract**. For example, the display of goods with prices in a shop window is an 'invitation to treat', a mere inducement for the shopper to make their own offer. This is not actually done until the shopper takes the goods selected to the cash desk. (See *Pharmaceutical Society of Great Britain* v. *Boots Cash Chemists (Southern) Ltd* [1953] (c), and *Harvey* v. *Facey* [1893] (d). A similar question arises in respect of advertisements: Most of these are invitations to treat and are not binding in law at that stage. In the case of employment contracts this is also true, although in the absence of other documentation such as a written contract where there is a legal dispute the court or tribunal may take into consideration the words used in a job advertisement to determine the content of the subsequent contract.

Generally, **acceptance of an offer to contract must be properly communicated and be absolute and unconditional**. A counter-offer is a rejection of the original offer. In most cases the acceptance of an offer must be accompanied by some overtly obvious sign of acceptance. For example, in *Felthouse* v. *Bindley* [1862] (e) the uncle of the owner of a horse wrote to his nephew saying: 'If I hear no more about him I consider the horse is mine at £30.75'. The nephew intended to sell the horse to his uncle but an auctioneer inadvertently sold the horse at auction along with some of the nephew's farm animals. The uncle sued the auctioneer, but the court said that there was no contract between him and his nephew because the latter had failed to communicate his acceptance of his uncle's offer.

Hyde v. *Wrench* [1840] (f)

The defendant offered his farm for sale at the price of £1000 to the plaintiff. The plaintiff responded by offering only £950. When this was rejected the plaintiff subsequently offered the original asking price of £1000. There was no contract between the parties. The original offer of £950 had been rejected. The new offer of £1000 was a new offer which had extinguished the original offer.

This principle is enshrined in law today: Any alteration to the terms of the offer will render the acceptance invalid.

An example applied to employment law

Suppose that an employer decides to make unilateral changes to the contracts of employment of his staff. The employer offers the new terms to the employees on a take it or leave it basis. The staff do nothing. The employer cannot assume that silence means they have accepted the new terms. In the absence of a good business reason for changing the contract terms any subsequent changes made will constitute a breach of contract and a dismissal for refusing to accept the new terms will be unfair dismissal.

The contract – additional points

Acceptance of the contract can be signified by the conduct of the party in question. Using the example of the employer making changes to contracts of employment, suppose that one of the new employees starts to voluntarily work under the new contractual conditions? This could include starting work earlier by one hour for the same rate of pay. This conduct could be argued as affirmation of (the new) contract by conduct.

Contracts, including contracts of employment, in common law do not have to be in writing and can be verbally made without the presence of witnesses. The Employment Rights Act 1996 (Section 1) requires that an employer give to a new employee a statement of the main contractual terms and conditions within two months of beginning employment. Section 4 of the same statute requires an employer to give to an existing employee a revised statement where certain terms and conditions have been changed. However, you should note that this 'statement' does not constitute the contract of employment and will not be treated by the courts as one in the absence of a written contract. But where this situation does occur the courts and tribunals will accept the 'statement' as evidence of contractual terms.

There are certain statutes that require specific contracts to be made in writing – for example, consumer credit agreements (Consumer Credit Act 1974) and the sale of land or property (Law of Property (Miscellaneous Provisions) Act 1989).

Illegality of contracts

Generally no contract can be enforced if it is based on or contains something illegal which is known to one of the parties. Examples include criminal activities, contracts contrary to public policy (such as those in restraint of trade) and those which offend accepted morality. This may be the case even where one party is entirely innocent and ignorant of the illegality.

12.7.2   Other factors that can affect the validity of the contract

Frustration of contract

This occurs when, without fault of either party, the contract becomes impossible or unlawful to perform, or commercially not viable, or where there has been such a change in the significance of the obligation that the performance of it would be fundamentally different from what the parties originally intended. If the contract is frustrated, it comes to an end automatically by operation of law and neither party will be in breach or be able to claim against the other, unless in an employment contract the claim is for wages due up to the date of frustration. The best examples of frustration are in employment contracts due to imprisonment or illness. However, the courts have been unwilling to find contracts frustrated in these circumstances because it may leave the employee without any remedy, and, moreover, it does not wish to undermine the statutory rights of the individual to claim unfair dismissal. A complication is that since 1996 employees may be covered by the Disability Discrimination Act 1995 which may render a dismissal for sickness absence disability discrimination. See Section 12.13.

12.7.3   Discharge by breach and remedies

Where one party fails to perform his obligations under the contract the other party may repudiate the contract and possibly seek damages for the loss suffered. Damages are a common law remedy which provide for financial redress for the injured party. The objective is to place the plaintiff in the position he or she would have been had the contract not been broken. The damages will be relative to actual loss suffered; the value ('measure' of the damages) will be objectively assessed, not determined by the value the plaintiff will put on his or her loss. Some contracts have penalty clauses in them so that the party responsible for a breach of contract pays the other party a pre-agreed sum. These are commonly known as clauses for liquidated damages. Damages are not confined to physical loss but can be obtained in respect of personal and psychological disturbance such as anxiety, frustration and inconvenience.

12.7.4   Specific performance and injunctions

These are remedies in equity and so will only be awarded by the courts where the circumstances render it fair and just to do so. Specific performance is a decree of the court requiring the defendant to perform his obligations under the contract, but it is not used where damages will provide an appropriate remedy, remembering that equity is there to remedy the defects in the common law, not replace it. As a principle of law the courts will not grant specific performance in respect of employment contracts. This is because the courts are extremely careful not to order something which is akin to slavery.

There are several types of injunctions, but the most commonly sought are prohibitory injunctions to stop or prevent one party from doing something. They are relatively common in employment disputes over disciplinary matters, recruitment decisions, misuse of confidential information or in collective disputes involving employer and trades union, usually where strike action has been called. The question of restraint clauses is considered in the next section.

12.8 Competition law

12.8.1 Contract law

A general principle is that clauses that seek to restrict trade are generally void. However, some restraint clauses may be legal if reasonable (taking account of trade custom), no wider than to protect the legitimate interests of the party and not contrary to the public interest. It is quite common for employees to voluntarily enter into a contract of employment with clauses that aim to restrict their behaviour during and after the termination of the contract. A restraint clause (or restrictive covenant) can be enforced for three reasons:

- Trade secrets, provided it is not excessive in scope or duration.
- Business connections, with the same provisos as above. Here the employee or former employee may not make contact with certain customers or clients in a private or new employed capacity.
- A former employee setting up in competition or working for a competitor within a time or geographical limit.

The employee is obliged by the implied duty of faithful and honest service not to divulge confidential information belonging to his employer nor permit a conflict of interest to arise. However, what of an ex-employee? In *Faccenda Chicken Ltd* v. *Fowler & ors* [1986] (g) the Court of Appeal laid down four tests:

- Did the nature of the job involve regularly handling confidential information?
- Was the information a trade secret or highly confidential? Only this type of information could be protected.
- Could the information be easily isolated from other information handled by the former employee?
- How far had the employer impressed on the employee the need for confidentiality?

In addition 'confidential' meant the information was not in the public domain and was not information that could be gained in a day-to-day manner without special access.

As well as the employer–employee relationship, restraint clauses may also be contractually provided with distributors, manufacturers, retailers and traders.

12.8.2 Public policy

As we have shown, the existence of a restraint clause may offend against public policy and be made void by the courts. Some contracts are prohibited by statute either implicitly or expressly. In the former situation it is for the judge to decide on the construction of the statute; for example, where a statute prohibits or excludes certain activities or requires conduct of a certain kind. In *Anderson Ltd* v. *Daniel* [1924] (h) a seller of artificial fertilizers was unable to recover the price of goods because he had failed to indicate in the invoice the chemical composition of the fertilizers supplied, which was required by Act of Parliament.

Express statutory prohibition

There is an enormous range of statutory provisions. One example is the Resale Prices Act 1976 where collective agreements between two or more persons to fix the price of goods which may be resold is unlawful, and the Crown may take civil proceedings including seeking an injunction to prevent the practice. The EU now has extensive legislation in this area. See Section 12.10.

12.9 The law of torts

The word 'tort' derives from the Norman-French meaning 'wrong'. A tort is a civil wrong which does not arise from a breach of criminal law or from contract. But like contract law the plaintiff may seek damages and/or an injunction. The general duty to refrain from committing a tort is imposed by the law of the land. There are many examples of torts, but the following are illustrative of the range:

- **Negligence:** Claims arise where the plaintiff claims the defendant had a duty of care, but the scope of a claim is broad and not always clear. However, it appears that this means that wherever one person is in a position to foresee that his or her act or omission may injure another the duty of care arises. This definition arises out of the famous case of *Donoghue* v. *Stevenson* [1932] (i) where the House of Lords upheld the decision that the manufacturer of a bottle of ginger beer should have ensured that a snail did not get into the bottle where it was reasonably foreseeable that a consumer might drink the contents of the bottle and be ill as a consequence.
- Careless misstatement and negligent misstatement, of which the latter may occur in drawing up a job reference.
- An occupier's liability to exercise reasonable care, although this duty is now augmented by statutory obligations.
- Trespass to both land and to the person; the latter may constitute assault and battery where an employer searches an employee without prior permission.
- False imprisonment – unlawfully restricting the freedom of another.
- Conversion of goods, so that the defendant deals with the plaintiff's goods in such a way that he calls the title of the goods into question.
- Trespass to goods – interference with the plaintiff's goods.
- Nuisance – this is governed by the rule of 'give and take' so that we must all bear certain inconveniences by virtue of living when and where we do.

Of key interest to employers is their liability in law for employees' stress at work. Following the *Walker* case in 1995 (j(i)) the Court of Appeal ruled in the *Hatton* case (j(ii)) that employers will only be liable in the tort of negligence where harm to the individual's health was reasonably foreseeable. Furthermore, that there are no occupations which are considered intrinsically dangerous to mental health. As part of their decision the Court laid down a series of guidelines on how liability should be determined.

Four torts specifically relevant to employment law are:

- Conspiracy to put unlawful pressure on the plaintiff. This tort has been used by employers in industrial disputes with trades unions where the latter have conspired to act in restraint of trade outside the common law immunities laid down in the Trade Union and Labour Relations (Consolidation) Act 1992 (TULR(C)A).

- Interference with the performance of a contract – this can be using lawful means to execute an unlawful act or where both means and act are unlawful. Again, the area of industrial disputes has presented a number of examples, such as striking workers through their union threatening to block supplies or services reaching an employer.
- Intimidation: There has been some doubt about the existence of this tort, but as a result of the case of *Rookes* v. *Barnard* [1964] (k) the Court of Appeal ruled it constituted violence or a threat. The TULR(C) Act 1992 did amend this situation to bring a threat to interfere with a contract in a trade dispute within the immunities provided the dispute is in 'contemplation or furtherance of a (defined) trade dispute'.
- Defamation: In the writing of a reference for an employee the employer makes a defamatory statement about the individual's character.

12.10   Consumer protection law

The scope of consumer protection law in the UK is very wide. The main statute protecting buyers of goods and services has been the Sale of Goods Act 1979. Together with competition law the legislation created a number of institutions and government bodies/ agencies. The most important are:

- The Office of Fair Trading (OFT). Under the **Enterprise Act 2002** and other statutes the Director-General of the OFT has wide powers to investigate and intervene in mergers, monopolies, restrictive practices and any trading practice considered unfair to consumers. In addition, the OFT can investigate any medium-sized or large company to determine whether it is engaging in anti-competitive practices. The bigger companies can be referred to the Competition Commission. The OFT can refer cases to the Restrictive Practices Court.
- The Competition Commission (formerly the Monopolies and Mergers Commission). Its main areas of investigation are price-fixing, the forming of cartels and the reduction of services or supply of goods contrary to the public interest by private and public-sector organizations. One of the most important roles is its powers to investigate mergers where the gross assets of the target company exceed £70 million. Many of these provisions dovetail with the government's policy of encouraging corporate governance best practice, e.g. by splitting the posts of chairman and chief executive (due to become effective in 2005).

12.11   Company law

This is a large and complex area of the law, and so we will be examining only the basic principles of company law. There are two basic types of company:

- **Public companies** are defined by the Companies Act 1985; they are limited by shares or limited by guarantee with a share capital stated in the memorandum of the company. At least two persons must become shareholders to form a public limited company as well as at least two directors. The name of the company will end with the letters plc. Under the Act the authorized capital must be at least £50 000. The Registrar of Companies (at Companies House) has the power under Section 117 to issue a certificate signifying its status as a plc. This permits the company to commence business and begin borrowing. The initial shareholders subscribe their names to a memorandum of association which must be provided for the Registrar before a certificate can be issued. The document will provide key information about the company such as its objectives, the type of business and where its registered office will be situated. It will also state the limit of its financial liability, £50 000 or over. A further document which must be drawn up is the articles of association. This regulates the internal organization and management of the company.

A public limited company limited by its share issue means that any outstanding corporate debts will be limited by the memorandum of association to the amount unpaid on shares held with the company. There are two main types of shares: preference shares which contain a fixed right to a dividend and the return of the share capital to the shareholder when the company is wound up. There are also ordinary shares which will not be protected in this way.

- **Private companies** can be formed by two or more and up to fifty persons under the Act, although the EU Twelfth Company Law Directive does allow (under certain circumstances) membership to be only one person. Numerous legislative provisions differentiate between small-, medium- and large-scale companies in respect of accounting rules, shares, profit and loss and financial failure involving 'winding up'. A private company can become incorporated under the 1985 Act, but may not involve members of the public through the holding of shares. In other words, the shareholders are private owners of the company, and will have their names entered into the register of members.

Once a year companies must hold an annual general meeting and directors elected. In addition to the legislation already discussed specific laws determine the role and responsibilities of company directors. Where a company is wound up it may either voluntarily or involuntarily go into liquidation, whereupon liquidators will be hired or appointed by the courts to oversee the sale of the assets of the company to pay off debts and preference shareholders.

12.12   Employment law

12.12.1   Introduction

As we have seen from earlier sections in this chapter, the role of the common law and statute are the principal sources of English law, and so it is with this special branch of the civil law. Nowadays, it is statute that is the predominate influence on legal rights and duties, particularly because of the influence of European Union law. When we talk of employment law we are, strictly referring to 'individual' law, whereas there is also 'collective' labour law. The differences and connections between the two are explained in Figure 12.3.

In the figure:

A   The individual employment relationship is based on the contract of employment. This relationship has been significantly strengthened for the employee by the introduction since 1963 of a broad 'floor of employment rights' provided by statute. Most employment rights for the individual and employers' obligations are now found in various pieces of legislation.

B   This part of the relationship reflects a collective one because the trade union represents the collective rights of its members *vis-à-vis* their employer. Obviously, the employer must 'recognize' the union for the purposes of collective bargaining for this three-way

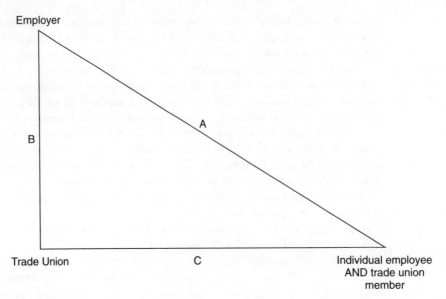

Figure 12.3. The three-way employment relationship of employer-employee/trade union member-trade union (based on the work of Lord Wedderburn[4])

relationship to exist as it is represented in the diagram. The introduction of the Employment Relations Act 1999 (which inserted many new provisions into the TULR (c) Act 1992), has arguably significantly strengthened the rights of trades unions to gain lawful recognition by employers. But even if the employer does not recognize the union concerned it may still attempt to represent its members' concerns to the employer, although there is no guarantee of success in these circumstances.

The collective relationship between employer and trades union based on recognition is normally enshrined in the collective agreement, a non-legally binding agreement which may determine the way in which the two parties deal with each other as well as the outcome of their negotiations. For the individual employee the key outcome will be such matters as increases in pay, improvements in terms and conditions and working practices, working environment, health and safety, equal opportunities, job security and the avoidance of compulsory redundancies. In law, the process of 'incorporation' permits the relevant terms of the collective agreement to be transferred to the individual's contract of employment; but for this to happen in the first place the contract must contain a clause which permits it to be changed from time to time as a result of collective agreements. There is, thus a direct connection between B and A in the diagram. You will note that the contract of employment is binding on employer/employee, but the collective agreement between employer and trade union is not legally binding. Except for the period 1971–1974 collective agreements have always been presumed in law **not** to be legally binding, but binding in 'honour only'. If you recall the earlier discussion of the UK's free-market economic framework in this chapter (in Section 12.4 and Chapter 8) you will appreciate that the environment in which trades unions and employers conducted their business throughout the late nineteenth century and the twentieth centuries was a voluntary one. Only during the years 1976 to 1980 was there any form of legally compulsory trade union recognition procedure, that is, until the introduction of the union recognition procedures in the Employment Relations Act 1999.

The basis on which trades unions continue to exist legally remains fundamentally unchanged since the 'golden formula' was put in place in 1906. Unions must continue to act within strict legal parameters or they will be acting outside their statutory framework and be liable to a number of common law torts. However, it is important to note that for economic and political reasons the UK government has intervened significantly in legislating these parameters, particularly since 1971.

C   Finally, there is the individual trade union membership relationship based on the person's contract of membership with his or her union. Obviously, this part of the relationship does not exist unless the individual is a union member. However, you should note that around 2 million workers in the UK who are not union members do have their terms and conditions determined by collective agreements between their employer and union(s) of which they are **not** members. In most cases the Union Rule Book is the contract of membership, and like all contracts can be enforced in the courts. Historically, it was interpreted in accordance with common law rules, but since 1984 it has been subject to substantial statutory regulation.

12.12.2   The contract of employment

Earlier in this chapter we discussed the basic law of contract with reference to employment examples. However, because it is the core of the employment relationship it is necessary to summarize its basic tenets.

Employment status

The contract of employment is still referred to as a 'contract *of service*', which reflects its origins in the days of 'master and *servant*'. The person employed under such a contract is defined an as '*employee*'. With the growth of flexible systems of work, particularly numerical and temporal, the numbers of people hired as self-employed has grown (see Section 5.8.3 and 12.4). In law we distinguish their relationship with the employer by defining them as '*workers*' who are engaged on a contract *for services*. For a large number of workers this reflects their genuine status as self-employed, but there is also a substantial number of individuals hired through agencies or on special contracts who are not really self-employed at all, and subsequently do not enjoy employment protection rights. Of course, employers have benefited from this situation, being able to manage employment costs, workforce headcounts and time-specific work projects in a much more efficient way. You should note that the European Union and the UK government are taking some steps to provide extra protection for these workers through the introduction of new statutes, such as the draft directive on working conditions of temporary workers, and regulations to amend the Employment Agencies Act 1973.

Where disagreement exists about an individual's status it will be for the tribunals and courts to decide the matter based on well-established common law rules. These will help to determine whether the individual is truly 'in business on their own account' (a worker who is self-employed) or employed on a 'contract of service' (employee).

The importance for the 'employee' is that he or she will enjoy statutory employment protection including statutory maternity pay, statutory sick pay, statutory redundancy pay and the right to claim unfair dismissal. Anti-discrimination law applies to both employees and workers. The benefit for the 'worker' is the payment of income tax through Schedule D at the end of each tax year whereby certain expenses can be offset against tax, as well as the freedom to work when, where and for whom they like.

Exercise

At a selection interview Larry is verbally offered the job based on certain terms and conditions including pay of £250 per week and six weeks' annual holiday. Larry verbally accepts the offer and the next day gives notice to his current employer. Ten days later Larry receives a letter from the new employer detailing terms and conditions, including pay of

£200 per week and five weeks' annual holiday. The employer explains there was a mistake at the interview and this reflects the true position. Is Larry in the position where he can either take it or leave it?

Feedback

No. The terms offered at the interview which Larry accepted are the contractual terms which now prevail. If the new employer refuses to honour them Larry could seek compensation in the employment tribunal for breach of contract on termination. After all, if the employer refuses to hire Larry on the originally agreed terms they are arguably breaking the contract. In *Sarker* v. *South Tees Acute Hospitals NHS Trust* [1997] (l) the EAT upheld the applicant's claim for breach of contract on termination when the terms of the offer letter to Sarker were unilaterally changed a few days after the original offer. The EAT said: 'the mere fact that the duties under [the] contract would not be performed until a subsequent date cannot take it outside the concept of a contract of employment'. Furthermore, the fact that Sarker's duties with the NHS Trust would be performed at a later date did not invalidate the existence of the contract that could be enforced by either party.

This case illustrates the importance of agreed terms whether they are in writing or not. Obviously, a sensible employer and employee will want to confirm the contractual terms in writing as soon as possible; this is often done in an 'offer letter'. Confusion often exists between the written contract and the statement of principal terms and conditions. The latter is a statutory requirement (Section 1: Employment Rights Act 1996) where the employee has worked for at least one month and who should receive the statement within two months of commencing work. The statement must contain key details of terms and conditions, such as the identity of the parties, the date of commencement of the contract, the level of remuneration, the hours and normal place of work, length of notice and holidays. See Section 12.15 below.

12.12.3   The sources of the contract

The contract of employment is a complex mixture of different sources. The sources shown in Figure 12.4 are shown in order of importance, e.g. 1 is the most important and so on.

The implied terms of the contract of employment

The importance of certain universal implied terms have already been discussed earlier in this section. In addition, there are a number of implied contract terms specific to the employer's and employee's role in the employment relationship such as:

The employer's obligations:

● **To pay wages:** Where the employee is 'ready and willing to work' the employer must pay the contractually agreed level of wages, even though there is no work to be done. The exception to this is where the contract expressly says otherwise.

The employee's obligations:

● **To exercise the duty of skill and care:** This involves undertaking any skill or knowledge in a way which is fully beneficial to the employer. To act negligently would be a breach of this duty. Moreover, the employee must not act in a way which could cause a health and safety risk to others.

Finally, there is the **mutual obligation of trust and confidence** – arguably, the most important of all the terms. Both parties must act in a courteous way which upholds a certain degree of respect for each other. In *Courtaulds Northern Textiles Ltd* v. *Andrew* [1979] (m) the court said that this term could be expressed so that the employer should not 'without

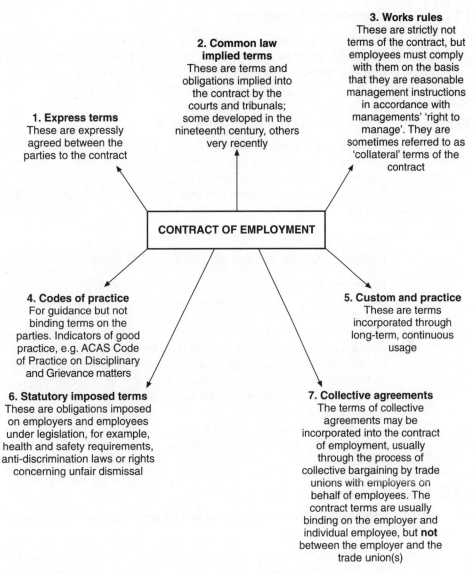

Figure 12.4. The seven sources of the contract of employment.

reasonable or proper cause, conduct themselves in a manner calculated or likely to destroy or seriously damage the relationship of mutual confidence and trust between the employer and the employee'.

A breach of this duty by the employer may lead to the employee claiming that there has been a constructive dismissal which may also be unfair. On the employee's part it could represent gross misconduct and lead to summary (instant) dismissal. Examples of a breach of this term by the employer would include:

- Swearing and insulting the employee
- Failing to hear a grievance
- Sexual or racial harassment
- Forcibly searching an employee

Obviously, these acts could also constitute other breaches of law.

12.12.4   Variation of contract

Without the consent of the other party this could also be a breach of mutual trust and confidence as well as a substantive breach by itself. The former would entitle the employee to resign without giving notice and claim constructive dismissal.

12.12.5   The employee's right to wages

Any failure by the employer to pay the employee the agreed level of wages is likely to be a breach of the express and implied terms. In addition it may also be a breach of the Employment Rights Act 1996 which makes it unlawful for the employer not to make payments due to the employee by making deductions not permissible under the contract or other legal provision.

National Minimum Wage (NMW) Act 1998 (amended 1999)

Every employee has the right not to be remunerated by his or her employer at a rate less than specified in the NMW Regulations accompanying the Act, depending on age and whether in training or employment. A complaint can be made to the employment tribunal for a failure to pay the NMW and where the individual has received some detriment for attempting to enforce his or her rights under the Act (e.g. dismissal). Inspectors appointed by the government have the powers to enter premises, inspect employers' records and instigate criminal action against those in breach of the statute.

In certain circumstances employees are entitled to statutory sick pay (SSP) and statutory maternity pay (SMP). Also, there are statutory rights to paid time off from work, for example to undertake duties as a trade union representative, a health and safety representative or a justice of the peace.

12.12.6   Termination of contract

The contract of employment can be brought to an end for a number of reasons:

By the employer:

(i)   Dismissal of the employee for one of the potentially five statutory fair reasons (Employment Rights Act 1996):
  * Misconduct
  * Redundancy
  * Some other substantial reason – SOSR (e.g. reorganization of the employer's business)
  * Incapability (e.g. ill health absence)
  * Statutory bar (that is, some statute prevents the employee from being employed, e.g. a driver of a lorry loses his driving licence because of a motoring offence and alternative work cannot be found for him).
(ii) Compulsory retirement of the employee (the employee may be able to claim an unfair dismissal, or sex discrimination where the retirement ages are based on gender).
(iii) A contract based on the completion of a task is completed by the performance of the task (if found fair by a tribunal this will be for SOSR).
(iv) A contract for a fixed-term expires on the given date (if found fair by a tribunal this too will be for SOSR).

(v) By frustration – this was discussed earlier, and you will see from that section that tribunals are reluctant to confirm termination by frustration because it undermines statutory rights indicated in (i) above.

(vi) As a result of the insolvency of the employer's business (dismissal may be fair or unfair).

By the employee:

(i) Resignation.

(ii) Voluntary retirement (although the employer must obviously consent).

Also, by mutual agreement.

The importance of giving notice

Not only should either party give the full contractual notice, but the employer must ensure that they give the minimum statutory notice period laid down in the Employment Rights Act 1996. After one month's service and up to two years' service, the employee is entitled to one week's notice. Thereafter, the employee is entitled to one additional week for every year of service up to a maximum of twelve weeks.

Types of dismissal

You will see from the above list that a number of common law terminations can give rise to different statutory dismissals. In addition, there is the common law **wrongful dismissal**; this is where the employer terminates the contract in breach of one or more of its terms. The most common example is failure to give proper contractual notice, in which case the employee may sue the employer for damages in the civil courts. Since 1994 the employee has had the statutory right to seek compensation for the same breach in the employment tribunal. In both jurisdictions there is no qualifying period to claim (see the *Sarker* case discussed earlier). A second common law term used is **summary dismissal**; this occurs where the employer is entitled to dismiss straight away because the employee has seriously breached an important term of the contract amounting to a repudiatory breach (usually one of the key implied terms is the most common reason). However, it is important to note that case law shows that even in these circumstances an employer should investigate the allegations against the employee who should be allowed to fully answer the charge made against them.

Unfair dismissal

This crucial employment right was introduced in 1971 to give employees a statutory right of complaint as well as costly and time consuming common law means of redress. The Employment Rights Act 1996 lays out five potentially fair reasons for dismissal that have already been listed under (i) of **termination of contract**. There are no qualifying hours to make a claim of unfair dismissal, but since 1 June 1999 the qualifying period of two years' continuous employment has been reduced to one year. Examples of where no qualifying period is required are dismissal on grounds of pregnancy, sex, race, disability, trade union membership or duties, or health and safety.

An employee bringing a constructive dismissal will also complain of there being an unfair dismissal in order to secure redress in the employment tribunal. Compensation for unfair dismissal (maximum award) is updated every year. In 2002 it was £52 600.

Exercise

Which of the following scenarios represents a constructive unfair dismissal?

1 A senior manager makes disparaging and insulting remarks in a loud voice about his (long-serving) secretary to another manager so that the secretary and several other employees overhear the remarks.
2 A manager says to an employee (who he has been bullying): 'if you don't resign I'll make sure you get sacked'.
3 Employee B who has worked for the employer for eight months has reminded him six times over the last three months about the unexplained shortages in her monthly salary. The deductions have still not been made good. B leaves her employment without giving notice.

Feedback

In both scenarios 1 and 2 there is a good chance that the employee will be able to successfully claim constructive unfair dismissal. The treatment is probably a breach of mutual trust and confidence permitting the employee to leave in circumstances which are unfair. In scenario 3 the employee cannot claim because she has only six months' service. However, with one year's service up to and including the last occasion on which she unsuccessfully tried to secure her shortages in pay she would be able to claim, probably successfully.

12.13   Anti-discrimination law

We have already provided examples of this legislation elsewhere in the chapter. Anti-discrimination law is the fastest growing area of employment law in the UK. Primarily, this is due to new EU directives coming onstream up to 2006. For over a quarter of a century in the UK we have had the Equal Pay Act 1970, the Sex Discrimination Act 1975, and the Race Relations Act 1976. Because the first two have been subject to EU law they have undergone important changes since being enacted.

Discrimination may be either direct or indirect; the former takes place where a person of one sex or of a particular racial or ethnic group is treated less favourably (wholly or partly) because of their sex or race. Indirect discrimination requires the complainant to show that although there may be no direct discrimination a 'provision, criterion or practice' applied by the employer disproportionately affects them on the ground of their sex (or race) and is to their detriment, unless the employer can objectively justify that treatment. Intention is not necessary on the part of the perpetrator to show unlawful discrimination. From October 2001 the burden of proof has shifted to the employer to positively rebut any charge of discrimination.

The Disability Discrimination Act 1995 has provided a powerful influence on employers to treat disabled people fairly. However, the workings of the statute in practice are complicated. To show disability the complainant must be suffering from (or suffered from) a complaint that has a substantial and long-term (i.e. 12 months or more) adverse affect on their ability to carry out their normal day-to-day activities. The disability must constitute a well-recognized illness and may be physical or mental. Once disability has been established the employer has a statutory duty to make a reasonable adjustment to accommodate that person in work, but failure to do so can be justified on objective grounds.

As we have mentioned, at the time of writing there are enormous changes underway in refining and developing anti-discrimination law. Significant changes will be made by the introduction of the EU's Employment Equal Treatment (Framework) Directive 2000. This will require employers to devise fresh policies covering all HR domains and re-consider the prevailing culture of their workplaces, mainly because of new areas of legislation (*). The coverage and timescales for implementation of the Directive in the UK are:

Religion (*), religious belief (*) and sexual orientation (*):	July 2003
Disability:	December 2004
Age (*):	December 2006.

In addition, a Race Directive became effective in July 2003.

12.14   Data protection

This legislative area of protection applies to consumers and private citizens as well as employees, although we will discuss it in the context of the latter. The Data Protection Act 1984 provided for rights for 'data subjects' (i.e. employees) and placed obligations on 'data users' (i.e. employers). A Data Protection Registrar was established to review and enforce the Act. The 1998 Data Protection Act has amended the law by applying statutory rules not only to data kept electronically on disk or tape, but also by manual means provided the data is retained in a 'relevant filing system' which means a method of storing data in a systematic way. Data processed automatically by operating equipment cannot be relied upon solely for the purpose of making decisions, such as automatic cv scanning for selection purposes. A responsible person must also take an independent decision. The 1998 Act brings together the eight data protection principles of the 1984 Act and several new ones:

Original principles:

(i)   The information on the data subject shall be processed fairly and lawfully.
(ii)   It shall be kept only for one or more specified and lawful purposes.
(iii) The data shall not be disclosed in a manner incompatible with the holding of the data.
(iv) The data held shall be accurate and kept up to date.
(v)   The data shall be adequate, relevant and not excessive in relation to the purposes for which the data is held.
(vi) The data shall not be kept for longer than necessary.
(vii) The data subject should be kept informed of data kept on them and have the right to correct or erase it where appropriate, and the data subject shall have access to the data.
(viii) Appropriate security measures must be taken in respect of the data.

The 1998 principles also state that:

(ix) The data subject must consent to the processing of the data under certain circumstances (e.g. in appraisals or in providing job references).

The Freedom of Information Act 2000 changed the title of the Data Protection Register to that of Information Commissioner who should be notified by data controllers of any data processing. The Commissioner has powers of enforcement and may institute legal proceedings as a result of any infringement of the Act or regulations made under it. In 2002 the first and second parts of a controversial four-part Employment Practices Code of Practice was published by the Commissioner.

12.15   Employment Act 2002

Several innovative legal provisions were introduced in this extensive piece of legislation. The following is a brief summary of these provisions:

- Statutory discipline and grievance procedures must now be used (on their own or as part of the employer's existing procedures). Any dismissal in contravention of the statutory disciplinary procedure will be automatically unfair. (Effective: April 2004)
- The procedures become part of every employee's contract of employment. The statement of terms and conditions issued under Section 1 Employment Rights Act 1996 must now contain the procedures or refer to a means by which full access may be obtained.
- Employment Tribunal proceedings are reformed.
- Changes to the law on using fixed-term contracts giving employees similar rights to 'permanent' employees.
- Extensive rights for working parents are introduced:
  - Paternity leave and pay
  - Adoption leave and pay
  - Extended maternity leave and pay
  - Rights to work flexibly, e.g. part-time work after returning from maternity leave, subject to reasonableness and practicality.

12.16   Collective law

This specialist branch of 'employment law' has already been introduced at the beginning of this chapter. You will have learnt that trades unions obtained a series of immunities from the common law torts through the so-called 'golden formula' legislation which was substantially amended by the Conservative governments 1979–96. However, the basic premise of the immunities remains, that is, provided the union concerned acts within the definition of a trade dispute (laid down in the TULR(C) Act 1992) it will not be liable for damages. The meaning of a trade dispute laid out in the TULR(C) Act defines the scope of any lawful dispute which the union can pursue; it is now carefully prescribed so that it must only be between the employees and their employer. Although unions have never been given a positive right to exist legally, in fact, they have been able to organize their members to associate with one another, enforce their own rules, collectively bargain with employers, make collective agreements, and call out their members to participate in industrial action even though as employees these members would render themselves liable to summary dismissal for misconduct.

The way in which a trade dispute is defined in the statute means that only a strike which is held following a fully secret postal ballot of the membership can guarantee immunity. The restriction of a dispute to the primary parties (employer and employees) in practice means that all so-called 'secondary' action and unofficial action is outlawed. Examples of this type of action include striking in sympathy with other workers (secondary action) and not calling for a proper ballot before striking (unofficial action). Lawful picketing is possible provided that it too is restricted to the primary dispute and the premises at which normally the striking employees carry out their work. A Code of Practice republished by the government in 1992 reiterates that a picket should consist of no more than six members at or near the entrance/exit of the workplace. The Code can be used in legal proceedings.

The Conservative government was, of course, opposed to trade union intervention in the running of the economy. They saw it both ideologically and practically as a brake on economic growth and global competitiveness. For this reason the period 1980–93 saw seven pieces of legislation with a collective element. Some curtailed the operation of unions at a macro-level in the economy, others eliminated the 'closed shop', that is, the obligation on the employer to employ only union members. The Trade Union Act 1984 legislated for the internal administration of unions.

The Employment Relations Act 1999 has mitigated for unions some of the worst effects of the Conservative legislation without substantially reducing the restricted definition of a trade dispute or affecting the basis on which the immunities apply. Two key developments are legislated for in the 1999 Act:

- First, a union may now seek compulsory recognition from an employer where at least 21 employees are involved in a discrete 'bargaining unit', and in a ballot a majority of the employees voting and at least 40 per cent of the members of the bargaining unit support recognition of the union. Disputes over recognition will be handled by the Central Arbitration Committee (CAC). Several complex rules apply to the recognition procedure, the meaning of a 'bargaining unit', collective agreements for recognition and subsequent disputes.
- Second, the nearest the UK has come to having an individual employee's positive right to strike is now law. Prior to 1999 an employee on strike could be fairly dismissed without any right to complain otherwise, unless there had been selective dismissal or re-engagement of strikers within a period of three months. Now, the employee may embark on a period of 'protected' industrial action for 8 weeks provided the industrial action itself is within the definition of a trade dispute and the union enjoys immunity. Any dismissal of the employee during the 8-week period under these circumstances will be automatically unfair. In order to dismiss after the termination of the 8-week period the employer must show that he or she has exhausted any collective disputes procedure in place in order for the dismissal to be fair.

Case study

ABC plc

In March 2003 ABC plc experienced an all-out strike by its 5000 workforce. There were three main reasons for this. First, the company had refused to continue to bargain collectively with the trade union (the Transport and General Workers Union TGWU) which it also de-recognized. Second, ABC plc informed the unions just before de-recognition that it was in negotiations with another company with a view to selling the whole company at the end of the year. Third, the union received anonymous information that ABC plc had provided the prospective buyer with personal details of the workforce with a view to 'dismissing unsatisfactory members of staff before the transfer, particularly union trouble makers'. The union believes this is unlawful for two reasons.

On 5 March the local TGWU branch called a workplace meeting of all the workforce and on a show of hands an immediate strike was called. In response the company warned all striking employees that if they did not return to work the next day they would all be dismissed. Because only 100 employees returned to work the next day all others were immediately dismissed. A picket of 2500 (now) former employees blocked the entrances to the company seven days a week preventing anybody from entering or leaving the premises. Fights broke out between some pickets, and local police were brought in to keep the entrances to the company's premises free of obstruction. The company took legal action against the union, which, for its part, took legal action against the company on the grounds that it was acting contrary to the Transfer of Undertakings (Protection of Employment) (TUPE) Regulations 1981.

> **Task**
>
> Identify the various sources of law involved in this dispute and isolate those laws that have been arguably broken by the union and the company. What courts or tribunals could hear the subsequent cases?

Feedback

Sources of law:

(i) **Civil law: Collective labour law:** Union recognition and entry into collective agreements continues to be voluntary unless they are subject to a declaration by the Central Arbitration Committee (CAC) under the compulsory union recognition rules introduced by the Employment Relations Act 1999. ABC's recognition of the TGWU is not subject to these rules and it can, therefore de-recognize the union whenever it wishes. Of course, such a move is detrimental to good industrial relations. Had the union recognition been subject to a CAC declaration this move and the dismantling of collective bargaining would have to be in accordance with a series of legal rules laid down by the 1999 statute, and which is now incorporated into the Trade Union and Labour Relations (Consolidation) Act 1992 (TULR(C)A).

(ii) **Transfer of Undertakings – Civil law:** This is a mixture of individual employment law and collective labour law. In respect of the former the TUPE Regulations exist to protect individual employees affected by a transfer. The TUPE Regulations also require employee representatives (or union(s)) to be consulted on behalf of the (collective) workforce. However, we do not know whether ABC plc will be taken over through the purchase of the majority of its shares. As a public limited company it is 'quoted' on the stock market and is subject to company law (Companies Act 1985). The TUPE Regulations do not apply to shares take-overs.

(iii) **The passing of information to the potential buyer of ABC plc.** The union is arguing this is in breach of the Data Protection Act 1998 which is civil (private) law. The second reason why the union believes this practice is unlawful is because any dismissal 'connected' with a transfer would be unlawful, and any dismissal of an employee because of his or her trade union membership, duties or activities is automatically an unfair dismissal under the Employment Rights Act 1996.

(iv) **Any dismissal of strikers** prior to the Employment Relations Act 1999 was automatically fair provided there was no selective dismissal or re-engagement within three months of the dismissals. Under the 1999 Act industrial action can be protected insofar as **any** dismissals are unlawful and unfair within a period of 8 weeks from the commencement of the industrial action. However, the action itself must be lawful – see next point. Any claim for unfair dismissal will be brought to the employment tribunal under the law laid down in the Employment Rights Act 1996.

(v) **The strike** organized by the local TGWU officials is unlawful under the TULR(C)A 1992. Arguably, a number of common law torts are being committed by the union membership.

(vi) Lastly, the **obstruction of the highway** by the pickets and their **fighting** with the police are criminal acts.

Laws that have been broken and the relevant courts and tribunals

(i) The directors of the company are perfectly entitled to sell it to others, but there are complications. ABC is a plc and, therefore the shareholders must be consulted under the 1985 Companies Act and other corporate legislation. They must give their approval to the sale at a meeting of the shareholders. If the purchasers are going to acquire the majority of shares they may do this in two ways: either buy up shares on the stock market or make an offer for the bulk purchase of the shares which the shareholders must agree to in sufficient numbers for the purchasers to acquire a majority of shares. The directors of ABC plc must, therefore, be careful about selling the company without proper authorization, otherwise a criminal breach will occur. The magistrates' court could hear the case for commital, and the case be referred thereafter to the Crown Court.

(ii) Similarly, the directors (with shareholder agreement) may proceed to sell the company so that the TUPE Regulations apply. However, the union is quite correct in its analysis of the situation: Any employee dismissed in 'connection' with the transfer would be automatically unfairly dismissed, unless there is an 'ETO' (i.e. economic, technical or organization) reason, which is not apparent here. Second, although the union is now de-recognized the employer must consult with 'employee representatives' on the transfer. These must be elected from among the workforce in a fair and democratic way. Both cases could be referred to the employment tribunal, the first type of cases brought by the individuals affected, and in the second type of cases by the union (on behalf of the individual employees) seeking a protective award for the employees. It is also possible that the union could seek an injunction from the High Court prohibiting the employer from proceeding with the sale until the consultation requirements have been satisfied. Finally, because the TUPE Regulations derive from the EU Acquired Rights Directive the superior appeal court will be the European Court of Justice.

(iii) **Data protection:** It is quite possible that the information conveyed to the prospective purchaser of the business is lawful. The seller of the business (transferor) can communicate to the purchaser (transferee) certain data about the workforce, e.g. numbers, grades, skills, age, gender profiles, etc. However, information of a personal nature (e.g. names, addresses, union association, etc.) would be a breach and unlawful at this stage. This type of information could only lawfully be transferred when the purchase is agreed. A complaint could initially be made to the Information Commissioner, who could seek an injunction in the High Court to prevent any further disclosures, and subsequently pursue a complaint there. The company could be fined.

(iv) The TGWU's strike has been called without a proper lawful ballot which should have been postal and, therefore secret. The industrial action, including the picket, although a primary dispute, is unlawful and takes the union outside the immunities of the TULR(C)A. It has now exposed itself to a number of common law economic torts, such as conspiracy, interference with the performance of a contract, trespass and intimidation. Initially, the company could seek an injunction in the High Court, and thereafter pursue an action for damages. The dismissal of strikers used to be automatically fair, but this has now been amended to take account of the 8-week 'protected' period of industrial action. Complaints must be submitted to the employment tribunal.

(v) Finally, the picket is supposed to be made up of six persons according to the 1992 Code of Practice. Moreover, the picket is involved in a number of criminal activities such as obstruction of the highway, causing an affray and a breach of the peace, and obstructing a police officer, to name but a few. Several criminal statutes could be broken and the pickets arrested and charged in the magistrates' court. It is important to note that in respect of (iv) the trade union could officially repudiate the action of its local officials and thereby avoid any legal penalties. Local union officials responsible for persisting with the strike and with the criminal acts would then take individual responsibility for any breaches.

Summary

In this chapter we have examined the important legal context for organizations. As you will have seen from the case study, the areas of law can interlink so that civil and criminal, individual and collective law will form part of employment disputes and corporate affairs. Suppose that matters relating to anti-discrimination law and alleged breaches of employment contracts by ABC plc had also been involved. The matter would have become legally very complex. Indeed, complexity and interlinking legal rights and duties will continue to increase in the foreseeable future making this area of management an important and difficult one for all managers, but particularly those in the HR profession. The main source of new law is the European Union's Social Policy Agenda; coupled with the growth in peoples' willingness to assert their rights in law, organizations must proactively address legal issues in order to manage both resources and all relationships successfully.

Examination questions for this chapter are given in Appendix 2.

Areas of law not covered in this chapter are:

Public law

- Constitutional and administrative law are not referred to in the sections on the administration of the law and employment law. Health and safety law is examined in Section 5.1.
- Criminal law
- Social security law
- Revenue law.

Private law

- The law of property
- Trusts
- Family law
- Succession law
- Bankruptcy.

References

1 Bradney, A. *et al.* (1991) *How to Study Law.* Sweet and Maxwell.
2 Hayek, F. A. (1962) *The Road to Serfdom.* Routledge and Kegan Paul.
3 Employment Law Flexible Learning Advanced Diploma (1999) Malpas Flexible Learning Ltd. (written by Peter Winfield).
4 Wedderburn, Lord (1986) *The Worker and the Law.* Pelican.

Table of statutes

UK primary legislation

1906	Trade Disputes Act
1964	Industrial Training Act
1968	Trades Descriptions Act
1970	Equal Pay Act as amended in 1983
1971	Industrial Relations Act
1972	Local Government Act

1972   Trades Descriptions Act
1974   Health and Safety at Work Act
1975   Sex Discrimination Act
1976   Race Relations Act
1977   Unfair Contract Terms Act
1984   County Courts Act
1984   Data Protection Act
1984   Trade Union Act
1985   Companies Act
1989   Law of Property (Miscellaneous Provisions) Act
1992   Trade Union and Labour Relations (Consolidation) Act
1995   Disability Discrimination Act
1996   Employment Rights Act
1998   National Minimum Wage Act and Amendment 1999
1998   Employment Rights (Dispute Resolution) Act
1998   Data Protection Act
1998   Human Rights Act
1999   Employment Relations Act
2000   Freedom of Information Act
2002   Employment Act
2002   Enterprise Act

Secondary legislation

1983   Equal Pay (Amendment) Regulations
1991   Transfer of Undertakings (Protection of Employment) Regulations
1993   Sex Discrimination and Equal Pay (Remedies) Regulations
1998   Working Time Regulations
1999   Control of Substances Hazardous to Health (SI no 1999/437)

European Union directives

1975   Equal Pay Directive
1976   Equal Treatment Directive and Amendment Directive 2002
1976   Collective Redundancies Directive
1977   Acquired Rights Directive
1980   Twelfth Company Law Directive
1992   Pregnant Workers Directive
1994   European Works Council Directive
1995   Working Time Directive
1996   Part-Time Workers Directive
1999   Fixed-term Work Directive
2000   Employment Equal Treatment (Framework) Directive

Treaties

1950   Convention on Human Rights and Fundamental Freedoms
1957   Treaty of Rome (Treaty of European Economic Community)
1997   Treaty of Amsterdam

List of cases

(a)   *Polkey* v. *AE Dayton Services Ltd* [1988] AC 344, HL

(b)   *R.* v. *Secretary of State for Employment, ex-parte Seymour-Smith & Perez* [1997] ICR 37, HL

(c)   *Pharmaceutical Society of Great Britain* v. *Boots Cash Chemists (Southern) Ltd* [1953] 1 QB 401

(d)   *Harvey* v. *Facey* [1893] AC 552

(e)   *Felthouse* v. *Bindley* [1862] 11 CB (NS) 869

(f)   *Hyde* v. *Wrench* [1940] 3. Beav.

(g)   *Faccenda Chicken Ltd* v. *Fowler & ors* [1986] ICR 297, CA

(h)   *Anderson Ltd* v. *Daniel* [1924] 1 KB 138

(i)   *Donoghue* v. *Stevenson* [1932] AC 562, HL

(j(i))   *Walker* v. *Northumberland County Council* [1995] IRLR 35

(j(ii))   *Hatton & ors.* v. *Sutherland & ors.* [2002] Times Law Report 12.2.2002, CA

(k)   *Rooks* v. *Barnard* [1964] AC 1129, *CA*

(l)   *Sarker* v. *South Tees Acute Hospitals NHS Trust* [1997] IRLR 328, EAT

(m)   *Courtaulds Northern Textiles Ltd* v. *Andrew* [1979]

Further reading

Anderman, S. D. (2000) *Labour Law – Management Decisions and Workers' Rights*. Butterworths.

Doyle, B. (2003) *Disability Discrimination: Law and Practice*. Jordans.

Hammonds (2003) *Family Friendly Rights*. CIPD.

Keenan, D. (2001) *Advanced Business Law*. Pitman Publishing.

Kenner, J. (2002) *EU Employment Law: From Rome to Amsterdam and beyond*. Hart.

Lewis, D. and Sargeant, M. (2002) *Essentials of Employment Law*. CIPD.

Smith, I. T and Thomas, G. H. (2000) *Industrial Law*. Butterworths.

Web-site addresses

Advisory Conciliation and Arbitration Service (ACAS): http://www.acas.org.uk

British employment law: http://www.emplaw.co.uk

Butterworths: http://www.butterworths.co.uk

Commission for Racial Equality: http://www.cre.gov.uk

Department of Trade & Industry: http://www.dti.gov.uk

Disability Rights Commission: http://www.drc.org.uk

Employment Tribunal Service: http://www.ets.gov.uk

Equal Opportunities Commission: http://www.eoc.org.uk

Equality: http://www.equalitydirect.org.uk

European Commission: http://www.ias-berlin.de/

European Union: http://www.europa.eu.int/index_en.htm

European Union Employment and Social Affairs:
   http://europa.eu.int/comm/employment_social/index_en.htm

Guidance on employment rights: http://www.tiger.co.uk

Health and Safety Executive: http://www.hse.gov.uk/hsehome.htm

Information Commissioner: http://www.dataprotection.gov.uk

Legal information: http://justask.org.uk

Legal Questions: http://www.legalquestion.com

Local Government Association Research: http://www.lga.gov/lga/research

Trades Union Congress: http://www.tuc.org.uk

UK Legal: http://uklegal.com.uk

13   The technological context of management

Chapter objectives

In this chapter you will:

- Review the development and applications of information technology
- Examine the implications of internet-related technology for business and management
- Consider the management of new technology at work and
- Assess the impact of new technology on society.

Chapter introduction

Technological change has been an integral part of the process of industrialization since the eighteenth century. From the 1970s onwards, however, commentators have viewed developments in computing and information technologies (IT) to be sufficiently different to justify the title 'the new technology'. There is little doubt that we are in the midst of a 'technological revolution', which is bringing about profound changes in the way we live and work. Indeed, it can be argued that internet-related technology has 'emerged as perhaps one of the key technological developments of the twentieth century' in terms of its radical effect on the way we work and organize economic activity.[1] For example, new technology is seen to be one of the forces driving globalization (see Chapter 8):

What is new about the modern global system is the spread of globalization in and through new dimensions of activity – technological, organizational, administrative and legal, among others – and the chronic intensification of patterns of interconnectedness mediated by the modern communications industry and the new information technology. Distant localities are now interlinked as never before. Globalization has reordered both time and space and has shrunk the globe.[2]

As the following extract suggests, this technology is likely to have far-reaching effects, many of which we are unable to predict:

Internet 'heralds new industrial revolution'

Stuart Miller, *The Guardian*, 16 June 1999

The internet is driving the biggest social and economic revolution since the 18th century, according to research published today.

Thirty years on from the birth of the internet, the ferocious pace of change it has started will have as great an impact on society as factory processing and the steam engine during the industrial revolution, the report claims.

The research, carried out by the Henley Centre for Forecasting, suggests that the internet is already having far-reaching effects on everyday life, with six times more men than women taking to shopping in cyberspace.

'The internet offers a male paradise for shopping, being quicker, less overt, more anonymous and currently offering products more suitable for them,' says the report.

Electronic retailing will be the main growth area for the internet, according to the research. While most people see it primarily as a source of information or a communications tool, more than 20% believe that on-line shopping will be its main application within five years. At the moment, only 2% of men and 6% of women are concerned about the potential for on-line fraud.

The research, commissioned by computing firm Cisco Systems, challenges conventional wisdom by claiming that the importance of the world wide web has been 'under-hyped'.

James Richardson, the company's president, said: 'If you thought the technology bubble was about to burst, think again. Everything you ever thought possible through internet working will pale into insignificance compared with what is to come in the next few years.'

The key to the internet's success has been the speed with which the technology became available. Cisco estimates that there will be 6,000 new users every day this year – a population equivalent to that of Britain going on-line every six months.

The report warns that the internet is only at the 'innovation' stage of its development. Advance in technology must move in the same direction as consumer needs. There is a feeling that people are overwhelmed by the amount of information available.

The report also predicts that the internet will only achieve its full potential if alternatives to the personal computer are developed, allowing greater access from home. Although the proportion of homes with PCs rose from 10% in 1995 to 30% last year, this expansion is likely to reach a ceiling at about 40% in the next five years, and is heavily concentrated in middle class homes.

In this chapter, we provide an overview of the current and some of the likely future effects of technological developments. We focus on the impact of new technology on business and in the workplace, but also consider its implications for individuals and for society as a whole.

13.1   Developments in technology

Case study

Technological change in the banking industry

Until relatively recently, the only way to deal with a bank was by visiting the local branch where people's accounts were held. The accounting side of banking was maintained through hand-written ledgers, the reconciliation of accounts being dependent on the arithmetic and handwriting skills of the banking staff. The advent of commercially available technology in the 1960s began a process of transformation in the banking industry, a process that continues today.

Over the last forty or so years, it is possible to identify six distinct phases of change in the industry, as follows.

Phase 1 – the early 1960s

This era witnessed a period of mechanization – using mechanical tools to perform manual tasks. For example, hand-held adding machines (the forerunner of the electric calculator) became widely available. These machines became critical to the processing of the work of the bank.

Phase 2 – the 1960s–1970s

This phase represents arguably the biggest single advance in the use of technology. Until this point, the accounts of the banks were calculated and hand-written in large books known as ledgers. The sheer effort and time involved in doing this meant that many accounts were reconciled only on a weekly basis. With the development of mainframe computers accounts could now be calculated in a fraction of the time. Customer accounts were updated daily with a much greater degree of accuracy. Also, the miniaturization of electronics meant that modern calculators now became commercially viable.

Phase 3 – the early 1980s

Up until this time, technology had replaced the 'arms and legs' of the staff. Now there was the potential for it to start to replace some of the 'intelligence'. A good example of this is the way in which the information about a customer could be analysed by a computer and a score calculated that would indicate the likelihood that a customer would default on the repayment of a loan. The computer could help the decision making of the managers who were responsible for giving loans to customers. The computer could also 'learn' by being updated with historical data and over time become more and more accurate in predicting the likelihood of default.

Phase 4 – the mid-1990s

As computer technology became ever more advanced, it increasingly supplemented the intelligence of the banking staff. Instead of just supporting the lending decisions, banks used this technology to automate the lending process for certain types of loans and customer groups. Effectively, the computers were deciding whether to lend the bank's money. As they were fed with more and data about default rates, their decision-making capabilities became better and better, thereby improving the lending profitability of the banks.

Phase 5 – the late 1990s

Having automated many of the traditional tasks involved in banking and applied the improved technology to replace the capability of the staff, the banking industry now started to apply technology to change the way in which banking was undertaken. Leisure time had become a priority and growing numbers of people did not want to visit their local branch of the bank. Many felt increasingly comfortable with the new technology and wanted to take advantage of the opportunities for managing their finances from home via computers or over the telephone. Banks, therefore, looked to technology to change the way in which they delivered their products and the way in which customers were able to transact with them. During this stage there was a massive increase in the use of telephone banking, which relied upon intelligent telephone call-handling systems and the ability to immediately access all the relevant information on a customer. The widespread availability of the internet provided another opportunity for banks to offer their products and services. The face of banking had changed forever. No longer was a physical presence on the high street a necessity. There are some banks that have only an internet capability.

Phase 6 – the present and the future

So where does banking go from here? The fact that technology now plays a large part in many of our lives presents a particular challenge to the banking industry. People are increasingly discerning about the way in which they wish to deal with banks and the products that they require. This means that nowadays, banks must use technology in a much more focused fashion. They have to consider the influence of technology on behaviour, market segmentation and product design. As an example, the use of mobile telephones in particular age groups presents both a challenge and an opportunity to banks as to how they deliver their products. We can envisage a significant growth in mobile banking in such customer groups. And society's attitude to internet shopping will similarly shape the extent of the future of internet banking. One thing is certain, the banking industry will continue to change in many new and different ways. And technology will be at the heart of that change.

(With thanks to Paul Sinnott of Barclays Bank plc.)

Exercise

How do you think technological change has impacted on people management in the banking sector?

Feedback

The impact has been far-reaching. Technological change has had a de-skilling effect in that computers now make decisions that were once made by bank employees (about the creditworthiness of customers, for example). Many roles have become obsolete during this period – the 'traditional' bank manager being a case in point – while certain uses of technology have created job opportunities (in the case of call-centres and the industry of systems development itself, for example). Existing employees have had to re-skill – for instance, bank staff learning sales and marketing techniques and being required to sell the banks' products rather than manage people's accounts – with major learning and development implications.

The net result of technological change has been large reductions in the numbers employed in the banking industry, and consequently banks have needed to formulate plans for employee release. Generally, banks have had to develop strategies for managing change throughout this period.

The significance of IT can best be appreciated if it is placed in the context of long-term developments in automation. Gill[3] identifies three phases in the development of manufacturing automation since the Industrial Revolution:

- **Primary mechanization** (up to the end of the nineteenth century) – the use of machinery driven by water or steam power to replace human manual labour in production

- **Secondary mechanization** (up to the middle of the twentieth century) – the use of power by electricity to run assembly lines
- **Tertiary mechanization** (since the Second World War) – the use of computing and IT to coordinate and control production.

In the service sector, according to Friedman and Cornford,[4] three phases of computerization can be discerned (note the distinct parallels with the phases of technological developments outlined in the case study):

- **Phase 1** (1940 to 1960s). During this period, the focus was on the development of mainframe computers, mainly for defence and university research. The technology was very costly and, by today's standards, lacked both processing power and reliability.
- **Phase 2** (mid-1960s to 1980s). In this period, the focus shifted to improvements in software.
- **Phase 3** (1980s to date). The emphasis is now on matching the hardware and software to the needs of the users.

McLoughlin and Clark[5] note that the latest stages in the automation of work involve 'the convergence of four lines of technological development: telecommunications, computing, electronics and broadcast'. The development of digital techniques and fibre optics technology means that telecommunications systems and broadcast can now be linked to computer systems. Resulting advances, such as the internet and interactive digital television, can arguably be seen as a 'fourth phase' of computerization.

13.2 The applications of information technology

The main capabilities of computers and IT are information capture, storage, manipulation and distribution. These features give computers the ability to:

Automate the control of service and production operations

- The equipment can provide feedback to the operator
- The equipment or process can be controlled by the computer through a predetermined sequence
- Deviations from standards can be measured and corrected by the computer.

Promote organizational integration by:

- Making information more accessible to different levels and areas
- Increasing the speed of communications
- Providing performance information
- Increasing management control by providing faster and more precise management information.

However, it is important to note that the control of work organizations is not completely automated in the sense that there is no need for any human intervention. The real distinguishing feature of the new technology is that it provides information about the underlying administrative and production processes of the organization.

Some of the most revolutionary implications of new information and computing technologies have been in the areas shown in Table 13.1.

Table 13.1 The applications of information technology in the workplace

Design and Manufacture

- **Computer-aided design and drafting** (CAD)
  - interactive computer graphics
- **Computer-aided manufacture** (CAM)
  - computer-numerical control (CNC)
  - robotics
  - flexible manufacturing systems
- **Computer-integrated manufacturing** (CIM)
  - Computer-aided design and manufacture (CAD/CAM)
  - computer-aided production planning (CAPP)
  - computer-aided measurement and test (CAMT)
  - materials requirement planning (MRP)
  - just-in-time production (JIT)
  - quality management (QM)

Administration

- **Computing**
  - on-line processing
  - real-time management information systems (MIS)
  - word processors, personal computers (PCs)
  - knowledge management
- **Telecommunications**
  - electronic mail
  - viewdata and on-line databases
  - private automatic branch networks (PABX)
  - local area networks (LAN)
  - broadcast
  - internet
  - intranets

Finance and retailing

- **Finance**
  - automated teller machines (ATMs)
  - electronic funds transfer (EFT)
  - internet banking
- **Retailing**
  - electronic point-of-sale machines (EPOS)
  - electronic retailing ('internet shopping')
- **Finance and retailing**
  - electronic funds transfer at point of sale (EFTPOS)
  - integrated circuit cards ('smart cards')
  - electronic data interchange (EDI)

Electronic commerce

Adapted from McLoughlin and Clark[5]

13.3   The information age

This section considers the place of new technology, and particularly internet-related technology, in today's commercial global environment. The term 'information age' has its origins in the 1980s and refers to the role of computer-generated information in creating and sustaining the global economy which has emerged at the end of the century. Information is seen as the major force driving economic growth and as being instrumental in creating the post-industrial state, where it is the source of wealth and business leadership.[6] The precipitous fall in the cost of information is a key factor in these developments, exemplified by the use of the internet for obtaining information services or software applications:

'In the past, the providers of the information/software would have to produce, in a physical form of one sort or another, a copy of the required information/software for each individual user. Nowadays the provider simply installs one copy of the software/information on their particular internet site. Users then wishing to access the information/software simply dial up the site and read it accordingly. The point is, it does not matter whether it is accessed by one user or 10 million. The cost of production and delivery to the provider are as much for the first user as they are for the last. Such a change in the costs of supply is revolutionary, to say the least . . .'[6]

The growth of IT in both the business and the domestic environments is due to the advances in microelectronics and complementary software applications. As a result, computers and computer-controlled devices are tackling ever more complex tasks at ever lower costs, allowing the spread of new technologies. This expansion of IT has been facilitated by non-technical factors such as the liberalization of the world's tele-communications industries and markets. It is the increased competition stimulated by the latter development which has brought prices down. Furthermore, organizations using significant levels of IT need a well-educated, flexible workforce. This requirement has seen national governments across the world prioritizing education and training.

Commercial internet working

Business technology at the turn of the century is dominated by the internet, which has emerged as a serious global trading/information system. The impact of internet technology on business is evidenced by the inclusion of proposed internet development plans in many company annual reports. In July 1999, 17 per cent of the UK population had internet access.[7]

Features of the internet

- There is no one government or organization in control of the internet. Consequently, it has no overall design strategy.
- **E-mail.** This is currently the main application on the internet. It is cheap, fast and secure.
- **The World Wide Web** (WWW, or 'the web'). This is the fastest developing sector on the internet. Its popularity is mainly due to its user-friendly navigation features (it is easy for users to find their way around, or 'surf', the web). The information itself appears in a structure known as a web page. The WWW is used by individuals and organizations as a point of contact. Communication is not only cheap and efficient, but because it is multimedia based, it is also interesting. The web has been particularly advantageous for smaller companies, who for a minimum capital outlay have been able to take advantage of these benefits in trading over the internet.

The economic and social impact of the internet

The internet is seen by some as the embodiment of the global free market, with traders making direct and instant contact in a system of 'frictionless capitalism'.[8] (We saw in

Chapter 8 that a lack of information is one of the barriers to the efficient operation of the free market.) One key effect of internet trading is to reduce the role of intermediaries: retailers, for example, are faced with increasing competition as consumers place direct orders with manufacturers and suppliers. Other implications for business include the following:

- **Education and training.** (E-learning) Learners can access information and courses without physical attendance; universities and colleges can deliver programmes through cyberspace and publicly funded research is becoming more accessible.
- **Virtual business communities.** E-mail, chat lines and the web have seen the emergence of business virtual communities. An example of such a 'community' in operation is firms in particular sectors are scanning the internet to identify contracts for which they can tender.
- **Government.** Traders can illegally bypass purchase taxes such as VAT by buying products from countries beyond the jurisdiction of their government. For example, a user can dial up a foreign website, place an order for products such as software, videos and music and pay via credit card. The website is unlikely to charge or collect a foreign tax and the user's government can do little about the delivery of the product down the telephone line.

Intranet technology

Corporate users have begun to employ web pages and web browsers to operate their own in-house networks. These 'intranets' can connect users to existing corporate databases and enable the pooling of information across the organization. Intranets are usually equipped with an internet 'gateway' (access to the WWW), but entry to the intranet by outside agents is restricted by a 'firewall'. Intranets are used for internal publishing and as a cost-effective communication link.

Teleworking

A 'teleworker' is a home-based office worker. The home is effectively their 'virtual office' and they communicate with their customers and/or employers via techniques such as fax, phone, electronic mail and video conferencing. The sorts of tasks that lend themselves to teleworking include clerical duties such as sales invoicing or payroll, processing insurance claims, and document translation. Other 'professional' roles are also suitable for teleworking, for example journalism and various design/drafting occupations.

Teleworking represents significant savings for organizations, particularly in relation to the on-costs of employment (office space, heating, lighting, etc.). It also appears to have a positive effect on performance and productivity. Research suggests that this is due to the absence of commuting and the ability of the teleworker to organize flexible work schedules. Teleworking also has advantages for the workforce, as discussed in Chapter 2. There are drawbacks, however, mainly associated with feelings of isolation due to lack of social contact and problems with management arising from lack of personal contact.

Nomad workers

Sophisticated portable computers with full internet connectivity mean that workers can be an integral part of an organization without being physically based at a particular site. These are skilled, mobile workers who follow the work, wherever it may be.

13.4 Making sense of technological change in the workplace

We now turn to an examination of how technological change affects organizations. There are a number of theoretical frameworks which can be used to analyse the impact of technological change on the workplace. Here we consider contingency theory, labour process theory, flexible specialization and the strategic choice approach.

Contingency theory

Contingency theory starts from the point that there is no one best way to organize and manage production; this is seen to depend upon (is 'contingent' on) factors such as product markets, labour markets, organization size and technology. On the basis of her research in the 1950s and 1960s, Joan Woodward[9] suggested that the form of organization (and the management control system adopted) is determined by the technology used in producing the firm's output. As McGloughlin and Clark[5] observe, 'she argued that advanced technological change would lead to "mechanical" and integrated forms of management control which were incorporated within the technology itself. This would relieve management of the need to direct and personally supervise the workforce, whose performance would be subject to control by machinery.' In other words, where production is highly automated it is the functioning of the technology itself which controls the workforce, leaving supervisors to support and coordinate the work groups under their control.

Labour process theory

This essentially Marxist perspective is associated with Braverman,[10] who claims that technology is introduced by management in order to deskill the content of jobs, thereby increasing management control over work. Management gains control over the labour process by the application of 'Taylorist' techniques to production, namely the separation of conception from the execution of work tasks. According to Braverman, it is the capitalist search for increased profitability and management concern for increased control over work which drive technological change.

This is a very different view from that of Woodward, who saw management as a process of trying to 'fit' systems of organization and control to the technology in use. She also assumed that employers, managers and the workforce would have a common interest in this process. Braverman, on the other hand, saw management control systems as an aspect of a wider class conflict.

Flexible specialization

This perspective sees industry as undergoing a transition from Fordist mass production as the dominant form of organization and a return to (skilled) craft production, or flexible specialization. In contrast to Fordism, flexible specialization is a strategy of permanent innovation involving the accommodation to ceaseless change, rather than an effort to control it. This strategy is based on flexible – multi-use – equipment; skilled workers; and the creation, through politics, of an industrial community that restricts the forms of competition to those favouring innovation. In these conditions, work is upskilled rather than deskilled and industrial relations are cooperative.[11]

This perspective has been criticized on a number of counts: first, that the changes taking place are 'no more than variations on a Fordist theme, that is "neo-Fordism" '[5]; second, the flexible specialization model is based on perceived changes in a shrinking manufacturing sector, and ignores the growing service sector; and third, that technological change has involved the upskilling of 'core' workers jobs and the deskilling of those at the periphery, resulting in a polarization between the two groups.

The strategic choice approach

This concept of technological change sees its outcomes as being determined by the organizational actors themselves. Thus 'the outcomes of technological change, rather than being determined by the logic of capitalist development, or external technical and product market imperatives, are in fact socially chosen and negotiated within organizations by organizational actors'. This implies that organizations will respond in different ways to the introduction of new technology, their particular responses depending on 'the manner in which managers, unions and workforce are able to intervene to influence outcomes'.[5]

The strategic choice approach is usually associated with Child,[12] who argues that decision making in organizations is a political process and decisions about whether, when and how to introduce new technology are made by a 'power-holding group' within the organization. Although these strategic choices are likely to be made by senior managers, they can be modified by the workforce (through collective action) and by middle managers (who are responsible for implementing strategy). The implications of this perspective are that whether the outcome of introducing new technology is the deskilling or upskilling of work is a result of choice and negotiation.

Managing technological change

Once the decision to introduce new technology has been taken and the required equipment obtained, choices need to be made about how the new equipment will be implemented at workplace level. In making choices, management can take either a participatory or a non-participatory approach: at one extreme, managers may decide to 'impose' the new technology on the workforce and that a minimum of information should be made available to employees; at the other, they may decide to communicate and consult fully with their employees.

Other decisions about introducing new technology centre around whether a 'top-down' or 'bottom-up' approach should be adopted. The advantage of a top-down approach, where the change is managed centrally by a project team or a single manager, is that it enables a high degree of senior management control over change. However, a disadvantage is that the 'end-users' of the technology (the middle and junior managers) will have little say over its introduction. The bottom-up approach involves delegating the responsibility for managing the change to line managers, who will ultimately be responsible for using the new technology. The drawback here is less control over the management of the change and a lack of continuity as managers give priority to operational responsibilities rather than to the management of change. McGloughlin and Clark[5] argue that the strategy adopted for implementing new technology is likely to emerge 'as a result of choice and negotiation within the organization', rather than as a rational selection from alternatives.

Research indicates that UK managers tend to see the introduction of new technology as a way of increasing managerial control. As we have seen, some commentators argue that this is achieved by deskilling work, along Taylorist lines; others hold that control will be achieved by upskilling through functional flexibility. However, as McGloughlin and Clark note:[5]

The empirical evidence . . . suggests that policies concerned with the management of human resources do not flow unproblematically from overall business strategies. Such decisions involve political processes of strategic choice within organizations, which cannot be explained exclusively in terms of technical or product market imperatives or the logic of the historical development of forms of capitalist control over labour. It is apparent that managers pursue a diverse range of objectives when new technology is introduced . . . Moreover, available evidence suggests that the introduction of new technology has not been accompanied by significant innovations in human resource policies, in particular those associated with increased flexibility.

13.5   The social implications of technological change

We have seen that technological change tends to be viewed in relation to the competitiveness of the economy in a global marketplace. New technology is seen to initiate increased productivity and economic competitiveness; advances in technology are perceived as inherently beneficial, or at least essential to remain competitive.

However, the speed of technological change has not only affected the corporate sector. It has also had an impact on individuals in the home and as consumers of products and services. People need to be able to understand and use new technology, and that involves learning. Once they have learned to use, say, a video recorder or a personal computer, they can learn about other things which may interest them. Thus, learning about and using new technology can help to build confidence to go on to further learning. Here technology becomes a powerful tool for self-directed learning and provides grounds for the development of learning resource centres (see Chapter 3, Section 3.6). The use of technology in open and distance learning can facilitate the widening of access to learning and the learner to become more autonomous. However, it should also be noted that this type of learning can be isolating for the individual. Also, as noted in the opening case study, the ownership of personal computers is mainly concentrated in middle-class homes. This suggests a split in society between the 'information-rich' and the 'information-poor'.

New technology has also affected politics. Some commentators argue that it has the effect of 'empowering' individuals:

Computers have transformed (political) campaigning but more fundamentally the reason that democracy is healthy is that citizens are empowered by education, information and communication which cannot be controlled from above. There can be no turning back to rule by unchallenged elites in most advanced countries in part because of the power of the computer. [13]

In brief

We began this chapter by considering the stages of technological change and the applications of information technology in the workplace. We continued by examining the developments of the 'information age', in particular the internet, and their impact on business and management. The next section dealt with the management of technological change in the workplace, and we concluded by assessing the impact of IT on society.

In conclusion, information technology has had a profound effect on the way we live, work and organize economic activity. Some commentators predict that the latest phase of technological development, namely internet-related technology, will be responsible for a 'new industrial revolution'. This remains to be seen.

Examination questions for this chapter are given in Appendix 2.

References

1 McLoughlin, I. (1999) *Creative Technological Change: Shaping technology and organizations.* Routledge.

2 Held, D. (1993) *Democracy and the New International Order.* IPPR.

3 Gill, C. (1985) *Work, Unemployment and New Technology.* Polity Press.

4 Friedman, A. and Cornford, D. (1989) *Computer Systems Development: History, Organization and Implementation.* Wiley.

5 McLoughlin, I. and Clark, J. (1994) *Technological Change at Work* (2nd edn). Open University Press.

6 Cleary, T. (1998) *Business Information Technology.* Financial Times/Pitman Publishing.

7 *The Guardian Online*, 8 July 1999.

8 Robson, W. (1997) *Strategic Management and Information Systems.* Financial Times/Pitman Publishing.

9 Woodward, J. (1980) *Industrial Organization: Theory and Practice* (2nd edn). Oxford University Press.

10 Braverman, H. (1974) *Labour and Monopoly Capital: The Degradation of Work in the Twentieth Century.* Monthly Review Press.

11 Piore, M. J. and Sabel, C. F. (1984) *The Second Industrial Divide: Possibilities for Prosperity.* Basic Books.

12 Child, J. (1985) Managerial strategies, new technology and the labour process. In *Job Redesign: Critical Perspectives on the Labour Process.* (eds Knights, D., Wilmott, H. and Collinson, D.). Gower.

13 Leadbetter, C., quoted in *The Guardian Online*, 8 July 1999.

14 Social responsibility and business ethics

Chapter objectives

In this chapter you will:

- Consider the key ethical issues in business
- Examine the idea of 'corporate social responsibility'
- Compare 'agency' and 'stakeholder' theories
- Examine the relationship between the various parties involved in corporate governance and
- Evaluate practical guidelines for establishing ethical priorities.

Chapter introduction

The spectacular collapses in 2002 of Enron and WorldCom, two leading American corporations, have fuelled the already lively UK debate about corporate social responsibility and business ethics. In Britain, people's perceptions have been influenced by a number of high-profile cases (including the BCCI failure, the Barings Bank 'rogue trader' fiasco, directors' pay and genetically modified food, for example) which have called into question the ethical standards of some companies. However, these instances should not allow us to lose sight of the fact that there is a long tradition of ethical behaviour in business. From the Quakers (who believed that it was morally unacceptable to exploit their workers to make money) to The Body Shop (with its championing of environmental causes), companies have sought to 'do the right thing'. This raises two questions for managers:

- What is 'the right thing' to do in business?
- How do we ensure that 'the right thing' is done?

As Nash[1] argues, 'business ethics is not a separate moral standard, but the study of how the business context poses its own unique problems for the moral person who acts as an agent for the system'. The issues, then, are:

- How managers respond to the moral challenges of business and
- What are the ground rules for defining which actions are permissible, and which are not?

According to Johnson and Scholes,[2] business ethics are concerned with:

- Ethical standards and behaviour of individuals
- Corporate social responsibility to the various stakeholders (particularly those with little power) and
- Corporate governance, particularly in relation to accountability.

The following case study highlights a number of key ethical issues in business which, along with other moral questions for managers, will be examined in this chapter.

**Case
study**

Did HR fuel the demise of Enron?

Jane Lewis examines the risk-taking, entrepreneurial work culture of the energy giant and shows how HR played a leading role.

Few companies have risen so quickly then burned down with such intensity as Enron. The collapse of the Texan energy giant, once hailed as a model for all 21st century companies, has shaken America to its roots – some commentators have even claimed its long-term impact, at least in terms of how the country views itself, may be stronger than that of 11 September.

This is not just because Enron, thought to owe a staggering $55bn, is the largest corporate bankruptcy in history; nor because so many thousands of its employees now face the misery of personal financial ruin. The real point about Enron is that it is a wound the US inflicted on itself – and there is no telling where else the gangrene may be lurking. If such a seemingly invincible powerhouse can be exposed as little more than a house of cards, who will be next? As one corporate anatomist has remarked, much of the US population is now suffering a mass epidemic of 'Enronitis': a nervous condition brought on by implausible company accounts.

But as Enron's leading managers brace themselves for a prolonged circus of Congressional hearings and investigations, it is increasingly clear that the cause of the company's downfall goes much deeper than improper accounting or alleged corruption at the top. The real problem that hastened Enron's demise, claim the many management experts now raking over its ashes, is the very same risk-taking, entrepreneurial culture that first propelled its high-octane growth. And if you believe that, says Martin Goodman, a consultant in Watson Wyatt's strategic change practice, it is but a short step to concluding that 'ultimately the responsibility must lie with HR'. Who else, he argues, was responsible for framing and policing Enron's corporate values, its recruitment policy, and the cut-throat performance processes that did so much to shape a culture in which the survival of the fittest, by any means necessary, came to be the paramount consideration?

But, as Goodman is the first to point out, Enron's HR department, while clearly responsible, should not bear the full burden of blame. Faced with a management board that not only condoned the subversion of accepted corporate ethics, but which often appeared actively to encourage malpractice, the department's hands were tied. 'You cannot expect people to act in an ethical manner, if those at the top of the business are not doing so,' he says.

What Enron represents, therefore, is the inherent conflict in the role of HR: a department responsible for corporate ethics, yet seemingly powerless to enforce them at the highest level. Above all, the scandal highlights one of the most fundamental questions that every HR practitioner should examine. Is the department merely an agent of senior management, or does it have a responsibility to act on behalf of the interests of the workforce as a whole? In Enron's case, as we will see, the path taken by HR was clear-cut. Which way would you go?

Culture and ethics

During Enron's glory period (*circa* 1995-August 2000, when shares hit a peak of $90), it was often remarked that this was a company in love with itself. CEO Kenneth Lay was only half joking when he suggested a fitting tribute to the 'coolest' corporation on the planet would be to wrap a giant pair of shades around its Houston HQ.

Enron employees were easily identifiable by their swagger. The rewards for those who performed well were high: bonus day at Enron became known in the city as car day because of the lines of shiny new sports cars cluttering up the streets; its most opulent suburb, River Oaks, looked in danger of becoming an Enron dormitory town. Anyone working for the company, in whatever capacity, was considered a person with prospects.

If the city of Houston was impressed by Enron's freewheeling, sassy culture it was nothing to the praise lavished by the armies of management experts who flocked to Texas. As the new economy model took off, Enron seemed to be doing everything by the book – indeed, from an HR perspective, the company was virtually writing the book. Enron, said management guru Gary Hamel, had achieved the holy grail of modern people management: it encouraged a 'hotbed of entrepreneurial activity' in which staff were encouraged to take risks and become career builders. Retaining talent was never an issue at Enron because the HR department modelled itself as a kind of internal employment agency and kept an up-to-date internal database of CVs that encouraged managers to recruit internally. 'If you make it easy for people to move inside the company, they are less likely to look outside,' said vice-president of HR, Cindy Olson last year. It was not unusual for high-flyers to change jobs two or three times in as many years. The point, she said, was to enable entrepreneurs to 'build something of their own within the company'. 'Everyone knew,' says another executive, that if [CEO Jeff Skilling] liked you 'the leash was very long'. But with hindsight, the downside of this approach is obvious: inexperienced young MBAs were routinely handed extraordinary authority to make multi-million dollar decisions without higher approval. And because they tended to move between businesses, rather than within them, experience was not made to count. 'If you move young people fast in senior-level positions without industry experience, and then allow them to make large trading decisions, that is a risky strategy,' says Jay Conger, a management professor at London Business School.

In many ways the culture at Enron could not have been more straightforward: make your numbers or else – and executives were particularly highly rewarded for originating money-making ideas. Women did especially well in this environment: two of Enron's most profitable trading centres – its weather derivatives business and online trading division – were begun by ambitious young female executives who were noisily proclaimed corporate heroines.

The counter-balance to this risk-centric culture was supposed to be a strong code of corporate ethics, written up in a 61-page booklet and centring on Enron's guiding principles of RICE (Respect, Integrity, Communication, Excellence). These were prominently displayed on wall-posters, key rings, mouse mats and T-shirts and all employees had to sign a certificate of compliance. In practice, however, the unrelenting emphasis on profit growth and individual initiative tipped the culture from one that awarded aggressive strategy to one that increasingly relied on unethical corner-cutting. The corporate ethics were in place, but they were rarely policed and frequently ignored if they stood in the way of the more 'important' business.

The lead for this came from the top. In an interview two years ago, Skilling recalled his impatience with the mundane business of approving expenses claims. 'You've got to be kidding me,' he said. Here was a new world of opportunities to be tapped 'and I'm going to sit here and go through an expense statement line-item by line-item?' Henceforth, he decreed, expense reports would be routinely approved without review.

The lesson to be gleaned from this is clear, says Goodman at Watson Wyatt: it is no use having a corporate ethics policy 'unless you have processes in place that ensure these codes are enforced'. If you want to prevent people taking 'expeditious routes' you need to 'spell out the penalties', even to those at the top.

The decline of corporate ethics at Enron was no sudden event, but rather the 'gradual erosion of standards'. This made it very easy to turn a blind eye to malpractice because, eventually, breaking the rules became the norm. As one employee points out: 'Towards the end everyone knew the company was a house of cards. But people thought if they were getting away with it now, they would get away with it forever.'

Performance management and incentives

One of Skilling's undoubted achievements at Enron was to put the notion of intellectual capital firmly on the map. His belief that the main engine driving the company's growth was talent meant he was prepared to go to almost any ends to nurture his growing pool of thrusting young MBAs – and discard anyone who failed to make the grade. Skilling claimed that Enron's ruthless system of performance evaluation – swiftly christened 'rank and yank' – was pivotal to forging a new strategy and culture, 'It is the glue that holds the company together,' he said. At a senior level, he presided over a peer-review process imported from management consultants McKinsey and Co. This was, in effect, a star chamber, consisting of some 20 executives who regularly sat in judgement over every vice-president in the company, ranking them numerically. The stakes were high: the top 5 per cent of 'superior' managers were typically rewarded with bonuses some 66 per cent higher than the next grade down. The process was also laborious, because the committee's decision had to be unanimous.

Skilling claimed the system helped eliminate a 'yes man' culture because 'it was impossible to kiss 20 asses'. In practice, the reverse became true. The best way to get a good rating, employees agreed, was to not 'object to anything'. Further down the company chain, rank and yank became even more cut-throat. Skilling decreed that every six months the bottom 10 per cent of the workforce was to be eliminated regardless of individual performance. The upshot was a regular frenzy as employees jostled to make their numbers by hook or by crook.

Although one of the criteria on which Enron staffers were supposed to be judged was team-work, in practice this became the first casualty of a dog-eat-dog system in which an individual's ability to 'add value' to the bottom line was paramount. Far from operating as a collective entity, says one commentator, Enron began to resemble 'a collection of mercenaries'. It became common practice, when working on a project, to bring in as few people as possible 'so you wouldn't have to split your bonus'.

This survival of the fittest system, while undoubtedly ruthless, may have had a certain efficacy while times were good. But as the new economy soured there was much less success to go around, and the process took on a new and highly corrosive viciousness. As employee denounced employee in a desperate attempt to survive selection for the chop, the system became more political and more crony-based. It also encouraged desperate pragmatism. Some managers lied, altering the records of colleagues they wanted removed, others made use of Enron's much-vaunted whistle-blowing system, to submit negative reviews against people they were competing against for rankings. One of the first casualties of this system was corporate transparency, and a sinister use of euphemism crept into the corporate vocabulary: employees scheduled for 'redeployment' were told they had 45 days to find a new job within the company. In reality there were no such jobs available: the HR department was instructed to deter managers from other divisions from hiring them.

In common with many of its new economy peers, Enron made a point of rewarding successful executives with stock options. The logic was unassailable: by linking performance with shareholder value, executives aligned their actions with the wider interests of company stakeholders. 'If you have incentives that aren't aligned, the risk is that executives operate in a manner that doesn't give the best return to shareholders,' says Duncan Brown, principal of Towers Perrin.

But at Enron, where the vast bulk of executive remuneration comprised stock options – senior chiefs cashed in some \$1bn in stock in the years immediately preceding the company's crash – the environment was ripe for abuse. The personal interest that senior managers had in keeping the share-price high at any cost encouraged corruption, greed and financial impropriety and discouraged transparency. Far from promoting the best behaviour, the incentive system at Enron frequently spawned the worst.

What lessons can be drawn from all this? It all depends, says Brown, on whether the investigation into Enron shows that an abuse of the system was to blame, rather than the system itself. But what happened at Enron should spell a clear warning to HR of the dangers of monitoring and rewarding performance by numbers alone – there is now widespread recognition that a more qualitative, well-rounded approach is needed. The benefits of using a balanced scorecard approach are plain.

Finally, although executive bonuses in the UK have yet to reach the exorbitant level of those routinely doled out in the US, HR needs to start asking tough questions now about whether executive pay rises can actually be justified objectively.

Pensions

Progressive HR management thinkers have long been vocal advocates of employee company ownership because of the huge benefits it offers in terms of employee buy-in, commitment and loyalty. But the miserable fate of the many thousands of Enron employees who lost everything when their company stock collapsed exposes the inherent danger of putting too many eggs in one basket.

Like many US companies, Enron had begun the process of shifting responsibility for its employees' retirement back on to the individual via the introduction of pension plans known as 401(k), which offered a diverse array of investments. But thousands of employees, still mired in their 'I'll be taken care of' mentality, ignored every alternative investment to plough 100 per cent of their pension plans into Enron stock, with disastrous results. In the UK, of course, the system is very different. But the already pronounced shift from defined purchase plans to Money Purchase Plans and Share Incentive Plans means employees are now more exposed to risk. The main lesson we must all learn from Enron is the importance of diversification. If your company matches your retirement savings with company shares, it makes sense not to invest in any additional stock, however tempting.

It is commonly agreed, however, that the real scandal revealed by the collapse of Enron was how the company's pension scheme was managed. Far from acting in the interests of plan participants, the fund's trustees – including HR vice-president Cindy Olson – consistently put the interests of the company first. This was most apparent in the decision to ban employees from selling their stock in the weeks before the company filed for bankruptcy. In the US, there is an active campaign to eliminate such abuse by insisting that companies which have traditionally selected their own trustees must now be required to appoint truly independent individuals. While the regulatory environment in the UK post the Robert Maxwell affair is undoubtedly much tighter than its US equivalent, it is clear that we can still draw some useful guidance from what happened at Enron, in particular, the suggestion that employees should have a greater input in selecting trustees.

Whistleblowing

Enron encouraged whistleblowers: its policy was to allow employees to complain anonymously about their co-workers. So why wasn't the whistle blown earlier about what we now know to be widespread malpractice in its accounting and financial departments?

In fact, financial executive Sherron Watkins was not the first voice to raise concerns within the company. Two years ago Enron's treasurer, Jeffery McMahon, questioned the propriety of some of CFO Andrew Fastow's 'partnerships' – and found himself swiftly 'promoted' out of the action to a post in London. It now emerges that Enron's corporate lawyer, Jordan Mintz, also questioned the partnerships and sought outside legal advice.

The answer, it is clear, lies in the autocratic system of hierarchy that (for all its boasts to the contrary) continued to prevail at Enron. Since whistleblowers appealing to the highest level of the company were discouraged, ignored and ultimately punished, what hope was there of being listened to further down the ranks? In many respects the climate prevailing at Enron was no different from that of most other companies: while catered for on paper, whistleblowers run a real risk of becoming corporate pariahs and damaging their careers for good. Frequently tarred as 'disgruntled', they continue to be seen as a risky hire even if they leave a company.

But it is not just fear of reprisal that prevents people speaking out. At Enron, as we have seen, the culture itself discouraged it. People became so identified with the organization and its practices that they stopped seeing that something was wrong.

As Goodman points out, it is the responsibility of HR to put in place a formal system – independent of senior managers – in which complaints and doubts can be freely expressed without fear. The failure of Enron's HR department to achieve this was the main reason why malpractice was allowed to flourish for so long. Employees knew the system was crooked, but felt powerless to change it. They were right. All Enron's whistleblowers behaved in an exemplarily fashion: they did not steal documents or go to the newspapers, they took their concerns to the top guy. And nothing happened.

Could the Enron scandal signal a new movement in corporate challengers? One US hot-line operator notes that calls to its centres have risen exponentially since the scandal broke. Cynics may argue that this is transitory – deep down most employees know the consequences for whistleblowers are usually grim. But what Enron has shown us above all is that ignoring misconduct can have truly terrible consequences for everyone. The most optimistic outcome of its fall from grace is that it may issue in a new era of employee empowerment.

Cindy Olson
Vice-president, HR
Olson, who became head of Enron's HR department last year, was a newcomer to the profession. Having spent 15 years as an accountant, she worked for three years in community relations before assuming the top HR job. Although privy to Sherron Watkins' August 2001 memo, she took no action, in her capacity as an 'independent' fiduciary and trustee of Enron's 401(k) pension plan, to alert fellow employees. She later told a congressional hearing she believed Watkins' assessment to be untrue. Even more controversially, she agreed to a moratorium last October, which banned employees from selling the Enron stock in their plans while it still retained some value. 'We didn't have a crystal ball,' she said. 'We didn't know where the stock was going to go.' Nonetheless, on the advice of her own financial advisor, she admitted to cashing in some $6.5m in Enron stock, most of it in the year before the company's collapse.

Personnel Today, 19 March 2002.

Exercise

What could the HR function have done to prevent the practices which contributed to Enron's downfall?

Feedback

As the article makes clear, HR was responsible for creating and reinforcing Enron's risk-taking entrepreneurial culture through framing both the supporting people management structures (in particular the performance management system and the recruitment policy) and the company's corporate values. HR was also responsible for ensuring that employees adhered to an explicit code of ethics.

So it appears that the HR function should shoulder some of the blame for the company's failure. However, as the author points out, HR practitioners were not in a position to counter the malpractice that was to all intents and purposes encouraged by senior management. HR's dilemma is summed up by Torrington *et al.*:[3]

The problem is that HR people do not have a separate professional existence from the management of which they are part. Human resource management must be a management activity or it is nothing. Doctors, lawyers and accountants, even when employed by a large organisation, can maintain a non-managerial professional detachment, giving advice that is highly regarded, even when it is unpopular. Furthermore they advise; they do not decide. HR specialists are employed in no other capacity than to participate closely in the management practice of a business. They can not, therefore, be expected to take up a full-fledged, independent professional stance. Were they to retreat to an ivory tower and maintain a purist position on ethical matters then theirs would be a voice in the management wilderness that nobody wanted to hear . . .

This would suggest that HR professionals put themselves in an untenable position if they simultaneously aspire to be 'business partners' with line managers and then look to claim the moral high ground when tough decisions have to be made. As Torrington *et al.*, argue, the way forward for HR is 'to make a strong business case for taking an ethical line wherever it is credible to do so'.

14.1   Ethics and business decisions

Many business decisions have an ethical element and managers need to be able to identify when ethical issues are involved. There are various ethical standpoints, derived from moral philosophy, which can be applied to ethical dilemmas in business. Thus, in making business decisions, managers could ask questions such as:

- Is this decision in accordance with both the law and the accepted rules of society?
- Are most people going to benefit from this decision?
- Do the ends justify the means?
- What is in the best interests of the business?

However, managers are not philosophers and cannot be expected to apply the generalized and sometimes conflicting principles implied by these questions to business decisions. The situation is further complicated by what is known as 'ethical relativism', which refers to the fact that morality is not a constant; it changes from society to society and from time to time, so what is right in one place or time could be wrong in another. Some would argue that this permits managers to work to different standards in different countries and cultures – a convenient principle for companies that operate internationally and competing against companies with different moral codes. This could justify corporate gift-giving (otherwise known as bribery).

There are definite business advantages of ethical behaviour. Companies such as Levi-Strauss, Marks & Spencer and Johnson & Johnson have an established ethical reputation and enjoy the business benefits which flow from this. However, there is a cost, in terms of time and resources, as they need to make substantial efforts to maintain this reputation. For example, Marks & Spencer took legal action against Granada TV when one of the latter's programmes accused the company of exploiting overseas suppliers; and Johnson & Johnson withdrew Tylenol from sale as soon as a defect was suspected.

The growing interest in business ethics, both as an area of concern for the business community and as a subject for academic enquiry, is evidenced by its higher profile in professional management programmes and on both undergraduate and postgraduate business and management courses. This reflects the fact that managers are increasingly being confronted with ethical challenges and need to be prepared to recognize and manage these as they arise. To assist managers in this, it is useful to think of ethical issues as having a number of dimensions (see Figure 14.1):

- **The employee dimension** – relations with employees. This relates to the way in which individual employees are treated. The issues which can be considered here include discrimination, confidentiality, loyalty and employee surveillance.
- **The customer dimension** – customer relations and marketing. Issues here include pricing, product safety and advertising.
- **The corporate dimension** – relations with other companies. This includes the payment of suppliers, the ethical standards of the suppliers themselves (e.g. do they mistreat their workforce?), mergers and acquisitions and insider trading.
- **The community dimension** – relations with the community. This includes cultural diversity, self-regulation, bribery, the physical environment and community relations.

The use of such a framework to examine ethical issues helps managers to recognize the broad context of business ethics, while allowing them to identify which issues are of particular concern at any one time.

Figure 14.1. The ethical dimensions of business.

The identification of an ethical context of business also highlights the fact that firms, as well as individuals, can be viewed as 'moral agents'.[4] Ethical lapses in business can arise at three levels:

- **Individual level** – arising from need, greed or 'sharp practice'.
- **Organization level** – arising from a corporate culture of excessive pressure for results, or of inadequate supervision (the Barings Bank collapse falls into this category), or from laziness or ignorance.
- **Industry level** – arising from a feature of the industry such as the payment of commission in the insurance industry, resulting in the mis-selling of policies.

It is important to note that ethical dilemmas tend not to be clear choices between good and bad. A good example of this principle is trade with South Africa in the apartheid era.

Looking back now on the controversy surrounding trade with South Africa can be salutary in this respect. Who was right: the companies that pulled out and supported the boycott and international disapproval of apartheid or the companies that stayed on and used the Sullivan principles and other strategies to erode apartheid from the inside, while also ensuring that there would be a viable economy after the revolution? There is, of course, no answer to this question. But it remains a good question. It suggests in this case that maybe both ethical approaches had right on their side and that each was effective in its own way.[4]

People tend to be uneasy with the idea of drawing attention to business ethics and would rather just get on with running a 'decent' business. Some feel that it is judgemental and moralizing. Therefore the term 'social responsibility' is preferred, partly because it is seen as less threatening when applied to business behaviour.

14.2 Corporate social responsibility

The starting point for an analysis of corporate responsibility is a consideration of the question: to whom is a company responsible?

14.2.1 'The business of business is business'

Some commentators, such as Milton Friedman, believe that managers should be guided in their actions by the economic imperative, i.e. profit maximization: 'There is only one social responsibility of business – to use its resources and engage in activities designed to increase profits so long as it stays within the rules of the game, and engages in open and free competition without deception or fraud.'[5]

Friedman stated that business should be conducted in conformity with the basic legal and ethical rules of society. He was criticizing the practice of diverting business from its proper role, as society's wealth-producing organ, and applying its resources to tackle social problems. The trend in the UK at this time was for government to expect businesses to demonstrate their credentials as 'good citizens' by encouraging them to become involved with various community projects. Friedman saw this as imposing unwarranted social obligations on business and substituting corporate philanthropy for government spending.

For Friedman, businesses provided sufficient social benefit by creating employment and wealth (by producing goods and services). For businesses to donate to philanthropic causes was effectively a self-imposed tax. Managers were employed to maximize shareholder value.

A business can be socially responsible by:

● Pursuing its economic objectives, involving:
  (i)   Making a profit
  (ii) Being a going concern
  (iii) Providing goods and services
  (iv) Creating employment
  (v)   Paying taxes
  (vi) Paying creditors
● Respecting and operating within the laws of the land
● Contributing to the solving of social problems and involvement in the community
● Treating its stakeholders fairly.

It is the third element that Friedman objects to on the grounds that it involves spending shareholders' and employees' money on what managers arbitrarily decide to be 'good causes'.

Others argue that businesses should not have a completely free hand to operate as they wish in pursuit of profit. Businesses operate within a framework of other social institutions on whom they depend for human, financial and physical resources. Business therefore needs to respond to society's own imperatives if it is to be accepted as part of that society.

(social responsibility) requires of the manager that he assume responsibility for the public good, that he subordinate his actions to an ethical standard of conduct, and that he restrain his self-interest and his authority wherever their exercise would infringe upon the common weal and upon the freedom of the individual.[6]

Those who subscribe to the idea of corporate social responsibility hold that the relationship between business and society is therefore characterized by mutual dependency and obligations.

As business changes over time, so do the expectations of society. As discussed in Chapter 11, people's attitudes change: for example, in relation to environmental issues or food standards.

14.2.2   'Enlightened self-interest'

To what extent does a desire by business to act in a socially responsible way originate from genuine philanthropic intentions or from enlightened self-interest? In reality, organizations with a reputation for taking an ethical stance attempt to combine business success with a socially responsible attitude. Anita Roddick of The Body Shop sums this up as follows:

I am no loony do-gooder, traipsing the world hugging trees and staring into crystals . . . I am also not one of those people who is opposed to trade or change . . . (but) I would rather be measured by how I treat weaker and frailer communities I trade with rather than by how great are my profits.

'Anita Roddick speaks out on corporate responsibility' (The Body Shop, 1994)

To summarize, there are arguments for and against corporate social responsibility: as shown in Table 14.1.

Table 14.1 Arguments for and against companies acting in a socially responsible way

For:	Against:
• Good for business	• Not management's job
• Enhances the public image of the company	• Distracts from the pursuit of profit – risk of reduced competitiveness
• May avoid government intervention	• Business lacks public accountability
• In the company's long-term interests	• Business does not have the skills to pursue social goals
	• Undermines the role of the state

14.3   Stakeholder theory

Friedman's views on the role of business in society are an example of agency theory. Here managers are the 'agents' of the shareholders, responsible only to the board of directors. Stakeholder theory, on the other hand, suggests that corporate decisions can be improved by considering those who have a significant stake or interest in the organization. This definition can be extended to include those who are in some way affected by corporate decisions.

An organization's responsibilities to its stakeholders can be characterized as follows:

- **Shareholders.** Managers' social responsibilities include safeguarding investments and the opportunity for shareholders to participate in policy decisions and question management on the affairs of the company. The prime objective of managers is to maximize profits in response to what they rightly assume to be shareholder priorities. Shareholders' attitudes to social responsibility will depend on their time horizons. If they adopt a short-term perspective, then they are unlikely to be concerned about whether the company in which they have invested is behaving in a socially responsible way. However, if they take a long-term view, then they may be willing to consider the argument that social responsibility pays off in terms of contributing to organizational performance. Also, the growth of ethical unit trusts provides evidence that there are those who value corporate social responsibility above maximizing their personal wealth.
- **Customers.** Research suggests that customers are now more aware of issues of corporate responsibility. They may boycott certain products if they feel that producers are behaving unethically, e.g. the consumer boycott on South African products during the apartheid era. A more recent example is many people's refusal to buy genetically modified food, resulting in retailers removing such products from their shelves.
- **Employees.** Stakeholder theory requires organizations to adhere to 'good employer' principles in relation to fair treatment and remuneration, personal development, job security, participation and consultation, job design.
- **Suppliers.** Conditions of purchase or sale and settlement dates should be honoured.
- **The community.** The growth of the footloose multinational corporation means that the link between producers and their community is not as strong as it once was. However, customers and employees live in these communities which are still important.
- **Society.** The corporate responsibility approach holds that society has the right to sanction business operations and will confront organizations who behave in a way which society deems to be unacceptable. One of the features of the latter years of the twentieth century saw growing concern for the environment. Some organizations are now taking the interests of society and communities into account when formulating strategy, as illustrated by the following cases.

Stakeholding BA seeks neighbourly trust

BAA, the privatized airport operator, will this week launch a 'contract with the community' programme designed to transform the business into a stakeholder corporation. It will put environmental and community issues at the heart of business development with the aim of avoiding the kind of lengthy and expensive battles which have continually delayed the approval of a new terminal at Heathrow. Sir John Egan, BAA chief executive, will tell the group's 150 senior managers at a conference on Thursday that they have to change the way they work if they are to achieve business objectives – including further expansion of airport capacity in the south-east of England. In future they will have to adopt the sustainability agenda of the government and environmentalists who have opposed Heathrow's terminal five and new runways at Gatwick and Stanstead.

BAA's mission statement previously referred to customer needs including safety, and continuous improvement in financial performance and service quality. After lengthy debate among management another was added, which commits the group to grow 'with the support and trust of our neighbours'. The chief executive will stress the importance of the mission at this week's conference. 'This is not just a set of words, it commits us to action' Sir John says. The new programme will be led by Janis Kong, Managing Director of Gatwick airport. The contract consists of ten commitments, including the integration of green and community issues into airport expansion strategies and continuous improvement of environmental performance. The pledges include lobbying through international bodies for wider environmental improvements and pressing suppliers and airlines to improve their performance.

Green reporting helps Tarmac profits grow

Green initiatives helped leading construction company Tarmac boost its profits, chief executive Sir Neville Simms says today, writes Tom McGhie. For the last five years Tarmac has been seeking to link reporting of its environmental performance with that of its financial results. Commenting on the annual report from the firm's environmental panel, Sir Neville says: 'The further improvement in our environmental performance in 1998 was particularly encouraging, with over 70 per cent of performance targets fully or substantially achieved, and with each of the challenges set by the environmental panel delivered in full.' Last year profits rose by 14 per cent to £131.4 million, with improved margins.

Reported in *The Guardian*, 17 May 1999

The principles of stakeholder analysis are that in formulating and implementing strategy, managers must take into account both the interests and the relative power of stakeholder groups (see Chapter 7). This raises a number of ethical issues for managers:

● Can managers be expected dispassionately to weigh the conflicting interests of stakeholder groups?
● Are managers accountable only to certain stakeholders – e.g. shareholders – and thereafter merely responsible for ensuring that decisions are acceptable to other stakeholders?

- Do managers make strategies to suit their own purposes and manage stakeholder expectations to ensure acceptance of these strategies?

Issues for individuals and managers include:

- What is the responsibility of an individual who believes that his or her organization's strategy is unethical or is not representing the interests of legitimate stakeholders? Should the individual leave the company or report the organization – a course of action now commonly known as *whistleblowing*?
- Managers are in a powerful position in relation to other stakeholders. This is because they have access to resources and information that are not available to other stakeholders. Johnson and Scholes[2] note that 'with this power comes the obligation to behave with *integrity*'.

The ethical challenge of stakeholder theory is to find a way of satisfying all the parties who have an interest in, or whose interests are seriously affected by, a firm's behaviour. The Royal Society of Arts report *Tomorrow's Company* identified that the UK's economic success was dependent on what it described as the 'inclusive company', that is, a company which can build constructive relationships with its stakeholders.

There is now also a political dimension to the idea of 'stakeholders'. This was popularized by commentators such as Will Hutton,[7] who talked of 'stakeholder capitalism'. The prime minister, Tony Blair, spoke of a 'stakeholder economy', as one in which there was increased employee participation in corporate decisions.

The main advantage of the stakeholder idea is that it provides a wider perspective for business by identifying all the groups in society who are affected by its actions. The disadvantages are that:

- Many stakeholders can be identified
- Stakeholder theory provides no way of arbitrating between conflicting stakeholder claims
- Attempts to prioritize between different classes of stakeholders are often of little practical use.

14.4 Corporate governance

Corporate governance has been defined as 'The system by which companies are directed and controlled'.[8] It relates to the process of supervising executive decisions and actions, accountability and the regulatory framework within which organizations operate. There are several groups (managers, directors, the board, shareholders and investment fund managers) that form a 'chain of governance' and have a legitimate influence on the organization's purposes – that is; they have formal 'rights' through the corporate governance framework. In all but the smallest of companies, ownership is now divorced from managerial control so that the managers who are driving the company's strategy may be very remote from the beneficiaries of the organization's performance, who will often have their interests guarded by intermediaries such as asset managers for pension funds. The complexity of corporate governance gives rise to conflicts of interest which need to be balanced by managers. A key issue here is whether managers are solely responsible to shareholders or to a wider range of stakeholders.

A key ethical issue is to increase management accountability to owners and to encourage shareholders to bear the full cost of ownership, over and above the financial risk involved. The problem here is that ownership is spread thinly and it is therefore difficult to conceive of individual shareholders bearing 'responsibility' for the company they partly own. However, recent years have seen the emergence of 'shareholder activism' in both the UK and the USA. For example, in the UK institutional shareholders have moved to control perceived excesses in executive remuneration; in doing so, they are reflecting society's concerns and thereby taking note of and exercising their social responsibilities.

The Cadbury Report, set up in the wake of the Robert Maxwell scandal, called on shareholders to ensure that companies follow best-practice guidelines on corporate governance. This includes measures such as disclosing the details of directors' remuneration packages in the company's annual report and the role of independent directors in overseeing corporate decisions. The Greenbury Report on executive pay made new recommendations on how directors should be paid.

Corporate governance has come to the fore in recent years because some groups would like to see shareholders become more active in the companies in which they invest. Furthermore, it is felt that companies should themselves take more notice of their other stakeholders whose interests need to be taken into account if the companies are to achieve long-term improvements in shareholder value.

An independent committee, appointed by the former Secretary of State for Trade and Industry Margaret Beckett to conduct a wide-ranging review of company law produced its interim report in February 1999. It recommended that companies face a requirement to report on their social and environmental performance as part of a broader approach to communications with stakeholders. The report stated that directors should be more 'inclusive' by considering the wider implications of a company's actions, rather than focusing exclusively on shareholder interests.

The ethical behaviour of employees can be influenced by specific organizational measures, some of which are outlined here.

14.5   Codes of ethics

A number of companies have developed codes of ethics and we saw in the opening case study how Enron's attempt to control people's behaviour in this way had signally failed. However, according to McDonald and Zepp,[9] the advantages of codes of ethics are:

- to clarify management's thoughts of what constitutes unethical behaviour
- to help employees think about ethical issues before they are faced with the reality of the situation
- to provide employees with the opportunity of refusing compliance with an unethical action
- to define the limits of what constitutes acceptable or unacceptable behaviour
- to provide a mechanism for communicating the managerial philosophy in the realm of ethical behaviour
- to assist the induction and training of employees

The disadvantages are:

- even a detailed list of guidelines cannot be expected to cover all the possible grey areas of potentially unethical practices

- codes of ethics are often too generalized to be of specific value
- rarely are codes of ethics prioritized; for example, 'loyalty to the company and to fellow employees' does not resolve the potential conflict when a colleague is seen to be acting contrary to company interest.
- as an individual phenomenon, ethical behaviour which has been guided by ethical codes of conduct will only be effective if the codes have been internalized and are truly belied by employees.

Ethical policy statements

Ethical policy statements promote ethical behaviour, but tend to suffer from the same defects as ethical codes.

Leadership

If employees do not perceive senior managers to be complying with ethical policy, they may tend not to comply themselves. While top management can influence ethical behaviour, other employees may not operate to the same ethical standards unless the ethical value system of the corporation is accepted by all members of the organization. Again, we saw how senior managers at Enron failed to comply with the company's own code of ethics.

Ethics committees

Organizations such as Motorola have used ethics committees to focus attention on business ethics. The committee membership is rotated among all employees, thereby exposing them to ethical problems submitted by managers and other employees. A decision by the committee provides clear guidelines for action.

Realistic performance and reward schemes

The pressure to perform can often override personal ethical standards. Measures such as cost-saving plans, performance-related pay and setting unrealistic objectives may unknowingly be rewarding unethical behaviour. This requires the organization to reassess its approach to performance management. Once again, Enron is a case in point.

Establishment of ethical corporate cultures

As McDonald and Zepp[9] note, 'the corporate culture will naturally affect the ethical values of its personnel, and the more an employee feels him/herself a member of the company team, the stronger will be the tendency to conform to the ethical standards of the company'.

14.6 A professional code of conduct for managers

There is a potential conflict for managers around what courses of action are best for their own career development and what strategies are in the longer-term interests of the organization. As Johnson and Scholes[2] note, integrity is the key ingredient of professional

Table 14.2 Extract from the Chartered Management Institute Code of Conduct[10]

As a Professional Manager you will:

- Pursue managerial activities with integrity, accountability and competence
- Disclose any personal interest which might be seen to influence managerial decisions
- Practise an open style of management so far as is consistent with business needs
- Keep up-to-date with developments in best management practice and continue to develop personal competence
- Adopt an approach to the identification and resolution of conflicts of values, including ethical values, which is reasonable and justifiable
- Safeguard confidential information and not seek personal advantage from it
- Exhaust all available internal remedies for dealing with matters perceived as improper, before resorting to public disclosure
- Encourage the development and maintenance of quality and continuous improvement in all management activities

management and is included in the code of conduct of professional bodies such as the Chartered Management Institute.

The code of conduct is binding on all corporate members of the Institute (see Table 14.2). Managers are expected to maintain certain standards of conduct in relation to:

- The individual manager
- Other members of the organization
- The organization
- Others external to but in direct relationship with the organization
- The wider community
- The Chartered Management Institute

Readers should also refer to the Chartered Institute of Personnel and Development Code of Conduct.

In brief

We began this chapter by examining the ethical issues surrounding one of the most notorious corporate failures in history and the extent to which HR was culpable for that episode. We continued with a discussion of the moral dilemmas facing managers and analysed various conceptions of 'corporate social responsibility'. Having discussed corporate governance, we then went on to evaluate the ways in which organizations try to influence the moral behaviour of employees, for example through producing codes of ethics.

Examination questions for this chapter are given in Appendix 2.

References

1 Nash, L. L (1994) Why business ethics now? In *Managing Business Ethics* (eds Drummond, L. and Bain, B.). Butterworth-Heinemann.
2 Johnson, G. and Scholes, K. (1999) *Exploring Corporate Strategy* (5th edn). Prentice Hall Europe.
3 Torrington, D., Hall, L. and Taylor, S. (2002) *Human Resource Management* (5th edn). Prentice Hall.

4 Mahoney, J. (1997) *Mastering Management*. Financial Times/Pitman Publishing.
5 Friedman, M. (1970) The social responsibility of business is to increase profits. *The New York Times Magazine*, 13 September.
6 Drucker, P. F. (1989) *The Practice of Management*. Heinemann Professional.
7 Hutton, W. (1995) *The State We're In*. Jonathan Cape.
8 The Cadbury Committee (1992) *The Financial Aspects of Corporate Governance*. Stock Exchange Council.
9 McDonald, G. M. and Zepp, R. A. (1994) In *Managing Business Ethics* (eds Drummond, L. and Bain, B.). Butterworth-Heinemann.
10 Chartered Management Institute (2002) Code of Professional Management Practice.

Further reading

Lavalette, M. and Pratt, A. (eds) (2001) *Social Policy – An Introduction*. Sage.

Web-site addresses

Chartered Institute of Personnel and Development: http://www.cipd.co.uk
Chartered Management Institute: http://www.managers.org.uk
Guardian newspaper: http://www.guardian.co.uk

Appendix 1

How the book and the CIPD syllabus link together

A cursory glance at the learning outcomes included here and in the contents page as well as the CIPD's own core management standards and new syllabus will inform the reader that the authors have closely followed the CIPD's own core management format. All three parts of this book mirror those in the CIPD syllabus, omitting Managing Information. Also, all the chapters reflect the CIPD's syllabus as well as the learning outcomes listed here. However, to add further clarity the following is a concise cross-reference of the CIPD's syllabus and the chapters/sections found in this book.

Core Management for HR Students and Practitioners		*CIPD standards/syllabus*
Part One	Managing People at Work	Managing people
Chapter 1	Individual Differences:	The Fundamental Characteristics of People

All elements of the syllabus are included except Learning Theory which has been included in Chapter 3, Section 3.6.

Chapter 2	People at Work	The Changing World of Work
Chapter 3	Managing People – Optimizing the People Contribution	Optimizing the People Contribution
Part Two	Managing Activities	Managing Activities
Chapter 4	Managerial Work	The Nature of Managerial Work
Chapter 5	The Work Organization	The Work Environment
Chapter 6	The Issue of Quality	Quality and Continuous Improvement
Part Three	Managing in a Business Context	
Chapter 7	The Strategic Framework of Management	The Strategic Framework

Managing Information is covered in a complementary text.

Appendix 2

Specimen examination questions and answers

Further questions and answers will be available on the Butterworth-Heinemann web-site.

Part One – Managing People at Work

Question

1 Drawing upon your knowledge of motivation theory, consider how would you advise any organization planning to introduce 'flexibility' into the workplace; specifically, you should consider the formulation and implementation of appropriate policies which would help the organization improve levels of employee trust and commitment.

Answer

This is not an easy question to answer! Firstly, you would have to provide an overarching definition of motivation (see Section 3.4.1), distinguishing between extrinsic and intrinsic motivation. However, you should not spend too much time on defining motivation because the question is how employers handle workplace flexibility in the light of motivation theory. Therefore, the next paragraph should briefly explain the main types of flexibility (see Section 2.3.5). Finally, you should indicate that trust/commitment will depend upon the strength of the psychological contract (see Section 2.1).

Once all these definitions are in place you should explain that functional flexibility is more likely to satisfy intrinsic motivational as well as extrinsic motivational needs if the job is of a high skill/competency level. However, the risk is that temporal and numerical flexibility could yield low levels of motivation because of the short-term and exploitative nature of both the legal and the psychological contract. Obviously, the type of workplace and its sector will be determining factors, but any employer should bear in mind that employee or worker responses will reciprocate what s/he provides by way of intrinsic and extrinsic motivators. Flexibility should go hand-in-hand with good job design.

Question

2 How can an understanding of the process of social perception be of assistance to the manager of human resources? Provide examples to support your argument.

Answer

This can be found in Section 1.1. The opening and the end-of-chapter case studies will provide you with clear guidelines on how to answer the question. Of course, the key to the answer is that the manager must realize that everyone has their own frame of reference by which they make judgements about everybody else. Upon this basis they make assumptions about their personality type, their behaviours and other personal attributes. In this way, people can be stereotyped. Ramifications are far-reaching, such as decisions about job selection and training, granting rewards and discipline and the way in which grievances are handled. There is a clear link with equal opportunities and discrimination. You should also note the link with the attitudes and personality of the person who is taking the view of others. Any organization serious about equal opportunities and diversity must tackle this underlying issue otherwise there is little chance of changing prevailing cultures.

Question

3 Briefly outline the main causes of workplace stress. What can employers do to reduce the effects of stress and remove its causes?

Answer

As you will have found from reading Section 2.4.4 the causes of workplace stress can be many and will be linked with factors such as the individual's personality, role(s) performed and work environment. Figure 2.7 summarizes the causes. When answering such a question it would be necessary to first furnish a short definition of stress. Some examples of the damaging ramifications of stress could also be supplied, such as physical: poor performance, or psychological: irrationality. The massive costs and negativity of workplace stresses must be emphasized. The second part of the question can be answered by examining Section 2.4.6. Again, the possibilities are very considerable, but must be tailored to the specific problems identified and comprise practical solutions, not just fine words. Organizations can help individuals identify and employ their own coping mechanisms. Ideally, the employer should attempt to eradicate the causes of stress, not just provide mechanisms to manage stress levels. For example, Employee Assistance Programmes, no matter how good, may only be part of the solution.

Question

4 What choices face a newly appointed team leader of a large work group about the styles of leadership he or she can adopt? How will the leader know whether he or she has chosen the most successful style(s)?

Answer

In Section 3.3 concepts and theories of leadership are discussed. The new team leader may be entering a very competitive environment where expectation are high for him or her to deliver results. It may be that some form of change management is required, in which case elements of transformational leadership could be needed. Critically, the team leader must adopt a style of leadership which is most appropriate to achieving results while generating a motivated work group. Perhaps 'style' theories will help, but a more focused approach is found in Vroom's Contingency Theory. This will require a lot of analysis of the situation by the team leader, he or she must be resilient enough if necessary to take tough decisions which may not induce popularity in the short term. Of critical importance in applying the theory is an analysis of the team leader's power base. The most successful style will be judged against four main criteria:

● Has the task(s) been achieved successfuly (e.g. in time and on budget)?
● Do the team members now respect and trust the leader? Would they be prepared to follow him or her?
● Has the team leader made best use of all the resources available?
● Has the team leader learnt from the experience?

Question

5 Identify and explain the key equal opportunities issues in generating positive employee attitudes towards work.

Answer

This subject arises in our discussion of flexibility in Section 2.3.4. The primary issue seems to be people's need to strike a work–life balance. Employers are finding that in introducing flexible working practices it is necessary to take account of the needs of working parents and those who wish to pursue a full private life outside work. Temporal and numerical flexibility cannot be one-sided to benefit only the employer in an exploitative way. In the section we not only provide several examples of the ways in which a mutual agenda can be established, but also links with issues such as racial segregation of workers and the employment of those with disabilities. Reality shows that many employers still have a long way to go despite the positive rhetoric. In answering this question a short explanation of the meaning of the words work attitude is necessary; also, a brief mention of the psychological contract and how it can be reforged in the light of family-flexible working.

Question

6 Before using any psychometric test for purposes of employee selection you would need to satisfy yourself as to the reliability and validity of the test. Explain what is meant by these two terms.

Answer

You will find a clear discussion of the meaning of these terms in Section 3.2.6. You will note that there are various types of validity, but predictive and construct validity are very important. The question could be broadened to include assessment centres and the necessary administrative steps of using tests effectively. Tests can be used not only for selection, but also for promotion, training, counselling and even redundancy purposes.

Question

7 Discuss the sources of power used in the workplace by the following:

    (a) The bully *vis-à-vis* his victims.
    (b) The informal leader *vis-à-vis* his or her followers
    (c) The HR manager *vis-à-vis* his or her staff.

Answer

Power and authority is discussed in Section 3.1. French and Raven, and Handy identified a series of power sources. The main power sources here are: (a) physical (coercive) (ALIENATIVE), (b) charismatic (or expert) (NORMATIVE), and (c) position (or resource) (CALCULATIVE). The power relationship is shown in capital letters according to Etzioni. Of course, it would be hoped that the HR manager would develop his or her charismatic and expert power sources; sole reliance on position or resource power is not indicative of high long-term trust levels or high levels of commitment.

Question

8 Why should employers be concerned about the existence and state of the psychological contract that exists between employers and their employees?

Answer

A full discussion of this subject is conducted in Section 2.1, particularly Sections 2.1.5–2.1.6. Before answering the question it is important to explain that the contract is the implicit agreement between the employer and the individual employee about the basis on which each party will make assumptions about each other and have expectations about how each party will treat the other. Psychological contracts will vary considerably depending upon the sector of industry, whether in the private or public sector, and the type of organization, which will provide different rewards and standards of behaviour. Employers should be concerned because a healthy and robust contract will demonstrate that employees are committed and trusting of the employer. The contract of employment is a legal and formal record of the basis of the relationship, but it fails to tell us exactly how the parties will behave towards each other. Organizations in which psychological contracts which are under strain might show poor employee relations, high levels of absenteeism and turnover and poor productivity.

You will note from Section 2.1.6 that there has been much discussion about a 'new' psychological contract, although this seems overstated.

Question

9 What are the potential components of a successful performance management system?

Answer

There are a number of possibilities, but several are considered in Section 3.5.4. Before directly answering this question you should define performance management indicating the key constituent elements that make up most performance management systems. The possible components are laid out in the final part of Section 3.5.4, but it would be necessary to cover key examples such as strategy, SMART objective-setting, incorporation of an effective performance review or appraisal system, and excellent feedback and review systems. Motivation theory (discussed in Section 3.4) underpins the concept of performance management. Increasingly sophisticated means are used by employers to systemize performance management and so link individual contribution, team contribution, corporate performance and fair/objective means of assessment and meaningful rewards.

Part Two – Managing Activities

Question

1 Henry Mintzberg and Rosemary Stewart both investigated the work of managers. Discuss their different findings.

Answer

This can be found in Sections 4.18 and 4.19. There is a need to describe the work that managers do according to both researchers. For example, Stewart talks about managers managing 'on the run' and Mintzberg refers to the regular duties a manager has to carry out. Further discussion is required of Stewart's categories of Emissaries, Writers, Discussers, Trouble-shooters and Committee Men, as well as describing Mintzberg's three role sets – Interpersonal, Information and Decisional.

Question

2 You have been recently appointed to a head a group of five employees. You are beginning to get to know them, and now you have to allocate work to them. Explain how you might go about this.

Answer

A framework that might help you as a manager to deal with this is described in Section 4.2.3 by asking the questions 'what, why, when, how and who' is best suited to do the work in question. By answering these questions we should be able to identify the individual's competence, availability, the methods used to accomplish the work and the time-frame(s) available for its completion.

Question

3 As a newly promoted manager you have been asked to bring together a number of different individuals to form a successful management team. Explain how you would go about this.

Answer

This can be found in Section 4.4.15. Here, you will find the different management team roles identified by Meredith Belbin. It is important not only to identify the roles, but also to note that these roles can be identified for best-fit purposes in individuals by psychometric testing (see also Section 3.2.60). When the roles performed by individuals are combined in certain ways they help produce a synergy that leads to an effective team.

Question

4 Health and safety policies are essential to the well-being of everyone in an organization. Explain how you would produce a health and safety policy using, wherever possible, evidence from your own experience to support your answer.

Answer

This can be found in Section 5.1.14. It is important to mention the need for a policy statement and to involve everyone as far as possible in its drafting. Remember, having a policy statement is a legal requirement for most employers. The support of all managerial staff should be emphasized. Good communication of the policy and any special procedures and specifications concerning health and safety should be clearly and effectively communicated. By involving as many people as possible at all levels of the organization a culture of safe working can be encouraged. This answer can be supported by practical examples from the student's own working environment.

Question

5 Communication has been described as: 'the transferring of meaning from one person to another'. Using examples from your own work experience describe the process of communication.

Answer

The basis for this answer can be found in Section 4.3.5. Using the model found there the student should be able to relate it to their own work. For example, the use of technical jargon when communicating to a non-technical person can cause misunderstandings and confusion. It is vital that the communicator pays attention to the elements contained in the model to ensure the recipient is absolutely clear and confident about the content and the true meaning of the message.

Question

6 'Customers come and go, but the company will always be there'. Using your knowledge of customer relations explain whether or not you think this is a true statement.

Answer

This can be found in Section 6.2. Customers are the reason for the existence of providers of goods and services, whether they be internal customers or external customers. Without external customers who purchase goods and services there is no need for the company to exist. It is important for organizations to attract and retain customers as well as giving them a voice through open communications. Retention of loyal customers is especially important since it is more cost effective to retain an existing customer than to attract a new one. Of course, new customers are critical for steady growth. Students should emphasize the key role of HR in this process, for example by ensuring customer contact staff are well trained, courteous and able to deal with not only satisfied customers but also dissatisfied ones in an effective way. Internal customers play an important part in the existence of the HR function because the latter has to 'sell' its various services to this group; increasingly such an internal relationship is placed on a commercial basis.

Part Three – Managing in a Business Context

Question

1 What are the forces driving globalization? How is globalization impacting on UK organizations?

Answer

- Define 'globalization' – the integration of national economies.
- Identify the 'forces' – the global spread of free-market ideology; the growing importance of developing countries; technological advances.
- Outline the 'impact' – a highly competitive commercial environment, resulting in a downward pressure on prices and costs; the need for organizations to be flexible and innovative; the need for employees to be functionally flexible; continuous improvement requires continuous learning.

Question

2 Distinguish between 'business ethics' and 'corporate social responsibility'.

Answer

- Define 'business ethics' – the moral standards and behaviour of individuals operating in a business context.
- Identify the ethical dimensions of business – employee, customer, corporate and community.
- Discuss the levels at which ethical lapses can occur – individual, organization and industry.
- Outline the problem with the concept of 'business ethics' – judgemental and moralizing, 'moral relativism'.
- Define 'corporate social responsibility' – to whom is the organization responsible?
- Discuss the different perspectives (Friedman, Drucker).
- Summarize the arguments 'for' and 'against' corporate social responsibility.

Question

3 What are the main arguments for and against European Monetary Union?

Answer

- Define 'European Monetary Union' – a single currency, a single monetary policy and a single bank for the EU.
- List the Treasury's 'five tests'.

For

- The elimination of the cost of converting currency.
- Increased competition and efficiency.
- The elimination of exchange rate uncertainties.

- Increased inward investment.
- Low inflation and interest rates.

Against

- The surrender of national economic and political sovereignty.
- The UK economic cycle differs from those of our EU partners.

Question

4 Distinguish between the planning, emergent and incremental approaches to developing strategy.

Answer

- Define 'strategy' – the long-term direction of an organization; an integrated plan to ensure the achievement of the organization's objectives.
- **Planning approach** – strategy as a highly systematic process, involving the extensive use of analytical tools and techniques and a rational sequence of steps.
- **Emergent approach** – describes how strategy is in fact formulated and implemented. Strategy 'emerges' as a result of trial, experimentation and small steps forward.
- **Incremental approach** – strategy has a political dimension, involving bargaining between stakeholders.

Question

5 Who are the main stakeholders in your organization? How can management reconcile their respective interests?

Answer

- Define 'stakeholders' – those who have an interest in the organization and may wish to influence its strategy and purpose.
- Distinguish between internal stakeholders (managers and other employees) and external stakeholders (shareholders, customers, suppliers, the community and so on).
- Highlight the fact that shareholder interests can conflict (give examples).
- Describe stakeholder mapping as a technique for reconciling stakeholder interests when developing strategy.

Question

6 Discuss the likely impact of changes in interest rates for your organization.

Answer

- Define 'interest rates' – the price of borrowing money.

Relatively low interest rates

- Stimulate demand.
- Can be inflationary.
- Lead to fall in the exchange rate, affecting international trade.
- Stimulate investment.
- Affect savings.

Relatively high interest rates

- Limit demand.
- Can be deflationary.
- Lead to a rise in the exchange rate, affecting international trade.
- Curb investment.
- Affect savings.

Question

7 Comment on the possible implications of an ageing population for organizations, with particular reference to your organization.

Answer

Discuss the following in relation to 'your organization':

- Change in the pattern of demand for goods and services.
- Higher dependency ratio.
- Increased call on welfare services.
- Increase in the tax burden on the working population.
- The implications of an ageing workforce.

Question

8 How has competition policy affected UK businesses?

Answer

Define 'competition policy' – legislation to limit the market power of monopolies and oligopolies through controlling monopolies, mergers and restrictive practices.

- Note that the consumer is not always exploited – firms can charge low prices because of economies of scale.
- Each case is therefore treated on its own merits – the emphasis is on how market power is used.
- It is argued that competition policy is weak and does not affect companies in a major way.

Question

9 Define the roles and functions of any three of the following: (a) the European Commission; (b) the Council of Ministers; (c) the European Parliament; and (d) the European Court of Justice.

Answer

The European Commission – the civil service of the EU which proposes legislation, ensures that EU treaties are respected and is responsible for policy implementation.
The Council of Ministers – the legislature of the EU, comprising ministers from the 15 states who are accountable to their own assemblies and governments.
The European Parliament – the elected body, primarily a scrutinizing assembly but has recently acquired legislative powers in a number of policy fields.
The European Court of Justice – interprets and adjudicates on European law.

Question

10 The sources of the contract of employment comprise different sources. What are these different sources and explain their importance and relevance for the contractual relationship between employer and employee?

Answer

Figure 12.4 provides an excellent overview of the seven key sources. Section 12.12.3 discusses the sources in some detail. You will see that the express terms are the essence of the contract and in that sense are the most important. Implied terms are next in importance because the law has implied a number of terms into contracts. However, it is important to note that no contract term irrespective of its source can over-ride any term inserted by virtue of statute (i.e. legislation passed by Parliament). The sources of the contract show the various duties and rights of both employer and employee.

Question

11 What do you understand by the term 'new technology'? Identify four ways in which new technology is impacting on organizations.

Answer

- Define 'new technology' – developments in computer and information technologies from the 1970s.
- Put 'new technology' into its historical context – successor to steam power and electricity.
- Discuss the business applications of IT – data storage and retrieval, communications (e-mail, Internet, intranet), automation of manufacturing and service provision, provision of management information, e-commerce, and so on.

Index